Lecture Notes in Artificial Intell

T0238679

Subseries of Lecture Notes in Compu

LNAI Series Editors

Randy Goebel
  University of Alberta, Edmonton, Canada
Yuzuru Tanaka
  Hokkaido University, Sapporo, Japan
Wolfgang Wahlster
  DFKI and Saarland University, Saarbrücken, Germany

LNAI Founding Series Editor

Joerg Siekmann
  DFKI and Saarland University, Saarbrücken, Germany

Chun-Yi Su Subhash Rakheja
Honghai Liu (Eds.)

Intelligent Robotics and Applications

5th International Conference, ICIRA 2012
Montreal, QC, Canada, October 3-5, 2012
Proceedings, Part III

 Springer

Series Editors

Randy Goebel, University of Alberta, Edmonton, Canada
Jörg Siekmann, University of Saarland, Saarbrücken, Germany
Wolfgang Wahlster, DFKI and University of Saarland, Saarbrücken, Germany

Volume Editors

Chun-Yi Su
Concordia University
Department of Mechanical and Industrial Engineering
Montreal, QC H3G 1M8, Canada
E-mail: cysu@alcor.concordia.ca

Subhash Rakheja
Concordia University
Department of Mechanical and Industrial Engineering
Montreal, QC H3G 1M8, Canada
E-mail: rakheja@alcor.concordia.ca

Honghai Liu
The University of Portsmouth
School of Creative Technologies
Portsmouth, PO1 2DJ, UK
E-mail: honghai.liu@port.ac.uk

ISSN 0302-9743   e-ISSN 1611-3349
ISBN 978-3-642-33502-0   e-ISBN 978-3-642-33503-7
DOI 10.1007/978-3-642-33503-7
Springer Heidelberg Dordrecht London New York

Library of Congress Control Number: 2012946931

CR Subject Classification (1998): I.2.8-11, I.5.3-4, I.4.8-9, K.4.2, J.2, J.3, C.3, C.2, G.1.10

LNCS Sublibrary: SL 7 – Artificial Intelligence

Typesetting: Camera-ready by author, data conversion by Scientific Publishing Services, Chennai, India

Printed on acid-free paper

Springer is part of Springer Science+Business Media (www.springer.com)

Preface

The Organizing Committee of the 5th International Conference on Intelligent Robotics and Applications aimed to facilitate interaction among participants in the field of intelligent robotics, automation, and mechatronics. Through this conference, the committee intended to enhance the sharing of individual experiences and expertise in intelligent robotics with particular emphasis on technical challenges associated with varied applications such as biomedical applications, industrial automations, surveillance, and sustainable mobility.

The 5th International Conference on Intelligent Robotics and Applications was most successful in attracting 271 submissions addressing state-of-the-art developments in robotics, automation, and mechatronics. Owing to the large number of submissions, the committee was faced with the difficult challenge of selecting the most deserving papers for inclusion in these lecture notes and for presentation at the conference, held in Montreal, Canada, October 3–5, 2012. For this purpose, the committee undertook a rigorous review process. Despite the high quality of most of the submissions, a total of 197 papers were selected for publication in 3 volumes of Springer's Lecture Notes in Artificial Intelligence, a subseries of Lecture Notes in Computer Science.

The selected articles were submitted by scientists from 25 different countries. The contribution of the Technical Program Committee and the referees is deeply appreciated. Most of all, we would like to express our sincere thanks to the authors for submitting their most recent work and the Organizing Committee for their enormous efforts to turn this event into a smoothly running meeting. Special thanks go to Concordia University for their generosity and direct support. Our particular thanks are due to Mr. Alfred Hofmann and the editorial staff of Springer-Verlag for enthusiastically supporting the project.

We sincerely hope that these volumes will prove to be an important resource for the scientific community.

July 2012

Chun-Yi Su
Subhash Rakheja
Honghai Liu

Conference Organization

International Advisory Committee

Jorge Angeles	McGill University, Canada
Suguru Arimoto	Ritsumeikan University, Japan
Hegao Cai	Harbin Institute of Technology, China
Tianyou Chai	Northeastern University, China
Clarence De Silva	University of British Columbia, Canada
Han Ding	Huazhong University of Science and Technology, China
Sabina Jeschke	RWTH Aachen University, Germany
Ming Li	National Natural Science Foundation of China, China
Zhongqin Lin	Shanghai Jiao Tong University, China
Ding Liu	Xi'an University of Technology, China
Jinping Qu	South China University of Technology, China
Bruno Siciliano	University of Naples, Italy
Mohammad Siddique	Fayetteville State University, USA
Mark W. Spong	University of Texas at Dallas, USA
Kevin Warwick	University of Reading, UK
Ming Xie	Nanyang Technological University, Singapore
Youlun Xiong	Huazhong University of Science and Technology, China

General Chairs

Chun-Yi Su	Concordia University, Canada
Rama B. Bhat	Concordia University, Canada
Xiangyang Zhu	Shanghai Jiao Tong University, China

Program Chairs

Subhash Rakheja	Concordia University, Canada
Jangmyung Lee	Pusan National University, South Korea
Camille Alain Rabbath	DRDC, Canada

Publicity Chairs

Tongwen Chen	University of Alberta, Canada
Li-Chen Fu	National Taiwan University, Taiwan
Shuzhi Sam Ge	National University of Singapore, Singapore

Naoyuki Kubota	Tokyo Metropolitan University, Japan
Kok-Meng Lee	Georgia Institute of Technology, USA
Ning Xi	City University of Hong Kong, Hong Kong
Xiaohua Xia	University of Pretoria, South Africa
Peter Xu	University of Auckland, New Zealand
Huayong Yang	Zhejiang University, China
Bin Yao	Purdue University, USA
Xinghuo Yu	Royal Melbourne Institute of Technology, Australia
Chaohai Zhang	Harbin Institute of Technology, China

Organized Session Chairs

Mirco Alpen	Helmut Schmidt University, Germany
Shengyong Chen	Zhejiang University of Technology, China
Weidong Chen	Shanghai Jiao Tong University, China
Xiang Chen	University of Windsor, Canada
Xinkai Chen	Shibaura Institute of Technology, Japan
Mingcong Deng	Tokyo University of Agriculture and Technology, Japan
Jun Fu	Massachusetts Institute of Technology, USA
Xin Fu	Zhejiang University, China
Haibo Gao	Harbin Institute of Technology, China
Yueming Hu	South China University of Technology, China
Yangmin Li	University of Macau, Macau, SAR China
Zhijun Li	South China University of Technology, China
Guangjun Liu	Ryerson University, Canada
Xinjun Liu	Tsinghua University, China
Daniel Schilberg	RWTH Aachen University, Germany
Yandong Tang	Shengyang Institute of Automation, CAS, China
Danwei Wang	Nanyang Technological University, Singapore
Enrong Wang	Nanjing Normal University, China
Caihua Xiong	Huazhong University of Science and Technology, China
Simon Yang	University of Guelph, Canada
Hongnian Yu	Staffordshire University, UK
Jianhua Zhang	Shanghai University, China
Youmin Zhang	Concordia University, Canada
Limin Zhu	Shanghai Jiao Tong University, China

Publication Chairs

Honghai Liu	University of Portsmouth, UK
Xinjun Sheng	Shanghai Jiao Tong University, China

Award Chair

Farhad Aghili   Canadian Space Agency, Canada

Registration Chairs

Zhi Li   Concordia University, Canada
Sining Liu   Concordia University, Canada

Finance Chair

Ying Feng   South China University of Technology, China

Local Arrangement Chairs

Wen-Fang Xie   Concordia University, Canada
Chevy Chen   Concordia University, Canada

International Program Committee

Amir Aghdam   Concordia University, Canada
DongPu Cao   Lancaster University, UK
Qixin Cao   Shanghai Jiao Tong University, China
Jie Chen   Beijing Institute of Technology, China
Mingyuan Chen   Concordia University, Canada
Zuomin Dong   University of Victoria, Canada
Guangren Duan   Harbin Institute of Technology, China
Shumin Fei   Southeast University, China
Gang Feng   City University of Hong Kong, China
Huijun Gao   Harbin Institute of Technology, China
Luis E. Garza C.   Tecnológico de Monterrey, México
Andrew A. Goldenberg   University of Toronto, Canada
Guoying Gu   Shanghai Jiao Tong University, China
Jason J. Gu   Dalhousie University, Canada
Peihua Gu   University of Calgary, Canada
Zhi-Hong Guan   Huazhong University of Science & Technology,
                              China
Shuxiang Guo   Kagawa University, Japan
Lina Hao   Northeastern University, China
Henry Hong   Concordia University, Canada
Liu Hsu   Federal University of Rio de Janeiro, Brazil

Huosheng Hu	University of Essex, UK
Qinglei Hu	Harbin Institute of Technology, China
Chunqing Huang	Xiamen University, China
Wei Lin	Case Western Reserve University, USA
Derong Liu	University of Illinois at Chicago, USA
Min Liu	Tsinghua University, China
Peter X. Liu	Carleton University, Canada
Jun Luo	Shanghai University, China
Tao Mao	Dartmouth College, USA
Daniel Miller	University of Waterloo, Canada
Yuichiro Oya	University of Miyazak, Japan
Hailong Pei	South China University of Technology, China
Juntong Qi	Chinese Academy of Sciences, China
Joe Qin	University of Southern California, USA
Yaohong Qu	Northwestern Polytechnical University, China
Lbrir Salim	The University of Trinidad and Tobago, Trinidad and Tobago
Inna Sharf	McGill University, Canada
Yang Shi	Victoria University, Canada
Gangbing Song	University of Houston, USA
Jing Sun	University of Michigan, USA
XiaoBo Tan	Michigan State University, USA
Yonghong Tan	Shanghai Normal University, China
Yong Tang	South China University of Technology, China
Gang Tao	University of Virginia, USA
Didier Theilliol	University of Lorraine, France
Hong Wang	University of Manchester, UK
Xingsong Wang	Southeast University, China
Pak Kin Wong	University of Macau, Macau, SAR China
Shaorong Xie	Shanghai University, China
Xin Xin	Okayama Prefectural University, Japan
Zhenhua Xiong	Shanghai Jiao Tong University, China
Bugong Xu	South China University of Technology, China
Jianxin Xu	National University of Singapore, Singapore
Deyi Xue	University of Calgary, Canada
Zijiang Yang	Ibaraki University, Japan
Dingguo Zhang	Shanghai Jiao Tong University, China
Guangming Zhang	Nanjing University of Technology, China
Yanzheng Zhao	Shanghai Jiao Tong University, China
Wenhong Zhu	Canadian Space Agency, Canada

List of Reviewers

We would like to acknowledge the support of the following people, who peer reviewed articles from ICIRA 2012.

Achint Aggarwal
Farhad Aghili
Jose Alarcon Herrera
Mirco Alpen
Nicolas Alt
Philippe Archambault
Ramprasad Balasubramanian
Mark Becke
Andrey Belkin
Francisco Beltran-Carbajal
Stanley Birchfield
Swetha Sampath Bobba
Hans-Joachim Böhme
Itziar Cabanes
Yifan Cai
Yang Cao
Zhiqiang Cao
Alberto Cavallo
Abbas Chamseddine
Mingyuan Chen
Xiang Chen
Wei Chen
Diansheng Chen
Xinkai Chen
Shengyong Chen
Yixiong Chen
Xiang Chen
Weidong Chen
Chaobin Chen
Shengyong Chen
Chevy Chen
Zhao Cheng
Yushing Cheung
Dong-Il Cho
Yunfei Dai
David D'Ambrosio
Krispin Davies
Hua Deng
Mingcong Deng
Wenhua Ding
Xuejun Ding
John Dolan

Mitchell Donald
Xiao-Gang Duan
Su-Hong Eom
Ole Falkenberg
Yuanjie Fan
Yongchun Fang
Wei Feng
Simon Fojtu
Gustavo Freitas
Klaus Frick
Zhuang Fu
Jun Fu
Xin Fu
Luis Garza
Shuzhi Sam Ge
Jason Geder
Hernan Gonzalez Acuña
Guo-Ying Gu
Tianyu Gu
Yongxin Guo
Zhao Guo
Roger Halkyard
Jianda Han
Lina Hao
Mohamed Hasan
Syed Hassan
Michal Havlena
Jiayuan He
Sven Hellbach
Abdelfetah Hentout
Katharina Hertkorn
Trent Hilliard
Johannes Höcherl
Joachim Horn
Mir Amin Hosseini
Qinglei Hu
Yonghui Hu
Jin Hu
Chunqing Huang
Jidong Huang
Aitore Ibarguren
Satoshi Iwaki

Markus Janssen
Qiuling Jia
Ying Jin
Balajee Kannan
Jun Kanno
Bijan Karimi
Mohammad Keshmiri
Sungshin Kim
Alexandr Klimchik
Yukinori Kobayashi
Tim Köhler
Naoyuki Kubota
Xu-Zhi Lai
Lin Lan
Marco Langerwisch
Jangmyung Lee
Sang-Hoon Lee
Min Lei
Yan Li
Shunchong Li
Jing Li
Zhijun Li
Hengyu Li
Nanjun Li
Yinxiao Li
Qingguo Li
Yangming Li
Zhi Li
Binbin Lian
Junli Liang
Guanhao Liang
Miguel Lima
Xinjun Liu
Han Liu
Chengliang Liu
Peter Liu
Chao Liu
Jia Liu
Sining Liu
Jun Luo
Xiaomin Ma
Yumin Ma
António Machado
Werner Maier
Jörn Malzahn

Mohamed Mamdouh
Ida Bagus Manuaba
Tao Mao
Farhat Mariem
Luis Mateos
Iñaki Maurtua
Aaron Mavrinac
Deqing Mei
Yi Min
Lei Mo
Abolfazl Mohebbi
Vidya Murali
Mahmoud Mustafa
Keitaro Naruse
Ashutosh Natraj
Myagmarbayar Nergui
Bin Niu
Scott Nokleby
Farzad Norouzi fard
Farzan Nowruzi
Ernesto Olguín-Díaz
Godfrey Onwubolu
Tomas Pajdla
Chang-Zhong Pan
Lizheng Pan
Ricardo Pérez-Alcocer
Andreas Pichler
Charles Pinto
Erion Plaku
Peter Poschmann
Radius Prasetiyo
Marius Pruessner
Juntong Qi
Xiaoming Qian
Guo Qiwei
Yaohong Qu
Mohammad Rahman
Ahmed Ramadan
Christian Rauch
Laura Ray
Hamd ul Moqeet Riaz
Martijn Rooker
Miti Ruchanurucks
Kunjin Ryu
Iman Sadeghzadeh

Thomas Schlegl
Christian Schlette
Sven Severin
Inna Sharf
Karam Shaya
Huiping Shen
Huimin Shen
Xinjun Sheng
Thierry Simon
Olivier Simonin
Dalei Song
Zhenguo Sun
Tadeusz Szkodny
XiaoBo Tan
Wenbin Tang
Yandong Tang
Alberto Tellaeche
Didier Theilliol
Christopher Tomaszewski
Abhinav Valada
Prasanna Velagapudi
Tianmiao Wang
Xiaoyan Wang
Xinmin Wang
Jingchuan Wang
Yancheng Wang
Xin Wang
Enrong Wang
Ralf Waspe
Zhixuan Wei
Graeme Wilson
Jonas Witt
Christian Wögerer
Pak Kin Wong
Olarn Wongwirat
Chong Wu
Yier Wu
Jianhua Wu
Min Wu
Xiaojun Wu
Baihua Xiao
Fugui Xie
Rong Xie
Shaorong Xie
Pu Xie
Wen-Fang Xie

Le Xie
Xin Xin
Jing Xin
Zhenhua Xiong
Rong Xiong
Caihua xiong
Bugong Xu
Bin Xu
Xiong Xu
You-Nan Xu
Deyi Xue
Zijiang Yang
Jie Yang
Chenguang Yang
Wenyu Yang
Jing Yang
Chang-En Yang
Lin Yao
Gen'ichi Yasuda
Michael Yeh
Zhouping Yin
Yong-Ho Yoo
Haoyong Yu
Xinghuo Yu
Mimoun Zelmat
Shasha Zeng
Jie Zhang
Zhengchen Zhang
Gang Zhang
Xiaoping Zhang
Jianjun Zhang
He Zhang
Dingguo Zhang
Yifeng Zhang
Xuebo Zhang
Yequn Zhang
Jinsong Zhang
Wenzeng Zhang
Chaohai Zhang
Yanzheng Zhao
Pengbing Zhao
Zhaowei Zhong
Hangfei Zhou
Li-Min Zhu
Asier Zubizarreta

Table of Contents – Part III

Robot Actuators and sensors

Robot Design, Development and Control

Robot Intelligence, Learning and Linguistics

Robot Mechanism and Design

Robot Motion Analysis and Planning

Robotic Vision, Recognition and Reconstruction

Planning and Navigation

Hands-Free Head-Motion Interface Using Air Pillow

Hajime Nakamura[1], Shouta Mikura[1], Satoshi Iwaki[1], Kazuhiro Taniguchi[1],
Manabu Motegi[2], Shin-you Mutou[2], and Toru Kobayashi[2]

[1] Graduate School of Information Sciences, Hiroshima City University,
3-4-1 Ohtsukahigashi, Asaminami-ku Hiroshima, Japan
iwaki@hiroshima-cu.ac.jp
[2] NTT Cyber Solution Laboratory, 1-1 Hikarinodai, Yokosuka, Japan

Abstract. To realize a non-invasive hands-free interface for use in daily life, we propose a head-motion interface using an air pillow. This air pillow consists of four air bags in a layered overlapping pattern whose air pressures are measured to control the cursor position as well as click-and-drag operations on a PC screen. In accordance with the initial condition of the pillow and the user's head movement ability, rapid and user-friendly cursor manipulation is implemented. Based on the throughput and click time performance indices, a comparison is made with an existing interface to evaluate the proposed method as a practical hands-free interface.

Keywords: pillow, hands-free interface, head motion, air.

1 Introduction

Recently, to support people with impaired arm or hand function who wish to express their intention, hands-free input interfaces using head movement have been actively studied [1-7]. To indicate to others a subject of interest, the user of the interface uses head movements to perform the mouse operations of a PC, such as cursor movement and clicks, and to control the direction of a physical pointing device.

Aida *et al.* proposed a system where the user mounts a three-dimensional motion sensor with a gyro sensor to assist voice input through head movement [1]. Nakazawa *et al.* proposed a system with a gyro sensor attached to the head, where head tilt controls the direction of cursor movement, and the modes of movement and of clicks are changed through the opening and closing of the mouth [2]. Nunoshita *et al.* proposed a method using an ultrasonic wave transmitter attached to the face in which head tilt controls the position of the cursor [3]. Ito proposed a method using an attached laser pointer, through which the curser is moved to the point irradiated on the display panel, and performed a detailed evaluation using quantitative evaluation parameters, namely, throughput and click time (CT) [4]. Tsukada proposed a method, which is similar to Ito's, in which the irradiated point and the cursor position are linked [5]. There is room for the improvement of the above-mentioned methods [1]-[5] because they require an attached sensor in order to detect head movement, resulting in an unnatural feel for the user. On the other hand, Kubo *et al.* proposed a

C.-Y. Su, S. Rakheja, H. Liu (Eds.): ICIRA 2012, Part III, LNAI 7508, pp. 1–12, 2012.

method of detecting eyeball position by using a camera and controlling the cursor position by letting head tilt control the direction of the cursor movement [6]. This is an excellent method in that a device attached to the face is not needed, offering the advantage of non-invasiveness, but the problem is that the user must close the eyelids for clicking, and, without a marker, image recognition of eyeballs may be difficult under some illumination conditions. Among the products on the market, TrackIR is a system in which infrared rays are irradiated from the top part of the display, reflected from a reflector affixed to the head, and then received and detected, with head tilt controlling the cursor position [7]. Operability is good near the screen center, but an expected problem is that the operability degrades as the user becomes distant from the screen.

The many proposals for head-movement interface described above have strong points and weak points, and it may be said that an ideal system like an optical mouse has not yet been established. Note that the evaluation criteria for a head-movement interface include many items such as pointer movement performance, instruction performance (click, drag, etc.), setup simplicity, portability, non-invasiveness, and cost; meeting all these requirements is difficult. The importance of a particular criterion depends on the user's head movement ability and also on the use environment. For example, operation performance and non-invasiveness may be important for long-time use, but setup simplicity may be more important if the period of operation is short. In addition, operation performance is critical for complex tasks, but setup simplicity and non-invasiveness become more important in relatively simple work.

In this study, we focus on the pillow, which is something almost everyone uses every day, in order to realize an interface that is extremely non-invasive. This is accomplished simply by remodeling the familiar pillow. In adopting a pillow, non-invasiveness is high because a special sensor or marker need not be attached to the head or face, and operation is easy because the system can be used in bed. In addition, the system is expected to be beneficial not only for users with impaired arm function, but also for users with normal arm function who can use the system if they need both hands for other purposes.

In this paper, Section 2 discusses the hardware and the basic air pillow system; Section 3 proposes methods based on preliminary tests for predicting the amount of manipulation, controlling the cursor speed, and implementing the event control; Section 4 presents the results of evaluation experiments and discussion including a comparison of performance with existing head-movement interfaces; and Section 5 presents conclusions and future problems.

2   Hardware Components and Basic Principles

2.1   Hardware Components

We focus on the pillow because it can be used in bed, simply by putting a pillow on the bed and the head on the pillow, where the back of the head is the only contact region, without the need to attach a sensor to the face. The ease of use and non-invasiveness of the pillow are high because pillows are widely used in daily life.

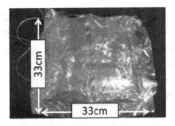

Fig. 1. Pillow interface overview

In this study, an air pillow with four plastic air bags [8] is proposed as a pressure sensor. Figure 1 shows a photograph of the air pillow, and Fig. 2 shows a schematic of the system. In the pillow interface, four air bags are placed in a layered overlapping pattern, and each air bag has an air pressure sensor whose signal is transmitted to PC via A/D converter. In this structure, the direction of the head weight can be detected from the air pressures of the air pillow units, and the user controls the mouse cursor position and click events through the air pressure of each air bag. The advantages of the proposed hardware components are as follows. Air pillows are lightweight with excellent portability and are widely used. Due to the layered overlapping structure, the height and hardness of the pillow, which are the main conditions needed for sound sleep, can be controlled independently; and there are even studies in which they are controlled separately [9-10]. Since the whole air pillow is the detection part of the sensor, we can detect a very small change of force, and the layered structure helps reduce the equipment area. In addition, the back of the head can easily be supported because there is a dent in the center of the pillow.

2.2 Basic Measurement Principles and Preliminary Tests

Let $p_i(i = 1, ..., 4)$ be the pressure in the four air bags. Figure 2 shows that, for example, p_2 increases and p_1 decreases, and p_3 and p_4 do not change when the head weight increases in the positive direction of the X-axis. On the other hand, if the head weight increases in the positive direction of the Y-axis, p_3 increases and p_4 decreases, and p_1 and p_2 do not change. In the layered overlapping structure, since

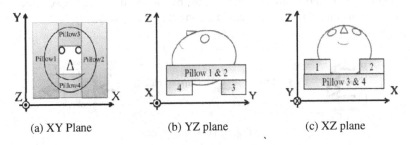

(a) XY Plane   (b) YZ plane   (c) XZ plane

Fig. 2. Pillow interface configuration

the increase and decrease pattern of the four pressures changes depending on the position of the head, the basic principle is that the direction of the weight on the XY plane is measured by detecting the pattern.

Thus, we can have the following relations;

$$f = \begin{pmatrix} f_x \\ f_y \end{pmatrix} = \begin{pmatrix} s_x(p_2 - p_1) \\ s_y(p_3 - p_4) \end{pmatrix} \tag{1}$$

where f_x, f_y denote head pushing force with respect to X, Y direction and s_x, s_y denotes coefficient with the dimension of area. Using f_x, f_y, we can calculate cursor position $c = (x, y)^T$ as follows;

$$c = \int f dt \tag{2}$$

If the cursor moves in the direction of the head weight movement and the weight does not change, it is expected that the cursor position right before the movement is maintained due to the integral effect. Implementing Eqs. (1) and (2) on a PC, preliminarily tests confirmed the results as expected [11,12]. However, there appeared to be a great difference of operation performance depending on the initial state and the user's ability to move the head. Therefore, in the following section, we propose, based on the preliminary tests, a method to deliver the best operation performance considering these factors.

3   Proposed Method

The basic principle as given by Eqs. (1) and (2) shall now be improved from the viewpoints of individual differences and operation performance enhancement. First, since the pillow interface is not a position-input device, but rather a force-input device, we pay attention to the cursor speed v just before outputting the cursor position.

In other words, the process flow between p_i and $c = (x, y)^T$ is divided into two steps as shown in Fig. 3, and the problem reduces to the problem of determining the two functions $f = S_1(p_i)$ and $v = S_2(f)$. The initial state and individual differences are handled by S_1, while S_2 handles operability improvement by using the generalized and normalized values. Thus, by clearly dividing between the design phases, we can control the parameters in a comprehensible way.

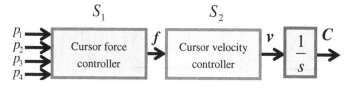

Fig. 3. Two-step process

3.1   Determination of Manipulation Amount f and S_1

To ease the influence of the initial state and individual differences, the function f is normalized in the preliminary adjustment work (calibration). In the calibration, the head is placed on the center of the pillow and then the head is moved from right to left or up and down in the preferred motion of the user. Note that the calibration is completed in only a few seconds.

Handling Variation of the Initial State
It is not guaranteed that the initial air volume or pressure of the air pillow is always constant, and the function f calculated by Eq. (1) is affected by the initial state due to differences in weight, shape, and center of gravity. To solve the problem, the initial air pressure p_{i0} is obtained in the static state where the head is placed on the central part of the pillow before use, and, during the use of the interface, instead of p_i in Eq. (1), we use the percent change d_i from the initial air pressure as given by

$$d_i = (p_i - p_{i0})/p_{i0} \qquad (3)$$

After the head is placed on the center of the pillow interface, Fig. 4 shows the change of f when the head is moved from right to left or up and down in the preferred stroke of the user. The use of Eq. (1) gives (a) while the use of Eq. (3) gives (b). Focusing on Fig. 4(a), the origin of the graph and the center of the variation of f differ due to the difference in the initial state. Focusing then on Fig. 4(b), we can confirm that the center of the variation of f almost agrees with the center of the graph. Thus, we can lessen the influence of the initial state by using the initial air pressure as the base.

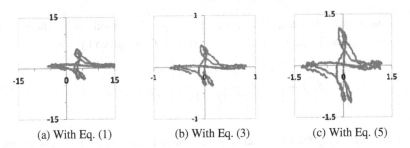

(a) With Eq. (1)   (b) With Eq. (3)   (c) With Eq. (5)

Fig. 4. Trajectories of f when moving head horizontally and vertically

Handling Different Head Motions Among Users
As shown in Fig. 4(b), the stroke width that the user favors differs according to directions, depending also on the differences in head shape and physical capability between individuals. Thus, there is a problem that the operational feel may become unstable depending on the direction and the user. To solve this, after the initial air pressure is extracted before use, the user is asked to move their head from right to left

and up and down in their preferred stroke, and the favored stroke width is obtained in each direction by using d_i at the time:

$$d_{up} = d_3 - d_4, \quad d_{down} = d_4 - d_3$$
$$d_{right} = d_1 - d_2, \quad d_{left} = d_2 - d_1 \tag{4}$$

In using the interface, the manipulation amount is defined by the ratio with respect to the favored stroke width in every direction, and the cursor position is controlled by using the following equation

$$f = \begin{pmatrix} f_x \\ f_y \end{pmatrix} = \begin{pmatrix} 1/d_x(d_2 - d_1) \\ 1/d_y(d_3 - d_4) \end{pmatrix} \tag{5}$$

where $d_x = d_{right} / d_{left}$ and $d_y = d_{up} / d_{down}$ vary with the input direction. For example, if the input direction is upper right ($d_3 > d_4$ and $d_1 > d_2$), we have $d_x = d_{right}$ and $d_y = d_{up}$, and $|f| = 1$ for the stroke width input at the time of calibration. Here, Fig. 4(c) shows the behavior of f when Eq. (5) is used. Note that the actual head motion is the same in all case of (a)-(c). In (b), the difference is more than two-fold for the maximum stroke between the downward and rightward directions, indicating that the preferred motion greatly varies. In (c), the maximum difference is about 1.2, indicating that the difference in input by direction is small. In this way, the operational feel becomes isotropic, and f is normalized to conform to the user stroke.

3.2   Determination of Cursor Speed v and S_2

Based on the preliminary test results and the proposed method for predicting the manipulation amount, Fig. 5 shows the designed $S_2(f)$ as given by

$$S_2(f) = \begin{cases} 0 & (|f| > r) \\ \dfrac{v_b \cdot (|f| - r)}{(1 - r)^2} \cdot (f - r) & (|f| \le r) \end{cases} \tag{6}$$

where $r = r \cdot (f_x / |f|, f_y / |f|)$, and v_b is the basic cursor speed, which is set such that $|v| = v_b$ (constant) when the input is made with the stroke used in calibration ($|f| = 1$). Thus, it becomes possible to arbitrarily control the speed depending on the user's favored stroke. Adopting a quadratic expression here, the low speed area extends so that a higher speed operation becomes possible with a smaller stroke. This allows the user to accurately point within small areas and make rapid movements to distant points.

Note that, in preliminary tests, we encountered unintended cursor movement or an unfavorable operational feel due to a subtle head tilt near the center of the pillow. To

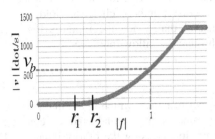
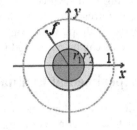

Fig. 5. Relation between cursor velocity and cursor force   **Fig. 6.** Dead zone characteristics

prevent this, a circular dead zone is placed around the origin of f (Fig. 6). However, although it is desirable to enlarge the dead zone to prevent unintended movement, the operability degrades if too much of the movable head area is assigned to the dead zone. Therefore, the radius r_2 of the dead zone during the rest time is set larger than the radius r_1 of the dead zone in the active time by using different dead zones for the rest period and the active time. In this process, a distinctive input is needed for the transition from the rest to the active and from the active to the rest period so that unintended movement can be prevented.

3.3   Event Control

To select among click events, we use the average $\bar{d}$ of the air pressure change rate d of the four air pillows, which corresponds to the force to push the whole pillow interface in the Z-axis direction in Fig. 2. Figure 7 shows the state transition diagram of click events. Here, $\bar{d}'$ is the derivative of $\bar{d}$, T_i is an arbitrary threshold, and *time* is the time after the state transition. In MOVE state, the cursor is moved through the integration using Eq. (2) of v, which is calculated using Eq. (6); the CLICK state performs the left click, and the EVENT OPT state performs event selection. Nothing occurs in the PUSH or PULL state. In other words, assuming that the cursor is in the rest state, the left click works if the pillow is pushed and brought back to its initial state over time, and event selection works if the head is lifted from the pillow and then returned to its initial position over time. In event selection, if the input is given in any of the upward, downward, leftward, and rightward directions, the event

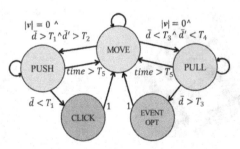

Fig. 7. State transition diagram of click events

corresponding to that direction shall be performed. Presently, *left* corresponds to W click, *right* corresponds to right click, *up* corresponds to click-and-hold, and *down* corresponds to drop. It is considered useful that, since the input is hierarchical, various events can be controlled simply through the pillow interface.

4   Experimental Evaluation

To quantitatively evaluate the operational performance, which is the main element of the evaluation criteria, comparative experiments were conducted to evaluate the operational performance with multiple participants using the pillow interface. Here, for the evaluation task and criteria, we adopted a procedure similar to the one in reference [4], where detailed evaluation results were presented. In the present study, the eight participants were healthy undergraduate and graduate students in their 20s.

4.1   Outline of Experiments

Lying in a supine position and monitoring the screen projected onto the ceiling (Fig. 8), the participant performs the evaluation task using the pillow interface. The task, as shown in Fig. 9, involves 30 targets placed at the center and circumferentially around it; the examinee clicks the central point and one of the other targets alternately as quickly as possible (60 times in total). On the screen, only the target to be subsequently chosen is shown, and the target once selected disappears. The window size is 1000×750 dots, and the target diameter is 26 dots, similar in size to the commonly used close button in a graphical user interface. The evaluation was performed three times by each participant using the pillow interface.

As the evaluation parameters, similarly to reference [4], we used throughput (the amount of work done within a certain period of time), which shows the cursor movement performance,

$$Throughput = \frac{log_2(\frac{D}{W} + 1)}{MT} \tag{7}$$

and CT [s], which shows the time before the click after the cursor reaches the target. Here, D is the distance between the starting point and the center of the target, W is the diameter of the target, and MT is the time for the mouse cursor to reach the target. Higher throughput means higher movement performance; the index value increases when less time is taken to reach a smaller, farther target.

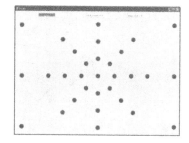

Fig. 8. Experimental setup   **Fig. 9.** Target marks for evaluation task

4.2   Experimental Results and Discussion

Evaluation of Throughput

Table 1 shows the average and standard deviation of out-bound and in-bound throughput for participants(A,...,H) using the pillow interface to point at 30 targets. Further, Fig. 10 compares the average of the out-bound and in-bound movements of all participants using the pillow interface with the data in [4]. The pillow interface shows better throughput by about 1%, 16%, and 9% for the out-bound, in-bound, and round-trip movements, respectively. Throughput is better in the in-bound movement probably because it is not necessary to establish the target position and thus the transition from click to movement takes less time (as similarly discussed in [4]). Further, the in-bound movement shows a greater difference than the out-bound movement probably because the movement speed presents itself more clearly in the in-bound movement where it is not needed to confirm the cursor position; note that the maximum speed is 1300 dots/s in the pillow interface, and 300 dots/s in [4]. On the other hand, the variation in the movement time was larger in the pillow interface where the cursor movement speed is set continuously between 0 and 1300 [dot/s], whereas the cursor movement speed takes only two values, 80 dots/s and 300 dots/s, in [4]. In operating a PC, except for games, the point to be targeted does not necessarily appear suddenly, but its position is often known in advance. In that case, the movement performance in operating a PC becomes closer to that of the out-bound movement, and it is reasonable that the movement performance of the pillow interface is superior.

Table 1. Pillow interface average throughput [bits/s]

	1st		2nd		3rd	
	Out	In	Out	In	Out	In
A	2.45	3.32	2.61	3.28	2.32	3.51
	±1.00	±1.25	±0.91	±1.18	±0.89	±1.37
B	1.92	1.60	1.57	1.77	2.04	1.70
	±0.98	±0.66	±0.55	±0.63	±0.83	±0.65
C	2.11	1.96	1.80	2.31	1.76	1.94
	±0.72	±0.54	±0.56	±1.03	±0.53	±0.59
D	2.13	2.48	2.13	2.09	2.32	2.33
	±0.73	±1.41	±0.96	±0.98	±1.01	±0.80
E	1.71	1.60	1.90	2.54	2.12	3.27
	±0.62	±0.54	±0.59	±1.22	±0.59	±2.41
F	2.48	2.28	2.27	2.36	2.29	2.46
	±0.83	±0.62	±1.13	±0.85	±0.94	±1.15
G	2.50	3.21	2.30	3.68	2.51	3.27
	±0.68	±1.60	±0.66	±2.63	±0.94	±1.59
H	3.31	4.04	3.25	4.25	2.98	3.59
	±1.13	±1.46	±0.83	±1.72	±0.83	±1.12

Table 2. Pillow interface CT average [s]

	1st		2st		3rd	
	Out	In	Out	In	Out	In
A	1.79	2.49	1.96	1.78	2.12	1.81
	±0.80	±1.37	±0.77	±0.71	±0.93	±1.10
B	3.23	4.05	2.69	2.57	3.03	1.97
	±1.94	±3.05	±2.73	±2.35	±2.31	±1.13
C	2.03	1.60	1.50	1.82	1.60	1.85
	±1.39	±1.12	±0.87	±1.30	±0.82	±0.82
D	2.23	2.29	1.35	1.28	1.65	1.08
	±1.62	±1.68	±0.87	±0.68	±1.06	±0.67
E	1.95	2.45	1.63	1.69	2.32	1.73
	±1.34	±1.98	±1.19	±1.00	±1.45	±1.64
F	1.62	1.40	1.21	1.47	1.31	1.28
	±1.04	±0.98	±0.70	±1.31	±0.85	±0.96
G	1.77	1.40	1.24	1.13	1.36	1.12
	±1.07	±0.77	±1.08	±0.71	±0.85	±0.50
H	1.05	0.92	1.00	0.93	1.09	0.92
	±0.69	±0.51	±0.50	±0.48	±0.90	±0.55

Evaluation of CT

Table 2 shows the result for the time, CT, before the participant finished the click after pointing at the target. Similarly to throughput, the average and the standard deviation of CT were evaluated for the out-bound and in-bound movements by using the 30 targets. Figure 11 compares the averages of all the participants using the pillow interface and the results in [4]. In CT, the pillow interface is inferior by about 85%, 99%, and 91% in the out-bound, in-bound, and round-trip movements, respectively, and the difference in time is about 0.6 s. This is probably because CT includes the time of minor adjustment after the overshooting the target and minor adjustment takes extra time. The average standard deviation of the pillow interface is 1 s, and the time required for minor adjustment would greatly affect the CT result. CT is considered to

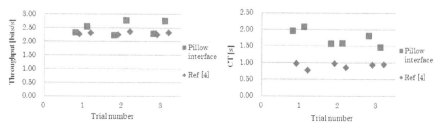

Fig. 10. Average throughput   **Fig. 11.** CT average

be about 0.5 s. Therefore, for clicking a sufficiently large target where overshoot is not likely to occur, we could realize a click time similar to that in [4].

Further, the trend of CT decreasing between trials, from first to second to third, seems to show that CT could be improved if the user gets used to the operation.

Overall Evaluation

With throughput and CT taken together, [4] shows better results for total operation time assuming the tasks here. However, from the fact that the pillow interface shows better throughput results, it is considered that higher operability could be achieved once the user masters the operation to reduce the number of overshoots and the adjustment time. However, as initially discussed, operability is merely one evaluation criterion of an interface. The advantage of our system is that it is not necessary to attach a cumbersome apparatus to the user's face, indicating non-invasiveness and convenience, light weight and portability, ready availability, and that, being a force-input-based system, the pillow interface can be operated with a small movement by the user. This suggests the effectiveness and practicality of using the proposed pillow interface in relatively simple and short operations.

5   Conclusion

Aiming at the development of a simple and noninvasive interface, we proposed a head-movement interface using an air pillow and a method for controlling the cursor position and events. By adopting the pillow as hardware, a highly noninvasive interface was obtained, characterized by portability and simplicity where it is only necessary for users to place their head on the pillow, without any sensor on the face. Further, the usefulness was verified by comparing the operability with existing research results.

In the future, through an evaluation by users with disabilities, we aim to improve operability by optimizing Eqs. (1)-(6), and to conduct a comprehensive investigation including the evaluation criteria. Further, we will explore the applicability of the system as a head-movement monitor for patients with sleep apnea syndrome.

References

1. Aida, T., et al.: A Voice Interface System with the Head Motion Sensor. Institute of Electronics, Information and Communication Engineers, IEICE Technical Report, TL2006-55 (2007)
2. Nakazawa, et al.: Interface for Operating a Personal Computer with Head Tilting and Mouth Open/Close Motions. Transactions of the Japan Society of Mechanical Engineers C 72(724), 3892–3898 (2006)
3. Nunoshita, et al.: Head Pointing System Based on Ultrasonic Position Measurement. Journal of the Institute of Image Information and Television Engineers 57(3), 403–408 (2003)
4. Ito: Light Spot Operated Mouse Pointing Device for Cervical Spinal-Cord Injured PC Users. IEICE Transactions on Information and Systems J90-D(3), 771–779 (2007)

5. Tsukada, et al.: Handsfree Pointing System for the Handicapped. IEICE Technical Report. MBE, ME and Bio Cybernetics 108(52), 1–6 (2008)
6. Kubo, et al.: A Mouse Emulation Tool Using Head Movement for the Handicapped. IEICE Technical Report, HCS, Human Information Processing 101(36), 35–42 (2001)
7. http://www.mikimoto-japan.com/beans/products/track_ir5/index.htm
8. Iwaki, et al.: Japanese patent publication number 2007-286903.
9. Iwaki et al.:Flexible Structure and Its Air Pressure Control Method. Japanese patent publication number 449036
10. Yamamoto, et al.: Open Loop Type Impedance Adjustment of the Air Pillow Using Piston Cylinder Transport. Transactions of the Society of Instrument and Control Engineers (SICE) 48(3), 167–174 (2012)
11. Nakamura, et al.: Head Movement Interface Using the Air Pillow I. In: 12th IEEE Hiroshima Student Symposium, Outstanding Paper Award / Best Presentation Award (2010)
12. Nakamura, et al.: Head Movement Interface Using the Air Pillow II. In: SICE System Integration 2010 (2010)

A Self-localization System with Global Error Reduction and Online Map-Building Capabilities

Karam Shaya, Aaron Mavrinac, Jose Luis Alarcon Herrera, and Xiang Chen[*]

Department of Electrical and Computer Engineering, University of Windsor,
Windsor, Ontario, Canada
{shayak,mavrin1,alarconj,xchen}@uwindsor.ca

Abstract. An economical self-localization system which uses a monocular camera and a set of artificial landmarks is presented herein. The system represents the surrounding environment as a topological graph where each node corresponds to an artificial landmark and each edge corresponds to a relative pose between two landmarks. The edges are weighted based on an error metric (related to pose uncertainty) and a shortest path algorithm is applied to the map to compute the path corresponding to the least aggregate weight. This path is used to localize the camera with respect to a global coordinate system whose origin lies on an arbitrary reference landmark (i.e., the destination node of the path). The proposed system does not require a preliminary training process, as it builds and updates the map online. Experimental results demonstrate the performance of the system in reducing the global error associated with large-scale localization.

1 Introduction

With the growing demand for autonomous robots in industrial, medical, domestic, and other domains, a large portion of research in the robotics industry has been geared toward the development and improvement of localization systems. For the purposes of this paper, existing localization systems in the literature will be divided into two categories: those that obtain their data from multiple sensors (e.g., [8], [1], [5]) and those that obtain them from a single sensor (e.g., [11], [15], [16]). The former type of system takes a sensor fusion approach. One major advantage of sensor fusion is the availability of multiple sources of data, through which the robot may verify the readings of its individual sensors and reduce the overall error of its pose estimates. The disadvantages of multiple sensors are added complexity (in the localization algorithm and hardware design), larger form factor, and increased cost. Conversely, systems that use single sensors tend to be simpler, smaller, and less expensive; however, they do not have the redundancy and fusion of multiple independent sensor measurements and must therefore use internal methods to reduce estimation error. The focus of our work is on reducing the estimation error of a single sensor localization system.

---

[*] This research is supported in part by NSERC-Discovery Grant to Prof. Xiang Chen.

C.-Y. Su, S. Rakheja, H. Liu (Eds.): ICIRA 2012, Part III, LNAI 7508, pp. 13–22, 2012.

Compared to the sensing modalities used in other solutions (e.g., odometry, sonar, and laser), two dimensional images provide a robot's localization algorithm with more data about the environment [9]. They can be used by a localization algorithm to detect, identify, and estimate the pose of objects in a scene.

The nature of the map-building process of visual localization yields two particular types of pose estimation errors: *local error* – which originates from error and noise in image capture and affects pose estimations made with respect to coordinate systems in the image – and *global error* – which arises from the accumulation of local error and affects pose estimations made with respect to a global coordinate system that may not necessarily be in the image. Due to the influence local error has on global error, reducing the former would result in a reduction of the latter. This may be achieved, for example, through markers (i.e., artificial landmarks) that can be accurately detected and discerned to help keep local error at a minimum [7], [4], [10].

In this paper, the problem will be approached from a different perspective. While local error reduction can be characterized as a low-level means of reducing global error, the proposed method will take on a more direct approach by representing the surrounding environment as a mathematical graph whose edge weights reflect the effects of local error. Graphical representation of similar vision-based pose estimation problems has previously been applied to such areas as multiview registration of 3D scenes [14] and large-scale extrinsic calibration of camera networks [3]. By applying a shortest path algorithm, the graph can be optimized to yield the paths of minimum global error (i.e., accumulated local error). To the best of the authors' knowledge, the minimization of global error in a localization system using the graphical approach outlined herein has not been presented in literature.

The remainder of this paper is organized as follows: Section 2 defines the preliminary concepts relating to pose composition, graphs, and the shortest path algorithm; Section 3 states the necessary assumptions and presents the proposed self-localization system's method and algorithm; Section 4 demonstrates the performance of the system in reducing the effect of global error; and Section 5 concludes the paper by providing reflections on the results.

2   Preliminaries

2.1   Pose Composition

A pose $P_{\alpha\beta}$ is a rigid three dimensional Euclidean transformation from the coordinate system of object α to the coordinate system of object β. This may be referred to as the pose of object α with respect to object β.

The inverse of pose $P_{\alpha\beta}$ may be denoted $P_{\alpha\beta}^{-1}$ or $P_{\beta\alpha}$. The former notation will be used here to emphasize that $P_{\alpha\beta}$ is the available direct estimate.

Successive pose transformations may be composed into a single pose:

$$P_{\alpha\gamma}(\mathbf{p}) = (P_{\alpha\beta} \circ P_{\beta\gamma})(\mathbf{p}) = P_{\beta\gamma}(P_{\alpha\beta}(\mathbf{p})) \tag{1}$$

Note that a left-composition convention is used to better illuminate the sequence of pose transformations.

The details of pose inversion and composition vary depending on the representation used. The reader is directed to any of the numerous texts on Euclidean geometry for a treatment appropriate to his or her working representation.

2.2 Relative Pose Calculation

Refering to Fig. 1, the relative pose transformation of a marker α with respect to another marker β is determined through pose composition to be

$$P_{\alpha\beta} = P_{\alpha c} \circ P_{\beta c}^{-1} \tag{2}$$

where $P_{\alpha c}$ and $P_{\beta c}$ are the poses of α and β with respect to the camera c (assumed to be available). Note that this calculation is made possible by the fact that both markers are in the camera's FOV (shaded area in Fig. 1) at the same time; more specifically, pose estimates are taken from the same captured camera frame.

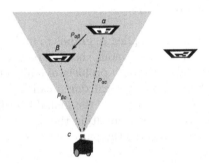

Fig. 1. Relative Pose Calculation - the camera can calculate the relative pose transformation between multiple markers by capturing them concurrently in its FOV

2.3 Marker Graph

The *marker graph* (based on the *calibration graph* introduced by Mavrinac et al. [12]) is a method of representing a set of markers as a topological map. It is a weighted, undirected graph $\mathcal{G}_M = (\mathcal{M}, E_M, \mathcal{W}_M)$, where $\mathcal{M}$ is the set of detected markers in the system, E_M is a set of edges, and $\mathcal{W}_M$ is the set of weights corresponding to the edges in E_M. The existence of an edge $\{\alpha, \beta\} \in E_M$ indicates that a relative pose transformation from marker α to marker β (or vice versa) is available.

Since it is trivial to invert a pose, the availability of $P_{\alpha\beta}$ implies availability of $P_{\beta\alpha}$. The edge weight $(w_{\alpha\beta} \in \mathbb{R}^+) \in \mathcal{W}_M$ is the estimation uncertainty of $P_{\alpha\beta}$.

A path $p = \langle \alpha, \ldots, \beta \rangle$ in $\mathcal{G}_M$, from node α to node β, represents a sequence of pose transformations which may be composed to yield $P_{\alpha\beta}$. If $p = \langle v_1, v_2, \ldots, v_n \rangle$,

$$P_{1,n} = P_{1,2} \circ P_{2,3} \circ \cdots \circ P_{n-1,n} \tag{3}$$

where $P_{i,j}$ is the pose transformation from v_i to v_j. If any $P_{i,j}$ is not available, $P_{i,j} = P_{j,i}^{-1}$. The aggregate error associated with this pose is

$$w_{1,n} = \sum_2^n w_{k-1,k} \tag{4}$$

which is the length of path p.

2.4   Localization Graph

The *localization graph* is essentially a marker graph that includes the camera c as an additional node. It is a weighted, undirected graph $\mathcal{G}_L = (\mathcal{L}, E_L, \mathcal{W}_L)$, where $\mathcal{L} = c \cup \mathcal{M}$, E_L is the set of edges between nodes $\mathcal{L}$, and $\mathcal{W}_L$ is, again, the set of associated edge weights. The localization graph is incrementally updated as the camera c moves through the environment. Note that $\mathcal{G}_L \supset \mathcal{G}_M$.

2.5   Shortest Path Algorithm

Shortest path algorithms can be applied to graphs to find the minimum topological path between two nodes. The famous shortest path algorithm by Dijkstra [6] solves the single-source shortest path problem of undirected graphs with non-negative edge weights. Since globally localizing a camera involves obtaining its pose with respect to a single source (i.e., the global coordinate system), Dijkstra's algorithm is appropriate for computing the shortest path of edges from said source to the camera. It returns the path yielding the minimum aggregate error defined in (4).

3   Global Localization

3.1   Assumptions

Internal Calibration and Pose Estimation. It is assumed that there exists some means by which a camera may estimate, from a single view, its relative three dimensional pose with respect to a calibration target of known structure [17], [2]. This normally implies that the camera is internally calibrated.

Marker Constraints. It is assumed that (i) if a marker $m \in \mathcal{M}$ is connected to an edge, it remains fixed in its position, and (ii) the selected reference node R corresponds to a marker that is available and detectable in the environment.

Map Updates. It is assumed that any operation that updates $\mathcal{G}_M$ simultaneously updates $\mathcal{G}_L$, and vice versa.

3.2   Problem Definition

The problem of global localization using computer vision is formalized as follows:

> Given a monocular camera c, a set of markers $\mathcal{M}$, and an arbitrary global
> reference frame $R \in \mathcal{M}$, find P_{cR} as c traverses the environment.

Let us further define a set of markers $\mathcal{V}$ which are in the camera's current FOV
(e.g., shaded area in Fig. 1). Then, it can be noted that P_{cR} may either be
obtained directly from R (when $R \in \mathcal{V}$) or indirectly from another marker $v \in \mathcal{V}$
(when $R \notin \mathcal{V}$), assuming there exists a path in $\mathcal{G}_L$ from c to R.

   It is additionally desirable to decrease the global error by using the path p
yielding the minimum aggregate error (as defined in (4)) for each estimated P_{cR}.

3.3   Self-localization Method

The method will be explained with the aid of an example. Suppose it is desired
to find the pose of a monocular camera c within an environment consisting of
markers $\mathcal{M} = \{W, X, Y, Z, R\}$, as shown in Fig. 2. In this case, R is selected as the
global reference frame, so the problem is to find P_{cR}. As mentioned previously,
there are two ways of finding P_{cR}: either directly through R (when R is in the
FOV) or indirectly through intermediate markers W, X, Y, Z (when R is not in
the FOV).

   As shown in Fig. 3, the localization graph is connected assuming that the
direct pose estimates in Fig. 2 are all available. Thus, the camera c can be
localized with respect to the common reference frame R using any of the markers
in the map.

   The minimum requirement to achieve global localization is that there must
exist a path from the current position of c to the reference frame R in $\mathcal{G}_L$.
Additional edges may yield shorter paths (i.e., pose compositions with lower
aggregate error). The positioning of the set of markers $\mathcal{M}$ should be chosen
appropriately. Note that there is no disadvantage, aside from additional effort
positioning and obtaining pose estimates, to increasing the size of $\mathcal{M}$.

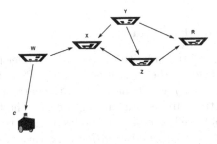

Fig. 2. Camera Pose Estimation - arrows indicate the direct pose estimate of one object
(camera or marker) with respect to another, where the pose of the object on the arrow's
tail is given with respect to that on the arrow's head

In this example, direct pose estimates P_{Wc}, P_{WX}, P_{YX}, P_{ZX}, P_{YZ}, P_{YR}, and P_{ZR} are obtained, along with their respective pose uncertainties. The availability of direct pose estimates is encapsulated in the localization graph of Fig. 3.

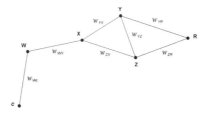

Fig. 3. Localization Graph for System in Fig. 2 - edge weights represent pose estimation uncertainty values

The solution is obtained through composition of the estimated poses, according to (3), where the shortest paths are computed using Dijkstra's algorithm or similar. As an example, suppose the shortest path from c to R in $\mathcal{G}_L$ is $\langle c, W, X, Y, Z, R \rangle$. Then,

$$P_{cR} = P_{Wc}^{-1} \circ P_{WX} \circ P_{YX}^{-1} \circ P_{YZ} \circ P_{ZR} \tag{5}$$

as per (3). The associated aggregate error is $w_{cR} = w_{Wc} + w_{WX} + w_{YX} + w_{YZ} + w_{ZR}$.

Map Updating. When there are multiple markers in the FOV, the relative poses between all possible pairs of markers in the frame are calculated and connecting edges (with associated weights) are created between them. If in a subsequent frame an edge is re-detected and is found to have a lower weight than the existing edge, its relative pose transformation and weight overwrite those corresponding to the existing edge. In this way, the edges of the graph maintain the minimum weights (and thus the relative poses with the least uncertainty) at all times.

3.4   Self-localization Algorithm

In the formal expression of the algorithm (Algorithm 1), let primed ($'$) variables represent calculations made in the current frame (e.g., P_{ij}' represents the relative pose between markers i and j as calculated from the current frame). Three previously undefined functions are used in this algorithm: The first, $calcw(\{\alpha, \beta\})$, calculates the weight of the edge connecting nodes α and β based on an appropriately derived error metric; the second, $con(\mathcal{G}, s, d)$, returns $True$ if there exists a path from s to d in $\mathcal{G}$; the third, $sp(\mathcal{G}, m, R)$, returns the shortest path p_s from m to R in $\mathcal{G}$ (using Dijkstra's algorithm) in the form defined in Section 2.3. The boolean variable n will be used to indicate that a map update has occurred.

Algorithm 1. Proposed Self-Localization Algorithm (Finding P'_{cR})

1: $\mathcal{M} \leftarrow \{R\}$
2: $E_M, \mathcal{W}_M, \mathcal{V} \leftarrow \emptyset$
3: $n \leftarrow False$
4: **loop**
5:     Capture frame
6:     **if** $\mathcal{V} \neq \emptyset$ **then**
7:         $\mathcal{M} \leftarrow \mathcal{M} \cup \mathcal{V}$
8:         **if** $|\mathcal{V}| > 1$ **then**
9:             **for all** $\{v_i, v_j\} \in \binom{\mathcal{V}}{2}$ **do**
10:                 $P'_{ij} \leftarrow P'_{ic} \circ P'^{-1}_{jc}$
11:                 $P'_{ji} \leftarrow P'^{-1}_{ij}$
12:                 **if** $\{v_i, v_j\} \notin E_M$ **then**
13:                     $E_M \leftarrow E_M \cup \{v_i, v_j\}$
14:                     $w_{ij}, w_{ji} \leftarrow \infty$
15:                     $\mathcal{W}_M \leftarrow \mathcal{W}_M \cup w_{ij}, w_{ji}$
16:                 **end if**
17:                 **if** $calcw'(\{v_i, v_j\}) < w_{ij}$ **then**
18:                     $w_{ij}, w_{ji} \leftarrow calcw'(\{v_i, v_j\})$
19:                     $P_{ij} \leftarrow P'_{ij}$
20:                     $P_{ji} \leftarrow P'_{ji}$
21:                     $n \leftarrow True$
22:                 **end if**
23:             **end for**
24:             **if** $n = True$ **then**
25:                 **for all** $\{m \in \mathcal{M} \mid con(\mathcal{G}_M, m, R)\}$ **do**
26:                     $p_s \leftarrow sp(\mathcal{G}_M, m, R)$
27:                     $P_{mR} \leftarrow P_{p_{s,1}, p_{s,2}}$
28:                     $w_{mR} \leftarrow w_{p_{s,1}, p_{s,2}}$
29:                     **for** $k = 2 \rightarrow |p_s| - 1$ **do**
30:                         $P_{mR} \leftarrow P_{mR} \circ P_{p_{s,k}, p_{s,k+1}}$
31:                         $w_{mR} \leftarrow w_{mR} + w_{p_{s,k}, p_{s,k+1}}$
32:                     **end for**
33:                 **end for**
34:             **end if**
35:         **end if**
36:         **if** $R \in \mathcal{V}$ **then**
37:             $P'_{cR} = P'^{-1}_{Rc}$
38:         **else if** $\exists \{v \in \mathcal{V} \mid con(\mathcal{G}_M, v, R)\}$ **then**
39:             $v_m \leftarrow \underset{v \in \mathcal{V}}{\operatorname{argmin}}(calcw'(\{v, c\}) + w_{vR})$
40:             $P'_{cR} \leftarrow P'^{-1}_{v_m c} \circ P_{v_m R}$
41:         **end if**
42:     **end if**
43:     $n = False$
44: **end loop**

---

4   Experimental Results

An experiment was performed in an indoor environment using an internally calibrated ICube NS4133BU Camera, a set of markers, a marker detection algorithm,
and the proposed self-localization algorithm. The purpose of the experiment is
to demonstrate the proposed algorithm's performance in reducing global error.

The metric used for quantifying the edge weights of the localization graph
is based on the findings of Schweighofer and Pinz [13]. In their paper, they
demonstrate that pose ambiguity of planar targets is affected by the change in
position and/or orientation of the target in the scene. For instance, the pose
ambiguity was found to increase with the distance between the camera and
the target. Based on this, a simple function $f(d)$, where d is the perpendicular
distance between the camera and a marker, can be used as a metric for the edge
weights. When the edge is defined by two markers, the function is applied to
each marker individually and the two results are averaged to obtain the weight
of the connecting edge.

The general procedure is outlined as follows:

- The markers are attached to a wall in the configuration shown in Fig. 4(a).
- The camera is traversed through the room (facing the markers throughout)
  while the marker detection and self-localization algorithms are running.
- A map with reference R is built and updated online by the self-localization
  algorithm (refer to Fig. 4(b)).
- The camera is positioned such that only marker Y is visible in its FOV.
- From this known position, the localization accuracy was compared between
  the shortest path obtained from our algorithm and the 35 other possible
  (simple) paths between markers Y and R.

Three types of functions for edge weights were tested on the map: linear ($f(d) = d$), quadratic ($f(d) = d^2$), and exponential ($f(d) = 3^d - 1$). Each function was
applied to the 36 possible paths from Y to R. In all the cases, the shortest path
corresponding to the minimum aggregate error (obtained from our algorithm)

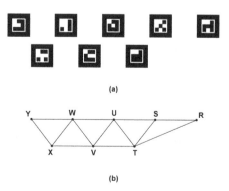

(a)

(b)

Fig. 4. Experimental Map - (a) arrangement of markers in the environment, (b) topological representation of the map

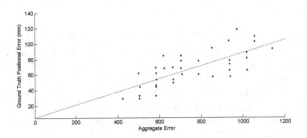

Fig. 5. Ground Truth vs. Aggregate Error - finding a correlation using exponential edge weight function $f(d) = 50^d - 1$

yielded the lowest ground truth positional error compared to the 35 other paths. The average, minimum, and maximum ground truth errors for the 36 paths were identical for all three functions: 67.9, 29.1, and 117.8 mm, respectively. Furthermore, it was observed that compared to the other two, the exponential function showed the best correlation between the aggregate error and the ground truth positional error. Fig. 5 shows this correlation in the form of a line of best fit with correlation coefficient $R \approx 0.74$, using the exponential function $f(d) = 50^d - 1$. The bottom left-most data point in this figure graphically shows how the minimum aggregate error corresponds to the minimum ground truth positional error of the 36 paths for the given metric.

The experiment was repeated using the same exponential error function, except the three lower markers were moved closer to the camera and tilted horizontally. In this case, the minimum ground truth error corresponded to the *third* least aggregate error and there was a *negative* correlation of $R \approx 0.47$ between the aggregate and ground truth errors. This indicates that this particular error function may not be suitable for all configurations of markers.

5   Conclusion

A proposed topological mapping approach is applied to a self-localization system to reduce global error and eliminate the need for an offline map-building mode. The map is incrementally built and updated as the camera moves through the environment. A shortest path algorithm is applied to the map to find the path of least aggregate error based on an appropriate edge weight metric. Experiments were done with online map-building and using a weight metric based on the perpendicular distance between the camera and each marker. The results demonstrate the effectiveness of the system in reducing global error but emphasize the importance of deriving an appropriate error metric for the edge weights.

References

1. Anjum, M., Park, J., Hwang, W., il Kwon, H., Hyeon Kim, J., Lee, C., Soo Kim, K., il Danr Cho, D.: Sensor data fusion using unscented kalman filter for accurate localization of mobile robots. In: 2010 International Conference on Control Automation and Systems (ICCAS), pp. 947–952 (October 2010)
2. Ansar, A., Daniilidis, K.: Linear pose estimation from points or lines. IEEE Transactions on Pattern Analysis and Machine Intelligence 25(5), 578–589 (2003)
3. Brand, M., Antone, M., Teller, S.: Spectral Solution of Large-Scale Extrinsic Camera Calibration as a Graph Embedding Problem. In: Pajdla, T., Matas, J(G.) (eds.) ECCV 2004. LNCS, vol. 3022, pp. 262–273. Springer, Heidelberg (2004)
4. Chen, X., Li, R., Wang, X., Tian, Y., Huang, Q.: A novel artificial landmark for monocular global visual localization of indoor robots. In: 2010 International Conference on Mechatronics and Automation (ICMA), pp. 1314–1319 (August 2010)
5. Choi, H., Kim, D.Y., Hwang, J.P., Kim, E., Kim, Y.O.: Cv-slam using ceiling boundary. In: 2010 the 5th IEEE Conference on Industrial Electronics and Applications (ICIEA), pp. 228–233 (June 2010)
6. Dijkstra, E.W.: A note on two problems in connexion with graphs. Numerische Mathematik 1(1), 269–271 (1959)
7. Fiala, M.: Artag, a fiducial marker system using digital techniques. In: IEEE Computer Society Conference on Computer Vision and Pattern Recognition, CVPR 2005, vol. 2, pp. 590–596 (June 2005)
8. Hwang, S.Y., Park, J.T., Song, J.B.: Autonomous navigation of a mobile robot using an upward-looking camera and sonar sensors. In: 2010 IEEE Workshop on Advanced Robotics and its Social Impacts (ARSO), pp. 40–45 (October 2010)
9. Kitanov, A., Bisevac, S., Petrovic, I.: Mobile robot self-localization in complex indoor environments using monocular vision and 3d model. In: 2007 IEEE/ASME International Conference on Advanced Intelligent Mechatronics, pp. 1–6 (September 2007)
10. Lim, H., Lee, Y.S.: Real-time single camera slam using fiducial markers. In: ICCAS-SICE, pp. 177–182 (August 2009)
11. Lv, Q., Zhou, W., Liu, J.: Realization of odometry system using monocular vision. In: 2006 International Conference on Computational Intelligence and Security, vol. 2, pp. 1841–1844 (Novemebr 2006)
12. Mavrinac, A., Chen, X., Tepe, K.: An automatic calibration method for stereo-based 3d distributed smart camera networks. Computer Vision and Image Understanding 114(8), 952–962 (2010)
13. Schweighofer, G., Pinz, A.: Robust pose estimation from a planar target. IEEE Transactions on Pattern Analysis and Machine Intelligence 28(12), 2024–2030 (2006)
14. Sharp, G., Lee, S., Wehe, D.: Multiview registration of 3d scenes by minimizing error between coordinate frames. IEEE Transactions on Pattern Analysis and Machine Intelligence 26(8), 1037–1050 (2004)
15. Van Hamme, D., Veelaert, P., Philips, W.: Robust monocular visual odometry by uncertainty voting. In: 2011 IEEE Intelligent Vehicles Symposium (IV), pp. 643–647 (June 2011)
16. Yu, Y., Pradalier, C., Zong, G.: Appearance-based monocular visual odometry for ground vehicles. In: 2011 IEEE/ASME International Conference on Advanced Intelligent Mechatronics (AIM), pp. 862–867 (July 2011)
17. Zhang, Z.: A flexible new technique for camera calibration. IEEE Transactions on Pattern Analysis and Machine Intelligence 22(11), 1330–1334 (2000)

Sensor Classification Methods Applied to Robotics

Miguel F.M. Lima[1] and J.A. Tenreiro Machado[2]

[1] CI&DETS and Dept. of Electrical Engineering, School of Technology,
Polytechnic Institute of Viseu, Campus Politécnico de Repeses, 3504–510, Viseu, Portugal
lima@mail.estv.ipv.pt
[2] Dept. of Electrical Engineering, Institute of Engineering,
Polytechnic Institute of Porto, Rua de S. Tomé, 4200–072, Porto, Portugal
jtm@isep.ipp.pt

Abstract. The data obtained from the robotic instrumentation can be redundant due to the multiplicity of sensors. Additionally, the study of the sensor's data can help in optimization the design of the manipulators. In this line of thought, this paper applies two distinct methods for classification of sensors used in robotics. One of the adopted methods leads to arrange the robotic signals in terms of identical spectrum behavior. The other method is the multidimensional scaling technique applied to the correlation of the signals in the time domain. Both methods conduct to similar results, obtaining three groups of signals: the group of "positions", the group of "currents" and the group of "forces, torques and accelerations".

1 Introduction

The robotic manipulators have several sensors and actuators in order to carry out the desired movements. Due to the multiplicity of sensors, the data obtained can be redundant because the same type of information may be seen by two or more sensors. Due to the price of the sensors, this aspect can be considered in order to reduce the cost of the system. On the other hand, the placement of the sensors is an important issue in order to obtain the suitable signals of the vibration phenomenon. Moreover, the study of these issues can help in the design optimization of the acquisition system. In this line of thought a sensor classification scheme is presented.

Several authors have addressed the subject of the sensor classification scheme. White [1] presents a flexible and comprehensive categorizing scheme that is useful for describing and comparing sensors. The author organizes the sensors according to several aspects: measurands, technological aspects, detection means, conversion phenomena, sensor materials and fields of application. Michahelles and Schiele [2] systematize the use of sensor technology. They identified several dimensions of sensing that represent the sensing goals for physical interaction. A conceptual framework is introduced that allows categorizing existing sensors and evaluates their utility in various applications.

Today's technology offers a wide variety of sensors. In order to use all the data from the diversity of sensors a framework of integration is needed. Sensor fusion,

C.-Y. Su, S. Rakheja, H. Liu (Eds.): ICIRA 2012, Part III, LNAI 7508, pp. 23–31, 2012.
© Springer-Verlag Berlin Heidelberg 2012

fuzzy logic, and neural networks are often mentioned when dealing with problem of combing information from several sensors to get a more general picture of a given situation. The study of data fusion has been receiving considerable attention [3, 4]. A survey of the state of the art in sensor fusion for robotics can be found in [5]. Henderson and Shilcrat [6] introduced the concept of logic sensor that defines an abstract specification of the sensors to integrate in a multisensor system.

The recent developments of micro electro mechanical sensors (MEMS), with unwired communication capabilities, allow a sensor network with interesting capacity. This technology was applied in several applications [7], including robotics. Cheekiralla and Engels [8] proposed a classification of the unwired sensor networks according to its functionalities and properties.

This work presents a development of a sensor classification scheme using two distinct statistical methods. One is based on the trendlines slopes of frequency spectrum of the signals. The other uses the multidimensional scaling technique (MDS) applied to the signals correlations.

Bearing these ideas in mind, this chapter is organized as follows. Section 2 describes briefly the robotic system enhanced with the instrumentation setup. Section 3 shows the experimental results. Finally, section 4 draws the main conclusions and points out future work.

2   Experimental Platform

The developed experimental platform has two main parts: the hardware and the software components. The hardware architecture is shown in Fig. 1 (left). Essentially it is made up of a robot manipulator (Scorbot ERVII from Eshed Robotec), a personal computer, and an interface electronic system.

The interface box is inserted between the robot arm and the robot controller, in order to acquire the internal robot signals; nevertheless, the interface captures also external signals, such as those arising from accelerometers and force/torque sensors.

The software package runs in a Pentium 4, 3.0 GHz PC and, from the user's point of view, consists of two applications: the acquisition application and the analysis package. The acquisition application is a real time program for acquiring and recording the robot signals.

After the real time data acquisition, the analysis package processes the data off-line in two phases, namely, pre-processing and processing. The preprocessing phase consists of the signal selection in time, and their synchronization and truncation. The processing stage implements several algorithms for signal processing such as the auto and cross correlation, Fourier transform (FT), window Fourier transform, time synchronization, etc.

In the experiments a flexible link is used, consisting of a long and round flexible steel rod clamped to the end-effector of the manipulator. In order to analyze the impact phenomena in different situations two types of beams are adopted: a thin and a gross rod. The robot motion is programmed in a way such that the rods move against a rigid surface. Figure 1 (right) depicts the robot with the flexible link and the impact surface.

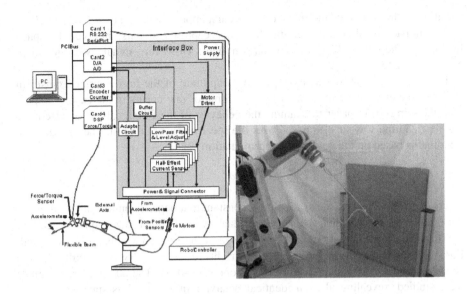

Fig. 1. The hardware: block diagram of the architecture (left) and the steel rod impact against a rigid surface (right)

During the motion of the manipulator the clamped rod is moved by the robot against a rigid surface. An impact occurs and several signals are recorded with a sampling frequency of $f_s = 500$ Hz. The signals come from several sensors, such as accelerometers $\{A_1, A_2\}$, force $\{F_x, F_y, F_z\}$ and torque $\{M_x, M_y, M_z\}$ sensor, position encoders $\{P_1, P_2, P_3, P_4, P_5\}$, and current sensors $\{I_1, I_2, I_3, I_4, I_5\}$.

In order to have a wide set of signals captured during the impact of the rods against the vertical screen thirteen distinct trajectories were defined. For each trajectory the motion of the robot begins in one point, moves against the surface and returns to the initial point. A parabolic profile was used for the trajectories.

Several sets of signals are captured corresponding to the cases: (*i*) without impact, (*ii*) the impact of the rod on a gross screen and (*iii*) the impact of the rod on a thin screen, using either the thin, or the gross rod.

3   Experimental Results

According to the platform described in Section 2 a set of experiments is developed. Based on the signals captured from the robot this section presents several results obtained both in the time and frequency domains.

3.1   Analysis of the Spectrum Trendlines Slopes

Figure 2 (left) shows the electrical currents $\{I_1, I_2, I_3, I_4, I_5\}$ of the robot's axes motors obtained for thin rod during one trajectory. The signals present clearly a strong variation at the instant of the impact that occurs, approximately, at $t = 3$ s. The effect of the impact is also reflected in the other captured signals, but due to space limitations these variables are not shown here. However, signals with identical behavior can be seen in [9].

Figure 2 (right) shows, as example, the amplitude of the Fast Fourier Transform (FFT) of the electrical current I_3 of the axis 3 motor that occurs in the case of impact with the thin rod. In order to examine the behavior of the FT signals, in a systematic way, a trendline was superimposed over the spectrum over, at least, one decade. The trendline is based on the power law approximation [9].

$$\left| F\left\{ f(t) \right\} \right| \approx c \omega^m \tag{1}$$

where F is the FT of the signal, $c \in \Re$ is a constant that depends on the amplitude, ω is the frequency, and $m \in \Re$ is the slope. For each type of signal, the frequency interval was defined approximately in the middle range of the frequency content of the signal. For the spectrum shown in Figure 2 (right) a trendline was calculated, and superimposed to the signal (case ii), with slope $m = -1.31$. The others current signals were studied, revealing also an identical behavior in terms of its spectrum spread, both under impact and no impact conditions, either for the thin rod or the gross rod. The spectrum was approximated by trendlines in a frequency range larger than one decade.

According to the robot manufacturer specifications [10] the loop control of the robot has a cycle time of $t_c = 10$ ms. This fact is observed approximately at the fundamental ($f_c = 100$ Hz) and multiple harmonics in all spectra of motor currents (see Fig. 2 right).

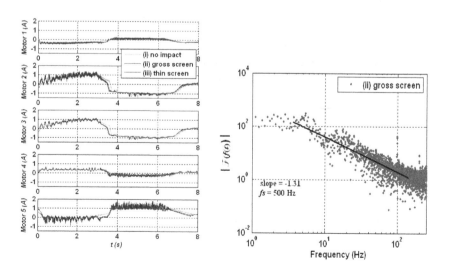

Fig. 2. Electrical currents of the robot's axes motors obtained for thin rod: $\{I_1, I_2, I_3, I_4, I_5\}$ (left); Spectrum of I_3 (right)

The positions, forces, torques and accelerations signals were studied also for the distinct test conditions, namely: impact, no impact, thin rod and gross rod. Their FFT amplitudes revealed also an identical behavior in terms of its spectrum spread for the tested conditions.

Based on the several values of the spectrum trendlines slopes several statistics can be performed. During each trajectory of the robot eighteen signals were captured. For each trajectory there are three cases: (*i*) without impact, (*ii*) the impact of the rod on a gross screen, and (*iii*) the impact of the rod on a thin screen. As referred before, thirteen trajectories were defined. Additionally, the same trajectories were executed with the thin rod and with the gross rod. In this work we present the results for the gross rod, which leads to a population of 702 slope values.

A box plot provides a visual summary of many important aspects of a data distribution. It indicates the median, upper and lower quartile, upper and lower adjacent values (whiskers), and the outlier individual points. Figure 3 shows a box plot of the spectrum trendlines slopes for the three cases of the gross rod impact. Moreover, Fig. 4 depicts the respective interquartile range (IQR) versus the median. The IQR is obtained by subtracting the lower (first) quartile value from the upper (third) quartile value. The IQR is a robust way of describing the dispersion of the data.

Based on the inter-distances of the signals, from Fig. 4 three groups of signals can be defined. The rounded rectangles depicted in the chart represent these groups. The forces $\{F_x, F_y, F_z\}$, moments $\{M_x, M_y, M_z\}$, accelerations $\{A_1, A_2\}$, and I_3 signals form one group. A deeper insight into the nature of this feature must be envisaged to understand the behavior of the I_3 signal. The positions $\{P_1, P_2, P_3, P_4, P_5\}$ signals are located on the left side of the Fig. 4. Finally, the other electrical currents $\{I_1, I_2, I_4, I_5\}$ are situated in the middle of the chart and near each other.

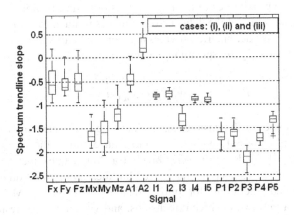

Fig. 3. Statistics of spectrum trendlines slopes for all the cases (*i, ii, iii*) using the gross rod

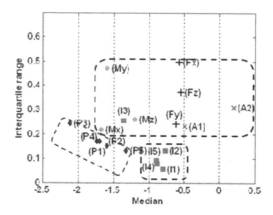

Fig. 4. IQR *versus* median for all the cases (*i, ii, iii*) using the gross rod

3.2   MDS Analysis

The MDS has its origins in psychometrics and psychophysics where is used as a tool for perceptual and cognitive modeling. From the beginning MDS has been applied in many fields, such as psychology, sociology, anthropology, economy, educational research, etc. In last decades this technique has been applied also in others areas, including computational chemistry [11], machine learning [12], concept maps [13] and wireless network sensors [14].

MDS is a generic name for a family of algorithms that construct a configuration of points in a low dimensional space from information about inter-point distances measured in high dimensional space. The new geometrical configuration of points, which preserves the proximities of the high dimensional space, allows gaining insight in the underlying structure of the data and often makes it much easier to understand.

The Minkowski distance metric provides a general way to specify the distance $d_{i,j}$, between the objects i and j, for quantitative data in a multidimensional space:

$$d_{ij} = \left(\sum_{k=1}^{m} w_k \left| x_{ik} - x_{jk} \right|^r \right)^{1/r} \tag{2}$$

where m is the number of dimensions, x_{ik} is the value of dimension k for object i and w_k is a weight. For $w_k = 1$, with $r = 2$, the metric equals the Euclidian distance metric, while $r = 1$ leads to the city-block (or Manhattan) metric. In practice, normally the Euclidian distance metric is used but there are several others definitions that can be applied, including for binary data [15]. Typically MDS is used to transform the data into two or three dimensions, and visualizing the result to uncover hidden structure in the data.

In practice several indices can be used to evaluate the relationship between the signals, including statistical, entropy and information theory approaches. In this work several indices are calculated, such as correlation, the mutual information and the entropy. The tests developed show that the correlation index seems to be more appropriate when comparing with the others. Therefore, in order to reveal some hypothetical hidden relationships between the signals the MDS technique is used with the signals correlations. Several metric and non-metric scaling MDS criteria were tested. The Sammon [16] metric scaling criterion revealed good results for the correlation. This criterion gives weight to small distances, which helps to detect clusters. Consequently, the Sammon criterion is adopted in this work.

In Fig. 5 is shown the 2D (left) and 3D (right) locus of sensor positioning based on the correlation measure between the signals for the case (*i*) using the gross rod. Three groups of signals can be defined. The ellipses depicted in the chart represent two of these groups. The positions $\{P_1, P_2, P_3, P_4, P_5\}$ signals are located close to each other. The electrical currents $\{I_1, I_2, I_3, I_4, I_5\}$ are situated on the left of the chart and near each other. Finally, the remaining signals form a big group composed by the forces $\{F_x, F_y, F_z\}$, moments $\{M_x, M_y, M_z\}$ and the accelerations $\{A_1, A_2\}$ situated at

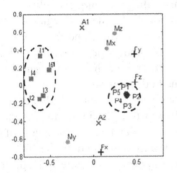 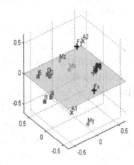

Fig. 5. Locus of sensor positioning based on the correlation measure between the signals for the case (*i*) using the gross rod: 2D (left); 3D (right)

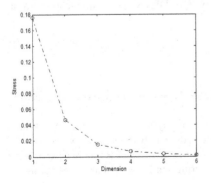 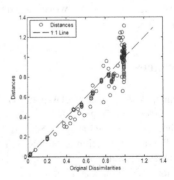

Fig. 6. Evaluation of MDS results based on correlation: Stress test (left); Shepard plot (right)

scattered positions away from each other. Fig. 6 shows two tests developed to evaluate the consistency of the results obtained by MDS analysis. The value of the stress function *versus* the dimension is shown in Fig. 6 (left), which allows the estimation of the adequate p–dimension. An "elbow" occurs at dimension three for a low value of stress, which corresponds to a substantial improvement in fit. Additionally, the Shepard plot (Fig. 6 right) shows the fitting of the 3D configuration distances to the dissimilarities.

4   Conclusion

In this work an experimental study was conducted to investigate several robot signals. Two methodologies were proposed for sensor classification. One of the adopted methodologies leads to arrange the robotic signals in terms of identical spectrum behavior, obtaining the groups of signals: the group of "positions", the group of "currents" and the group of "forces, torques and accelerations". The other methodology is based on the multidimensional scaling technique applied to the correlation of the signals in the time domain. Although the methodologies used for classification are distinct and applied to different domains (time and frequency), the results obtained are similar. Both adopted methodologies revealed hidden relationships between the robotic signals and leads to arrange them in the same three groups. This fact can reveal the adequacy of the methods proposed.

The results merit a deeper investigation as they give rise to new valuable concepts towards instrument control applications. In this line of thought, in future, we plan to pursue several research directions to help us further understand the behavior of the signals. In this stage of the work, the classification presented based on the MDS was obtained for an experiment corresponding to one trajectory. In future this approach should be applied for all the thirteen trajectories referred before. Additionally, the methodologies used in this work should be applied to others signals of different nature.

Acknowledgment. This work is supported by CI&DETS and Fundação para a Ciência e Tecnologia (FCT).

References

1. White, R.M.: A sensor classification scheme. IEEE Trans. on Ultrasonics, Ferroelectrics and Frequency Control 34(2), 124–126 (1987)
2. Michahelles, F., Schiele, B.: Sensing opportunities for physical interaction. In: Workshop on Physical Interaction of Mobile HCI Conference, Udine, Italy (September 2003)
3. Esteban, J., Starr, A., Willetts, R., Hannah, P., Bryanston-Cross, P.: A review of data fusion models and architectures: towards engineering guidelines. Neural Computing & Applications 14(4), 273–281 (2005)
4. Luo, R., Kay, M.: A tutorial on multisensor integration and fusion. In: IEEE 16th Annual Conf. of Industrial Electronics Society, pp. 707–722 (1990)

5. Hackett, J., Shah, M.: Multi-sensor fusion: a perspective. In: Proc. IEEE Int. Conf. on Robotics & Automation, pp. 1324–1330 (1990)
6. Henderson, T., Shilcrat, E.E.: Logical sensor systems. J. of Robotic Systems 1(2), 169–193 (1984)
7. Arampatzis, T., Manesis, S.: A Survey of Applications of Wireless Sensors and Wireless Sensor Networks. In: Proc. IEEE Int. Symp. on Intelligent Control, pp. 719–724 (2005)
8. Cheekiralla, S., Engels, W.: A functional taxonomy of wireless sensor network devices. In: 2nd International Conference on Broadband Networks IEEE, vol. 2, pp. 949–956 (2005), doi:10.1109/ICBN.2005.1589707
9. Lima, M., Machado, J., Crisóstomo, M.: Experimental Signal Analysis of Robot Impacts in a Fractional Calculus Perspective. Journal of Advanced Computational Intelligence and Intelligent Informatics 11(9), 1079–1085 (2007)
10. Robotec, E.: Scorbot ER VII, User's Manual, Eshed Robotec (1996) ISBN 9652910333
11. Glunt, W., Hayden, T.L., Raydan, M.: Molecular conformation from distance matrices. J. Computational Chemistry 14, 114–120 (1993)
12. Tenenbaum, J., de Silva, V., Langford, J.: A global geometric framework for nonlinear dimensionality reduction. Science 290(5500), 2319–2323 (2000)
13. Martinez–Torres, M., BarreroGarcia, F., ToralMarin, S., Gallardo, S.: A Digital Signal Processing Teaching Methodology Using Concept-Mapping Techniques. IEEE Transactions on Education 48(3), 422–429 (2005), doi:10.1109/TE.2005.849737
14. Mao, G., Fidan, B.: Localization Algorithms and Strategies for Wireless Sensor Networks. Igi-Global (2009) (ebook) ISBN 978-1-60566-397-5
15. Cox, T., Cox, M.: Multidimensional scaling, 2nd edn. Chapman & Hall/CRC (2001) ISBN 1584880945
16. Sammon, J.: A nonlinear mapping for data structure analysis. IEEE Trans. Computers C-18(5), 401–409 (1969)

Design and Simulation of Bio-inspired Flexible Tactile Sensor for Prosthesis

Guanhao Liang, Deqing Mei[*], Yancheng Wang, Yu Dai, and Zichen Chen

The State Key Lab of Fluid Power Transmission and Control,
Department of Mechanical Engineering,
Zhejiang University, Hangzhou, Zhejiang, 310027, P.R. China
medqmei@zju.edu.cn

Abstract. In human hand skin, there are four kinds of mechanoreceptors with different sensing mechanisms to detect both gentle touch and high pressure. In this study, an integrated bio-inspired tactile sensor array, which consists of a capacitive layer and a pressure-sensitive-rubber (PSR) based layer, is designed for prosthesis application. The capacitive layer can detect the low-pressure, while the PSR-based layer is designed to detect the high-pressure. The capacitive layer and PSR-based layer are integrated together with space resolution of 2 mm and 1 mm, respectively. For the designed sensor array, the finite element analysis (FEA) is conducted to study the effects of the dimensions of polyimide in capacitive layer and the Young's modulus of the conductive rubber in PSR-based layer on the sensing performance. The simulation results show that the developed bio-tactile sensor array is highly sensitive in both low and high pressure range.

Keywords: Bio-inspired, Tactile Sensor, Capacitive, Pressure-sensitive-rubber (PSR).

1 Introduction

The fields of the intelligent prosthesis and micro-sensors have witnessed tremendous growth and progress in bio-mechatronics during the past decades. The prosthesis mounted with many types of sensors has been developed to improve the amputees' lives. To detect external environmental information, many sensors have been presented and integrated into the prosthesis mechanism. But still now, many problems need to be solved. For example, in order to obtain accurate tactile information when prosthesis is contacting with the objects, the tactile sensor with high sensitivity and flexibility is needed.

For tactile sensor, there exist several sensing mechanisms, such as resistive, capacitive, piezoelectric, and organic field-effect transistors (OFETs) sensor, etc [1-6].

Generally, human hand tactile perception can be divided into two types: the gentle touch with the pressure < 10 kPa and the objective manipulation with the pressure range from 10 to 100 kPa [7]. High sensitivity and wide sensing range are two design

---

[*] Corresponding author.

C.-Y. Su, S. Rakheja, H. Liu (Eds.): ICIRA 2012, Part III, LNAI 7508, pp. 32–41, 2012.

criterions to evaluate the performance of the tactile sensors. At present, most of the developed tactile sensors cannot detect the pressure in a wide range with high sensitivity. Therefore, according to the haptic mechanism of human skin, this study will propose an idea that two kinds of tactile sensing elements will be integrated into one sensing element. One kind of the element is high sensitive and aimed at low-pressure sensing in small measuring range. The other one is relatively low sensitive and aimed at high-pressure sensing in large measuring range. In this study, a capacitive layer is designed for low-pressure sensing, and a pressure-sensitive-rubber (PSR) based layer is designed for high-pressure sensing. Then, the capacitive layer and the PSR-based layer will compose a two-layer tactile sensor array. The ratio of space resolution of the capacitive layer and PSR based layer is 2:1 according to the characteristics of the human skin. In order to make each layer of the sensors detect the pressure in their own measuring range, the finite element analysis will be done to optimize the dimension of the polyimide in the capacitive layer and the Young's modulus of the conductive rubber in the PSR-based layer. The optimized sensor array shows high sensitivity in a wide pressure range by simulation.

2   Design of the Tactile Sensor

In the past decades, many researchers have designed many tactile sensors based on the characteristics of human skin. However, many of the preceding studies mimic little characteristics from human skin. Aiming to improve the performance of the bio-inspired tactile sensor, a novel design idea of the tactile sensor will be proposed.

2.1   Haptic Mechanism of Human Skin

The human skin consists of three layers: epidermis, dermis and subcutanea. The subcutanea is mainly composed of thick fat that can absorb sudden shocks. The dermis is a soft layer outside of the subcutanea and the outer layer is epidemis which is a hardest one in the three layers, aiming at protecting the tissues beneath and improving the pressure sensing performance.

There are four mechanoreceptors that response to pressure within the dermis layer and the subcutanea layer. They are Meissner corpusde, Pacinian corpusde, Ruffini organ and Merkel disks. Meissner corpusde locate superficially in the dermis, so they are sensitive to vibration and gentle touch. Pacinian corpusde, which are most sensitive to vibration, locate deep into the subcutanea. The above two mechanoreceptors (Meissner corpusde and Pacinian corpusde) are sensitive to dynamic force and gentle touch while the Ruffini organs and Merkel disks are sensitive to static force. The Merkel disks locate superficially in dermis and can sense pressure which is normal to the skin, but the Ruffini organs are sensitive only when the skin is stretched.

Table 1 has figured out the receptive field and distribution density of the four mechanoreceptors. From Table 1, it can be seen that the mechanoreceptors which occupy larger receptive field have lower distribution density and locate deeper. Thus, when designing tactile sensor, the layer located deeper should have lower distribution density.

Table 1. Characteristics of the skin mechanoreceptors [9]

Receptor	Receptive Field (mm^2)	Receptors per cm^2
Pacinian corpusde	10–1000	21
Meissner corpusde	1–100	140
Ruffini organ	10–500	49
Merkel disks	2–100	70

2.2   Structural Design of Tactile Sensor

According to the haptic mechanism of human skin, the Pacinian corpusde, i.e. the mechanoreceptors which are most sensitive to vibration and gentle touch, are located deep in the human skin. On the contrary, the Merkel disks, which are sensitive to the static or high pressure, locate superficially. The distribution density of the Pacinian corpusde and the Merkel disks is 21 and 70 per cm^2, respectively, as shown in Table 1. Thus, the ratio of the space resolution of the Pacinian corpusde and the Merkel disks can be calculated as follows:

$$\text{ratio of the space resolution} = \frac{\sqrt{70}}{\sqrt{21}} = 1.823:1 \tag{1}$$

By emulating the Pacinian corpusde and the Merkel disks, the tactile sensors should consist of a low-pressure sensing layer and a high-pressure sensing layer, the ratio of whose space resolution is configured as 2:1. The two layers are designed as capacitive layer and pressure-sensitive-rubber (PSR) based layer, respectively. The capacitive layer is composed of capacitance array aiming at low-pressure sensing with the space resolution of 2 mm, while the PSR-based layer is composed of conductive rubber aiming at high-pressure sensing with space resolution of 1 mm. The capacitive layer should be placed beneath the PSR-based layer. The total view of one element of the sensor is shown in Fig. 1(a), and the detailed structure of the sensor from bottom to top is the PDMS substrate, the capacitive layer, the PSR-based layer and the PDMS bump.

Fig. 1(b) shows the structure of the capacitive layer. The two copper plates are fabricated on polyimide thin film, forming a capacitance. And a rectangle-hollowed PDMS supporter is sandwiched between the two plates, forming a rectangle air gap which serves as the dielectric layer of the capacitance. The thickness of the air gap is 15 μm. The whole capacitive layer gets support from the PDMS substrate with 100 μm in thickness.

Fig. 1(c) shows the structure of the PSR-based layer, the thickness of which is 100 μm. The upper electrodes and the lower electrodes are fabricated on the upper side and the lower side of a polyimide thin film, respectively, forming an orthogonal matrix circuit. All the electrodes will be fabricated directly on the polyimide by micro contact printing (μCP) [10], by which the electrodes can be designed smaller and can be more complicated. Then, the cylinder-shaped conductive rubbers are laminated on the electrodes. And a layer of PDMS protector surrounding the conductive rubber is fabricated in order to protect the conductive rubber.

The PDMS bump is used to concentrate stress on the pressure sensing layers, which can make the sensor easy to be deformed.

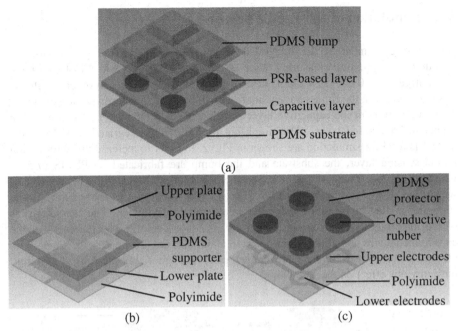

Fig. 1. Structure of the tactile sensor. (a) Total view of the tactile sensor. (b) Structure of the capacitive layer. (c) Structure of the PSR-based layer.

2.3   Working Principle of the Tactile Sensor

When a low-pressure is applied normal to the surface of the PDMS bump, the change of the strain of the capacitive layer is much larger than that of the PSR-based layer, so the capacitive can keep high sensitivity during the low-pressure sensing. The air gap in capacitive layer will be compressed (as shown in Fig. 3), resulting in the distance decrease between the two capacitance plates. Thus, the capacity will increase. The variation of the capacity is related to the amplitude of the pressure applied. By detecting the variation of the capacity, the pressure applied can be obtained.

When a high-pressure is applied, the air gap in the capacitive layer has been compressed too much and it is difficult to continue being compressed. At this time, the conductive rubber in PSR-based layer shows its advantage of high-pressure sensing, representing higher sensitivity than the capacitive layer. The resistance of the conductive rubber decreases when it deforms due to the applied pressure. By detecting the variation of the resistance, the pressure applied can be obtained.

Actually, the boundary of low-pressure and high-pressure is vague. So in the design process of the tactile sensor, we need to make definition of the pressure range. From Ref. [12], pressure lower than 10 kPa is comparable to gentle touch of the human skin. However, for tactile sensor, taking 0 – 10 kPa as low-pressure would be inappropriate for the materials we used are far harder than the human skin. So we define 0 – 35 kPa (about 0.05 N on a 2 mm × 2 mm sensing element) as low-pressure and 35 kPa – 1400 kPa (about 2 N on a 2 mm × 2 mm sensing element) as high pressure.

3   Simulation of the Tactile Sensor

One sensing element of the integrated sensor will be taken out to optimize its structure. The pressure measuring range of the capacitive layer and PSR based layer are configured as 0 – 35 kPa and 35 kPa – 1400 kPa, respectively. In order to achieve this configuration, the finite element analysis will be done to determine the dimension of the polyimide in the capacitive layer and the Young's modulus of the conductive rubber in PSR based layer. The simplified profile of the integrated sensor and the materials used for simulation are shown in Fig. 2. In order to increase the deformation of the sensing layer, the substrate and the bump are fabricated by PDMS (7.5:1), which has higher Young's modulus, and the protector is fabricated by PDMS (20:1), which has lower Young's modulus. The PDMS used in the fabrication of the supporter is 10:1 composition, which is a common configuration. The characteristics of the materials used in the simulation are listed in Table 2. The thickness of the capacitance plates and all the electrodes are about 200 nm, to simplify the simulation, all the electrodes including the capacitance plates are ignored because it is too thin to have obvious effect on the simulation.

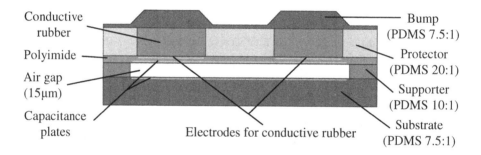

Fig. 2. Simplified profile of the integrated sensor

Table 2. Characteristics of the materials used in the simulation [11]

Material	Young's modulus (MPa)	Poisson's ratio
PDMS(7.5:1)	1.254	0.45
PDMS(10:1)	1.119	0.45
PDMS(20:1)	0.58	0.45
Polyimide	3500	0.335
Conductive rubber	1.5-6	0.45

3.1   Optimization of the Capacitive Layer

The initial state of the capacitive layer is shown in Fig. 2. When pressure is applied on the surface of the sensor, the induced pressure from the bottom of the PSR-based layer will lead to the deformation of the polyimide as shown in Fig. 3. As the pressure

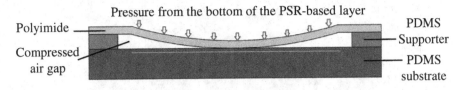

Fig. 3. Deformed capacitive layer

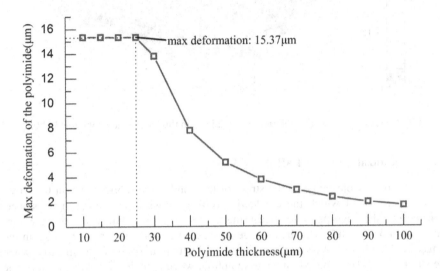

Fig. 4. Polyimide thickness effect on the maximum deformation of the polyimide

getting higher, the deformation of the polyimide will get larger, and the polyimide will finally contact with the PDMS substrate as shown in Fig. 3. It is obvious that before the polyimide contact with the substrate the deformation is changing rapidly, which will lead to the high sensitivity of the pressure sensing, but when the polyimide begin to contact with the substrate the deformation becomes difficult, and the sensing sensitivity will get lower when the contact area get larger. To guarantee that the capacitive layer is sensitive in the defined low-pressure range of 0 – 35 kPa, the optimization objective is to find an appropriate thickness of the polyimide, the maximum deformation of which is 15 μm when the sensor is applied 35 kPa pressure.

The pressure fixed at 35 kPa, several simulations that choosing different thickness of polyimide have done. Fig. 4 shows the maximum deformations of the polyimide of different thickness. In Fig. 4, it can be seen that when the thickness of polyimide decreases from 100 μm, the maximum deformation of the polyimide increases. The deformation reaches 15.37 μm when the thickness of the polyimide is 25 μm, and Fig. 5 shows the distribution of the deformation. When the polyimide is thinner than 25 μm, the maximum deformation increases slowly (or no longer increase) because the polyimide has contacted with the substrate. According to the optimization objective mentioned above, the thickness of the polyimide is configured as 25 μm.

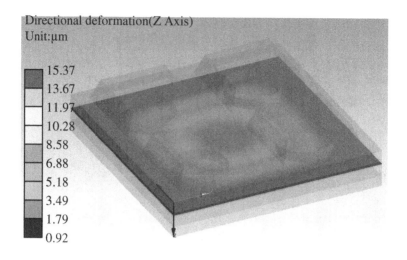

Fig. 5. Deformation of the polyimide with 25 μm in thickness when applying 35 kPa

3.2   Optimization of the PSR Based Layer

Generally, the usable range of the strain of the conductive rubber is about 0 – 40%, out of the range of which the conductive rubber shows little change in resistance. Considering the high-pressure measuring range, we hope that when the pressure varies from 35 to 1400 kPa, the average strain of the conductive rubber varies in the range of 0 – 40%. Assuming that the conductive rubber deform linearly when the strain is 0 – 40%. Based on the assumption, when applying 700 kPa pressure, the average strain of the conductive rubber is about 20%, which is used as optimization objective of the Young's modulus of the conductive rubber.

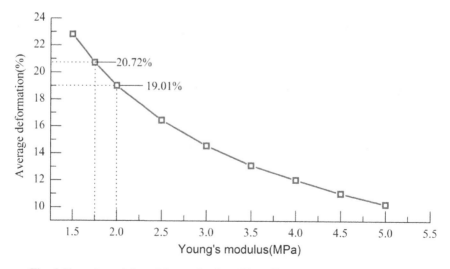

Fig. 6. Young's modulus of the conductive rubber effects on the average deformation

Fig. 6 shows the effect of Young's modulus of the conductive rubber on the average deformation of the conductive rubber. In Fig. 6, it can be seen that when the Young's modulus is 1.75 MPa and 2 MPa, the average deformation of conductive rubber is 20.72% and 19.01%, respectively. Considering that the larger Young's modulus leads to the larger pressure sensing range, the Young's modulus of the conductive rubber is configured as 2 MPa and Fig. 7 shows the distribution of the deformation.

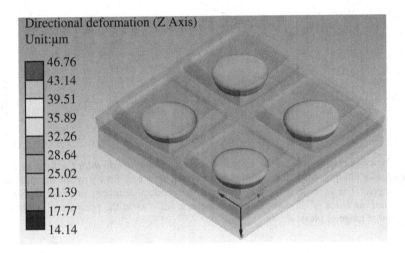

Fig. 7. Deformation of the conductive rubber with Young's modulus of 2 MPa when applying 700 kPa

3.3   Pressure Sensing Performance of the Tactile Sensor

The thickness of the air gap affects the sensing capacity and average deformation of the conductive rubber further related to the resistance. For 25 μm thickness of the polyimide in capacitive layer and 2 MPa of the Young's modulus of the conductive rubber in PSR-based layer, the results of the compression of the air gap and the average deformation of the conductive rubber when applying different pressures, are shown in Fig. 8. In order to reduce the non-linear effect of the PDMS and conductive rubber, the pressure is applied in the range of 0 – 700 kPa, in which the PDMS and conductive rubber can be considered as linear materials.

From Fig. 8, it can be seen that the compression rate of the air gap increases sharply in the range of 0 – 35 kPa and varies slowly when pressure is larger than 35 kPa. On the contrary, the deformation of the conductive rubber shows little change in 0 – 35 kPa but increase linearly in large range of pressure and by tuning the concentration of the conductive nanoparticles in the conductive rubber, the change of the resistance of the conductive rubber can be as linear as possible in the designed range of pressure. That means the capacitive layer is sensitive to low pressure and PSR based layer is sensitive to high pressure. The result conforms to the design objective that the integrated sensor performs well in wide range of pressure sensing.

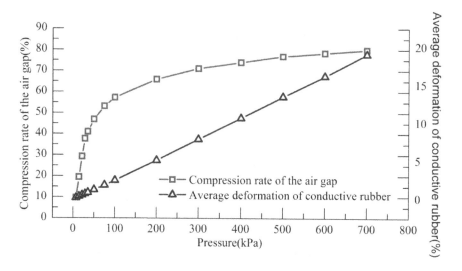

Fig. 8. The compression rate of the air gap (*reduced volume divide initial volume of the air gap*) increases sharply when the pressure is low and increases slowly when the pressure is getting larger. The average deformation rate of the conductive rubber (*average deformation divide initial thickness of conductive rubber*) increase little when the pressure is low but keep linear in large range of pressure.

4   Conclusions and Future Work

Inspired from human skin's structure and haptic mechanism, an integrated bio-inspired tactile sensor for prosthesis is proposed, which can detect both low-pressure and high-pressure. The designed bio-inspired tactile sensor consists of a capacitive layer and PSR-based layer. The simulation and optimization have been performed for the integrated bio-inspired tactile sensor. Based on the optimization results, the thickness of the polyimide in capacitive layer is configured as 25 μm and the Young's modulus of the conductive rubber in PSR-based layer is configured as 2 MPa. Then, the simulation has performed to analyze the pressure sensing performance of the integrated sensor. The result shows that the capacitive layer of the integrated sensor plays major role in low-pressure sensing while the PSR-based layer of the integrated sensor plays major role in high-pressure sensing. So the conclusion can be drawn that the integrated sensor has performed well in wide range of pressure.

For future works, we will focus on the bio-tactile sensor's manufacturing method and process, followed by experimental tests and validation.

Acknowledgments. The author would like to acknowledge the supports from the National Basic Research Program (973) of China under Grant No. 2011CB013300, the National Natural Science Foundation of China under Grant No. 51105333, and the Postdoctoral Science Foundation of China under Grant No. 2011M500995.

References

1. Noda, K., Hoshino, K., Matsumoto, K., Shimoyama, I.: A shear stress sensor for tactile sensing with the piezoresistive cantilever standing in elastic material. Sens. Actuators A: Phys. 127, 295–301 (2006)
2. Yu, S., Chang, D., Tsao, L., Shih, W., Chang, P.: Porous nylon with electro-active dopants as flexible sensors and actuators. In: Proceedings of the IEEE 21st International Conference on Micro Electro Mechanical Systems (MEMS), Tucson, AZ, USA, pp. 908–911 (2008)
3. Kawaguchi, H., Someya, T., Sekitani, T., Sakurai, T.: Cut-and-paste customization of organic FET integrated circuit and its application to electronic artificial skin. IEEE J. Solid-State Circ. 40(1), 177–185 (2005)
4. Lee, H., Chung, J., Chang, S., Yoon, E.: Normal and shear force measurement using a flexible polymer tactile sensor with embedded multiple capacitors. J. Microelectromech. Syst. 17, 934–942 (2008)
5. Hosoda, K., Tada, Y., Asada, M.: Anthropomorphic robotic soft fingertip with randomly distributed receptors. Robotics and Autonomous Systems 54, 104–109 (2006)
6. Dahiya, R.S., Valle, M., Metta, G., Lorenzelli, L.: Bio-inspired tactile sensing arrays. In: Proceedings of Bioengineered and Bioinspired Systems IV, Dresden, Germany, SPIE, 73650D-9 (2009)
7. Mannsfeld, S.C.B., Tee, B.C., Stoltenberg, R.M., Chen, C.V.H., Barman, S., Muir, B.V.O., Sokolov, A.N., Reese, C., Bao, Z.: Highly sensitive flexible pressure sensors with microstructured rubber dielectric layers. Nat. Mater., 859–864 (2010)
8. Hoshino, K., Mori, D.: Three-dimensional tactile sensor with thin and soft elastic body. In: Proceedings of the IEEE Workshop on Advanced Robotics and Its Social Impacts, ARSO 2008, pp. 1–6 (2008)
9. Dargahi, J., Najarian, S.: Human tactile perception as a standard for artificial tactile sensing-a review. Int. J. Medical Robotics and Computer Assisted Surgery 1(1), 23–35 (2004)
10. Xia, Y., Whitesides, G.M.: Soft Lithography. Annu. Rev. Mater. Sci. 28, 153–184 (1998)
11. Bin, W.: Fabrication and Adhesion Study of Biomimetic Viscous Material. Nanjing University of Aeronautics and Astronautics, China (2010)
12. Dellon, E.S., Mourey, R., Dellon, A.L.: Human pressure perception values for constant and moving one- and two-point discrimination. J. Plast. Reconstr. Surg. 90, 112–117 (1992)

A Monitoring Network Based on Embedded Vision Nodes Suitable for Robotic Systems

Jile Jiao[1], Shuguang Ye[2], Zhiqiang Cao[1], Yuequan Yang[3], Xilong Liu[1], and Min Tan[1]

[1] State Key Laboratory of Management and Control for Complex Systems,
Institute of Automation, Chinese Academy of Sciences, Beijing 100190, China
[2] JiangSu King Source Electric Co., Ltd., Jiangsu, 225200, China
[3] College of Information Engineering, Yangzhou University, Yangzhou 225009, China
{jile.jiao,zhiqiang.cao,xilong.liu,min.tan}@ia.ac.cn,
yeshuguang2000@163.com, yangyq@yzu.edu.cn

Abstract. A visual monitoring network suitable for robotic systems is presented in this paper. The monitoring network is composed of embedded vision nodes. By interacting with an upper computer as well as the robotic system, the monitoring network provides an important supplement, which may accelerate the task execution. Each embedded vision node captures and processes images independently, and it is easy to install with compact size. The vision node contains a S3C2440 processor as the main processing module, a CMOS camera as the image capturing module and a zigbee module for wireless communication. The detection based on frame difference or color feature is used to determine the mass center of moving object. On this basis, the object information from one vision node may also be sent to another one for stereo vision localization with stereo vision model and least square method. Application examples are demonstrated to testify the monitoring network.

Keywords: monitoring network, embedded vision node, zigbee, stereo vision localization.

1   Introduction

With the expansion of robotic applications[1], some tasks may require the robotic system with more information that is beyond the sensing ability of the system itself. A better way is to deploy some nodes in the environment to provide environmental information. Network Robot System (NRS) [2] that combines the robotic system with wireless sensor network may expand the sensing ability of robotic system by interacting with environments. NRS has become an important research direction and received many attentions. The URUS project designs a network robot system interacting with human beings and the environment in a cooperative way to carry out tasks such as guiding, assisting, transporting materials and monitoring[3]. APE project [4] verifies how robots actively participate in a dynamic sensor network reconfiguration. PEIS ecology project [5] explores a solution to build intelligent robotic systems in the service of people by putting together insights from the fields of autonomous robotics and of ambient intelligence. NRS project [6] aims at enabling

C.-Y. Su, S. Rakheja, H. Liu (Eds.): ICIRA 2012, Part III, LNAI 7508, pp. 42–51, 2012.
© Springer-Verlag Berlin Heidelberg 2012

user-friendly interaction between humans and networked environments. Visible robots provide information to people while observation and recognition of people are mainly handled by the sensors embedded in the environment.

The recognition and localization of objects are an important aspect in the field of NRS. By providing the related information about the objects, the more reasonable decision may become possible. For common object information acquisition, the vision, RFID, laser scanner, etc. have been used. Among them, the vision is broadly utilized for its abundant information, low cost and agility for use[7]. Kassebaum et al.[8] proposes a distributed camera network localization approach based on a large number of feature points. A visual servo controller comprises classical image-based visual servo and machine learning approach for robust grasping is presented in [9]. Shi et al.[10] proposes a framework for network multi-robot system, and conducts the localization research in indoor environment with CCD cameras whose image data are transformed through wireless modules. [11] designs a stereo vision system and an improved active search method is used to locate and track the end-effector in unknown and dynamic environment.

At present, the computer is the commonly used for image processing in the vision monitoring network. The huge image data from cameras may be transmitted to computers by wired or wireless way. For wired transmission, the position of camera is limited around the computer, whereas the wireless transmission may lead to a heavy communication burden. In this case, it is necessary to develop a network with many vision nodes having the capability to process its image information independently, and then the communication amount will be reduced. The vision node has a compact hardware that consumes little power. As a consequence, many researchers have developed embedded vision systems. Sawasaki et al. [12] develops an embedded vision system to perform vision based navigation on a mobile service robot, and the embedded vision system can accelerate the image processing functions with low power consumption. Spampinato et al. [13] presents an embedded vision system based on FPGA and two CMOS cameras to perform stereo image processing and 3D mapping for autonomous navigation. [14] designs an embedded stereo vision system that provides flexible baseline for robots of compact size. A real-time robotic embedded vision system based on CMOS cameras providing visual information for a control scheme of mobile manipulation is presented in [15]. [16] designs a middleware that integrates CMUcam3 CMOS camera module and SunSPOT sensor module for a wireless vision sensor node, which is used for object tracking through foreground detection.

In this paper we provide a monitoring network based on embedded vision nodes and each vision node may process its image data independently with compact hardware that features low power consumption and easy installation. And then we focus on the recognition and localization of the object by employing two vision nodes that always see the moving object. The rest of the paper is organized as follows. In section 2, we describe the monitoring network framework based on embedded vision nodes as well as the structure diagram of the vision node. Section 3 gives the localization of moving object. The application examples are demonstrated in section 4 and section 5 concludes the paper.

2   The Monitoring Network Based on Embedded Vision Nodes

The framework for monitoring network is shown in Fig. 1 and it includes a number of embedded vision nodes, which are arranged according to the task to be executed by robotic system, actual environment and the node itself. Each embedded vision node performs image gathering as well as image processing independently. By the relaying of a series of vision nodes, the object is observed continuously, and even the localization is also implemented. The related information provided by monitoring network is transferred to an upper computer, which is in charge of information integration and sends related task command to robotic system. The vision node may also directly exchange information with nearby robot. By interacting with the upper computer and robotic system, the monitoring network provides an important supplement, which is beneficial to the task.

When the moving object is required to be localized, a group of two vision nodes is utilized. Take embedded vision node EVN1 and EVN2 in Fig. 1 as an example to show the work flow of localization. $O_W X_W Y_W Z_W$ is the world coordinate system, and (u_1, v_1) and (u_2, v_2) are image coordinates of mass center of object I in CMOS cameras

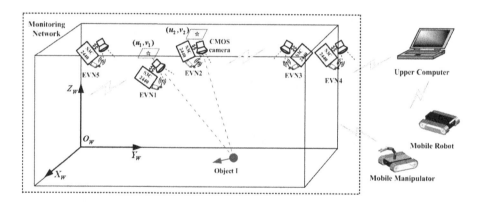

Fig. 1. The framework of monitoring network based on embedded vision nodes

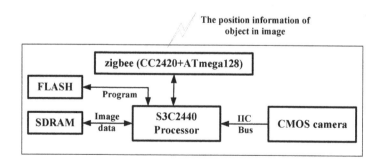

Fig. 2. Structure diagram of embedded vision node

of EVN1 and EVN2, respectively. When one node gets the image information of the moving object I, if it also receives the object information from the other node in the meantime, it will synthesize the information for localization.

For each embedded vision node, a CMOS camera OV9653 for image capturing is used, and related image data will be stored into SDRAM memory through IIC Bus and processed by a S3C2440 processor based on ARM9. This processor calls the start-up code and application program from FLASH memory and executes the corresponding image processing based on image data read from SDRAM memory. The communication among vision nodes is realized by a zigbee module, which mainly includes RF chip CC2420 and an ATmega128 processor. Fig. 2 illustrates its architecture.

3   Moving Object Localization

Moving object localization includes two parts, mass center detection of moving object and stereo vision localization. For the former part, we may adopt frame difference or color feature based method for moving object detection. The latter generates the space position of the moving object with least square method, according to stereo vision model and the coordinates of moving object in two cameras.

3.1   Mass Center Detection of Moving Object

(1) Frame Difference Based Detection

The foreground is extracted by frame difference method. The foreground image is

$$D_{i,j} = \begin{cases} 1 & if \ |\mu(i,j) - y(i,j)| \geq T \\ 0 & |\mu(i,j) - y(i,j)| < T \end{cases}$$, where $\mu(i,j)$ and $y(i,j)$ are image pixel values of

point (i, j) in current frame and previous frame, and T is the threshold to distinguish foreground and background. Then, a 5×5 pixels object region detection template is

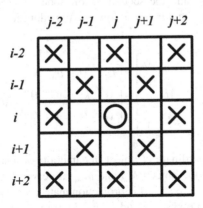

Fig. 3. 5×5 object region detection template

utilized to filter the noise and non-object region points. For the purpose of reducing the calculation amount, the image is scanned every three lines and three columns. If one foreground region point is detected, we may decide whether the point is object region point according to the 12 sparse points shown in Fig. 3. According to equation (1), if $M(i, j) > 9$, the point (i, j) is object region point. Based on the object region points generated, the mass center of moving object is obtained.

$$M(i, j) = \sum D_{i \pm m, j \pm n} + \sum D_{i \pm k, j \pm l} - 1 \, (m = 0,2; n = 0,2; k = l = 1). \tag{1}$$

(2) Color Feature Based Detection

Although color feature is widely used to identify object, the light conditions often affect the recognition quality, which makes the fixed threshold be unsatisfactory to the requirement. In this case, self-adaptive threshold becomes meaningful.

Take red feature as an example. For red identifier, its red intensity is surely bigger than its green intensity and blue intensity. Firstly, we employ a loose threshold to find the rough red region of current image as well as the average value R_{ave} of red intensity. Re-scan the image by using the threshold $T = R_{ave}$. For a pixel point (i, j), if $R(i, j) > T \&\& R(i, j) > K_r G(i, j) \&\& R(i, j) > K_r B(i, j)$, where $K_r = 1.7$, the pixel point is red, where $R(i, j)$, $G(i, j)$, $B(i, j)$ represent the values of red intensity, green intensity and blue intensity of (i, j), respectively. Next, a 3×3 template is adopted to filter noise points and finally the image coordinate of mass center of red identifier is obtained by averaging all red pixel points.

3.2   Stereo Vision Localization

Two embedded vision nodes are required for coordination for stereo vision localization. After these two vision nodes get coordinates of the object mass center in current image, one vision node will only acquire the information and send the information to the other, and the second vision node is responsible for solving the space position, which is given in the following. We adopt the camera model of [7] as follows:

$$z_c \begin{bmatrix} u \\ v \\ 1 \end{bmatrix} = M_{in} M_{out} \begin{bmatrix} x_t \\ y_t \\ z_t \\ 1 \end{bmatrix} = M \begin{bmatrix} x_t \\ y_t \\ z_t \\ 1 \end{bmatrix} = \begin{bmatrix} k_x & 0 & u_0 & 0 \\ 0 & k_y & v_0 & 0 \\ 0 & 0 & 1 & 0 \end{bmatrix} \begin{bmatrix} R_{3\times3} & P \\ 0^T & 1 \end{bmatrix} \begin{bmatrix} x_t \\ y_t \\ z_t \\ 1 \end{bmatrix}. \tag{2}$$

where z_c is the z axis coordinate of object in camera coordinate system, and $[u, v]$ is the image coordinate of the object; M_{in} and M_{out} are camera intrinsic parameters and external parameters, respectively; M is projection matrix; $[x_t, y_t, z_t]$ is the coordinate of object in world coordinate system, and k_x and k_y are magnification coefficients of x axis direction and y axis direction, respectively; $[u_0, v_0]$ is the image coordinate of intersection point of optical axis center line and image plane, $R_{3 \times 3}$ is the rotation matrix and P is the position of camera in world coordinate system.

According to the image coordinate (u_1, v_1) and (u_2, v_2) of object's mass center, combined with camera model mentioned above, we acquire an overdetermined set of equations shown in Eq. (3). The space position of the object in world coordinate system is gained by solving Eq. (3) with the least square method.

$$\begin{cases} z_{c1}u_1 = m_{11}x_t + m_{12}y_t + m_{13}z_t + m_{14} \\ z_{c1}v_1 = m_{21}x_t + m_{22}y_t + m_{23}z_t + m_{24} \\ z_{c2}u_2 = m'_{11}x_t + m'_{12}y_t + m'_{13}z_t + m'_{14} \\ z_{c2}v_2 = m'_{21}x_t + m'_{22}y_t + m'_{23}z_t + m'_{24} \end{cases} \tag{3}$$

where $\begin{cases} z_{c1} = m_{31}x_t + m_{32}y_t + m_{33}z_t + m_{34} \\ z_{c2} = m'_{31}x_t + m'_{32}y_t + m'_{33}z_t + m'_{34} \end{cases}$, $\begin{bmatrix} m_{11} & m_{12} & m_{13} & m_{14} \\ m_{21} & m_{22} & m_{23} & m_{24} \\ m_{31} & m_{32} & m_{33} & m_{34} \end{bmatrix}$ and

$\begin{bmatrix} m'_{11} & m'_{12} & m'_{13} & m'_{14} \\ m'_{21} & m'_{22} & m'_{23} & m'_{24} \\ m'_{31} & m'_{32} & m'_{33} & m'_{34} \end{bmatrix}$ are the projection matrixes of two cameras. The calibration

procedure is performed by using the camera calibration toolbox of Matlab[17].

4   Experiment

Fig. 4 shows the designed embedded vision node. It mainly includes a CMOS camera, an image interface expansion board, an ARM core board, a power board, and a zigbee module as well as Lithium battery. The size of vision node assembled is 107mm×74mm×40mm. In the following experiments, two embedded vision nodes are utilized for moving object localization/manipulator grabbing operation.

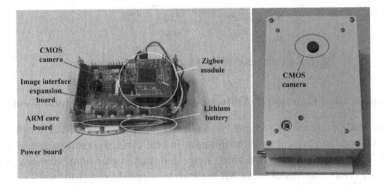

Fig. 4. Embedded vision node

4.1   Application Example I: Moving Object Localization

In this experiment, we adopt frame difference for the moving object detection. Set the threshold $T=30$, the projection matrixes of two CMOS cameras are as follows:

$$M_1 = \begin{bmatrix} 231.76 & 101.75 & 407.68 & 26884 \\ 178.35 & -213.08 & -1.4002 & 119300 \\ 0.94698 & 0.25639 & -0.19364 & 1155 \end{bmatrix},$$

$$M_2 = \begin{bmatrix} 289.3 & -44.509 & 384.16 & 24195 \\ 44.386 & -276.13 & -12.259 & 202530 \\ 0.92398 & -0.26566 & -0.27511 & 1038.8 \end{bmatrix}.$$

Let an object move along the direction that parallel to the x axis of the world coordinate system from the starting position So to goal position Go. Fig.5 shows the moving trajectory of the object in space, where *Real Trajectory* is the real trajectory of the object, *Trajectory1* and *Trajectory2* are two measuring trajectories of moving object by stereo vision localization. It is seen that these two measuring trajectories obtained are nearly coincide with the real trajectory, which shows the feasibility of embedded vision localization scheme.

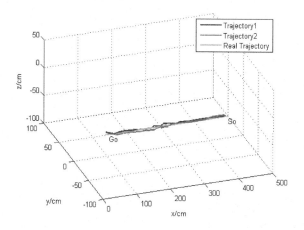

Fig. 5. Experiment result of moving object localization

4.2   Application Example II: Object Localization and Manipulator Grabbing

The color feature is used for moving object detection in this example. After the object position information is sent to a manipulator in real time, the manipulator estimates whether the object is within its grabbing range and start to grab in appropriate time.

The projection matrixes of two CMOS cameras adopted are as follows:

$$M_1 = \begin{bmatrix} -246.71 & 10.566 & 253.42 & 101310 \\ -135.14 & 336.6 & -69.689 & 80151 \\ -0.91044 & 0.024326 & -0.41293 & 778.05 \end{bmatrix},$$

$$M_2 = \begin{bmatrix} -246.23 & -10.716 & 254.99 & 105220 \\ -150.72 & 342.79 & -62.684 & 50184 \\ -0.88978 & 0.021614 & -0.45588 & 779.74 \end{bmatrix}.$$

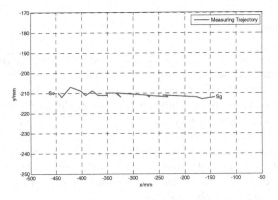

Fig. 6. Experiment result of moving object localization

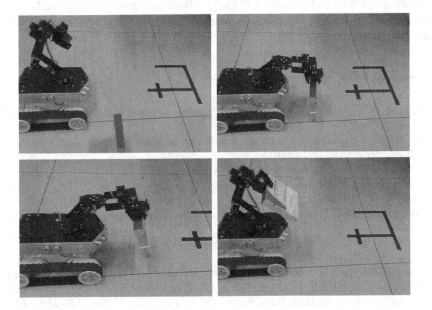

Fig. 7. Manipulator grabbing operation

The object moves along the direction that parallel to the x axis of world coordinate system. It has a red identifier on the top and it is dragged manually. When the object is close enough and suitable to be grabbed by a manipulator that is equipped with a static robot, the manipulator executes the grabbing operation. Fig. 6 shows the measuring trajectory of the object in X-Y coordinate system from So to Sg where it is grabbed, and the next grabbing operation is shown in Fig. 7. We can see that the manipulator may fulfill the task smoothly based on the information of moving object provided by embedded vision system.

5   Conclusion

This paper presents a monitoring network composed of embedded vision nodes and each vision node captures and processes images independently. The moving object may be recognized, and its space position may also be acquired by integrating the information from two vision nodes with stereo vision model and least square method. The related information provided by monitoring network may be sent to an upper computer or the corresponding robot, which is beneficial to the task. The experiments of moving object localization/manipulator grabbing operation have been implemented. The ongoing and future work includes multi-object recognition in complex environments as well as the coordination among embedded monitoring network, upper computer and robotic system.

Acknowledgments. This work is supported in part by the National Natural Science Foundation of China under Grants 61175111, 60805038, and in part by the National High Technology Research and Development Program of China (863 Program) under Grant 2011AA041001.

References

1. Tan, M., Wang, S., Cao, Z.Q.: Multi-robot Systems. Tsinghua University Press (2005) (in Chinese)
2. Sanfeliu, A., Hagita, N., Saffiotti, A.: Network robot systems. Robotics and Autonomous Systems 56(10), 793–797 (2008)
3. Ubiquitous Networking Robotics in Urban Settings, http://urus.upc.es/index.html
4. Amigoni, F., Brandolini, A., Caglioti, V., et al.: Agencies for Perception in Environmental Monitoring. IEEE Transactions on Instrumentation and Measurement 55(4), 1038–1050 (2006)
5. PEIS Ecology, http://aass.oru.se/~peis/frameset_page.html
6. http://www.irc.atr.jp/en/
7. Ma, S.D., Zhang, Z.Y.: Computer Vision. Tsinghua University Press (2005) (in Chinese)
8. Kassebaum, J., Bulusu, N., Feng, W.C.: 3-D Target-Based Distributed Smart Camera Network Localization. IEEE Transactions on Image Processing 19(10), 2530–2539 (2010)
9. Wang, Y., Lang, H.X., de Silva, C.W.: A Hybrid Visual Servo Controller for Robust Grasping by Wheeled Mobile Robot. IEEE Transactions on Mechatronics 15(5), 757–769 (2010)

10. Shi, K., Cao, Z.Q., Jiao, J.L., et al.: A Framework for Network Multi-robot System and the Localization Research in Indoor Environment. In: Proceeding of International Colloquium on Computing, Communication, Control, and Management (CCCM), pp. 316–319 (2010)
11. Pajpar, A.H., Huang, Q., Pang, Y.T., et al.: Location and Tracking of Robot End-effector Based on Stereo Vision. In: Proceeding of IEEE International Conference on Robotics and Biomimetics (ROBIO), pp. 1140–1145 (2006)
12. Sawasaki, N., Nakao, M., Yamamoto, Y., Okabayashi, K.: Embedded Vision System for Mobile Robot Navigation. In: Proceeding of IEEE International Conference on Robotics and Automation (ICRA), pp. 2693–2698 (2006)
13. Spampinato, G., Lidholm, J., Ahlberg, C., et al.: An Embedded Stereo Vision Module for 6D Pose Estimation and Mapping. In: IEEE/RSJ International Conference on Robots and Systems (IROS), pp. 1626–1631 (2011)
14. Ben-Tzvi, P., Xu, X.: An Embedded Feature-Based Stereo Vision System for Autonomous Mobile Robots. In: IEEE International Workshop on Robotic and Sensors Environments (ROSE) (2010)
15. Andrain, H., Song, K.T.: Embedded CMOS Imaging System for Real-Time Robotic Vision. In: IEEE/RSJ International Conference on Robots and Systems (IROS), pp. 1096–1101 (2005)
16. Casares, M., Vuran, M.C., Velipasalar, S.: Design of a Wireless Vision Sensor for object tracking in Wireless Vision Sensor Networks. In: Second ACM/IEEE International Conference on Distributed Smart Cameras (2008)
17. Bouguet, J.Y.: Camera Calibration Toolbox for Matlab (EB/OL) (2010), http://www.vision.caltech.edu/bouguetj/calib_doc/

Conceptual Design and Kinematic Analysis
of a Parallel Rotational Robot

Fray J. Herrera[1], Hernan Gonzalez Acuña[1], Omar Lengerke[1], and Max Suell Dutra[2]

[1] Research Group in Control and Mechatronics, Mechatronics Engineering Program,
Universidad Autonoma de Bucaramanga, Bucaramanga, Colombia
{fherrera2,hgonzalez3,olengerke}@unab.edu.co
[2] Research Group in Machine Design and Robotics, Department of Mechanical Engineering,
COPPE, UFRJ, Federal University of Rio de Janeiro, Rio de Janeiro, Brazil
max@mecanica.coppe.ufrj.br

Abstract. This paper presents the conceptual design and simulation of a rotational parallel robot. This robot is used to reproduce movement; the robot workspace, inverse kinematic study and a simulation of the system in a trajectory were analyzed. Computational tools were used to resolve equations, create a virtual design and conduct simulation in the conceptual design. The rotational parallel robot used 6 servomotors and 6 links with spherical joints that provide 360^0 rotational capabilities on its axis. This is a big flexibility in comparison with Stewart platform but the workspace is smaller than that of the Stewart platform.

Keywords: parallel robot, inverse kinematics, conceptual design.

1   Introduction

Parallel robots are mechanical structures with a closed chain mechanism where the end effect is attached to the base by at least two independent kinematic chains [1]. It has features like a better ratio load-weight, high precision, better dynamic performance, better stiffness and effect of coupling between joints. However, these platforms have a relatively small workspace. The development of the parallel mechanism was the first step in the creation of parallel robots. In [2], the first parallel robot of 5 degrees of freedom for paint spraying operation was presented. The Stewart platform, [3] the most famous parallel robot of 6 dof applied in flight simulation, arouses our interest to build autonomous machines.

The applications of parallel robots are: handling tools, precision tasks, medical applications, micro-manipulation, humanoid robotics with driving simulators, ship simulators [4] and flight simulators used by companies like TOYOTA and CAE among the most common.

Some parallel robots with new design are presented in [5], [6] and robots with 6 dof constructed with revolute joints are called Rotopods [7],[8]. This configuration can move on a circular rail. The rotational parallel robot design was modeled on Rotopod, created by the PRSCO Company. This robot has 6 links with a constant length joining the top part to the base; these links have spherical joints to allow end

C.-Y. Su, S. Rakheja, H. Liu (Eds.): ICIRA 2012, Part III, LNAI 7508, pp. 52–61, 2012.
© Springer-Verlag Berlin Heidelberg 2012

effector motion. All the links are on a slider driven by a servomotor through a ring providing end effector motion. Perfect synchronization between all servomotors is necessary to produce the desired movement. In comparison with the Stewart platform, this robot can rotate more than $360°$ in yaw because its base is not fixed. However it has disadvantages like a reduced workspace and a complex control system.

2   Rotopod Structural Analysis

Given the configuration presented in Figure 1, freedom degree calculation for this type of robot is determined by Grüber's equation (1).

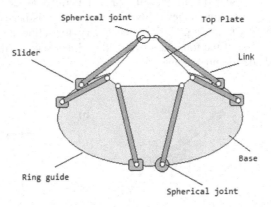

Fig. 1. Rotopod platform with revolution joints

$$m = \lambda(n - j - 1) + \sum_{i=1}^{j} f_i - l_f \tag{1}$$

Where:

m = Number of system's degrees of freedom.
λ = Degrees of freedom of the space housing the mechanism. $\lambda = 3$, for two-dimensional case and $\lambda = 6$ spatial case.
n = Number of fixed links of the mechanism including the base and the mobile part.
j = Number of joints of the mechanism.
f_i = Degrees of relative movement of the mechanism.
l_f = Number of degrees of freedom passive mechanism. The values for the equation terms are: $\lambda = 6$, n = 14, j = 18, $f_i = 3$, (spherical joints), $f_i = 1$, (prismatic joints) and $l_f = 6$.

Replacing the values in the equation (1) we obtain

$$m = 6(14 - 18 - 1) + \sum_{i=1}^{12} 3 + \sum_{i=1}^{6} 1 - 6 = 6$$

3   Rotopod Analysis

3.1   Rotopod Inverse Kinematic

In comparison with serial robots, parallel robots have relatively complex direct kinematics, as compared with inverse kinematics. Inverse kinematics of the Rotopod platform is used to calculate the necessary position of each servomotor that determines the position and orientation of the top. This position is measured in angles from $0°$ to $360°$ in a ring that allows the movement of each slider with the link. This movement is used in trajectory generation of applications that require control and precision or movement strictly limited to factors such as speed and acceleration or even operating factors such as those presented in Merlet [9], Liu [10], Perng & Hsiao [11].

To develop the inverse kinematics of the moving plate, it is necessary to calculate top geometry, as shown in Fig. 2. It is necessary to define such mathematical restrictions as the shape of the top and lengths of the links because these are constant elements and the shapes do not change.

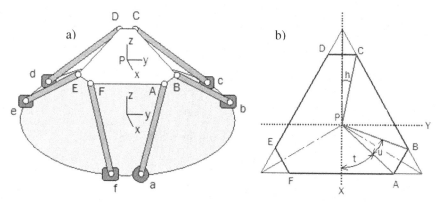

Fig. 2. a) Coordinate system of the Rotopod   b) Real geometry of the top shape
            platform.   platform.

These coordinates are calculated with the length of $\overline{AF}$ and $\overline{AB}$, the geometry relations of an equilateral triangle. The incircled radio is calculated with the regular polygon $\overline{ABCDEF}$ and the distance between the center of the top to any point defined in the geometry $A - F$. This can be calculated with equations (2) and (3).

$$\overline{PA} = \sqrt{\left(\frac{(\overline{AF} + 2\,\overline{AB})\sqrt{3}}{6}\right)^2 + \left(\frac{\overline{AF}}{2}\right)^2}$$

$$\angle t = \tan^{-1}\left(\frac{\dfrac{\overline{AF}}{2}}{\dfrac{(\overline{AF} + 2\,\overline{AB})\sqrt{3}}{6}}\right)$$

(2)

$$\angle u = \cos^{-1}\left(1 - \frac{\overline{AB}^2}{2\overline{PA}^2}\right)$$

$$\angle h = \sin^{-1}\left(\frac{\frac{\overline{AF}}{2}}{\overline{PA}}\right) \tag{3}$$

The coordinates of each point of the geometry presented in Fig. 2 are given in Table 1.

Table 1. Relation of coordinates of the platform

Angle	Relation	Components
A	$\angle t$	$\overline{Ax} = \overline{PA}\cos(A)$ $\overline{Ay} = \overline{PA}\sin(A)$
B	$\angle t + \angle u$	$\overline{Bx} = \overline{PA}\cos(B)$ $\overline{By} = \overline{PA}\sin(B)$
C	$180 - \angle h$	$\overline{Cx} = \overline{PA}\cos(C)$ $\overline{Cy} = \overline{PA}\sin(C)$
D	$180 + \angle h$	$\overline{Dx} = \overline{PA}\cos(D)$ $\overline{Dy} = \overline{PA}\sin(D)$
E	$360 - (\angle t + \angle u)$	$\overline{Ex} = \overline{PA}\cos(E)$ $\overline{Ey} = \overline{PA}\sin(E)$
F	$360 - \angle t$	$\overline{Fx} = \overline{PA}\cos(F)$ $\overline{Fy} = \overline{PA}\sin(F)$

Given the above, the platform's geometry can be raised through X and Y coordinates, based on the original point P that is located in the plane XYZ. In this way one condition of point of reference P in the three axes of study, determines the displacement and orientation of the platform. This condition concerns simple homogeneous transformation matrix (4), as shown below:

$$T = \begin{bmatrix} T_{11} & T_{12} & T_{13} & T_{14} \\ T_{21} & T_{22} & T_{23} & T_{24} \\ T_{31} & T_{32} & T_{33} & T_{34} \\ 0 & 0 & 0 & 1 \end{bmatrix} \tag{4}$$

With
$$T_{11} = c(\gamma)\big(c(\beta)c(\delta) - s(\alpha)s(\beta)s(\delta)\big) - c(\alpha)s(\gamma)s(\delta)$$
$$T_{12} = -s(\gamma)\big(c(\beta)c(\delta) - s(\alpha)s(\beta)s(\delta)\big) - c(\alpha)c(\gamma)s(\delta)$$
$$T_{13} = c(\delta)s(\beta) + c(\beta)s(\alpha)s(\delta)$$
$$T_{14} = c(\delta)Tx - s(\delta)Ty$$
$$T_{21} = c(\gamma)\big(c(\beta)c(\delta) + c(\delta)s(\alpha)s(\gamma)\big) + c(\alpha)c(\delta)s(\gamma)$$
$$T_{22} = c(\alpha)s(\gamma)s(\delta) - s(\gamma)\big(c(\beta)s(\delta) + c(\delta)s(\alpha)s(\beta)\big)$$

$T_{23} = s(\beta)s(\delta) + c(\beta)c(\delta)s(\alpha)$
$T_{24} = s(\delta)Tx + c(\delta)Ty$
$T_{31} = s(\alpha)s(\gamma) - c(\alpha)c(\gamma)s(\beta)$
$T_{32} = c(\gamma)s(\alpha) + c(\alpha)s(\beta)s(\gamma)$
$T_{33} = c(\alpha)c(\beta)$
$T_{34} = Tz$

Where $s = Sen, c = Cos, \alpha = \angle x, \beta = \angle y, \gamma = \angle z$ y $\delta = \angle z$

Once the platform's geometry within the workspace is defined, iteration software with stop condition $abs(\varrho - L) \leq \Delta\varepsilon$, calculates the position of the slider so that the distance meets the boundary conditions of the system, like circular guide radius, lengths of the links (L) and distances of the arcs previously defined, equations (5). These limits are really important to find the minimum and maximum points of dislocation, velocities and acceleration rates of the shape.

$$\varrho = \sqrt{(A_{xi} - P_{xi})^2 + \left(A_{yi} - P_{yi}\right)^2 + (A_{zi} - P_{zi})^2} \qquad (5)$$

3.2   Rotopod's Workspace

The irregular solid shown in the upper part of Fig. 3, represents the workspace of the Rotopod platform. The irregular solid was determined through an iteration program which solves the possible positions of the platform having as its boundary the maximum link length. As shown, the workspace is small and reduced, and depends on the guide ring of the ground base and the length of the bars.

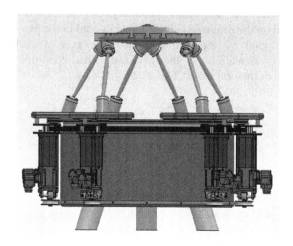

Fig. 3. Rotopod workspace

3.3   Results of Inverse Rotopad Kinematics

Since inverse kinematic allows construction and simulation of trajectories, 2 trajectories have been determined to see the angular displacement of each of the sliders. Fig. 4 shows displacement and rotation values in X, Y and Z using in the top movement, considering a constant velocity.

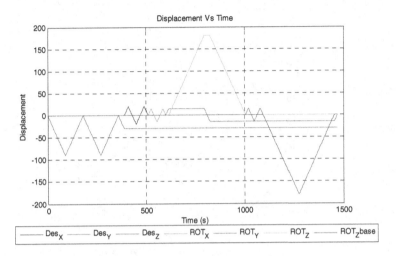

Fig. 4. Platform translation and rotation movements of the base sliders in three axes

In Fig. 5 records the sequence of the angular position of each of the sliders for the movement presented in the Fig. 4, appreciating therefore the non-linearity of motion.

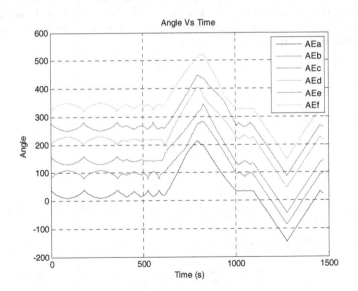

Fig. 5. Slider's angular position

Below is the analysis of one circular and spatial trajectory, Fig. 6. The dimensions of this ring have been calculated according to the workspace thus concluding that the maximum and minimum dimensions of one closed path are in the order of [-20 mm, 20 mm] in the X and Y axis. However, for the Z axis displacement can reach between [10mm, 50mm].

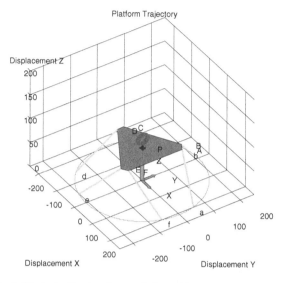

Fig. 6. Circle inclined trajectory followed by the platform

The trajectory of Fig. 6 contains a variable acceleration component and consequently the displacement in each axis and the change of their rotations can be seen in the Fig. 7. The acceleration in this trajectory is variable to achieve a more realistic motion simulation.

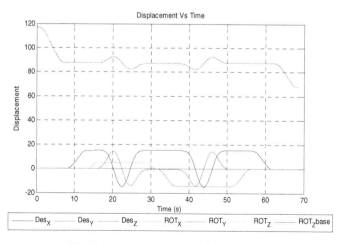

Fig. 7. Cause displacement of the trajectory

The graph above shows that the displacements in the *X* and *Y* axis start at zero, while the *Z* axis has an initial value of 117 mm, maximum value of height at which the platform can limit its rotations to values not exceeding [1° 2°](roll, pitch, yaw).

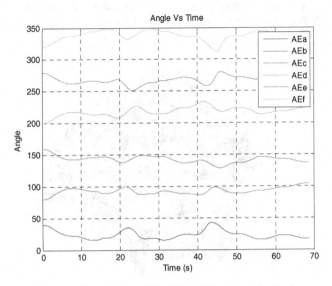

Fig. 8. Angular position of the sliders (Circular trajectory)

Knowing the values of angles during the trajectory it is possible to register the angular velocities w, Fig. 9, they are useful to determine the necessary power of the actuators to track the movement or be used as setpoint in control of trajectories.

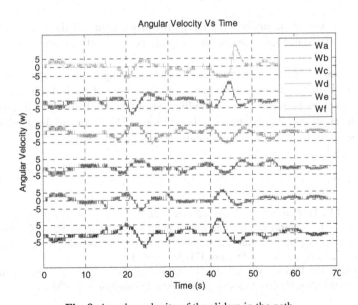

Fig. 9. Angular velocity of the sliders in the path

4   Cad Design of a Rotopod Robot

The figure below presents a physical approach of a Rotopod, as well as its components: top shape, sliders, ring rail, pair of universal joints at both ends, and actuators with their respective mechanical coupling systems to develop movement on the sliders.

Fig. 10. CAD design of a robot Rotopod

5   Conclusions

By means of kinematic analysis of the platform we obtained the graphs of position and angular speed needed to assess the possible behavior of the actuators in a defined path.

The workspace of the platform is limited according to the relation between the ratio of the diameter of the circular guide and the length of the links. Therefore, it can achieve distances between [-15 15] millimeters of the path in a displacement of its three axes. However, this range may change depending on the angles *Roll, Pitch and Yaw* adjacent to the platform at any point.

References

1. Merlet, J.P.: Parallel Robots, 2 edn. Springer (2006).
2. Pollard, W.L.V.: Spray painting machine. United States Patent N° 2.213.108 (1940)
3. Stewart, D.: A platform with 6 degrees of freedom. In: Proceedings of the Institution of Mechanical Engineers, vol. 180, pp. 371–386 (1965)
4. Gonzalez, H.: Projeto Mecatrônico De Uma Plataforma Stewart Para Simulação Dos Movimentos Nos Navios. Universidade Federal de Rio de Janeiro (2009)

5. Zabalza, I., Ros, J., Gil, J., Pintor, J., Jimenez, J., Scott, T.: A new kinematic structure for a 6-dof decoupled parallel manipulator. In: Proceedings of the Workshop on Fundamental Issues and Future Research Directions for Parallel Mechanisms and Manipulators, pp. 12–15 (2002)
6. Yime, E., Moreno, H., Saltaren, R.: A Novel 6 dof Parallel Robot with Decoupled Translation and Rotation. In: 13th World Congress in Mechanism and Machine Science (2011)
7. Schmitt, D.J., Benavides, G.L., Bieg, L.F., Kozlowsk, D.M.: Analysis of the Rotopod: An All Revolute Parallel Manipulator. Sandia National Laboratories (1998)
8. Bieg, L.F.: Six Degrees of Freedom Multi-Axis Positioning System, U.S. Patent 5901936
9. Merlet, J.P.: Kinematics of the wire-driven parallel robot marionet using linear actuators. In: Proceedings of the IEEE Int. Conf. Robotics and Automation, pp. 3857–3862 (2008)
10. Liu, K.F., Lewis, J.M.: Kinematic Analysis of a Stewart plataform Manipulator. IEEE Transactions on Industrial Electronics 40(2), 282–293 (1993)
11. Perng, M.H., Hsiao, L.: Inverse kinematic Solutions of a fully parallel Robot with singularity robustness. The International Journal of Robotics Research 18(6), 575–583 (1999)

Attitude Control of the Unicycle Robot Using Fuzzy-Sliding Mode Control

Yan Li, Jae-Oh Lee, and Jangmyung Lee[*]

Department of Electrical Engineering, Pusan National University, South Korea
{lyagmj,jaeoh,jmlee}@pusan.ac.kr

Abstract. This paper proposes an attitude control of a single wheel balanced robot. The unicycle robot is controlled by two independent control laws: the mobile inverted pendulum control for pitch axis and the reaction wheel pendulum control for roll axis. It is assumed that both roll and pitch dynamics are decoupled. Therefore the roll and pitch dynamics are obtained independently considering the interaction as disturbances to each other. Each control law is implemented by a controller separately. The unicycle robot has two DC motors to rotate the disk for roll and to drive the wheel for pitch. Experimental results show the performance of the controller and verify the effectiveness of the proposed control algorithm.

Keywords: Unicycle Robot, Fuzzy Logic, Sliding Mode Control.

1 Introduction

This paper proposes an attitude and direction control algorithm for a single-wheel (unicycle) robot. The unicycle robot is controlled following two independent control laws which including mobile inverted pendulum for pitch axis and reaction wheel pendulum for roll axis. The angle data of the unicycle robot is obtained by the gyro and the accelerometer attached on the robot. And a fuzzy sliding controller is applied to control the robot.

Researches on the unicycle robot have been down for more than 20years since the 1980's in the U.S. and Japan. A. Schoonwinkel of Stanford University first proposed the motion control of a unicycle robot in his Ph.D. thesis in 1987 [1]. Prof. Yamafujii of Tokyo University implemented PI control to robot dynamic model as an upper turntable and a lower rotating wheel in 1997 [2]. In 2005, Minh-Quan DAO and Kang-Zhi LIU of Chiba University maintained the roll balance using two gyroscopes and an actuator, and the pitch balance using a rotating wheel [3].

In this paper, a simplified controller design is implemented based on a simplified dynamics model of unicycle robot. First of all, the roll and the pitch axes control of the unicycle robot dynamics model are assumed to be decoupling with each other. Then the pitch axis is modeled as an inverted pendulum while the roll axis is modeled as a reaction wheel pendulum. In this process, the coupled terms of the pitch and the

---

[*] Corresponding author.

C.-Y. Su, S. Rakheja, H. Liu (Eds.): ICIRA 2012, Part III, LNAI 7508, pp. 62–72, 2012.

roll axes are considered as their own disturbance, and a robust fuzzy sliding mode controller designed in this paper is applied to overcome these disturbances. The unicycle robot consists of two DC motors for pitch and roll axes separately. Besides that, a 2-axis gyro and a 3-axis accelerometer are utilized to measure the angle data of the robot. In the former papers, the reaction force was used to control the direction of robot by a rotor rotation follow yaw axis to implement the direction control.

The paper is organized as follows. Section 2 presents the dynamics of the unicycle robot, and a fuzzy sliding mode control method is illustrated in section 3. In section 4, experiments are conducted to assess the performance of the method. Finally, discussion and conclusions are provided in section 5.

2   Dynamic Modeling

In this section, how to derive the dynamic model of the unicycle robot by using the Lagrangian method is discussed. Figure 1 depicts the unicycle robot developed in this research. As shown in Figure 1, the unicycle robot consists of three main parts: rotating disk, a robot body and a rotating wheel. And the mass of the rotating disk, the robot body, and the rotating wheel are represented as m_d, m_b and m_w respectively.

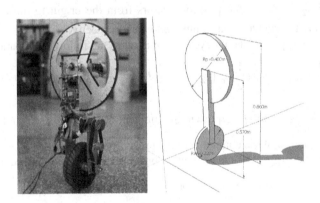

Fig. 1. Model of the Unicycle robot

2.1   Dynamics for Roll Axis

The rotation wheel and the robot body are considered as a compound object which is modeled as a reaction wheel pendulum [4].

Figure 2(a) illuminates the coordinate system for the roll dynamics. L_2 and L_{br} represent the length from the ground to the center of the rotation disk and the center of mass of the rotation wheel-robot body compound object respectively. θ_b and θ_w represent the angle of the roll axis and the angle of the rotation disk

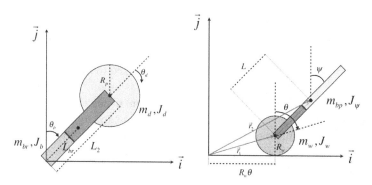

Fig. 2. Model of the Unicycle robot for (a) Roll and (b) Pitch

respectively. R_p is the radius of the rotation disk. And m_{br} is denoted as the sum of m_b and m_w. The position vectors are set as the following equations

$$\vec{r}_1 = L_{br} \sin \theta_b \vec{i} + L_{br} \cos \theta_b \vec{j} \tag{1-a}$$

$$\vec{r}_2 = L_2 \sin \theta_b \vec{i} + L_2 \cos \theta_b \vec{j} \tag{1-b}$$

where $\vec{r}_1$ and $\vec{r}_2$ represent the position vectors from the origin to the center of the rotation disk and the center of the compound object respectively.

The kinetic energy T of the unicycle robot is set as the following equations

$$T = \frac{1}{2} m_{br} \left(\vec{v}_1 \cdot \vec{v}_1 \right) + \frac{1}{2} m_d \left(\vec{v}_2 \cdot \vec{v}_2 \right) + \frac{1}{2} J_b \dot{\theta}_b^2 + \frac{1}{2} J_d \left(\dot{\theta}_b + \dot{\theta}_d \right)^2 \cos \theta_b \vec{j} \tag{2}$$

where $\vec{v}_i = \dfrac{d\vec{r}_i}{dt}$. J_d and J_b represent the moment of inertia of the rotation disk and the moment of inertia of the compound object respectively.

The potential energy V of the unicycle robot is set as the following equation.

$$V = m_{br} g L_{br} \cos \theta_b + m_d g L_2 \cos \theta_b \tag{3}$$

Therefore, the Lagrange equation L can be represented as

$$L = T - V = \frac{1}{2} m_{br} \left(\vec{v}_1 \cdot \vec{v}_1 \right) + \frac{1}{2} m_d \left(\vec{v}_2 \cdot \vec{v}_2 \right) + \frac{1}{2} J_b \dot{\theta}_b^2$$
$$+ \frac{1}{2} J_d \left(\dot{\theta}_b + \dot{\theta}_d \right)^2 \cos \theta_b \vec{j} - m_{br} g L_{br} \cos \theta_b - m_d g L_2 \cos \theta_b \tag{4}$$

Substituting equation 4 in Lagrange equation as equation 5, the dynamics for roll axis can be obtained as equation 6.

$$\frac{d}{dt} \frac{\partial L}{\partial \dot{\mathbf{q}}} - \frac{\partial L}{\partial \mathbf{q}} = \tau_q \quad where, \mathbf{q} = \begin{bmatrix} \theta_b & \theta_d \end{bmatrix}^T \tag{5}$$

$$\left(J_b + L_{br}^2 m_{bw} + L_2^2 m_d \right) \ddot{\theta}_b - g \left(L_{br} m_{br} + L_2 m_d \right) \sin \theta_b = -\tau_r \tag{6-a}$$

$$J_d \ddot{\theta}_d = \tau_r \tag{6-b}$$

Where, τ_r denotes the torque generated by rotational disk motor. And it applied to the pendulum as the same magnitude in the opposite direction.

2.2   Dynamics for Pitch Axis

The rotation disk and the robot body are considered as a compound object which is modeled as an inverted pendulum [5].

Figure 2(b) illuminates the coordinate system for the pitch dynamics. L represents the length from the center of the rotation wheel to the center of mass of the rotation disk-robot body compound object respectively. R_w represents the radius of the rotation wheel. θ and ψ represent the angle ranges of the rotation wheel and pitch axis respectively. m_w and m_{bp} denote the mass of the rotation wheel and the mass of the rotation disk-robot body compound object respectively. The position vectors are set as the following equations

$$\vec{r}_1 = R_w \theta \vec{i} + R_w \vec{j} \tag{7-a}$$

$$\vec{r}_2 = (R_w \theta + L \sin \psi) \vec{i} + (R_w + L \cos \psi) \vec{j} \tag{7-b}$$

where $\vec{r}_1$ and $\vec{r}_2$ represent the position vectors from the origin to the center of the rotation wheel and the center of the compound object respectively.

The kinetic energy T of the unicycle robot is set as the following equations

$$T = \frac{1}{2} m_w (\vec{v}_1 \cdot \vec{v}_1) + \frac{1}{2} m_{bp} (\vec{v}_2 \cdot \vec{v}_2) + \frac{1}{2} J_w \dot{\theta}^2 + \frac{1}{2} J_\psi \dot{\psi}^2 + \frac{1}{2} n^2 J_m (\dot{\theta} - \dot{\psi})^2 \tag{8}$$

where $\vec{v}_i = \dfrac{d\vec{r}_i}{dt}$. J_w and J_ψ represent the moment of inertia of the rotation wheel and the moment of inertia of the compound object respectively. J_m and n represent the moment of inertia of the motor and the gear ratio of it.

The potential energy V of the unicycle robot is set as the following equation.

$$V = m_w g R_w + m_{bp} g (R_w + L \cos \psi) \tag{9}$$

Therefore, the Lagrange equation L can be represented as

$$L = T - V = \frac{1}{2} m_w (\vec{v}_1 \cdot \vec{v}_1) + \frac{1}{2} m_{bp} (\vec{v}_2 \cdot \vec{v}_2) + \frac{1}{2} J_w \dot{\theta}^2$$
$$+ \frac{1}{2} J_\psi \dot{\psi}^2 + \frac{1}{2} n^2 J_m (\dot{\theta} - \dot{\psi})^2 - m_w g R_w - m_{bp} g (R_w + L \cos \psi) \tag{10}$$

Substituting equation 10 in Lagrange equation as equation 11, the dynamics for pitch axis can be obtained as equation 12.

$$\frac{d}{dt}\frac{\partial L}{\partial \dot{q}} - \frac{\partial L}{\partial q} = \tau_q \quad where, \mathbf{q} = \begin{bmatrix} \theta & \psi \end{bmatrix}^T \tag{11}$$

$$J_1\ddot{\theta} + J_3\ddot{\psi} + Lm_{bp}R_w \sin\psi\dot{\psi}^2 = -\tau_p \tag{12-a}$$

$$J_2\ddot{\theta} + J_4\ddot{\psi} - gLm_{bp}\sin\psi = \tau_p \tag{12-b}$$

where $J_1 = J_w + J_m n^2 + (m_w + m_{bp})R_w^2$, $J_2 = Lm_{bp}R_w \cos\psi - J_m n^2$,

$J_3 = Lm_{bp}R_w \cos\psi - J_m n^2$, $J_4 = J_\psi + L^2 m_{bp} + J_m n^2$. τ_p denotes the torque generated by rotational wheel motor. And it applied to the pendulum as the same magnitude in the opposite direction.

3   Controller Design

In this section, the controllers for the roll and pitch axes described in section 2 are designed and concurrently applied for the control of the robot at the same time.

3.1   Design of the Sliding Mode Controller for Roll Axis

In order to design the sliding mode controller, the sliding mode controller is set as follows

$$s(t) = k_1 e(t) + \dot{e}(t) \tag{13}$$

where, k_1 is a constant. $e(t)$ as shown as equation 14 is the difference between the real angle θ_b for roll axis and the reference angle θ_{ref}.

$$e(t) = \theta_b(t) - \theta_{ref}(t) \tag{14}$$

To obtain an equivalent control input u_{eq}, $\dot{s}$ can be obtained as follows

$$\dot{s} = k_1\dot{e} + \ddot{e} = k_1\dot{e} - \ddot{\theta}_{ref} + \ddot{\theta}_b = k_1\dot{e} - \ddot{\theta}_{ref} + \frac{1}{Den_r}\left(g(L_{br}m_{br} + L_2 m_d)\sin\theta_b - \tau_r\right) \tag{15}$$

where, $\ddot{\theta}_b$ can be obtained by the equation 6 and $Den_r = J_b + L_{br}^2 m_{br} + L_2^2 m_d$. The control input u_{eq} can be selected to satisfy the condition $\dot{s} = 0$ such that the control state variables of $e(t)$ and $\dot{e}(t)$ gradually approach to 0 [6].

$$u_{eq} = k_1\dot{e} - \ddot{\theta}_{ref} + \frac{1}{Den_r}g(L_{br}m_{br} + L_2 m_d)\sin\theta_b \tag{16}$$

To keep the system states on the sliding surface, the control input u can be set as

$$u = u_{eq} + \gamma_1 \cdot \text{sgn}(s) \tag{17}$$

where, $\gamma_1 > 0$ and $\text{sgn}(s)$ is defined as equation 18.

$$\text{sgn}(s) = \begin{cases} -1 & if \ s < 0 \\ 1 & if \ s > 0 \end{cases} \tag{18}$$

The Lyapunov function is $V = \frac{1}{2}s^2$, and the equation 19 can be obtained after substituting the control input u into $\dot{V} = s\dot{s}$.

$$\dot{V} = s\dot{s} = s\left[k_1\dot{e} - \ddot{\theta}_{ref} + \frac{1}{Den_r}g(L_{br}m_{br} + L_2 m_d)\sin\theta_b \right.$$
$$\left. -\left(k_1\dot{e} - \ddot{\theta}_{ref} + \frac{1}{Den_r}g(L_{br}m_{br} + L_2 m_d)\sin\theta_b \right) - \gamma_1 \cdot \text{sgn}(s) \right] \tag{19}$$
$$= s \cdot -\gamma_1 \frac{|s|}{s} \le 0$$

The control strategy adopted here will guarantee the system trajectories move toward and stay on the sliding surface $s = 0$ to satisfy the condition $\dot{V} = s\dot{s} \le 0$ [7].

3.2   Design of the Sliding Mode Controller for Pitch Axis

The design of the sliding mode controller for pitch axis is the same as that for roll axis described above. The sliding mode controller is set as follows.

$$s(t) = k_2 e(t) + \dot{e}(t) \tag{20}$$

where, k_2 is a constant. $e(t)$ as shown in equation 21 is the difference between the real angle ψ for roll axis and the reference angle ψ_{ref}.

$$e(t) = \psi(t) - \psi_{ref}(t) \tag{21}$$

To obtain an equivalent control input u_{eq}, $\dot{s}$ can be obtained as follows

$$\ddot{\psi} = \frac{1}{Den_p}\left[-\left(J_w + m_w R_w^2 + m_{bp}R_w^2 + Lm_{bp}R_w\cos\psi \right)\tau_p + \right.$$
$$\left. g\left(J_w Lm_{bp} + J_m Lm_{bp}n^2 + Lm_w m_{bp}R_w^2 + Lm_{bp}^2 R_w^2 \right)\sin\psi - Lm_{bp}R_w\left(-J_m n^2 + Lm_{bp}R_w\cos\psi \right)\sin\psi \dot{\psi}^2 \right] \tag{22}$$

where,
$$Den_p = J_w L^2 m_{bp} + J_m J_w n^2 + J_m L^2 m_{bp}n^2 + L^2 m_w m_{bp}R_w^2 + L^2 m_{bp}^2 R_w^2 + J_m m_w n^2 R_w^2$$
$$+ J_m m_{bp}n^2 R_w^2 + J_\psi(J_w + J_m n^2 + (m_w + m_{bp})R_w^2) + 2J_m Lm_{bp}n^2 R_w\cos\psi - L^2 m_{bp}^2 R_w^2\cos^2\psi$$

The control input u_{eq} can be selected to satisfy the condition $\dot{s} = 0$ such that the control state variables of $e(t)$ and $\dot{e}(t)$ gradually approach to 0 [6].

$$u_{eq} = \frac{Den_p}{\alpha}\left(k_2\dot{e} - \ddot{\psi}_{ref}\right) + \frac{1}{Den_p}g\left(J_w Lm_{bp} + J_m Lm_{bp}n^2 + Lm_w m_{bp}R_w^2 + Lm_{bp}^2 R_w^2\right)\sin\psi$$
$$-\frac{1}{Den_p}Lm_{bp}R_w\left(-J_m n^2 + Lm_{bp}R_w\cos\psi\right)\sin\psi\dot{\psi}^2 \tag{23}$$

where, $\alpha = J_w + m_w R_w^2 + m_{bp}R_w^2 + Lm_{bp}R_w\cos\psi$.

To keep the system states on the sliding surface, the control input u can be set as

$$u = u_{eq} + \gamma_2 \cdot \text{sgn}(s) \tag{24}$$

where, $\gamma_2 > 0$. The Lyapunov function is $V = \frac{1}{2}s^2$, and the equation 25 can be obtained after substitute the control input u into $\dot{V} = s\dot{s}$.

$$\dot{V} = s\dot{s} = s\left(k_2\dot{e} - \ddot{\psi}_{ref} + \frac{1}{Den_p}\left[-\left(J_w + m_w R_w^2 + m_{bp}R_w^2 + Lm_{bp}R_w\cos\psi\right)\tau_p\right.\right.$$
$$+g\left(J_w Lm_{bp} + J_m Lm_{bp}n^2 + Lm_w m_{bp}R_w^2 + Lm_{bp}^2 R_w^2\right)\sin\psi \tag{25}$$
$$\left.\left.-Lm_{bp}R_w\left(-J_m n^2 + Lm_{bp}R_w\cos\psi\right)\sin\psi\dot{\psi}^2\right]\right) = s \cdot -\gamma_2\frac{|s|}{s} \le 0$$

The control strategy adopted here will guarantee the system trajectories move toward and stay on the sliding surface $s = 0$ to satisfy the condition $\dot{V} = s\dot{s} \le 0$.

3.3   Design of the Fuzzy-Sliding Mode Controller

In this section, the fuzzy-sliding mode controller will be introduced [8]. The optimal sliding mode controller can be designed easily if the control input u_{eq} presented above obtained accurately. However, it is very difficult to obtain the control input accurately in real system. Therefore, the fuzzy logic system is implemented in our research to obtain the close control input [9]. The fuzzy rules as same as follows

$$\text{Rule } i: \textbf{IF} \text{ error is } F_e^i \textbf{ AND} \text{ change- of- error is } F_c^i \textbf{ THEN} \text{ ouput is } \delta_i \tag{26}$$

where, $\delta_i, i = 1, 2, ..., m$ are singleton values. F_e^i and F_c^i are fuzzy sets for the error and the derivative of the error, respectively. The triangular membership functions are used for both the IF and THEN parts. The fuzzy rules are summarized in Table 1.

The parameters of the unicycle robot are shown in table 2.

Both of error and change of error are labeled by a linguistic term such as "negative huge (NH)", "negative large(NL)","negative big (NB)", "negative medium(NM)", "negative small (NS)" ,"zero (ZO)","positive small(PS)", "positive medium (PM)", "positive big (PB)", "positive large(PL)"and "positive huge (PH)".

Table 1. Two input one output fuzzy rule for δ

δ		Change of error									
		NH	NL	NB	NM	NS	ZO	PS	PM	PB	PL	PH
	NH	PH	PH	PH	PH	PH	PH	PL	PB	PM	PS	Z
	NL	PH	PH	PH	PH	PH	PL	PB	PM	PS	Z	NS
	NB	PH	PH	PH	PH	PL	PB	PM	PS	Z	NS	NM
	NM	PH	PH	PH	PL	PB	PM	PS	Z	NS	NM	NB
E	NS	PH	PH	PL	PB	PM	PS	Z	NS	NM	NB	NL
R R O R	ZO	PH	PL	PB	PM	PS	Z	NS	NM	NB	NL	NH
	PS	PL	PB	PM	PS	Z	NS	NM	NB	NL	NH	NH
	PM	PB	PM	PS	Z	NS	NM	NB	NL	NH	NH	NH
	PB	PM	PS	Z	NS	NM	NB	NL	NH	NH	NH	NH
	PL	PS	Z	NS	NM	NB	NL	NH	NH	NH	NH	NH
	PH	Z	NS	NM	NB	NL	NH	NH	NH	NH	NH	NH

For the defuzzification, the center of gravity method was used as

$$u_{fz} = \frac{\sum_{i=1}^{m} w_i \cdot \delta_i}{\sum_{i=1}^{m} w_i} \tag{27}$$

where, w_i is the weight for the ith rule.

To determine the stability of this fuzzy-sliding mode algorithm, the roll dynamics in the equation 6-a can be defined as

$$\ddot{\theta}_b = f_{roll}(q) - u \tag{28}$$

where, $f_{roll}(q)$ includes the uncertain time varying and nonlinear terms in the roll dynamics. From the equation 17, for the control input u, u_{eq} is replaced by u_{fz} and the result is substituted into the equation 19 for $\dot{V} = s\dot{s}$.

$$\dot{V} = s\dot{s} = s\left(k_1\dot{e} - \ddot{\theta}_{ref} + f_{roll}(q) - u\right) = s\left(k_1\dot{e} - \ddot{\theta}_{ref} + f_{roll}(q) - u_{fz1} - \gamma_1 \operatorname{sgn}(s)\right) \tag{29}$$

where, the condition $u_{fz1} = k_1\dot{e} - \ddot{\theta}_{ref} + f_{roll}(q)$ is satisfied by the fuzzy rules which guarantee the stability condition for $\dot{V} = s\dot{s} \leq 0$.

As same as roll dynamics, the pitch dynamics in the equation 12-a can be defined as

$$\ddot{\psi} = f_{pitch}(q) - u \tag{30}$$

where, $f_{pitch}(q)$ includes the uncertain time varying and nonlinear terms in the pitch dynamics. From the equation 24, for the control input u, u_{eq} is replaced by u_{fz} and the result is substituted into the equation 25 for $\dot{V} = s\dot{s}$.

$$\dot{V} = s\dot{s} = s\left(k_2\dot{e} - \ddot{\psi}_{ref} + f_{pitch}(q) - u\right) = s\left(k_2\dot{e} - \ddot{\psi}_{ref} + f_{pitch}(q) - u_{fz2} - \gamma_2\operatorname{sgn}(s)\right) \quad (31)$$

where, the condition $u_{fz2} = k_2\dot{e} - \ddot{\psi}_{ref} + f_{pitch}(q)$ is satisfied by the fuzzy rules which guarantee the stability condition for $\dot{V} = s\dot{s} \le 0$.

4   Experiments and Results

The unicycle robot used in our research is shown in figure 1. The gyro and accelerometer which were used to measure the angle were installed in the middle position of the robot. The microcontroller and the motor driver were installed on the upper part and the bottom part of robot body respectively. The NTARS of NTREX Corp. and the processor ARM Cortex-M3(LM3S8962) were used to obtain the angle of robot. The DC motors by MAXON Corp. were used and the angular data obtained by encoders. For the motor drives, NT-DC20A H-bridge types were used.

The DC motor for pitch drive was connected with the wheel by timing belt. The reason is to keep the structure of the roll axis balance than the case connecting the motor with the wheel directly. However, the motor for roll drive was connected with the rotation disk directly. The bluetooth module was installed on the top part of robot body to communicate with computer.

Table 2. Parameters of the unicycle robot

Symbol	Value	Symbol	Value	Symbol	Value
m_d	$1.225[kg]$	R_w	$0.110[m]$	J_d	$0.0402\left[kg\,m^2\right]$
m_b	$3.664[kg]$	R_p	$0.200[m]$	J_b	$0.5295\left[kg\,m^2\right]$
m_w	$1.300[kg]$	L_2	$0.570[m]$	J_ψ	$0.7208\left[kg\,m^2\right]$
m_{br}	$4.889[kg]$	L_{br}	$0.285[m]$	J_w	$0.0079\left[kg\,m^2\right]$
m_{bp}	$4.964[kg]$	L	$0.330[m]$	J_m	$0.0001\left[kg\,m^2\right]$

For the two inputs of ramp and ladder shapes, the robot's angles and positions were measured to evaluate the performance of the proposed decoupled control scheme.

4.1   Ramp Input

A ramp input was applied to the unicycle robot for a distance about 3.3m while measuring the angle, velocity and distance data of robot. In figure 3(a) the solid line and the dotted line represent the real movement distance and the reference input respectively. And the dotted line represents the difference between them. Figure 3(b) illustrates roll and pitch angle errors of the robot which represented by the dotted line and the solid line respectively. The results show that roll and pitch angular errors were kept within approximately ±1° and ±2° respectively while the unicycle robot traveling.

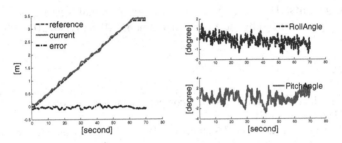

Fig. 3. (a) Tracking for rotational angle of wheel, (b) The angle of robot for (a)

4.2   Ladder Input

A ladder input was applied to the unicycle robot for moving forward a distance about 1.1m and returning to the start point while measuring the angle, velocity and distance data of robot. In figure 4(a) the solid line and the dotted line represent the real movement distance and the reference input respectively. And the dotted line represents the difference between them. Figure 4(b) illustrates the roll and pitch angle errors of the robot which represented by the dotted line and the solid line respectively. The results show that the roll and pitch angular errors were kept within approximately ±2° and ±4° respectively while the unicycle robot traveling.

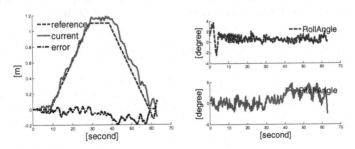

Fig. 4. (a) Tracking for rotational angle of wheel, (b) The angle of robot for (a)

5   Conclusions

In this paper, we researched on the attitude control method of the unicycle robot. The roll and the pitch axes controls of the unicycle robot dynamics model were assumed to be decoupling with each other, and established based on Lagrange function separately. In this process, the coupled terms of the pitch and the roll axes are considered as their own disturbance, and a robust fuzzy sliding mode controller designed in this paper is applied to overcome these disturbances. The performance of the fuzzy-sliding controller proposed in this paper was superior, which was proved by simulations and experiments.

Acknowledgements. This study was supported by National Research Foundation of Korea (NRF) grant funded by the Korea government (MEST) (No. 2010-0027360).

References

1. Schoonwinkel, A.: Design and test of a computer stabilized unicycle. Ph. D. dissertation, Stanford Univ., CA (1987)
2. Sheng, Z., Yamafuji, K.: Postural Stability of a Human Riding a Unicycle and Its Emulation by a Robot. IEEE Trans. Robotics and Automation 13(5), 709–720 (1997)
3. Dao, M.Q., Liu, K.Z.: Gain-Scheduled Stabilization Control of a Unicycle Robot. JSME International Journal 48(4), 649–656 (2005)
4. Block, D., Åström, K., Spong, M.: The Reaction Wheel Pendulum. Synthesis Lectures on Control and Mechatronics. Morgan & Claypool Publishers, Princeton (2007)
5. Technical report of LEGO Mindstorm,
   http://www.mathworks.com/matlabcentral/fileexchange/19147
6. Han, S.I., Kong, J.H., Shin, D.W., Kim, J.S.: Precise Control for Servo Systems Using Sliding Mode Observer and Controller. Journal of the Korean Society of Precision Engineering 19(7), 154–162 (2002)
7. Bui, V.P., Kim, Y.B.: Design of Sliding Mode Controller for Ship Position Control. Journal of Institute of Control, Robotics and Systems 17(9), 869–874 (2011)
8. Seo, S.J., Kim, D.S., Kim, D.W., Park, G.T.: Control of Hydraulic Excavator Using Self Tuning Fuzzy Sliding Mode Control. Journal of Institute of Control, Robotics and Systems 11(2), 160–166 (2005)
9. Ryu, S.H., Park, J.H.: Auto-tuning of Sliding Mode Control Parameters Using Fuzzy Logic. In: Conference of the Korean Society of Precision Engineering (2000)

Evaluation of Response Models to a Series of Commands in a Telerobotics Supervisory Control System

Ida Bagus Kerthyayana Manuaba[1,2], Ken Taylor[2], and Tom Gedeon[1]

[1] Research School of Computer Science, The Australian National University
[2] Commonwealth Science and Industrial Research Organisation ICT Centre, Australia
{bagus.manuaba,tom.gedeon}@anu.edu.au, ken.taylor@csiro.au

Abstract. In contrast to direct manual control of manipulators, telerobotic interaction based on human supervisory control allows human operators to plan the movement of the remote machine by entering a series of commands as pre-defined positions. There are two possible kinds of response movements from executing this series of commands. Firstly, the robot moves towards the newly defined position immediately; or, secondly, the robot moves to achieve all the queued series of positions one by one. This paper describes an experiment to test the performance of the two kinds of response movements under varying visual feedback scenarios. By applying a mixed reality environment as the telerobotics interface, this experiment makes use of virtual objects to provide additional information for planning and monitoring the process. The highest productivity was achieved using a queue based model of interaction with additional visual cues. This was also compared to direct manual control and found to be considerably superior.

Keywords: Human Supervisory Control, Telerobotics, Multi-defined position, Response Movement, Virtual Information.

1 Introduction

The advancement of telerobotics technology allows a move from manual operation to full automation. This transformation can reduce human workload and increase productivity. However, unlike factory or industrial areas which utilise machines to perform a repeatable task [1], in mining areas most scenarios are varied and require human operators to make decisions in performing the task. Therefore, direct manual control is most commonly applied in mining areas.

Human supervisory control is proposed to shift the control model toward automation without eliminating the role of the human operator in the operating process. This technology is an alternative to manual operation that minimises human operator involvement without interfering with the machine performance [2][3]. Supervisory control systems are used by a human operator who acts as the supervisor of the intelligent system, which allows them to plan, monitor and intervene in the process when needed.

In telerobotics with supervisory control, the human operator can define a series of input commands, which will be carried out automatically by the machine. There are

C.-Y. Su, S. Rakheja, H. Liu (Eds.): ICIRA 2012, Part III, LNAI 7508, pp. 73–84, 2012.
© Springer-Verlag Berlin Heidelberg 2012

two possible response movements namely "Adaptation" and "Queue". In general, the Adaptation model works by moving the manipulator immediately to a new position. The Queue model works by making sure the manipulator reaches all intermediate positions one by one before reaching the final position.

Another important aspect in telerobotics is the ability of the interface (system) to provide information on the remote location to the end user. From previous work[4][5], we developed a telerobotics user interface by utilising a mixed reality environment that integrates information between a 3D virtual environment and a live video. The advantage of using the virtual environment is the ability to create a number of virtual objects to provide visual feedback information, which is useful in planning, monitoring and performing the task.

This paper describes an experiment that was conducted to test a telerobotics system utilising human supervisory control based on response movements from a series of input commands in a mixed reality interface. The key questions of the experiment were:

a. Based on the completion time and success rate, how do the performance of the Adaptation and Queue models compare?
b. Could the visual planning information improve the operator performance in task completion?
c. Would the human supervisory control model be able to replace manual/direct control for this experiment design task?

The rest of this paper describes related works on human supervisory control (section 2); the introduction of two models of response movement (section 3); the prototype implementation of our telerobotics system (section 4); the evaluation of the experiment (section 5) and the experimental results (section 6). The paper is concluded with a discussion of the results (section 7 and 8).

2   Related Work

The term supervisory control (SC) has emerged in most areas of the industry, from auto-pilot [6] to smart-phones [7][8]. In general, human supervisory control can be defined as an interaction between a human, who acts as the supervisor, and the machine/system, which acts as the subordinate. Tendick [9] said that human supervisory control is a system where a human operator acts as a supervisor who has the abilities to plan, monitor and interrupt the process during the execution carried out by machines. In telerobotics, human supervisory control can also be a preference to direct/manual control[1–3]. Human supervisory control has a number of advantages such as the ability to improve the reliability of the machine's performance without total human involvement [1]; simplify the control process by defining movements and goals rather than fully controling the process; minimise the effect of time delay in communication between human and teleoperator [3][10][11]; and eliminate the requirement for continual human attention, therefore reducing the operator workload.

Based on its definition, human supervisory control has three generic supervisory functions, which are known as planning, monitoring and intervening (interrupting).

Sheridan [1] states that the important aspect in telerobotics supervisory control is the ability of the system (computer) to package consolidated information in a visual display to the human operator. This information is useful for planning and examining the task performance and for making a quick decision to override the process when needed.

3   The Model of Response Movement

The experiment was a continuation of our previous work in telerobotics using a Mixed Reality Interface [4][5]. We conducted the experiment by testing human supervisory control as an alternative input model to direct/manual control. As mentioned above, human supervisory control allows the human operator to input a series of commands when defining target positions. In this experiment, we grouped the possible kinds of response movements into two models as follows:

a. Adaption Model

This response model has the ability to respond to the operator's commands by moving to a new position immediately. The algorithm in the adaptation model forced the 3D model or the manipulator to cancel the current process, update its target according to the new position determined, and continue the process towards the new target. This model gives human operators more control in supervising the manipulator's movement.

b. Queue Model

This response model adopts the logic of queuing services. The queuing services works by following a FIFO (First-In-First-Out) concept where the system needs to complete servicing one entity before continuing to the next entity. This system is shown in Fig.1 where the 3D model or the manipulator moves to reach all the positions one by one.

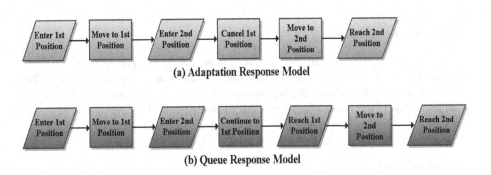

(a) Adaptation Response Model

(b) Queue Response Model

Fig. 1. Diagram of Adaptation and Queue response model

4   Prototype Implementation

We built a closed loop client server communication between the operator–interface
(as client) and the server/remote machine (as manipulator). The overall system is
illustrated in Fig.2.

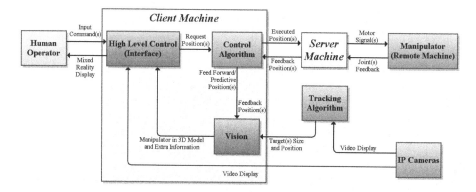

Fig. 2. Diagram Telerobotics System Implementation (Overall System)

4.1   Our Telerobotics System

We developed an interface using a gaming engine called unity3D for user interaction.
A 3D model of a robot arm was inserted into this virtual environment to show the real
time position feedback from the robot arm. In applying the mixed reality concept and
provide all information in a single screen, we also added video streaming from the IP
camera which was installed at the remote location. At the remote location a server
was built to convey any information between the robot arm and the end user. Further,
the server is also connected to the IP camera to track the positions of the target objects
(blocks) and update these positions on the end user interface.

4.2   Features Available

Our user interface provided all the information, including the previous information
(feedback), current information (monitoring) and future information (planning). In the
unpredictable situation where the manipulator is stuck before reaching the target
positions or where the human operator needs to change/cancel the robot's movement,
they can override the process instantly. There are a number of features available on
this system to enhance the performance of human supervisory control.

a. Stop Functions

In emergency situations, the system provides a number of functions that can be used
to override the current process and take control of the movement. These functions are
temporary stop (TS) and full stop (FS). Firstly, the temporary stop (TS) is a function

which works by suspending the predicted model and robot's movement temporarily by holding a key button, and allowing them to continue moving to the target when the operator releases the button. This function allows the operator to suspend movement while they evaluate the situation. Secondly, the full stop (FS) function works by stopping the robot's movement and at the same time cancelling all subsequent targets.

b. Path Finding Algorithm

Our user interface represents detected block as 3D models each of which can be defined as a target block. However, it was designed so that only one block can be selected as a target object. When a model block is selected as a target, the remaining blocks will serve as obstacles to the manipulator. Accordingly, a function is added into the system, which is adopted from A*(read: A-star) path-finding algorithm, to create paths which allow the robot to avoid the obstacles automatically.

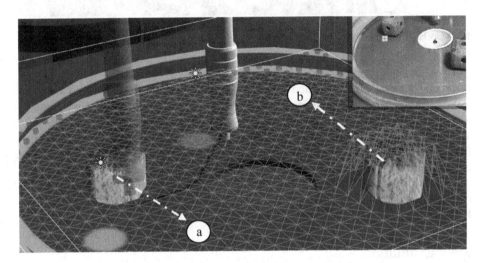

Fig. 3. Path generating from A*(A-star) algorithm in (a) selected block and (b) unselected block model

c. Visual Planning Information

A mixed reality concept combines information gained from the virtual environment and live video [4][5]. The telerobotics user interface allows the computer to provide virtual objects as prediction or feedback information. These virtual objects can be utilised for planning, monitoring and intervening in processes. Below are four examples of the virtual objects which have been used (See Fig.4).

A "green circle" object serves as planning information to help the operator by showing the series of target positions. It appears when a target position for the robot is defined. Each green circle had a diameter of 4mm indicating that the error tolerance for the model/robot to reach the destination target was 0 – 2mm. Another virtual object that was used is the "shadow TIP". It gave a prediction of the position of the

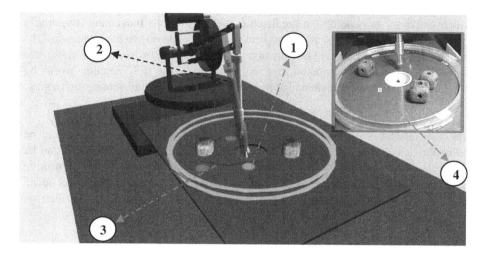

Fig. 4. Visual informations (1) Green circles. (2) Shadow TIP, (3) Line path, and (4) Overlay pointer.

manipulator model and replicated the shape of the robot arm TIP model by using a transparent texture. The "line path" was another virtual object. This line pointed towards the TIP shadow object to predict the path of the manipulator model. The last virtual object is the "overlay pointer". It was presented as a cross symbol and showed the predicted position of the TIP on the video display. The overlay pointer applied the concept of augmented reality by enhancing virtual object overlays on the live video.

In order to analyse the performance of this visual planning information, each response movement model (Adaptation and Queue) was tested with and without this feature.

5   Evaluation

The objective of this experiment was to analyse the performance of two movement response models by using additional virtual information in the planning and monitoring process. In order to test the advantages of human supervisory control, direct control was used as a performance comparison with the best human supervisory control.

Participants were asked to test the program and evaluate its performance. Result of our previous research in utilising mixed reality for a telerobotics interface [5] was applied to this interface. We continue to investigate telerobotics system control in terms of objective and subjective measures for both human supervisory and direct control.

5.1   Experimental Setup

In this experiment, the telerobotics interface and the supervisory functions were built into a gaming engine. A gaming engine offers a sophisticated environment, which enables us to create the replica models of a remote machine, including the kinematics; to have integrated input devices and sensors (e.g. joystick, keyboard + mouse, haptics); to provide an immersive environment for the operators; and to allow client server communication. Therefore, this experiment setting was divided into two areas, the user interface at a client site and remote manipulator at a server site.

In the client site, a 32" monitor was used as the main screen with a resolution of 2560 x 1600 pixels, which showed the telerobotics mixed reality interface (including the 3D model and live video) from the remote location to the participants. A standard keyboard and mouse was used as the input devices to deliver commands from the human operator to the interface (client machine). A computer server was located at the remote location to communicate with the user interface, and a robot arm used as a manipulator was connected to the server. An IP camera was also attached at the remote location to capture video information and provide it for the interface. Besides providing video streaming information, this camera was also connected to the server to work as a tracking system to provide updates on the position of the target objects through image analysis.

5.2   Participants

The experiment was conducted with a total of 24 participants. They were selected by using participants driven sampling with a snow-ball sampling method. The participants consist of 79% male and 21% female with ages ranging from 16 – 37 years old (mean = 22.75, SD = 5.75 years old). All the participants have a background in university education. Most of them were computer users (13% used a computer less than 7 hours per week, 26% between 7 to 21 hours per week, and 61% used computers for more than 21 hours per week) and played computer games (50% played computer games for less than 7 hours per week, 25% between 7 to 21 hours per week, and the remaining 25% played for more than 21 hours per week). None of them had any background knowledge on telerobotics and were new to this prototype interface/system design.

5.3   Experimental Design and Procedure

The main task in this experiment was choosing a block and pushing it into a hole by following a generated path arrow. The initial robot and blocks positions were the same for each participant. All participants were required at the start to select one block by clicking its model. They were allowed to change their block by clicking on another block model which would automatically assign the remaining blocks as obstacles.

Based on the response movement models and visual planning information described, we grouped the experiment into four different models. They are the (1) Adaptation model with planning information; (2) Adaptation model without planning information; (3) Queue model with planning information; and (4) Queue model without planning information. The participants were randomly assigned to model-test sequences. Prior to the experiment, the participants received an explanation (10-15 minutes) regarding the aims of the experiment, the differences between the models and the task scenario. Participants did not practice prior to the experiment. A maximum of 180 seconds was allocated to perform the task for each model. During the experiment, a successful result was counted when the participants followed the path assigned and sunk a block into the hole during the time allocated. Completion times were also recorded when the participant sank the block in the hole. These variables were noted as objective measurements in analysing the performance of each model. Either prior or subsequent to the requested task with the supervisory control model, the participants were also asked to perform the same task using the manual/direct control model to be later compared with the best supervisory control model. A questionnaire using a 7 point *Likert* scale and open-ended questions were used as subjective measurements.

6   Results

6.1   Objective Measurement

Completion time was the first objective meassurement recorded in the experiment. The average completion time for successful result in four models tested was 77.35 seconds (SD = 38.41 seconds) with detail for each model shown in table 1.

Table 1. Completion time for successful result using each model tested

Model Tested	Mean	SD	Min	Max
Adaptation with Info	91.49 s	39.61 s	32.6 s	150.7 s
Adaptation non Info	73.75 s	36.58 s	30.2 s	163.0 s
Queue with Info	75.15 s	37.66 s	19.4 s	165.1 s
Queue non Info	71.41 s	27.55 s	27.8 s	125.4 s

This experiment showed that there was a relation between the probability of success and the completion time with the correlation coefficient of -0.62. To further study this relationship, we grouped the completion time into 3 groups, 0-60 seconds, >60-120 seconds, and >120-180 seconds. As shown in table 2, there was a significant relationship (p=0.000) between completion time and result of the experiment (success or failure).

Table 2. The distribution proportion of result experiment by group of time

Completion Time (seconds)	Result of experiment		p	χ^2
	Failure N(%)	Success N(%)		
0 – 60	2 (5.88)	32 (94.12)	0.000	35.29
>60 – 120	0 (0.00)	34 (100.00)		
>120 – 180	15 (53.57)	13 (46.43)		

Logistic regression was performed to analyse this relationship more deeply, and the results showed that the participants who took longer than 120 seconds to complete the task have a much lower probability of success compared to those groups who completed the task more quickly (OR=0.05, p=0.000). Detailed logistic regressions for each model are shown in Fig.6.

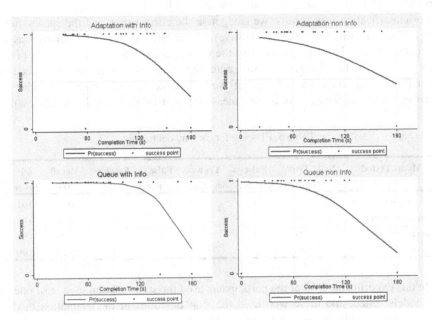

Fig. 6. Logistic regression showing the relationship between the probability of success and completion time

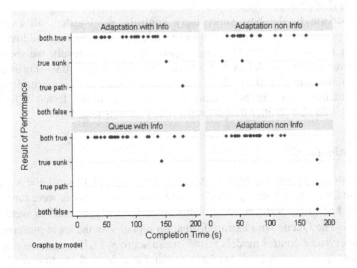

Fig. 7. Scatter plot – result of performance and completion time for four supervisory model tested

In this experiment, we recorded two variables, path and sunk, as indicators of the result of the experiment.

Based on Rijsbergen's equation [12], we used the F1-score to test the harmonic mean between precision and recall variable, in order to measure the performance from each model tested. The F1-score can be interpreted as a weight average of these two variables, with the best value at 1 and worst score at 0.

For classification task results, we categorise the correct path and the successfully sunk rocks as a correct result (True positive), the incorrect path with a sunk rock as an unexpected result (False positive), only the path is correct as a missing result (True negative) and the last category, neither path and sunk was correct as an absence of result (False negative). Then, by using these variables we calculated the value of precision and recall for each model and measured the F1-score (See Table 3 below).

Table 3. F1-score for each model tested

Model Tested	N	True positive	False positive	True negative	False negative	Precision (p)	Recall (r)	F1 Score
Adaptation with Info	24	20	1	3	0	0.95	0.87	0.91
Adaptation non Info	24	19	2	3	0	0.90	0.86	0.88
Queue with Info	**24**	**21**	**1**	**2**	**0**	**0.95**	**0.91**	**0.93**
Queue non Info	24	19	1	3	1	0.95	0.86	0.90

In this experiment, 83% of the participants used the stop function in at least one of the models tested, and these who used the stop functions in the adaptation model, were 8.4 times more likely to succeed compared with those who did not used these functions (p=0.05). On the contrary, there is no significant relationship between the utilization of stop function and result of experiments (success or failure) in the queue model (OR=0.66, p=0.6).

In comparison to the best supervisory control model tested, all twenty four participants performed an additional sub experiment to test the manual/direct control model using the same design task and experiment. As the result, we measure the precision value for this model as 0.70 where the recall value is 0.94. Further the F1-score for manual control is 0.80 which means the F1-score performance for the direct model is smaller than the best supervisory control model tested (Queue with Information), and also smaller than all supervisory models tested.

6.2   Questionnaire

Based on our participants' opinion, most of them agreed that all the supervisory models tested were user friendly (modus score for the four models were ranging from 5 to 7) and had good performance (modus score for the four models were ranging from 4 to 6). The Queue with extra information model was the most preferred out of the four supervisory control models tested (mean score = 4.67, modus ranging from 5 to 7). In addition, participants also agreed that the extra information in the model interface helped them in performing the task.

7   Discussion

The result showed that the Queue model perform slightly better than the Adaptation model (higher F1 score). In the Queue model, it seems that the participants had more control in their movement's planning. Even though in some situations they intervened by changing the path plan, it can easily be done with the available stop functions. Compared with the queue model, the stop functions were more helpful in the adaptation model since each time this model defined a new target position, the robot directly moved to the new target. In this scenario, the stop functions were useful to provide a condition for checking or cancelling the planning process. We also found that in performing either with the Adaptation or Queue model, most participants can successfully finish the task (by following the correct arrow and sink the block) less than 120 seconds, with the highest success under the Queue model with visual planning information.

The experimental results also showed that the models tested with visual planning information performed better than those without. The planning information, which was not sourced from the remote location, is useful in helping the participant to perform the scenario task, especially for the Queue model.

Comparing the performance between the best supervisory model (Queue with info model) and Manual/Direct control, participant using the supervisory model did better in following the path and sinking the block than participants using the manual/direct model. The movement planning function appeared to be an important feature which needed to be provided for telerobotics especially for the supervisory control model.

In addition to the objective measurement, we also asked our participants several open-ended questions about the interface performance. Participants were asked which features they were most attracted to and their suggestions for improving the interface performance. Based on the collected data, some of our participants said that the interface was enjoyable and fun. We thus argue that the gaming environment has played a significant role in creating an immersive atmosphere contributing to the participants' satisfaction. When asked about the features of the interface, most mentioned that they liked the functionality of the interface in providing information. As mentioned by one of our participants, "The mixture of 3D and video interface was useful for me because I can cross-check between each interface." This showed that the combination of 3D virtual and video view had assisted them in performing the task.

Moreover, three participants mentioned that they liked all features of our interface. Based on comments that we received from other participants, the viewpoint control, the graphic display and the additional information provided (e.g. green circle and lines) made our interface likeable. Furthermore, 17.6% of our participants emphasized that the most interesting feature for them was being able to use or control the interface easily, as expressed by the following response, "..... The use of the gaming key helped me to better control the robot arm and manage the 3D interface .... ".

8   Conclusion

The four supervisory models tested in this experiment showed better performance than direct/manual control. The queue response movement with visual planning information performed best. The visual planning information provided improved task performance. However, visual planning information did not have a large impact on performance in the Adaptable model probably because the participants do not plan very far ahead.

Even though the models tested showed good performance and received positive response from our participants, a number of suggestions for improvements in several aspects of the interface were provided. Most of the participants focused their comments on the 3D virtual views' performance. When they tried to operate the interface, they found several weaknesses in our 3D views, such as the precision, time delay and the stability of the 3D graphic. Due to these problems, our participants had a tendency to rely more on the video camera than they otherwise would have: "…. There were circumstances when we could see the robot arm touching the object on the video … but this could not be seen in the 3D model". This emphasises the need for mixed reality in interfaces to provide a mechanism that allows human interpretation to be applied where inaccurate sensing has introduced model errors. In practical telerobotics applications, incomplete models are common as a process that can be accurately modelled is probably amenable to fully automated control.

References

1. Sheridan, T.B.: Telerobotics, Automation, and Human Supervisory Control. The MIT Press Cambridge, Massachusetts, London, England (1992)
2. Ho, Y.F., Masuda, H., Oda, H., Stark, L.W., Fellow, L.: Distributed Control for Tele-Operations 5(2), 100–109 (2000)
3. Blackmon, T., Stark, L.: Model-based supervisory control in telerobotics. Presence 5(2), 205–223 (spring 1996)
4. Manuaba, I.B.K., Taylor, K., Gedeon, T.: Comparison between Two Mixed Reality Environments for Teleoperation Interface. In: IEEE International Conference on Robotics and Automation (ICRA 2011), Shanghai, China, pp. 1335–1340 (May 2011)
5. Manuaba, I.B.K., Taylor, K., Widzyk-capehart, E.: Building Effective Teleoperation Interfaces Applications By Utilising Mixed Reality For Mining. In: 22nd World Mining Congress & Expo, Instambul, Turkey, September 11-16 (2011)
6. Sheridan, T.B.: Human and Automation. A John Willey & Sons, Inc., Santa Monica (2002)
7. Fong, T., Thrope, C., Baur, C.: Active Interfaces for Vehicle Teleoperation. Robotics and Machines Perception, SPIE's International Technical Group Newsletter 10(1) (2001)
8. Fong, T., Conti, F., Grange, S., Baur, C.: Novel interfaces for remote driving: gesture, haptic and PDA (2000)
9. Tendick, F., Voichick, J., Tharp, G., Stark, L.: A supervisory telerobotic control system using model-based vision feedback, Sacramento, CA, April 9-11, vol. 3, pp. 2280–2285 (1991)
10. Lin, Q., Kuo, C.: Applying Virtual Reality to Underwater Robot Tele-operation and Pilot Training. The International Journal of Virtual Reality 5(1), 19 (2001)
11. Reichenbach, T., Miclic, D., Kovacic, Z.: Supervisory Control by Using Active 3D Models in-the-loop (2006)
12. Rijsbergen, C.J.: Information Retrieval. Butterworth-Heinemann (1979)

An Embedded Control System
for Automatic Guided Vehicle

Xiaoming Qian and Peihuang Lou

College of Mechanical and Electrical, Nanjing University of Aeronautics and Astronautics
Nanjing, Jiangsu, China 210016
drqian@nuaa.edu.cn

Abstract. An embedded control system with a Real-Time Operating System (RTOS) is designed and developed for a vision based Automatic Guided Vehicle (AGV) in this paper. In order to get high performance and reliability, the dual-core processor embedded system is used, including a main-controller for vehicle motion control, and a sub-controller for vision navigation. The embedded RTOS uC/OS-II is used to construct a software development platform, by which tasks schedule and system services software are realized.

Keywords: Embedded System, Automatic Guided Vehicle, Real-Time Operating System.

1 Introduction

Automatic Guided Vehicle (AGV) is a 年 intelligent equipment used for logistics handling [1]. The hardware system of most AGV is using industrial computer as the controller with multi-function cards for extended module while the software system is generally based on Windows operating system [2]. It is convenient to develop control system with different function cards for an industrial computer, and easy to get driver for various devices under Windows OS. However, there are also some unavoidable disadvantages for this universal solution [3]. Unnecessary functions in the system charge additional payment from users. Power dissipation is another problem because real time execution in universal system requires CPU with high performance [4]. Besides, it is difficult for Windows system to achieve real time completely [5].

AS for AGV, it has many strict requirements for hardware control system. First, it needs real time motion control and navigation [6]. Second it requires reduction in size of components and circuits of the hardware to lower the power dissipation and reduce signal propagation delays [7]. With the development of embedded systems, ARM, DSP and FPGA have become more and more popular for mobile robot like AGV. The ARM and DSP are used widely to accomplish motion control [8], and sometimes also applied for complex algorithm, such as image processing.

A multi-processor control system with master-slave distributed architecture for a vision based AGV is designed and developed in this paper. This multi-processor controller consists of a main-controller with ARM LPC2210, and a sub-controller for

C.-Y. Su, S. Rakheja, H. Liu (Eds.): ICIRA 2012, Part III, LNAI 7508, pp. 85–92, 2012.

vision navigation with DSP TMS320DM642. All functions related to the AGV can be classified as different tasks. Image processing for guideline acquisition is developed by the sub-controller DSP, which can get path errors (distance and angle errors) according to a guideline on the ground.

The remaining part of this paper is organized as follows. A hardware structure of the dual-core control system is presented in section 2. Design of software structure and development of multitask programming based on the RTOS uC/OS- II are discussed concretely in section 3. A physical AGV is introduced in section 4. In the end, the conclusion and future work are outlined in section 5.

2   Hardware of Control System for AGV

2.1   Mechanical Structure of AGV

The mechanical structure of the AGV is shown in Fig. 1. Two wheels in middle of the AGV are driven wheels, which are actuated separately by two DC motors. Two optical encoders are mounted respectively to each driven wheel shaft for position and speed feedback. Other two wheels are universal wheels to support AGV. There are two trajectories of line and arc for AGV. The center of linking line between two driven wheels is the kinematics origin of AGV. A CCD camera is in front of the AGV. Two ultrasonic sensors are installed to detect obstacles and measure the distance. Two photoelectric sensors are fixed both in front and back of it to find obstacles in a close distance. Four contact switches are distributed around it to monitor collision.

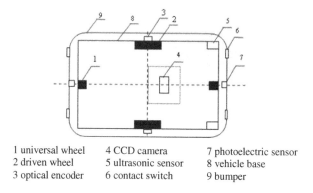

1 universal wheel	4 CCD camera	7 photoelectric sensor
2 driven wheel	5 ultrasonic sensor	8 vehicle base
3 optical encoder	6 contact switch	9 bumper

Fig. 1. Mechanical structure of AGV

2.2   Dual-Core Embedded Control System of AGV

The dual-core embedded control system of AGV is divided into six parts as show in Fig.2, including DSP TMS320DM642 for image processing and RFID information collecting, ARM LPC2210 for task manager, power regulation, sensors input, output for motor control and wireless communication. Each part is separately designed as function board and assembled by a connection board.

In order to get higher performance and better task schedule for AGV control, there are two processors called dual-core for the embedded control system. The controller consists of a main-controller with ARM LPC2210, and a sub-controller for vision navigation with DSP TMS320DM642. All functions related to the AGV can be classified as different tasks. Image processing for guideline acquisition are developed by the sub-controller DSP, which can extract two path errors (distance and angle errors) according to a guideline on the ground. All the other tasks are implemented by the main-controller ARM.

The DSP TMS320DM642 is excellent in image processing application. With performance of up to 5760 million instructions per second at a clock rate of 720 MHz, The DSP has the operational flexibility of high-speed controller and the numerical capability of array processor which is widely used for image processing algorithms. Moreover, additional on-chip peripherals set includes: three configurable video ports;

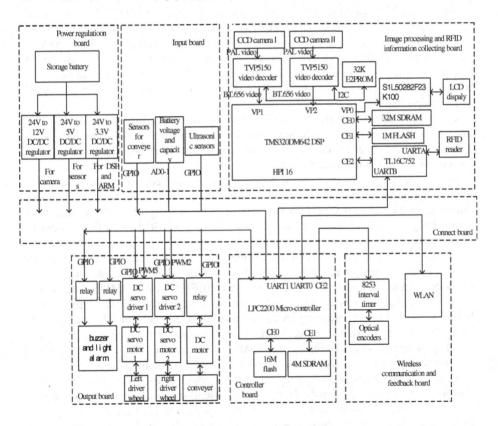

Fig. 2. Embedded system constructure of AGV

a management data input/output module; the I2C Bus module; three 32-bit general-purpose timers; a user-configurable 16-bit or 32-bit host-port interface; a 16-pin general-purpose input/output port with programmable interrupt/event generation modes; and a 64-bit external memory interface, which is capable of interfacing to two synchronous SDRAM and asynchronous FLASH program memories with 1M bytes.

Each of these configurable video ports consists of two channels — A and B with a 5120-byte capture/display buffer. CCD camera I and II export PAL format analog video signal, VP1 and VP2 operate as video capture ports, which provide interface to common video decoders TVP5150AM with horizontal and vertical sync signals. Each line capture completed event automatically informs Enhanced Direct Memory Access to transfer data to specified SDRAM address without DSP controller which saving the time of image processing. VP0 with the ability to output raw RGB data and horizontal/vertical sync signals is configured as video display mode, which has the necessary functionality to seamlessly interface to TFT LCD controllers.

E2PROM stores necessary data of system state, which isn't lost when system is power off. To communicate with RFID reader, the DM642 needs a UART interface to transmit data. The extended UART transmitter and receiver TLP16C752 is adopted to realize bidirectional conversation between serial and parallel data form.

LPC2210 is based on a 16/32 bit CPU with real-time emulation and embedded trace support. With its 144 pin package, low power consumption, various 32-bit timers, 8-channel 10-bit ADC, PWM channels and up to 9 external interrupt pins, this microcontroller is particularly suitable for industrial control. That is why it is adopted as the main-controller of the AGV.

Connection board is a passive device that supplies other functional boards with mutual interfaces & ports, which are defined by several signal lines or bus for every functional board. Specific definition of every interface is introduced later when the corresponding functional board is discussed.

Power board contains two sets of power supply system considering kinds of anti-interference requirements between the control system and the driving system. The interface for power board includes two sets of power supply of 12V, 5V, and 3.3V respectively, and an input signal line to send an alarm to ARM when faults occur in the power supply system.

Kernel board is a platform with a minimum system of the ARM LPC2210, which provides various peripheral devices for other functional boards related to it. The memory system contains a 16Mbit flash SST39LF160 and a 4Mbit static RAM IS61LV 25616, which is able to satisfy capacity requirements of the sophisticated hybrid algorithm of path tracking based on this embedded platform. The interface for kernel board consists of address & data bus, analog inputs, PWM outputs, GPIO, and serial communication interfaces, such as UART, I^{2}C, and SPI.

Input board provides several analog signal interfaces for ultrasonic sensors, and two-state signal interfaces for photo-electric sensors, contact switches, and other sensors. The two-state signals from contact switches will cause an immediate response from ARM by using the external interruption pin when a collision happens. Other input signals are processed periodically in a small time slot due to their lower demand on real time.

Output board has two kinds of control means: PWM and two-state switch outputs. The PWM outputs are utilized to control DC servo drivers, which amplify control signals from ARM, and actuate DC servomotors. The switch outputs are used to control two-state actuators and other output devices. In order to avoid power interference from the driving system to the control system, circuits are used to isolate control signals from the driving signals.

Encoder & wireless communicator board contains data & address bus, Uart1 with modem interface, and SPI1. In order to estimate the position and speed of the AGV, a decoding and counting interface circuit is used to count pulses and discern direction, which is based on the decoder/counter interface. Then ARM can read the value of the counter by address & data bus. Wireless communication is a perfect solution for information exchange between a mobile robot and a ground host computer. In order to reduce the processing burden on ARM, a microcontroller is responsible for wireless communication on the cooperation of a FSK receiver/transmitter chip.

3 Software Design for AGV

3.1 The Software for Main-Controller

An embedded RTOS for the main-controller ARM LPC2210 is able to simplify software development greatly by dividing the application into a series of tasks, and improve system reliability by ensuring real time performance.

The AGV control and management software running on LPC2210 is developed with uC/OS-II. All control functions are classified as ten tasks and one external interrupt, as shown in Fig. 3. Eight event control blocks, including semaphores, mailboxes, and a queue, provide inter-task communication and shared data protection.

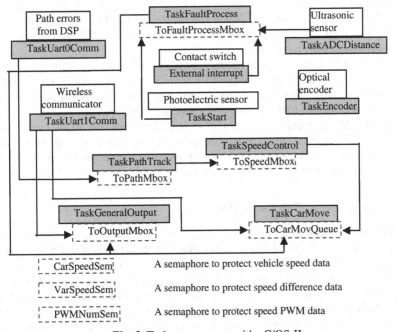

Fig. 3. Task management with uC/OS-II

The initial task TaskStart is the first and only task created by the main function, which is used to initialize the objective hardware, set device parameters, and create other nine tasks. A queue ToCarMovQueue with fixed-sized memory partitions is designed for TaskCarMove. Four mailboxes are assigned to four tasks respectively for inter-task communication. Three semaphores are used to protect shared data for data integrality. An event that some obstacles approach will trigger a message sent to the mailbox of TaskFaultProcess.

The communication task TaskUart0Comm is responsible for the path errors acquisition from DSP. In a fixed time slot, LPC2210 inquires the path errors actively and DSP provides the status data passively. Then the path errors are sent as a message to the mailbox of TaskPathTrack.

With the wireless controller STC12LE2052, another communication task TaskUart1Comm is involved in information exchange with the ground host computer. This task receives the command information from STC2052 by the serial port UART1, and then allocates them as messages to the different tasks according to the operation.

The Analog/Digital conversion task TaskADCDistance transforms periodically a 4-20mA current output of ultrasonic sensors to a 0-3.3V voltage that describes a distance between the AGV and a possible obstacle.

The TaskEncoder reads the count number and direction of the pulse from the IC HCTL-2021 by address & data bus. The vehicle speed is calculated according to the accumulated pulse number in the current interval.

The TaskFaultProcess estimates the running state of the V-AGV according to the feedback information from kinds of sensors. Once some accident occurs, this task commands the TaskGeneralOutput and TaskCarMove to run or stop output devices immediately. Until all faults are removed a command to cancel the alarm is sent out.

The TaskPathTrack implements the hybrid algorithm of path tracking control for the AGV. Speed difference for two driven wheels is calculated to adjust the AGV for eliminating two path errors when it moves along the guideline. The hybrid algorithm is carried out when path errors occur.

The driven wheel speed control task TaskSpeedControl converts the speed difference output to the voltage output, which controls the servomotor drivers directly. An expert PID algorithm is used for the wheels servo control in PWM way. The PWM number is sent to the mailbox of TaskCarMove.

The TaskCarMove provides a series of control functions for AGV movements, such as start, stop, speed change, etc. A queue is used to store temporarily the messages from other tasks in order to avoid possible information loss when a time delay occurs for smoothing sudden speed change.

3.2   The Software for Sub Controller

Fig. 4 shows the workflow of the sub controller DSP. DSP/BIOS is a real-time kernel for applications that require real-time scheduling and synchronization, host-to-target communication, or real-time instrumentation. First, the reset interrupt vector of DSP/BIOS is setup to branch after reset, stack is set up sequentially. BIOS_init is called to initialize the modules used by system. After all modules have completed their initialization procedures, the main routine is called for hardware interrupts initialization. Then BIOS_start is called, which is responsible for enabling the

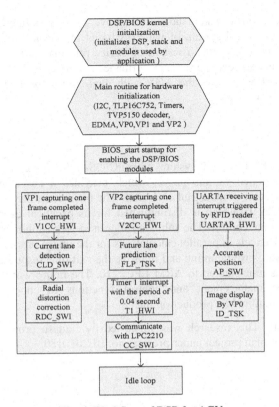

Fig. 4. Workflow of DSP for AGV

DSP/BIOS modules and invoking the MOD_startup macro for each DSP/BIOS. At last, the task scheduler runs TSK_idle which calls IDL_loop.

High performance algorithms are designed to accurately detect the artificial guide line. Image captured by camera I is processed using median filters that particularly effective in the presence of impulse noise. Segmenting, edge detecting algorithms and the method of least square is used to calculate equation of path line. Image captured by camera II is used for predict lane information of the future moment. Especially when AGV running speed exceed 1.5m/s. horizontal and vertical direction Hough transform is used to predict straight and turning way.

Fig. 5. Physical AGV

The embedded control system advanced above is a cost-effective solution for AGV, the previous control system of which is based on an industrial computer and several extended function cards. The aim of device reformation is to implement the similar functions and achieve the same performance at a much lower cost by using the embedded system. Fig.5 shows the AGV with dual-core embedded control system designed in this paper.

4   Conclusion

A dual-core embedded control system with uC/OS-II for a vision based AGV is designed and developed in this paper, which provides a cost-effective solution, compared to the system of industrial computer. The main-controller of AGV is based on the ARM LPC2210, which is distinguished for its excellent capability of event handling and real time control. The sub-controller used for vision navigation is based on the DSP, which excels in parallel calculations for the image processing. In order to simplify the software programming and improve the real time response, an embedded RTOS uC/OS-II is transplanted to ARM LPC2210. The future work focuses mainly on extending the management and control functions to cooperate with other equipments in the automobile production line.

Acknowledgments. This research was supported by Jiangsu province science and technology support plan project under projects no. BE2010189.

References

1. Martinez-Barbera, H., Herrero-Perez, D.: Development of a flexible AGV for flexible manufacturing systems. Industrial Robot 37(5), 459–468 (2010)
2. Armesto, L., Tornero, J.: Automation of industrial vehicles: a vision-based line tracking application. In: 2009 IEEE 14th International Conference on Emerging Technologies & Factory Automation, ETFA (2009)
3. Maalouf, E., Saad, M., Saliah, H.: A higher level path tracking controller for a four-wheel differentially steered mobile robot. Robotics and Autonomous Systems 54, 23–33 (2006)
4. Tomoya, F., Jun, O., Tamio, A.: Semi-Guided Navigation of AGV through Iterative Learning. In: International Conference on Intelligent Robots and Systems, Mani, Hawaii, USA, October 29-November 03 (2001)
5. Borangiu, T., Anton, F.D., Anton, S.: Open architecture for robot controllers. In: 19th International Workshop on Robotics in Alpe-Adria-Danube Region, RAAD 2010 - Proceedings, pp. 181–186 (2010)
6. Azimi, P., Hale, H., Alidoost, M.: The selection of the best control rule for a multiple-load AGV system using simulation and fuzzy MADM in a flexible manufacturing system. Modelling and Simulation in Engineering, 821701–821711 (2010)
7. Yamamoto, H., Yamada, T.: Intelligent AGV control of autonomous decentralized FMS by oblivion and memory. Key Engineering Materials, 447–448, 326–330 (2010)
8. Yahyaei, M., Jam, J.E., Hosnavi, R.: Controlling the navigation of automatic guided vehicle (AGV) using integrated Fuzzy logic controller with programmable logic controller (IFLPLC) - Stage 1. International Journal of Advanced Manufacturing Technology 47(5-8), 795–807 (2010)

Predictive Delay Compensation for Camera Based Oscillation Damping of a Multi Link Flexible Robot

Jörn Malzahn, Anh Son Phung, and Torsten Bertram

Institute of Control Theory and Systems Engineering, Technische Universität Dortmund,
D-44221 Dortmund, Germany
{Joern.Malzahn,AnhSon.Phung,Torsten.Bertram}@tu-dortmund.de
http://www.rst.e-technik.tu-dortmund.de

Abstract. For oscillation damping of a multi link flexible arm under gravity this paper exploits the image data already acquired by an eye-in-hand camera used for visual servoing. It replaces commonly applied distributed strain measurements in a model free oscillation damping control concept. Based on simulations and experiments the paper compares three predictive signal processing approaches to compensate for the sensor inherent delay. Damping results for oscillations induced by joint motions as well as sudden load changes are presented in three different unstructured scenes.

Keywords: Multi link flexible robots, visual oscillation damping, delay compensation.

1 Introduction

1.1 Related Work

Eye-in-hand visual servoing controllers accurately position the end-effector of multi link flexible robots in the presence of configuration and load dependent static deflections. A video demonstrating this fact is available on the internet[1]. The underlying oscillation damping controller is frequently realized with multiple strain gauges along the kinematic chain [1]. Actually, during visual position control the single camera already acquires the information about the superposed oscillations on all links. The idea behind this contribution is to exploit the present information in order to replace the set of distributed strain sensors.

The feasibility constraints imposed by the camera projection, frame rate and oscillation amplitudes are investigated in [2]. The image acquisition and processing adds a delay, which can destabilize the oscillation damping controller. The authors of [3] employ an extended Kalman filter with a full dynamics model of the flexible link robot to compensate the delay for motion induced oscillations. Especially with varying payloads accurate dynamics models of multi link flexible arms are hard to derive. In this paper predictive signal processing approaches infer the actual delay free feedback signal from a sliding window of recorded signal samples. They involve only minimum knowledge about the excitation source and plant dynamics. In [4] auto-regression as well as functional modelling are both termed linear prediction methods and constitute

---

[1] http://www.youtube.com/watch?v=V2NnEU6yGEA

C.-Y. Su, S. Rakheja, H. Liu (Eds.): ICIRA 2012, Part III, LNAI 7508, pp. 93–102, 2012.

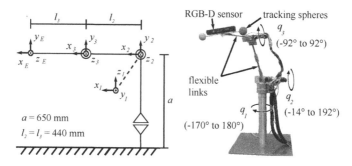

Fig. 1. TUDOR - Technische Universität Dortmund Omnielastic Robot

an alternative to the Discrete Fourier Transform (DFT). The Linear Predictive Coding is an auto-regression technique originally applied in audio signal processing [5]. The sinusoidal-regression approach with an adaptive window length belongs to the functional modelling methods and assumes the signal to be composed of an a priori known number of sinusoids. The authors of [6] investigate the sinusoidal-regression for camera based damping of a flexible link arm with a single dominant eigenfrequency. In this contribution multiple frequencies are considered.

After the introduction to the experimental rig the next section illustrates the camera based oscillation sensing. Section 3 introduces the extrapolation based on the discrete Fourier series and the two linear prediction methods. The delay deliberated oscillation signals replace the distributed strain measurements in a model free control scheme contained in section 5. The Experimental setup and damping results with oscillations excited by joint motions as well as environment interactions are given in section 6. The paper ends with conclusions and gives an outlook in section 7.

1.2   Experimental Rig TUDOR

The experimental rig TUDOR is depicted in Fig. 1. The three rotary joints consist of brushless DC motors with high ratio planetary ceramic gears. The left of Fig. 1 shows their arrangement in the joint zero configuration of the equivalent rigid body kinematics. The material of the two flexible links is spring steel with rectangular cross sections. Their lengths are denoted by l_2 and l_3. The cross section height h_y is 4 mm while the width h_z amounts to 15 mm. Each flexible link has two strain gauge pairs applied as reference. A video illustrating the undamped oscillation amplitudes is available online[2]. The end-effector carries the RGB-D camera (450 g), which provides per pixel depth measurements in addition to a conventional RGB image.

2   Oscillation Sensing

At the time step τ an image Jacobian based on the subpixel image coordinates u_k and v_k of the point feature at time step $\tau - 1$ together with the calibrated focal length λ computes to:

---

[2] http://www.youtube.com/watch?v=pmnX4wpgB_E

Fig. 2. Experimental test scenes with extracted features. The average feature depths amount to: 3.99 m (*a*), 1.65 m (*b*) as well as 2.33 m (*c*). The standard deviations of the feature depths are: 1.25 m (*a*), 0.23 m (*b*) and 0.77 m (*c*). Compared to (*a*) and (*b*) scene (*c*) is sparsely textured.

$$
\mathbf{J}_{I,k} = \begin{bmatrix} \frac{\lambda}{z_k}, & 0, & -\frac{u_k}{z_k}, & -\frac{u_k\,v_k}{\lambda}, & \frac{\lambda^2+u_k^2}{\lambda}, & -v_k \\ 0, & \frac{\lambda}{z_k}, & -\frac{v_k}{z_k}, & -\frac{\lambda^2+v_k^2}{\lambda}, & \frac{u_k\,v_k}{\lambda}, & u_k \end{bmatrix}. \tag{1}
$$

The camera translation **t** and rotation $\boldsymbol{\omega}$ are reconstructed from multiple point features:

$$
\begin{bmatrix} \mathbf{t} \\ \boldsymbol{\omega} \end{bmatrix} = \mathbf{J}_{I,n_k}^{\dagger} \left[\Delta u_1, \Delta v_1, \Delta u_2, \Delta v_2, \cdots \Delta u_{n_k}, \Delta v_{n_k} \right]^{\mathrm{T}}, \tag{2}
$$

where the Jacobian $\mathbf{J}_{I,n_k}$ is the line-by-line composition of (1) for each point feature extracted on the real world office environment scenes in Fig. 2. The pseudo-inverse of $\mathbf{J}_{I,n_k}$ is denoted by $\mathbf{J}_{I,n_k}^{\dagger}$. During image acquisition the detection of periodic light impulses triggered from the robot real-time operating system verifies the time $t_T = 72$ ms to be inherent to the camera and image processing.

3   Predictive Delay Compensation

This contribution contrasts three predictive signal processing approaches to account for the delay t_T. All three require just minimal assumptions about the actual plant dynamics and no prior knowledge about the oscillation source. They operate on a sliding data window with a finite number of n_τ signal samples recorded from an arbitrary oscillation signal $\mu(t_k)$ with $t_k = k\,T_s$. T_s denotes the sampling time.

3.1   Fourier Extrapolation

The Fourier analysis models any signal as weighted sum of sines and cosines. The complex weights are computed from a set of n_τ discrete signal samples via the Discrete Fourier transform (DFT):

$$
c(f_k) = \sum_{t_k=1}^{n_\tau} \mu(t_k)\, \exp\left[-\frac{2\pi\mathrm{i}}{N}(t_k - 1)(f_k - 1)\right], \tag{3}
$$

where i denotes the imaginary unit and the f_k represent equidistant discrete frequencies. The DFT is bijective and has the inverse:

$$\mu(t_k) = \frac{1}{n_\tau} \sum_{f_k=1}^{n_\tau} c(f_k) \exp\left[\frac{2\pi i}{N}(t_k - 1)(f_k - 1)\right]. \tag{4}$$

The complex weights $c(f_k)$ and their corresponding frequencies f_k represent a model of the currently observed signal. With the sampling time T_s bound to the camera frame rate a large sliding window size n_τ improves the frequency resolution but reduces the reactivity to signal changes. Prediction is done by evaluating the series (4) at $t_k + t_T$.

The influence of measurement noise is reduced by setting weights outside the frequency band of interest to zero. The same applies to weights, which have an absolute value below a percentage c_σ of the maximum frequency peak.

3.2 Sinusoidal-Regression

From modal analysis the number and the non-equidistant values of the arm eigenfrequencies are approximately known. In [6] the model for the oscillation signal of a flexible link with a single dominant frequency is the trigonometric polynomial:

$$\hat{\mu}(t_k) = a_0 + \sum_{j}^{n_j} a_j \cos(2\pi f_j t_k) + b_j \sin(2\pi f_j t_k) \tag{5}$$

with $n_j = 1$. Depending on the joint configuration and payload the first eigenfrequencies of both flexible links can be found in the spectra of the strain measurements on each link of TUDOR. Hence: $n_j > 1$. The authors of [6] propose a two stage identification of the model parameters. An M-estimator with Tukeys weighting function is used to identify the oscillation frequency based on the zero-crossings detected within the entire sliding window. From this first stage the frequency is assumed to be known and the amplitude parameters a_0, a_1 and b_1 are estimated by linear regression performed on smaller adaptive sliding window. The prediction is done by evaluating (5) for $t_k + t_T$.

The presence of multiple signal frequencies renders the zero-crossing based frequency estimation infeasible. In this contribution the authors apply the Levenberg-Marquardt algorithm to estimate the signal frequencies by minimizing the objective function:

$$e_\mu = \sum_{t_k=1}^{n_\tau} (\mu(t_k) - \hat{\mu}(t_k))^2. \tag{6}$$

For the assumed number n_j of relevant frequencies the expression of the objective Jacobian used during minimization is derived analytically. In every Levenberg-Marquardt iteration step the current amplitude parameter estimates for a_0, a_j and b_j enable the approximation of the numeric values of this Jacobian.

3.3 Auto-Regression

The Linear Predictive Coding approach [5] describes the estimation error within a sliding window by an auto-regressive process model represented by the finite impulse response filter (FIR):

$$G_e(z) = \frac{e_\mu(\tau)}{\mu(\tau)} = 1 - \sum_{\gamma=1}^{n_\gamma} a_\gamma z^{-\gamma}, \tag{7}$$

so that $\mu(\tau)$ can be reconstructed by filtering with the infinite impulse response filter (IIR):

$$G_P(z) = \frac{1}{G_e(z)} \tag{8}$$

For online identification of the filter coefficients the Burg algorithm [7] is used, which guarantees filter stability. The prediction is done by initializing the filter states with the number of n_τ samples and iteratively evaluating (8) with zero input. Assuming the prediction horizon to be fixed the analytical expression derived from this recursion can also be used.

The minimum filter order to predict a sinusoidal signal with a total of n_j frequencies and time varying amplitudes is $2\,n_j$. The window size n_τ and the filter order n_γ always satisfy: $n_\tau > n_\gamma + 1$.

4 Predictor Analysis and Comparison

The influence of the sliding window size n_τ, signal noise σ_μ as well as the method specific parameters on the prediction is investigated in simulations with a stationary oscillation signal:

$$\mu(t) = 30 \sin(2\pi\,2\text{Hz}\,t) + 10 \sin(2\pi\,6\text{Hz}\,t). \tag{9}$$

It approximates the frequencies and amplitudes observed in the reconstructed camera rotation ω_x on TUDOR. All three methods are finally compared based on real measurements with transient as well as damped amplitudes.

The prediction error is computed as the Root Mean Squared Error between the prediction and the shifted input signal. The error is normalized to the signal standard deviation (NRMSE). The standard deviation of the prediction error σ_e is related to the added signal noise σ_μ by the ratio: $\sigma_{\text{rel}} = \sigma_\mu/\sigma_e$. Large values of σ_{rel} indicate a slim error distribution.

4.1 Prediction Error Comparison

The NRMSE and the relative standard deviation σ_{rel} in the presence of signal noise and different window sizes n_τ are illustrated in Fig. 3. With the window size $n_\tau > 30$ the Fourier extrapolation error steps up to more than 60 %. Independent of the window size the NRMSE for all methods linearly increases with the noise level. For the sinusoidal-regression the relative error distribution σ_{rel} grows proportionally with the window size. This results in a smoother prediction the larger the window size is chosen. For the other two approaches the relative error distribution shows no dependence on the window size. For both metods σ_{rel} saturates at a certain noise level, which can be interpreted as limited smoothing capabilities of these predictors.

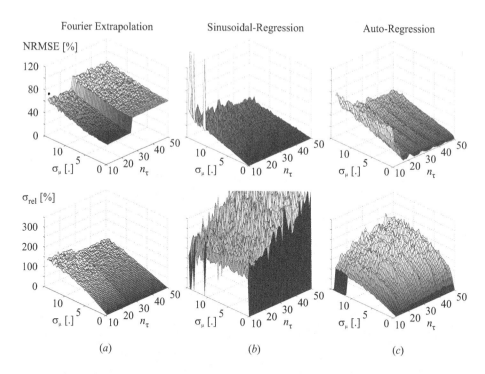

Fig. 3. Simulated NRMSE and relative standard deviation for all three predictors

4.2   Method Specifc Parameters

Fig. 4 (a) shows the relative standard deviation σ_{rel} of the Fourier extrapolation and a varying noise level σ_μ as well as smoothing parameter c_σ. For $c_\sigma < 0.2$ the relative standard deviation saturates at $\sigma_\mu > 5$. For $c_\sigma > 0.2$ it keeps linearly growing with the noise level, which preserves the smoothing effect of this threshold. The value $c_\sigma = 0.2$ at a window size of $n_\tau = 16$ is chosen for the remainder of the paper.

Fig. 4 (b) depicts the NRMSE for different window sizes n_τ and errors Δf of the initial signal frequency guess. The plot clearly shows a valley with a width of 0.4 Hz. Within this valley the NRMSE remains below 5 %. Outside this valley the prediction error abruptly increases to 40 %. The need of a proper initial guess of the signal frequencies is a major drawback of this method. The minimum window size of $n_\tau = 10$ is chosen in this paper.

Fig. 4 (c) contains the NRMSE computed from simulations with varying number of filter coefficients n_γ and window sizes n_τ. For large values of both parameters the prediction error remains below 5 %. A smaller window size improves the reactiveness of the predictor. Together with the window size also the possible filter order decreases. For $n_\gamma < 10$ the prediction error significantly steps up. The autoregressive predictor is tuned to $n_\gamma = 11$ and $n_\tau = 16$.

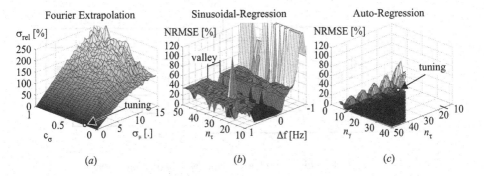

Fig. 4. Analysis of method specific parameters

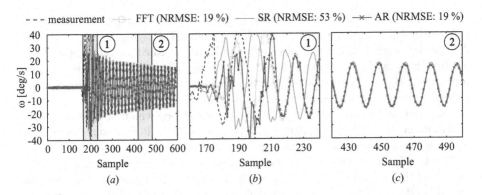

Fig. 5. Prediction of oscillation measurements with transient and damped amplitudes

4.3 Transients and Damping

The prediction error in the presence of transient as well as exponentially decaying oscillation amplitudes is evaluated with real measurements based on the test scenes in Fig. 2. The shifted time series of the reconstructed and predicted camera rotation ω_x is shown in Fig. 5. The close-up Fig. 5 (b) illustrates that the high NRMSE for the sinusoidal-regression emerges right after transient amplitude change. For this approach, it takes more than 80 samples (2.3 s) to converge. The auto-regression and Fourier extrapolation techniques readily converge after 40 samples. During exponential decay in Fig. 5 (c) the sinusoidal-regression slightly overestimates the amplitude in comparison to the other methods.

Considering all test scenes, the auto-regression method always has a prediction error below 20 %. The Fourier extrapolation error is generally up to 2 % larger than the auto-regression error.

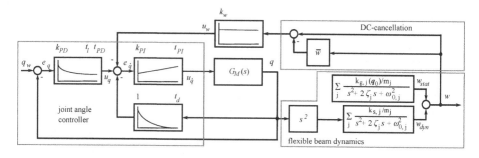

Fig. 6. Independent joint control architecture with oscillation feedback

5   Control Architecture

The contribution follows a cascaded independent joint control strategy, where the robot is interpreted as a sequence of SISO joint-link modules. The high gear ratios allow the dynamic couplings between the individual modules to be treated as disturbances.

The dynamics of the current controlled joints are modelled by a standard linear transfer function $G_M(s)$ including the effective inertia and viscous friction. The finite difference of the incremental encoder signals is smoothed with a time constant t_d to allow for the quasi continuous design of a PI velocity control loop with time constant t_{PI} as well as the controller gain k_{PI}. For angular position control a $\mathrm{PDT_1}$ controller with the time constant t_{PD}, gain k_{PD} and lag t_l is designed.

The flexible link dynamics are mathematically described via modal analysis [8]. For the robot being in a quasi-static joint configuration $\mathbf{q_0}$, the procedure results in a set of n_j independent transfer models for the deflection $w(x,t)$, observed at an instant t and a distance x from the hub:

$$w_j(x_s, s) = \frac{q(s)\, k_{s,j}(x_s)/m_j\, s^2}{m_j\, s^2 + d_j\, s + c_j} + \frac{k_{g,j}(\mathbf{q_0})/m_j}{m_j\, s^2 + d_j\, s + c_j}, \tag{10}$$

where n_j is the number of assumed oscillation modes. The quantities m_j, d_j and c_j represent the modal mass, damping and stiffness. The gain $k_{s,j}(x_s)$ belongs to the dynamic deflection part w_{dyn}, while $k_{g,j}(x_s, \mathbf{q_0})$ is the configuration and payload dependent gain of the static deflection part w_{stat}.

In [1] the deflection is inferred from equivalent per link strain measurements. The cancellation of the static part by subtracting the moving average $\bar{w}(x_s, t)$ from the measurement enables the Evans root locus method to tune a proportional feedback gain k_w. The feedback shifts the poles of n_j superposed second order systems to root locus regions of higher damping. The modified closed loop dynamics cause oscillations originating from joint movements, pendulum motions of supply and communication cables as well as environment interactions to decay equally fast.

The image processing provides the deflection velocity $\begin{bmatrix} {}^0\mathbf{t}_E, {}^0\boldsymbol{\omega}_E \end{bmatrix}^{\mathrm{T}}$ at the endeffector transformed to the robot base frame. The differential relation to the joint velocities $\dot{\mathbf{q}}$ as well as the deflection rates $\dot{\mathbf{w}} = \begin{bmatrix} {}^2\dot{w}(l_2, t), {}^3\dot{w}(l_3, t) \end{bmatrix}^{\mathrm{T}}$ of individual links is given by the robot Jacobian:

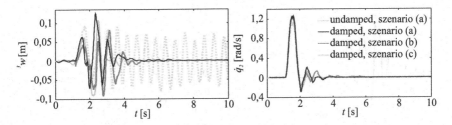

Fig. 7. Approximate deflection of the end-effector (*left*) and joint angular velocity of the second joint (*right*) after a step motion from $\mathbf{q}_1 = [90°, 20°, 10°]^T$ to $\mathbf{q}_2 = [90°, 50°, 40°]^T$

$$\mathbf{J}_R(\mathbf{q}, \mathbf{w}) = \left[\mathbf{J}_q(\mathbf{q}, \mathbf{w}), \mathbf{J}_w(\mathbf{q}, \mathbf{w})\right]. \tag{11}$$

The rearrangement under the assumption of small deflections yields the estimate of the deflection rates:

$$\dot{\mathbf{w}} = \mathbf{J}_w^\dagger(\mathbf{q}) \left[\left[{}^0\mathbf{t}_E, {}^0\boldsymbol{\omega}_E\right]^T - \mathbf{J}_q(\mathbf{q})\,\dot{\mathbf{q}}\right]. \tag{12}$$

The numerical integration yields the camera based replacement for the oscillation signal used in [1]. In this case the subtraction of the moving average also compensates for the accumulated estimation errors. The complete control architecture shown in Fig. 6 waives the need to actually compute the robot dynamics at runtime.

6 Experimental Setup and Damping Results

The controller parameters are fixed for all experiments. The damping results are illustrated with the reconstructed deflection of the third link as well as the joint velocity of the second joint.

6.1 Damping Motion Induced Oscillations

The oscillation damping results for an upwards directed step motion beginning at $t = 1$ s are depicted in Fig. 7. The experiment is performed in front of the three scenes depicted in Fig. 2 and compared to the undamped case acquired in front of scene (*a*). In all scenarios the oscillations are nearly settled after $t = 4$ s. The damping action can be seen from the harmonic modification to the joint velocity signal in the left of Fig 7.

6.2 Damping External Disturbances

The independent joint control scheme derived in section 5 influences the closed loop system dynamics by shifting the flexible poles of each individual beam to regions of higher damping within the complex s-plane. This dampens oscillations independent of the excitation source such as joint movements or environment interactions. This is experimentally verified by the sudden placement of a ceramic cup of 390 g on a metal plate at the end-effector. The abrupt payload increase of 86 % excites the oscillations visible in Fig. 8. They decay as fast as the motion induced oscillations before.

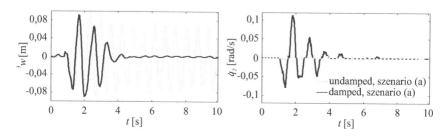

Fig. 8. Approximate deflection of the third link (*left*) and joint angular velocity of the second joint (*right*) after a sudden placement of a ceramic cup (390 g) at the end-effector in the joint configuration $\mathbf{q}_2 = [90°, 50°, 40°]^T$

7   Conclusions and Outlook

The paper replaces conventional strain gauges by a single eye-in-hand mounted camera sensor for oscillation damping of a multi link flexible robot arms under gravity. Among Fourier extrapolation, sinusoidal-regression and auto-regression the auto-regression is the most robust and precise predictive delay compensation approach. During experiments in a real world office environment the proposed control concept dampens oscillations originating from joint motions as well as sudden payload changes. The damping results are achieved without the actual computation of the robot dynamics at runtime. Model predictive approaches may further reduce the settling times in future works.

Acknowledgments. This work is supported by the German Research Foundation (DFG, BE 1569/7-1) and DAAD MOET (project 322).

References

1. Malzahn, J., Phung, A., Hoffmann, F., Bertram, T.: Vibration Control of a Multi-Flexible-Link Robot Arm under Gravity. In: International Conference on Robotics and Biomimetics, Phuket, Thailand. IEEE (2011)
2. Malzahn, J., et al.: Markerless Visual Vibration Damping of a 3-DOF Flexible Link Robot Arm. In: 41st International Symposium on Robotics (ISR) and 6th German Conference on Robotics (ROBOTIK), pp. 401–408. VDE (2010)
3. Jiang, X., Konno, A., Uchiyama, M.: A vision-based endpoint trajectory and vibration control for flexible manipulators. In: International Conference on Robotics and Automation, pp. 3427–3432. IEEE (2007)
4. Koehl, P.: Linear prediction spectral analysis of nmr data. Progress in Nuclear Magnetic Resonance Spectroscopy 34(3), 257–300 (1999)
5. Kauppinen, I., Roth, K.: Audio signal extrapolation–theory and applications. In: Proceedings of the 5th Int. Conference on Digital Audio Effects, pp. 105–110 (2002)
6. Dubus, G., David, O., Measson, Y.: A vision-based method for estimating vibrations of a flexible arm using on-line sinusoidal regression. In: International Conference on Robotics and Automation (ICRA), pp. 4068–4075. IEEE (2010)
7. Burg, J.: Maximum Entropy Spectral Analysis, Stanford University. PhD thesis (1979)
8. Srinivas, R.: Textbook of Mechanical Vibrations. PHI Learning Pvt. Ltd. (2004)

Control of an Ostrich-Like Knee Joint for a Biped Robot Based on Passive Dynamic Walking

Hiroya Yamamoto and Keitaro Naruse

University of Aizu

Abstract. Ostriches are the fastest of all bipedal walking animals, with a knee joint that bends in the opposite direction to the human knee. We investigate the various gaits of a bipedal model of an ostrich, developed according to the notion of passive dynamic walking, and compare them with the walking gaits of a human model. In particular, by controlling the model, we can identify relationships between the leg angles, the walking speed, the trajectory of foot points and the energy consumption. Numerical experiments show that the angle of touching the ground is closer to the vertical for the ostrich model than for the human model, which can be better for high-speed walking.

1 Introduction

In recent years, many bipedal walking robots have been developed, with particular attention being paid to passive dynamic walking (PDW) robots. Together with the use of gravity, PDW uses energy only to generate an initial velocity, which is very energy efficient. Moreover, the walking gait of PDW robots appears more natural. The idea of PDW was introduced by McGeer [1]. The simplest walking model (SWM) was introduced by Garcia [2]. Double-pendulum models, also called compass models, and point-foot models were studied by Goswami [3] [4]. Asano introduced virtual PDW [5] [6] [7], which makes walking on a level surface possible. Asano further investigated human models with an added upper body [8]. However, ostriches are the fastest of all bipedal walking animals, with a unique knee joint that bends in the opposite direction to the human knee. We can speculate that this joint mechanism is the key to its walking and running speed. To date, an ostrich-like knee-joint model has been investigated by Lim [9], [10], based on the concept of the zero moment point (ZMP). However, an ostrich-like knee-joint model based on PDW has yet to be developed.

The objective of this paper is to investigate the gaits of bipedal robots with ostrich-like knee joints. We model an ostrich walking, and develop a control method for it. To achieve energy-efficient walking, we introduce a simple controller and evaluate the gaits of the model in terms of PDW. We carry out numerical experiments on the ostrich model and on a human model. Comparing their gaits, we find that the angle of contact with the ground is closer to the vertical for the ostrich model than for the human model, which may be better for high-speed walking.

C.-Y. Su, S. Rakheja, H. Liu (Eds.): ICIRA 2012, Part III, LNAI 7508, pp. 103–112, 2012.

2   The Ostrich Walking Model

2.1   The Link Model

The models used in this paper are based on the 3-link model introduced by Ikemata [11]. Figure 1 shows the model, with its two legs and three joints. The leg that is in contact with the sloping ground is called the contact leg. The other leg is called the swing leg. The bottom and top joints are called the ankle joint and the hip joint, respectively. The joint between the ankle and hip joints is called the knee joint. The leg angles θ, ϕ_1 and ϕ_2 are defined in Figure 1. When the swing leg contacts the slope, it undergoes a completely inelastic collision. At that instant, the two legs switch roles, with the swing leg becoming the contact leg and vice versa. We assume that the leg switching happens instantaneously, with time being ignored.

When the swing leg straightens, the knee locks, as shown in Figure 2. The knee joint remains locked until it returns to being the swing leg. For each leg, its 3-link phase is when its knee joint is free, with its 2-link phase being when its knee joint is locked.

The model has a mass M at the hip joint. For the swing leg, the mass and length of its upper and lower links are m_1, l_1 and m_2, l_2, respectively. For the contact leg, we have a single link of mass m and length l. The position of the mass in the link is specified by a and b. We assume that M is much larger than m (i.e. $M \gg m$), where $m = m_1 + m_2$. In the model, g refers to the gravitational force, γ to the angle of the slope and $u_1, u_2 and u_3$ are the torques at the ankle, hip and knee joints, respectively.

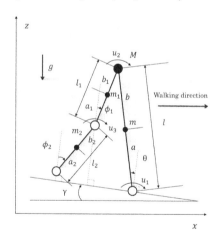

Fig. 1. The 3-link Model

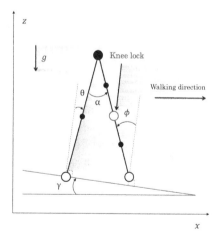

Fig. 2. The 2-link Model

Two walking models are examined in this paper. The model with knee joints rotating in the "human" direction (the human-like model) is shown in Figure 3. The model with knee joints rotating in the "ostrich" direction (the ostrich-like model) is shown in Figure 4.

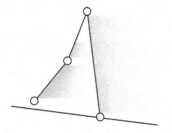

Fig. 3. A Human-like Model

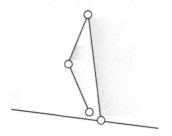

Fig. 4. An Ostrich-like Model

2.2 Dynamic Equations

The two walking models considered in this paper alternate between their 3-link and 2-link phases. For the 3-link phase, the equations of motion (1) to (4) are defined as follows.

$$M_K(\theta_K)\ddot{\theta}_K + H_K(\theta_K, \dot{\theta}_K) + G_K(\theta_K, \gamma) = E_K \tau_K. \tag{1}$$

$$M_K(\theta_K) = \begin{bmatrix} l^2 & 0 & 0 \\ -(b_1 l + p l l_1)\cos(\theta - \phi_1) & b_1^2 + p l_1^2 & p b_2 l_1 \cos(\phi_1 - \phi_2) \\ -b_2 l \cos(\theta - \phi_2) & b_2 l_1 \cos(\phi_1 - \phi_2) & b_2^2 \end{bmatrix}. \tag{2}$$

$$H_K(\theta_K, \dot{\theta}_K) = \begin{bmatrix} 0 \\ (b_1 l + p l l_1)\sin(\theta - \phi_1)\dot{\theta}^2 + p b_2 l_1 \sin(\phi_1 - \phi_2)\dot{\phi}_2^2 \\ b_2 l \sin(\theta - \phi_2)\dot{\theta}^2 - b_2 l_1 \cos(\phi_1 - \phi_2)\dot{\phi}_1^2 \end{bmatrix}. \tag{3}$$

$$G_K(\theta_K, \gamma) = \begin{bmatrix} -l\sin(\theta + \gamma) \\ (b_1 + p l_1)\sin(\phi_1 + \gamma) \\ b_2 \sin(\phi_2 + \gamma) \end{bmatrix} g, \quad E_K = \begin{bmatrix} 1 & 0 & 0 \\ 0 & 1 & -p \\ 0 & 0 & 1 \end{bmatrix}, \quad \tau_K = \begin{bmatrix} u_1/M \\ u_2/m_1 \\ u_3/m_2 \end{bmatrix}. \tag{4}$$

Here, p is the mass ratio given by $p = m_2/m_1$ and θ_K is the angle vector given by $\theta_K = [\theta, \phi_1, \phi_2]^T$.

After a knee lock, the model enters its 2-link phase, for which the equations of motion are as follows.

$$M_C(\theta_C)\ddot{\theta}_C + H_C(\theta_C, \dot{\theta}_C) + G_C(\theta_C, \gamma) = E_C \tau_C. \tag{5}$$

In this equation, the matrices M_K, H_K, G_K, E_K and τ_K are defined in (6), (7), (8) and (9).

$$M_C(\theta_C) = \begin{bmatrix} l^2 & 0 \\ -(1 + p)bl \cos(\theta - \phi) & \bar{I} + (1 + p)b^2 \end{bmatrix}. \tag{6}$$

$$H_C(\theta_C, \dot{\theta}_C) = \begin{bmatrix} 0 \\ (1+p)bl\sin(\theta - \phi)\dot{\theta}^2 \end{bmatrix}. \tag{7}$$

$$G_C(\theta_C, \gamma) = \begin{bmatrix} -l\sin(\theta + \gamma) \\ (1+p)b\sin(\phi + \gamma) \end{bmatrix} g. \tag{8}$$

$$E_C = \begin{bmatrix} 1 & 0 \\ 0 & 1 \end{bmatrix}, \qquad \tau_C = \begin{bmatrix} u_1/M \\ u_2/m_1 \end{bmatrix}. \tag{9}$$

Here, θ_C is the angle vector $\theta_C = [\theta, \phi]^T$, ϕ is the angle when the knee locks, $\bar{I} = I/m_1$ and $I = m_2(l_2 - b_2 - a)^2 + m_1(l_2 + a_1 - a)^2$.

Switching Legs. When switching legs, the angle and angular velocity change as shown by equations (10), (11), (12) and (13).

$$\phi_1^+ = \theta^-, \quad \phi_2^+ = \theta^-, \quad \theta^+ = \phi^-. \tag{10}$$

$$Q^+(\alpha)\dot{\theta}_C^+ = Q^-(\alpha)\dot{\theta}_C^-. \tag{11}$$

$$Q^+(\alpha) = \begin{bmatrix} l^2 & 0 \\ -bl\cos(\alpha) & b^2 + \frac{\bar{I}}{1+p} \end{bmatrix}. \tag{12}$$

$$Q^-(\alpha) = \begin{bmatrix} l^2\cos(\alpha) & 0 \\ -ab + \frac{\bar{I}}{1+p} & 0 \end{bmatrix}. \tag{13}$$

Here, the index "$-$" means just before switching legs, "$+$" means just after switching legs and α is the angle between the contact leg and the swing leg, where $\alpha = \theta + \phi$.

Knee Locking. When the knee locks, the angle and angular velocity change as shown by equations (14) and (15).

$$\phi^+ = \phi_1^- = \phi_2^-, \quad \dot{\theta}^+ = \dot{\theta}^-. \tag{14}$$

$$\dot{\phi}^+ = \frac{(b_1^2 + pl_1^2 + pl_1b_2)\dot{\phi}_1^- + (pb_2^2 + pb_2l_1)\dot{\phi}_2^-}{b_1^2 + p(l_1 + b_2)^2}. \tag{15}$$

2.3   Controls

Without external control, the 3-link model cannot descend a slope by itself because scuffing occurs. As an appropriate control method, we describe a proportional–differential (PD) control method in this paper. The "P" term adds a torque proportional to the difference between the current angle and the target angle and the "D" term adds a torque proportional to the current angular velocity. In this research, PD control is applied only to the knee joint. Therefore,

Table 1. Specification of Control Gains

θ_f	k_{os}	k_{hs}	k_{od}	k_{hd}
2.08[rad]	0.625	0.0	0.1	0.1

Table 2. Specification of Parameter Values

M	m	m_1	m_2	l	l_1	l_2	a
14.0 [kg]	1.40 [kg]	1.0 [kg]	0.4 [kg]	0.7 [m]	0.35 [m]	0.35 [m]	0.35 [m]
b	a_1	b_1	a_2	b_2	g	γ	Δt
0.35[m]	0.175 [m]	0.175 [m]	0.175 [m]	0.175 [m]	9.8 [m/s^2]	0.019 [rad]	0.0001 [s]

Table 3. Specification of Initial Parameter Values

θ	ϕ_1	ϕ_2	$\dot{\theta}$	$\dot{\phi}_1$	$\dot{\phi}_2$
0.225 [rad]	-0.225 [rad]	-0.225 [rad]	0.9 [rad/s]	1.07 [rad/s]	1.07 [rad/s]

$u_1 = u_2 = 0$. The control equation for the ostrich-like model is then given by equation (16).

$$u_3 = \begin{cases} -k_{os}((\phi_2 - \phi_1) + \theta_f) - k_{od}\dot{\phi}_2 & (switching\ legs) \\ 0 & (otherwise) \end{cases} \qquad (16)$$

In contrast, the control equation for the human-like model is as follows.

$$u_3 = \begin{cases} -k_{hs}((\phi_2 - \phi_1) - \theta_f) - k_{hd}\dot{\phi}_2 & (switching\ legs) \\ 0 & (otherwise) \end{cases} \qquad (17)$$

Here, k_{os}, k_{od}, k_{hs} and k_{hd} are control gains and θ_f is a target angle. These torques are applied to the knee joint when switching legs for only 0.17 seconds, in opposite directions for the ostrich and human models. The human model avoids scuffing by undergoing a staggering swing. On the other hand, the ostrich model bends its knee joints in an opposite direction to the human model. We set the control parameters as indicated in Table 1.

3   Numerical Experiments

3.1   Simulation Setup

In the numerical experiments described below, the differential equations were solved by the Runge–Kutta method. The step size for time was specified as $\Delta t = 0.0001$ seconds. The simulations each ran for 10 seconds. The other parameters were set as indicated in Table 2. The initial parameters were set as indicated in Table 3. These parameter values were chosen following Ikemata [11]. For both the human model and the ostrich model, we investigated the angles of each leg, the energy consumption by the controller, the trajectories of foot positions, walking speeds, clearances, step length and velocity vectors.

3.2   Motion Snapshots

Figures 5 and 6 show stick diagrams for the human model and the ostrich model. The figures show the first step of each model for a time step of 0.1 seconds, indicating that both models can walk on a level surface when the proposed controller is used.

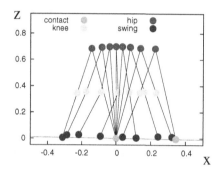
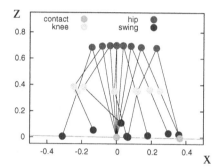

Fig. 5. Stick Diagram for the Human-like Model

Fig. 6. Stick Diagram for the Ostrich-like Model

3.3   Angles

Figure 7 shows the trajectories of the angles in the human model over a five-second period. Figure 8 shows those for the ostrich model. In comparing them, we find that the ostrich model walks with longer steps. Over these five seconds, the human model walks seven and a half steps and the ostrich model walks six and a half steps. The angle of the knee joint ϕ_2 has a different trajectory for each model. The human ϕ_2 bends in the "+" direction, whereas the ostrich ϕ_2 bends in the "−" direction and involves a greater change in angle.

3.4   Energy Consumption by Controller

Figures 9 and 10 show the energy consumption required for control. The ostrich model needs more than the very little torque needed by the human model because the ostrich's knee bends in the opposite direction to that of a human knee.

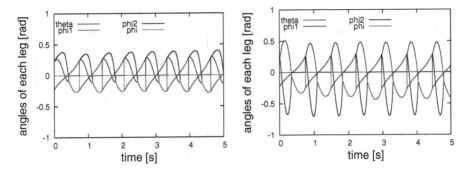

Fig. 7. Angle for the Human-like Model   **Fig. 8.** Angle for the Ostrich-like Model

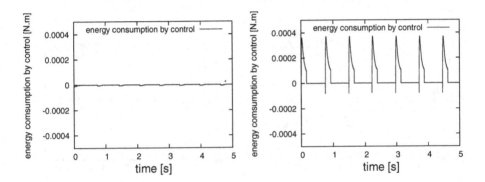

Fig. 9. Energy in the Human-like Model   **Fig. 10.** Energy in the Ostrich-like Model

3.5   Trajectories of Foot Positions

Figures 11 and 12 show the trajectories of foot positions during a few steps following the first step. The ostrich model has an interesting feature, namely that it avoids scuffing by having a high leg swing. Conversely, the contact point of the foot in the human model is very close to the slope. In Figures 11 and 12, the first step is shown in red, the second in blue, the third in green and the fourth in pink.

3.6   Walking Speeds

Walking speed is measured as an average speed, which is 0.52 m/s for the ostrich model and 0.56 m/s for the human model. The human model is faster than the ostrich model because the human model has a smaller swing.

3.7   Velocity Vectors

Figures 13 and 14 show the velocity vectors for each of the models. In these figures, the first step is in red and the next step is in blue. The green arrows

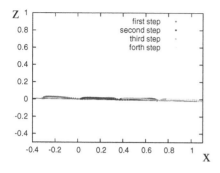

Fig. 11. Trajectory in the Human-like Model

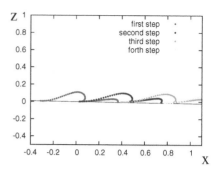

Fig. 12. Trajectory in the Ostrich-like Model

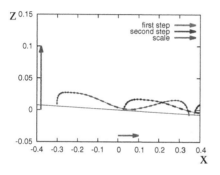

Fig. 13. Velocity Vector for the Human-like Model

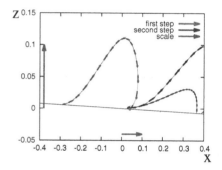

Fig. 14. Velocity Vector for the Ostrich-like Model

show the scale size. Focusing on the moment of contact, note that the ostrich model strikes the slope almost vertically, whereas the human model strikes it obliquely.

3.8   Step Length

The step length for one step is specified as shown in Figure 15. Figure 17 shows the value for step lengths in each of the models untill the end of steps. For each step, the ostrich model has a longer step length and a greater period.

3.9   Clearances

The clearance h of the foot with respect to the slope is specified as shown in Figure 16. Table 4 gives the average and maximum values for h in each of the models, showing that the ostrich model involves a greater clearance.

Table 4. Clearance Values

	Ostrich-like Model	Human-like Model
h (average)	0.041 [m]	0.016 [m]
h (maximum)	0.087 [m]	0.031 [m]

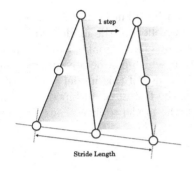

Fig. 15. Specification of Stride Length

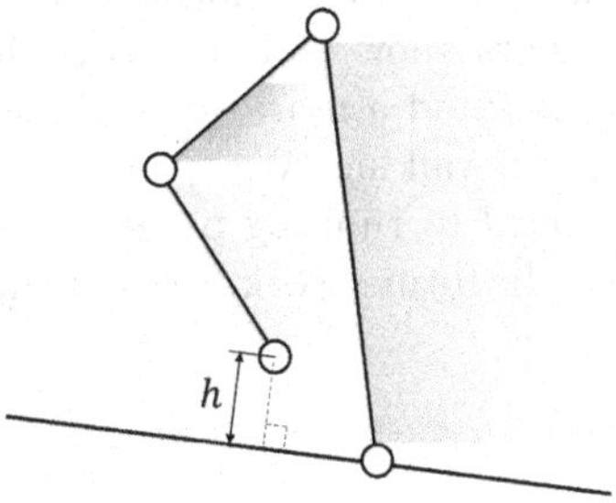

Fig. 16. Specification of Clearance

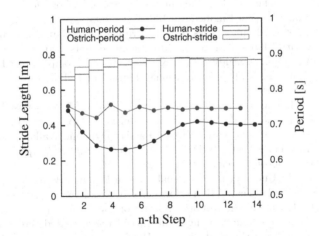

Fig. 17. Stride and Period for Each Step

4   Discussion

Firstly, the ostrich model needs more torque than the human model because the ostrich knee bends backwards with respect to the walking direction. Secondly, the leg-swing motions for the ostrich model are greater than for the human model. Therefore, its walking speed is reduced and the gait is unstable because the center of gravity is higher. However, the ostrich model avoids scuffing more easily because of the greater clearance. In general, it is efficient for the swing leg to contact the slope vertically because this does not reduce the horizontal speed. The ostrich model can therefore offer higher energy efficiency because the human model reduces the horizontal speed on contact.

5   Conclusion and Future Work

The objective of this paper is to investigate ostrich walking gaits. We have modeled the ostrich walk and have developed a controller for the model. Numerical experiments show that the ostrich model has a greater foot clearance above the ground and a more vertical contact with it, which can be advantageous for high-speed walking. We speculate that the best use of this model will occur if it is applied to running because the ostrich is the fastest of all bipedal walking animals. In future work, we will therefore use the model to investigate running.

References

1. McGeer, T.: Passive Dynamic Walking. The International Journal of Robotics Research 9(2), 62–82 (1990)
2. Garcia, M., et al.: The Simplest Walking Model: Stability, Complexity, and Scaling. Journal of Biomechanical Engineering 120(281) (1998)
3. Goswami, A., et al.: Limit Cycles in a Passive Compass Gait Biped and Passive-Mimicking Control Laws. Journal of Autonomous Robots 4(3), 272–286 (1997)
4. Goswami, A., et al.: A study of the passive gait of a compass-like biped robot – symmetry and chaos. The International Journal of Robotics Research 17(12), 1282–1301 (1998)
5. Asano, F., et al.: Gait Generation and Control for Biped Robots Based on Passive Dynamic Walking. Journal of the Robotics Society of Japan 22(1) (2004)
6. Asano, F., et al.: Underactuated Virtual Passive Dynamic Walking using Rolling Effect of Semicircular Feet –(I) On Driving Mechanisms of Compass-like Models. Journal of the Robotics Society of Japan 25(4) (2007)
7. Asano, F., et al.: Underactuated Virtual Passive Dynamic Walking using Rolling Effect of Semicircular Feet –(II) Performance Analyses and Extension to Redundant Models. Journal of the Robotics Society of Japan 25(4) (2007)
8. Asano, F., et al.: Dynamic Walking Analyses of Underactuated Biped Robot That Added Upper Body by Means of Bisecting Hip Mechanism. Journal of the Robotics Society of Japan 26(8) (2008)
9. Lim, H., et al.: Ostrich-like Robot with Passivity and Activity Element. Journal of the Japan Society of Mechanical Engineers (2-6), 66–67 (2002)
10. Lim, H., et al.: Walking Control of Ostrich-like Robot. Journal of the Japan Society of Mechanical Engineers (3-4), 117–118 (2003)
11. Ikemata, Y., Sano, A., Fujimoto, H.: Generation and Local Stabilization of Fixed Point based on a Stability Mechanism of Passive Walking. Journal of the Robotics Society of Japan 24(5), 632–639 (2006)

Adaptive Neural Network Control of Robot with Passive Last Joint*

Chenguang Yang[1], Zhijun Li[2,4,**], Jing Li[1,3], and Alex Smith[1]

[1] School of Computing and Mathematics, Plymouth University, UK
[2] Department of Automation , Shanghai Jiao Tong University, Shanghai, China
[3] Department of Mathematics, Xidian University, China
[4] College of Automation Science and Engineering,
South China University of Technology, China
zjli@ieee.org

Abstract. Adaptive control of a robot manipulator with a passive joint (which has neither an actuator nor a holding brake) is investigated. With the aim to shape the controlled manipulator dynamics to be of minimized motion tracking errors and joint accelerations, we employ a linear quadratic regulator (LQR) optimization technique to obtain an optimal reference model. Adaptive neural network (NN) control has been developed to ensure the reference model can be matched in finite time, in the presence of various uncertainties.

Keywords: model reference control, neural network, robot manipulator.

1 Introduction

Underactuated robots have received considerable research attention in the last two decades ([1]-[7]). In contrast to conventional robots, for which each joint has one actuator and the degrees of freedom is equal to the number of actuators, an underactuated robot has passive joints equipped with no actuators. Though the passive joints are not actuated they can be controlled by using the dynamic coupling with the active joints, i.e., these passive joints can be indirectly driven by other active joints. The underactuation structure makes it possible to reduce the weight, energy consumption and cost of a manipulator, which is an advantage for tasks involving an impact, e.g., hitting or hammering an object, as damage to the joint actuators is reduced. It can also contribute to fault tolerance of fully-actuated manipulators in cases where joint actuators can fail.

The zero torque at the passive joints results in a second-order nonholonomic constraint. This method allows the control of more joints than actuators. Since

---

* This work is supported by the Marie Curie International Incoming Fellowship H2R Project (FP7-PEOPLE-2010-IIF-275078), the Natural Science Foundation of China under Grants (60804003, 61174045, 61111130208), the International Science and Technology Cooperation Program of China (0102011DFA10950), and the Fundamental Research Funds for the Central Universities (2011ZZ0104).
** Corresponding author.

C.-Y. Su, S. Rakheja, H. Liu (Eds.): ICIRA 2012, Part III, LNAI 7508, pp. 113–122, 2012.

these robots usually have nonholonomic second-order constraints, the control problems are challenging (see e.g.,[1]-[2]). In robotics, nonholonomic constraints formulated as nonintegrable differential equations containing time-derivatives of generalized coordinates (velocity, acceleration etc.) are regularly studied.such constraints include the following: 1) Kinematic constraints which geometrically restrict the direction of mobility; 2) Dynamic constraints due to dynamic balance at passive degrees of freedom where no force or torque is applied. Examples of mechanical systems which have constraints of the former type include trailers [5] and manipulators with nonholonomic gears [6]. These systems commonly have fewer control inputs than the number of generalized coordinates. Therefore, it is necessary to combine the limited number of inputs skillfully in order to control all the coordinates.

2   Neural Network Approximation

Higher order neural networks (HONN) satisfy the conditions of the Stone-Weierstrass Theorem and can therefore approximate any continuous function over a compact set [8]. The structure of HONN is expressed as

$$\phi(W, z) = W^T S(z)$$
$$S(z) = [s_1(z), \ s_2(z), \ \ldots, \ s_l(z)]^T$$
$$s_i(z) = \prod_{j \in I_i} [s(z_j)]^{d_j(i)}, \quad i = 1, 2, \ldots, l \tag{1}$$

where $z \in \Omega_z \subset R^m$ is the input to HONN, l the NN nodes number, $\{I_1, I_2,...,I_l\}$ a collection of l not-ordered subsets of $\{1, 2, ..., m\}$, e.g., $I_1 = \{1, \ 3, \ m\}$, $I_2 = \{2, \ 4, \ m\}$, $d_j(i)$ are nonnegative integers, W an adjustable synaptic weight vector, and $s(z_j)$ a monotonically increasing and differentiable sigmoidal function. In this paper, it is chosen as a hyperbolic tangent function, i.e., $s(z_j) = \frac{e^{z_j} - e^{-z_j}}{e^{z_j} + e^{-z_j}}$. For a smooth function $\varphi(z)$ over a compact set $\Omega_z \subset R^m$, given a small constant real number $\mu^* > 0$, if l is sufficiently large, there exist a set of ideal bounded weights W^* such that $\max |\varphi(z) - \phi(W^*, z)| < \mu(z)$, $|\mu(z)| < \mu^*$.

For convenience of approximation of a nonlinear matrix function with each element a unknown scalar function, we use the following block matrix operators as introduced in [9]. We define block matrices $\{W\}$ and $\{S\}$ as follows:

$$\{W\} \triangleq \begin{bmatrix} W_{11} & W_{11} & \cdots & W_{1m} \\ W_{21} & W_{11} & \cdots & W_{1m} \\ \vdots & \vdots & \ddots & \vdots \\ W_{n1} & W_{11} & \cdots & W_{nm} \end{bmatrix} \in R^{nl \times m}, \quad \{S\} \triangleq \begin{bmatrix} S_{11} & S_{11} & \cdots & S_{1m} \\ S_{21} & S_{11} & \cdots & S_{1m} \\ \vdots & \vdots & \ddots & \vdots \\ S_{n1} & S_{11} & \cdots & S_{nm} \end{bmatrix} \in R^{nl \times m}$$

with each block $W_{ij} \in \mathbf{R}^l$ a column vector of NN weight and $S_{ij} \in \mathbf{R}^l$ a column vector of NN basis function. A "transpose" operation $\langle T \rangle$ of the block matrix $\{W\}$ is defined in such a way

$$\{W\}^{\langle T \rangle} \triangleq \begin{bmatrix} W_{11}^T & W_{11}^T & \cdots & W_{1m}^T \\ W_{21}^T & W_{22}^T & \cdots & W_{2m}^T \\ \vdots & \vdots & \ddots & \vdots \\ W_{n1}^T & W_{n2}^T & \cdots & W_{nm}^T \end{bmatrix} \in R^{n \times ml} \tag{2}$$

that each block of the column vector is transposed to a row vector while the relative location of each block in the matrix $\{W\}$ is not changed. Furthermore, we define block matrix multiplication between $\{W\}^{\langle T \rangle}$ and S as

$$\{W\}^{\langle T \rangle} \langle \cdot \rangle S \triangleq \begin{bmatrix} W_{11}^T S_{11} & W_{12}^T S_{12} & \cdots & W_{1m}^T S_{1m} \\ W_{21}^T S_{21} & W_{22}^T S_{22} & \cdots & W_{2m}^T S_{2m} \\ \vdots & \vdots & \ddots & \vdots \\ W_{n1}^T S_{n1} & W_{n2}^T S_{n2} & \cdots & W_{nm}^T S_{nm} \end{bmatrix} \in R^{n \times m} \tag{3}$$

3   Dynamics of Underactuated Robot Manipulator

The partition of generalized coordinate vector q as $q = [q_a^T, \quad q_b^T]^T$ with $q_a = [q_1, q_2, \ldots, q_{n-1}]$ and $q_b = q_n$ such that

$$q_a = I_0 q, \quad I_0 = [I_{[n-1,n-1]}, 0_{[n-1,1]}] \in R^{(n-1) \times n}, \tau_a = [\tau_1, \tau_2, \ldots, \tau_{n-1}] \tag{4}$$

The dynamics model of robot manipulator with a passive last joint is described as follows:

$$\begin{bmatrix} M_a & M_{ab} \\ M_{ba} & M_b \end{bmatrix} \begin{bmatrix} \ddot{q}_a \\ \ddot{q}_b \end{bmatrix} + \begin{bmatrix} C_a & C_{ab} \\ C_{ba} & C_b \end{bmatrix} \begin{bmatrix} \dot{q}_a \\ \dot{q}_b \end{bmatrix} + \begin{bmatrix} g_a \\ g_b \end{bmatrix} + \begin{bmatrix} \tau_{d_a} \\ \tau_{d_b} \end{bmatrix} = \begin{bmatrix} \tau_a \\ 0 \end{bmatrix} \tag{5}$$

Defining

$$M = \begin{bmatrix} M_a & M_{ab} \\ M_{ba} & M_b \end{bmatrix} \quad C = \begin{bmatrix} C_a & C_{ab} \\ C_{ba} & C_b \end{bmatrix} \quad g = \begin{bmatrix} g_a \\ g_b \end{bmatrix} \quad \tau_d = \begin{bmatrix} \tau_{d_a} \\ \tau_{d_b} \end{bmatrix} \tag{6}$$

Then (5) can be written in a compact form as

$$M\ddot{q} + C\dot{q} + g + \tau_d = I_0^T \tau_a \tag{7}$$

Note the matrix M is symmetric and positive definite. Therefore, the blocks M_a and M_b are also invertable and the inverse of the matrix M exists:

$$M^{-1} = \begin{bmatrix} S_b^{-1} & -M_a^{-1} M_{ab} S_a^{-1} \\ M_b^{-1} M_{ba} S_b^{-1} & S_a^{-1} \end{bmatrix} \tag{8}$$

where S_a and S_b are Schur complements of M_a and M_b, respectively, defined as

$$S_a = M_b - M_{ba} M_a^{-1} M_{ab}, \; S_b = M_a - M_{ab} M_b^{-1} M_{ba} \tag{9}$$

Multiplying $I_0 M^{-1}$ on both sides of (7) gives us

$$\ddot{q}_a + I_0 M^{-1} C\dot{q} + I_0 M^{-1} g + I_0 M^{-1} \tau_d = I_0 M^{-1} I_0^T \tau_a = S_b^{-1} \tau_a \tag{10}$$

Then, multiplying S_b on both sides of the above equation, we have

$$S_b\ddot{q}_a + S_b I_0 M^{-1} C\dot{q} + S_b I_0 M^{-1} g + S_b I_0 M^{-1} \tau_{da} = \tau_a \tag{11}$$

Defining $\mathcal{M} \triangleq S_b \in \mathbf{R}^{(n-1)\times(n-1)}$, $\mathcal{C} \triangleq S_b I_0 M^{-1} C = [\mathcal{C}_a, \mathcal{C}_b] \in \mathbf{R}^{(n-1)\times n}$ with $\mathcal{C}_a \in \mathbf{R}^{(n-1)\times(n-1)}$, $\mathcal{C}_b \in \mathbf{R}^{(n-1)\times 1}$, and $\mathcal{G} = (S_b I_0 M^{-1} g + S_b I_0 M^{-1} \tau_{da})$, then we have q_a-subsystems as follows

$$\Sigma_{q_a} : \mathcal{M}\ddot{q}_a + \mathcal{C}_a\dot{q}_a + \mathcal{C}_b\dot{q}_b = (\tau_a - \mathcal{G}) \tag{12}$$

We assume there exists two positive constants $\underline{\mathcal{M}}$ and $\bar{\mathcal{M}}$ such that $\underline{\mathcal{M}} \le |\mathcal{M}| \le \bar{\mathcal{M}}$. If we further define $\underline{m} = \frac{1}{\bar{\mathcal{M}}}$ and $\bar{m} = \frac{1}{\underline{\mathcal{M}}}$, then we can obtain $\underline{m} \le |\mathcal{M}^{-1}| \le \bar{m}$. At the same time, we obtain the q_b-subsystem as follows:

$$\Sigma_{q_b} : M_b\ddot{q}_b + C_b\dot{q}_b + g_b + \tau_{db} + M_{ba}\ddot{q}_a + C_{ba}\dot{q}_a = 0 \tag{13}$$

4   Control of Subsystem Σ_a

4.1   Subsystem Dynamics

For convenience, define $\bar{q}_a = [q_a^T, \dot{q}_a^T]^T$, $\bar{q}_b = [q_b, \dot{q}_b]^T$, and $\bar{q} = [q_a^T, q_b, \dot{q}_a^T, \dot{q}_b]^T$, we then rewrite (12) as

$$\dot{\bar{q}}_a = A_a\bar{q}_a + A_b\bar{q}_b + B\mathcal{M}^{-1}(\tau_a - \mathcal{G}) \tag{14}$$

where

$$A_a = \begin{bmatrix} 0_{[n-1,n-1]} & I_{[n-1,n-1]} \\ 0_{[n-1,n-1]} & -\mathcal{M}^{-1}\mathcal{C}_a \end{bmatrix} = \begin{bmatrix} 0_{[n-1,n-1]} & I_{[n-1,n-1]} \\ A_{a1} & A_{a2} \end{bmatrix} \in \mathbf{R}^{2(n-1)\times 2(n-1)}$$

$$A_b = \begin{bmatrix} 0_{[n-1,1]} & 0_{[n-1,1]} \\ 0_{[n-1,1]} & -\mathcal{M}^{-1}\mathcal{C}_b \end{bmatrix} = \begin{bmatrix} 0_{[n-1,1]} & 0_{[n-1,1]} \\ A_{b1} & A_{b2} \end{bmatrix} \in \mathbf{R}^{2(n-1)\times 2}$$

$$B = \begin{bmatrix} 0_{[n-1,n-1]}, I_{[n-1,n-1]} \end{bmatrix}^T \tag{15}$$

For clarity, here and hereafter, the argument $\bar{q}$ of $A_a, A_b, \mathcal{M}$ and $\mathcal{G}$ is omitted.

Optimal Reference Model. The control objective is to control the subsystem dynamics (14) to follow a given reference model

$$\dot{\bar{q}}_m = A_m\bar{q}_m + BM_d^{-1}r_m \tag{16}$$

where $\bar{q}_m \in R^{2(n-1)\times 2(n-1)}$ is the desired response of the system, and

$$A_m = \begin{bmatrix} 0_{[n-1,n-1]} & I_{[n-1,n-1]} \\ A_{m1}(\bar{q}_m) & A_{m2}(\bar{q}_m) \end{bmatrix} = \begin{bmatrix} 0_{[n-1,n-1]} & I_{[n-1,n-1]} \\ -M_d^{-1}K_d & -M_d^{-1}C_d \end{bmatrix} \tag{17}$$

$$r_m = -F_\eta(q_d, \dot{q}_d), \quad \bar{q}_m = [q_m^T, \dot{q}_m^T]^T$$

Actually, the reference model (16) is just a transformation of the following second order system

$$M_d\ddot{q}_m + C_d\dot{q}_m + K_d q_m = -F_\eta(q_d, \dot{q}_d) \tag{18}$$

where M_d, C_d, K_d are the desired inertia, damping and stiffness matrices, respectively, and F_η can be regarded as an artificial force. As the control objective is to make the closed-loop dynamics of the controlled subsystem (14) match the dynamics of the reference model (18), we should choose suitable parameters for the reference model such that it not only guarantees the motion tracking but also handles the manipulator's performance. In order to choose the optimal values of the reference model parameters, we introduce the performance index:

$$P_I = \int_{t_0}^{t_f} \left(e_m^T Q e_m + \ddot{q}_m^T M_d \ddot{q}_m \right) dt. \tag{19}$$

which minimizes both the motion tracking error $e_m = q_m - q_d$ and the joints' angular accelerations. We aim to minimise manipulator jerk by reducing any unnecessary angular accelerations, while at the same time to ensure motion tracking performance. Now let us consider how to minimize the performance index I_P by suitably designing C_d, K_d and F_η. In order to apply the LQR optimization technique, we rewrite the reference model (18) as

$$\dot{\bar{q}}_m = A_d \bar{q}_m + Bu \tag{20}$$

with

$$\bar{q}_d = [q_d^T, \ \dot{q}_d^T]^T \in \mathbf{R}^{2(n-1) \times 2(n-1)}, A_d = \begin{bmatrix} 0_{[n-1,n-1]} & I_{[n-1,n-1]} \\ 0_{[n-1,n-1]} & 0_{[n-1,n-1]} \end{bmatrix}, \tag{21}$$

$$Q = \begin{bmatrix} q_1 & 0 & \cdots & 0 \\ 0 & q_2 & \cdots & 0 \\ \vdots & \vdots & \ddots & \vdots \\ 0 & 0 & \cdots & q_{n-1} \end{bmatrix}, u = -M_d^{-1}[K_d, \ C_d]\bar{q}_m - M_d^{-1} F_\eta(q_d, \dot{q}_d) \tag{22}$$

Noting that $u = \ddot{q}_m$ and introducing $\bar{Q}$ defined as $\bar{Q} = \begin{bmatrix} Q & 0_{[n-1,n-1]} \\ 0_{[n-1,n-1]} & 0_{[n-1,n-1]} \end{bmatrix}$, we can then rewrite the performance index (19) as

$$P_{\bar{I}} = \int_{t_0}^{t_f} \left((\bar{q}_m - \bar{q}_d)^T \bar{Q} (\bar{q}_m - \bar{q}_d) + u^T M_d u \right) dt \tag{23}$$

If we regard u as the control input to system (20), then the minimization of (23) subject to dynamic constraints (20) becomes a typical LQR control design problem. According to the LQR optimal control technique [12], the solution of u that minimizes (23) is

$$u = -M_d^{-1} B^T P \bar{q}_m - M_d^{-1} B^T s \tag{24}$$

where P is the solution of the following differential equation

$$-\dot{P} = P A_d + A_d^T P - P B M_d^{-1} B^T P + \bar{Q}, \quad P(t_f) = 0_{[2(n-1),2(n-1)]} \tag{25}$$

and s is the solution of the following differential equation

$$-\dot{s} = (A_d - B M_d^{-1} B^T P)^T s + \bar{Q} \bar{q}_d, \quad s(t_f) = 0_{[2(n-1)]} \tag{26}$$

Comparing equations (22) and (24), we can see that the matrices K_d and C_d can be calculated as $[K_d, C_d] = B^T P$, $F_\eta = B^T s$.

4.2   NN Control and Model Matching

According to $\mathcal{M}$'s nonsingularity and from the state feedback control for linear systems, we conclude that there must exist $K(\bar{q}) \in \mathbf{R}^{(n-1)\times2(n-1)}$, $L(\bar{q}) \in \mathbf{R}^{(n-1)\times2}$, $T(\bar{q}) \in \mathbf{R}^{(n-1)\times(n-1)}$, $G(\bar{q}) \in \mathbf{R}^{(n-1)\times1}$ such that the control law can be chosen as

$$\tau_a = G(\bar{q}) + K(\bar{q})\bar{q}_a + L(\bar{q})\bar{q}_b + T(\bar{q})r_m, \tag{27}$$

the closed-loop system is the same as the reference model (16). By substituting the control law (27) into the system equation (14), the closed-loop system is given by

$$\dot{\bar{q}}_a = [A_a + B\mathcal{M}^{-1}K(\bar{q})]\bar{q}_a + [A_b + B\mathcal{M}^{-1}L(\bar{q})]\bar{q}_b$$
$$+ B\mathcal{M}^{-1}T(\bar{q})r_m + B\mathcal{M}^{-1}[G(\bar{q}) - \mathcal{G}] \tag{28}$$

Comparing it to match the reference model (16), we obtain

$$A_a + B\mathcal{M}^{-1}K(\bar{q}) = A_m, A_b + B\mathcal{M}^{-1}L(\bar{q}) = 0_{[2(n-1),2]}$$
$$\mathcal{M}^{-1}T(\bar{q}) = M_d^{-1}G(\bar{q}) - \mathcal{G} = 0_{[n-1]} \tag{29}$$

By the definitions of $A_a, A_b, B, A_m, \mathcal{G}$, we have

$$K(\bar{q}) = \mathcal{M}([A_{m1} \ A_{m2}] - [A_{a1} \ A_{a2}]), L(\bar{q}) = -\mathcal{M}[A_{b1} \ A_{b2}] \tag{30}$$
$$T(\bar{q}) = \mathcal{M}M_d^{-1}, G(\bar{q}) = \mathcal{G} \tag{31}$$

Unfortunately, the dynamic matrices $A_a, A_b, \mathcal{M}, \mathcal{G}$ are not available during practical implementation, and the exact values of the desired gains $K(\bar{q}), L(\bar{q}), T(\bar{q})$ and $G(\bar{q})$ are also unknown. Consider employing the high order neural network (HONN) to approximate the controller gains as follows

$$K(\bar{q}) = K^*(\bar{q}) + \varepsilon_K, \ L(\bar{q}) = L^*(\bar{q}) + \varepsilon_L, \ T(\bar{q}) = T^*(\bar{q}) + \varepsilon_T, \ G(\bar{q}) = G^*(\bar{q}) + \varepsilon_G$$

with $K^*(\bar{q}) = [W_K^{\langle T \rangle}\langle\cdot\rangle S_K(\bar{q})]$, $T^*(\bar{q}) = [W_T^{\langle T \rangle}\langle\cdot\rangle S_T(\bar{q})]$, $L^*(\bar{q}) = [W_L^{\langle T \rangle}\langle\cdot\rangle S_L(\bar{q})]$, $G^*(\bar{q}) = [W_G^{\langle T \rangle}\langle\cdot\rangle S_G(\bar{q})]$. $W_{Ki,j} W_{Li,k}, W_{Ti,s}, W_{Gi} \in \mathbf{R}^{l\times1}$ are the NN ideal weights for $K_{i,j}(\bar{q}), L_{i,k}(\bar{q}), T_{i,s}(\bar{q}), G_i(\bar{q})$, respectively ($i = 1, \cdots, n-1; j = 1, \cdots, 2(n-1); k = 1, 2; s = 1, \cdots, n-1$), l is the number of the neurons. $S_K(\bar{q}), S_L(\bar{q}), S_T(\bar{q}), S_G(\bar{q})$ are the outputs of the bounded basis functions, and $\varepsilon_K, \varepsilon_L, \varepsilon_T, \varepsilon_G$ are the NN approximation errors. For a fixed number of nodes, we know that $\|\varepsilon_K\|, \|\varepsilon_L\|, \|\varepsilon_T\|, \|\varepsilon_G\|$ are bounded, W_K, W_L, W_T, W_G are unknown constant parameters.

Consider the following NN based control law

$$\tau_a = \hat{K}(\bar{q})\bar{q}_a + \hat{L}(\bar{q})\bar{q}_b + \hat{T}(\bar{q})r_m + \hat{G}(\bar{q}) + \tau_r$$
$$= [\hat{W}_K^{\langle T \rangle}\langle\cdot\rangle S_K(\bar{q})]\bar{q}_a + [\hat{W}_L^{\langle T \rangle}\langle\cdot\rangle S_L(\bar{q})]\bar{q}_b + [W_T^{\langle T \rangle}\langle\cdot\rangle S_T(\bar{q})]r_m$$
$$+ [W_G^{\langle T \rangle}\langle\cdot\rangle S_G(\bar{q})] + \tau_r \tag{32}$$

where τ_r is a robust control term for closed-loop stability which will be defined later to compensate for the approximation errors of the NNs. Define $e_a = \bar{q}_a - \bar{q}_{am}$,

$\tilde{W}_K = \hat{W}_K - W_K$, $\tilde{W}_L = \hat{W}_L - W_L$, $\tilde{W}_T = \hat{W}_T - W_T$, $\tilde{W}_G = \hat{W}_G - W_G$
Substituting the control law (32) into the subsystem dynamics (14), and using NN approximations (32)-(32) and recalling (29), we obtain the following error equation

$$\dot{e}_a = A_m e_a + B\mathcal{M}^{-1}(\tau_r - \varepsilon_K \bar{q}_a - \varepsilon_L \bar{q}_b - \varepsilon_T r_m - \varepsilon_G) \tag{33}$$

$$+ B\mathcal{M}^{-1}[\tilde{W}_K^{\langle T \rangle} \langle \cdot \rangle S_K(\bar{q})] \bar{q}_a + B\mathcal{M}^{-1}[\tilde{W}_L^{\langle T \rangle} \langle \cdot \rangle S_L(\bar{q})] \bar{q}_b$$

$$+ B\mathcal{M}^{-1}[\tilde{W}_T^{\langle T \rangle} \langle \cdot \rangle S_T(\bar{q})] r_m + B\mathcal{M}^{-1}[\tilde{W}_G^{\langle T \rangle} \langle \cdot \rangle S_G(\bar{q})]$$

For stable A_m of the reference model, let P_m be the symmetric positive definite solution of the Lyapunov equation $P_m A_m + A_m^T P_m = -Q_m$ where Q_m is symmetric positive definite.

Theorem 1. *For the system (14), consider the NN based control laws (32). If the updating laws of the weights of the adaptive NNs are given by*

$$(\dot{\hat{W}}_{Ki}^{\langle T \rangle})^T = -\Gamma_{Ki} \langle \cdot \rangle S_{Ki}(\bar{q}) \bar{q}_a e_a^T P_m (B)_i, \quad (\dot{\hat{W}}_{Ti}^{\langle T \rangle})^T = -\Gamma_{Ti} \langle \cdot \rangle S_{Ti}(\bar{q}) r_m e_a^T P_m (B)_i$$

$$(\dot{\hat{W}}_{Li}^{\langle T \rangle})^T = -\Gamma_{Li} \langle \cdot \rangle S_{Li}(\bar{q}) \bar{q}_b e_a^T P_m (B)_i, \quad \dot{\hat{W}}_{Gi} = -\Gamma_{Gi} S_{Gi}(\bar{q}) \bar{q}_b e_a^T P_m (B)_i \tag{34}$$

and

$$\tau_r = -k_r \operatorname{sgn}(B^T P_m e_a) - k_2 e_a, k_r = k_1 + k_{r1} + k_{r2} \tag{35}$$

where $(B)_i$ stands for the $i-th$ column of B, k_1, k_2 are the positive constants, $k_{r1} \geq \|\varepsilon_K \bar{q}_a + \varepsilon_L \bar{q}_b + \varepsilon_T r_m + \varepsilon_G\|, k_{r2} \geq \|[\tilde{W}_K^{\langle T \rangle} \langle \cdot \rangle S_K(\bar{q})]\| \|\bar{q}_a\| + \|[\tilde{W}_L^{\langle T \rangle} \langle \cdot \rangle S_L(\bar{q})]\| \|\bar{q}_b\| + \|[\tilde{W}_T^{\langle T \rangle} \langle \cdot \rangle S_T(\bar{q})]\| \|r_m\| + \|[\tilde{W}_G^{\langle T \rangle} \langle \cdot \rangle S_G(\bar{q})]\|, \Gamma_{Ki} \in \mathbf{R}^{(2(n-1) \cdot l) \times (2(n-1) \cdot l)}, \Gamma_{Ti} \in \mathbf{R}^{((n-1) \cdot l) \times ((n-1) \cdot l)}, \Gamma_{Li} \in \mathbf{R}^{(2l) \times (2l)}, \Gamma_{Gi} \in \mathbf{R}^{l \times l}$ are the symmetric positive definite matrices, then the adaptive NN controller ensures that all states of the system are bounded, and the matching error e_a will converge to zero in finite time, i.e., there exist a finite time t_e such that $\|e_a\| = 0, t > t_e \ll t_f$.

Proof. Choose the following Lyapunov function $V_1 = U_1 + U_2$ with

$$U_1 = \frac{1}{\bar{m}} e_a^T P_m e_a, U_2 = \sum_{i=1}^{n-1} \tilde{W}_{Ki}^{\langle T \rangle} \Gamma_{Ki}^{-1} (\tilde{W}_{Ki}^{\langle T \rangle})^T + \sum_{i=1}^{n-1} \tilde{W}_{Li}^{\langle T \rangle} \Gamma_{Ki}^{-1} (\tilde{W}_{Li}^{\langle T \rangle})^T$$

$$+ \sum_{i=1}^{n-1} \tilde{W}_{Ti}^{\langle T \rangle} \Gamma_{Ti}^{-1} (\tilde{W}_{Ti}^{\langle T \rangle})^T + \sum_{i=1}^{n-1} \tilde{W}_{Gi}^T \Gamma_{Gi}^{-1} \tilde{W}_{Gi}. \tag{36}$$

Differentiating the Lyapunov candidate along (33) and noting $\underline{m} \leq |\mathcal{M}^{-1}| \leq \bar{m}$, then substituting the adaptive laws (34) and τ_r from (35), we have

$$\dot{V}_1 = -\frac{1}{\bar{m}} e_a^T Q_m e_a - 2(k_1 + k_{r2}) e_a^T P_m B \operatorname{sgn}(B^T P_m e_a) - 2k_2 e_a^T P_m B e_a \tag{37}$$

$$\leq -k_0 \|e_a\| < 0, \|e_a\| \neq 0, \tag{38}$$

with $k_0 = 2k_1 \|P_m B\| > 0$. Expression (37) means both U_1 and U_2 are bounded and consequently $e_a, \tilde{W}_K, \tilde{W}_T$ are bounded; then e_a asymptotically converges to zero. At the same time, we also derive that

$$\dot{U}_1 \leq -k_0 \|e_a\| = -c_0 U_1^{1/2} \tag{39}$$

According to the finite time stability theorem, there exist a finite time t_e such that $\|e_a\| = 0$, $t > t_e$. This completes the proof.

5   Reference Trajectory Generator for q_b Subsystem

As above discussed, after finite time, q_a will exactly track q_{ad}, such that the dynamics (13) becomes as follows:

$$\ddot{q}_b = -M_b^{-1}(C_b\dot{q}_b + g_b - M_b^{-1}\tau_{db} + M_{ba}\ddot{q}_{ad} + C_{ba}\dot{q}_{ad}) \tag{40}$$

Let $\varphi = [\varphi_1, \varphi_2]^T = [q_b, \dot{q}_b]^T$, $\phi = [\phi_1^T, \phi_2^T]^T = [q_{ad}^T, \dot{q}_{ad}^T]^T$ and $v = \ddot{q}_{ad}$. Then, equation (40) can be rewritten as

$$\dot{\varphi}_1 = \varphi_2, \quad \dot{\varphi}_2 = f(\varphi, \phi, v) \tag{41}$$

with $f(\varphi, \phi, v) = -M_b^{-1}M_{ba}v - M_b^{-1}(C_b\varphi_2 + g_b + \tau_{db} + C_{ba}\phi_2)$ and $\dot{\phi}_1 = \phi_2, \dot{\phi}_2 = v$. Consider the desired forward position and velocity of the manipulator as q_{bd} and $\dot{q}_{bd}$, respectively. Then, our design objective is to construct a v (subsequently ϕ_1 and ϕ_2) such that φ_1 and φ_2 of system (41) follow φ_{1m} and φ_{2m} generated from the following reference model:

$$\dot{\varphi}_{1m} = \varphi_{2m}, \dot{\varphi}_{2m} = f_m(q_{bd}, \dot{q}_{bd}, \varphi_m) \tag{42}$$

where $\varphi_m = [\varphi_{1m}, \varphi_{2m}]^T$ and $f_m(q_{bd}, \dot{q}_{bd}, \varphi_m) = -k_1(\varphi_{1m} - q_{bd}) - k_2(\varphi_{2m} - \dot{q}_{bd}) + \ddot{q}_{bd}$. It can be easily checked that the reference model (42) ensures that $\varphi_{1m} \to q_{bd}$ and $\varphi_{2m} \to \dot{q}_{bd}$, with positive k_1 and k_2 to be specified by the designer. It should be mentioned that optimization has also been widely applied in robotic trajectory planning [14], and the LQR based optimization method used in Section 4.1 can also be used here to choose optimal values for k_1 and k_2, but for simplicity we ommit further discussion here. According to implicit function theorem based neural network design [15], there must exist a function f_v

$$v^* = f_v(q_{bd}, \dot{q}_{bd}, \varphi, \phi) \tag{43}$$

such that $f(\varphi, \phi, v^*) = f_m(q_{bd}, \dot{q}_{bd}, \varphi)$ Employing the high order neural network (HONN), we see that there exists the ideal HONNs weight vectors such that

$$v^* = [W_v^{*\langle T \rangle}\langle\cdot\rangle S_v(z)] + \epsilon_v, \quad z = [q_{bd}, \dot{q}_{bd}, \varphi^T, \phi^T]^T \tag{44}$$

where $\epsilon_v \in \mathbf{R}^{(n-1)\times 1}$ is the neural network approximation error vector. Let us employ HONNs to approximate v^* as follows:

$$\hat{v} = \hat{W}_v^{\langle T \rangle}\langle\cdot\rangle S_v(z) \tag{45}$$

with $\hat{W}_v^{\langle T \rangle} = [\hat{W}_{v1}^T, \hat{W}_{v2}^T, \cdots, \hat{W}_{v(n-1)}^T]$ where $\hat{W}_{vi}^T \in \mathbf{R}^{l\times 1}(i = 1, 2, \cdots, n - 1)$ are the neural network weight vectors. Substituting $\hat{v}$ into (41) and using $f(\phi, \varphi, v^*) = f_m(q_{bd}, \dot{q}_{bd}, \varphi)$, we have

$$\dot{\varphi}_1 = \varphi_2, \quad \dot{\varphi}_2 = f_m(q_{bd}, \dot{q}_{bd}, \varphi) - M_b^{-1}M_{ba}([\tilde{W}_v^{\langle T \rangle}\langle\cdot\rangle S_v(z)] - \epsilon_v) \tag{46}$$

where $\tilde{W} = \hat{W} - W^*$. Define $\tilde{\varphi}_1 = \varphi_1 - \varphi_{1m}$ and $\tilde{\varphi}_2 = \varphi_2 - \varphi_{2m}$ such that $\tilde{\varphi} = \hat{\varphi} - \varphi$. Then, the comparison between (42) and (46) yields

$$\dot{\tilde{\varphi}}_1 = \tilde{\varphi}_2, \quad \dot{\tilde{\varphi}}_2 = -k_1\tilde{\varphi}_1 - k_2\tilde{\varphi}_2 - M_b^{-1}M_{ba}([\tilde{W}_v^{\langle T\rangle}\langle\cdot\rangle S_v(z)] - \epsilon_v) \qquad (47)$$

Theorem 2. *Consider the following weight adaptation law for HONN employed in (45):*

$$\dot{\hat{W}}_{vi} = \Gamma_{vi}S_{vi}(z)\tilde{\varphi}^T P_W [0 \ \ 1]^T - \sigma\Gamma_{vi}\hat{W}_{vi} \qquad (48)$$

where $\Gamma_{vi} \in \mathbb{R}^{l\times l}$ and σ are suitably chosen as a symmetric positive definite matrix and a positive scalar, respectively. Then, the tracking errors $\tilde{\varphi}_1$ and $\tilde{\varphi}_2$ in (47) will be eventually bounded into a small neighborhood around zero.

Proof. Let us rewrite the error dynamics (47) as

$$\dot{\tilde{\varphi}} = A_W\tilde{\varphi} - M_b^{-1}M_{ba}([\tilde{W}_v^{\langle T\rangle}\langle\cdot\rangle S_v(z)] - \epsilon_v)[0 \ \ 1]^T \qquad (49)$$

$$= A_W\tilde{\varphi} - [0 \ \ 1]^T M_b^{-1}\sum_{i=1}^{n-1} M_{bai}(\tilde{W}_{vi}^T S_{vi}(z) - \epsilon_{vi}) \qquad (50)$$

where M_{bai} represents the i-th element of vector M_{ba}, $A_W = \begin{bmatrix} 0 & 1 \\ -k_1 & -k_2 \end{bmatrix}$ satisfies the Lyapunov equation $A_W^T P_W + P_W A_W = -Q_W$. Consider a Lyapunov function $V_2(t) = \tilde{\varphi}^T P_W\tilde{\varphi} + M_b^{-1}\sum_{i=1}^{n-1} M_{bai}\tilde{W}_{vi}^T\Gamma_{vi}^{-1}\tilde{W}_{vi}^T$ and the closed-loop dynamics (49) with the update law (48), we can derive that

$$\dot{V}_2(t) \leq -\lambda_{Q_W}\|\tilde{\varphi}\|^2 - 2\sigma M_b^{-1}|M_{ba}|\|\tilde{W}_v^{\langle T\rangle}\|^2 + \varepsilon^2\|\tilde{\varphi}\|^2$$

$$+\varepsilon^2\|\tilde{W}_v^{\langle T\rangle}\|^2 + \frac{1}{\varepsilon^2}\epsilon_0^2 M_b^{-1}|M_{ba}|^2\|P_W[0 \ \ 1]^T\|^2 + \frac{1}{\varepsilon^2}\sigma^2 M_b^{-1}|M_{ba}|^2\|W_v^{*\langle T\rangle}\|^2$$

where $|\epsilon_v| \leq \epsilon_0$, λ_{Q_W} is the minimum eigenvalue of Q_W, ε is any given positive constant and we can choose it sufficiently small. Furthermore, we can choose suitable Q_W and σ making $\lambda_{Q_W} \geq \varepsilon^2$, $2\sigma M_b^{-1}|M_{ba}| \geq \varepsilon^2$, and it follows that $\dot{V}_2(t) \leq 0$ in the complementary set of a set S_b defined as $S_b \triangleq$ $\left\{(\tilde{\varphi}, \tilde{W})\Big|\frac{\|\tilde{W}_v^{\langle T\rangle}\|^2}{\bar{a}^2} + \frac{\|\tilde{\varphi}\|^2}{\bar{b}^2} - 1 \leq 0\right\}$, $\bar{a} = \frac{1}{\varepsilon}M_b^{-1}|M_{ba}|\frac{\sqrt{\epsilon_0^2\|P_W[0,1]^T\|^2 + \sigma^2\|W_v^{*\langle T\rangle}\|^2}}{\sqrt{\lambda_{Q_W} - \varepsilon^2}}$, $\bar{b} = \frac{1}{\varepsilon}M_b^{-1}|M_{ba}|\sqrt{\epsilon_0^2\|P_W[0, \ \ 1]^T\|^2 + \sigma^2\|W_v^{*\langle T\rangle}\|^2}/\sqrt{2\sigma M_b^{-1}|M_{ba}| - \varepsilon^2}$. Obviously, the set S_b defined above is compact. Hence, by LaSalle's theorem, it follows that all the solutions of (49) are bounded.

6 Conclusion

In this paper, adaptive NN control has been designed for the robot with a passive last joint. The dynamics of the the actuated subsystem has been shaped to follow a reference model, which is derived using the LQR optimization technique to minimize both the motion tracking error and the transient acceleration. The tracking performance of the unactuated subsystem is achieved by generating a suitable reference trajectory. The proposed control method considers the presence of various uncertainties including both parametric and functional uncertainties.

References

1. Acosta, J.A., Ortega, R., Astolfi, A., Mahindrakar, A.D.: Interconnection and damping assignment passivity-based control of mechanical systems with underactuation degree one. IEEE Transactions on Automatic Control 50(12), 1936–1955 (2005)
2. Reyhanoglu, M., van der Schaft, A., McClamroch, N.H., Kolmanovsky, I.: Dynamics and control of a class of underactuated mechanical systems. IEEE Transactions on Automatic Control 44(9), 1663–1671 (1999)
3. Cui, R., Yan, W., Xu, D.: Synchronization of multiple autonomous underwater vehicles without velocity measurements. Science China Information Sciences (2012), doi:10.1007/s11432-012-4579-6
4. Cui, R., Yan, W.: Mutual synchronization of multiple robot manipulators with unknown dynamics. Journal of Intelligent & Robotic Systems (2012), doi:10.1007/s10846-012-9674-9
5. Sampei, M., Tamura, T., Kobayashi, T., Shibui, N.: Arbitrary path tracking control of articulated vehicles using nonlinear control theory. IEEE Trans. Control Systems Technology 3(1), 125–131 (1995)
6. Sodalen, O.J., Nakamura, Y., Chung, W.J.: Design of a nonholonomic manipulator. In: Proc. IEEE Int. Conf. Robot. Automat., pp. 8–13 (1994)
7. Brockett, R.W., Millman, R.S., Sussmann, H.J.: Asymptotic stability and feedback stabilization. In: Differential Geometric Control Theory, pp. 181–191. Birkhäuser (1983)
8. Kosmatopoulos, E.B., Polycarpou, M.M., Christodoulou, M.A., Ioannou, P.A.: High-order neural network structures for identification of dynamical systems. IEEE Transactions on Neural Networks 6(2), 422–431 (1995)
9. Ge, S.S., Lee, T.H., Harris, C.J.: Adaptive Neural Network Control of Robotic Manipulators. World Scientific, London (1998)
10. Gupta, M.M., Rao, D.H.: Neuro-Control Systems: Theory and Applications. IEEE Press, New York (1994)
11. Polycarpou, M.M., Ioannou, P.: Learning and convergence analysis of neural-type structured networks. IEEE Transactions on Neural Networks 3(1), 39–50 (1992)
12. Anderson, B.D.O., Moore, J.B.: Optimal Control. Prentice Hall, London (1989)
13. Siciliano, B., Sciavicco, L., Villani, L., Oriolo, G.: Robotics: Modelling, Planning and Control. Springer (2008)
14. Cui, R., Gao, B., Guo, J.: Pareto-Optimal Coordination of Multiple Robots with Safety Guarantees. Autonomous Robots 32(3), 189–205 (2012)
15. Yang, C., Ge, S.S., Xiang, C., Chai, T., Lee, T.H.: Output Feedback NN Control for two Classes of Discrete-time Systems with Unknown Control Directions in a Unified Approach. IEEE Transactions on Neural Networks 19(11), 1873–1886 (2008)

4M-Model Based Bionic Design of Artificial Skeletal Muscle Actuated by SMA

Jianjun Zhang[1] and Jianying Zhu[2]

[1] State Key Laboratory of Mechanism System and Vibration, Institute of Robotics,
Shanghai Jiao Tong University, Shanghai 200240, China
zhangjianjun@sjtu.edu.cn
[2] Mechatronics Research Institute, Nanjing University of Aeronautics and Astronautics,
Nanjing 210016, China

Abstract. This paper presents a novel 4M-model based artificial skeletal muscle (AM) actuated by shape memory alloy (SMA) wires. Different from Hill- and Huxley- model, the 4M-model is developed based on the microscopic working mechanism of molecular motor (4M), which is the origin of muscle contraction. Overlapped SMA wires and custom made passive composite (CMPC) of the AM were used to mimic biomechanical characteristics of skeletal muscle, which mainly refers to force-length relationship. Experimental results of the AM demonstrate the desired performance.

Keywords: Shape memory alloy, Artificial skeletal muscle, 4M-model, Bionic design.

1 Introduction

Skeletal muscle is the source of human body motion. For decades, many scholars have conducted and are still conducting research on artificial skeletal muscle (AM) to imitate the form and function of skeletal muscle. However, two key challenges hamper the development of the AM. One challenge is inaccurate biomechanical model of skeletal muscle. A wide variety of skeletal muscle models have been proposed for their important values in biomechanics and bionics engineering [1]. The most representative model is Hill-model originating with macroscopic experiments [2]. The model didn't consider microscopic properties of muscle contraction. Another representative muscle model is Huxley-model originating at the molecular level [3] without considering muscle macroscopic contraction properties. Different from Hill- and Huxley- model, 4M-model is developed based on the collective microscopic working mechanism of molecular motor (4M) with a statistical mechanics method [4-7], and builds the relationship between micro- and macro- biomechanics of skeletal muscle, which is more accurate for the bionic design of the AM.

Another key challenge is the muscle-like actuator. Many actuator devices (such as electric motors, hydraulics and pneumatics) and smart materials (such as EAP and SMA) have been put forth as AM. Conventional actuator devices, such as DC motor

C.-Y. Su, S. Rakheja, H. Liu (Eds.): ICIRA 2012, Part III, LNAI 7508, pp. 123–130, 2012.
© Springer-Verlag Berlin Heidelberg 2012

[8-12] and hydraulics [13] are hard to imitate skeletal muscles because of their low power density and large volume. Pneumatic artificial muscles [14] can imitate the performance of natural muscle, but they are noisy and require a separate pump to provide the energy. EAP-based artificial muscle has been developed recently [15], but the generated force is small and the operating voltage is too high (>1000V) to be of practical use. SMA wires have high energy density similar to skeletal muscle, further, SMA wires have many other muscle-like properties, such as unidirectional actuating, flexibility and silent operation. Besides, SMA wires can be driven directly by low-voltage. Thus, it is feasible to realize SMA-based artificial skeletal muscle [16].

The motivation of this paper is to develop an artificial skeletal muscle. An important step in the development is to identify the properties and performance that the AM is expected to achieve. The 4M-model is used to describe the performance of skeletal muscle. The model serves as a means for comparison with the AM. In the development of the AM, parallel SMA wires and custom made passive composite (CMPC) are used to mimic both the active and passive force properties of skeletal muscle. Experimental results demonstrate that the AM presents muscle-like performance in terms of force-length properties.

2   4M-Model of Skeletal Muscle

The first step in designing an AM is to identify the skeletal muscle properties to be imitated. However, muscle properties vary widely not only between species but also within a species. The approach used here is to present the 4M-model as a guideline to specify the muscle properties for bionic design of the AM.

The skeletal muscle consists of muscle fibers surrounded by connective tissue. Each fiber contains hundreds of parallel myofibrils, and each myofibril comprises hundreds of series sarcomeres. The sarcomere is the basic unit of skeletal muscle. Each sarcomere comprises thin and thick filaments called actin and molecular motor (myosin). The force of skeletal muscle is produced by the overlap and interaction of actin and molecular motor. Besides, the total force F generated by skeletal muscle comprises the active force F_a and the passive force F_p (see Eq. (1))[6].

$$F = F_a + F_p \tag{1}$$

2.1   Active Force-Length Properties of Skeletal Muscle

The active force is produced by the collective working of numerous molecular motors. According to 4M-model, the active force of a whole skeletal muscle satisfies the following equation:

$$F_a = \frac{A\alpha\beta n_0 c}{s} \int_0^L x\rho(x,t)dx \tag{2}$$

Where α is the overlap degree between thin and thick filaments. β is the activation degree of sacromere. $\beta = 1$ represents the muscle contracts at tetanical state. c is the elasticity coefficient of molecular motor. An_0/s represents the total number of molecular motors in the skeletal muscle. $\int_0^t x\rho(x,t)dx$ represents the average displacement of molecular motor on thin filaments, which can be considered as a constant. Note that, the active force for a certain given skeletal muscle is a function of the overlap degree and the activation degree, because the other parameters can be considered as constants. Besides, the overlap degree satisfies Eq. (3) because of the symmetry structure of sarcomere.

$$\alpha = e^{-(l-l_0)^2/\sigma^2} \tag{3}$$

Where l is the length of skeletal muscle and l_0 is the resting length of skeletal muscle. Thus the active force of a certain given skeletal muscle is a function of the muscle length and the activation degree. The dimensionless active force to length curves at different activation degree are shown in Fig.1 (a), where F_0 is the maximal active force at the resting length.

2.2 Passive Force-Length Properties of Skeletal Muscle

The passive force is produced by the visco-elastic tissue of skeletal muscle, which satisfies the following equation:

$$F_p = k_m \Delta l + \gamma \dot{l} \tag{4}$$

Where k_m is the nonlinear elasticity coefficient and γ is the drag coefficient of the muscle. Δl is the contraction length and $\dot{l}$ is the contraction velocity of the muscle. The dimensionless passive force to length curve is shown in Fig. 1 (b). The dimensionless total force produced by the sum of active and passive muscle force is shown in Fig.2.

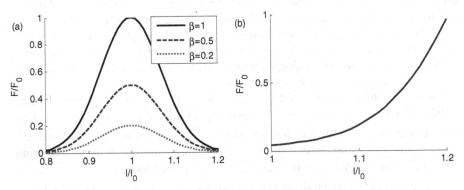

Fig. 1. Relationship between active (a) and passive (b) force and muscle length

3   Bionic Design Method of AM

The stated objective of this research is to develop a muscle-like artificial muscle. Thus the artificial muscle should mimic both the active force-length and passive force-length properties of muscle. While some investigators have proposed the use of commercially available actuators, such as DC motor, pneumatic actuator. We propose the use of SMA wires as the active element due to its active contractile function similar to muscle fibers.

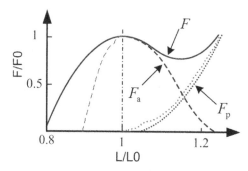

Fig. 2. Dimensionless relationship between total (solid), active (dashed), passive (dotted) force and length for skeletal muscle compared with a fully heated SMA wire (red dashed) and the CMPC (red dotted)

3.1   Design of Active Muscle Element

SMA mainly has two phases, namely martensite (M), austenite (A). When being activated by heating, a SMA wire shortens its length from M to A. Subsequent cooling returns the wire to its longest length (equal to non-activated "resting" length) from A to M under enough applied load. In order to mimic the active force properties of skeletal muscles, we conducted a series of force-length experiments on a single SMA wire. The experiment method, as shown in Fig.3, is similar to the classical muscle contraction experiment. The SMA wire is mounted between a load cell and a slider. The slider position, corresponding to the SMA wire length, is measured by the LVDT. The SMA wire is activated by current, and the contraction force is measured by the load cell. A computer equipped with a data acquisition card (NI USB-6211) is used to store and process all the measured data.

When the fully heated SMA wire contracts over a range of lengths ($0.9L_0 < L < L_0$), the force-length relationship can be determined by measuring the force output against the length of the SMA wire, as shown in Fig. 2 (red dashed). The force increases from zero at the SMA wire's minimum length to the maximum value F_0 when the SMA wire is at resting length L_0. The dimensionless force-length curve has a similar parabolic shape to the active force-length curve of skeletal muscles when the SMA wire length is less than the resting length, which is caused by SMA

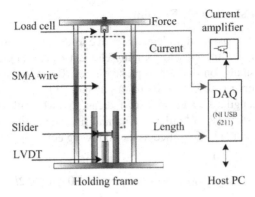

Fig. 3. Configuration of the experimental setup

phase transformation. However, the strain of SMA wire (10%) is smaller than muscle (40%). Besides, the SMA wire cannot be stretched beyond the resting length. Otherwise plastic deformation will occur [17].

The main design principle of the AM is to imitate mechanical properties of skeletal muscles while maintaining simplicity. In our AM design, mechanically parallel while electrically series SMA wires are used to output the desired contraction force. The more the number of parallel SMA wires, the larger the contraction force can be achieved. Besides, a simple but effective method for the solution of the low strain problem is proposed, as shown in Fig.4 (a). The parallel SMA wires are arranged in overlapping pattern by using a custom made muscle frame. The muscle frame mainly comprises a rigid aluminum tube combining with two resin circular plate. The overlapped SMA wires can enhance the AM strain from 10% to 19% while maintaining the large force capability. 8 parallel overlapped SMA wires with diameter of 0.25mm are selected. The AM with total length of 250mm can provide a maximum contraction force of 115N and a maximum contraction length of 47.5mm.

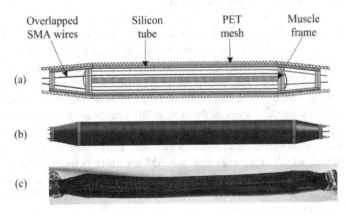

Fig. 4. Schematic (a), CAD model (b) and picture (b) of the artificial muscle

3.2   Design of Passive Muscle Element

It is hard to mimic the passive muscle element due to the nonlinear elastic properties. According to 4M-model, the muscle damping element can be neglected without loss of accuracy, for its small contribution to passive force. Besides, the passive force is 0 when the muscle length is less than the resting length. When the muscle is stretched beyond the resting length, the passive force increases slowly with small stiffness and then fast with large stiffness. 3rd order polynomial function is used to fit the passive-length curve. Thus Eq. (4) is simplified as the following equation:

$$F_p = \begin{cases} 0 & \text{for } x \le 0 \\ ax^3 + bx^2 + cx + d & \text{for } 0 < x \le 0.2l_0 \end{cases} \tag{5}$$

Where a, b, c and d are coefficients of the polynomial function. Besides, the passive force varies depending on how much connective issue the muscle contains, which is assumed proportional to active force. Thus, the maximal passive force can be considered to be equal to the maximal active force.

In order to mimic the passive properties, we used a custom made passive composite (CMPC), which comprises a silicon tube and a polyethylene terephthalate (PET) mesh, as shown in Fig.4 (a). The small stiffness is provided by the silicon tube and the larger stiffness is provided by the PET mesh. The PET mesh wrapped outside the silicon tube can create a nonlinear muscle-like passive force-length relationship. By changing the diameter, wall thickness of the silicon tube and the length of the PET mesh, the desired force-length relationship can be gained. After a series test on different tube and PET mesh combinations, we determined a silicon tube with length of 250mm, outer diameter of 10mm and wall thickness of 1.5mm and a PET mesh with maximal length of 263mm at last in our design. The experimental dimensionless force-length curve (red dotted) of CMPC is shown in Fig.2, which presents a good similarity with that of skeletal muscle obtained from Eq. (5) (black dotted).

4   Force- Length Properties of the AM

The whole designed artificial muscle with the CMPC wrapped and fixed outside the SMA wires are shown in Fig.4 (a-c). In order to explore the force-length properties of the AM, a series of isometric contraction experiments are implemented under different activation degree. The activation degree of the AM refers to the heating temperature of the SMA, which can be represented by heating current. The isometric dimensionless force-length curves of the AM at different heating current are shown in Fig.5. The experimental data are fitted using 6th order polynomial function. When the heating current is 600mA, the SMA wires are fully heated with the highest contraction force, which represents that the AM are fully activated. As the heating current decreases, the contraction force decreases gradually, but the passive force doesn't change. Because the passive force of the CMPC is independent of the active force of SMA wires.

Compared the force-length curves of Fig.5 with that of Fig.2. The AM have a similar force-length properties with skeletal muscle except for the strain restrained by SMA wires. Actually the AM maximal contraction strain of 19% is comparable to that of skeletal muscles at normal contraction degree.

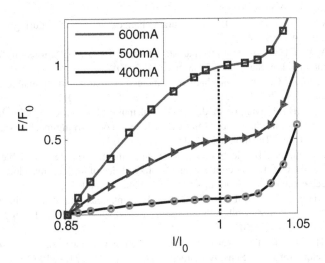

Fig. 5. Experimental results of isometric dimensionless force-length curves of the AM

5   Conclusion

We designed an SMA-actuated artificial skeletal muscle based on the 4M-model. Overlapped parallel SMA wires are used to output the desired active force and increase the AM contraction strain. Besides, the custom made passive composite has a good muscle-like passive force-length property. Experimental results have demonstrated that the artificial muscle can basically mimic the force-length properties of skeletal muscle except for the limited strain. Another main drawback of the AM is the slow response speed caused by SMA slow heat transfer rate. Faster speed can be achieved by improving the cooling speed, or using thinner SMA wires. In future, the AM dynamic contraction properties will be explored and an AM actuated robotic ankle-foot will be developed.

Acknowledgment. This work was supported by the National Natural Science Foundation of China (61075101,60643002), the National Basic Research Program of China (2011CB013203),the Science and Technology Intercrossing and the Medical and Technology Intercrossing Research Foundation of Shanghai Jiao Tong University (LG2011ZD$_1$06,YG2010ZD$_1$01).

References

1. Yin, Y.H., Guo, Z., Chen, X., Fan, Y.J.: Studies on Biomechanics of Skeletal Muscle Based on the Working Mechanism of Myosin Motors: An Overview. Chin. Sci. Bull. (2012)
2. Hill, A.V.: The heat of shortening and the dynamic constants of muscle. Proc. R Soc. Lond. B 126, 136–195 (1938)
3. Huxley, A.F., Niedergerke, R.: Structural changes in muscle during contraction. Nature 173, 971–973 (1954)
4. Guo, Z., Yin, Y.H.: Coupling mechanism of multi-force interactions in the myosin molecular motor. Chin. Sci. Bull. 55, 3538–3544 (2010)
5. Yin, Y.H., Guo, Z.: Collective mechanism of molecular motors and a dynamic mechanical model for sarcomere. Sci. China-Technol. Sci. 54, 2130–2137 (2011)
6. Guo, Z., Yin, Y.H.: A dynamic model of skeletal muscle based on collective behavior of myosin motors—Biomechanics of skeletal muscle based on working mechanism of myosin motors (I). Sci. China-Technol. Sci. 55, 1589–1595 (2012)
7. Yin, Y.H., Chen, X.: Bioelectrochemical control mechanism with variable-frequency regulation for skeletal muscle contraction—Biomechanics of skeletal muscle based on the working mechanism of myosin motors (II). Sci. China-Technol. Sci. 55, 2115–2125 (2012)
8. Yin, Y.H., Fan, Y.J., Xu, L.D.: EMG and EPP-integrated human-machine interface between the paralyzed and rehabilitation exoskeleton. IEEE T. Inf. Technol. Biomed. 16(4), 542–549 (2012)
9. Yin, Y.H., Hu, H., Xia, Y.C.: Active tracking of unknown surface using force sensing and control technique for robot. Sens. Actuators A: Phys. 112(2-3), 313–319 (2004)
10. Yin, Y.H., Zhou, C., Chen, S., Hu, H., Lin, Z.: Optimal design of micro-force sensor for wire bonding with high acceleration and frequent movement Sens. Sens. Actuators A: Phys. 127(1), 104–118 (2006)
11. Yin, S., Yin, Y.H.: Study on virtual force sensing and force display device for the interactive bicycle simulator. Sens. Actuators A: Phys. 140(1), 65–74 (2007)
12. Fan, Y.J., Guo, Z., Yin, Y.H.: SEMG-based neuro-fuzzy controller for a parallel ankle exoskeleton with proprioception. Int. J. Robot. Autom. 26(4), 1–11 (2011)
13. Alfayad, S., Ouezdou, F.B., Namoun, F., Gheng, G.: High performance integrated electro-hydraulic actuator for robotics. Part I: Principle, prototype design & first experiments. Sens. Actuators A: Phys. 169(1), 115–123 (2011)
14. Konishi, S., Kawai, F., Cusin, P.: Thin flexible end-effector using pneumatic balloon actuator. Sens. Actuators A: Phys. 89(1-2), 28–35 (2001)
15. Cohen, Y.B.: Electroactive polymer (EAP) actuators as artificial muscles: reality, potential, and challenges. SPIE press (2004)
16. Zhang, J.J., Yin, Y.H.: SMA-based bionic integration design of self-sensor–actuator-structure for artificial skeletal muscle. Sens. Actuators A: Phys. 181, 94–102 (2012)
17. Lagoudas, D.C.: Shape Memory Alloys: Modeling and Engineering Application. Springer, New York (2008)

Design Considerations of a Robotic Head
for Telepresence Applications

Wee Ching Pang[1], Burhan[1], and Gerald Seet[2]

[1] BeingThere Centre, Institute for Media Innovation, Nanyang Technological University
BeingThere Centre, Institute for Media Innovation, Research Techno Plaza,
XFrontier Block Level 03-01, 50 Nanyang Drive, Singapore 637553
{WEECHING,BURHAN}@ntu.edu.sg
[2] Robotics Research Centre, School of Mechanical and Aerospace Engineering
Nanyang Technological University, 50 Nanyang Avenue, N3-01a-01, Singapore 639798
MGLSEET@ntu.edu.sg

Abstract. This work attempts to enhance telepresence by empowering nonverbal communication i.e. head gestures communication with an implementation of a robotic rear-projection head device. The feature of this implementation which is considered to be novel is the containment of all the necessary components for rear-head projection within the volume of a typical human head. This provides a natural look to the rear-projection head and facilitates interaction. The resultant head is capable of accurately projecting human facial features.

Keywords: Rear-Projection, Robotic head, Telepresence, Face robot, Human-robot interaction.

1 Introduction

Since humans began interacting with one another, direct face-to-face interaction has invariably been the interaction mode of choice. In addition to facilitating communication via speech, face-to-face interaction allows facial expressions or gestures to provide subliminal information that augment conscious communication efforts [1] [2]. When gestures are used in conjunction with speech, information is conveyed via the visual as well as the auditory sensory channels. In this manner, communication can become more efficient and easily understood. Such use of the visual and auditory sensory channels to effectively convey information has also been applied in user interface design for human interaction with rescue robots [3].

While speech is one of the first things to come to mind when considering face-to-face interaction, it is worth noting that a typical human face provides an array of visual information such as age, gender, ethnicity, line-of-work, status as well as moods and emotions. Small variations in expressions and gestures can significantly affect communication. Furthermore, eye movements and gazes [4] can also signal our perceptions of the people we are interacting with.

C.-Y. Su, S. Rakheja, H. Liu (Eds.): ICIRA 2012, Part III, LNAI 7508, pp. 131–140, 2012.

With the prevalence of the internet culture and the advances of technology, there is resurgence in the desire to replace direct face-to-face interaction with one that can make do without the need for time consuming international travel. Telepresence [5] [6] refers to a set of technologies that enables geographically separated individuals to interact effectively with all the sensations and advantages of actually being at the remote site. This has been demonstrated by the use video-mediated communications such as video conferences [7] [8] within boardrooms [9] and desktop video interaction tools such as Skype and Google Talk[10]. Although such communication via video screen provides a richer interaction experience, it lacks a number of spatial and perceptual cues. It is not easy to notice peripheral cues, control the floor when interacting with a large audience, have side conversations, point to things and manipulate real-world objects when communicating via video [11] .

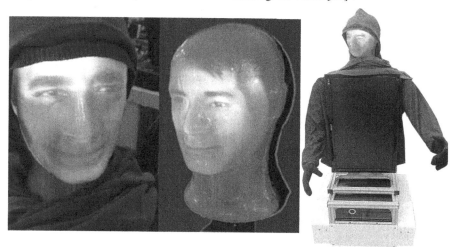

Fig. 1. Rear-Projection Robotic Head for MAVEN

Our work attempts to further enhance telepresence by empowering two aspects of nonverbal communication, i.e. head and hand gestures communication, as shown in Fig. 1. In this paper, the focus is on the implementation of a robotic head device capable of expressing basic human emotions and head gestures. Whilst a flat video image can convey facial gestures, viewing of a physical 3D head with the addition of textual features can be expected to provide a more rewarding experience. The ability to view the sides of the head coupled by its physical motion appears to be favored over a flat video image. In other words, a robotic head can provide a flexible solution for facial representations and expressions as well as head gestures during communication, taking into advantage the advancements of image processing techniques over mechanically controlled head.

The scope of this paper includes the engineering realization of hardware - that is a "complete" rear-projection robotic head for telepresence communication, as well as the reconstruction of face texture from a 2D image. The development of the robotic head is part of a larger effort for developing a humanoid robot for telepresence applications. Currently, a mobile holonomic platform called MAVEN (Mobile Avatar for Virtual Engagement by NTU) has been developed [12]. Navigation with the

MAVEN platform is possible via tele-operation as well as with autonomy. MAVEN can display the human operator (or inhabitor) on a flat screen TV mounted on the robot. The robotic head would provide an alternative to this if mounted on MAVEN as it would then be possible to project the inhabitor's facial features onto the head's face as shown in Fig. 1.

2   Related Work

Among the various attempts to build a robotic head or face, Ishiguro [13] and Hanson [14] have tried to use solid silicon elastomers to build robotic heads that emulate human faces realistically. Facial expressions and emotions are articulated via pneumatic actuators and electro-actuated polymers respectively. However, such robotic android head is not generic, it has to be custom-made to look like a particular person and others will not be able to use the same head to represent themselves during a conversational communication. Furthermore, the implementation cost, as well as the maintenance cost of these realistic robotic heads is exorbitant.

Therefore, an alternative to robotic android head is to project an imagery of a face onto a surface that shaped like a human head. Disneyland™ [15] has pioneered the use of a front projection technique in its Haunted Mansion™ attraction to animate the Madam Leota figure. The front projection technique involves projecting the film imagery of a face directly onto the front of the head bust from a projector in front of the face. Academically, Lincoln et al. [16] has implemented an animatronics shader lamps avatar head using the front projection technique as well. Rather than projecting an animated or filmed imagery of a human, their system uses cameras to capture the appearance of a human user and map onto a Styrofoam head. The head is mounted on a pan-tilt gimbal such that the head's movement is driven by the actual head movement of the human user.

The disadvantage of a front-projection robotic head is that any movement of the head with respect to the projector will cause the projection to be out of focus or mismatched. Another drawback of a front projection head is that there must be a clear path between the projector and the head because any object that block the path of projection will cast a shadow on the head. This makes it impractical for communicating or interacting purposes. Several groups have tried to implement the projection head technique by designing a rear projection head such that the imagery of a face is projected onto the back of a translucent head. Typically, to project an image to a small projection surface (about 33cm width), the throw distance between the projector and screen surface would be very long depending on throw ratio. However, installing the projector at a large distance from the back of the face will not solve the shadow casting problem faced by frontal projection; it also results in an unnatural and irregular shaped head. Therefore, there is a motivation to hide the projector within the head or as near to the face as possible.

One of the earliest rear projection head is the "Talking Head Projection" [17] [18] implemented as an experimental work in telepresence in 1980. A large plane mirror is mounted behind the head, adapting to keep the projector near the head while projecting an image on the face. The head movement, as well as the audio video information, of a human user is first recorded on film, before being played back onto the head that has a face-shaped screen mounted in a pan-tilt unit. Instead of using mirrors, Delaunay et al. [19] discussed the potential of using a small pico-projector with shorter throw ratio while the Disneyland™ [15] and Mask-bot [20] have installed a wide angle lens and fish-eye lens within their rear-projection heads to adjust the focusing as well as the throw distance of the projection respectively. All of the above mentioned rear-projection heads used the head as a device to play back recorded film (e.g. [17] [18]) or to display an animated cartoon (e.g. [15], [19]) or texture face (e.g. [20]). All these rear-projection heads, except that by Disneyland, are still constrained by a couple of outstanding issues needing resolution. The projector and lens configurations invariably require the rear of the robot head to be extended beyond the physical limits attributed to a human head. The rear of the head is incomplete and typically masked by scarf, providing for an unnatural setting.

3   Hardware Configuration of the Rear-Projection Head

There is a motivation to produce a natural and realistic head that can be used to represent any human user during a telepresence interaction session. This would mean that the head is "completed" with the entire projection module encapsulated within the head and have no protruding components. This is expected to make the head look more natural. An overview of the hardware configuration can be seen in Fig. 2.

The hardware consists of three main components: the head screen, the projector system, and the motor-controlled base. Fig. 2(b) illustrates the resultant head when a reference image is projected on the head screen. The various head landmarks are also labeled on the figure.

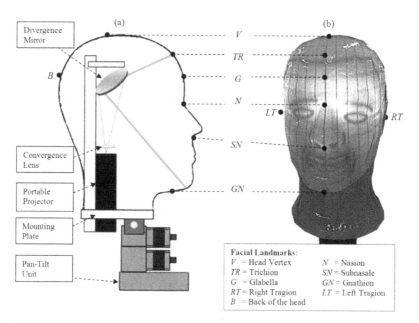

Fig. 2. (a) Hardware configuration of the rear-projection head system (b) Resultant head when a reference image is projected on the head screen

3.1   Head Screen

The head screen has been developed using the vacuum forming technique on transparent APET (Amorphous Polyethylene Terephthalate) sheets. After the vacuum forming process with the mould of a face, a coat of matt paint has been applied to the inner surface of the head. This is to diffuse the light from the projector. The rear of the head was made by vacuum forming a black APET sheet with a mould of the back of a head. Because the APET sheets are thin, a frame in the shape of the head has been cut out of sheet plastic of approximately 2 cm in thickness to provide rigidity. Both the head screen and the back of the rear projector head have been mounted onto this frame.

Table 1. Anthropometric measurements of the rear-projection robotic head

Symbol	Description	Tool	Measurement (mm)
G-B-G	**Head circumference:** Surface distance from above the ridges of the eyebrows and around the back of the head	Tape	635
V-GN	**Head Length:** Axial distance between the top of the head and the chin	Caliper	211
B-G	**Head Depth:** Axial distance between the back of the head and the glabella landmark.	Caliper	230
LT-SN-RT	**Bitragion subnasale arc:** Surface distance between the left and right tragion landmarks across the bottom of the nose	Tape	277
LT-GN-RT	**Bitragion chin arc:** Surface distance between the left and right tragion landmarks across the anterior point of the chin	Tape	343
LT-G-RT	**Bitragion frontal arc :** Surface distance between the left and right tragion landmarks above the ridges of the eyebrows	Tape	280
TR-GN	**Face Length:** Axial distance between the hairline to the chin	Caliper	167
LT-RT	**Face Width:** Axial distance between the left and right tragion landmarks	Caliper	146

The summary of the anthropometric measurements of the head screen is as illustrated in the Table 1. A pair of calipers is used to measure the shortest distance between two facial landmarks, while a plastic measuring tape is used to measure surface distance between two landmarks. The depth of the head, measured from the back of the head (B) to the glabella landmark (G), is 23 cm. It is 4 cm longer than that of an average male head because of the additional plastic frame. The circumference of the head is around 63 cm while the length of the head is about 21 cm. The head length is measured from the top of the head (*V*) to the chin (*GN*) along the y-axis of the canonical coordinate as shown in Fig. 2. All equipments must be aligned suitably within the volume defined by the circumference, depth and length of the head. The length of the face, on the other hand, is measured from the hairline (*TR*) to the chin (*GN*). It is 16.7 cm, implying that the height of the projection area should be around 17 to 21cm.

The width of the projected face image must cover the width of the face. The face width (bitragion length) is measured as 14.6 cm along the x-axis of the canonical coordinate, while the various bitragion arc lengths such as the bitragion subnasale arc, bitragion frontal arc and bitragion chin arc are 27.7 cm, 28 cm and 34.3 cm respectively. Therefore, it is concluded that the width of the projection area should be around 27 cm to 35 cm.

3.2   Projector System

The projector used in this effort is the MP160 pocket projector from the 3M Corporation. It is capable of displaying at 32 ANSI lumens and weighs 0.3 kg. The dimension is 15cm by 6cm by 3cm. The throw distance of the projector ranges from 20 cm to 240 cm, and the diagonal of the projected image can range from 17 cm to 200 cm. Hence, to project an image within a short distance to suit the current application, some modification of the optics was necessary.

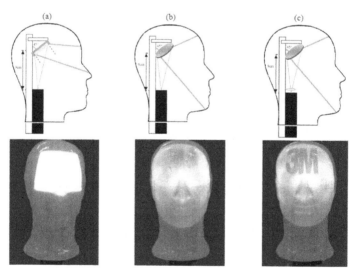

Fig. 3. Projector Setup and the projected image on the screen when (a) a normal mirror is used (b) a divergence mirror is used and (c) a divergence mirror is used with convergence lens

In this effort, the modification was performed by first increasing the projected image's distance from the projector to the head screen with the aid of a small mirror as shown in Fig. 3(a). The mirror is inclined at an angle of 45° from the vertical support bar. The distance between the center of the mirror and the projector lens is 9 cm and the distance between the center of the mirror and the head screen is 17 cm. In this manner, the throw distance is 26 cm and this would result in a projected area where its width is equal to 21 cm and its height is 13 cm as shown in Fig. 3(a).

As the projected area does not fit the entire face, a divergence spherical mirror is used, instead, to assist in magnifying the projected image so that it fits the screen. The mirror is of round shape and its diameter is 10 cm. The curvature is approximately 5 cm and the focal length of the mirror is estimated to be 5.5 cm. The result is as shown in Fig. 3(b).

The magnification of the mirror, M, is calculated to be 1.57, where $M = -\frac{image\ distance}{object\ distance} = -\frac{D_i}{D_o} = -\frac{-14.14}{9} = 1.57$ since $\frac{1}{D_i} = \frac{1}{D_o} - \frac{1}{f} = \frac{1}{9} - \frac{1}{5.5} = -0.07$ and therefore $D_i = -14.14$. The height of the projected screen is about 20 cm and the width of the projected screen is about 33 cm. However, magnifying the image diminishes its quality as shown in Fig. 3(b). To address this, a convergence lens has been added to focus the image. The convergence lens is approximately 3 cm wide and has a focal length of 25 cm. It is mounted 1 cm above the projector lens. The final projection result is as illustrated in Fig. 3(c).

3.3   Motor-Controlled Base (Pan-Tilt Unit (Model PTU-D47))

The above head assembly has been installed on a pan-tilt unit (PTU) to allow for motion and gesturing. The PTU used is the PTU-D47 from the Directed Perception Corporation. Control of the PTU is achieved with a laptop computer via a serial connection.

4   Construction of the Human Face Texture

A texture of a human face has been rendered for display from the rear of the projection head. As the screen on the head is in the shape of a human face, it is not a flat 2D screen and there is a need to warp the texture of any human face image to fit the screen's contours. The process to this involves two key stages.

The first stage involves the generation of a reference image. This requires three steps. Firstly, markings are made on the outer surface of the rear projection head's screen. These markings will note locations on the screen that correspond to facial features such as the hairline, eyebrows, eyes, the cheekbones, the nose and the mouth. The second step involves the display of a grid from the projector within the rear-projection head onto the head's screen. The third step in generating the reference image is to note the corresponding locations of the facial features on the displayed grid. To do this, an image editor is used to make markings on the grid. The aim is to match the markings on the grid to correspond with those made previously on the head's screen. The marked grid then becomes the reference image. Fig. 2(b) illustrates the result when the reference image is projected on the head's screen.

The second stage is the morphing of the source image using the reference image for accurate display on the head's screen. A source image is basically the texture image of a person's face. Features on a source image will be corresponded to those on the reference image. The source image is then warped, via linear mapping, to produce the resultant image. This resultant image is then displayed on the head's screen, as shown in Fig. 1 and Fig. 4. To display another person's face, only stage two has to be repeated. Therefore, features on the new source image are then to be corresponded to those on the reference image and a new resultant image is produced.

The display of the human face texture described so far only allows for the display of a static image. That means that movements on the face such as those for eyelids and lips when a user blinks or talks are not shown on the screen. As such, the morphing of specific parts of the resultant image has also been developed. Such morphing of the eyes and mouth of the resultant image produces movements on the screen to mean blinking or speech. At this point, work is being conducted to track facial movements on the inhabitor so that blinks and mouth movements made by him or her in real time can be correspondingly displayed with the face texture.

5   Result and Discussion

A rear-projection robotic head has been constructed for the purpose of telepresence communication, as shown in Fig 4. This head would be used to represent any male human user during a telepresence interaction session. The main strengths of this rear-projection head are its cost of manufacture as well as its flexibility. The cost of designing and building the rear-projection face is considerably low, due to rapid prototyping and vacuum forming production techniques used for making the translucent head mask, as well as the inexpensive commercially-off-the-shelf portable projection technology. The face of the robot head can be changed flexibly to represent any human user by changing the face texture projected on the head. Figure 4 illustrates the comparison of the implemented rear-projection robotic head with other robotic heads.

  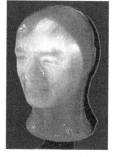

| Mechanical Head from Hanson Robotics [14] that can be used to represent one person only. | Mask-bot [20] Rear-Projection head with protruding components, making the head look unnatural | The resultant rear-projection head, with all components concealed within the head. It is able to represent more than one person. |

Fig. 4. The resultant rear-projection robotic head in comparison to the other robotic heads

5.1   Issues and Potential Problems

One potential issue with this rear-projection robotic head is that the projector used is a small portable projector which uses LED technology. Although LEDs are commonly used as a lighting solution, the brightness of LEDs constrains most of their applications to indoor environments. Furthermore, the light power of the projector is of 32 lumens which is relatively low when compared to a normal projector which typically have a light power of over 1000 lumens. This causes a dimmer projection and details of the face, such thin wrinkles, freckles or any small facial markings, to be lost during projection. This level of detail can be argued to be unnecessary in most applications.

The technology and design of this rear-projection head would require free space between the head screen and the projector. No opaque objects, such as sensors, can be used or fitted within this space as these would block the projected beam and cause a shadow on the head screen.

Lastly, as the shape of the head is rigid, accurately representing different faces could be difficult. It may be a challenge to recognize people whose faces are more rounded or thinner through the projection on the robotic head. Nevertheless, it is believed that with some training, users should be able to recognize people more easily through the projected face.

6   Conclusion

In this paper, the design and development of a rear-projection head for the purpose of telepresence has been presented. The feature of this implementation which is considered to be novel is the containment of all the necessary components for rear-head projection within the space of the head. This provides a natural look to the rear-projection head and facilitates interaction. The result has shown that the developed head is capable of accurately projecting human facial features. The implemented design is expected to be useful for designers of telepresence robots seeking a way to accurately display the features of a human head. The future work includes experimental evaluation to determine the accuracy in using the rear-projection robot head to represent a human face as well as to determine the effectiveness of using the head to enhance interaction. Future work also includes implementation of a software system to extract facial expressions rather than the user's entire facial texture for display over a generic facial texture on the screen. This will do away with the need for a camera to always point straight towards the user's face.

Acknowledgment. This research, which is carried out at BeingThere Centre, is supported by the Singapore National Research Foundation under its International Research Centre @ Singapore Funding Initiative and administered by the IDM Programme Office.

References

[1] Goldin-Meadow, S.: Beyond words: The importance of gesture to researchers and learners. Child Development 71, 231–239 (2000)

[2] Knapp, M.L., Hall, J.A.: Nonverbal communication in human interaction. Wadsworth Pub. Co. (2009)

[3] Wong, C.Y., Seet, G.L., Sim, S.K., Pang, W.C.: A hierarchically structured collective of coordinating mobile robots supervised by a single human. In: Mobile Ad Hoc Robots and Wireless Robotic Systems: Design and Implementation. IGI Global (2012)

[4] Argyle, M., Cook, M.: Gaze and mutual gaze. Cambridge U Press, Oxford (1976)

[5] Minsky, M.: Telepresence. Omni 2, 45–52 (1980)

[6] Sheridan, T.B.: Musings on telepresence and virtual presence. Presence: Teleoperators and Virtual Environments, 120–126 (1992)

[7] Turletti, T., Huitema, C.: Videoconferencing on the Internet. IEEE/ACM Transactions on Networking (TON) 4, 340–351 (1996)

[8] Buxton, W.: Telepresence: integrating shared task and person spaces. In: Proceedings of Graphics Interface, vol. 92, pp. 123–129 (1992)

[9] Szigeti, T., McMenamy, K., Saville, R., Glowacki, A.: Cisco Telepresence Fundamentals. Cisco Systems (2009)

[10] Sat, B., Wah, B.W.: Analysis and evaluation of the Skype and Google-Talk VoIP systems. In: IEEE International Conference on Multimedia and Expo., pp. 2153–2156 (2006)

[11] Isaacs, E.A., Tang, J.C.: What video can and cannot do for collaboration: a case study. Multimedia Systems 2, 63–73 (1994)

[12] Seet, G.G.L., Pang, W.C., Burhan: Towards the Realization of MAVEN - Mobile Robotic Avatar. In: The 25th International Conference on Computer Animation and Social Agents, Singapore (2012)

[13] Ishiguro, H.: Android science–Toward a new cross-interdisciplinary framework. In: CogSci-2005 Workshop: Toward Social Mechanismsof Android Science, Stresa, Italy, vol. 28, pp. 1–6 (2005)

[14] Oh, J.H., et al.: Design of android type humanoid robot Albert HUBO. In: 2006 IEEE/RSJ International Conference on Intelligent Robots and Systems, pp. 1428–1433 (2006)

[15] Liljegren, G.E., Foster, E.L.: Back Projected Image Using Fiber Optics. USA Patent US Patent# 4, 978, 216 (1990)

[16] Lincoln, P., Welch, G., Nashel, A., Ilie, A., Fuchs, H.: Animatronic Shader Lamps Avatars. In: 8th IEEE International Symposium on Mixed and Augmented Reality, ISMAR 2009, Orlando, FL, pp. 27–33 (2009)

[17] Lobel, I.: Inna Lobel. (December 2010),
http://www.innalobel.com/projects/talkingHeads.html

[18] Naimark, M.: Talking Head Projection (1980),
http://www.naimark.net/projects/head.html

[19] Delaunay, F., de Greeff, J., Belpaeme, T.: Towards retro-projected robot faces: an alternative to mechatronic and android faces. In: The 18th IEEE International Symposium on Robot and Human Interactive Communication, RO-MAN 2009, Toyama, Japan, pp. 306–311 (2009)

[20] Kuratate, T., Matsusaka, Y., Pierce, B., Cheng, G.: Mask-bot: A life-size robot head using talking head animation for human-robot communication. In: 11th IEEE-RAS International Conference on Humanoid Robots (Humanoids), Bled, Slovenia, pp. 99–104 (2011)

Scaling Studies for an Actively Controlled Curvature Robotic Pectoral Fin

Jason D. Geder[1], Ravi Ramamurti[1], John Palmisano[2], Marius Pruessner[3],
Banahalli Ratna[3], and William C. Sandberg[4]

[1] Naval Research Laboratory, Laboratory for Computational Physics and Fluid Dynamics,
4555 Overlook Ave SW, Washington, DC 20375
[2] NOVA Research, Inc., Naval Research Laboratory Contractor, 4555 Overlook Ave SW,
Washington, DC 20375
[3] Naval Research Laboratory, Center for Bio-molecular Science and Engineering,
4555 Overlook Ave SW, Washington, DC 20375
[4] Science Applications International Corporation, Modeling and Analysis Division,
1710 SAIC Dr, McLean, VA 22102

Abstract. Scaling studies for an actively controlled curvature robotic pectoral
fin are presented in detail. Design, development, and analysis of the fin are
conducted using a combination of computational fluid dynamics tools and
experimental tests. Results include a Generation 2 (Gen2) fin design with
approximately 3x more surface area and a slightly larger aspect ratio compared
with our Generation 1 (Gen1) version. The Gen2 fin demonstrates 9x more
thrust production than the Gen1 fin, validating the computational studies.
Additionally, changes to the structural design of the ribs and actuation of the rib
angles leads to a power savings and a more efficient fin.

Keywords: bio-inspired, pectoral fin, active curvature control, UUV,
station- keeping.

1   Introduction

Despite the broad range of missions enabled by traditional propeller-driven
underwater vehicles, there still exists a maneuverability gap between what these
current systems offer and what is needed in many dynamic near-shore environments.
In these regions where precise positioning and small radius maneuvers are required,
fish have demonstrated the agility needed to effectively operate. As such, researchers
have studied the fin mechanisms of various fish species [1][2]. Within fish
swimming, articulation of the pectoral fins has been shown to produce forces and
moments ideal for high-maneuverability in low-speed and hovering operations [3].
Several investigators have developed and adapted passively deforming robotic
pectoral fins onto unmanned underwater vehicles (UUVs) [4][5][6][7], whereas others
have pursued the development of active control deformation pectoral fins
[8][9][10][11].

C.-Y. Su, S. Rakheja, H. Liu (Eds.): ICIRA 2012, Part III, LNAI 7508, pp. 141–150, 2012.
© Springer-Verlag Berlin Heidelberg 2012

To enable unmanned vehicle missions in near-shore underwater environments, we have studied the swimming mechanisms of a particular coral reef fish, the Bird wrasse (*Gomphosus varius*). Inspired by the pectoral fin of this species, we have designed a robotic fin based on computational fluid dynamics (CFD) studies of the forces and moments generated by the flapping fins [9]. The resulting robotic fin uses active curvature control through actuation of individual ribs to produce desired propulsive forces [12].

Results of implementation and testing of this Generation 1 (Gen1) robotic fin on an unmanned vehicle platform have demonstrated the capabilities of the fin [13], and have also validated our computational models [9]. However, this original vehicle design lacked additional mission-enabling payload space, and the force production capability of the fins was insufficient for operations in targeted near-shore environments. To facilitate an upgrade to a vehicle capable of precise maneuvering and station-keeping in complex near-shore environments such as in harbors and around piers, we investigate issues in fin scaling as well as necessary changes to fin construction and actuation.

Initial fin redesign was driven by CFD analysis of thrust production as well as structural consideration for selection and placement of actuators. The most important factors in this redesign are fin area and aspect ratio, fin rib rigidity, and actuator performance. Based on the CFD results and actuator performance studies, a Generation 2 (Gen2) fin is built and experimental tests are conducted to demonstrate thrust production improvement over the Gen1 fin and to validate our CFD tool for studying fin geometry changes.

2   Scaling Motivation

In developing a UUV for a general class of operations, one design constraint is that the vehicle must have the propulsion and control authority to achieve desired maneuvering performance. The NRL Pectoral Fin UUV (PFUUV) is intended for low-speed operations in near-shore environments where station-keeping and precise positioning are essential performance criteria. The vehicle must be able to hold position in the presence of wave and current flow disturbances in areas such as harbors and shallow channels. Looking at flow velocity data from various potential operating locations, the PFUUV should be able to counter flows of up to 2.0 knots (1.0 m/s) [14][15]. The Gen1 vehicle demonstrated a top speed performance of 0.8 knots (0.4 m/s), indicating a need to scale up the fin design for improved thrust capability.

In addition to fin thrust, the second major design constraint is vehicle payload capacity. While the Gen1 vehicle has onboard space limited to electronics for basic vehicle operation, a mission capable vehicle requires additional space for payloads such as sonar, a ballast system, and modular mission-specific equipment. Discussion of the UUV sizing and payload requirements are beyond the scope of this paper, but a Gen2 vehicle hull design has been selected (Figure 1) and drag characteristics are modeled for fin scaling studies.

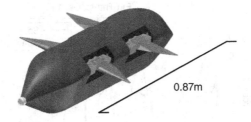

0.87m

Fig. 1. Gen2 vehicle hull design with four-fin actuation. CFD was used to design for low drag based on volumetric constraints.

3   Computational Studies of Fin Scaling

Computational studies were performed to investigate changes to the fin in both spanwise rib rigidity and fin surface area. To limit our parameter search, we constrained the fin flapping frequency, f, and stroke amplitude, Φ_B, to values achieved in the Gen1 fin [13]. The computational results provided the basis for the Gen2 fin design.

3.1   Spanwise Rib Rigidity

The Gen1 fin was designed with individual, spanwise-directed ribs that are deflected using a push-pull actuation at the rib base [9]. However, finite element stress analysis determined as the fin length scales up linearly, rib base actuator torque must increase exponentially to retain desired curvature. For a fin twice the length of the Gen1 fin, and factoring in compliant structure design modifications of the ribs, the push-pull actuating servos would require 6x the torque of the Gen1 rib servos. This would necessitate much larger motors, and also presented a large efficiency loss. To aid in a redesign that would mitigate this size and power burden, a study of spanwise rib flexibility was conducted. It has been determined that chordwise, or leading edge to trailing edge direction, curvature in the fin is needed to produce the force-time histories for desired thrust generation [16]. However, the effect of spanwise, or fin root to fin tip direction, curvature on thrust generation was not previously studied.

The computational results of a comparison of fin gaits, identical in all respects except rib rigidity, show that spanwise curvature of the ribs does have an effect on fin thrust production for a set of kinematics designed to produce forward thrust. Figure 2 shows thrust comparison for two fins of equal surface shape, surface area, stroke amplitude, stroke frequency, and rib tip deflection. The only difference in fin motion is the curvature of the ribs from base to tip. For this set of fin kinematics, the fin with spanwise rigid ribs actually demonstrates a thrust benefit over the fin with spanwise flexible ribs. The change from spanwise flexible to spanwise rigid ribs results in more fluid being displaced in the chordwise direction than in a spanwise direction, which in turn generates the higher peak thrust seen during the midstroke.

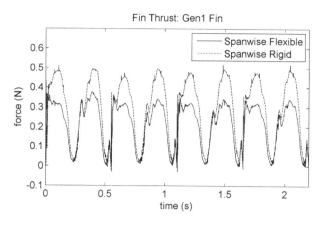

Fig. 2. Gen1 fin thrust-time histories for a fin with stroke frequency $f = 1.8$ Hz and $\Phi_B = 85$ degrees

3.2   Fin Surface Area

Computational studies of both drag on the notional Gen2 vehicle hull and thrust from scaled fin models are performed to determine the Gen2 fin design that will enable the required vehicle performance of 1 m/s forward speed (or holding position in a 1 m/s flow).

Gen2 vehicle drag at 1 m/s was computed as 0.3 N (Figure 4) for a smooth hull. However, up to 4 N of drag occurs at this same speed if the portholes where the fins are anchored are completely open to the flow due to large stagnation points inside the portholes. Practical construction of the Gen2 vehicle will not allow for completely solid, closed portholes, but mechanical designs are being investigated to negate this issue.

Based on Gen1 fin thrust results, we scaled the fin surface area using Equation 1 where F_T is the fin generated thrust, ρ is fluid density, V_{tip} is the instantaneous tip velocity of the fin leading edge, A_{fin} is the fin area, and C_T is the coefficient of thrust. Researchers have studied the effects of Reynold's number (Re) and Strouhal number (St) on the thrust coefficient of flapping mechanisms [17][18]. They have found that for a forward thrust producing kinematics set, the effect of Re is minimal in the range considered, and that forces collapse for the same St. Further, we have found in past research that for a flapping fin at zero freestream flow ($U_\infty = 0$), the thrust coefficient is constant for a given set of rib kinematics, and fin thrust scales proportional to fin surface area and to the square of fin tip velocity [19].

$$F_T = \tfrac{1}{2}\rho V_{tip}^2 A_{fin} C_T \ . \tag{1}$$

Using Equation 1, the Gen2 fin geometry was scaled up in span length from 0.10 m to 0.18 m, and in chord length from 0.060 m to 0.095 m. The width of the ribs at the base is also increased, and these changes correspond to a 3x increase in fin area and a 1.8x increase in fin tip speed. This leads to an estimated fin thrust increase for the Gen2 fin of 9.2x over the Gen1 fin. Computational results yield an 8.4x increase, and this difference from the analytical results is seen in Figure 3 which shows the computational force-time history of the Gen2 fin results compared with the Gen1 fin results scaled by area and tip speed. The Gen1 fin benefited from a thrust peak just after stroke reversal due to a wake capture effect that the Gen2 fin does not experience.

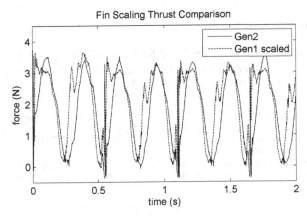

Fig. 3. Gen2 fin thrust-time history compared with scaled thrust-time history of Gen1 fin (scaled by 3.0x fin area and 1.8x fin tip velocity). Results are presented for a fin at $U_\infty = 0$ with $f = 1.8$ Hz, $\Phi_B = 85$ degrees.

The fin thrust for four fins ($f = 1.8$ Hz, $\Phi_B = 85$ degrees) at various flow speeds is shown in Figure 4 along with the computed hull drag. These results indicate that the Gen2 vehicle will reach a maximum speed, where thrust forces equal drag forces, of 0.9 m/s (1.8 knots) with open fin portholes. However, even modest reduction in vehicle drag by partially closing the portholes will allow for the desired two knot vehicle speeds (Figure 4).

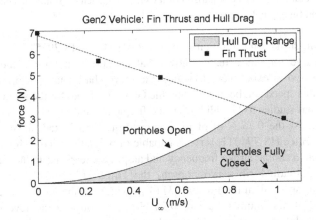

Fig. 4. Gen2 four-fin thrust for $f = 1.8$ Hz and $\Phi_B = 85$ degrees, compared with Gen2 vehicle hull drag

4   Fin Redesign and Construction

Using the results of the computational analysis, a Gen2 mechanical fin was designed to match the fin stroke and rib deflection frequencies and amplitudes of the Gen1 fin. Improvements in structural and materials robustness were also desired.

4.1   Actuator Selection

An actuator selection process for the Gen2 fin identified two servos, one for fin bulk rotation and one for individual rib rotation, capable of matching the frequency response characteristics of the Gen1 fin (Figure 5).

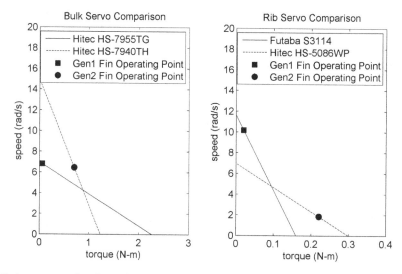

Fig. 5. Average rotational speed comparison of the Gen1 and Gen2 fins and ribs based on servo specifications and fin applied torque

The Gen1 fin stroke bulk rotation is driven by a Hitec HS-7955TG servo and the speed-torque curve for this actuator shows that at 0.06 N-m torque (the maximum torque on the servo in experimental testing) the servo shaft rotates at 6.7 rad/s. It is important that this speed can be matched by the Gen2 fin stroke for the scaling results of the computational studies to be valid as stroke frequency and amplitude were assumed to be the same. At the 0.75 N-m of maximum torque anticipated on the Gen2 bulk stroke axis, the Hitec HS-7940TH servo is capable of 6.5 rad/s speed. This will provide the Gen2 fin with a similar stroke frequency and amplitude response to the Gen1 fin.

The Gen2 individual rib servo chosen, the Hitec HS-5086WP, has a slower anticipated shaft speed than the Futaba S3114 provided on the Gen1 fin ribs, but the 1.8 rad/s speed at maximum torque of 0.24 N-m is enough to achieve the desired 15-20 degree rib deflection changes during the fin stroke. Additionally, the Hitec HS-5086WP consists of a waterproof design that will reduce failures during operation.

4.2   Fin Ribs and Skin

As computational results show fin thrust is not negatively affected by more spanwise-rigid ribs, the Gen2 fin ribs have been designed for direct actuation of rotation angle. This is different from the push-pull mechanism of the Gen1 ribs (Figure 6). This direct actuation allows for 20% greater rib tip deflection for equal servo axis rotation, significantly reduces the torque required to hold the rib in place, and eliminates the concerns commonly associated with material fatigue.

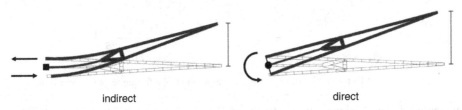

indirect   direct

Fig. 6. Indirect push-pull actuation of a fin rib compared with direct actuation of a fin rib. The indirect actuation puts more stress on fragile points near the base of the rib, and also requires more torque to move the rib and hold in position.

5   Experimental Results

Our initial set of experiments on the Gen2 fin focused on forward thrust production from a set of fin kinematics defined as the forward gait [9]. While an exact comparison cannot be made between the Gen1 and Gen2 fins due to changed rib structure and different servo characteristics, our results offer experimental evidence on the effects of fin scaling. Our goal for the Gen2 design was not to exactly mimic the fin on a larger scale, but to create a fin that produces enough thrust to propel a vehicle in excess of 2 knots. For the results shown here, the Gen1 and Gen2 fins have matching commanded rib tip deflections and curvature-time histories.

Forward gait experiments were conducted for both fins over a series of stroke frequencies and amplitudes. A six degree-of-freedom force and torque sensor from ATI Industrial Automation (Nano17 IP68) was used to measure the fin forces.

Figure 7 shows fin thrust as function of actual stroke frequency and commanded stroke peak-to-peak amplitude. Maximum average thrust for the Gen2 fin is 1.1 N, and occurs at $f = 1.4$ Hz and $\Phi_{B,c} = 100$ degrees ($\Phi_B = 90$ degrees), where $\Phi_{B,c}$ is commanded peak-to-peak stroke amplitude. At the same frequency and rotation for the Gen1 fin, average thrust is 0.13 N. This represents an 8.5x increase in thrust production from Gen1 to Gen2 fin with equal (or very similar) stroke parameters.

While the Gen2 fin produces 8.5x greater thrust than the Gen1 fin, power consumption only increases 23%, from 12.0 W to 13.5 W, demonstrating a 7x improvement in thrust efficiency. These results do not fully indicate if the efficiency savings was gained from changing the rib drive from indirect push-pull actuation to direct angular actuation (Figure 6), fin size scaling, or a combination of these two factors. Further studies would need to be done to determine the specific cause of

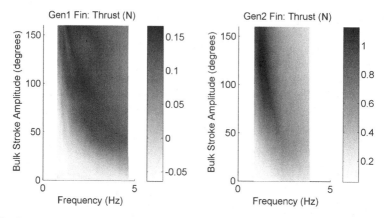

Fig. 7. Gen1 and Gen2 single fin thrust over a range on stroke frequencies and amplitudes

increased thrust efficiency. It has, however, been experimentally determined that the servos used in the Gen2 design are 2x more efficient than those in the Gen1 design.

Figure 8 shows the experimental force-time history of thrust and lift for the Gen1 and Gen2 fins at $f = 1.4$ Hz and $\Phi_{B,c} = 100$ degrees. In addition to the 8.5x increase in mean thrust, peak-to-peak thrust increases by 8.0x. Average lift for the forward gait in both the Gen1 and Gen2 fins is zero as the stroke is symmetric about the horizontal plane. Peak-to-peak lift increases by 4.0x.

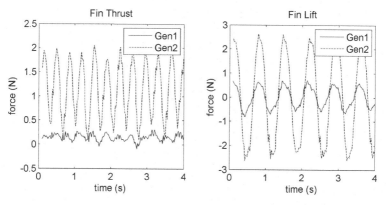

Fig. 8. Gen1 and Gen2 single fin experimental thrust and lift compared for $f = 1.4$ Hz and $\Phi_{B,c}$ = 100 degrees

6   Discussion and Conclusions

The experimental work presented in this paper highlights that even though we have not built a perfectly representative scaled version of the Gen1 fin, the results obtained demonstrate the effects of fin scaling. Both computational analyses and the mechanical design produced a Gen2 fin that generates the desired thrust for our specific mission requirements.

The results in Fig. 7 show not only the stroke frequency and amplitude where maximum average thrust is achieved, but also the full range of fin thrusts at different operating points. One noticeable difference between thrust results of the forward gait for the Gen1 and Gen2 fins is that the Gen1 fin has a peak average thrust at a higher flapping frequency than the Gen2 fin. This could indicate a larger envelope of operating points in the frequency-amplitude domain for the Gen1 fin, which in turn points to differences in the fin curvatures caused by a combination of the rigid ribs and to differences in the fin and rib actuators. In nature, we see that as organisms increase in size and weight, the frequency of their flapping decreases [20].

For the forward gait presented in Figure 8, where both the Gen1 and Gen2 fins are actuated at $f = 1.4$ Hz and $\Phi_{B,c} = 100$ degrees ($\Phi_B = 90$ degrees for both fins), we can make a comparison of the fin improvement to that seen in the computational studies. The 8.5x increase in experimentally measured thrust from Gen1 to Gen2 fins matches well with the 8.4x increase seen in CFD, and serves to validate our computational models. The experimental and CFD runs have been carried out at slightly different operating conditions ($f = 1.4$ Hz for experimental, $f = 1.8$ Hz for computational), but scaling laws apply as shown in previous studies [18].

Also for the case presented in Figure 8, the power consumed by the Gen1 fin is 12.0 W, and the portion of that attributed to the bulk stroke servo is 2.5 W. The power consumed by the Gen2 fin is 13.5 W, 7.0 W of which is for the bulk stroke servo. Predictably, the power consumed by the bulk stroke servo is a greater percentage of the total power in the Gen2 fin than in the Gen1 fin. In fact, the total power consumed by all the individual rib servos decreases from 9.5 W in the Gen1 fin to 6.5 W in the Gen2 fin, even though the servos in the Gen2 fin need to hold position under higher dynamic pressures. This total decrease in rib servo power consumption indicates a combination of reduced mechanical losses in the servos and smaller torque on the servos in the Gen2 fin than the Gen1 fin.

In summary, a fin scaling study was presented which demonstrates the use of computational studies in scaling up an actively controlled curvature robotic pectoral fin for increased thrust production. This study was limited to looking at forward thrust generating kinematics, but experimental analysis validated the computational approach to design. Further, improvements in fin rib design and actuation yielded a Gen2 fin that produced 8.5x more thrust than a Gen1 fin while only increasing power consumption by 23% leading to a fin that is 7x more efficient in thrust production.

Acknowledgments. The authors would like to acknowledge the Naval Research Laboratory and the Office of Naval Research for sponsoring this research.

References

1. Colgate, J.E., Lynch, K.M.: Mechanics and Control of Swimming: A Review. IEEE Journal of Oceanic Engineering 29, 660–673 (2004)
2. Bandyopadhyay, P.R.: Trends in biorobotic autonomous undersea vehicles. IEEE Journal of Oceanic Engineering 30, 109–139 (2005)

3. Walker, J., Westneat, M.A.: Labriform propulsion in fishes: kinematics of flapping aquatic flight in the bird wrasse, Gomphosus varius. Journal of Experimental Biology 200, 1549–1569 (1997)
4. Kato, N.: Hydrodynamic Characteristics of a Mechanical Pectoral Fin. ASME Journal of Fluids Engineering 121, 605–613 (1999)
5. Kato, N.: Control Performance of a Fish Robot with Mechanical Pectoral Fins in the Horizontal Plane. IEEE Journal of Oceanic Engineering 25(1), 121–129 (2000)
6. Hobson, B., Murray, M., Pell, C.A.: PilotFish: Maximizing Agility in an Unmanned-Underwater Vehicle. In: Proceedings of the International Symposium on Unmanned Untethered Submersible Technology, Durham, NH (1999)
7. Licht, S., Polidoro, V., Flores, M., Hover, F.S., Triantafyllou, M.S.: Design and Projected Performance of a Flapping Foil AUV. IEEE Journal of Oceanic Engineering 29(3), 786–794 (2004)
8. Ando, Y., Kato, N., Suzuki, H., Ariyoshi, T., Suzumori, K., Kanda, T., Endo, S.: Elastic Pectoral Fin Actuators for Biomimetic Underwater Vehicles. In: Proceedings of the 16th International Offshore and Polar Engineering Conference, pp. 260–267 (2006)
9. Palmisano, J., Ramamurti, R., Lu, K.J., Cohen, J., Sandberg, W.C., Ratna, B.: Design of a Biomimetic Controlled-Curvature Robotic Pectoral Fin. In: IEEE Int. Conf. on Robotics and Automation, Rome, Italy (2007)
10. Moored, K.W., Smith, W., Chang, W., Bart-Smith, H.: Investigating the thrust production of a myliobatoid-inspired oscillating wing. In: 3rd International CIMTEC Conference, Acireale, Italy (2008)
11. Tangorra, J., Davidson, N., Hunter, I., Madden, P., Lauder, G., Dong, H., Bozkurttas, M., Mittal, R.: The Development of a Biologically Inspired Propulsor for Unmanned Underwater Vehicles. IEEE Journal of Oceanic Engineering 32(3), 533–550 (2007)
12. Geder, J.D., Ramamurti, R., Palmisano, J., Pruessner, M., Ratna, B., Sandberg, W.C.: Dynamic Performance of a Bio-Inspired UUV: Effects of Fin Gaits and Orientation. In: Proceedings of the 17th International Symposium on Unmanned Untethered Submersible Technology, Portsmouth, NH (2011)
13. Geder, J.D., Ramamurti, R., Palmisano, J., Pruessner, M., Sandberg, W.C., Ratna, B.: Four-fin Bio-inspired UUV: Modeling and Control Solutions. In: ASME International Mechanical Engineering Congress and Exposition, International Mechanical Engineering Congress and Exposition, 2011-64005 (2011)
14. National Oceanic and Atmospheric Administration Tides and Currents Information, http://tidesandcurrents.noaa.gov/
15. Clem, T.: Oceanographic Effects on Maritime Threats: Mines and Oil Spills in the Strait of Hormuz. Master's Thesis, Naval Postgraduate School, Monterey, CA (2007)
16. Ramamurti, R., Sandberg, W.C.: Computational Fluid Dynamics Study for Optimization of a Fin Design. In: Proceedings of the 24th AIAA Applied Aerodynamics Conference, San Francisco, CA. AIAA-2006-3658 (2006)
17. Bozkurttas, M., Mittal, R., Dong, H., Lauder, G.V., Madden, P.: Low-dimensional models and performance scaling of a highly deformable fish pectoral fin. Journal of Fluid Mechanics 631, 311–342 (2009)
18. Ramamurti, R., Sandberg, W.: Simulation of Flow About Flapping Airfoils Using Finite Element Incompressible Flow Solver. AIAA Journal 39(2), 253–260 (2002)
19. Ramamurti, R., Geder, J.D., Palmisano, J., Ratna, B., Sandberg, W.C.: Computations of Flapping Flow Propulsion for Unmanned Underwater Vehicle Design. AIAA Journal 48(1), 188–201 (2010)
20. Azuma, A.: The Biokinetics of Flying and Swimming. Springer, Tokyo (1992)

Control of a Passive-Dynamic-Walking-Based Biped Model with Semicircular Feet for a Small Stair Step

Jun Kanno and Keitaro Naruse

University of Aizu

Abstract. Because a passive dynamic walking (PDW) robot can walk down shallow slopes using only an initial velocity and gravity, PDW robots are energy efficient. To date, they have been investigated only for shallow slopes and flat surfaces. This paper extends the walking environment to include a small stair step. Here, we use virtual PDW for a biped walking model with semicircular feet. This model has many advantages over the simple PDW model. We analyze the relationships between the height of the small stair step and the model's torque values, and between the height and the time taken to return to stable walking. This enables us to characterize the model's walking capability for a small stair step.

1 Introduction

Various biped robots have been developed in recent years. It is important to control such robots with as little energy as possible. A method for controlling the robot with minimal energy is passive dynamic walking (PDW), which was introduced by McGeer [1]. PDW robots can walk down a shallow slope using only gravity and the energy required to produce an initial velocity. They have no actuators and are energy efficient. Some of PDW models have compass-like legs, which move like a pendulum. PDW is achieved by recovering the mechanical energy that is otherwise lost by contact of a leg with the ground under gravity.

To date, PDW robots have been investigated only for shallow slopes and flat surfaces. To characterize the model in more realistic environments, we should consider how robots walk on steep slopes and stairs. We believe that this has yet to be investigated sufficiently.

The objective of the paper is to investigate the walking capability of a PDW-based biped model with semicircular feet with respect to a small stair step. A semicircular foot enables the model to include a rolling effect in its gait. The rolling effect becomes an impelling force for forward motion. Moreover, the energy loss during ground contact is better controlled, and faster walking can be achieved. These effects were shown by Asano [2], and we speculate that these effects will help the PDW model to negotiate a small stair step. We therefore performed two experiments with the model walking down and up the step. We simulated by computer the walking of a kneeless compass model using its hip-joint torque. We examined the relationship between the torque and the height of

C.-Y. Su, S. Rakheja, H. Liu (Eds.): ICIRA 2012, Part III, LNAI 7508, pp. 151–160, 2012.

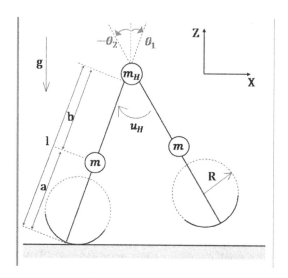

Fig. 1. Biped model with semicircular feet

the small stair step, and the relationship between the height and the time taken to return to stable walking [3].

2   The Robot and Its Control

2.1   Robot Model

In this paper, we use a PDW-based biped walking model with semicircular feet. Figure 1 shows the model, with its two legs and hip joints. One leg is the "support leg," which contacts the ground during a step. The other leg is the "swing leg," which moves like a pendulum. The angle of the support leg is θ_1 and that of the swing leg is θ_2. The feet are semicircular and the model can walk with a rolling gait. The foot performs a completely inelastic collision when it contacts the ground. At that moment, the swing leg becomes the support leg, the support leg becomes the swing leg, and the next step begins. We assume that the leg switching happens instantaneously, with any time taken being ignored.

The length of each leg is l and its mass is m. The distance from the hip joint to the leg's center of mass is b and the length from that point to the foot is a. The radius of the foot's semicircle is R. The gravitational acceleration is g. Because the legs have the same length, scuffing occurs when the swing leg passes alongside the support leg. However, we ignore the scuffing problem at this stage.

Motion equation (1) is used for our experiments using a PDW-based biped walking model with semicircular feet. Here, the generalized coordinates are $[\theta_1 \; \theta_2]^T$, the hip torque is u_H, and the relative angle between θ_1 and θ_2 is θ_H.

$$M(\theta)\ddot{\theta} + C(\theta, \dot{\theta})\dot{\theta} + g(\theta) = S u_H = \begin{bmatrix} 1 \\ -1 \end{bmatrix} u_H. \tag{1}$$

Details of the matrices and vectors are as follows.

$$M(\theta) = \begin{bmatrix} M_{11} & M_{12} \\ M_{21} & M_{22} \end{bmatrix}, C(\theta, \dot{\theta}) = \begin{bmatrix} C_{11} & C_{12} \\ C_{21} & C_{22} \end{bmatrix}, \tag{2}$$

$$M_{11} = m(R^2 + (a - R)^2 + 2R(a - R)\cos\theta_1) \tag{3}$$
$$+ (m_H + m)(R^2 + (l - R^2) + 2R(l - R)\cos\theta_1),$$

$$M_{12} = M_{21} = -mb(R\cos\theta_2 + (l - R)\cos\theta_H), \tag{4}$$

$$M_{22} = mb^2, \tag{5}$$

$$C_{11} = -mR(a - R)\dot{\theta}_1\sin\theta_1 - (m_H + m)R(l - R)\dot{\theta}_1\sin\theta_1, \tag{6}$$

$$C_{12} = mb\dot{\theta}_2(R\sin\theta_2 - (l - R)\sin\theta_H), \tag{7}$$

$$C_{21} = mb(l - R)\dot{\theta}_1\sin\theta_H, \tag{8}$$

$$C_{22} = 0, \tag{9}$$

$$g(\theta) = \begin{bmatrix} -(m_H l + ml + ma - MR)g\sin\theta_1 \\ mbg\sin\theta_2 \end{bmatrix}. \tag{10}$$

The legs switch roles when the swing leg hits the ground. The condition for both legs to contact the ground is expressed by equation (11). Here, S_H is the height of the small stair step, O_Z are the coordinates for Z, the center point of the semicircular foot on the swing leg. Equation (11) is satisfied when $\theta_1 = 0$ and $\theta_2 = 0$. However, switching between legs happens in this case and involves scuffing.

$$\begin{cases} S_H - (O_Z - R) = 0 & when \;\; steps = 1 \\ \theta_1 - \theta_2 = 0 & otherwise \end{cases}. \tag{11}$$

Equations (12) and (13) are about changing angles and angular velocities. The angles of the legs change when the switch occurs. Here, the index "−" means just before the foot contact and "+" means just after the foot contact.

$$\theta_1^+ = -\theta_2^-, \tag{12}$$

$$\theta_2^+ = -\theta_1^-. \tag{13}$$

Moreover, angular momentum is conserved during the leg switch, leading to the angular velocity equations (14) to (16).

$$Q^+(\alpha)\dot{\theta}^+ = Q^-(\alpha)\dot{\theta}^-. \tag{14}$$

$$Q^+(\alpha) = \begin{bmatrix} m_H l^2 + ma^2 + ml(l - b\cos 2\alpha) & mb(b - l\cos 2\alpha) \\ -mbl\cos 2\alpha & mb^2 \end{bmatrix}, \tag{15}$$

$$Q^-(\alpha) = \begin{bmatrix} (m_H l^2 + 2mal)\cos(2\alpha) - mba & -mba \\ -mba & 0 \end{bmatrix}. \tag{16}$$

2.2   Control

A simple PDW robot cannot walk on a flat surface. To enable walking on a flat surface, we use a virtual PDW [2], as developed by Asano. This simulates a small virtual gravity point and the effect on each leg mass produces hip torque. We can therefore simulate walking on a flat surface. The torque is expressed by equations (17) and (18).

$$u_H = \frac{Mg \tan \phi \dot{X}_g}{\dot{\theta}_H}.$$
(17)

$$\dot{X}_g = R\dot{\theta}_1(1 - \cos\theta_1)$$
$$+ \frac{(m_H l + ma + ml)\dot{\theta}_1 \cos\theta_1 - mb\dot{\theta}_2 \cos\theta_2}{M}.$$
(18)

Equation (17) shows that the value of the torque is determined by ϕ, which is a virtual angle and the control parameter. Moreover, equation (17) shows that the torque increases in proportion to any increase in the value of ϕ. The coordinates of the virtual gravity point are X_g.

3   Results

3.1   Experimental Procedure

Our experiments involve computer simulation. The parameter values are set as shown in Tables 1 and 2, in accordance with Asano's paper [2]. With these parameter values, a PDW-based biped walking model with semicircular feet was able to walk on a flat surface.

Table 1. Modelparameters

g [m/s²]	m [kg]	m_H [kg]	a [m]	b [m]	l [m]	R [m]
9.8	5.0	5.0	0.5	0.5	1.0	0.5

Table 2. Initial parameters

θ_1 [rad]	θ_2 [rad]	$\dot{\theta}_1$ [rad/s]	$\dot{\theta}_2$ [rad/s]
-0.3	0.3	1.15	0.75

First, we make the PDW-based biped walking model with semicircular feet walk down a small stair step and examine the relationship between its height and the control parameter ϕ. If the model can walk for 10 seconds, we define this as "can walk" in this paper.

Second, we give three examples of changing the control parameter ϕ, and examine the relationship between the height of the small stair step and the time taken to return to stable walking. We define "stable walking" as motion that follows equations (19) and (20) in this paper. θ_{1k} and θ_{2k} are the angles of the legs when the legs switch for the k-th time.

$$\theta_{1k} - \theta_{1k-1} < \epsilon, \tag{19}$$

$$\theta_{2k} - \theta_{2k-1} < \epsilon. \tag{20}$$

We set $\epsilon = 0.01$ in this paper. We then perform the same set of experiments for the model walking up the small stair step.

3.2 Situations

The height of a small stair step should be low in comparison to the length of the leg, and the flat surface should be sufficiently long. The surface is noncontinuous, as for stairs. The height of the small stair step is increased from 0.001 [m] to 0.150 [m] in increments of 0.001 [m]. The state when the support leg contacts the stair edge, as shown to the left in Figure 2, is the initial position for walking down. The initial position for walking up is shown in Figure 3. When the model walks down and up the small stair step, the swing leg hits the edge of the stair step. Collisions between this edge and the swing leg are ignored in this research.

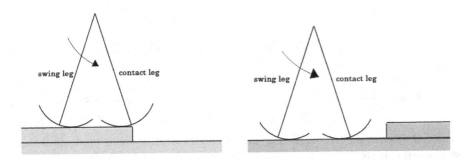

Fig. 2. Initial position when walking down   **Fig. 3.** Initial position when walking up

3.3 Height and the Control Parameter ϕ

The PDW-based biped walking model with semicircular feet walks as shown in Figure 4 when walking down and walks as shown in Figure 5 when walking up. Figure 6 shows the maximum heights for the small stair step that the model can negotiate for various values of ϕ. In Figure 6, the blue trajectory indicates walking down and the red indicates walking up. Figure 6 shows that the maximum step height that the model can walk down occurs when ϕ is 0.011 [rad]. In addition, Figure 6 shows that the maximum step height when walking up is

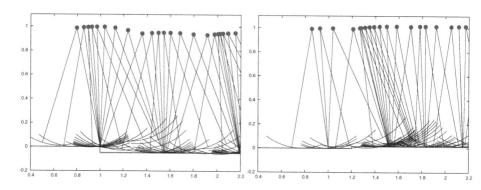

Fig. 4. Stick diagram when walking down   **Fig. 5.** Stick diagram when walking up

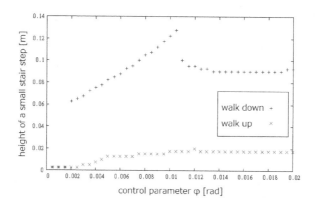

Fig. 6. Relationship between height and ϕ when walking down and up

achieved when ϕ is 0.012 [rad]. The model cannot walk down or up a small stair step when ϕ is small.

3.4   Height and Return to Stable Walking

Figures 7 and 8 show the relationship between the height of the small stair step and the time taken to return to stable walking. If the model cannot return to stable walking, the time is shown as zero. Figures 7 and 8 show examples of walking down and up, respectively. In Figures 7 and 8, the red trajectory indicates $\phi = 0.005$ [rad], the blue indicates $\phi = 0.010$ [rad], and the purple indicates $\phi = 0.020$ [rad]. Figures 7 and 8 show that a return to stability takes proportionally longer as the height of the small stair step increases. Furthermore, these figures show that the model cannot return to stable walking at all if $\phi = 0.005$.

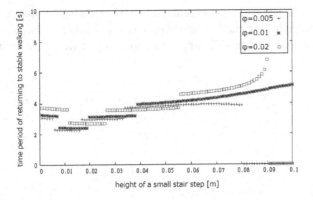

Fig. 7. Relationship between time and height when walking down

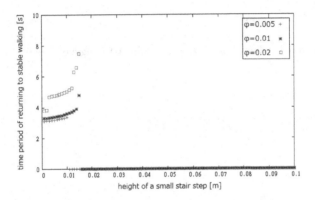

Fig. 8. Relationship between time and height when walking up

4 Discussion

4.1 Height and Control Parameter ϕ

It was found that the PDW-based biped walking model with semicircular feet reaches the maximum height that the model can walk down when $\phi = 0.011$ [rad], whereas the model reaches the maximum height that the model can walk up when $\phi = 0.012$ [rad]. If ϕ is greater than 0.011 [rad], the maximum heights are lower or unchanged when walking down. If ϕ is greater than 0.012 [rad], the maximum height is lower when walking up. Therefore, it is important to find the optimal parameter values for efficient walking.

4.2 Height and Return to Stable Walking

It was found that it takes longer to return to stable walking as the value of ϕ increases. However, Figures 7 and 8 indicate points where this time is shorter. We speculate that the criterion for returning to stable walking involves the switching of legs. For example, the model can return to stable walking four steps before a gap occurs, whereas the model can return to stable walking three steps after a gap occurs.

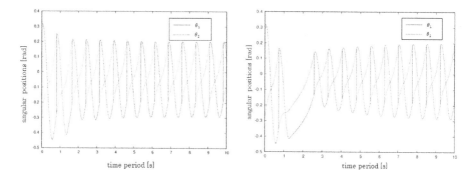

Fig. 9. Angle of legs when walking down   **Fig. 10.** Angle of legs when walking up

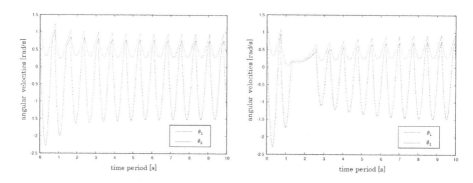

Fig. 11. Angular velocities when walking down   **Fig. 12.** Angular velocities when walking up

For walking down or up a small stair step, the control parameter ϕ is important. We found that $\phi = 0.010$ [rad] gives the best results in the experiments, because the model can negotiate a relatively high stair step and can take a relatively short time to return to stable walking.

The maximum height for walking down is greater than for walking up, as shown in Figure 6. Figures 9 and 10 show the angles of the legs when walking down and up, respectively, where the height of the small stair step is 0.015 [rad]. Figures 11 and 12 show the angular velocities of the legs when walking down and up, respectively. These figures show that the changes in these parameters when walking up are greater than those when walking down, and that it takes longer to return to stable walking. These results show numerically that walking up is more difficult than walking down. Figures 10 and 12 show that the model takes longer for the two steps that include the step after walking up the small stair step. At this time, the model opens its leg using the torque and moves forward with a rolling effect. Asano indicated that this motion occurs when m_H/m is small. We think that the model was able to walk up the small stair step by an impelling force for which the semicircular feet have a rolling effect. From these results, we think that the rolling effect is particularly important when walking up a small stair step.

5 Conclusions and Future Work

This paper shows that a PDW-based biped walking model with semicircular feet designed for flat surfaces can walk down and up a small stair step. The torque required is not proportional to the height of the small stair step. The higher the small stair step and the larger the torque, the longer the model takes to return to stable walking. These results show that it is important to set the control parameter ϕ appropriately for stable walking. If ϕ is too small, the maximum height that the model can negotiate is very small. On the other hand, if ϕ is too big, it takes a long time to return to stable walking.

The scuffing problem and the collision between the stair edge and the swing leg were ignored in this paper. However, these problems cannot be ignored in the real world. Models with knees or elastic legs may be able to solve these problems. The initial positions and some parameter values are fixed in this paper. If we can find better matching for parameter values, walking may become more effective. Moreover, if the PDW robots can return to stable walking more quickly, these robots will be able to negotiate staircases.

References

1. McGeer, T.: Passive Dynamic Walking. The International Journal of Robotics Research 9(2), 62–82 (1990)
2. Asano, F., Luo, Z.: Underactuated Virtual Passive Dynamic Walking using Rolling Effect of Semicircular Feet – (I) On Driving Mechanisms of Compass-like Models. Journal of the Robotics Society of Japan 25(4), 566–577 (2007)
3. Garcia, M., Chatterjee, A., Ruina, A., Coleman, M.: The Simplest Walking Model: Stability, Complexity, and Scaling. Journal of Biomechanical Engineering 120, 281–288 (1998)
4. Asano, F., Luo, Z.: Underactuated Virtual Passive Dynamic Walking using Rolling Effect of Semicircular Feet – (II) Performance Analyses and Extension to Redundant Models. Journal of the Robotics Society of Japan 25(4), 578–588 (2007)
5. Asano, F., Luo, Z., Yamakita, M.: Dynamic Gait Generation and Control based on Mechanical Energy Restoration. Journal of the Robotics Society of Japan 23(7), 821–830 (2005)
6. Asano, F., Luo, Z., Yamakita, M.: Gait Generation and Control for Biped Robots based on Passive Dynamic Walking. Journal of the Robotics Society of Japan 22(1), 130–139 (2004)

7. Goswami, A., Espiau, B., Keramane, A.: Limit cycles in a passive compass gait biped and passivity-mimicking control laws. Autonomous Robots 4(3), 273–286 (1997)
8. Ikemata, Y., Sano, A., Fujimoto, H.: A Stability Mechanism of the Fixed Point in Passive Walking. Journal of the Robotics Society of Japan 23(7), 839–846 (2005)
9. Asano, F., Luo, Z.: Parametrically Excited Dynamic Walking Control of Telescopic Legged Robots. Journal of the Robotics Society of Japan 23(7), 910–918 (2005)
10. McGeer, T.: Principles of Walking and Running. Advances in Comparative and Environmental Physiology 11, 113–139 (1992)
11. Lui, N., Li, J., Wang, T.: Passive walker that can walk down steps: simulations and experiments. Acta Mechanica Sinica 24(5), 569–573 (2008)
12. Tehrani Safa, A., Saadat, M., Naraghi, M.: Principles of Walking and Running. Mechanism and Machine Theory 42(10), 1314–1325 (2007)

Evaluation of a Proposed Workspace Spanning Technique for Small Haptic Device Based Manipulator Teleoperation

Mohamed Mamdouh[1], Ahmed A. Ramadan[2], and Ahmed A. Abo-Ismail[2]

[1] Egypt-Japan University for Science and Technology, New Borg ElArab, Alexandria, Egypt
[2] On leave from Tanta university
{mohamed.elshormbably,ahmed.ramadan,aboismail}@ejust.edu.eg

Abstract. This paper presents an evaluation of a new proposed workspace spanning technique for master/slave system teleoperation which is still a challenging task. This new technique integrates position control and a modified rate control methods to solve the problem of workspace mapping of two kinematically dissimilar robots used in teleoperation system. The slave device is having a large workspace in most cases while the master device is usually having a physically limited workspace. The workspace mapping of a small haptic device based robot should be handled carefully without disturbing the user perception of continuous teleoperating the robot movement in a natural and precise way. The proposed technique referred to as Positioning with Modified Rate Control is simple and overcomes the drawbacks of other techniques like indexing, rate control, ballistic control, and drift control. It depends on switching between rate control with constant speed for coarse motion and position control for accurate movements. Experimental setup based on phantom premium haptic device as a master and RV-2AJ Mitsubishi robot arm as a slave is used to evaluate the feasibility of the proposed technique. Experimental results demonstrate that the operator can easily navigate through the whole workspace of an industrial robot using a small haptic device while achieving accurate positioning. Besides, the proposed technique is judged against the scaling technique in performing a prescribed task to evaluate its performance.

Keywords: Workspace mapping, Teleoperation, Haptic device.

1 Introduction

Teleoperators are electromechanical systems which enable the operator to remotely control a robot (slave) interacting with the environment, using another robot (master). Teleoperation systems found a wide range of application in remote environments like space, underwater or telesurgery and for manipulating hazardous materials in nuclear stations or in unreachable places like mines [8, 10].

The two robots used in teleoperation systems may be similar in size and kinematics [1], [3] or are different in kinematics and/or size; which is the case when using a haptic device as a master and an industrial robot manipulator to act as a slave [2, 12]. In the latter case the master haptic device workspace is physically limited compared to the workspace of the slave industrial robot. For this case, teleoperation tasks are

C.-Y. Su, S. Rakheja, H. Liu (Eds.): ICIRA 2012, Part III, LNAI 7508, pp. 161–170, 2012.

performed based on Cartesian space using the inverse kinematics of the robot manipulator. This requires a suitable and efficient mapping technique to allow the operator to span the whole workspace of the slave without holding off or disconnecting the haptic device – like in the case of computer mouse - while at the same time offers accurate positioning. Different techniques have been proposed to solve this problem [2, 3, 5, 9]:

- **Indexing method** which is inspired by the computer mouse, except it is implemented in 3D space. This technique depends on directly mapping the end effector displacement of the master haptic device to displacement of the end effector of the slave robot until it reaches its mechanical limit, then break the coupling between the two devices and relocate the master device back to its origin position. Despite its simplicity, this method causes an interruption of the teleoperation tasks at the time of indexing. Also, if the ratio of the two workspaces is large, frequent indexing will be required.

- **Positioning or scaling control** in which the displacement of the master device is multiplied by a constant factor, then mapped to the slave side. With large scale factor the resolution of the slave displacement is adversely affected and fine manipulation cannot be accomplished.

- **Ballistic control method** depends on changing the scaling factor in proportional to the speed of the master device. So if the operator moves the master device slowly this means that he/she is performing fine manipulation and unity or small scale factor is used. And, if he/she moves fast this means that he/she performs coarse motion, so large scale factor is used. The main problem is the displacement offset arises when the operator tries to move to a position slowly and then moves rapidly back in the opposite direction.

- **Rate control method** does not present direct physical mapping between the two workspaces. Instead it moves the slave robot with a speed proportional to the displacement of the master device from its origin position, which could be suitable for coarse motion only. So, the master device can be held steady at certain position while the slave robot is in motion at a given speed.

- **Drift control method** depends on repositioning the workspace of the haptic device while the user moving it. This method relies on the fact that the human operator is greatly influenced by what he perceives visually and often doesn't notice small deviations of his hand unless those small deviations have visual reflection. So, depending on the speed of the operator, a drift force tries to continuously move the workspace of the master device. This force should be guaranteed not to be felt by the operator to avoid interfering with the feedback force from the slave robot. Also, the adjustment of the drift factor is not easy as it is correlated to the operator sensing and the type of haptic device.

There are other techniques that depend on combining two or more of the previously mentioned methods together. A sophisticated technique was proposed in [11] that is using a combination of position and rate control, and is implemented using two wrists based on Lorentz magnetic levitation; one as a master and the other is attached to the end effector of an elbow manipulator. Also a combined position and rate control method was introduced in [4] named the bubble technique which is proposed to explore large workspace in virtual reality. Another technique combines the drift control with ballistic control is proposed in [2].

This paper presents a simple yet efficient method to solve the mapping problem based on virtually partitioning the workspace of the slave robot to overlapped regions with the same volume as the haptic device workspace. Inside each region, the scaling factor can be set to unity or less to allow fine manipulation. And for moving from one region to another, this will be implemented using a switch in the haptic device without causing interruption of the coupling between the master device and the slave robot. So it could be seen as there are two modes of operation; fine motion mode (the switch is released) and coarse motion mode (pressing and holding the switch). This is referred to as Positioning with Modified Rate Control technique.

The paper is organized as follow: Section 2 explains the concept of the new proposed Positioning with Modified Rate Control technique. Section 3 describes the experimental setup used to test and evaluate the proposed method. The experimental results of using the proposed technique are presented in section 4. Section 5 shows the performance results of the proposed technique against the scaling method in drawing the correct path inside a maze. Finally, section 6 concludes the paper.

2   Positioning with Modified Rate Control

The previously mentioned mapping techniques are either having drawbacks like interruption of the operation, offset, reducing control accuracy or of complicated nature. So the main objective of this research is to introduce a simple and efficient technique to accomplish the task of workspace mapping of kinematically dissimilar robots in a continuous yet easy way. This method is inspired by a technique named the bubble technique used in virtual reality for spanning large virtual workspace [4].

The concept of the technique is illustrated in Fig. 1. The position of the slave robot end effector is determined according to eq. (1):

$$\vec{X_e} = K\,\vec{X_h} + \vec{X_w} \tag{1}$$

where X_e, X_w, X_h represent the position of the robot end effector, the virtual workspace position relative to the world frame, and the haptic device cursor position

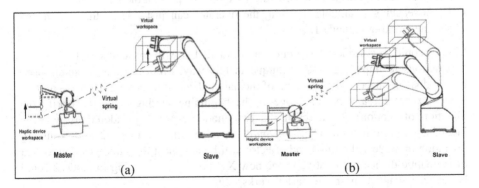

Fig. 1. Schematic of the proposed technique operation modes. (*a*) Mode 1 and (*b*) Mode 2

relative to the haptic device frame respectively. The constant K is a scaling factor that should be equal to or less than unity. In our case, it is chosen to be unity.

The operation can be divided into two modes as in Fig. 1:

— **Mode 1 fine manipulation mode:** in which the virtual workspace position X_w remains fixed. As moving the haptic device, the same displacement is mapped to the robot arm relative to X_w. With unity scale factor, the operator can fine manipulate a workspace volume equal to that of the master haptic device. This is typically a position control scheme. In this mode the stylus switch is released.

— **Mode 2 coarse motion mode:** that should be switched to when it is desired to work in an area in the slave robot workspace that cannot be reached with the current value of the virtual workspace position X_w. To accomplish this, the stylus switch in the haptic device is pressed and held. As a result the virtual workspace position X_w is updated as described in the following:

- Just after the switch is pressed the position of the haptic device X_i is recorded.
- After this, any small movement of the haptic device X_f is recorded.
- By knowing X_i and X_f points of the guiding vector, a unit vector in the same direction can be computed using eq. (2).

$$\vec{U} = \frac{\vec{X_f} - \vec{X_i}}{\left\| (\vec{X_f} - \vec{X_i}) \right\|} \tag{2}$$

where U represents a unit vector in the direction of guiding vector and X_i and X_f represent the starting and ending points of this guiding vector respectively.

- Next, the virtual workspace position X_w is updated according to eq. (3).

$$\vec{X_w} = \vec{X_w} + v \cdot \vec{U} \tag{3}$$

where v is a constant that represents the speed by which the virtual workspace position X_w is moving.

- The former equation is updated with same rate of the haptic device scheduler which is 1 KHz. This in turn shifts the virtual workspace of the slave robot.
- Upon reaching a suitable location, the operator can just release the switch and resume working in mode 1.

Mode 2 could be considered as a rate control mode but with constant speed. There are two reasons to implement the technique in this way. *Firstly*, using constant speed almost does not need a displacement of the haptic device for moving in coarse motion mode (except for a very small one at the beginning of this mode to specify the direction of motion). As a result the two modes can be considered as working independently from each other. *Secondly*, after the end of mode 2 and resuming operation in mode 1 the robot end effector will be at almost the same position as that of the haptic device but relative to the new X_w position. Switching to mode 2 could be realized at any point in the master workspace.

3   Experimental Setup

In order to check the feasibility of the new proposed Positioning with Modified Rate Control technique, an experimental setup as in Fig. 2 is established. The details of the hardware, software, and bilateral control approach used are as following.

3.1   Hardware

The hardware used are Phantom premium 1.5 haptic device, RV-2AJ Mitsubishi robot arm with its CR1-571 servo controller, PC and communication channel. The Phantom haptic device (SensAble technology) is used as a master device. It is a 6-DOF haptic device with force feedback capability for the x-,y-,and, z-directions and torque feedback for roll, pitch and yaw rotation directions. Its nominal exertable force is 6.2 N and its workspace is 381mm (W)×267mm (H)×191mm (D) [6].

As a slave device, RV-2AJ 5-DOF robot arm (Mitsubishi Electric industrial robot arm) is used. CR1-571 is the robot servo controller through which the position command is executed and the current position could be monitored.

Communication between the robot controller and the PC which represent the controller of the haptic master device is established via LAN communication and UDP protocol is used to exchange the position information between both of them using C++.

3.2   Software

Starting with a sample program for external control of the robot arm [13], a C++ program was developed to establish communication between the robot arm and the PC under windows OS. This program is used in commanding the joints angle position, and monitoring the current position and orientation of the robot in real time (the control time is 7.1 msec). Then the haptic device library (hdu.lib) is linked to the program in order to communicate with the haptic device and update its states by a rate of 1 KHZ.

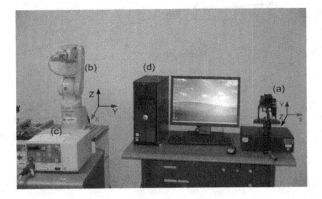

Fig. 2 Experimental setup (a) *Phantom premium 1.5 haptic device* (b) RV-2AJ Mitsubishi robot arm (c) *CR1-571 robot controller* (d) *Personal computer*

3.3   Bilateral Control

Bilateral teleoperation control is implemented on the two robots. After reading the position and orientation (only roll and pitch are used) of the phantom device, the reference position of the slave robot end effector is calculated. Then using the inverse kinematics of the robot arm, the command joint angles are calculated and transmitted to CR1-571 controller which execute the command and send back the arm current position. The concept of virtual spring is applied to ensure coupling between the two devices [7]. Also, the force applied to the phantom is calculated according to eq. (4).

$$\vec{F} = K_{vir}(\overrightarrow{X_a} - \overrightarrow{X_e}) \qquad (4)$$

where K_{vir} represents the virtual spring constant, X_a is the current arm position and X_e represents the reference position for the robot arm.

It should be noticed that both of these two positions depend on the virtual workspace position X_w, so the subtraction in (4) expresses the error in position between the haptic device tip position in the physical haptic workspace and the position of the robot arm end effector in the virtual haptic workspace. Also using this method enables the operator to feel the boundary of the slave robot.

4   Experimental Results

The following scenario was used experimentally to illustrate the two modes of operation of the proposed technique. Starting from the origin of the phantom device, the switch is pressed and a little displacement in the positive X axis of the phantom was made. This forces the virtual workspace position X_w and as a result the robot arm to move in Y axis direction of the robot arm end effector (It should be noticed that the

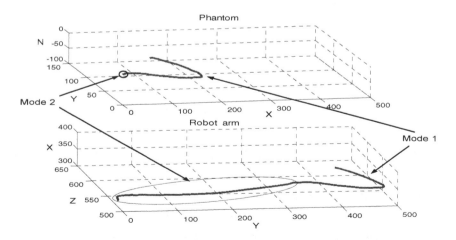

Fig. 3. Motion of the phantom device and robot controller in the two mode of operation

direction of the orthogonal axes of both the haptic device and the robot arm are not identical, this is illustrated in Fig. 2). This represents mode 2 of coarse motion. Then after about 8 seconds the switch is released and mode 1 of fine manipulation starts in which the robot arm end effector follows the movement of the haptic device tip.

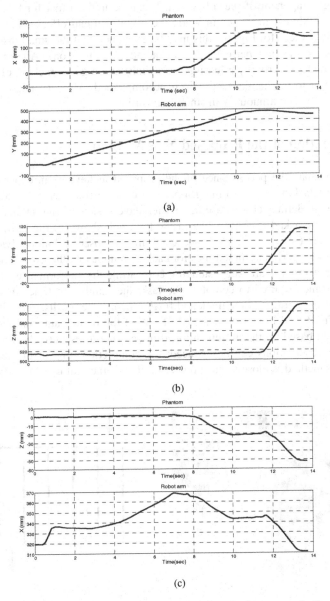

Fig. 4. Position change in phantom device tip and robot arm end effector

Fig. 3 illustrates the resultant motion profile of both the haptic master and the slave robot devices. It should be noticed that while the haptic device begins from its origin, the robot arm begins from its initial virtual workspace position (X_w) which is arbitrary set in this experiment to position [319.5, 0,513.9]. Fig. 4 illustrates the changes of the x, y and z components of each point in the path of the haptic device, with the corresponding component of the robot arm. It can be noticed that for 8 seconds the haptic device is almost in its origin while the robot arm end effector moves with a constant speed (except for Fig. 6c, this may be explained that the small displacement in the beginning was not perfectly in the intended x direction). After 8 seconds, operation in mode 1 starts (by releasing the switch) and a good tracking of the robot arm end effector to the haptic device tip is accomplished. Also, it should be noticed that the operation is continuous with smooth transition.

5   Evaluation of the Proposed New Method

In order to evaluate the performance of the proposed technique, an experiment was performed by attaching a pen to the gripper of the slave robot as in Fig.5 (a). After explaining the guidelines how to use the master/slave system, different and untrained five persons were asked to draw a line inside the track shown in Fig.5 (b) using the scaling technique (with a scale of 5) and using the proposed technique. Each one of them repeats the experiment three times for each technique and the average result was recorded. Three criteria are suggested for comparing the performance of the two methods; the time required to complete the task, the number of times in which the person crosses the borders of the track and finally the number of discontinuities in the line drawn. Fig. 6 and Fig. 7 show a trial of one of the participants and the average results obtained based on the aforementioned three criteria respectively. From which the following observations can be deduced; the completion time of the scaling and proposed new method is close to each other and that of the scaling time is faster with some persons.

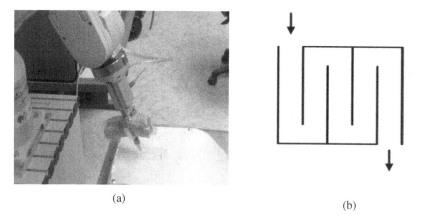

(a)   (b)

Fig. 5. Experimental test *(a) slave robot with pen attached (b) Border of the track used*

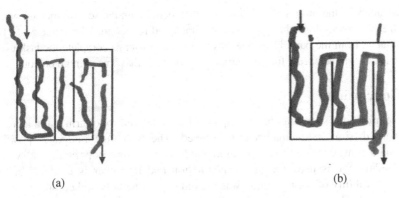

(a)   (b)

Fig. 6. Experimental results (a) *Scaling method* (b) *Proposed method*

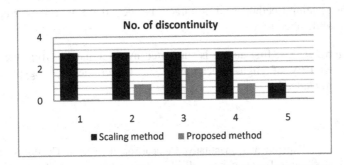

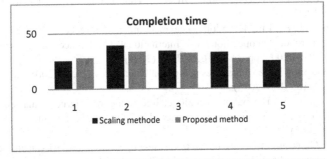

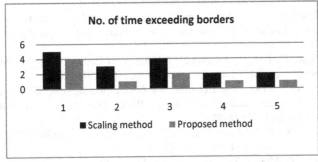

Fig. 7. Statistics results

The accuracy of the proposed technique is much better than the scaling method which enables the persons to draw the line inside the track and reduce the discontinuities. The feedback taken from the participants ensures that it was easier to complete the task using the proposed technique except for one participant who feels that it need more practice.

6   Conclusion

A new technique for spanning the workspace of an industrial robot arm using a haptic device with dissimilar kinematics is developed. The technique integrates position control and a constant speed rate control methods. It depends on operating the system in two modes; one is used for fine manipulation and the other is used for coarse motion. The validity of the technique was proved experimentally and compared to the scaling method. The results ensure the efficiency of the technique in spanning a large area of the slave workspace in one mode and good tracking characteristics in the other mode. The comparison illustrates that the proposed method has the advantages of the speed of the scaling method and accuracy besides there is no interruption or discontinuity while operation.

Acknowledgement. The first author is supported by a scholarship from the Mission Department, Ministry of High Education of the Government of Egypt which is gratefully acknowledged.

References

1. Aliaga, I., et al.: Experimental Quantitative Comparison of Different Control Architectures for Master–Slave Teleoperation. IEEE Transactions on Control Systems Technology 12(1), 2–11 (2004)
2. Chotiprayanakul, P., Liu, D.: Workspace mapping and force control for small haptic device based robot teleoperation. In: International Conference on Information and Automation, ICIA 2009, pp. 1613–1618. IEEE (2009)
3. Conti, F.: Spanning large workspaces using small haptic devices. In: 2005 and Symposium on Haptic, pp. 183–188 (2005)
4. Dominjon, L., et al.: The bubble technique: Interacting with large virtual environments using haptic devices with limited workspace. In: 2005 and Symposium on Eurohaptics Conference (2005)
5. Passenberg, C., et al.: A survey of environment-, operator-, and task-adapted controllers for teleoperation systems. Mechatronics 20(7), 787–801 (2010)
6. Pérez, A., Rosell, J.: An assisted re-synchronization method for robotic teleoperated tasks. In: 2011 IEEE International Conference on Robotics and Automation (ICRA), pp. 886–891. IEEE (2011)
7. RodrIguez-Seda, E., Lee, D.: Experimental comparison study of control architectures for bilateral teleoperators. IEEE Transactions on 25(6), 1304–1318 (2009)
8. Salcudean, S., et al.: Design and control of a force-reflecting teleoperation system with magnetically levitated master and wrist. IEEE Transactions on Robotics and Automation 11(6), 844–858 (1995)
9. Song, G., Guo, S.: A Tele-operation system based on haptic feedback. In: 2006 IEEE Information Acquisition, pp. 1127–1131 (2006)
10. Mitsubishi-Electric Manual, Ethernet interface, Art. no: 13231

Prior Knowledge Employment Based on the K-L and Tanimoto Distances Matching for Intelligent Autonomous Robots

Andrey Belkin[1] and Jürgen Beyerer[1,2]

[1] Vision and Fusion Laboratory (IES),
Karlsruhe Institute of Technology (KIT)
Adenauerring 4, 76131 Karlsruhe, Germany
belkin@kit.edu
[2] Fraunhofer Institute of Optronics, System Technologies
and Image Exploitation (IOSB)
Fraunhoferstraße 1, 76131 Karlsruhe, Germany
juergen.beyerer@iosb.fraunhofer.de

Abstract. Modern autonomous robots are performing complex tasks in a real dynamic environment. This requires real-time reactive and pro-active handling of arising situations. A basis for such situation awareness and handling can be a world modeling subsystem that acquires information from sensors, fuses it into existing world description and delivers the required information to all other robot subsystems. Since sensory information is affected by uncertainty and lacks for semantic meaning, the employment of a predefined information, that contains concepts and descriptions of the surrounding world, is crucial. This employment implies matching of the world model information to prior knowledge and subsequent complementing of the dynamic descriptions with semantic meaning and missing attributes. The following contribution describes a matching mechanism based on the Kullback-Leibler and Tanimoto distances and direct assignment of the prior knowledge for the model complementation.

Keywords: prior knowledge, world model, matching, Kullback-Leibler, Tanimoto, metric, intelligent, autonomous, robot.

1 Introduction

Modern autonomous robots are challenged by more and more complex tasks. Moreover, these tasks demand real-time handling in a real-life dynamic environment. Some of the tasks imply interaction or even cooperation with other robots or humans. Such complex activities require reactive and pro-active handling of arising situations. A basis for such situation awareness and handling is often a *world modeling* subsystem [1], which acquires information from sensors and fuses it into existing world description by means of *data association and fusion* [2], [1]. The world modeling subsystem serves then as a central information hub to all other robot subsystems, such as context recognition and

C.-Y. Su, S. Rakheja, H. Liu (Eds.): ICIRA 2012, Part III, LNAI 7508, pp. 171–180, 2012.
© Springer-Verlag Berlin Heidelberg 2012

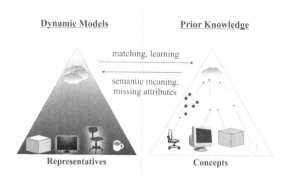

Fig. 1. Prior knowledge employment [1]

pro-active planning [3], [4]. The information acquired from sensors is affected by uncertainty and lacks for *semantic meaning*. Moreover, due to combinatorial complexity, the dynamic model should be as slim as possible, containing only vital information during the operational time. The solution to these issues is a *dynamic employment* of predefined information – *prior knowledge* – that contains concepts and descriptions of the surrounding world. This dynamic employment implies matching of the world model information to prior knowledge and subsequent complementing of the world model with semantic meaning and missing attributes as shown in Fig. 1. In this analysis we define a matching mechanism based on the *Kullback-Leibler* and *Tanimoto distances* for the matching process and direct assignment of the prior knowledge for the information complementation. The Kullback-Leibler distance is widely used in the classification domain (e. g., heart signals classification [5], similarity of ontology elements [6] or word clustering in text classification [7]) but is not employed for the direct connection of prior knowledge to dynamic models of autonomous systems. Similarly, the Tanimoto distance is widely used for comparison of finite sets (e. g., structural similarity search for biomolecule classification [8] or land cover detection [9]) but the prior knowledge employment in dynamic modeling of autonomous systems is left intact.

The rest of the paper is organized as follows: the Section 2 gives a short overview of a world modeling system. Next, a detailed analysis of the matching process between world model information and prior knowledge is given in the Section 3. A brief overview for a direct prior knowledge assignment is given in the following Section 4. An experimental set-up with an example workflow is described in the Section 5. A conclusion is presented in the last Section 6.

2   Information Representation

Before defining the prior knowledge employment mechanism, it is vital to describe the information representation used in this analysis. Each entity of a dynamic world model represents some element of the real world and thus is called *representative*. Each entity of the prior knowledge represents either a generalization of real world entities, called *class concept*, or a description of some specific entity (e. g., *person Alexey, white coffee cup*), called *entity concept*. Both representatives and concepts contain attributes, which describing entity or class properties. During the information association and fusion, representative's attributes are updates upon receiving new sensory information [10], [11]. On the other hand, class attributes are predefined offline by prior knowledge experts based on known statistical distributions [1].

Since sensory and prior information contains uncertainty, each attribute is described by a continuous or discrete probability distribution. The advantages of the *Degree-of-Belief* (DoB) interpretation of probability distributions were discussed in [1], [2]. In practice, each continuous DoB distribution is given by a *Gaussian mixture approximation*. This approximation represents a weighted sum of M component Gaussian densities as given in Eq. 1:

$$p(x|\omega, \mu, \Sigma) = \sum_{i=1}^{M} \omega_i g\left(x|\mu_i, \Sigma_i\right), \tag{1}$$

where x denotes a D-dimensional continuous data vector, ω_i are the normalized mixture weights with $\sum_{i=1}^{M} \omega_i = 1$, and $g\left(x|\mu_i, \Sigma_i\right)$ are the component Gaussian densities.

Both dynamic model and prior knowledge are organized in a graph structure. The model representatives are connected by relations into multiple semantic networks [10]. The prior knowledge is usually represented by an *ontology* [10], [12].

3   Matching Process

The employment of prior knowledge starts with matching of a world model representative to prior knowledge concepts. Since these class and entity concepts describe the whole surrounding world, the exact structure of the prior knowledge ontology can be sophisticated. The concepts are connected to each other with relations of different types, forming complex graphs [12] as shown in Fig. 2. Some subgraphs can form semantic hierarchies (e. g., "*is a*" generalization tree). For normalization reasons, each hierarchy level is supplemented by a *dummy concept* that includes everything, except already presented on that level (e. g., *fruit* → *apple, pear, dummy* (other fruits)). Matching of representatives to complex graphs is complicated and computationally hard. Thus, only one hierarchy is analyzed at each moment as shown in Fig. 2.

3.1   Depth-First Search

After marking out one given tree, it is processed with a *depth-first search* (DFS) algorithm, finding concepts similar to the representative under consideration with the similarity higher than a threshold (Fig. 3). At the end, all concepts

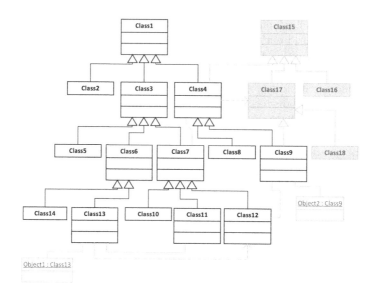

Fig. 2. A graph of concepts: concepts are depicted as threefold boxes and dummies as unary boxes. The marked out *"is a"* generalization tree is black and excluded subgraphs are gray.

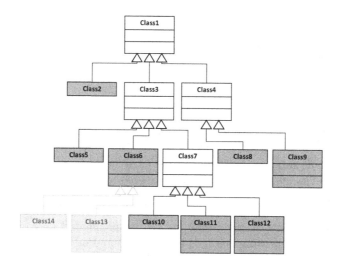

Fig. 3. The resulting leaves of the depth-first search algorithm (green) after finding concepts similar to the given representative

similar to the representative are marked as candidates. The representative is assigned to these concepts by means of probability distribution, based on the similarity score, as shown in Fig. 4.

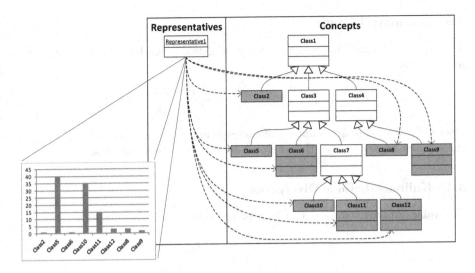

Fig. 4. The assignment of concepts to the given representative

3.2 Similarity Comparison

The similarity comparison of the representative to the prior knowledge concepts is performed by a *structural and probability distributions analysis*. The structural analysis finds the intersection between representative's attributes set and concept's attribute set, i.e., how many attributes are observed out of all possible attributes defined for this concept. The probability distribution analysis compares each representative's attribute (in form of Degree-of-Belief distribution) to the corresponding concept's attribute. The matching DoB distribution is written as $P(r|c)$, where r denotes the representative under consideration and $c \in C_r$ – concepts marked out by the depth search. Each matching can be expressed by some metric $d(r,c)$ that quantifies the similarity of r and c. A normalization of the metric d can be done by some monotonously increasing function f, projecting all metric values onto the range of $[0;1]$. So, the final matching DoB distribution is formalized as follows:

$$P(c|r) \propto P(r|c)P(c), \tag{2}$$

$$P(r|c) := f(d(r,c)), \tag{3}$$

$$f(d(r,c)) : [0;\infty) \to [0;1], \tag{4}$$

$$\sum_{c \in C_r} P(c|r) = 1, \tag{5}$$

$$d(r,c) = \underbrace{d(A^r, A^c)}_{\substack{\text{structural} \\ \text{similarity}}} + \lambda \cdot \underbrace{d_{A^r \cap A^c}}_{\substack{\text{value (DoB)} \\ \text{similarity}}}, \tag{6}$$

where $P(c)$ denotes the prior DoB distribution of the concepts, A^r and A^c are the representative's and concept's attributes, and λ is a weighting factor.

3.3 Tanimoto Distance

The structural similarity component of the metric d can be calculated by Tanimoto distance:

$$d_{Tanimoto}(A^r, A^c) = \frac{N_{A^r} + N_{A^c} - 2N_{A^r \cap A^c}}{N_{A^r} + N_{A^c} - N_{A^r \cap A^c}}, \qquad (7)$$

where N_{A^r} and N_{A^c} are numbers of corresponding attribute sets and $N_{A^r \cap A^c}$ is the number of elements of the intersection of two corresponding sets.

3.4 Kullback-Leibler Divergence

The value similarity $d_{A^r \cap A^c}$ can be represented by the following sum:

$$d_{A^r \cap A^c} = \sum_{A \in A^r \cap A^c} g_A \cdot d_{DoB}(A), \qquad (8)$$

where g_A is a weighting factor for the attribute A and $d_{DoB}(A)$ is a metric for the difference between $P(A^r)$ and $P(A^c)$ DoBs of the attribute A with a value a. The metric $d_{DoB}(A)$ is usually calculated by Kullback-Leibler equation:

$$d_{DoB}(A) = d_{K-L}(P, Q) = \sum_a P(a) \log \frac{P(a)}{Q(a)}, \qquad (9)$$

$$d_{DoB}(A) = d_{K-L}(P, Q) = \int_{-\infty}^{\infty} p(a) \log \frac{p(a)}{q(a)} da, \qquad (10)$$

where P and p denotes posterior and Q and q prior Degree-of-Belief distribution. It is important to note that p and q are normalized to 1.

3.5 Best Match

In the case of "hard" decision for the matching (i.e., only the best assignment has to be given), the Maximum A Posteriori (MAP) classification is employed. In MAP classification, the $P(c|r)$ is interpreted as a posterior DoB for the matching and the best match is calculated as follows:

$$\hat{c}_{MAP} := \arg \max_{\gamma \in C_r} P(\gamma|r) = \arg \min_{\gamma \in C_r} d(r|\gamma). \qquad (11)$$

4 Prior Knowledge Assignment

As soon as a representative is matched to a prior knowledge concept, the predefined semantic meaning is assigned for this representative. For example, if the assigned concept is *table*, the autonomous system is informed that it is used as a placeholder for other entities – as an *"is on"* surface with corresponding relations to other representatives. This information can be used further by assigning well-known *table height* to all entities laying on it. Second, the robot is informed that this surface can be used for placing things onto it. Third, this surface can be considered further as a search location. The knowledge about this location can be extended by a statistical distribution of how often specific things are found there. Later on it can be used for searching, e. g., by the command *"bring me the apartment keys and the mobile phone"*).

In addition to semantic meaning, missing attributes can be delivered from the prior knowledge to the representative under consideration. That means, all attributes that were not yet observed by sensors or contain large uncertainty are delivered to the representative attributes set. In the case of class concepts, the prior attributes are defined based on a statistical distribution over possible values. For example, table length can be assigned to the length probability distribution based on the length values of all tables in the building. In the case of entity concepts, the representative's attributes can be rewritten by attributes from the prior knowledge, since predefined values are more precise than those measured by sensors. In this case, the exact texture, 3D point clouds and other attributes are delivered as soon as the entity is recognized.

5 Experimental Set-Up

The described above prior knowledge employment was developed and tested within several projects. One of the notable projects, dedicated to intelligent autonomous robots, is the *DFG SFB 588*.

5.1 SFB 588 "Humanoid Robots"

The German Science Foundation (DFG) Collaborative Research Center (SFB) 588 "Humanoid Robots – Learning and Cooperating Multimodal Robots" [13] is dedicated to humanoid robots ARMAR designed with the purpose of helping humans in a household environment. For this, the humanoid robot needs a comprehensive state of knowledge on its environment. To this end, the described world modeling with prior knowledge employment has been developed. Figure 5 shows two humanoid robots in a kitchen scenario.

5.2 Example Workflow

One of the simplest scenarios is an exploration of entities on a table during a coffee break. The table has a constant size and location, which can be predefined in the prior knowledge. The ARMAR robot is equipped with stereo cameras allowing 3D spacing of the scene, though with a large uncertainty. A typical spatial uncertainty for a coffee machine placed 1.5 m in front of the robot is around 0.1 m depending on the angular calibration and the angle of sight [14]. For simplification, this scenario allows entity types of only two types: a coffee machine and a variety of coffee cups. Moreover, the only attributes involved into matching process are the size along the x-axis and sounds.

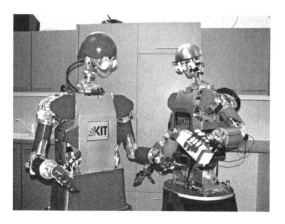

Fig. 5. Two ARMAR-III robots in a test environment

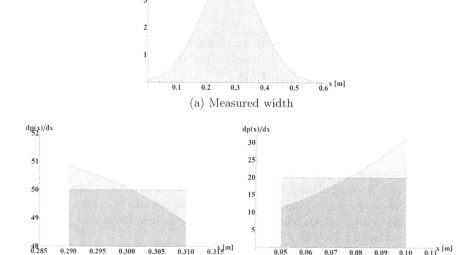

(a) Measured width

(b) K-L for coffee machine

(c) K-L for coffee cups

Fig. 6. Kullback-Leibler distance between an entity width (a) and the known coffee machine (b) or all possible cups (c)

At the first moment, the robot discovered an entity on the table with microphones and stereo cameras. The microphones subsystem has delivered loud sounds from the entity. The stereo cameras subsystem has delivered a measured width of approximately 28 cm as shown in Fig. 6(a). The prior knowledge contains information about:

- a coffee machine entity concept of the width of 30±1 cm and with an acoustic marker;
- a coffee cups class concept with the uniformly distributed width of [5; 10] cm.

The Tanimoto distances for the coffee machine and coffee cups are:

$$d_{Tanimoto}(A^r, A^{cm}) = \frac{2 + 2 - 2 \times 2}{2 + 2 - 2} = 0, \tag{12}$$

$$d_{Tanimoto}(A^r, A^{cc}) = \frac{2 + 1 - 2 \times 1}{2 + 1 - 1} = 0.5. \tag{13}$$

The Kullback-Leibler distances are 6.8×10^{-5} (Fig. 6(b)) and 4.2×10^{-2} (Fig. 6(c)) correspondingly.

Both distances show preference to the coffee machine, even without employment of the weighting factor λ and normalization functional $f(d(r, c))$. Thus, the beast match would be the coffee machine.

6   Conclusion

The analysis presented in this paper allows the dynamic employment of the prior knowledge. This knowledge is used to enrich dynamic models with semantics and missing information. For this, each dynamic model element is compared to prior knowledge elements based on the value and structural similarity. The value similarity is calculated based on the Kullback-Leibler distance of the posterior Degree-of-Belief distribution to possible prior distributions. The structural similarity is calculated with Tanimoto distance, measuring attribute sets of the dynamic model to possible attributes. The comparison to prior knowledge elements is performed by the ontology depth search algorithm. Additionally, several auxiliary ideas, like the best matching possibility and the direct assignment of prior knowledge, were described. The overall information representation and management system was developed on the SFB 588 humanoid robot ARMAR and presented on the example workflow.

Acknowledgments. This work has been supported by the German Science Foundation (DFG) within the Collaborative Research Center (SFB) 588 "Humanoid Robots – Learning and Cooperating Multimodal Robots".

References

1. Belkin, A., Kuwertz, A., Fischer, Y., Beyerer, J.: World Modeling for Autonomous Systems. In: Innovative Information Systems Modelling Techniques, vol. 1. InTech – Open Access Publisher (May 2012)
2. Baum, M., Gheţa, I., Belkin, A., Beyerer, J., Hanebeck, U.D.: Data Association in a World Model for Autonomous Systems. In: Proceedings of the 2010 IEEE International Conference on Multisensor Fusion and Integration for Intelligent Systems, pp. 187–192. Omnipress. IEEE (2010)

3. Belkin, A.: Information Management in World Modeling. In: Beyerer, J., Huber, M. (eds.) Proceedings of the 2010 Joint Workshop of Fraunhofer IOSB and Institute for Anthropomatics, Vision and Fusion Laboratory. Karlsruher Schriften zur Anthropomatik, vol. 7, pp. 187–199. KIT Scientific Publishing (2011)

4. Gheţa, I., Heizmann, M., Belkin, A., Beyerer, J.: World Modeling for Autonomous Systems. In: Dillmann, R., Beyerer, J., Hanebeck, U.D., Schultz, T. (eds.) KI 2010. LNCS (LNAI), vol. 6359, pp. 176–183. Springer, Heidelberg (2010)

5. Chung, Y.-J.: Using Kullback-Leibler Distance in Determining the Classes for the Heart Sound Signal Classification. In: Fyfe, C., Kim, D., Lee, S.-Y., Yin, H. (eds.) IDEAL 2008. LNCS, vol. 5326, pp. 49–56. Springer, Heidelberg (2008)

6. Zamanifar, K., Alamiyan, F.: A new similarity measure for instance data matching. In: Proceedings of the International Conference on Computer Communication and Management (2011)

7. Dhillon, I.S., Mallela, S., Kumar, R.: Enhanced word clustering for hierarchical text classification. In: Proceedings of the Eighth ACM SIGKDD International Conference on Knowledge Discovery and Data Mining, pp. 191–200. ACM (2002)

8. Karakoç, E., Cherkasov, A., Sahinalp, S.C.: Distance based algorithms for small biomolecule classification and structural similarity search. In: ISMB (Supplement of Bioinformatics) 2006, pp. 243–251 (2006)

9. Yang, Z.: A study of land cover change detection with tanimoto distance. In: Association of American Geographers Annual Meeting, Washington, DC, USA (April 2010)

10. Belkin, A.: Object-Oriented World Modelling for Autonomous Systems. In: Beyerer, J., Huber, M. (eds.) Proceedings of the 2009 Joint Workshop of Fraunhofer IOSB and Institute for Anthropomatics, Vision and Fusion Laboratory. Karlsruher Schriften zur Anthropomatik, vol. 4. KIT Scientific Publishing (2010)

11. Kühn, B., Belkin, A., Swerdlow, A., Machmer, T., Beyerer, J.B., Kroschel, K.: Knowledge-Driven Opto-Acoustic Scene Analysis based on an Object-Oriented World Modeling approach for Humanoid Robots. In: Proceedings of the 41st International Symposium on Robotics and the 6th German Conference on Robotics (ISR/ROBOTIK). VDE Verlag GmbH (June 2010)

12. Belkin, A.: Dynamic World Modeling with Prior Knowledge Matching for Autonomous Systems. In: Proceedings of the 2011 Joint Workshop of Fraunhofer IOSB and Institute for Anthropomatics, Vision and Fusion Laboratory. Karlsruher Schriften zur Anthropomatik. KIT Scientific Publishing (2012)

13. DFG SFB 588: Humanoid robots – learning and cooperating multimodal robots (2001-2012), http://www.sfb588.uni-karlsruhe.de

14. Belkin, A., Beyerer, J.: Information Entropy and Structural Metrics Based Estimation of Situations as a Basis for Situation Awareness and Decision Support. In: 2012 IEEE International Multi-Disciplinary Conference on Cognitive Methods in Situation Awareness and Decision Support (CogSIMA 2012), pp. 111–116. IEEE, New Orleans (2012)

Interactive Features for Robot Viewers

Thomas Hulin, Katharina Hertkorn, and Carsten Preusche

Institute of Robotics and Mechatronics, DLR (German Aerospace Center),
Muenchner Str. 20, D-82234 Wessling, Germany
{firstname.lastname}@dlr.de
http://www.dlr.de/rm

Abstract. Robot viewers are an important tool for robot developers, programmers and users. This article presents interactive visual features that can be used for robot viewers, including rotating arrows for torque controlled serial robots and special positioned textfields for numerically displaying joint parameters. The presented features support intuitive interaction modes such that the displayed content can be switched or their visibility can be toggled. With these features the DLR SeRo-Viewer has been developed, which aims at minimizing the efforts for integrating new robots in the visualization system, and at the same time being flexible enough to visualize various robotic systems. The SeRo-Viewer has already been successfully applied on several robotic systems.

Keywords: robot viewer, visualization features, torque controlled robots.

1 Introduction

A robot viewer is a useful tool for robot developers, programmers and users, since it provides an intuitive view on the robot's movements. In combination with a robot simulator, it improves efficiency of system tests in simulations, and diminishes hardware stress. Due to these advantageous reasons there are many robot viewers with different capabilities for numerous robotic systems. Most of them are based on libraries like Coin or Qt and are easy to use within the provided framework. Well-known robot viewers are

- RVIZ, the visualization tool for ROS [1]. It supports several display types (e.g. Axes, Grid, Map, Point Clouds) and special views for navigation and localization. Moreover, it enables diverse interaction possibilities with a computer mouse.
- the visualization of OpenRave [2], which provides a python interface, and supports the XML file format. It also includes additional interaction possibilities with a computer mouse.
- GraspIt! [3], a common tool for grasp planning where the simulated robot, or the robotic hand, is specified using XML. The fingers can be moved by mouse commands as well.
- OpenHRP, an integrated software platform for (humanoid) robot simulations and software developments [4] using a python interface. The user is provided with special views useful for humanoid simulations.

C.-Y. Su, S. Rakheja, H. Liu (Eds.): ICIRA 2012, Part III, LNAI 7508, pp. 181–193, 2012.

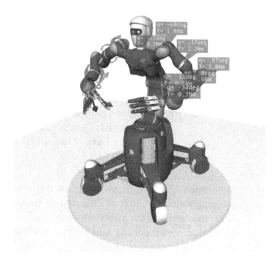

Fig. 1. Visualization of Rollin' Justin with rotating arrows and billboards. The wide torque arrows on the left robot arm indicate intuitively an external force applied to the robot.

There are also numerous other visualization tools that are framework independent. One famous example is Peekabot [5], which is a generic open source library for all POSIX compliant platforms. Other widespread commercial software tools for robot visualization are developed by robot companies, like the RobotStudio from ABB [6], or the KUKA.Sim package [7] from KUKA. These are powerful tools for offline programming of robots, and they contain sophisticated algorithms for robot simulation, such as collision detection or reachability checks. A generic example for a robot programming framework using scripting languages and including visualization of robots and its cells is COSIMIR [8]. Also at our institute diverse visualization tools have been developed over the years, e.g. [9,10,11].

The research focus of our institute is on torque controlled robotic systems which are equipped with torque sensors. Thus, they are able to perceive external forces on the robot structure and are therefore well suited for direct human-machine interaction. New requirements and challenges for robot visualization system arise with this new field of application for robots. On the one hand critical parameters must be presented intuitively, such that a user, who might not be familiar with a robotic system, is able to react reliable and fast on possible errors. On the other hand the user must be able to switch between the numerous parameters of such robotic systems, so that the relevant parameters can be selected for visualization while the view is not overloaded.

This paper presents visualization features for robot visualization systems meeting the challenging requirements of torque controlled robots and direct human-machine interaction, Sect. 2. Based on these features a proof of concept robot viewer – the DLR SeRo-Viewer – is presented in Sect. 3. This viewer is based on the open X3D standard [12] and is currently implemented for the InstantPlayer [13]. The authors provide the X3D files of the DLR SeRo-viewer upon request. It is free to use for research purpose. Five applications of the viewer in our institute are given in Sect. 4. Finally, the paper concludes in Sect. 5.

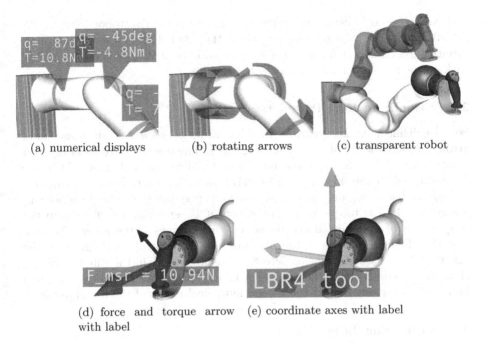

(a) numerical displays   (b) rotating arrows   (c) transparent robot

(d) force and torque arrow   (e) coordinate axes with label
with label

Fig. 2. Interactive visual features

2   Visual Features

This section presents five visual features for robot viewers. These features have three important properties in common. They are

- intuitive, such that the displayed information is self-explanatory,
- interactive, such that an interaction device (e.g. a computer mouse or touch screen) can be used to toggle between displayed parameters or switch the visualization mode, and
- co-located, which means that these features provide information directly at the respective location to which the information belongs.

The following subsections describe the visual features in detail. An exemplary implementation is detailed in Sect. 3.

2.1   Visualizing Numerical Parameters

Billboards are 3d objects that are always facing the camera of a virtual scene. In a robot viewer they are well suited for displaying numerical parameter values, such as joint angles or joint torques, as shown in Fig. 2(a). If they are placed in front of the respective joint, occlusions by the robot structure can be prevented, and furthermore they appear closer to the borders of the visualization window because of the perspective view on virtual scenes. Billboards can be equipped with an arrow to indicate their affiliation to the respective robot joint. Additionally, they may be semitransparent such that they do not obscure the robot. Intuitive interaction is enabled by toggling visibility of the billboards by mouse click on the robot structure or on the billboards.

2.2   Visualizing Joint Parameters

For visualizing joint accelerations or joint torques, this article suggests round arrows around the robot joints, see Fig. 2(b). These arrows are rotating with constant speed. By altering the arrows' rotating direction and arrow width, the direction and magnitude of the respective joint parameter can be intuitively presented. They were originally designed to display the proximity to robot singularities [14]. For torque controlled robots it is especially useful to map the torque error of commanded and measured joint torques to the arrows, because first this difference indicates the direction and amount of acceleration of the robot joint, and second it helps detecting possible errors in the robotic system, either in the controller or the sensors. A mouse click onto an arrow will cause a billboard to appear showing the precise numerical values of the round arrow.

2.3   Visualizing Target Poses

Transparent robots doubles are well suited for visualizing target poses of robots, Fig. 2(c). In particular, when robots are driving to initial positions, their transparent counterparts can not only indicate their final configuration, but also anticipate the path robots will move. Through the transparency the actual robot position is not occluded. Parameter values of the transparent counterparts are visualized by the numerical displays described in previous subsection 2.1.

2.4   Visualizing Interaction Forces and Torques

Arrows are a widespread utility and are used by most robot viewers to indicate the desired or measured forces, torques, or velocities. This article suggests smart arrows, which – like usual arrow – represent the direction and magnitude of a parameter, but in addition have interactive properties. As soon as they are clicked by an interaction device, a billboard appears that is showing the name and the numerical value of the respective parameter. This additional property upvalues traditional arrows, especially for those cases in which the exact parameter value is needed.

2.5   Visualizing Coordinate Axes

Similarly to force arrows, coordinate axes are part of many robot viewers, and are suggested here as smart axes. Smart axes are clickable and can show their names in a billboard. This functionality is especially useful when having complex robotic systems with dozens of degrees of freedom such as Justin (see Fig. 1), for which some axes have the same position but different orientation.

3   Proof of Concept – The DLR SeRo-Viewer

The requirements for visualizing torque controlled robots and for direct human-machine interaction demand more than the pure implementation of the introduced visual features. With rising complexity of robotic systems, it becomes quite costly and time consuming to include those visual features, implement a communication interface, and integrate the kinematics for each robot one wants to visualize.

In this section we present the DLR SeRo-Viewer. It is a proof of concept viewer that combines extensive functionality and ease of use, while being as generic as required for visualizing all kind of robotic systems. The SeRo-Viewer is a pure visualization tool without robot simulation algorithms which emphasizes the generic approach of the concept. The main properties of the presented tool are:

- easy to implement new robot-scenes taking almost zero effort
- flexible communication interface via UDP or shared memory
- intuitive visual feedback (see Sect. 2)
- script based interface without need to compile plugins
- intuitive usage
- extensible
- platform independent (Linux, Windows, ...)

The software concept is currently implemented for the InstantPlayer [13] and based on the open X3D standard [12]. The intuitive usage of the viewer is built-in in the software concept by providing two components that may be interpreted as classes following the object oriented paradigm: One component providing a shared memory and UDP interface as communication gateway and the other creating a serial robot encapsulating several features that are introduced in Sect. 2. They can be instantiated in a virtual scene and interact with each other. This modularity fits with two essential features of the X3D standard: The definition of own objects that are encapsulated in so-called protos, and the routing concept, which allows routing signals from one X3D node to another.

Each proto has a declaration part (see examplary Fig. 3) where the fields and datatypes of the user interface are defined, and an implementation part that contains the functionality of the proto (not shown here). Using different instances of a proto the scene description can be short and nevertheless include many features (see Fig. 7). These protos are loaded by the visualization toolkit (in our case the InstantPlayer), which also builds the specified scene graph and renders the 3d models.

The next subsections introduce the two main components of the SeRo-Viewer: the SerialRobot proto in the next subsection and the communication concept in Sect. 3.2. At last, an example code for visualizing a light-weight robot is given showing a realization of a complete scene description in a few lines of code.

3.1   Visualization

In the following, the concept of creating a serial robot providing several features is introduced. Fig. 3 shows the interface to the SerialRobot proto. With this

```
PROTO SerialRobot [
  # robot parameters:
  field SFString name "robot"
  field MFVec4f dhParams [0,0,0,0]
  field SFString directory ""
  field MFString filenames [""]
  exposedField SFMatrix4f baseFrame   1 0 0 0  0 1 0 0  0 0 1 0  0 0 0 1
  exposedField SFMatrix4f flangeFrame 1 0 0 0  0 1 0 0  0 0 1 0  0 0 0 1
  exposedField MFFloat jointAngles [0]
  exposedField MFNode children [ ]
  eventOut SFMatrix4f fwdKinFromBaseToFlange
  # additional visualization features:
  exposedField SFBool enableTouchSensor TRUE
  field MFVec3f offsetsToCenterOfJoints [0,0,0]
  exposedField SFBool showAxes FALSE
  field SFFloat axesSize 0.2
  exposedField SFFloat axesTransparency 0
  exposedField SFBool showArrows FALSE
  field SFFloat arrowRadius 0.1
  field SFFloat arrowWidthScale 0.01
  eventIn MFFloat torques
  exposedField SFBool showBillboards FALSE
  field SFFloat billboardScale 0.05
  eventIn MFFloat billboardValues
]
```

Fig. 3. The SerialRobot proto

interface the features contained in the proto (see Sect. 2) are customized to the current scene and parameterize the visualized robot. Due to the modular concept, the features can also be used without the encapsulation in the proto.

The first design choice is the format of the scene graph to be built. There are two possibilities to include the kinematics of the robot: either by building a flat hierarchy, see Fig. 4(a), or by representing the kinematic structure in the scene graph, see Fig. 4(b). In a flat hierarchy each link i of the robot is child of the root node ($i \in [0, N - 1]$, N is the total number of joints). Each pose of a link is calculated (represented by the node "forward kinematics" in the figure) and set accordingly. If a nested structure is chosen each link i is parent of the link $i + 1$ and the direct computation of the forward kinematics is avoided.

In our concept, the flat hierarchy is chosen as it provides the user with the transformation from base joint to the flange, which is not directly available in a nested structure. Using this transformation as an output of the proto, it helps to overcome one problem of visualization tools independent of e.g. the robotic control, a simulator or a planner: the consistency between the scenes which now can easily be checked.

The hierarchy is built as follows: For each name in `filenames` a transformation node (in the figure called "link") is created and serves as a parent node. The 3d geometry data of the robot links are loaded from the specified `filenames` in the `directory` as children of that parent nodes. To provide the different features more children are created by instantiating the protos for coordinate axis, billboards, rotating arrows and the touch sensor. More features can be included by adding other children. In the node "forward kinematics" the forward kinematics given by the DH-Parameters is calculated and each resulting transformation

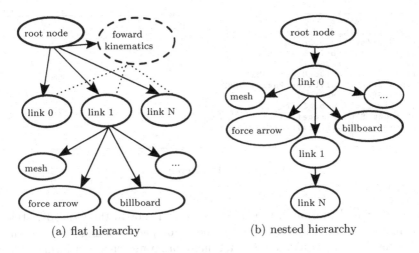

(a) flat hierarchy   (b) nested hierarchy

Fig. 4. Hierarchies of a scene graph

matrix is routed to the respective link (see the dotted lines in Fig. 4(a)). As the kinematic of a robot starts at the location of the robot base in the world, this transformation can be set using the `baseFrame`. The transformation from the last joint to the flange of the robot can be specified with the `flangeFrame`. The eventOut `fwdKinFromBaseToFlange` returns the transformation from base to flange, such that the user has access to the calculated forward kinematics.

Thus, a robotic tool can be simply added to the robot flange by routing that transformation to the tool's location. There is an even simpler possibility of adding tools to the robot flange, namely by adding them as `children` to the robot. In both cases the added objects are moving according to the robot's movements. To customize the features of the SerialRobot the according fields can be set if they vary from the initial values. The field `offsetsToCenterOfJoints` is used to move the display of the rotating arrows and billboards from the location defined by the `dhParameters`.

Although the SerialRobot-proto is built for serial robots, parallel kinematics can be implemented using several robots with serial kinematics.

3.2 Communication

The SeRo-Viewer is designed to receive robot data from external programs or X3D nodes. This section introduces the concept of a UdpReceiver proto: It receives UDP-packets and generates X3D events that can be directly routed to the virtual robot. In order to cover most of the various requirements of external programs, numerous parameters can be set (see Fig. 5). The most important parameter `structure` defines the structure of the UDP-packets as string. Different events are generated depending on the structure's definition. The UdpReceiver proto supports events for values, vectors, and homogenous transformation

```
PROTO UdpReceiver [
  field SFString structure ""
  field SFInt32 udpport 0
  field SFInt32 bufferOffset 0
  field SFBool isDouble TRUE
  field SFBool columnMajor TRUE
  field SFBool onlyLatestPacket TRUE
  field SFFloat scale 1.0
  field SFInt32 debuglevel 1
  eventOut SFBool receiving
  eventOut SFBool receiveTrigger
]
```

Fig. 5. The UdpReceiver proto

matrices. The definition of the UDP-structure is not in the C-header style, for two main reasons. First, it is much more compact defining the structure as string inside an X3D file, and second many programs choose a format different to C when defining their UDP-structure, such as the well-known Matlab toolbox Simulink.

Similarly to the UdpReceiver proto the SeRo-Viewer contains the ShmReader proto that communicates via shared memory, which has the advantage of reducing communication delays compared to UDP.

3.3   Example

With the two protos introduced in previous sections visualizing robots becomes quite easy. The following lines present an example for visualizing the DLR/KUKA light-weight robot (LWR) [15], which is equipped with position and torque sensors in each joint allowing the robot being operated impedance controlled. The code for visualizing the LWR as shown in Fig. 6 is listed below in Fig. 7.

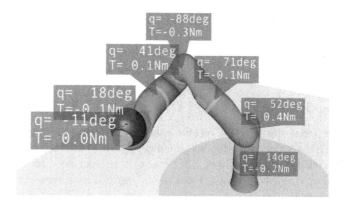

Fig. 6. Visualization of the light-weight robot obtained with the example code

This code has ten important lines, five for specifying the properties of the LWR, three for defining the communication parameters, and two for routing the communication events to the LWR. These lines of code are sufficient for visualizing a robot that is moving according to the data of the UDP-packets and for using all the features of the SeRo-Viewer, which will be described in detail in the following section. The only precondition is having the geometry data of the robot links positioned and oriented according to Craig's Denavit-Hartenberg notation [16], which means that the origin of each single joint is given such that its z-axis is coaxial with the rotational direction.

```
#X3D V3.0 utf8
Scene{
    EXTERNPROTO SerialRobot [] "PROTO_serialRobot.wrl"
    EXTERNPROTO UdpReceiver [] "PROTO_udpReceiver.wrl"
    children [
        DEF lwr SerialRobot {
            filenames [ "base.wrl", "link1.wrl", "link2.wrl", "link3.wrl", ↵
                "link4.wrl", "link5.wrl", "link6.wrl", "link7.wrl" ]
            directory "3dModels/robots/lwr/wrl/"
            dhParams [ 0 0 0 0.31, 1.5708 0 0 0, -1.5708 0 0 0.4, -1.5708 0 0 0, ↵
                1.5708 0 0 0.39, 1.5708 0 0 0, -1.5708 0 0 0 ]
            offsetsToCenterOfJoints [ 0 0 -0.2, 0 0 0, 0 0 -0.2, 0 0 0, 0 0 ↵
                -0.2, 0 0 0, 0 0 0.1 ]
        }
        DEF udpProto UdpReceiver {
            structure "7F7F"
            udpport 32000
        }
        # insert here other scene-elements
    ]
    ROUTE udpProto.values0 TO lwr.jointAngles
    ROUTE udpProto.values1 TO lwr.torques
    # insert here other routings
}
```

Fig. 7. An X3D file for visualizing the light-weight robot

4   Applications

The SeRo-Viewer can be used for visualizing various robots. This section presents five applications to different robots of our research institute.

4.1   Rollin' Justin

DLR's Rollin' Justin is the combination of a humanoid upper body called Justin [17] and a mobile platform with a variable base [18]. Although the platform with its four wheels has a parallel kinematics, it can be visualized using the SerialRobot proto, see Fig. 1. The overall system has a total amount of 51 degrees of freedom (DoF) where the upper body has 43 DoF: five DoF for the torso and head, 14 DoF for both arms and 24 DoF for the two four-fingered DLR Hands II.

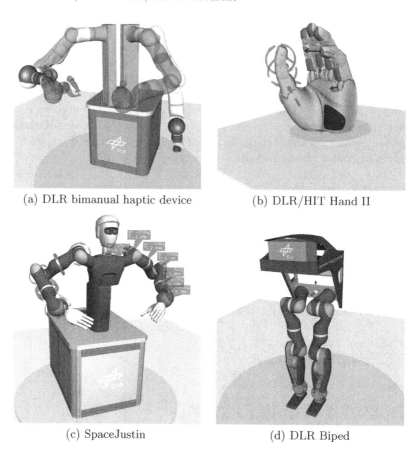

(a) DLR bimanual haptic device   (b) DLR/HIT Hand II

(c) SpaceJustin   (d) DLR Biped

Fig. 8. Applications

4.2   The DLR Bimanual Haptic Device

The DLR bimanual haptic device [19] is a haptic device consisting of two LWRs. It is used for interaction with haptic feedback with remote environments and virtual reality scenes. The user sits between the robots that are mounted behind him and which can be operated torque and position controlled. If they are position controlled the desired position should be visualized. If they are torque controlled, not only for security reasons, it is crucial to know which torque is applied at the moment. Activating the robot with high torque errors leads to a high acceleration of the robot and poses a risk for the user.

Both requirements are met by using the SerialRobot proto. The visualization of the haptic device in torque mode is similar to the one shown in Fig. 8(c) or Fig. 1. In Fig. 8(a) the visualization in position mode is shown where the green transparent robot shows the commanded desired positions. The shift between both modes is toggled using the UdpReceiver proto.

4.3   The DLR/HIT-Hand II

The DLR/HIT-Hand II is an anthropomorphic hand with five fingers [20] and 15 DoF. All fingers are equal having three degrees of freedom and three finger links where the last two links are coupled with a 1:1 ratio. The hand is visualized using five instances of the SerialRobot proto, one instance representing one finger. Especially the torque arrows are very useful while grasping and manipulating to display the current grasp forces. During grasp planning the object can be included in the scene as it is done e.g. in [21].

4.4   SpaceJustin

DLR's telepresence system consists of the bimanual haptic device (see Sect. 4.2) and a humanoid upper body (see Fig. 8(c)). SpaceJustin has three DoF for the torso and the head, seven DoF for each arm and 15 DoF for each hand, resulting in a 47 DoF robotic system. Monitoring commanded torques and positions intuitively in this complex system makes visualization mandatory. Axes labels clarify the use of different base and flange frames in the system.

4.5   The DLR Biped

Another application of the SerialRobot is the DLR Biped [22]. It is based on the technology of the torque controlled LWRs as they are used e.g. for the bimanual haptic device or Rollin' Justin. Similar to the arms, each leg has seven DoF.

5   Conclusions and Future Work

Torque-controlled robots create new challenges for robot viewers, because they open new areas of application while having at the same time considerably more measured parameters. This article presented new intuitive, interactive and co-located visual features for such robots. Based on these features a proof of concept viewer, the SeRo-Viewer has been introduced.

The SeRo-Viewer is a tool for visualizing robotic systems with focus on three key aspects: ease of use (clickable visual features), easy to implement (only couple of lines needed to code), and generic (arbitrary UDP and shared memory packages). Since the SeRo-Viewer follows the open X3D standard, all the functionality of available X3D viewers can be accessed, such as various stereo-visualization modes, augmented reality features, vision based tracking, humanoid animation, physics engines, and interfaces to dozens of interaction devices. Furthermore, X3D viewers can be extended by new protos or plugins, allowing to integrate new functionality easily.

The presented SeRo-Viewer including the new visual features have already been proven to visualize five different robotic systems of our institute while intuitively presenting robotic data. Future developments will enhance the functionality and the interfaces of the introduced protos. Exemplarily alternative definitions to the DH-parameter specification for robot kinematics is planned to be integrated.

Acknowledgment. We would like to acknowledge the excellent support from the Fraunhofer Institute for Computer Graphics Research (IGD), specifically from Sabine Webel, Uli Bockholt and Johannes Behr.

References

1. Quigley, M., Conley, K., Gerkey, B.P., Faust, J., Foote, T., Leibs, J., Wheeler, R., Ng, A.Y.: ROS: an open-source robot operating system. In: IEEE Int. Conf. on Robotics and Automation (ICRA) Workshop on Open Source Software (2009)
2. Diankov, R.: Automated Construction of Robotic Manipulation Programs. PhD thesis, Carnegie Mellon University, Robotics Institute (2010)
3. Miller, A., Allen, P., Santos, V., Valero-Cuevas, F.: From robot hands to human hands: A visualization and simulation engine for grasping research. Industrial Robot 32, 55–63 (2005)
4. Hirukawa, H., Kanehiro, F., Kajita, S.: OpenHRP: Open architecture humanoid robotics platform. In: Jarvis, R., Zelinsky, A. (eds.) Robotics Research. Springer Tracts in Advanced Robotics, vol. 6, pp. 99–112. Springer, Heidelberg (2003)
5. http://www.peekabot.org (2011)
6. ABB Robotics: Operating Manual RobotStudio, Västerås, Sweden (2007)
7. KUKA Robotics Corporation: Robotic simulation (2006) white paper
8. Freund, E., Hypki, A., Pensky, D.: New architecture for corporate integration of simulation and production control in industrial applications. In: Proc. of the IEEE Int. Conf. on Robotics and Automation (ICRA), pp. 806–811 (2001)
9. Brunner, B., Landzettel, K., Schreiber, G., Steinmetz, B., Hirzinger, G.: A universal task level ground control and programming system for space robot applications - the MARCO concept and it's application to the ETS VII project. In: Proc. of the Int. Symp. on Artifical Intelligence, Robotics, and Automation in Space (iSAIRAS), Noordwijk, The Netherlands (1999)
10. Zacharias, F., Borst, C., Hirzinger, G.: Capturing robot workspace structure: representing robot capabilities. In: Proc. IEEE/RSJ Int. Conf. on Intelligent Robots and Systems (IROS), Nice, France, pp. 3229–3236 (2007)
11. Bellmann, T.: Interactive simulations and advanced visualization with modelica. In: Casella, F. (ed.) Proc. of the Int. Modelica Conference, vol. 7, Linköping University Electronic Press, Como (2009)
12. Brutzman, D., Daly, L.: X3D: extensible 3D graphics for Web authors. Morgan Kaufmann series in interactive 3D technology. Elsevier/Morgan Kaufmann (2007)
13. Behr, J., Dähne, P., Jung, Y., Webel, S.: Beyond the web browser - X3D and immersive VR. In: Proc. of IEEE Symp. on 3D User Interfaces (3DUI), Charlotte, North Carolina, USA (2007)
14. Hulin, T., Schmirgel, V., Yechiam, E., Zimmermann, U., Preusche, C., Pöhler, G.: Evaluating exemplary training accelerators for programming-by-demonstration. In: Proc. IEEE Int. Symp. In: Robot and Human Interactive Communication (RoMan), Viareggio, Italy, pp. 467–472 (2010)
15. Hirzinger, G., Sporer, N., Schedl, M., Butterfaß, J., Grebenstein, M.: Torque-controlled lightweight arms and articulated hands: Do we reach technological limits now? The International Journal of Robotics Research 23, 331–340 (2004)
16. Craig, J.J.: Introduction to Robotics Mechanics and Control, 2nd edn. Addison-Wesley Publishing Company, Inc., USA (1989)

17. Borst, C., Ott, C., Wimböck, T., Brunner, B., Zacharias, F., Bäuml, B., Hillen-brand, U., Haddadin, S., Albu-Schäffer, A., Hirzinger, G.: A humanoid upper body system for two-handed manipulation. In: Proc. of the IEEE Int. Conf. on Robotics and Automation (ICRA)., vol. 2, pp. 2766–2767 (2007)

18. Borst, C., Wimböck, T., Schmidt, F., Fuchs, M., Brunner, B., Zacharias, F., Gior-dano, P.R., Konietschke, R., Sepp, W., Fuchs, S., Rink, C., Albu-Schäffer, A., Hirzinger, G.: Rollin' justin - mobile platform with variable base. In: Proc. of the IEEE Int. Conf. on Robotics and Automation (ICRA), pp. 1597–1598 (2009)

19. Hulin, T., Hertkorn, K., Kremer, P., Schätzle, S., Artigas, J., Sagardia, M., Zacharias, F., Preusche, C.: The DLR bimanual haptic device with optimized workspace. In: Proc. of the IEEE Int. Conf. on Robotics and Automation (ICRA), Shanghai, China, pp. 3441–3442 (2011)

20. Liu, H., Meusel, P., Hirzinger, G., Jin, M., Liu, Y., Xie, Z.: The modular multisen-sory DLR-HIT-Hand: Hardware and software architecture. IEEE/ASME Transac-tions on Mechatronics 13, 461–469 (2008)

21. Roa, M.A., Hertkorn, K., Borst, C., Hirzinger, G.: Reachable independent contact regions for precision grasps. In: Proc. of the IEEE Int. Conf. on Robotics and Automation (ICRA), Shanghai, China, pp. 5337–5343 (2011)

22. Ott, C., Baumgärtner, C., Mayr, J., Fuchs, M., Burger, R., Lee, D., Eiberger, O., Albu-Schäffer, A., Grebenstein, M., Hirzinger, G.: Development of a biped robot with torque controlled joints. In: Proc. of the IEEE-RAS Int. Conf. on Humanoid Robots (Humanoids), Nashville, Tennessee, USE, pp. 167–173 (2010)

Searching Energy-Efficient Route in Rough Terrain for Mobile Robot with Ant Algorithm

Anuntapat Anuntachai and Olarn Wongwirat

Embedded System Research and Development Laboratory
Facutly of Information Technology, King Mongkut's Institute of Technology Ladkrabang
1 Soi Chalongkrung 1, Ladkrabang, Bangkok, Thailand
{anuntapat,olarn}@it.kmitl.ac.th

Abstract. Recently, the ant algorithm has been widely used to solve the problem for searching optimized route from various different paths. It can be applied for searching an appropriate route that consumes less energy in mobile robot area as well. However, the previous optimized routes resulting from the ant algorithms considered only in flat terrain environment. They did not mention rough terrain environment. For the rough terrain, the optimized results might not be optimized in term of energy, due to slopes contained inside. This paper presents the application of ant algorithms for searching energy-efficient route of mobile robot in the rough terrain environment. The conventional ant colony optimization (ACO) algorithm and the adapted ACO algorithm are used to find the optimized routes in terms of distance and energy for comparison. The experimental results showed that, by using the speed with distance weighting factor, the adapted ACO yielded the optimized distance and energy in the flat terrain. In the rough terrain, the adapted ACO could also provide the energy-efficient routes better than the flat terrain. However, it could not be comparable with the ACO in some case and is required further improvement.

Keywords: Energy-efficient route, Rough terrain, Mobile robot, Ant algorithm.

1 Introduction

The problem for searching optimized route, or shortest path, can be solved by several algorithms. The ant colony optimization (ACO) is one of the most algorithms used for solving such the problem. For instance, in [1], the ACO algorithm was used to solve the travelling salesman problem (TSP). The research aimed to find the most appropriate and efficient route among several paths to all cities where the salesman used to visit. In [2], the Q-learning algorithm was applied with the ACO, called Ant-Q, for solving the TSP. The results implied that the Ant-Q yielded the shortest path with less data variation efficiently, when comparing with the ACO alone. In [3], the ACO was improved to find the shortest route among symmetric and asymmetric paths in the TSP. The symmetric and asymmetric paths in this work meant that the forward and backward costs among the two cities were unequal.

As in the TSP, searching for optimized route is also one of the major challenges in mobile robot area. However, not only should the distance be optimized in the route,

C.-Y. Su, S. Rakheja, H. Liu (Eds.): ICIRA 2012, Part III, LNAI 7508, pp. 194–204, 2012.
© Springer-Verlag Berlin Heidelberg 2012

but the energy for mobile robot as well. The energy is a limited resource in mobile robot applications and needs to be considered. This comes from the fact that the mobile robot deploys motors to traverse along the paths and requires the energy to drive. If the mobile robot could find the optimized, or shortest, route, it could save the energy and perform the task more efficiently.

There are research works in mobile robot area that apply the ACO algorithm for searching the optimized route. Some of them focus not only the shortest route, but also the operational efficiency in term of energy consumption. For instance, the research in [4] used the ACO to solve the mobile robot path planning problem. The work focused on finding the most appropriate route and shortest distance possible from the maps that consisted of static obstacles and walls in different arrangements. The results expressed that the proposed ACO produced better solutions. In [5], the ant-like robot system was introduced. The mobile robot was simulated to work like ants in this work. The dispatching algorithm was applied to distribute the robots along the unknown area. The work aimed to spread the robots over the entire area as much as possible by using efficient energy and time, when comparing with the number of robots. Our research work in [6] proposed the adapted ACO to find the energy-efficient route for mobile robot. The adapted ACO included the speed and distance as local information for weighting. The optimized route was converted into energy for comparison. The simulation results showed that, when using the speed and distance as the weighting factors, the adapted ACO could provide the shortest route consuming less energy.

Although the ACO algorithms involved the optimization in terms of distance and energy, those research works considered only in flat terrain environment. For the rough terrain, the optimized result might not be optimized in term of energy due to slopes contained inside. The research in [3] could be similar to rough terrain environment, in term of slopes among the two cities, but it did not mention in the work. This paper presents the application of ACO algorithms for searching energy-efficient route of mobile robot in rough terrain environment. Conventional ACO and our adapted ACO are used to find the optimized routes in terms of distance and energy for comparison. The paper is organized as follows: In section 2, the ACO algorithms used in this work are explained. Section 3 expresses the motion paths of mobile robot in rough terrain environment, including the energy consumption model. Experimental set and result discussion are presented in section 4. Finally, the conclusion is provided in section 5.

2   Related ACO Algorithms

2.1   Conventional ACO Algorithm

The conventional ACO algorithm is used to solve the problem for searching optimized, or shortest, route, e.g., TSP. The principle of ACO algorithm is started by generating the initial pheromones $\tau_{ij}(0)$ for each path (i, j) between city i and j randomly with the low positive values, i.e., $\tau_{ij}(0) \sim U(0, max)$. Then, the artificial ant k, where $k \in 1, ..., M$, is released at the beginning point, or city. After that, the $T+$ is assigned as the shortest path and the $L+$ is the distance of the shortest path. Each artificial ant k creates the route $T^k(t)$ by choosing the next city for $N - 1$ times with the probability $\Phi_{ij}^k(t)$, as in equation (1),

$$\Phi_{ij}^k(t) = \begin{cases} \dfrac{\tau_{ij}(t)^\alpha}{\tau_c(t)} & j \in C_i^k \\ 0 & j \notin C_i^k \end{cases} . \tag{1}$$

The parameter k is the artificial ant, $\tau_{ij}(t)$ is the amount of pheromones on path (i, j), and α is a constant. The C_i^k is a set of city that the ant k has not been visited, counted from town i, and $\tau_c(t)$ is the sum of pheromones in all C_i^k direction, as in equation (2).

$$\tau_c(t) = \sum_{c \in C_i^k} \tau_{ic}(t)^\alpha . \tag{2}$$

Then, the travel distance $L^k(t)$ of the artificial ants k is calculated. If the better path is found, it is recorded instead of $T+$ and $L+$. The pheromone of each path is adjusted by equation (3),

$$\tau_{ij}(t + 1) = (1 - \rho)\tau_{ij}(t) + \Delta\tau_{ij}(t) . \tag{3}$$

The $\Delta\tau_{ij}(t)$ is the sum of pheromones emitted by each ant k and can be found by equation (4) and (5).

$$\Delta\tau_{ij}(t) = \sum_{k=1}^{M} \Delta\tau_{ij}^k(t) . \tag{4}$$

$$\Delta\tau_{ij}^k(t) = \begin{cases} \dfrac{Q}{L^k(t)} & (i,j) \in T^k(t) \\ 0 & (i,j) \notin T^k(t) \end{cases} . \tag{5}$$

The Q in (5) is the system parameter. The constant ρ is called the forgetting factor that represents the fading of pheromone over time, where $\rho \in [0, 1]$. The probability of routing can be improved by adding local information η_{ij} of the town wanting to visit from city i to j, as in equation (6).

$$\Phi_{ij}^k(t) = \frac{\tau_{ij}(t)^\alpha \eta_{ij}^\beta}{\sum_{c \in C_i^k} \tau_{ic}(t)^\alpha \eta_{ij}^\beta} . \tag{6}$$

The α and β are the system parameter that controls the weight of pheromone. The η_{ij} can be found from equation (7),

$$\eta_{ij} = \frac{1}{d_{ij}}. \tag{7}$$

The parameter d_{ij} is the Euclidean distance between city i and j in the two dimensional plane. It can be observed that, at the same city, the value of Φ^k_{ij} might be different from each ant. This is due to individual ants that might be arrived at that city by using different routes. Finally, define the period $t = 1$ to t_{max} for the number of rounds of algorithm to loop.

The most important parameter of ACO algorithm is the forgotten factor and the number of artificial ants in the system. The other important parameters are α and β. If β is equal to 0, it means the system used only information from the pheromone. This may lead to the answers that are not the best. If α is equal to 0, it means the system does not use pheromones at all. Thus, the searching result becomes just a greedy algorithm [7], [8], and [9].

2.2   Adapted ACO Algorithm

The adaptation of ACO algorithm for mobile robot is emphasized on energy efficiency, i.e., finding the shortest distance to move the robot along the paths with less energy [6]. In our adapted ACO algorithm, the speed is added as the local information for weighting. This factor is used to present the local information in equation (7) and (6) instead. The speed parameter is related to the distance and time, as defined by equation (8).

$$v = \frac{d}{t'}. \tag{8}$$

The parameter v is the speed in meter per second (m/s), and t' is the time in second (s). By using the relationship in (9), the adapted ACO has two weighting factors, i.e., speed (v) and speed with distance ($v + d$), for searching the optimization. Therefore, the additional weighting factor in term of speed V_{ij} is given by equation (9).

$$V_{ij} = \frac{1}{v_{ij}}. \tag{9}$$

2.3   Travelling Salesman Problem

The traveling salesman problem (TSP) is one of the well-known and extensively studied problems in discrete or combinational optimization. The TSP aims to find the shortest roundtrip of minimal total cost for each given city (or node) where the salesman visited exactly once. A graph theory is used to define the problem as finding the Hamiltonian cycle with the least weight for a given complete weighted graph. The complete weighted graph $G = (N, E)$ can be used to represent the TSP, where N is the set of n cities and E is the set of edges (paths) fully connecting all cities. Each edge $(i,j) \in E$ is assigned the cost d_{ij}, which is the distance between cities i and j. The d_{ij} can be defined in the Euclidean space in (7) and is given by equation (10).

$$d_{ij} = \sqrt{(x_i - x_j)^2 + (y_i - y_j)^2} . \tag{10}$$

The parameter x and y are the coordinates of cities, or nodes. In typical TSP, the only coordinate (x, y) is implied the normal flat terrain environment.

3   Rough Terrain and Energy Consumption Models

3.1   Motion Path in Rough Terrain Model

The motion path of mobile robot to traverse in rough terrain environment is modeled in Fig. 1. As can be observed, the rough terrain contains three different paths between the nodes i and j. These paths include the flatting edge (d_f) and the slopes of rising edge (d_r) and falling edge (d_l).

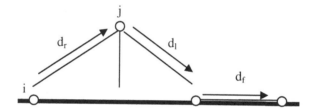

Fig. 1. Route between node i and j in rough terrain environment

In the flat terrain environment, the optimization result from ACO algorithms is in term of shortest route, or distance, among the nodes. The energy is derived by the distance in accordance with the shortest route directly. Thus, the optimized route consumes less energy, or energy-efficient route [6]. However, this is not the case for rough terrain that contains many slopes inside. The optimized route having a lot of raising edges is not optimized in term of energy, when comparing with the route containing the falling or flatting edges. Although the distance is equal, the energy is totally different. This is due to the fact that the mobile robot uses energy, or electrical power, to drive the motors. Therefore, in rough terrain environment, the optimization in term of shortest distance is not the same as energy, particularly for the raising edge. This will be verified and compared in section 4.

As the coordination between nodes i and j is different from the flat terrain, the Euclidean distance d_{ij} in the rough terrain can be defined by equation (11) instead.

$$d_{ij} = \sqrt{(x_i - x_j)^2 + (y_i - y_j)^2 + (z_i - z_j)^2} . \tag{11}$$

The parameter x, y, and z are the coordinate of nodes in rough terrain environment, where z represents the height of each node. Thus, the total distance in rough terrain is also given by equation (12).

$$d_{T_{ij}} = \sum d_{r_{ij}} + \sum d_{l_{ij}} + \sum d_{f_{ij}}. \tag{12}$$

3.2   Energy Consumption Model

As mentioned in section 3.1, the mobile robot traverses along the path by using motors that consume energy in term of electrical power. The motors transform electrical energy into mechanical energy. The power consumption of the motors is the sum of the mechanical output power and the transforming loss [10]. The motion power can be modeled as the function of speed, acceleration, and mass, as defined by equation (13).

$$p_m(m, v, a) = p_l + m(a + g\mu)v. \tag{13}$$

The p_m is the motion power in watts (W) and p_l is the transforming loss. The parameter m in (13) is the robot's mass, and μ is the ground friction constant. The variable v is the speed of mobile robot, a is the acceleration, and g is the gravity constant. The term $m(a + g\mu)$ is a traction force. Thus, when the robot traverses, the output mechanical power can be found in term of $m(a + g\mu)v$.

4   Experiment and Result Discussion

4.1   Experimental Set

The experiment is set to verify and compare the results between the ACO algorithm and the adapted ACO algorithm for searching the energy-efficient route in rough terrain environment by using equations and models in section 2 and 3. We imitate the problem as the TSP domain but include coordinate z for the height of each node, as in (11). The two random groups are generated for 50 nodes and 100 nodes representing the cities in TSP.

The group of 50 nodes includes coordinates x, y in the range of 1-80 m and coordinate z in the range of 1-3 m. This z range represents the low, middle, and high levels of terrain. The coordinates x, y, z are used to find the distance d_{ij} in (11) and (8). Then, the time t' is generated in the range of 10-100 minutes, which is used to find the speed v in (8). The group of 100 nodes is created in similar manner with 1-1,000 m for coordinates x, y, 1-3 m for z, and 100-1,000 minutes for t'. The start pheromone on the paths is 0.001. The parameter Q and α are set to 1, and the β is equal to 2. In the experiment, the number of ants employed is equal to the number of nodes, as in [5] and [9].

In each round of the experiment, the ant is released for 1,000 times to observe the result [11]. The experiment is repeated 100 times to find the optimized result in terms of distance and energy consumption in (13). In our experiment, the transforming loss p_l is considered insignificant and set to 0. The mass of robot m is normalized to 1 kilogram (kg). The acceleration a is set to 1 for the rising edge d_r, -1 for the falling edge d_l, and 0 for the flatting edge d_f, respectively. These values reflect the constant acceleration on rising and falling edge, including the constant speed on fatting edge. The ground friction constant is 0.8 for the rubber wheel. The results will be used to compare in terms of optimized distance and energy in the rough terrain environment.

4.2   Experimental Result and Discussion

Fig. 2 and Fig. 3 show the optimized distances resulting from the simulation experiment for 50 and 100 nodes, respectively. Fig. 2 (a), (c), (e) and Fig. 3 (a), (c), (e) express the result in x-y plane, or flat terrain. Fig. 2 (b), (d), (f) and Fig. 3 (b), (d), (f) show the result in x-y-z plane indicating the terrain slopes. Fig. 2 (a) and Fig. 3 (a) express the optimized distance from the ACO using the distance as the weighting factor. Fig. 2 (c), (e) and Fig. 3 (c), (e) express the optimized distance from the adapted ACO using the speed and the speed with distance as the weighting factors. Table 1 summarizes the optimized distances resulting from the routes in Fig. 2 and 3. Table 2 expresses the motion paths generated in rough terrain environment for the 50 and 100 nodes. Table 3 shows the energy consumption resulting from the optimized distances and routes in x-y plane and x-y-z plane for the 50 and 100 nodes.

The optimized distances in Table 1 are used to calculate the energy consumption in term of power in (13) by counting the number of edges in Table 2. The results are expressed in Table 3. As in Table 1, the adapted ACO using the speed with distance weighting factor provides better optimized distance than the conventional ACO, i.e., 541.390 m and 11,311.50 m for 50 and 100 nodes, respectively. However, for the speed weighting factor, the result is worse. When considering in term of energy optimization in Table 3, the adapted ACO using the speed with distance weighting factor yields better result for the x-y plane, i.e., 6.954 w and 12.864 w, respectively. Again, the result is worse for the speed weighting factor. When considering the x-y-z plane, the adapted ACO also gives better energy optimization than the x-y plane in case of speed with distance weighting factor, i.e., 6.799 w and 12.428 w, respectively. However, the conventional ACO provides better energy results in the x-y-z plane than the adapted ACO for 50 nodes, i.e., 6.658 w.

The results implied that, in the x-y plane, the motion path is considered as the flat terrain. The acceleration on each path among the nodes is equal to 0 in this case. Therefore, the speed is constant for all paths and the power consumption in (13) is directly depended on the distance, as the relationship expressed in (8). As the result, the energy consumption of mobile robot by using the adapted ACO is better for the speed with distance weighting factor.

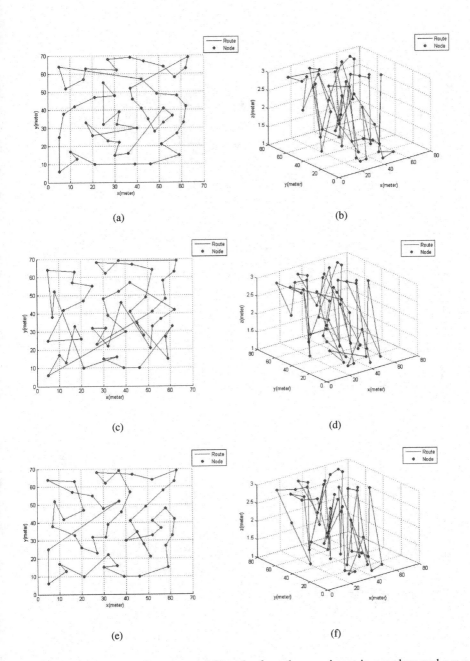

Fig. 2. The optimized, or best, route of 50 nodes from the experiment in x-y plane and x-y-z plane. (a) and (b) from the distance weighting factor. (c) and (d) from the speed weighting factor. (e) and (f) from the speed with distance weighting factors.

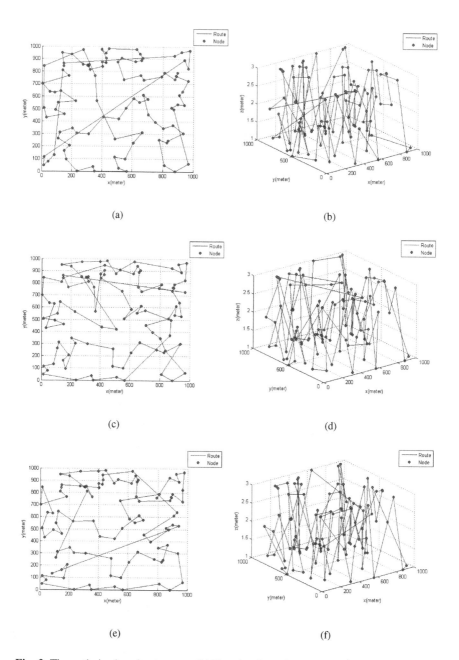

(a)

(b)

(c)

(d)

(e)

(f)

Fig. 3. The optimized, or best, route of 100 nodes from the experiment in x-y plane and x-y-z plane. (a) and (b) from the distance weighting factor. (c) and (d) from the speed weighting factor. (e) and (f) from the speed with distance weighting factors.

Table 1. Summary of the optimized distances for 50 and 100 nodes

Type	Weighting factor	Best distance (m)	
		50-node	100-node
ACO	Distance	542.023	11,639.20
Adapted ACO	Speed	711.900	12,163.88
	Speed + distance	541.390	11,311.50

Table 2. Motion paths in rough terrain environment

Type	Weighting factor	Number of falling, raising, and flatting edges					
		50-node			100-node		
		d_l	d_r	d_f	d_l	d_r	d_f
ACO	Distance	16	14	20	34	33	33
Adapted ACO	Speed	16	15	19	32	33	35
	Speed + distance	19	16	15	33	33	34

Table 3. Energy consumption from the routes in x-y plane and x-y-z plane

Type	Weighting factor	Power (w)			
		50-node		100-node	
		x-y plane	x-y-z plane	x-y plane	x-y-z plane
ACO	Distance	6.979	6.658	13.024	12.891
Adapted ACO	Speed	6.733	6.980	12.768	14.114
	Speed + distance	6.954	6.799	12.864	12.428

For the x-y-z plane, the motion path is similar to the rough terrain. In this case, the power consumption in (13) is relied not only on the speed but also the acceleration of mobile robot in each path. Consequently, the acceleration in rough terrain is depended on the number of slopes in the motion paths, as in Table 2. Therefore, the adapted ACO could yield better result for energy optimization, or the energy-efficient route, if there is a few rising edges in the path. As the result, the adapted ACO could not provide the optimized energy when comparing with the ACO in 50 node case. Furthermore, there is no local information related to the rough terrain included in the adapted ACO for weighting as well. However, the results expressed that the adapted ACO could provide the optimized energy in the rough terrain but could not be applied in general. This is due to the slopes inside the terrain that required more power of mobile robot to drive the motors.

5   Conclusion

This paper presented the adapted ACO algorithm used to search the energy-efficient route of mobile robot in rough terrain environment, in comparison with the conventional ACO algorithm. The background of both ACO algorithms was explained, including the TSP used. The motion path of mobile robot representing the slopes in rough terrain environment was modeled, including the energy consumption in term of electrical power. The experiment was also set by applying the TSP to verify the optimization results in terms of distance and energy for comparison between the conventional ACO and the adapted ACO.

The result of experiment expressed that the adapted ACO could provide the optimized distance and energy better than the ACO in flat terrain. For the rough terrain, the adapted ACO also yielded better optimized energy, or energy-efficient route, than the flat terrain. However, it depended on the factor of slopes inside that the mobile robot required more electrical power to drive the motors. There was also no local information related to the rough terrain counted for weighting. Thus, the optimized result of adapted ACO could not be comparable with the ACO in some case. In our future work, the rough terrain factors will be studied and used to adjust the adapted ACO algorithm for further improvement.

References

1. Hlaing, Z.C.S.S., Khine, M.A.: An Ant Colony Optimization Algorithm for Solving Traveling Salesman Problem. In: International Conference on Information Communication and Management, pp. 54–59 (2011)
2. Gambardella, L.M., Dorigo, M.: Ant-Q: A reinforcement learning to the traveling salesman problem. In: 12th International Conference on Machine Learning, Tahoe City, CA, pp. 252–260 (1995)
3. Gammbardella, L.M., Dorigo, M.: Solving Symmetric and Asymmetric TSPs by Ant Colonies. In: IEEE Conference on Evolutionary Computation, pp. 622–627 (1996)
4. Cong, Y.Z., Ponnambalam, S.G.: Mobile Robot Path Planning using Ant Colony Optimization. In: IEEE/ASME International Conference on Advanced Intelligent Mechatronics, pp. 851–856 (2009)
5. Chang, H.J., Lee, C.S.G., Lu, Y.H., Hu, Y.C.: Energy-time-efficient Adaptive Dispatching Algorithms for Ant-like Robot Systems. In: IEEE International Conference on Robotics and Automation, pp. 3294–3299 (2004)
6. Wongwirat, O., Anuntachai, A.: Searching Energy-Efficient Route for Mobile Robot with Ant Algorithm. In: International Conference on Control, Automation and Systems, pp. 1072–1075 (2011)
7. Artit, S.: Computational Intelligence, 1st edn., Suranaree U, Nakronrajchasrima (2009)
8. Dorigo, M., Birattari, M., Stutzle, T.: Ant Colony Optimization: Artificial Ant as a Computational Intelligence Technique. IRIDIA Technical report Series, University Libre De Bruxelles, Belgium (2006)
9. Dorigo, M.: The Ant System: Optimization by a Colony of Cooperating Agents. IEEE Transactions on Systems, Man, and Cybernetics Part B, Cybernetics 26(2), 1–13 (1996)
10. Mei, Y., Lu, Y.H., Hu, Y.C., Lee, C.S.G.: Deployment of Mobile Robot with Energy and Timing Constraints. IEEE Transactions on Robotics 22(3), 507–522 (2006)
11. Yoshikawa, M., Nagura, T.: Adaptive Ant Colony Optimization Considering Intensification and Diversification. In: International MultiConference of Engineer and Computer Scientists, vol. 1, pp. 200–203 (2009)

Real-Time Recognizing Human Hand Gestures

Alberto Cavallo

Dipartimento di Ingegneria dell'Informazione
Seconda Università di Napoli
via Roma 29, 81031 Aversa, Itay
alberto.cavallo@unina2.it

Abstract. The development of a system for classifying and interpreting human hands motion is considered in this paper. This is obtained by locally approximating motion data with rank-1 structures. The approximation is obtained in two steps: first the time series is decomposed into simpler sub-series (segmentation), then each subseries labelled by a unique vector.

The effectiveness of the proposed strategy is shown on sensory data from a data-glove when a human picks a tin can and a pencil. The strategy proves to be simple and reliable, even in the presence of unknown data corrupted by noise, and can be used as a basis for real-time automated recognition and interpretation of human gesture.

Keywords: Data segmentation, Features classification, Motion interpretation, Singular value decomposition, Gesture recognition.

1 Introduction

Detecting and interpreting human motion automatically from sensory data is a challenging and intriguing issue. Applications include different fields as security (surveillance), medical (physical damages detection), sport (optimized athlete training), support for impaired (lipreading, sign language interpretation), computer animation and, of course, prosthetic [1–3]. During the years, different measurements have been added to images, as in the case of cyberglove [4, 5], where other features related to hand-anatomy are measured. The availability of different sensory data is highly desirable, but also leads to the problem of data synchronization and data fusion. However, in many human hand motion activities data are strongly correlated due to coordination, kinematic and anatomical constraint [6]. This motivates the search of simple approximation, at least locally, of the time series. It is reasonable to model the whole time series as a sequence of simpler and smoother subsequences (data "segments" or "elementary actions"), that can be assembled together to reconstruct the original time series.

Thus, the notion of "elementary actions" arises naturally from the data. Moreover, each data segment can be given a label (classification of elementary actions). A taxonomy and a dictionary of elementary actions result from these operations, defining the knowledge-base of an automatic motion interpretation

C.-Y. Su, S. Rakheja, H. Liu (Eds.): ICIRA 2012, Part III, LNAI 7508, pp. 205–215, 2012.
© Springer-Verlag Berlin Heidelberg 2012

machine (see also [7] for a similar approach). A possible application of this strategy is to define and assemble elementary trajectories an anthropomorphic robot must follow to imitate human actions.

Usually, time segmentation is based on data time derivative [7, 8]: roughly speaking local minima of the velocity [9] are sought, and the data are segmented accordingly. This approach however presents two drawbacks: first, the data must be carefully synchronized to be coherently classified; second, same actions performed with different speed may be classified as different actions, unless a suitable (and rather critical) time scaling is performed.

On the contrary, the approach presented in this paper is unsensitive to time, hence repetitions of the same action executed by different subjects (with different speed and personal style) can be usefully employed as different realizations of the same action, reinforcing the learning phase during build-up of the dictionary.

Another possibility for automatic segmentation comes from the local approximation of the time series with simpler data structures, e.g., piecewise linear local approximations, as in [10], or polynomial approximations, as in [11]. However, in the cited papers only monovariate time series are considered, while in the proposed approach multivariate time series are addressed. Also in [12] only monovariate time series are considered, but the problem of segmentation and classification are considered *together*, that is an effective approach, from our point of view.

Recognition and classification of hand gestures in real-time have been investigated in [13], where Recursive Neural Networks (RNN) both continuous and discrete, are considered and compared. The authors of [13] find a best solution in mixing information from RNN and the continuous version of the HMM. In [13] a set of 5 gestures had to be recognized, and the focus was on generalization, so that the same gesture performed in different ways (e.g., by different actors) could be recognized as the same gesture. All the above strategies are rather complex and cannot be used for online classification or interpretation of time series.

Recently, an automated strategy for both segmentation and classification based on the use of the Singular Value Decomposition (SVD) has been proposed and applied to the classification of human hand movements [14, 15]. This paper goes on the direction of [14, 15], and proposes further developments.

2 Mathematical Preliminaries

It is well known that any matrix $A \in \mathbb{R}^{n \times m}$ with rank $r \leq \min(n, m) = m$ has a Singular Value Decomposition $A = U\Sigma V^{\mathrm{T}}$, where

$$U = (u_1, \ldots, u_n), V = (v_1, \ldots, v_m), \tag{1}$$

are square orthogonal matrices with u_i and v_i column vectrs and Σ is a $n \times m$ matrix with only r nonzero, positive elements on the main diagonal (singular values, σ_i), all the other entries being zero.

The following Theorems have been proved in [14, 15] and are here reported without proof for the sake of clarity. They are useful to quickly update the computation of singular values when only one row is appended to (or removed from) a given matrix.

Theorem 1. *Consider a matrix $A \in \mathbb{R}^{n \times m}$ and let $A = U \Sigma V^{\mathrm{T}}$ be its SVD. Consider a vector $0 \neq a \in \mathbb{R}^{m}$ and let*

$$\tilde{A} = \begin{pmatrix} A \\ a^{\mathrm{T}} \end{pmatrix}. \tag{2}$$

Then the singular values $\tilde{\sigma}_i$, $i = 1, \ldots, m$ of $\tilde{A}$ have the "forward interlacing" property

$$\sigma_1 \leq \tilde{\sigma}_1 < \sqrt{\sigma_1^2 + \|a\|^2} \tag{3}$$

$$\sigma_i \leq \tilde{\sigma}_i \leq \sigma_{i-1}, \qquad i = 2, \ldots, m \tag{4}$$

and the right singular vectors of $\tilde{A}$ are

$$\tilde{v}_i = \frac{\bar{v}_i}{\|\bar{v}_i\|}, \quad \bar{v}_i = V \left(\Sigma^2 - \tilde{\sigma}_i^2 I \right)^{-1} V^{\mathrm{T}} a. \tag{5}$$

Theorem 2. *With the same notation as Theorem 1, let the matrix $\hat{A}$ to be obtained from A by removing the first row a^{T}. Then the singular values $\hat{\sigma}_i$, $i = 1, \ldots, m$ of $\hat{A}$ have the "backward interlacing" property*

$$\sigma_{i+1} \leq \hat{\sigma}_i \leq \sigma_i, \qquad i = 1, \ldots, m - 1 \tag{6}$$

$$0 \leq \hat{\sigma}_m \leq \sigma_m \tag{7}$$

and the right singular vectors of $\hat{A}$ are

$$\hat{v}_i = \frac{\check{v}_i}{\|\check{v}_i\|}, \quad \check{v}_i = V \left(\Sigma^2 - \hat{\sigma}_i^2 I \right)^{-1} V^{\mathrm{T}} a. \tag{8}$$

As suggested by Theorems 1 and 2, the singular values of a matrix when a row is appended *or* deleted can be computed very quickly and efficiently by simply employing a bisection algorithm to the scalar function $f(\lambda) = \det(\lambda I - A^{\mathrm{T}} A)$. Although it is possible to merge the two Theorems into a single one considering simultaneously adding and removing a row, this would cause the loss of the very important interlacing property, and the computational simplicity of always having *only one* singular value in a known interval would be lost. By resorting to well-known properties of the bisection algorithm it is easy to give an estimate of the number of required iterations for a prescribed absolute or relative error of the estimated singular value [15], and the update can be done in real time.

3   Segmentation

Suppose that at the generic time instant t, n samples of m-dimensional data x have been collected into a $n \times m$ matrix

$$X(t) = \begin{pmatrix} x^{\mathrm{T}}(t - n + 1) \\ x^{\mathrm{T}}(t - n + 2) \\ \vdots \\ x^{\mathrm{T}}(t) \end{pmatrix} \tag{9}$$

with $t \geq n$.

Now we define a "segmentation index", i.e., a function depending on the data such that its value is below a given threshold when the data belong to a unique elementary action. Thus, the criterion for segmenting a block of data is to check wether the current value of the segmentation index $J(t)$ exceeds a prescribed threshold θ.

3.1   Segmentation Index 1

It is well known that the truncated SVD dyadic expansion of a matrix $A \in \mathbb{R}^{n \times m}$

$$A_q = \sum_{i=1}^{q} u_i \sigma_i v_i^{\mathrm{T}}, \ q < r. \tag{10}$$

has the well-known property of approximating the matrix A with prescribed error $\|A - A_q\|_2 = \sigma_{q+1}$, where $\| \cdot \|_2$ is the induced 2-norm.

Thus, the second singular value is the absolute error in approximating a matrix with the first term of the dyadic expansion, and the ratio second-to-first singular value is the relative error:

$$\frac{\sigma_2}{\sigma_1} = \frac{\|A - u_1 \sigma_1 v_1^{\mathrm{T}}\|_2}{\|A\|_2}. \tag{11}$$

This suggests a segmentation index J_1

$$J_1(t) = \frac{\sigma_2(t)}{\sigma_1(t)}, \ t = \tau, \tau + 1, \ldots, \tag{12}$$

where τ is any starting index of the time sequence and $\sigma_1(t)$, $\sigma_2(t)$ are the first two singular values of the matrix $X(t)$ in eqn. (9). The starting index τ is a further degree of freedom.

3.2   Segmentation Index 2

A second segmentation strategy is derived from the first and is aimed to further reduction of the computational burden. Basically, the idea is that instead of computing the singular values, it is easier to compute the sum of the squared singular values, which is simply the trace of the matrix $A^{\mathrm{T}}A$.

Since

$$\mathrm{tr}(A^{\mathrm{T}}A) - \sigma_1^2 = \sum_{i=2}^{m} \sigma_i^2 \leq (m-1)\sigma_2^2 \tag{13}$$

one has

$$\frac{1}{m-1}\left(\frac{\mathrm{tr}(A^{\mathrm{T}}A)}{\sigma_1^2} - 1\right) \leq \frac{\sigma_2^2}{\sigma_1^2} \leq \frac{\mathrm{tr}(A^{\mathrm{T}}A)}{\sigma_1^2} - 1 \tag{14}$$

Thus a possible segmentation index is

$$J_2(t) = \sqrt{\frac{\mathrm{tr}(X^{\mathrm{T}}(t)X(t))}{\|X^{\mathrm{T}}(t)X(t)\|} - 1} \tag{15}$$

It is clear that the indices coincide when the sum of the higher singular values is small related to the first two. Note that this index is simpler from the computational point of view, since only the first singular value has to be computed.

Obviously, the square root and the subtraction of one may be avoided in order to further simplify computation, but expression (15) simplifies the interpretation of the index as a relative error, thus simplifying the selection of the threshold θ.

3.3   Data Accumulation Strategy

Some considerations are now in order on the selection of the number of rows of the data matrix $X(t)$ at each time instant t. Basically, two are the possibilities: either fix the number of rows n, and at each step append a new row, while removing the first according to a FIFO strategy; or accumulate data by simply appending the current data to the matrix until the threshold is exceeded, then reset the data matrix. In the first strategy, a "sliding window" is applied to the data, and the procedure has a sort of "fading memory", so it is devoted to temporal changes in the data structure. The latter strategy results into matrices of different size for each segment and is suitable when outliers and noisy data are present, due to the robustness properties of the SVD[1].

4   Classification and Implementation Issues

Having defined data segments, the next step is to assign the segment a single (and unique) identifier, as can be a singular vector that uniquely identifies the segment.

In the case of human motion classification, it is important that the training data are as "natural" as possible, so as to confer the procedure the highest degree of generality when human movement have to be detected and recognized. Thus, different human trainees are used, executing the same operations with different speed and style. With traditional approaches, different execution speed would require data synchronization, e.g., by detecting reference points in data (e.g., extremal values) where to align signals. Obviously, this would prevent real-time operations, data have to be treated off-line, unless time duration of the series is accurately constrained, thus resulting in unnatural maneuvres. On the contrary, with the proposed strategy only the right singular vectors have to be averaged, or, more generally, clustered.

In order to cluster left-singular vectors for same maneuvres executed by different actors, a k-means clustering [16] strategy has been used, where the number of cluster centers, k is selected as the number of data segment, at the most (some segments could be repeated, thus using less clusters makes sense). This also gives an upper bound on the number of clusters and can be used in conjunction with techniques for choosing the optimal number of clusters.

---

[1] Note that if the "sliding window" approach is used, *all* the eigenvalues have to be computed, since after row removal according to Theorem 2 the lower bound for the updated i-th eigenvalue requires the knowledge of the old $(i + 1)$-th eigenvalue.

The following algorithm can be used to obtain segmentation and classification of actions using the proposed approach in the resetting version. The algorithm works with any of the proposed segmentation indices.

Algorithm 1. *Segmentation and classification of actions (resetting version).*

- *Step 0: Initialization. Select a segmentation index J_i, $i \in \{1, 2\}$ and a threshold $\theta > 0$; let $t = 1$;*
- *Step 1: New segment. Store the first data vector $x(t)$ in the $1 \times m$ matrix $X(t)$. $\sigma_1(t) = \|x(t)\|$, $\sigma_i(t) = 0$, $i > 1$. Let $J_i(t) = 0$.*
- *Step 2: Input. Increase t by 1; read a new data $x(t)$.*
- *Step 3: Update. Append the new data to the matrix $X(t)$; update the singular values and singular vectors of $X(t)$ by using Theorem 1 if J_1 has been selected, only the first singular value and the trace if J_2 has been chosen.*
- *Step 4: Check and repeat. If $J_i(t) < \theta$ go to Step 2.*
- *Step 5: End segment. The complete segment is the set of data from the initial to the current one; classification complete; the current first right singular vector "labels" uniquely the elementary action.*
- *Step 6: Resetting and new segment. Increase t by 1 and go to Step 1.*

In the above algorithm the right singular value representative of the data segment is that of the last block of data.

As far as the sliding widow strategy is concerned, the last parameter to be discussed is the windows length n, whose choice is far from trivial. Roughly speaking, it is clear that too long a window reduces sensitivity of segmentation, while too short reduces robustness to outliers and noise.

The following algorithm describes the windowing strategy.

Algorithm 2. *Segmentation and classification of actions (windowing version).*

- *Step 0: Initialization. Select the length n of the SVD window, an index J_i, $i \in \{1, 2\}$, a threshold $\theta > 0$; let $t = n$; accumulate the first n data in the $n \times m$ matrix $X(n)$ and compute the SVD $X^T(t)X(t) = V(t)\Sigma^2(t)V^T(t)$.*
- *Step 1: Input. Increase t by 1; read a new data $x(t)$.*
- *Step 2: Update. Append the new data to the matrix $X(t)$; update the squared singular vales and singular vectors according to Theorem 1; remove the first row from the matrix $X(t)$; update the SVD according to Theorem 2.*
- *Step 3: Check and repeat*
    - *Step 3.1: if $J_i(t) < \theta$ and $J_i(t-1) > \theta$, Start segment: store t as the beginning of a new segment;*
    - *Step 3.2: if $J_i(t) \geq \theta$ and $J_i(t-1) < \theta$, End segment; go to Step 4.*
    Go to Step 1.
- *Step 4: Segmentation complete; the complete segment is the set of data from the beginning (Step 3.1) to the current one (Step 3.2); classification complete; the current first right singular vector identifies the elementary action;*
- *Step 5: go to Step 1.*

Note that in the above algorithm, only the last n data contribute to classification. This has the advantage of storing always a prescribed number of samples. If a variable number of samples is desired, e.g., in order to increase robustness, it is possible to compute the singular vectors from the initial sample defined in Step 3.1 to the final one in Step 3.2.

5 Case Study

The experimental set-up used in this paper is devoted to the real-time analysis of hand gestures. The objective is recognition of two actions, i.e., the act of grasping a tin can and grasping a pen.

For the captures a performer wears a glove of non-reflective material (i.e., black lycra). The device configuration consist of 18 markers attached to the glove: 3 markers for each finger and 3 markers for a base reference system located on the back of the hand, as shown in Fig. 1.

Fig. 1. Data-glove

Each marker gives $3D$ data so, $n = 54$ features have been used for the characterization of the entire set of movements. After the phases of system calibration and subject calibration, global coordinates can be obtained at about 60 frames per second for any motion.

The use of five cameras (Vicon cameras and the related Vicon iQ Workstation software) allowed us to derive a set of data that are independent of the orientation of the hands with respect to the cameras. Indeed, if less cameras are used out-of-plane rotations may destroy the accuracy of gesture recognition [13]. Missing data due to occlusions are roughly reconstructed by means of interpolation. Also high-frequency unwanted vibrations of the hand are filtered out by using a low-pass filter. The data from the reference system are only used for frame compensation and are not used in segmentation and classification. Thus, after pre-filtering phase they are discarded, and only 45 features are retained for the algorithm (i.e. data related to the markers on the fingers). Sampling rate is 60Hz.

In a first set of experiments the action of grasping and releasing a tin can is considered. By using one of the two proposed algorithms, the motion is segmented into different primitives. The value of $\theta = 4\%$ has been preliminarily found by looking for a compromise between accuracy and number of segment produced (the smaller the relative error, the more the number of segments).

The same action is repeated four times by different operators (Datasets 1 to 4) in order to increase generalization capability. For each execution, the segmentation algorithm is used, and segments and first singular vectors are stored. Then a whole data matrix V_0 is formed from the first singular vectors for each segment and each execution, and finally a k-means clustering is applied to V_0, producing *prototypes* for each elementary action. Then each segment is classified according to the closest prototype. The selected number of cluster is $k = 3$, based on physical considerations, although optimal clustering strategies may be applied.

In order to test the windowing approach, a window of length $n = 45$ samples is considered. The results of this strategy are presented in Fig. 2 (left).

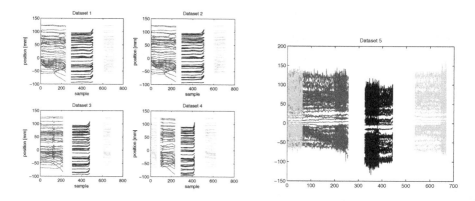

Fig. 2. Segmentation of four repetitions of can grasping (windowing, index J_1) and validation

In the figure, different colors denote different elementary actions, namely: object approaching, hand half-closed (red), object holding, hand closed (black) and object released, hand open (yellow). Note the presence of "gaps" due to transition between adjacent clusters. Finally, different executions of the same maneuver may be composed of different elementary action, especially those related to "rest", which is very reasonable from a physical point of view (see Dataset 4 in Fig. 2, left). The result makes sense, even though it has been obtained without human intervention.

In order to validate the effectiveness of the proposed strategy, a *new* dataset is presented to the classifier, and the classification capability is validated. Moreover, a Gaussian noise with zero mean and standard deviation equal to 10% the maximum absolute value for each signal is added on each sensor. The result of

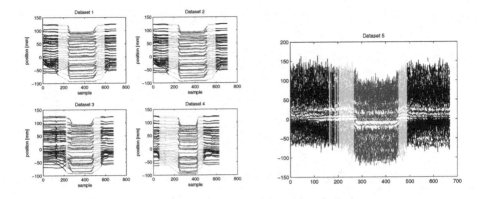

Fig. 3. Segmentation of four repetitions of can grasping (resetting strategy, index J_2) and validation

the classification is shown in Fig. 2 (right). Note that, due to the noise, the gap between elementary action may vary.

Next, the resetting strategy is tested. By using the segmentation index J_2 and the same repetitions of the can grasping, the results in Fig. 3 (left) are obtained.

Again, colors denote different elementary actions (completely different from the previous ones, and the color code has changed). The physical interpretation of the resetting strategy is even simpler than the windowing. The elementary actions are: hand open (black), hand closing or opening (yellow), hand closed (red). Obviously, there is no gap in proposed classification. Moreover, opening and closing of the hand are the same elementary action, only with time reversed. Next, dataset 5 with Gaussian noise as above has been presented to the trained classifier, producing the results in Fig. 3 (right). Note that, due to the noise, some elementary actions may switch with relatively high frequency during transient phases. This confirms the relatively low robustness of the resetting strategy to noisy data.

Finally, the *global* discriminant capacity of the proposed approach has to be assessed. The proposed procedure is preliminarily applied to a different grasping action, namely the grasping of a pencil. Although the measured values have similar limits, the way the grasp is executed is different (e.g., small finger does not play any role in this case), thus different results are produced. Training phase produce results similar to the tin case, and is not reported here for brevity. A *complete* library of elementary actions is constructed by collecting the prototypes of elementary actions learned with the can and those learned with the pencil. Finally, a new pencil grasping is proposed to the classifier. Segmentation and first singular vectors are computed, and elementary actions are classified according to the closest prototype in the database. The result in Fig. 4 shows that both the correct segmentation and the correct elementary actions, from the set related to pencil grasping, are automatically selected.

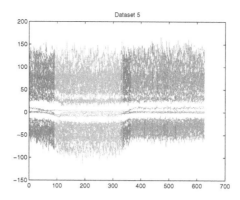

Fig. 4. Correctly recognized pencil grasping

6   Conclusions

In this paper a new approach to online data segmentation and classification has been presented. Segmentation refers to the capability to split blocks of data into atomic units, called elementary actions. Two different segmentation indices has been proposed, their possible usage in real-time discussed, along with their mathematical properties. Next, two different approaches to data acquisition have been considered. Algorithms have been presented for both strategies, and their properties discussed.

The methodology is applied to a different hand gestures, namely grasping of a tin can and of a pencil. The recognition capacity of the classifier is assessed even int he presence of noisy data. Work in progress deals with adding data from further sensors (e.g., force data) to recognize complex manipulation tasks.

References

1. Cédras, C., Shah, M.A.: Motion Based Recognition: A Survey. Image and Vision Computing 13(2), 129–155 (1995)
2. Buxton, H.: Learning and understanding dynamic scene activity: a review. Image Vision Comput. 21(1), 125–136 (2003)
3. Poppe, R.: A survey on vision-based human action recognition. Image Vision Comput. 28(6), 976–990 (2010)
4. Sturman, D.J., Zeltzer, D.: A Survey of Glove-based Input. IEEE Comput. Graph. Appl. 14(1), 30–39 (1994)
5. Kessler, G.D., Hodges, L.F., Walker, N., Neff: Evaluation of the CyberGlove as a whole-hand input device. ACM Trans. Comput.-Hum. Interact. 2(4), 263–283 (1995)
6. Santello, M., Flanders, M., Soechting, J.F.: Postural synergies for tool use. Journal of Neuroscience 18, 10105–10115 (1998)
7. Fod, A., Matarić, M.J., Jenkins, C.: Automated Derivation of Primitives for Movement Classification. Autonomous Robots 12, 39–54 (2002)

8. Gould, K., Rangarajan, K., Shah, M.: Detection and representation of events in motion trajectories. In: Gonzalez, Mahdavieh (eds.) Advances in Image Processing and Analysis. Optical Engineering Press (1992)

9. Nakazawa, A., Nakaoka, S., Shiratori, T., Ikeuchi, K.: Analysis and synthesis of human dance motions. In: Proc. of IEEE International Conference on Multisensor Fusion and Integration for Intelligent Systems, pp. 83–88 (2003)

10. Keogh, E., Chu, S., Hart, D., Pazzani, M.: An online algorithm for segmenting time series. In: Proceedings 2001 IEEE International Conference on Data Mining, pp. 289–296 (2001)

11. Fuchs, E., Gruber, T., Nitschke, J., Sick, B.: Online Segmentation of Time Series Based on Polynomial Least-Squares Approximations. IEEE Trans. on Pattern Analysis and Machine Intelligence 32(12), 2232–2245 (2010)

12. Wang, Z.J., Willett, P.: Joint segmentation and classification of time series using class-specific features. IEEE Transactions on Systems, Man, and Cybernetics, Part B, 1056–1067 (2004)

13. Ng, C.W., Ranganath, S.: Real-time gesture recognition system and application. Image and Vision Computing 20(13-14), 993–1007 (2002)

14. Cavallo, A.: Primitive Action Extraction for a Human Hand by using SVD. In: 9th IEEE International Symposium on Intelligent Systems and Informatics (SISY 2011), Subotica, Serbia (September 2011)

15. Cavallo, A.: Using SVD for Segmentation and Classification of Human Hand Actions. In: Tenth IEEE International Conference on Machine Learning and Applications (ICMLA 2011), Honolulu, Hawaii (December 2011)

16. Hastie, T., Tibshirani, R., Friedman, J.: The Elements of Statistical Learning: Data Mining, Inference, and Prediction. Springer (2003)

Safe Robot Learning by Energy Limitation

Sigurd Mørkved Albrektsen and Sigurd Aksnes Fjerdingen

Dept. of Applied Cybernetics, SINTEF ICT, Norway
{sigurd.morkved.albrektsen,sigurd.aksnes.fjerdingen}@sintef.no

Abstract. Online robot learning has been a goal for researchers for several decades. A problem arises when learning algorithms need to explore the environment as actions cannot easily be anticipated. Because of this, safety is a major issue when using learning algorithms.

This paper presents a framework for safe robot learning by the use of region-classification and energy limitation. The main task of the framework is to ensure safety regardless of a learning algorithm's input to a system. This is necessary to allow a learning robot to explore environments without damaging itself or its surroundings. To ensure safety, the state-space is divided into fatal, supercritical, critical and safe regions, depending on the energy of the system.

To show the adaptability of the framework it is used on two different systems; an actuated swinging pendulum and a mobile platform. In both cases obstacles with unknown locations must are avoided successfully.

1 Introduction

Taking advantage of knowledge about previous actions, and using this information to improve performance, is a task that researchers have tried to accomplish for decades. In robotics today, many applications make a robot perform the same task over and over again, following a preplanned trajectory. As long as the programmer's assumptions hold, and the environment is known, the robot will safely perform its task every time it executes. A problem here, however, is that the performance of this task would never improve, as the trajectory is never changed. To improve the performance of such systems one of two things are usually done. One approach is to specialize the used algorithm, and use much time and resources to perfect the movement manually so that a sufficiently good result for that specific task is reached. This is tedious and expensive and moves from a generalized solution that works on many different systems, towards a specialized solution that only works on very few systems. This increases the cost of introducing new products, as the specialization process must be repeated for every change of the system.

A more future oriented approach is to use robot learning that utilizes knowledge about previous experiences to gradually achieve better and better results. As robot learning systems must be able to explore the environment, it is difficult to ensure that the system will be able to perform its task, and that it will operate safely.

C.-Y. Su, S. Rakheja, H. Liu (Eds.): ICIRA 2012, Part III, LNAI 7508, pp. 216–225, 2012.
© Springer-Verlag Berlin Heidelberg 2012

This paper presents a framework that allows a combination of the best parts from the traditional approach and the robot learning approach. To be able to explore the environment, while still ensuring safe operation, is vital for a learning robotic system. If the exploration criteria are not fulfilled, the system can never improve its behavior, and if the safety criteria are not fulfilled the system might damage itself or its environment and will therefore not be accepted by industry. The approach in this paper consists of a framework that modifies the input so that safety is ensured independently of the system's original input.

The framework is then applied to two different cases that show the diversity of the approach: an inverse pendulum and a mobile platform. In both these cases obstacles must be avoided. The locations of the obstacles are not known before the algorithm executes, and they must be detected and then avoided if they are sufficiently close.

The rest of the paper is organized as follows: First, in section 2, the concepts of robot learning, *safe* robot learning are introduced in addition to a general presentation of the energy limitation framework. Then, the pendulum case and the moving platform case are presented in sections 3 and 4 respectively, along with results from simulations of each of the cases. A discussion of these results is found in section 5, and finally conclusive remarks and comments on future work are presented in section 6.

2   Safe Robot Learning

Robot learning is the process of using information from previously performed executions in combination with exploration to improve future results. Robot learning as a whole is often divided into two major disciplines: supervised learning, unsupervised learning. In supervised learning a human being will tell the robot if it is performing the correct action or not and thereby guide the robot through the learning phase. In unsupervised learning on the other hand, the robot has to be able to understand autonomously whether the performed action was correct or not.[1] There are also a division between offline and online learning. Offline learning is to first train an algorithm to act in a certain way when the system is in a certain state, while online learning is to learn more optimized approaches as the system executes. There also approaches that combines supervised and unsupervised learning (often referred to as semi-supervised learning[2]), and combination of offline learning and online learning.[3] As we focus on robots operating in unknown environments without human intervention, we will focus on online unsupervised learning for the rest of this paper.

Reinforcement learning is a popular robot learning approach where which is based on optimizing results from a reward function.[4] Reinforcement learning can be compared to training an animal, if the animal does what you want it to do, you give it a treat. The reward function is what defines the "treat" based on which action is performed in which state, and the algorithm tries to calculate how to get the most reward using a certain *policy*. The reward function is typically a measure of how well the system performs. For example "Have the system reached the goal state?" or "How far is the system from the goal state?". A policy is what defines which action to take in which state, and the policy can change multiple times during execution.

The two key elements of robot learning are *exploration* and *exploitation*. By exploring actions that have not been previously attempted, the algorithm can learn a new and improved way of solving the problem. When this improved solution of the problem is found, the algorithm exploits this solution to yield better results. There is a trade-off between exploration and exploitation. If an algorithm always explores, it will never utilize what it has learned, and if it never explores it does not learn anything new. Kaelbling et al. [5] points out that the longer the system will execute, the worse the consequences of converging to a sub-optimal result. Thus can the algorithm explore more if it is expected to execute for a longer period of time. Typically will an algorithm explore much in the initial phases of execution, and exploit more and more of the results when execution is finished. A problem with exploration when applied to robotic systems is that as the system has not previously attempted that exact execution, it can not necessarily guarantee that the new result is safe. This is where *safe* robot learning is needed.

The *safe* part of safe learning covers two topics: stable operation and operation that ensures that the robot does not damage the surrounding environment. There are several approaches to ensure safe operation in known environments, for example using Lyapunov analysis. A problem arises when a significant part of the environment is unknown before the robot starts execution of the control system. If this is the case the Lyapunov analysis can not guarantee safe operation without a very restrictive control scheme.

The idea behind the framework is to provide a safe arena where a learning algorithm can explore without endangering safety of the system, which is similar to what is done by Gillula et al.[6] Gillula et al. use a method where they define a *reachable set* where the system can act safely, and therefore explore safely, as long as it remains inside the set. Instead of using reachable sets, the framework presented in this paper is inspired by the safety function of Hans et al. [7]. Hans et al. give states one of the following labels: safe, critical, supercritical and fatal. A *fatal* state is a state where the system fails to operate correctly and might damage itself or its environment. A *supercritical* state is a state where no policy can guarantee that the system does not enter a fatal state. A *critical* state is a state which, depending on the input, can lead to a supercritical state, and a *safe* state is a state that is neither critical, supercritical nor fatal. This paper expands Hans's framework by creating safe, supercritical, critical and fatal *regions*, which do not have to be discrete and can be defined outside the Markov decision process (MDP) scheme used by Hans et al. These terms extend the work by Gillula et al., where an analogy would be to define the safe states as the states in the reachable sets, and the rest as critical.

To allow operation in unknown environments, another region type is created: the unknown region. This region must be treated as a critical region until it is detected by a sensor. Only then can the region be labeled as a definite "safe" or "critical" region.

The main task of the framework is to allow a learning algorithm to experiment in the environment, while still ensuring safety. The algorithm can then learn optimal parameters to improve execution using for example reinforcement learning. This allows Lyapunov based learning approaches such as that of Fjerdingen et al. [8] to operate in unknown environments.

The framework can be adapted to a variety of systems, and in this paper two example usages are shown: an inverse pendulum and a moving platform. The examples were chosen to show that the framework works with fundamentally different systems.

3   Case 1: Swinging Pendulum

The swinging pendulum case is a classical control engineering example where the goal is to move a pendulum pointing downwards to an upright position. It is an interesting case as it is a non-linear system with system dynamics that are easily described and therefore easily implemented. The control problem is, however, non-trivial. There are several variations of this problem based on for example the characteristics of the motor. If the motor is strong enough to move the pendulum from the downward position to the upright position in one swing the control problem is highly simplified.

In the case in this paper the parameters of the motor are chosen so that the pendulum needs several swings to increase its speed enough to get upright. In addition, an obstacle is placed at an unknown position. To detect the obstacle, the pendulum is equipped with a sensor that gives a response when the pendulum is closer than θ_d to an obstacle. The sensor is binary, so it can only detect if there is an obstacle closer than θ_d, not the distance to it.

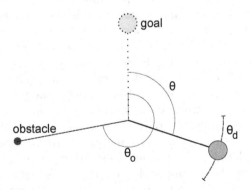

Fig. 1. The pendulum system with an obstacle on the left side, the angle shown as θ, the obstacle placement shown as θ_o and the detection distance shown as θ_d

The swinging pendulum consists of a ball with mass 1, connected to a frictionless actuator using a massless rod of length 1. The strength of gravity is set to 1 and there is no damping. The system dynamics are described as:

$$\ddot{\theta} = \sin(\theta) + u \qquad (1)$$

$$|u| < u_{max} \qquad (2)$$

As equation 1 shows, the control input u only affects the angular acceleration ($\ddot{\theta}$) directly. The control variable u is bounded by equation 2, hence the pendulum cannot stop instantaneously. The control problem is to find the appropriate u that swings the pendulum from a downward position to an upward position.

The energy function associated with the system, is the total mechanical energy of the system, i.e. the sum of the potential energy (E_p) and kinetic energy (E_k):

$$E_k = \frac{1}{2}m\dot{\theta}^2, \quad E_p = mg(\cos(\theta) + 1), \quad E = E_k + E_p = \frac{1}{2}\dot{\theta}^2 + \cos(\theta) + 1 \quad (3)$$

To allow safe control of the pendulum using the presented framework, and to solve the control task, the following requirements need to be met: 1) the sensor detection distance must not be too short, 2) the environment must be static, 3) there must exist a trajectory from the starting-state to the goal state, and 4) the actuator must be sufficiently powerful. As the pendulum needs time to decrease the speed to a halt in the distance between the sensor and the obstacle, the detection distance must be sufficiently large. The environment, including the obstacle, must remain static, as the pendulum requires several swings to reach an upwards position, and the speed at the downward position must be higher the second time than the first. Assuming that these requirements hold, one can define a critical angular velocity (ω_{crit}) that the system cannot exceed when moving outside the known environment. The third requirement is to ensure that there are not obstacles on both sides of the pendulum, in which case the pendulum can not swing upright. The fourth requirement is necessary to ensure that the pendulum can swing up even if an obstacle is placed close to the downright position. The closer to the starting state an obstacle is placed, the more powerful the actuator needs to be to swing the pendulum upright. If not requirement 1 and 2 are fulfilled, safe control can not be ensured. If requirements 3 and 4 are not fulfilled, the control task is impossible, although safety is still assured.

Using the vocabulary introduced in section 2, the safety regions become as follows: A small area around the obstacle is defined as the fatal region, as the pendulum must avoid this region to ensure collision-free motion. Assuming that the obstacle is not placed at the pendulum's starting position, which would yield an infeasible problem, the starting position is marked as "safe". Every other state is marked as "unknown". Furthermore the state of moving out of a known region with a speed greater than on ω_{crit} is marked as supercritical, as the framework cannot guarantee that the pendulum stops before it crashes into an obstacle.

To ensure that the supercritical state is never reached, the framework must increase the maximal allowed energy ($E_{allowed}$) by sufficiently small steps. The

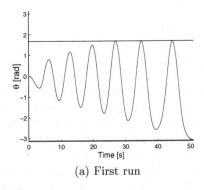
(a) First run

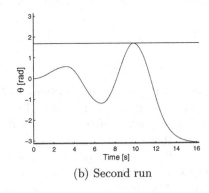
(b) Second run

Fig. 2. The figure shows the pendulum behaviour with an obstacle placed at $\theta_O = 0.65\pi \approx 2.04$. The obstacle spans 0.1 radians, so that it covers the area $[2.04 \pm 0.1]$, and the detection distance is set to 0.4. The lines above and below the graph show the maximal and minimal angles of the pendulum.

size of these energy increase steps depends on u_{max} and the detection distance, as the actuator must be able to break from ω_{crit} to a halt before it enters a fatal region. The increase in $E_{allowed}$ is performed every time the pendulum gains the maximal allowed energy in the left half plane. When an obstacle is detected, the energy of the system at that point (E_{crit}) is registered and the system's controller applies a maximal breaking force. That point now defines a critical region. This region cannot be entered with a greater energy than E_{crit}. If it would have done so, the framework could not guarantee that the pendulum would stop before hitting the obstacle, hence the system would have entered a supercritical region.

Figure 2 shows the output of an example run using a "modified energy ascent" (MEA) controller, presented by Perkins et al.[9]. Note that the y-scale has been modified to show 0 when the pendulum points downwards, and π at the goal to clarify the results. When the framework has identified the obstacle, it can use information about the maximal allowed energy to execute more efficiently in the same environment. This can be seen in figure 2, where the first reaches the goal position in 50.9203 seconds, while the second run reaches the same position in 16.2508 seconds. Note that the position never surpasses the detected safe position of 1.6843, which is well inside the interval $[2.04 - 0.1, 2.04 - 0.4]$.

4   Case 2: Mobile Platform

The mobile platform case consists of a platform that can move in a 2D-space. It has three degrees of freedom: position (x, y) and direction (θ), and two inputs: acceleration $(\dot{v})$ and angular velocity $(\dot{\theta})$.

The dynamics of the platform is described as:

$$\dot{x} = v \cdot \sin(\theta), \quad \dot{y} = v \cdot \cos(\theta)$$
$$\dot{v} = u_1, \quad \dot{\theta} = u_2 \tag{4}$$
$$0 \leq v \leq v_{max}, \quad |u_1| \leq u_{1,max}, \quad |u_2| \leq u_{2,max}$$

The goal of the platform is to move as fast as possible from a starting position to a given point in the 2D-space. Every point in the 2D-space is classified as either an obstacle or free space. Obstacles in the environment are static, and to detect these obstacles, the platform has an attached omnidirectional vision sensor with a limited range. To ensure safe operation, the platform cannot move faster than a certain speed. This speed depends on the detection distance of the sensor, and the maximal acceleration $u_{2,max}$. If the framework knows from prior experimentation that the area does not contain any obstacles, the speed can be increased.

The fatal regions in this case is to have a too high velocity towards an obstacle when the platform is close to it. Therefore, a maximal speed is set when the platform moves in an unknown environment, and the speed is increased when it moves in an area that it has visited earlier and marked as safe. For the framework be applicable, we need a certain sensor detection distance and static environment as in the previous case.

As we want to reduce the velocity when the platform is close to an obstacle, we define E_i as the energy associated with each obstacle obs_i, and the energy function is set to:

$$E_i = \begin{cases} E_{zero} + v_i/d_i & \text{if } obs_i \text{ is sufficiently close} \\ E_{zero} & \text{otherwise} \end{cases}$$

$$E = \begin{cases} \min(E_{zero} - d_c/v_c, 0) & \text{if the robot is in a safe region and } v_c > 0 \\ \min\left(\max_{i \in obs} E_i, \, E_{zero}\right) & \text{otherwise} \end{cases} \tag{5}$$

In equation 5, obs is the set of detected obstacles, and d_i is the distance between the mobile robot and obs_i. The variable v_i denotes the part of the robot's velocity in the direction towards obs_i. If the energy associated with any obstacle is greater than a given threshold (which depends on u_{max} and v_{max}), the framework limits the input so that the energy decreases. The variables d_c and v_c denote the distance to the closest critical region that the robot moves towards, and the velocity towards that region respectively. E_{zero} is introduced as a constant value, to keep the energy non-negative for all possible outcomes while still allowing the speed to be increased in safe areas.

The controller of the mobile platform the tries to regulate the system towards E_{zero} (a constant value that always keeps the energy of the system non-negative), so that if the robot is in a safe region, the velocity can be increased depending on d_c. As the maximal velocity of the platform is specified, a threshold is defined so

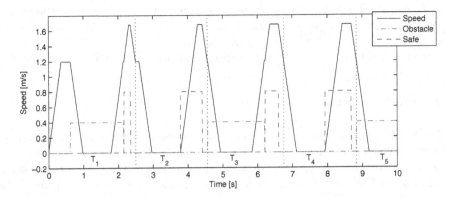

Fig. 3. A 1D-example of the worst case scenario where the platform moves at maximum speed towards an obstacle. The robot's speed, obstacle sensor and the area where the robot knows that it is safe are shown. The robot first moves toward an obstacle, then, at every T_n it turns 180°. Note that when the robot is safe (dashed line), the speed can increase to $v_{max,high}$, but when an obstacle is detected (the dash-dotted line), the speed is guaranteed to have decreased to $v_{max,default}$. The event when the robot is no longer exceeding $v_{max,default}$ is marked with a dotted vertical line.

that if d_c is larger than this threshold, a higher velocity ($v_{max,high}$) is allowed. If the platform is not in a safe region, the velocity is kept to the limit specified by E_{zero}, and if an obstacle is detected, the maximal allowed velocity is decreased to the default velocity ($v_{max,default}$). This behavior is shown in figure 3.

Figure 3 shows the robot's speed in the worst case scenario; where the robot runs at maximum speed towards an obstacle. The simulation consists of 5 steps, each ending with a 180° turn:

0 to T_1: The robot increases its speed to $v_{max,default}$, moves towards the obstacle, detects it and stops.

T_1 to T_2: The robot moves away from the obstacle. When the obstacle is no longer detected the robot knows that it is in a safe region and increases the speed. At approximately 2.5s the robot has moved to the start position, and as the region further away from the obstacle is unknown, the speed is slowed to the default max-value. At approximately 2.7s the robot stops and turns towards the obstacle.

T_2 to T_3: The robot moves towards the obstacle again. As the region from where it starts and to a given distance before the obstacle now is marked as safe, the speed is increased to $v_{max,high}$. When moving out of the safe region, the robot enters the worst case scenario; decreasing the speed from $v_{max,high}$ to $v_{max,default}$. Because of this, the obstacle is detected as the exact moment when the speed is decreased to $v_{max,default}$. As the speed of the robot has decreased to $v_{max,default}$ as the obstacle is detected, the rest of this step is equal to the first step.

T_3 to T_4: This is similar to the second step, but a larger part of the area is marked as safe. This is due to the fact that in step 2, the robot went further away from the obstacle than the start position.

T_4 to T_5: The robot increases the speed and stops before the obstacle.

5   Discussion

The results from section 3 and section 4 show that the energy limiting approach works well for the cases presented in this paper. In section 3 the pendulum never reaches the critical value and therefore avoids collision with the obstacle regardless of the input from the system's original controller. The results also show that when the obstacle handler has learned where the obstacles are, the framework allows efficient execution with very good results.

As can be seen from figure 3, the framework limits the maximal speed in the case of the moving platform as well. Even when it allows the speed to be increased when safety is assured, the platform always slows down enough to avoid obstacles. This is a feature that allows optimal behavior in safe cases, while still ensuring the safety of the system in difficult cases. The framework thus creates a safe, optimized arena which is vital when using learning algorithms.

There are, however, some limitations with this approach. Gillula et al. [6] mention, that calculating reachable sets in the general case suffers the "curse of dimensionality" - that is, it might be a challenging task to solve for large systems. This is true for the energy limitation approach presented in this paper as well, especially in cases where a loose lower-bound of the critical region is not good enough, such as navigation in a very narrow corridor.

Another limitation with the framework is that it might be difficult to detect that the system is in a critical state. This could be because the system is not aware of some hidden state in the system dynamics, or errors due to approximations. To compensate for such errors, the critical regions might be extended with a certain safety-margin, so that some of the safe region is marked at critical around hard limits. This could, however, lead to problems as the solution might lie on this border or even inside a critical region.

Although the approximation of the critical or safe regions might be looked upon as a limitation, upper or lower bounds of a system are often easier to find than tight bounds. In many systems one can use upper or lower bounds, instead of a tight bound, and still have sufficiently good results. The presented framework supports this approximation.

6   Conclusion

In this paper we have presented a framework for use with learning systems that ensures safety by limiting the allowed energy of the system. As learning systems need to explore the environment by acting in ways not yet attempted, the safety of the system might be compromised. As long as the presented framework is used properly, safety of the system is ensured and a learning algorithm can explore and optimize the results freely.

To classify the actions in different regions, safety terms are presented, and the appropriate actions in each of the regions are defined. This is done to clarify the safety of each state on another level of abstraction than the dynamic states provide directly, thus the control of the system is simplified.

The two implemented cases show that the framework works well with fundamentally different systems. This indicates that the safety-regions framework and the energy limitation concept are adaptable. As long as the energy is properly defined, the assumptions so that the framework knows how to handle the critical regions, safety is ensured for both of the cases. This allows a safe arena for a learning controller to explore.

As this framework now has been shown to work in simulations, real-life experiments are planned to be performed in near future for both cases. This will show how the framework will allow a robot to compensate for uncertainties for example from sensor data while still ensuring safety.

Further extensions to the framework are also planned. By allowing safe regions to only be valid for a certain amount of time, one can allow a slow-moving dynamic environment. The framework can also be extended to allow objects that move in specified patterns, such as with a linear speed, and then assign a special type of energy to these objects. We will also look into a more sparse representation of critical regions using estimators with convergence properties, to be able to efficiently handle big environments.

References

1. Connell, J.H., Mahadevan, S.: Introduction to Robot Learning. Springer (1993)
2. Olivier Chapelle, A.Z., Schölkopf, B.: Semi-Supervised Learning. The MIT Press (2006)
3. Gelly, S., Silver, D.: Combining online and offline knowledge in uct. In: Proceedings of the 24th International Conference on Machine Learning, ICML 2007, pp. 273–280. ACM, New York (2007)
4. Sutton, R.S., Barto, A.G.: Reinforcement learning. Journal of Cognitive Neuroscience 11(1), 126–130 (1999)
5. Kaelbling, L.P., Littman, M.L., Moore, A.W.: Reinforcement learning: A survey. Journal of Artificial Intelligence Research 4, 237–285 (1996)
6. Gillula, J.H., Tomlin, C.J.: Guaranteed safe online learning of a bounded system. In: IROS 2011, pp. 2979–2984 (September 2011)
7. Hans, A., Schneegaß, D., Schäfer, A.M., Udluft, S.: Safe exploration for reinforcement learning. In: European Symposium on Artificial Neural Network, pp. 143–148 (April 2008)
8. Fjerdingen, S.A., Kyrkjebø, E.: Safe reinforcement learning for continuous spaces through Lyapunov-constrained behavior. In: Frontiers in Artificial Intelligence and Applications, pp. 70–79 (May 2011)
9. Perkins, T.J., Barto, A.G.: Lyapunov design for safe reinforcement learning. J. Mach. Learn. Res. 3, 803–832 (2003)

Motion Recovery of Parallel Manipulators Using Task-Decomposition Approach

Vahid Nazari and Leila Notash

Department of Mechanical and Materials Engineering, Queen's University
Kingston, Canada
{nazariv,notash}@me.queensu.ca

Abstract. In this paper, the motion recovery of parallel manipulators is investigated. To achieve the desired performance, a failure recovery based on decomposing the task space of manipulator into the major and secondary subtasks is presented. The major subtasks are more important than the other subtasks and must be accomplished as precisely as possible. The secondary subtasks with less significance can be compromised to achieve secondary criteria such as optimizing measures of fault tolerance, singularity avoidance and obstacle avoidance. The task-decomposition approach minimizes the least square error of the vector of the major subtasks and at the same time optimizes the secondary criterion.

Keywords: Parallel manipulators, failure recovery, task space decomposition.

1 Introduction

Solid-link parallel manipulators, Fig. 1(a), are closed-loop mechanisms in which the mobile platform is connected to the base platform through a number of legs/branches. Each leg contains links and active and passive joints.

Failure is defined as any event in the components, subsystems or systems which makes the manipulator unable to perform its assigned function properly. When a joint is locked, it cannot move and as a result the failed joint is unable to contribute to the manipulator task. From the kinematics point of view, the failure recovery deals with retrieving the lost mobile platform motion due to failure in the manipulator through adjusting the velocity of the remaining joints. One approach in failure recovery of manipulators is incorporation of redundancy into design. By adding redundancy, the manipulator may still be able to perform its task even if one or more joints fail.

The failure recovery of parallel manipulators has been studied by a number of researchers. A methodology for investigating the effect of active joint failures on the force/moment (wrench) capabilities of parallel manipulators was presented in [1]. Criteria based on projecting the lost joint force/torque onto the orthogonal complement of the null space of the reduced Jacobian matrix were established to examine if the lost wrench due to failure of joints and actuators could be fully or partially retrieved. This

C.-Y. Su, S. Rakheja, H. Liu (Eds.): ICIRA 2012, Part III, LNAI 7508, pp. 226–235, 2012.
© Springer-Verlag Berlin Heidelberg 2012

methodology was also applied to wire-actuated parallel manipulators [2]. As well, the effect of the joint failure on the motion performance of parallel manipulators was investigated in [3], in which a methodology was presented for recovering the lost motion of the mobile platform due to zero or different/limited joint velocity. A recovery algorithm for both serial and parallel manipulators was proposed in [4] to reduce the internal shock when a failure occurs and to accomplish the continued trajectory tracking. Procedures for minimizing the jump in the norm of joint velocity vector of serial manipulators after single locked joint failure were presented in [5]. The velocity of the healthy joints was redistributed such that the mobile platform velocity jump was minimized. In [6] the degrees of freedom of platform were divided into those with higher importance as major degrees of freedom and those with less significance as secondary degrees of freedom. Based on the differential kinematics and static force models, the major subtasks were controlled as precisely as possible and at the same time the secondary goal was optimally achieved. The Moore-Penrose inverse of the Jacobian matrix was used to derive the active joint velocity vector and the unit inconsistency in the vector of the joint velocities was not taken into account. Furthermore, the condition in which the major subtasks were fully or partially accomplished was not discussed.

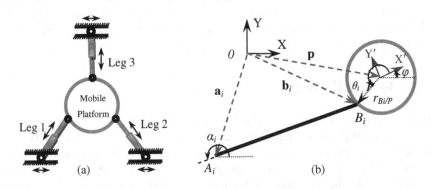

Fig. 1. (a) Planar parallel manipulator, (b) Parameters of planar parallel manipulator [3]

In this paper, the motion recovery of parallel manipulators for known locked joint failure using task space partitioning is studied. The differential kinematic model of the parallel manipulators is presented in Section 2. The failure recovery based on retrieving the lost motion of the mobile platform due to locked joint(s) reported in [3] is presented in Section 3. To improve the performance of the manipulator in retrieving the lost motion, the task space of the mobile platform is partitioned into the major and secondary subtasks in Section 4 so as to minimize the least square error of the major subtasks while optimizing the secondary criterion. The kinematic modeling of a planar parallel manipulator and simulation results are reported in Section 5. Finally, the conclusion and discussion is given in Section 6.

2   Differential Kinematics

For parallel manipulators, considering leg i with l active and passive joints, the $l \times 1$ joint velocity vector, ${}^i\dot{\mathbf{q}}$, and the mobile platform velocity vector, $\mathbf{V}$, are related by the $m \times l$ Jacobian matrix of the leg, ${}^i\mathbf{J}$, as [3]

$$\mathbf{V} = {}^i\mathbf{J}\ {}^i\dot{\mathbf{q}} = [\ {}^i\mathbf{J}_1 \quad {}^i\mathbf{J}_2 \quad \dots \quad {}^i\mathbf{J}_h \quad \dots \quad {}^i\mathbf{J}_{l-1} \quad {}^i\mathbf{J}_l\ ]\ {}^i\dot{\mathbf{q}} \tag{1}$$

where $l \geq m$. In redundant manipulators the Jacobian matrix ${}^i\mathbf{J}$ is not square, and hence, its generalized (Moore-Penrose) inverse, ${}^i\mathbf{J}^{\#} = {}^i\mathbf{J}^T ({}^i\mathbf{J}\ {}^i\mathbf{J}^T)^{-1}$, is used to solve for the joint velocity vector

$$ {}^i\dot{\mathbf{q}} = {}^i\mathbf{J}^{\#}\mathbf{V} + {}^i\widetilde{\mathbf{J}}\lambda \tag{2}$$

where ${}^i\widetilde{\mathbf{J}} = (\mathbf{I} - {}^i\mathbf{J}^{\#}\ {}^i\mathbf{J})$, $\mathbf{I}$ is an $l \times l$ identity matrix, λ is an arbitrary l-vector, the first term on the right-hand side of equation (2) is the minimum norm or particular solution to achieve the desired mobile platform velocity and the second term is the homogeneous solution that maps λ to the null space of ${}^i\mathbf{J}$.

One of the main challenges in redundant manipulators is that there are infinite solutions for joint velocities for a given mobile platform velocity. Hence, selecting a unique solution among infinite solutions is complicated and requires several considerations such as minimizing joint velocities, reliability enhancement, singularity avoidance, obstacle avoidance, optimizing fault tolerant measures and joint limit avoidance.

3   Failure Recovery

In this section, the effect of failure of active and/or passive joints on the motion performance of parallel manipulators reported in [3] is briefly reviewed. When a joint is locked, its velocity is zero which cannot contribute to the motion of the mobile platform. When joint h (active or passive) on leg i is locked, the mobile platform velocity will be different than the required value if the desired velocity of the failed joint is not zero. The velocity of the mobile platform after failure is calculated as

$$\mathbf{V}_f = {}^i\mathbf{J}\ {}^i\dot{\mathbf{q}}_f \tag{3}$$

where ${}^i\dot{\mathbf{q}}_f = [\ {}^i\dot{q}_1 \quad {}^i\dot{q}_2 \quad \dots \quad 0 \quad \dots \quad {}^i\dot{q}_{l-1} \quad {}^i\dot{q}_l\ ]^T$. If the desired velocity in joint h is not zero, the change in the mobile platform velocity will be $\Delta\mathbf{V}_f = \mathbf{V} - \mathbf{V}_f = {}^i\mathbf{J}\ ({}^i\dot{\mathbf{q}} - {}^i\dot{\mathbf{q}}_f) = {}^i\mathbf{J}_h\ {}^i\dot{q}_h$. ${}^i\mathbf{J}_h$ corresponds to column h of the Jacobian matrix for leg i and ${}^i\dot{q}_h$ is the desired velocity in joint h before the failure occurs. When joint h of leg i is locked, the velocity in the remaining healthy joints should be adjusted so as to compensate for the lost motion partially or completely. The correctional velocity is defined as

$$\Delta {}^i\dot{\mathbf{q}}_{corr} = [\Delta {}^i\dot{q}_1 \quad \Delta {}^i\dot{q}_2 \quad \dots \quad 0 \quad \dots \quad \Delta {}^i\dot{q}_{l-1} \quad \Delta {}^i\dot{q}_l]^T \tag{4}$$

where entry h is replaced by zero. For more than one locked joint, the entries of the vector of the correctional velocity corresponding to the failed joints are set to zero. Then the recovered velocity of the mobile platform will be [3]

$$V_r = {}^i J \, {}^i \dot{q}_f + {}^i J \Delta^i \dot{q}_{corr} = {}^i J \, {}^i \dot{q}_f + {}^i J_f \, \Delta^i \dot{q}_{corr} \tag{5}$$

where the reduced Jacobian matrix of leg i is defined as ${}^i J_f = [{}^i J_1 \;\; {}^i J_2 \; ... \; 0 \; ... \; {}^i J_{l-1} \;\; {}^i J_l]$. The change in the mobile platform velocity after applying the correctional velocity will be

$$\Delta V_r = V - V_r = {}^i J (\, {}^i \dot{q} - {}^i \dot{q}_f) - {}^i J_f \, \Delta^i \dot{q}_{corr} = \Delta V_f - {}^i J_f \, \Delta^i \dot{q}_{corr} \tag{6}$$

To fully compensate for the lost motion, ΔV_r should be equal to zero. If the lost motion ΔV_f belongs to the range space of the reduced Jacobian matrix ${}^i J_f$, then the lost motion could be fully recovered. The correctional velocity from the remaining healthy joints is formulated using equation (6). Therefore

$$\Delta^i \dot{q}_{corr} = {}^i J_f^{\#} \, {}^i J (\, {}^i \dot{q} - {}^i \dot{q}_f) + {}^i \tilde{J}_f k_1 \tag{7}$$

Where ${}^i \tilde{J}_f = (I - {}^i J_f^{\#} \, {}^i J_f)$ and ${}^i J_f^{\#} = {}^i J_f^T (\, {}^i J_f \, {}^i J_f^T)^{-1}$ is the generalized inverse of ${}^i J_f$ and $k_1 \in R^l$ is an arbitrary vector. If the joint velocity vector is not physically consistent, e.g., leg i has both revolute and prismatic joints, when ${}^i J_f$ has full row-rank a weighting matrix is required for calculating the generalized inverse of ${}^i J_f$ as ${}^i J_f^{\#} = W_{\dot{q}} \, {}^i J_f^T (\, {}^i J_f W_{\dot{q}} \, {}^i J_f^T)^{-1}$. The weighting matrix, $W_{\dot{q}}$, is selected so that ${}^i \dot{q}^T (W_{\dot{q}}^{-1} \, {}^i \dot{q})$ becomes physically consistent.

4   Task Space Decomposition

Following the concept of the task priority in [6, 7], provided the task/application allows, the mobile platform velocity could be divided into major DOFs (MDOF), which are critical in performing the task, and secondary DOFs (SDOF), which are less significant. Selection of the major and secondary DOFs depends on the application purposes of the manipulators.

Considering the task priority, the required velocity of the mobile platform can be ordered so that $V = [V_m \; V_s]^T$, where vector $V_m \in R^{m_1}$ denotes the components of the mobile platform velocity corresponding to MDOFs and $V_s \in R^{m_2}$ represents the remaining components of the mobile platform velocity corresponding to SDOFs and $m_1 + m_2 = m$. Hence, the differential kinematic model in equation (1) can be rearranged as

$$\begin{bmatrix} V_m \\ V_s \end{bmatrix} = \begin{bmatrix} {}^i J_m \\ {}^i J_s \end{bmatrix} {}^i \dot{q} \tag{8}$$

where ${}^i J_m \in R^{m_1 \times l}$ represents m_1 rows of the Jacobian matrix of leg i corresponding to MDOF, ${}^i J_s \in R^{m_2 \times l}$ represents the remaining m_2 rows of ${}^i J$ corresponding to SDOF and ${}^i \dot{q}$ contains both active and passive joints. For a given joint velocity, the mobile platform velocity is determined using equation (8). However, in many applications, the mobile platform trajectory is specified and the joint velocities need to be calculated to generate the desired velocity. For redundant manipulators, there are infinite solutions for equation (2). The first term on the right-hand side of equation (2) gives the joint velocity vector with minimum 2-norm which minimizes the least square solution of the mobile platform velocity. In the task decomposition method, achieving the desired MDOF is more preferable than the SDOF motion. Accordingly, instead of inverting the Jacobian matrix, i.e., ${}^i\mathbf{J}^\#$, which minimizes the mobile platform velocity across all DOFs, the proposed method handles the MDOF and SDOF motions separately. MDOF motions will be tracked if the desired velocity, $\mathbf{V}_m$, belongs to the range space of ${}^i\mathbf{J}_m$. Otherwise, a solution minimizing the 2-norm error of MDOF motion will be determined. SDOF motions will be sacrificed to achieve secondary criteria without compromising MDOF motions [6].

In differential kinematic model (1), a desired mobile platform velocity, $\mathbf{V}= [\mathbf{V}_m$ $\mathbf{V}_s]^T$, is given and the joint velocity vector in leg i is found so that $\mathbf{V}_m = {}^i\mathbf{J}_m{}^i\dot{\mathbf{q}}$. The minimum 2-norm solution of the joint velocity vector is ${}^i\dot{\mathbf{q}} = {}^i\mathbf{J}_m^\#\mathbf{V}_m$. Considering the number and type of MDOF, if $m_1 < l$ and ${}^i\mathbf{J}_m$ has full row-rank and all entries are physically consistent, then the generalized inverse of ${}^i\mathbf{J}_m$, i.e., ${}^i\mathbf{J}_m^\# = {}^i\mathbf{J}_m^T({}^i\mathbf{J}_m{}^i\mathbf{J}_m^T)^{-1}$, is used. A weighting matrix would be required for calculating the generalized inverse of ${}^i\mathbf{J}_m$ as ${}^i\mathbf{J}_m^\# = \mathbf{W}_{\dot{q}}{}^i\mathbf{J}_m^T({}^i\mathbf{J}_m\mathbf{W}_{\dot{q}}{}^i\mathbf{J}_m^T)^{-1}$ if the vector of joint velocity is not physically consistent [3]. The correctional velocity of the healthy joints in equation (7) can be rewritten as

$$\Delta{}^i\dot{\mathbf{q}}_{corr} = {}^i\mathbf{J}_{mf}^\#\Delta{}^i\mathbf{J}_m{}^i\dot{\mathbf{q}} + {}^i\tilde{\mathbf{J}}_{mf}\mathbf{k}_1 \qquad (9)$$

where ${}^i\tilde{\mathbf{J}}_{mf} = (\mathbf{I} - {}^i\mathbf{J}_{mf}^\#{}^i\mathbf{J}_{mf})$, $\Delta{}^i\mathbf{J}_m = {}^i\mathbf{J}_m - {}^i\mathbf{J}_{mf} = [\mathbf{0} \quad \mathbf{0} \quad \dots \quad {}^i\mathbf{J}_h \quad \dots \quad \mathbf{0} \quad \mathbf{0}] \in R^{m_1 \times l}$, ${}^i\mathbf{J}_{mf}$ is the m_1 rows of the reduced Jacobian matrix of leg i, in which column h is replaced by a zero vector and ${}^i\mathbf{J}_{mf}^\#$ is the generalized inverse of ${}^i\mathbf{J}_{mf}$. The first term on the right-hand side of equation (9) gives a solution which minimizes the 2-norm of the correctional velocity of the healthy joints to achieve the major subtasks. Also, when there is no exact solution to satisfy zero error in the MDOF after recovery, $\Delta\mathbf{V}_{mr} = {}^i\mathbf{J}({}^i\dot{\mathbf{q}} - {}^i\dot{\mathbf{q}}_f) - {}^i\mathbf{J}_{mf}\Delta{}^i\dot{\mathbf{q}}_{corr} = 0$, this term provides an approximate solution that minimizes the least square error of major subtasks. The second term on the right-hand side of equation (9) represents the redundancy left, which is specified by the secondary criterion, after performing the major subtasks. The relation between the joint velocity vectors after and before the locked joint failure is

$${}^i\dot{\mathbf{q}}_f = ({}^i\mathbf{J}_{mf}^\#{}^i\mathbf{J}_{mf}){}^i\dot{\mathbf{q}} \qquad (10)$$

In this paper, the error in the SDOF motion is defined as the secondary criterion $\|\mathbf{W}_1(\mathbf{V}_{sr} - \mathbf{V}_s)\|_2^2$. The weighting matrix $\mathbf{W}_1$ is used to avoid unit inconsistency because adding terms with different units gives a physically meaningless sum. The arbitrary vector $\mathbf{k}_1$ in equation (9) is formulated so that the secondary criterion is optimized while the major subtasks are as close to the desired mobile platform velocity as possible. Knowing that $\mathbf{V}_{sr} = {}^i\mathbf{J}_{sf}({}^i\dot{\mathbf{q}}_f + \Delta{}^i\dot{\mathbf{q}}_{corr})$ and ${}^i\dot{\mathbf{q}}= {}^i\mathbf{J}_m^\#\mathbf{V}_m$ and substituting equations (9) and (10) in $\mathbf{V}_{sr}$ and rearranging, the secondary criterion results in

$$W_1(V_{sr} - V_s) = W_1 \, {}^iJ_{sf}(\, {}^i\dot{q}_f + \Delta \, {}^i\dot{q}_{corr}) - W_1V_s = W_1 \, {}^iJ_{sf}(\, {}^iJ_{mf}^{\#} \, {}^iJ_{mf} \, {}^iJ_m^{\#}V_m + $$
$$ {}^iJ_{mf}^{\#}\Delta \, {}^iJ_m \, {}^iJ_m^{\#}V_m + \, {}^i\tilde{J}_{mf}k_1) - W_1V_s \tag{11}$$

where ${}^iJ_{sf}$ is the m_2 rows of the reduced Jacobian matrix of leg i, ${}^iJ_f$. By setting this equation equal to zero and rearranging, the secondary criterion$\|W_1(V_{sr} - V_s)\|_2^2$ is minimized if and only if

$$k_1 = {}^iA^{\#}(W_1V_s - {}^iBV_m) + {}^i\tilde{A}k_2 \tag{12}$$

where $k_2 \in R^l$ is an arbitrary vector and

$$\begin{aligned} {}^iA &= W_1 \, {}^iJ_{sf} \, {}^i\tilde{J}_{mf} \\ {}^i\tilde{A} &= I - {}^iA^{\#} \, {}^iA \\ {}^iB &= W_1 \, {}^iJ_{sf}(\, {}^iJ_{mf}^{\#} \, {}^iJ_{mf}) \, {}^iJ_m^{\#} + W_1 \, {}^iJ_{sf}J_{mf}^{\#}\Delta \, {}^iJ_m \, {}^iJ_m^{\#} \end{aligned} \tag{13}$$

Substituting (12) into (9) yields

$$\Delta \, {}^i\dot{q}_{corr} = (\, {}^iJ_{mf}^{\#}\Delta \, {}^iJ_m \, {}^iJ_m^{\#} - \, {}^i\tilde{J}_{mf} \, {}^iA^{\#} \, {}^iB)V_m + \, {}^i\tilde{J}_{mf} \, {}^iA^{\#}W_1V_s + \, {}^i\tilde{J}_{mf} \, {}^i\tilde{A}k_2 \tag{14}$$

which indicates that $\left\|\Delta \, {}^i\dot{q}_{corr}\right\|_2^2$is minimized if and only if

$$k_2 = -(\, {}^i\tilde{J}_{mf} \, {}^i\tilde{A})^{\#}[(\, {}^iJ_{mf}^{\#}\Delta \, {}^iJ_m \, {}^iJ_m^{\#} - \, {}^i\tilde{J}_{mf} \, {}^iA^{\#} \, {}^iB)V_m + \, {}^i\tilde{J}_{mf} \, {}^iA^{\#}W_1V_s] + y \tag{15}$$

which is obtained by setting $\Delta \, {}^i\dot{q}_{corr}$ of equation (14) equal to zero. In equation (15), $y = [I - (\, {}^i\tilde{J}_{mf} \, {}^i\tilde{A})^{\#} \, {}^i\tilde{J}_{mf} \, {}^i\tilde{A}]\lambda$ belongs to the null space of ${}^i\tilde{J}_{mf} \, {}^i\tilde{A}$. Since $I - (\, {}^i\tilde{J}_{mf} \, {}^i\tilde{A})^{\#} \, {}^i\tilde{J}_{mf} \, {}^i\tilde{A}$ is symmetric and idempotent [7], then $(\, {}^i\tilde{J}_{mf} \, {}^i\tilde{A})y = 0$. Substituting (15) into (14) and rearranging leads to

$$\begin{aligned} \Delta \, {}^i\dot{q}_{corr} = &\left[I - {}^i\tilde{J}_{mf} \, {}^i\tilde{A}(\, {}^i\tilde{J}_{mf} \, {}^i\tilde{A})^{\#}\right](\, {}^iJ_{mf}^{\#}\Delta \, {}^iJ_m \, {}^iJ_m^{\#} - \, {}^i\tilde{J}_{mf} \, {}^iA^{\#} \, {}^iB)V_m \\ &+ \left[I - {}^i\tilde{J}_{mf} \, {}^i\tilde{A}(\, {}^i\tilde{J}_{mf} \, {}^i\tilde{A})^{\#}\right](\, {}^i\tilde{J}_{mf} \, {}^iA^{\#}W_1V_s) \end{aligned} \tag{16}$$

5   Case Study

The planar parallel manipulator of Fig. 1(a) with three legs and one degree of kinematic redundancy in each leg, modeled and investigated in [3], is used as a case study. Each leg has two active prismatic joints and two passive revolute joints. The parameters and coordinates of the planer parallel manipulator are depicted in Fig. 1(b). Each leg is connected to the base and mobile platform through joints at A_i and B_i, respectively. A fixed coordinate system $\Psi(X, Y)$ with origin at point 0 is attached to the base and the moving coordinate system $\Gamma(X',Y')$ is assigned to the mobile platform, with origin at the center of mass of the mobile platform, point P.

The position vectors of points A_i and B_i in the fixed coordinate system $\Psi(X, Y)$ are $a_i = [a_{ix} \; a_{iy}]^T$ and $^\Psi b_i = [b_{ix} \; b_{iy}]^T$ for $i = 1,..., 3$, respectively. The angular position of points B_i on the mobile platform relative to the moving coordinate system is represented by angles θ_i. The position vector of point B_i in the moving coordinate system $\Gamma(X',Y')$ is $^\Gamma\mathbf{b}_i = [r_{Bi/P}\cos\theta_i \quad r_{Bi/P}\sin\theta_i]^T$ where $r_{Bi/P}$ is the length of the line connecting P to B_i. The position of B_i relative to the base frame, $^\Psi\mathbf{b}_i = [b_{ix} \quad b_{iy}]^T$, is calculated by $[^\Psi\mathbf{b}_i^T \quad 1]^T = \mathbf{A}_{\Psi,\Gamma}[^\Gamma\mathbf{b}_i^T \quad 1]^T$ using the homogenous transformation matrix relating $\Gamma(X',Y')$ to $\Psi(X,Y)$

$$\mathbf{A}_{\Psi,\Gamma} = \begin{bmatrix} \cos\varphi & -\sin\varphi & p_x \\ \sin\varphi & \cos\varphi & p_y \\ 0 & 0 & 1 \end{bmatrix} \tag{17}$$

The position and orientation of the moving coordinate system relative to the base coordinate system is represented by position vector $\mathbf{p} = [p_x \quad p_y]^T$ and angle φ which can be represented in terms of the joint displacements of leg i, $^i\mathbf{q} = [d_i \quad \alpha_i \quad l_i \quad \beta_i]^T$ (m, rad), for $i = 1,...,3$

$$\begin{bmatrix} p_x \\ p_y \\ \varphi \end{bmatrix} = \begin{bmatrix} a_{ix} + d_i - l_i\cos\alpha_i - r_{Bi/P}\cos(\alpha_i + \beta_i) \\ a_{iy} - l_i\sin\alpha_i - r_{Bi/P}\sin(\alpha_i + \beta_i) \\ \alpha_i + \beta_i - \theta_i \end{bmatrix} \tag{18}$$

The velocity of the mobile platform is related to the joint velocity vector of leg i, through the 3×4 Jacobian matrix of leg i as

$$\begin{bmatrix} v_x \\ v_y \\ \dot{\varphi} \end{bmatrix} = \begin{bmatrix} 1 & l_i\sin\alpha_i + r_{Bi/P}\sin(\alpha_i + \beta_i) & -\cos\alpha_i & r_{Bi/P}\sin(\alpha_i + \beta_i) \\ 0 & -l_i\cos\alpha_i - r_{Bi/P}\cos(\alpha_i + \beta_i) & -\sin\alpha_i & -r_{Bi/P}\cos(\alpha_i + \beta_i) \\ 0 & 1 & 0 & 1 \end{bmatrix} \begin{bmatrix} \dot{d}_i \\ \dot{\alpha}_i \\ \dot{l}_i \\ \dot{\beta}_i \end{bmatrix} \tag{19}$$

The coordinates of the base attachment points, A_i, $i = 1, ..., 3$, in the fixed coordinate system are $[-2 \quad -1.5]^T$(m), $[2 \quad -1.5]^T$ (m) and $[0 \quad 1.5]^T$(m), respectively. The position of connection points B_i on the platform, $^\Gamma\mathbf{b}_i$, is set at a constant radius of $r_{Bi/P} = 0.25$ meters. The angular coordinates, θ_i, $i = 1, ..., 3$, of the leg connections to the mobile platform are $-150°$, $-30°$ and $90°$, respectively. As reported in [3], when the mobile platform pose is $\mathbf{p} = [0 \quad -1.5]^T$ (m) and $\varphi = -30°$ the joint displacements of leg 1 are $^1\mathbf{q} = [0.0 \quad -180° \quad 1.750 \quad 0.0°]^T$ (m, rad). Then the Jacobian matrix of leg 1 will be

$$^1\mathbf{J} = \begin{bmatrix} 1.0 & 0.0 & 1.0 & 0.0 \\ 0.0 & 2.0 & 0.0 & 0.25 \\ 0.0 & 1.0 & 0.0 & 1.0 \end{bmatrix} \tag{20}$$

The task space velocity may be partitioned so as the components of the linear velocity, v_x and v_y, are considered as the major DOF and the angular velocity, $\dot{\varphi}$, is set to be the secondary DOF. Hence, $\mathbf{J}_m$ consists of the first two rows of $\mathbf{J}$ and $\mathbf{J}_s$ contains the last row of $\mathbf{J}$. For the desired mobile platform velocity of $\mathbf{V} = [1 \quad 1 \quad 0]^T$, i.e., for a linear velocity of $[1 \quad 1]^T$ m/s and zero angular velocity about Z direction, using the generalized inverse of $\mathbf{J}_m$ with an identity weighting matix, the minimum norm vector of the joint velocity is $^1\dot{\mathbf{q}} = {}^1\mathbf{J}_m^\#\mathbf{V}_m = [0.500 \quad 0.492 \quad 0.500 \quad 0.062]^T$(m/s, rad/s). When the first active joint ($h = 1$) of leg 1 ($i = 1$) is locked, i.e., has zero velocity, the remaining healthy joints have the velocity of $^1\dot{\mathbf{q}}_f = [0.0\;\;\;0.492\;\;\;0.500\;\;\;0.062]^T$ (m/s, rad/s), and the velocity of the mobile platform is calculated as $\mathbf{V}_{mf} = {}^1\mathbf{J}_m{}^1\dot{\mathbf{q}}_f = [0.500$ $1.000]^T$ m/s and $\mathbf{V}_{sf} = {}^1\mathbf{J}_s{}^1\dot{\mathbf{q}}_f = 0.554$ rad/s. The projections of $\mathbf{V}_m$ and $\mathbf{V}_s$ onto the range space of $\mathbf{I} - {}^1\mathbf{J}_{mf}{}^1\mathbf{J}_{mf}^\#$ and $\mathbf{I} - {}^1\mathbf{J}_{sf}{}^1\mathbf{J}_{sf}^\#$ are both zero vectors which indicate that the failure of the first active joint could be fully recovered. It should be noted that the correctional velocity should not lead to a joint velocity exceeding the limit.

For identity weighting matrices $\mathbf{W}_{\dot{q}}$ and $\mathbf{W}_1$ and using $\mathbf{k}_1 = [0.0\;\;0.079\;\;0.0\;\;-0.633]^T$ which minimizes the 2-norm error $\|\mathbf{W}_1(\mathbf{V}_{sr} - \mathbf{V}_s)\|_2^2$, the correctional velocity provided by the healthy joints will be

$$\Delta{}^i\dot{\mathbf{q}}_{corr} = {}^i\mathbf{J}_{mf}^\#\Delta{}^i\mathbf{J}_m{}^i\dot{\mathbf{q}} + {}^i\tilde{\mathbf{J}}_{mf}\mathbf{k}_1 = [0.0\;\;0.079\;\;0.500\;\;-0.633]^T \qquad (21)$$

As noted in [3], the overall joint velocity will be $^1\dot{\mathbf{q}}_f + \Delta{}^1\dot{\mathbf{q}}_{corr} = [0.0\;\;\;0.571\;\;1.000\;\;-0.571]^T$. Adjusting the healthy joints velocity produces the desired mobile platform velocity of $\mathbf{V} = {}^1\mathbf{J}({}^1\dot{\mathbf{q}}_f + \Delta{}^1\dot{\mathbf{q}}_{corr}) = [1.000\;\;\;1.000\;\;\;0.0]^T$.

For this manipulator, different cases of failures were analyzed and compared with the results of [3]. Simulation results indicate that depending on the configuration and task of the manipulator, MDOFs and SDOFs selection, the lost motion due to locked joint(s) failure will be fully or partially recovered. Two cases of [3] are investigated here and are reported in Tables 1 and 2, which correspond to the mobile platform pose of $\mathbf{p} = [1.0\;\;0.5]^T$ meters and $\varphi = -30°$ and joint displacements of $^1\mathbf{q} = [0.0\;\;\;-143.973°$ $3.400\;\;\;-36.027°]^T$ (length parameters are in meters). The desired mobile platform velocity is $\mathbf{V} = [1.0\;\;\;2.0\;\;\;0.873]^T$ (m/s, rad/s). In case 1, when both passive revolute joints are locked, the two prismatic joints cannot recover the lost angular velocity of the mobile platform in both methods. In case 2, following the failure of the first two

Table 1. Example joint failures using task-decomposition approach

$^1\dot{\mathbf{q}}_{ch}$	Case 1: $\dot{q}_{c2} = 0$, $\dot{q}_{c4} = 0$	Case 2: $\dot{q}_{c1} = 0$, $\dot{q}_{c2} = 0$
$^1\dot{\mathbf{q}} = {}^1\mathbf{J}_m^\#\mathbf{V}_m$	$[0.902\;\;0.423\;\;1.166\;\;0.186]^T$	
$\mathbf{V}_f = \begin{bmatrix} {}^1\mathbf{J}_m & {}^1\mathbf{J}_s \end{bmatrix}^T {}^1\dot{\mathbf{q}}_f$	$[1.845\;\;0.686\;\;0.0]^T$	$[0.943\;\;0.732\;\;0.186]^T$
$\Delta{}^1\dot{\mathbf{q}}_{corr} = {}^1\mathbf{J}_{mf}^\#\Delta{}^1\mathbf{J}_m{}^1\dot{\mathbf{q}} + {}^1\tilde{\mathbf{J}}_{mf}\mathbf{k}_1$	$[-2.652\;\;0.0\;\;2.234\;\;0.0]^T$	$[0.0\;\;0.0\;\;2.112\;\;0.687]^T$
$^1\dot{\mathbf{q}}_f + \Delta{}^1\dot{\mathbf{q}}_{corr}$	$[-1.75\;\;0\;\;3.40\;\;0]^T$	$[0.0\;\;0.0\;\;3.278\;\;0.873]^T$
$\mathbf{V}_r = \begin{bmatrix} {}^1\mathbf{J}_m \\ {}^1\mathbf{J}_s \end{bmatrix}({}^1\dot{\mathbf{q}}_f + \Delta{}^1\dot{\mathbf{q}}_{corr})$	$[1.0\;\;2.0\;\;0.0]^T$	$[2.651\;\;2.147\;\;0.873]^T$
$\Delta\mathbf{V}_r = \begin{bmatrix} {}^1\tilde{\mathbf{J}}_{mf}{}^1\mathbf{J}_m \\ {}^1\tilde{\mathbf{J}}_{sf}{}^1\mathbf{J}_s \end{bmatrix}({}^1\dot{\mathbf{q}} - {}^1\dot{\mathbf{q}}_f)$	$[0.0\;\;0.0\;\;0.873]^T$	$[-1.651\;\;-0.147\;\;0.0]^T$

Table 2. Example joint failures for leg 1 of parallel manipulator [3]

${}^1\dot{\mathbf{q}}_{ch}$	Case 1: $\dot{\mathbf{q}}_{c2} = 0$, $\dot{\mathbf{q}}_{c4} = 0$	Case 2: $\dot{\mathbf{q}}_{c1} = 0$, $\dot{\mathbf{q}}_{c2} = 0$
${}^1\dot{\mathbf{q}} = {}^1\mathbf{J}^{\#}\,\mathbf{V}$	$[0.914\ 0.409\ 1.118\ 0.464]^T$	
$\mathbf{V}_f = {}^1\mathbf{J}\,{}^1\dot{\mathbf{q}}_f$	$[1.818\ 0.658\ 0.0]^T$	$[0.904\ 0.774\ 0.464]^T$
$\Delta\,{}^1\dot{\mathbf{q}}_{corr} = {}^1\mathbf{J}_f^{\#}\,{}^1\mathbf{J}({}^1\dot{\mathbf{q}} - {}^1\dot{\mathbf{q}}_f)$	$[-2.664\ 0.0\ 2.283\ 0.0]^T$	$[0.0\ 0.0\ 0.715\ 0.575]^T$
${}^1\dot{\mathbf{q}}_f + \Delta\,{}^1\dot{\mathbf{q}}_{corr}$	$[-1.75\ 0\ 3.40\ 0]^T$	$[0.0\ 0.0\ 1.881\ 0.761]^T$
$\mathbf{V}_r = {}^1\mathbf{J}\,{}^1\dot{\mathbf{q}}_f + {}^1\mathbf{J}_f\,\Delta\,{}^1\dot{\mathbf{q}}_{corr}$	$[1.0\ 2.0\ 0.0]^T$	$[1.482\ 1.337\ 1.039]^T$
$\Delta\mathbf{V}_r = {}^1\tilde{\mathbf{J}}_f\,{}^1\mathbf{J}({}^1\dot{\mathbf{q}} - {}^1\dot{\mathbf{q}}_f)$	$[0.0\ 0.0\ 0.873]^T$	$[-0.482\ 0.663\ -0.166]^T$

joints, no components of the mobile platform velocity could be retrieved based on the method in [3] as this method produces the minimum 2-norm solution for the correctional velocity. However, if minimizing the error of the angular velocity of the mobile platform is taken as the secondary criterion, using the method presented in this paper, the velocities of the last two healthy joints are adjusted such that the secondary criterion is minimized while the 2-norm of the vector of joint velocities is kept as low as possible. However, the 2-norm of vector $\Delta\mathbf{V}_r$ using the task space decomposition method is greater than that in [3].

6   Discussion and Conclusion

A failure recovery method was discussed in this paper for a known locked joint(s). The task of the mobile platform was broken down into major and secondary subtasks, which enabled the manipulator to minimize the least square error of the MDOFs and optimize the secondary criterion. By selecting some components of the mobile platform velocity as MDOFs and the remaining ones as the SDOFs, the Jacobian matrices corresponding to MDOFs and SDOFs were obtained for the leg comprising locked joint(s). The weighted generalized inverse of the reduced Jacobian matrix corresponding to the MDOFs was used to solve for the correctional joint velocity of the healthy joints and to avoid unit inconsistency. The velocity of the healthy joints was adjusted such that the least square error of the vector of MDOFs was achieved and simultaneously the secondary criterion was optimized. Full or partial recovery of the lost motion mainly depended on the manipulator configuration and task and MDOFs and SDOFs assignment. In cases that the lost mobile platform task corresponding to MDOF did not belong to the range space of the reduced major Jacobian matrix of the leg with failed joint(s), the components of MDOF would not be entirely recovered. The failure recovery method presented in this paper is also applicable to serial manipulators.

References

1. Notash, L.: A Methodology for Actuator Failure Recovery in Parallel Manipulators. Mechanism and Machine Theory 46, 454–465 (2011)
2. Notash, L.: Failure Recovery for Wrench Capability of Wire-Actuated Parallel Manipulators. Robotica (in press), doi:10.1017/S0263574711001160
3. Notash, L.: Motion Recovery after Joint Failure in Parallel Manipulators. Special Edition of the Trans. Can. Soc. Mech. Eng. 35(4), 559–571 (2011)
4. Ting, Y., Tosunoglu, S., Tesar, D.: A Control Structure for Fault-tolerant Operation of Robotic Manipulators. In: Proceedings of IEEE International Conference on Robotics and Automation, Atlanta, GA, vol. 3, pp. 684–690 (1993)
5. Abdi, H., Nahavandi, S.: Joint velocity redistribution for fault tolerant manipulators. In: Proceedings of the IEEE Conference on Robotics, Automation and Mechatronics, Singapore, pp. 492–497 (June 2010)
6. Chen, Y., McInroy, J.E., Yi, Y.: Optimal, Fault-Tolerant Mappings to Achieve Secondary Goals without Compromising Primary Performance. IEEE Transactions on Robotics and Automation 19(4), 680–691 (2003)
7. Nakamura, Y.: Advanced Robotics: Redundancy and Optimization. Addison-Wesley (1991)

Derivation of Dynamic Equations of Serial Robot Manipulators with Coupled Ideal Joint Motion

Mark Becke and Thomas Schlegl

Regensburg University of Applied Sciences, Department of Mechanical Engineering,
Galgenbergstr. 30, 93053 Regensburg, Germany
{Mark.Becke,Thomas.Schlegl}@hs-regensburg.de

Abstract. The objectives of this work are the general derivation of a formal description of the equations of motion for a serial robot manipulator with ideal stiff joints subject to kinematic constraints such as complex mechanical couplings between actuator coordinates and joint coordinates. Therefore, the Lagrangian formalism is deployed for generation of the equations of motion. For evaluation, the feasibility and costs of coupling-induced change from general manipulator configuration description within joint space into actuator space are investigated at various stages during generation of equations of motion.

Keywords: Mechanical Coupling, Redundantly Driven Joints, Equations of Motion, Lagrangian Formalism, Serial Robot Manipulator.

1   Introduction

The derivation of the equations of motion (EoM) for geared serial robot manipulators with n degrees of freedom (DoF) are a well studied field of engineering. Various publications address this topic deploying several modifications of Lagrangian formalism, e.g., [1, 2], or of recursive Newton-Euler algorithm, e.g., [3, 4], and approved methods are covered in standard text books, e.g., in [5–7]. Most reported general methods are derived for non-redundant motion of stiff or elastic joints, i.e., each manipulator joint is driven by one actuator via one gearbox. In case of reported system-specific derivation of EoM for manipulators with redundantly driven joints, i.e., the motion of one joint is caused by two or more actuators due to mechanical couplings, motions are regarded both in joint configuration space and actuator space, e.g., in [8, 9]. In case of non-stiff joints, both coordinate sets subject to their kinematic constraints are kept for manipulator control, and in case of stiff joint behavior, joint coordinates are eliminated by replacing them by actuator coordinates. EoM are derived directly in remaining coordinate spaces, and especially in latter case, direct replacing actually means an early stage departing from general description of joint configuration. The effort of forming equations, from which EoM can be generated, increases directly with complexity of manipulator structure, e.g., for pairs of joints realized with differential gearboxes as reported in [9], or more general, e.g., in [10–12], even assuming ideal joint behavior by neglecting flexible joint structure or dissipative

C.-Y. Su, S. Rakheja, H. Liu (Eds.): ICIRA 2012, Part III, LNAI 7508, pp. 236–247, 2012.
© Springer-Verlag Berlin Heidelberg 2012

losses. Hence, a formal description of the coupling-induced impacts on EoM for simple change from general manipulator configuration description within joint space into actuator space would be useful, especially for further work regarding manipulator design as mentioned in [13, 14].

In this work, the Lagrangian formalism is used for a general derivation and formal description of the EoM for serial robot manipulators with ideal joints subject to kinematic constraints such as mechanical couplings. Furthermore, the feasibility and costs of change from joint space to actuator space are investigated at various stages of EoM generation.

2 General Manipulator Dynamics

In this section, a Lagrangian formalism is applied for hands-on generation of the EoM for a serial robot manipulator with n DoF, and n independent actuators, feasible to position in n_p DoF and to orientate in $n_o = n - n_p$ DoF. Application of Lagrangian formalism provides the packed EoM as generalized forces depending on joint configuration $q \in \mathbb{R}^n$ and its time derivative $\dot{q} = dq/dt$.

2.1 Manipulator Energy

Kinetic Energy. The kinetic energy of a manipulator with n rigid links and n actuators (drives) with non-elastic joint characteristics is the sum of the kinetic energy of all links, T_l, and of all drives, T_d, respectively.

For formulation of the kinetic energy of all links, one can separate the energy into translational and rotary components,

$$T_l = \frac{1}{2} \sum_{i=1}^{n} \left(m_{l_i} \dot{p}_{\mathrm{lcm}_i}^\top \dot{p}_{\mathrm{lcm}_i} + \dot{o}_{\mathrm{lcm}_i}^\top I_{\mathrm{lcm}_i} \dot{o}_{\mathrm{lcm}_i} \right), \tag{1}$$

with translational velocity of the link center of mass, $\dot{p}_{\mathrm{lcm}_i}(\dot{q}, q) \in \mathbb{R}^{n_p}$, and rotational velocity of the link center of mass frame, $\dot{o}_{\mathrm{lcm}_i}(\dot{q}, q) \in \mathbb{R}^{n_o}$, as time derivatives of joint configuration dependent operational space position and orientation, $p_{\mathrm{lcm}_i}(q)$ and $o_{\mathrm{lcm}_i}(q)$, respectively, both referenced to manipulator base frame. There, m_{l_i} is the mass of the whole structure of link i and the moment of inertia tensor of the i-th link center of mass, $I_{\mathrm{lcm}_i}(q) \in \mathbb{R}^{n_o \times n_o}$, is referenced to the base system.[1]

Since the operational space velocity, $\dot{w} \in \mathbb{R}^n$, is related with the joint space velocity via the Jacobian, $J \in \mathbb{R}^{n \times n}$, the velocity of an arbitrary point p located on a link is

$$\dot{w}_p(\dot{q}, q) = \begin{pmatrix} \dot{p}_p(\dot{q}, q) \\ \dot{o}_p(\dot{q}, q) \end{pmatrix} = \begin{pmatrix} J_p^{\langle p \rangle}(q) \\ J_o^{\langle p \rangle}(q) \end{pmatrix} \dot{q} = J^{\langle p \rangle}(q) \, \dot{q}. \tag{2}$$

---

[1] The tensor transformation from arbitrary frame f to base frame 0 applies to $I_f(q) = I_f^0(q) = R_f^0(q) I_f^f R_f^{0\top}(q)$ with rotation matrix $R_f^0(q) \in \mathbb{R}^{n_o \times n_o}$ describing the orientation of frame f w.r.t. to base frame.

Though, the analytic derivation of the Jacobian, J, less the Jacobian for position, $J_p \in \mathbb{R}^{n_p \times n}$, but in particular the Jacobian for orientation, $J_o \in \mathbb{R}^{n_o \times n}$, is not easy, especially due to not always unique description of orientation angles such as, e.g., RPY angles. A more convenient method uses geometric system properties [7]. With $j = 1, \ldots, i$, the j-th columns of the Jacobians of link i depending on the joint type are for a

revolute joint j: $J_{p_j}^{\langle lcm_i \rangle} = z_{j-1} \times (p_{lcm_i} - p_{j-1})$, $J_{o_j}^{\langle lcm_i \rangle} = z_{j-1}$;   (3)

prismatic joint j: $J_{p_j}^{\langle lcm_i \rangle} = z_{j-1}$, $J_{o_j}^{\langle lcm_i \rangle} = 0$.   (4)

Here, $p_{lcm_i}(q)$ and $p_{j-1}(q)$ are the position vectors of the center of mass of link i and the origin of the $(j-1)$-th frame, respectively, and $z_{j-1}(q)$ denotes the third column of $R_{j-1}(q)$. So, the center of mass Jacobian of link i based on geometric considerations assembles as

$$J^{\langle lcm_i \rangle} = \begin{pmatrix} J_p^{\langle lcm_i \rangle} \\ J_o^{\langle lcm_i \rangle} \end{pmatrix} = \begin{pmatrix} J_{p_1}^{\langle lcm_i \rangle} & \cdots & J_{p_{i-1}}^{\langle lcm_i \rangle} & J_{p_i}^{\langle lcm_i \rangle} & 0 \ldots 0 \\ J_{o_1}^{\langle lcm_i \rangle} & \cdots & J_{o_{i-1}}^{\langle lcm_i \rangle} & J_{o_i}^{\langle lcm_i \rangle} & 0 \ldots 0 \end{pmatrix}.$$ (5)

Finally, the combination of (1) and (5) yields an exploitable expression of the kinetic energy of the manipulator links,

$$T_l(\dot{q}, q) = \frac{1}{2} \dot{q}^\top \sum_{i=1}^{n} \left(m_{l_i} J_p^{\langle lcm_i \rangle \top}(q) J_p^{\langle lcm_i \rangle}(q) + \ldots \right.$$

$$\left. \ldots + J_o^{\langle lcm_i \rangle \top}(q)\, I_{lcm_i}(q)\, J_o^{\langle lcm_i \rangle \top}(q) \right) \dot{q} = \frac{1}{2} \dot{q}^\top M_l(q) \dot{q}.$$ (6)

For the sake of simplicity for formulation of (rotary) motor and gear kinetic energy, a few assumptions are made. So, for each motor, and gear, respectively, it is assumed that the center of gravity of the rotary parts lies on the according rotational axis and the rotor is rotational symmetric about that axis, i.e., the z-axis of the frame of the particular drive unit part.[2] The drives are supposed to be stiff and backlash-free and there are no dissipative losses. The general case and the case of using linear actuators is omitted here for shortness and can be found, e.g., in [7].

Since the translational and rotational velocity in operational space of one drive is

$$\dot{p}_{dcm_i} = J_p^{\langle dcm_i \rangle}(q)\dot{q}, \qquad \dot{o}_{dcm_i} = J_o^{\langle dcm_i \rangle}(q)\dot{q} + J_o^{*\langle dcm_i \rangle}(q)\dot{q},$$ (7)

with the Jacobians

$$J_p^{\langle dcm_i \rangle} = \begin{pmatrix} J_{p_1}^{\langle dcm_i \rangle} & \cdots & J_{p_{h-1}}^{\langle dcm_i \rangle} & J_{p_h}^{\langle dcm_i \rangle} & 0 \ldots 0 \end{pmatrix},$$ (8)

$$J_o^{\langle dcm_i \rangle} = \begin{pmatrix} J_{o_1}^{\langle dcm_i \rangle} & \cdots & J_{o_{h-1}}^{\langle dcm_i \rangle} & J_{o_h}^{\langle dcm_i \rangle} & 0 \ldots 0 \end{pmatrix},$$ (9)

---

[2] Then, the drive rotor inertia tensor w.r.t. principal axis frame of the drive is $I_{dcm_i}^{dcm_i} = \mathrm{diag}(I_{d_{i_{xx}}}, I_{d_{i_{yy}}}, I_{d_{i_{zz}}})$, with $I_{d_{i_{xx}}} = I_{d_{i_{yy}}}$.

where (8) and (9) are derived analogously to (5) for the i-th drive center of mass located on link h. Introducing $S = \mathrm{diag}(1/i_{g_1}, \ldots, 1/i_{g_n})$, containing (in this case non-redundant) relations between actuator space with actuator coordinates $\boldsymbol{\theta} \in \mathbb{R}^n$ and operational space, $\boldsymbol{q} = \boldsymbol{S}\boldsymbol{\theta}$, the Jacobian $\boldsymbol{J}_{\mathrm{o}}^{*\langle \mathrm{dcm}_i \rangle} \in \mathbb{R}^{n_{\mathrm{o}} \times n}$ considers the drive rotation about the spinning axis on motor side with

$$\boldsymbol{J}_{\mathrm{o}}^{*\langle \mathrm{dcm}_i \rangle} = \left(\boldsymbol{0} \ldots \boldsymbol{0} \; \boldsymbol{J}_{\mathrm{o}_i}^{*\langle \mathrm{dcm}_i \rangle} \; \boldsymbol{0} \ldots \boldsymbol{0} \right) \boldsymbol{S}^{-1}, \qquad \boldsymbol{J}_{\mathrm{o}_i}^{*\langle \mathrm{dcm}_i \rangle} = \boldsymbol{z}_{\mathrm{d}_i}. \tag{10}$$

With these, the kinetic energy of the drives assembles to

$$T_{\mathrm{d}}(\dot{\boldsymbol{q}}, \boldsymbol{q}, \dot{\boldsymbol{\rho}}) = \frac{1}{2} \dot{\boldsymbol{q}}^{\mathsf{T}} \left(\boldsymbol{M}_{\mathrm{d}}(\boldsymbol{q}) + 2\boldsymbol{H}(\boldsymbol{q}) + \boldsymbol{B} \right) \dot{\boldsymbol{q}}, \tag{11}$$

where the mass/inertia matrix of the drives, $\boldsymbol{M}_{\mathrm{d}} \in \mathbb{R}^{n \times n}$, is derived analogously to $\boldsymbol{M}_{\mathrm{l}}$ in (6) w.r.t. drive masses and inertias, and according centers of masses and principal axes, respectively. Due to special structure of $\boldsymbol{J}_{\mathrm{o}}^{*\langle \mathrm{dcm}_i \rangle}$, the inertia coupling matrix, $\boldsymbol{H} \in \mathbb{R}^{n \times n}$, is

$$\boldsymbol{H}(\boldsymbol{q}) = \sum_{i=1}^{n} \boldsymbol{J}_{\mathrm{o}}^{\langle \mathrm{dcm}_i \rangle \mathsf{T}}(\boldsymbol{q}) \, \boldsymbol{R}_{\mathrm{dcm}_i}(\boldsymbol{q}) \, \mathrm{diag}\left(0, 0, I_{\mathrm{d}_{i_{zz}}} \right) \boldsymbol{R}_{\mathrm{dcm}_i}^{\mathsf{T}}(\boldsymbol{q}) \, \boldsymbol{J}_{\mathrm{o}}^{*\langle \mathrm{dcm}_i \rangle}(\boldsymbol{q}), \tag{12}$$

and the matrix of motor-sided drive inertia, $\boldsymbol{B} \in \mathbb{R}^{n \times n}$, is

$$\boldsymbol{B} = \sum_{i=1}^{n} \boldsymbol{J}_{\mathrm{o}}^{*\langle \mathrm{dcm}_i \rangle \mathsf{T}}(\boldsymbol{q}) \, \boldsymbol{R}_{\mathrm{dcm}_i}(\boldsymbol{q}) \, \mathrm{diag}\left(0, 0, I_{\mathrm{d}_{i_{zz}}} \right) \boldsymbol{R}_{\mathrm{dcm}_i}^{\mathsf{T}}(\boldsymbol{q}) \, \boldsymbol{J}_{\mathrm{o}}^{*\langle \mathrm{dcm}_i \rangle}(\boldsymbol{q})$$
$$= \boldsymbol{S}^{-\mathsf{T}} \, \mathrm{diag}\left(I_{\mathrm{d}_{1_{zz}}}, \ldots, I_{\mathrm{d}_{n_{zz}}} \right) \boldsymbol{S}^{-1} = \mathrm{const}, \tag{13}$$

where $I_{\mathrm{d}_{i_{zz}}}$ consists of inertias of drive unit parts w.r.t. to according principal axis frame.[3]

Combining (6) and (11) yields finally the kinetic energy of the whole system,

$$T(\dot{\boldsymbol{q}}, \boldsymbol{q}) = \frac{1}{2} \dot{\boldsymbol{q}}^{\mathsf{T}} \left(\boldsymbol{M}_{\mathrm{l}}(\boldsymbol{q}) + \boldsymbol{M}_{\mathrm{d}}(\boldsymbol{q}) + 2\boldsymbol{H}(\boldsymbol{q}) + \boldsymbol{B} \right) \dot{\boldsymbol{q}} = \frac{1}{2} \dot{\boldsymbol{q}}^{\mathsf{T}} \boldsymbol{M}(\boldsymbol{q}) \dot{\boldsymbol{q}}. \tag{14}$$

Considering the case that masses and inertias of the drive stators and rotors are already defined within the structure of the links, e.g., by numerical computation by CAD software, the combined mass matrix of the link and drives is

$$\boldsymbol{M}_{\mathrm{c}}(\boldsymbol{q}) = \sum_{i=1}^{n} \left(m_{\mathrm{c}_i} \boldsymbol{J}_{\mathrm{p}}^{\langle \mathrm{ccm}_i \rangle \mathsf{T}}(\boldsymbol{q}) \boldsymbol{J}_{\mathrm{p}}^{\langle \mathrm{ccm}_i \rangle}(\boldsymbol{q}) + \ldots \right.$$
$$\left. \ldots + \boldsymbol{J}_{\mathrm{o}}^{\langle \mathrm{ccm}_i \rangle \mathsf{T}}(\boldsymbol{q}) \, \boldsymbol{I}_{\mathrm{ccm}_i}(\boldsymbol{q}) \, \boldsymbol{J}_{\mathrm{o}}^{\langle \mathrm{ccm}_i \rangle \mathsf{T}}(\boldsymbol{q}) \right) = \boldsymbol{M}_{\mathrm{l}}(\boldsymbol{q}) + \boldsymbol{M}_{\mathrm{d}}(\boldsymbol{q}). \tag{15}$$

---

[3] For drives with non-parallel relative orientation of motor and gear rotational axes, $\boldsymbol{z}_{\mathrm{m}_i} \neq \boldsymbol{z}_{\mathrm{g}_i}$, (11) has to be calculated for motor and gear parts separately.

Potential Energy. The derivation of the potential energy of the manipulator consequently is the sum of all potential energy portions of each link $i = 1, \ldots, n$,

$$V(q) = \sum_{i=1}^{n} V_i(q) = \sum_{i=1}^{n} -m_{l_i} g^\top p_{\text{lcm}_i}(q), \tag{16}$$

with the vector of gravitational acceleration, $g = (0, 0, -g)^\top$. Since the motor drives can be considered to be part of the link structure, their masses can already be taken into account here.

2.2   Application of Lagrangian Formalism

Once the kinetic and potential energy portions of the manipulator are determined, the Lagrangian formalism can be applied to derive the EoM. Composing the Lagrangian, $L = T - V$, and applying the formalism yields the generalized forces, $Q \in R^n$, or

$$Q(\ddot{q}, \dot{q}, q) = \frac{d}{dt} \frac{\partial L(\dot{q}, q)}{\partial \dot{q}} - \frac{\partial L(\dot{q}, q)}{\partial q} = M(q)\ddot{q} + C(\dot{q}, q)\dot{q} + G(q), \tag{17}$$

with the positive definite mass/inertia matrix, $M = M^\top \in \mathbb{R}^{n \times n}$, the centrifugal and Coriolis matrix, $C \in \mathbb{R}^{n \times n}$, and the gravity vector, $G \in \mathbb{R}^n$.

Although M is easy to extract from (14), and G is due to its dependence only on joint configuration $G(q) = \partial V(q)/\partial q$, some formulation for the combined centrifugal and Coriolis matrix is still required. Therefore, Christoffel symbols are deployed to derive C in such manner, that

$$C_{ij}(\dot{q}, q) = \sum_{k=1}^{n} c_{ijk}(q)\dot{q}_k = \sum_{k=1}^{n} \frac{1}{2} \left(\frac{\partial M_{ij}(q)}{\partial q_k} + \frac{\partial M_{ik}(q)}{\partial q_j} - \frac{\partial M_{jk}(q)}{\partial q_i} \right) \dot{q}_k. \tag{18}$$

Further, C can be decomposed into one centrifugal and one Coriolis part. The centrifugal matrix, $Ce \in \mathbb{R}^{n \times n}$, and the Coriolis matrix, $Co \in \mathbb{R}^{n \times n}$, are defined in a way in which the formulation

$$C(\dot{q}, q) \cdot \dot{q} = Ce(q) \cdot (\dot{q} \circ \dot{q}) + Co(\dot{q}, q) \cdot \dot{q} \tag{19}$$

holds, where $\dot{q} \circ \dot{q} = \left(\dot{q}_1^2, \ldots, \dot{q}_n^2\right)^\top$ describes the Hadamard product. Using the middle part of (18) for reformulation of the left hand side of (19), one can show by partitioning w.r.t. quadratic and bilinear velocities that

$$C_{ij}(\dot{q}, q)\dot{q}_j = \left(\sum_{k=1}^{n} c_{ijk}(q)\dot{q}_k \right) \dot{q}_j = c_{ijk}(q)\dot{q}_k^2 \big|_{k=j} + \sum_{k=1}^{n} c_{ijk}(q)\dot{q}_k \bigg|_{k \neq j} \dot{q}_j. \tag{20}$$

So, the elements of centrifugal matrix, and Coriolis matrix, respectively, are

$$Ce_{ij}(q) = c_{ijj}(q), \tag{21}$$

$$Co_{ij}(\dot{q}, q) = \sum_{k=1}^{n} c_{ijk}(q)\dot{q}_k \bigg|_{k \neq j}. \tag{22}$$

3 Ideal Joints with Linear Motion Constraints

Since in the previous section the relation of kinematics and dynamics between joint space and operational space of manipulators with one independent drive per joint are covered, here the effects of coupled motion of redundantly driven joints on the kinematics are outlined, e.g., for joints driven redundantly by two actuators of two consecutive links. So, time dependent coupled joint coordinates, $q \in \mathbb{R}^n$, as linear function of motor coordinates, $\theta \in \mathbb{R}^m$, may be written as

$$q_i(\theta(t)) = \sum_{j=1}^{m} S_{ij}\theta_j(t) \quad \forall i \in [1;n] \wedge S_{ij} = \text{const}. \tag{23}$$

However, the actual number of actuators participated within a coupled drive train per joint does not change the principal problem as long as they are coupled linearly. For that case, the problem is now analyzed generally.

The general linear coupling relation between the coordinates of n joints, $q(\theta) \in \mathbb{R}^n$, and the coordinates of $m \geq n$ motor drives, $\theta \in \mathbb{R}^m$, is defined in a structure matrix[4], $S \in \mathbb{R}^{n \times m}$, that is the constant Jacobian

$$S = \begin{pmatrix} S_{11} & \dots & S_{1m} \\ \vdots & \ddots & \vdots \\ S_{n1} & \dots & S_{nm} \end{pmatrix} = \frac{\partial q(\theta)}{\partial \theta} = \frac{\partial \dot{q}(\dot{\theta})}{\partial \dot{\theta}} = \frac{\partial \ddot{q}(\ddot{\theta})}{\partial \ddot{\theta}} = \text{const}, \tag{24}$$

and so for joint coordinates it applies $q = S\theta$, and analogously to velocities and accelerations. Referring to [10, 11], a well defined structure matrix possesses at least following properties:

1. The structure matrix has full rank, $\text{rank}(S) = n$. In case of $m = n$, the determinant is nonzero, $\det(S) \neq 0$, otherwise the redundantly driven joint is uncontrollable. Hence, the inverse relation between joint and gear coordinates is at least given by Moore-Penrose inverse, $\theta = S^+ q$.[5]
2. There cannot exist one ore more zero elements between any two nonzero elements within a column of S since the driven joints, or links, respectively, are consecutive due to the serial manipulator structure.
3. If there exist k further coordinate spaces $\{\theta_i\}_{i=1}^{k}$ between θ and q, then there exist $k+1$ structure matrices $\{S_i\}_{i=1}^{k+1}$, where $\theta_1 = S_1\theta, \theta_2 = S_2\theta_1, \dots, q = S_{k+1}\theta_k$. Then, the overall structure matrix holds $S = S_{k+1}\cdots S_2 S_1$.

4 Coupling-Induced Modifications on the Equations of Motion

All formulations in the following, are derived for the special case of equal number of actuators and redundantly driven joints, $m = n$, due to shortage of space. The EoM are modified, which is indicated with a tilde for comparison with unmodified terms.

---

[4] S might also be called transmission matrix [8], or transformation matrix [9, 10].

[5] For $m = n$, $S^+ = S^{-1}$, and for $m > n$, $S^+ = S^\top \left(SS^\top\right)^{-1}$. The cases of $m < n$ or of $\text{rank}(S) < n$ are not discussed here.

4.1   Modified Jacobian

In comparison to $J(q) \in \mathbb{R}^{n \times n}$ for links with independent joint motion, which was derived upon geometric considerations, the basic analytic derivation of the new coupled Jacobian depending on motor coordinates, $\tilde{J}(\theta) \in \mathbb{R}^{n \times n}$, holds the relation

$$\tilde{J}(\theta) = \frac{\partial w(q(\theta))}{\partial \theta} = \frac{\partial w(q)}{\partial q}\bigg|_{q=S\theta} \cdot \frac{\partial q(\theta)}{\partial \theta} = J(q)|_{q=S\theta} S, \qquad (25)$$

which, of course, also holds for the new sub-matrices $\tilde{J}_{\mathrm{p}}(\theta) \in \mathbb{R}^{n_{\mathrm{p}} \times n}$ and $\tilde{J}_{\mathrm{o}}(\theta) \in \mathbb{R}^{n_{\mathrm{o}} \times n}$. The operator $(\cdot)|_{q=S\theta}$ indicates substitution of q by $S\theta$, and $(\cdot)|_{(q=S\theta,\ldots)}$ substitutions also regarding the time derivatives. Figure 1 illustrates in context of changing coordinate space the coordinate configuration of actuator space, joint space, and operational space.

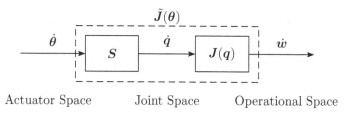

Actuator Space   Joint Space   Operational Space

Fig. 1. General configuration of actuator space, joint space, and operational space

Notable is the property, that one can exploit already derived geometric Jacobians, as long as all components of q are substituted by their corresponding components of $S\theta$ and subsequent post-multiplication of the structure matrix.

Since a well-defined structure matrix S is invertible, also the relation (25) is. For change from joint space to actuator space, the inverted relation is

$$J(q) = \tilde{J}(\theta)\Big|_{\theta=S^{-1}q} S^{-1}. \qquad (26)$$

4.2   Modifications on Lagrangian

In order to obtain the modified EoM in actuator space for the general case in form of $\tilde{Q} = \tilde{M}\ddot{\theta} + \tilde{C}\dot{\theta} + \tilde{G}$, it can be derived directly using the chain rule and componentwise substitution of q by $S\theta$ and their time derivatives. The vector of generalized forces of the linearly coupled system in actuator space and the one in joint space are correlated as following,

$$\tilde{Q}(\ddot{\theta}, \dot{\theta}, \theta) = \frac{d}{dt}\frac{\partial \tilde{L}(\dot{q}(\dot{\theta}), q(\theta))}{\partial \dot{\theta}} - \frac{\partial \tilde{L}(\dot{q}(\dot{\theta}), q(\theta))}{\partial \theta} \qquad (27)$$

$$= S^{\top} \left(\frac{d}{dt}\frac{\partial L(\dot{q}, q)}{\partial \dot{q}} - \frac{\partial L(\dot{q}, q)}{\partial q} \right)\bigg|_{(q=S\theta,\ldots)} \qquad (28)$$

$$= S^{\top} \left(M(q)|_{q=S\theta} S\ddot{\theta} + C(\dot{q}, q)|_{(q=S\theta,\ldots)} S\dot{\theta} + G(q)|_{q=S\theta} \right). \qquad (29)$$

The expressions for the coupled versions of mass matrix, generalized centrifugal and Coriolis matrix, and gravity vector, within actuator space follow directly from (29),

$$\tilde{M}(\theta) = S^\top \, M(q)|_{q=S\theta} \, S \,, \tag{30}$$

$$\tilde{C}(\dot{\theta}, \theta) = S^\top \, C(\dot{q}, q)|_{(q=S\theta,\ldots)} \, S \,, \tag{31}$$

$$\tilde{G}(\theta) = S^\top \, G(q)|_{q=S\theta} \,, \tag{32}$$

where $\tilde{M}, \tilde{C} \in \mathbb{R}^{n \times n}$, and $\tilde{G} \in \mathbb{R}^n$. From (11), (14) and (30) it follows for the drive inertia matrix $\tilde{B} = \mathrm{diag}\left(I_{\mathrm{d}_{1_{zz}}}, \ldots, I_{\mathrm{d}_{n_{zz}}}\right)$. Again, prior derived components can be exploited, only by substituting the components of q by $S\theta$ and their time derivatives and appropriate pre- and post-multiplication of $S^\top$ and S, respectively.

The reversed coordinate space change of (30), (31) and (32) is done by application of $(\cdot)|_{(\theta=S^{-1}q,\ldots)}$, and appropriate pre- and post-multiplication of $S^{-\top}$ and S^{-1}, respectively. Since the coordinate space change is possible in both directions, in the following and without loss of generality only the change from joint space into actuator space is presented.

Let $P_{ij} \in \mathbb{R}^{n \times n}$ be the dyadic product of the i-th and j-th row of S,

$$P_{ij} = \left(S_{i1} \ldots S_{in} \right)^\top \left(S_{j1} \ldots S_{jn} \right) = P_{ji}^\top \,. \tag{33}$$

Then, the (g, h)-th entry of P_{ij} is indicated as $(P_{ij})_{gh}$. With this definition, one can derive some properties and correlations of the matrices (30) and (31).

Expanding the right hand side of (30) and collecting the single entries of M, the entries of S form a coefficient matrix consisting of the dyadic product of rows of S,

$$\left(S^\top M S \right)_{gh} = \sum_{i,j=1}^{n} M_{ij} S_{ig} S_{jh} = \sum_{i,j=1}^{n} M_{ij} \left(P_{ij}^\top \right)_{gh} \,. \tag{34}$$

Since M is symmetric, in

$$\tilde{M}(\theta) = \sum_{i,j=1}^{n} M_{ij}(q)|_{q=S\theta} \, P_{ij} \,, \tag{35}$$

all entries of M are comprised twice, except those lying on main diagonal. So, after partitioning (35) w.r.t. main diagonal and non-diagonal elements of M, and considering $M_{ij} = M_{ji}$ and $P_{ij}^\top = P_{ji}$, it yields

$$\tilde{M}(\theta) = \sum_{i=1}^{n} M_{ii}(q)|_{q=S\theta} \, P_{ii} + \sum_{i=1}^{n-1} \sum_{j=i+1}^{n} M_{ij}(q)|_{q=S\theta} \left(P_{ij} + P_{ij}^\top \right) \,. \tag{36}$$

Analogously to (34), the combined matrix of centripetal and Coriolis terms for the linearly coupled system in (31) is the sum

$$\tilde{C}(\dot{\theta}, \theta) = \sum_{i,j=1}^{n} C_{ij}(\dot{q}, q)|_{(q=S\theta,\ldots)} \, P_{ij} \,. \tag{37}$$

5 Discussion of Results

For evaluation of the derived formulas subject to nominal efforts of changing coordinate space, in this context the efforts could be surveyed on the one side subject to aspects of variable substitutions and symbolic simplifications (inner costs), or subject to additional arithmetic operations due to simple application of the derived formulas (outer costs) on the other side. Since the evaluation of inner costs depends highly on structural complexity of the regarded manipulator design, for evaluation of nominal extra costs here only the outer costs are considered. Yet, for demonstration of formula implementation, the EoM of a 6 DoF serial robot manipulator (see Fig. 2) are transferred exemplary from joint into actuator space and the required times are evaluated.[6]

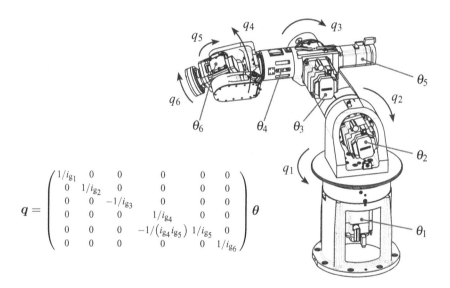

$$q = \begin{pmatrix} 1/i_{g_1} & 0 & 0 & 0 & 0 & 0 \\ 0 & 1/i_{g_2} & 0 & 0 & 0 & 0 \\ 0 & 0 & -1/i_{g_3} & 0 & 0 & 0 \\ 0 & 0 & 0 & 1/i_{g_4} & 0 & 0 \\ 0 & 0 & 0 & -1/(i_{g_4}i_{g_5}) & 1/i_{g_5} & 0 \\ 0 & 0 & 0 & 0 & 0 & 1/i_{g_6} \end{pmatrix} \theta$$

Fig. 2. Configuration of actuators and joints (both represented by according actuator and joint space coordinates, θ and q, respectively) of a 6 DoF robot manipulator designed for test purposes as described in [13]. The 5th joint is driven redundantly by actuators 4 and 5.

The nominal outer extra costs for change of coordinate space of the terms within the EoM and required times for both symbolic computation and simplification with numeric parameters of the 6 DoF robot manipulator are listed in Table 1. Evidently, least computational outer costs for change from joint configuration space into actuator space appear at the computation of $\tilde{M}$ from M

---

[6] For all calculations Matlab R2011b 64bit was used on a Windows 7 64bit system with Intel Core i7 CPU@3.40 GHz and 16 GB RAM.

using (36). However, computation using (36) is actually little slower than (30), but its symbolic simplification is 12 times faster. Although usage of (35) requires most time for computation, its simplification is also nearly 10 times faster than simplification of (30). Computation of $\tilde{C}$ from C using (37) is also slower than using (31), but again its simplification takes less time.

Table 2 contains the times for both symbolic computation with numerical parameters and simplification of centrifugal and Coriolis terms of the 6 DoF robot manipulator. Both, computation and simplification, require less time in joint space than in actuator space.

Figure 3 illustrates finally the relations between derived formulas of joint space and actuator space and depicts the sequence of least computational costs. Hence, although it is possible to transfer from C from joint space to actuator space using (37), it is more convenient to transfer only M with (36) and derive $\tilde{C}$ by applying (18) on $\tilde{M}$ w.r.t. actuator space coordinates, just as calculation of $\tilde{C}e$ and $\tilde{C}o$. G has to be transferred into actuator space separately anyway.

Table 1. Nominal (scalar) outer extra costs for changing EoM between coordinate spaces and required time for both symbolic computation and simplification for the exemplary 6 DoF robot manipulator

| Equation | Nominal extra costs (scalar) | | Required time ($n = 6$) | | |
	Additions	Multiplications	Computation	Simplification	Total
$M \to \tilde{M}$ (30)	$\sim (n^2 - 1)n^2$	$\sim n^6$	0.23 s	112.20 s	112.43 s
$M \to \tilde{M}$ (35)	$\sim (n^2 - 1)n^2$	$\sim n^6$	0.38 s	11.34 s	11.72 s
$M \to \tilde{M}$ (36)	$\sim (n^2 + n - 2)\frac{n^2}{2}$	$\sim n^6$	0.32 s	9.11 s	9.43 s
$C \to \tilde{C}$ (31)	$\sim (n^2 - 1)n^2$	$\sim n^6$	1.88 s	422.24 s	424.12 s
$C \to \tilde{C}$ (37)	$\sim (n^2 - 1)n^2$	$\sim n^6$	2.64 s	405.97 s	408.61 s
$G \to \tilde{G}$ (32)	$\sim (n - 1)n$	$\sim n^2$	0.02 s	0.01 s	0.03 s

Table 2. Required time for both symbolic computation and simplification for calculation of centrifugal and Coriolis terms in joint and actuator space for the exemplary 6 DoF robot manipulator

| Equation | Required time ($n = 6$) | | |
	Computation	Simplification	Total
$M \to C$ (18)	1.60 s	64.08 s	65.68 s
$\tilde{M} \to \tilde{C}$ (18)	1.50 s	91.48 s	92.98 s
$M \to Ce, Co$ (21), (22)	1.41 s	67.43 s	68.84 s
$\tilde{M} \to \tilde{C}e, \tilde{C}o$ (21), (22)	1.50 s	93.95 s	95.45 s

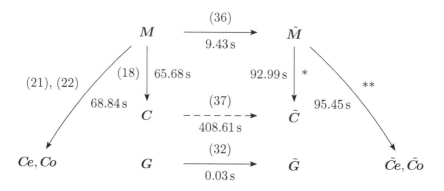

Fig. 3. Relations between derived formulas of changing between joint space (left) and actuator space (right). The derivation from top to bottom in actuator space is analogous to joint space, however, w.r.t. actuator coordinates instead of joint coordinates. For each formula, the total required time is given for the exemplary 6 DoF robot manipulator.

6   Conclusions

In this work, several formulas have been derived as formal description of the coupling-induced impacts on the EoM for serial robot manipulators with redundantly driven joints and ideal stiff joint behavior. The effects of linear kinematic constraints on terms of the EoM at various generation steps have been investigated and formulated for an equal number of actuators and driven joints. Based upon this, the feasibility and costs for a simple change from general manipulator configuration description within joint space into actuator space at each of the generation stages have been investigated. Additionally, the implemented formulas have been evaluated for an exemplary robot manipulator and a preferred generation sequence with least costs has been proposed. Though, due to shortage of space, derived formulas are restricted to joints redundantly driven by an equal number of actuators and with non-elastic and friction-less behavior. Hence, it is essential to extend the derived formal descriptions to cover less simplified cases with spring-damper characteristics as well.

References

1. Burdick, J.: An Algorithm for Generation of Efficient Manipulator Dynamic Equations. In: Proceedings of the IEEE International Conference on Robotics and Automation, vol. 3, pp. 212–218 (1986)
2. Cui, K., Haque, I., Thirumalai, M.: On Configurations of Symbolic Equations of Motion for Rigid Multibody Systems. Mechanism and Machine Theory 30(8), 1149–1170 (1995)
3. Featherstone, R., Orin, D.: Robot Dynamics: Equations and Algorithms. In: Proceedings of the IEEE International Conference on Robotics and Automation, ICRA 2000, vol. 1, pp. 826–834 (2000)

4. Mata, V., Provenzano, S., Valero, F., Cuadrado, J.I.: Serial-Robot Dynamics Algorithms for Moderately Large Numbers of Joints. Mechanism and Machine Theory 37(8), 739–755 (2002)

5. Murray, R.M., Li, Z., Sastry, S.S.: A Mathematical Introduction to Robotic Manipulation. CRC Press, Boca Raton (1994)

6. Siciliano, B., Khatib, O. (eds.): Springer Handbook of Robotics. Springer, Berlin (2008)

7. Siciliano, B., Sciavicco, L., Villani, L., Oriolo, G.: Robotics: Modelling, Planning and Control. Springer, London (2009)

8. Waiboer, R.R., Aarts, R.G.K.M., Jonker, J.B.: Application of a Perturbation Method for Realistic Dynamic Simulation of Industrial Robots. Multibody System Dynamics 13, 323–338 (2005)

9. Le Tien, L., Schäffer, A.A., Hirzinger, G.: MIMO State Feedback Controller for a Flexible Joint Robot with Strong Joint Coupling. In: IEEE International Conference on Robotics and Automation, pp. 3824–3830 (2007)

10. Chang, S.-L., Tsai, L.-W.: Topological Synthesis of Articulated Gear Mechanisms. IEEE Transactions on Robotics and Automation 6(1), 97–103 (1990)

11. Chen, D.-Z., Shiue, S.-C.: Topological Synthesis of Geared Robotic Mechanisms. Transactions of the ASME 115, 230–239 (1998)

12. Liu, C.-P., Chen, D.-Z., Chang, Y.-T.: Kinematic Analysis of Geared Mechanisms Using the Concept of Kinematic Fractionation. Mechanism and Machine Theory 39(11), 1207–1221 (2004)

13. Becke, M., Schlegl, T.: Toward an Experimental Method for Evaluation of Biomechanical Joint Behavior under High Variable Load Conditions. In: 2011 IEEE International Conference on Robotics and Automation (ICRA), pp. 3370–3375 (2011)

14. ManuCyte: Modular Manufacturing Platform for Flexible, Patient-Specific Cell Cultivation. Fraunhofer Institute for Manufacturing Engineering and Automation (IPA). Nobelstr. 12, D-70569 Stuttgart, http://www.manucyte-project.eu/

Mechatronics Design Applied to the Concept of Service Robot to Clean Storage Tanks

Hernan Gonzalez Acuña, Fausto J. Samiento Esparza, and Omar Lengerke

Research group in Control and mechatronics, Mechatronics Engineering program,
Universidad Autonoma de Bucaramanga, Bucaramanga, Colombia
{hgonzalez3,fsarmiento2,olengerke}@unab.edu.co

Abstract. This paper proposes a methodology of Mechatronics design applied to the concept of a service robot to clean storage tanks. Through this methodology, the system static analysis is done first, followed by dynamic analysis, and finally robot design. In some cases the cleaning process is done manually, but in tall oil tanks, workers need scaffolding or cranes. The principal, most popular cleaning method used is sandblasting, but it can give the workers health problems like acute silicosis. This is why a robot capable of working with sandblasting is proposed, changing the traditional cleaning method and improving the life quality of workers, with reduced cleaning time and improved service quality.

Keywords: Cleaning, storage tanks, climb, methodology, robot, sandblasting.

1 Introduction

In the petrochemical industry, storage tanks are some of the most important pieces of static equipment, used to hold sufficient amounts of supply products for later use. Given that storage tanks, generally made of steel, are exposed to such environmental conditions as rain, temperature variations, acidic, alkaline and neutral soils, and sea sand [1], maintenance is called for to keep their mechanical properties. The main maintenance activity is cleaning of external walls to remove corrosion and paint. The principal cleaning processes of external walls of storage tanks are: dryiceblasting [2], sandblasting [3], hydrosandblasting [4], hydroblasting [5] and sodablasting [6].

This industry uses many robots to help in the cleaning process of tanks. These robots can climb vertical walls by using one of the methods known, such as chemical, magnetic [7], pneumatic [8], [9], mechanical and electrostatic adhesion [10], [11]. However for the cleaning process, the most widely used methods are the magnetic, mechanical and pneumatic methods because the adhesion force they provide is higher than that provided by the others. Companies do not sell these robots because it is more profitable to provide the cleaning services. For this reason the companies handling storage tanks aim to develop their own cleaning robots so as to save money. Urakami R&D Co., is one of the companies with the most robots developed by themselves [12]. Fig. 1 shows their ultra-high pressure water-jet robot, which uses vacuum adhesion to adhere to the surface and suction dirt.

C.-Y. Su, S. Rakheja, H. Liu (Eds.): ICIRA 2012, Part III, LNAI 7508, pp. 248–257, 2012.
© Springer-Verlag Berlin Heidelberg 2012

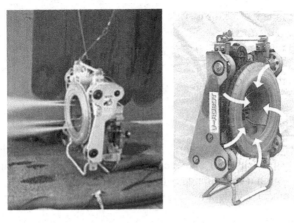

Fig. 1. Water jet robot by Urakami research company

Flow Water Jet, another important company, developed Hydrocat, shown in Fig. 2 This robot operates at a pressure of 40,000 psi and can suction water and remove solids in the cleaning operation.

Fig. 2. Hydrocat by Flow water jet

2   Analysis of Forces

= Friction force in the wheel, for n=1...4.
= Reaction force in the wheel, for n=1...4.
=Adhesion force.
= Weight of the robot and the hoses.
= Reaction force of the water jet.
= Coefficient of static friction between rubber and steel.
= Coefficient of dynamic friction between rubber and steel.

T_n= Static torque in the motor, for n=1...4.
r= Radio of the wheels.
i = Gear reduction ratio ($rev_{motor}/rev_{gearshaft}$).
n_{motor} = Motor Speed (rpm).
n_{load} = Load speed (rpm).

2.1   Reaction Force

Displacement speed of this kind of robots is low; in [13] it is concluded that top speed must be 1 mm/s to prevent wall damage. To ensure good quality cleaning process these robots work within a speed range between 30 mm/s and 60 mm/s. Given the low speed and displacement acceleration rate of this kind of robots, dynamic force is small.

The hydroblasting process to clean external walls in storage thanks works in a range of pressure between 345 bar (5,000 psi) and 2,800 bar (40,000 psi). The reaction force is given by the equation (1), when the water hits wall surfaces; it was first presented at a water jet conference [14].

$$Fr_{wj}(lb) = 0.052 \times Q \times \sqrt{P} \qquad (1)$$

Where: Q is the flow in *gpm and P* is the pressure in *psi*.

Using the equation (2) and working with 40,000 *psi* and 10 *gpm* the reaction force is:

$$Fr_{wj} = 104 \; lbf$$
$$Fr_{wj} = 462.6151 \; N \qquad (2)$$

Adhesion force will be 1,2 times reaction force by water jet, $F_{adh} = 555.13812N$. Fig. 3 shows the variation in the reaction force when the inclination angle of the water jet changes between 0° and 45° for a pressure of 40,000 *psi* and flow of 10 *gpm*.

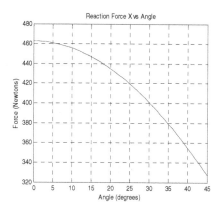

Fig. 3. Reaction force variation

2.2   Static Analysis

Static analysis calculates the minimal adhesion force necessary for the robot to keep equilibrium; such force is created by the vortex system, [15]. Static analysis only covers the position of the robot on the wall, [16].

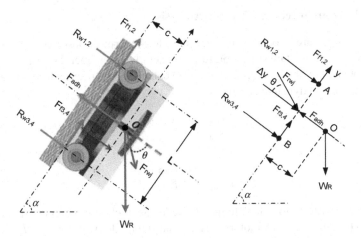

Fig. 4. Free Body diagram of the cleaning robot

Adhesion force is located in the middle of length L, and the position of the reaction force for sandblasting flow is calculated with (3):

$$\Delta y = c \times \tan \theta \tag{3}$$

The robot's symmetry allows torque equilibrium to be reached around point F in (4), and torque is calculated in the middle of the robot:

$$\sum T_F = 0 +\circlearrowleft$$

$$Fr_{wj} \cos \theta \left(\frac{L}{2} - \Delta y\right) + R_{w3}L + R_{w4}L + W_R \cos\alpha \frac{L}{2} = \frac{L}{2} F_{adh} + W_R \sin\alpha \times c \tag{4}$$

From (4), we can obtain the reaction force in wheels 3 and 4 in the rear of the robot. By symmetry Rw_3 and Rw_4 are equal and they are calculated with (5).

$$R_{w3,4} = \frac{1}{2L}\left(\frac{L}{2}(F_{adh} - W_R\cos\alpha) - Fr_{wj}\cos\theta\left(\frac{L}{2} - \Delta y\right) + W_R\sin\alpha \times c\right) \tag{5}$$

Calculating the reaction forces in wheels 1 and 2 calls for the value of the sum of forces in X, (6)

$$\sum F_x = 0$$

$$F_{adh} = R_{w1} + R_{w2} + R_{w3} + R_{w4} + Fr_{wj}\cos\theta + W_R\cos\alpha \tag{6}$$

As in Rw_3 and Rw_4 the reaction forces in Rw_1 and Rw_2 are equal because of symmetry, (7)

$$R_{w1,2} = \frac{1}{2}\left(F_{adh} - W_R\cos\alpha - Fr_{wj}\cos\theta - R_{w3} - R_{w4}\right) \tag{7}$$

2.3   Friction Forces and Torque Analysis

Friction forces are necessary to keep the cleaning robot positioned on the vertical walls of the storage tanks; friction forces generally counteract the forces of weight of the robot and the hoses, W_R. Equation (8) calculates the friction forces in each wheel for the static and dynamic coefficient.

$$\begin{aligned} Ff_{1,2} &= u_s R_{w1,2} \\ Ff_{3,4} &= u_s R_{w3,4} \\[1em] Ff_{1,2} &= u_d R_{w3,4} \\ Ff_{3,4} &= u_d R_{w3,4} \end{aligned} \tag{8}$$

Then it is necessary to calculate the torque, so as to choose motors torque using such value. The robot has two motors, M1 for the right side, with torques T_1 and T_3, and M2 for the left side, with torques T_2 and T_4. This static torque can be calculated with the simple equation (9):

$$\begin{aligned} T_{1,3} &= R_{w1} \times r + R_{w3} \times r \\ T_{2,4} &= R_{w2} \times r + R_{w4} \times r \end{aligned} \tag{9}$$

2.4   Dynamic Analysis

Some studies present the minimal conditions to have motion in the robot,[17]. The dynamic analysis is given by the profile of motion in the cleaning robot [18]. This profile has a time of acceleration, constant speed and deceleration. Fig. 5 presents the mechanism type used to transmit the motion to the robot shaft.

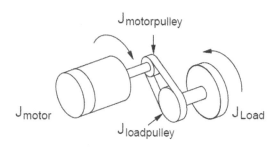

Fig. 5. Belt drive mechanism motion

The motor's velocity is given by equation (10).

$$n_{motor} = n_{load} \times i \qquad (10)$$

Total load inertia value is given by equation (11), where it is necessary to calculate the inertia of each element.

$$J_{total} = J_{motor} + J_{motorpulley} + \frac{J_{loadpulley} + J_{load}}{i^2} \qquad (11)$$

Finally, the torque necessary to accelerate or decelerate the load can be calculated by equation (12).

$$T_{motor} = J_{total} \times \left(\frac{\Delta speed}{\Delta time}\right)\left(\frac{2\pi}{60}\right) \qquad (12)$$

3   Adhesion Method

A vortex is a turbulent flow with spiral motion around a center. The speed and rate of rotation of the fluid in a vortex are greatest at the center, and decrease progressively with distance from the center, while the speed of a forced vortex is zero at the center and increases proportionally to the distance from the center. Mathematically, vorticity $\vec{w}$ is defined as the curl of fluid velocity $\vec{u}$, (13). Tangential velocity (v_θ) is given by equation (13), where Γ is the circulation and r is the radial distance from the center of the vortex.

$$\vec{w} = \nabla \times \vec{u}$$
$$v_\theta = \frac{\Gamma}{2\pi r} \qquad (13)$$

In [19], a system called vortex attractor is presented; this system presents the use of a centrifugal impeller into a cup to produce the air flow that creates vortex adhesion. Fig. 6 shows how the air flow enters through the center of the centrifugal impeller and is expelled in the radial direction. This flow of air goes to the walls of the cup, creating continuous flow between the air expelled and the air entering.

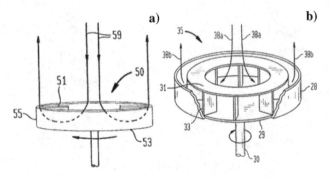

Fig. 6. (a) Air flow in the impeller (b) Centrifugal impeller used in the vortex attractor

4   Experimental Tests

Two experimental robots were built to test the adhesion system. Table 1 shows some technical specifications: robot weight, speed used along the test, and the adhesion force level reached at that speed.

Table 1. Test robots specifications

Robot	Weight (kgf)	Motor Speed (rpm)	Adhesion Force (Kgf)
1	0.6	9,000	1.1
2	3	25,000	10

Fig. 7 shows the first test robot on two different surfaces. The first surface, Fig. 7.a, is a concrete wall and the second surface, Fig. 7.b is a wooden door, and it can be observed that the robot keeps balance as it negotiates its way on the level change provided by a piece of wood of 1 cm in height, with the robot keeping its grip.

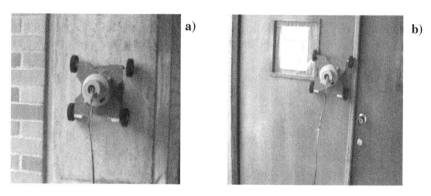

a)   b)

Fig. 7. Climbing robot, RLT V1

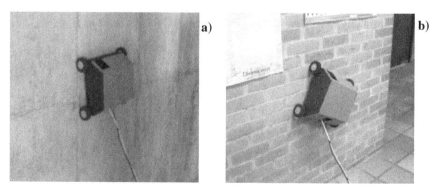

a)   b)

Fig. 8. Climbing robot RLT V2

Fig. 8. shows the second version of the cleaning robot undergoing testing for adhesion. In Fig. 8.a, the robot is climbing a regular surface on a concrete wall, and in Fig. 8.b, the robot is climbing an irregular bricks wall without loss of adhesion force.

5   Robot Design

Fig. 9 shows the basic components of the parts of the cleaning robot. There are four main parts: a) First part: the drive motors, in a configuration of differential robot, one motor on each side. b) Second part: the suction cup that is in charge of creation of an adhesion zone for the robot. c) Third part: water jet nozzle, where the reaction force is generated. d) Fourth part: vortex mechanism: this part is in charge of creating the air flow for suction of rust and water.

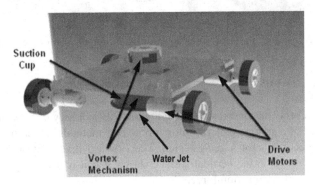

Fig. 9. Climbing robot components

Fig. 10.a shows the cleaning service robot; it is possible to see the red cup where vortex adhesion is generated; the water jet system to clean the walls can be seen connected in the upper part, and in the middle of the cup are the suction hoses for recycling of water used and suction of rust.

Fig. 10. Cleaning robot concept

Fig. 11 shows front and rear views of the isometric figure of the cleaning robot. All of the cleaning robot's components can be viewed in these pictures: the motors for transmission of motion, suction cup, water hoses and hoses for suction of recycling water and rust, as well as the rack and pinion mechanism, in charge of painting the clean parts of storage tank walls.

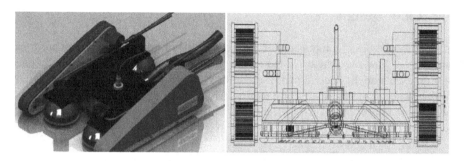

Fig. 11. a) Isometric figure of the cleaning robot. b)   Front view of the cleaning robot.

6   Conclusions

This paper presents the first results applying the methodology of mechatronics design to the concept of a storage tank cleaning robot. This methodology allows definition of the features necessary for a good design. The first test made with the vortex system for fixing the robot on the vertical surface shows that it is necessary to use 4 vortex units to withstand the reaction force.

References

1. Owate, I.O., Ezi, C.W.I., Avwiri, G.: Impact of environmental conditions on sub-surface storage tanks. Journal of Applied Sciences & Environmental Management 6(2), 79–84 (2002)
2. Tough, ice cold and with real pressure cleaning with dry ice. Messer Magazine, On air, pp. 8-11 (February 2007)
3. Work safe, Safe sandblast cleaning, bulletin 153 (April 1999)
4. Hidrojet brochure, Hidrosandblasting, pp. 40,41 (March 2007)
5. International marine coatings, Hydroblasting Standards, pp. 2–5
6. Dyer's Soda Blasting & Sandblasting, Bulleting: The Advantages of Soda Blasting
7. Fischer, W., Tâche, F., Siegwart, R.: Magnetic Wall Climbing Robot for Thin Surfaces with Specific Obstacles. In: Laugier, C., Siegwart, R. (eds.) Field and Service Robotics, pp. 551–561. Springer, Heidelberg (2008)
8. Zhang, H., Zhang, J., Wei Wang, W., Liu, R., Zong, G.: A series of pneumatic glass-wall cleaning robots for high-rise buildings. Industrial Robot: An International Journal, 150–160 (2007)
9. Miyake, T., Ishihara, H., Yoshimura, M.: Application of Wet Vacuum-based Adhesion System for Wall Climging Mechanism, pp. 532–537. IEEE (2007)

10. Marques, L., Almeida, A., Tokhi, M.O., Virk, G.S.: Advances in mobile Robotics. World Scientific (2008)
11. Longo, D., Muscato, G.: Adhesion techniques for climbing robots: state of the art and experimental considerations. CLAWAR (2008)
12. Urakami Research and Developed Co., V-Robo Systems
13. Wright, D., Wolgamott, J., Zink, G.: Inc StoneAge, Waterjet Cleaning Of Steel Process Lines Without Damage To The Steel Wall, WJTA Jet News (April 2006)
14. Working safe BC. High Pressure Washing Safe Work Practices, p. 51, ISBN 978-0-7726-6028-2
15. Li, J., Gao, X., Fan, N.: BIT Climber: A Centrifugal Impeller-Based Wall. In: IEEE International Conference on Mechatronics and Automation, Changchun, China, August 9-12 (2009)
16. González, H., Quintero, R., Ortiz, R., Montes, J., Hernando González, A.: Design of a mobile robot for clean the external walls of oil tanks, book: Mobile Ad Hoc Robots and Wireless Robotic Systems: Design and Implementation (2012)
17. Wang, X., Yi, Z., Gong, Y., Wang, Z.: Optimum Dynamic Modeling of a Wall Climbing Robot for Ship Rust Removal. In: Xie, M., Xiong, Y., Xiong, C., Liu, H., Hu, Z. (eds.) ICIRA 2009. LNCS (LNAI), vol. 5928, pp. 623–631. Springer, Heidelberg (2009)
18. Sureservo™, Selecting the servo system. AC Servo Systems User Manual
19. Illingworth, L., Reinfeld, D.: Vortex Attractor, United states Patent No 6.595.753 (July 22, 2003)

Research on the Impact of the Number of Wheels and Layouts to the Performances of Omni-Directional Chassis

Sheng-bin Huang, Dian-shen Chen, and Hao-qing Gong

Room A607, New main building, Beihang University, Xue Yuan Road 37th,
Hai dian district, Beijing, China, 100191
569509971@qq.com, {chends,gonghaoqinzl}@163.com

Abstract. The Omni-directional mobile chassis is a kind of mobile device which can travel in any direction under the premise of a fixed body posture, and can guarantee a zero radius of gyration when rotating. It shows different performances with different number of wheels or layouts. Based on the robot chassis functional requirements: mobility and stability, this article, through the theoretical analysis/ADAMS simulation and experiment to the three-wheel and four-wheel chassis proposals respectively, compares their two types of performances and finally gets their advantages and weaknesses. The conclusion of this paper provides some reference on the application of different Omni-directional mobile chassises in different situations.

Keywords: Omni-directional chassis, wheels, layout.

1 Introduction

With the development of robot technology, there has been a variety of robot chassises for different occasions. Depend on its intrinsic merits, the Omni-directional chassis based on Omni-directional wheels, in recent years has been widely noted. The Yaskawa Electric company developed an assisting living robot named Smart Pal which used a three-wheel Omni-directional chassis[1]. MKR (Muratec Keio Robot), an autonomous Omni-directional transfer robot system for hospital applications, uses a platform with four Omni-directional wheels[2]. The Omni-directional chassis has many forms, the three-wheel and four-wheel schemes are most familiar, but one scheme also has different layouts, the number of wheels and the layout can both affect the performances of the chassis. Most of the literatures about Omni-directional chassis focus on the mechanical structure[3] and performance parameters[4] of a specific scheme. There is no paper which deals with a systematic comparative analysis of these different options. Therefore, this paper attempts to do this work by theoretical analysis, simulation and experimental tests.

C.-Y. Su, S. Rakheja, H. Liu (Eds.): ICIRA 2012, Part III, LNAI 7508, pp. 258–267, 2012.
© Springer-Verlag Berlin Heidelberg 2012

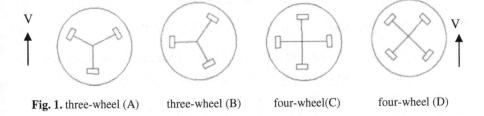

Fig. 1. three-wheel (A)   three-wheel (B)   four-wheel(C)   four-wheel (D)

2   The Theoretical Analysis of Chassis Mobility Parameters

The mobility parameters of chassis, such as maximum velocity, accelerating time, maximum acceleration are very important indicators to evaluate chassis performance. For example, the mobility of the soccer robot platform, to a certain extent, represents the level of performance of the robot chassis[6].

2.1   Velocity Analysis Translator Motion for the Three-Wheel Chassis

It is assumed that the mobile platform dose translator motion with α degrees angle deviating from the positive direction, the three-wheel platform move at a speed of V. The three Omni-directional wheel line speed are V_A, V_B and V_C. The velocity decomposition diagram is shown as Fig.2.

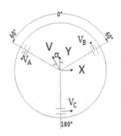

Fig. 2. Three-wheel platform velocity decomposition diagram

Fig. 3. Three-wheel platform velocity distribution diagram

Through analyzing the decomposed velocity, speeds of the three wheels are [5]:

$$V_A=V\times \cos(150° - \alpha), V_B=V\times \cos(30° - \alpha), V_C=V\times \cos (270° - \alpha) \qquad (1)$$

And： $V_A\in[- V_{max}, V_{max}]$ 、 $V_B\in[- V_{max}, V_{max}]$ 、 $V_C\in[- V_{max}, V_{max}]$, V_{max} is the maximum motor speed, then according to the relationship between the three

Omni-directional wheels speed can be deduced as follow:

$$V=\min\{V_A/\cos(150°-\alpha), V_B/\cos(30°-\alpha), V_C/\cos(270°-\alpha)\} \tag{2}$$

Angle α is between $0°$ and $360°$. The three-wheel platform velocity distribution diagram is displayed as Fig.3 according to formula (2). The radius of the circle is the maximum line speed of the three Omni-directional mobile platform, and the maximum speed is $2V_{max}/\sqrt{3}$, which turns up six times between $0°$ and $360°$.

2.2   Force Analysis of Translator Motion for the Three-Wheel Chassis

It is assumed that the mobile chassis starts accelerating from a static state with α degrees angle deviating from the positive direction, the amount external force that the three-wheel chassis suffered is F. The driving forces of the three Omni-directional wheel are F_A, F_B, F_C. The decomposition is shown as Fig.4.

Fig. 4. Three-wheel chassis forces decomposition diagram

Fig. 5. Three-wheel chassis resultant force distribution diagram

The resultant force of chassis in the moving direction can be expressed as:

$$F=-F_A \cos(30°+\alpha)+F_B \cos(30°-\alpha)-F_C \sin\alpha \tag{3}$$

The resultant force of chassis in the direction vertical to the moving direction is zero, consequently the system does not do rotary motion, then M=0:

$$F_A \sin(30°+\alpha) +F_B \sin(30°-\alpha)-F_C \cos\alpha =0 \tag{4}$$

$$F_A R+F_B R+F_C R=0 \tag{5}$$

$F_{A, B, C} \in [-F_{max}, F_{max}]$, F_{max} is the maximum driving force that one single wheel can reach, The resultant force F distribution diagram of the chassis on the relative coordinate system is shown as Fig.5, the maximum resultant force $F=\sqrt{3}F_{max}$, will turn up 6 times between $0°$ and $360°$.

2.3 Mobility Comparison between Three-Wheel and Four-Wheel Program

Analysis the velocity of the four-wheel scheme in the same way of which the three-wheel program, and get their velocity graphs(Fig.6) which changes with the angle α.

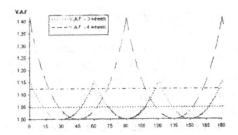

Fig. 6. The velocity graphs of three-wheel and four-wheel program [7]

It can be found that the maximum speed of four-wheel chassis is greater than that of three-wheel one.

3   Analysis of Motion Stability Factors for the Chassis

In order to ensure the accuracy of the robot localization and navigation, the robot chassis must have good motion stability. The motion stability of the chassis is related to many factors including the structure of wheel, the number of wheels, layout of chassis, machining and installation precision of chassis parts, accuracy of motor controlling and so on.

3.1   The Impact of Wheel Structure to Stability

The Omni-directional wheel used in this article has two teams of rollers which can alternately keep touch with the ground, making the wheel move smoothly. But the touching points are staggered both inside and outside, which makes the chassis drift off the moving direction, As a result, the center of robot mass will fluctuate and it is doomed to affect the move stability of the robot.

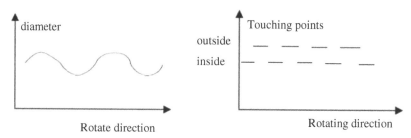

Fig. 7. Diameter change diagram   **Fig. 8.** Touching points change diagram

3.2   The Impact of the Number of Wheels and Layouts

The symmetrical arranging of driving wheels makes the chassis easy to control and the power source balanced and equally utilized. which will reduce the movement error. The four wheels of the four-wheel programs can not touch the ground together at same time, there will be a driving wheel hanging in the air, but this will make the robot move more stable because the pitching motion can relieve impact. In addition, motor has a speed up process. When the speed of the robot is given, speeds assigned to the three wheels may be different, therefore the acceleration time will be different. As a consequence, the robot will deviate from the predetermined direction since the start. From a design perspective, adding a driving wheel can improve the situation[8]. According to the analysis above, the four-wheel program has better stability than the three-wheel program.

4   The ADAMS Kinematics Simulation Analysis

In this paper, using the ADAMS software to do kinematics simulation, the chassis models can be predigested, and the machining errors of the parts, assembly errors and motor control errors of other non-research factors can be ignored In the ADAMS surrounding[9-10]. Each of the driving motor speed is set to N = 300deg/s in program A, C and D, the wheel diameter d=0.152m, so the wheel linear velocity is V=(N/360)πd=0.40m/s. In order to ensure a straight-line movement of chassis in scheme B, the two right wheel speeds are set to (1/2)N, the theoretical velocity of chassis is V.

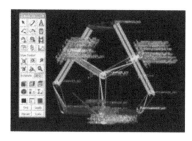

Fig. 9. The three-wheel chassis model

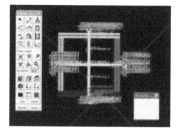

Fig. 10. The four-wheel chassis model

4.1   The Results of Translator Motion Simulation

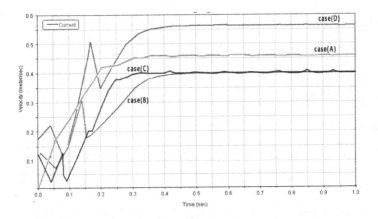

Fig. 11. The Velocity graphs of chassis (A)(B)(C)(D)

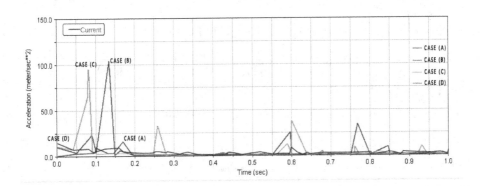

Fig. 12. The instantaneous Acceleration graphs of chassis (A)(B)(C)(D)

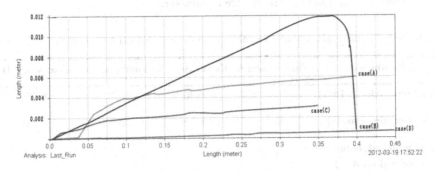

Fig. 13. The mass center trajectory graphs of chassis (A)(B)(C)(D) （move along X-axis）

4.2   The Results of Rotary Motion Simulation

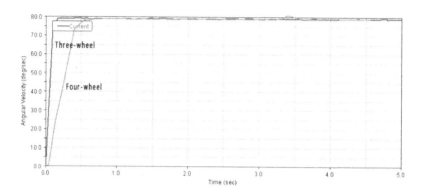

Fig. 14. The angular velocity graphs of chassis that do rotator motion

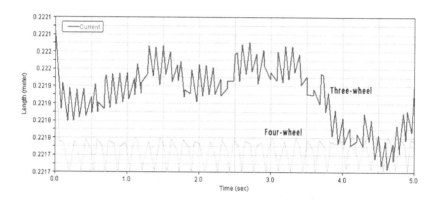

Fig. 15. The mass center displacement graphs of chassis

4.3   The Comparison of Performance Parameters

Table 1. The comparison of performance parameters of translator motion of the chassis

Parameter	Three-wheel A	Three-wheel B	Four-wheel C	Four-wheel D
Maximum velocity [m/s]	0.47	0.40	0.40	0.57
Accelerating time [s]	0.46	0.35	0.32	0.43
Maximum instantaneous acceleration[m/s^2]	16	105	93	10
Deviation rate (s_y/s_x)	0.006/0.4= 0.015	0.012/0.4= 0.003	0.00275/0.35= 0.008	0.0005/0.46= 0.001

Table 2. The data of performance parameters of rotator motion for the chassis

Parameter	Three-wheel	Four-wheel
Maximum angular velocity [deg/s]	78	78
Deviation of mass center[m]	0.0004	0.0002

5   Experimental Test

We use the robot physical prototype, stopwatch, tape measure to test performance parameters of the   four   chassis   programs and   record   the   data.   Through the experiments, we tested and   verified the theory analysis and simulation results and confirmed the performance characteristics of the four chassis layouts .

5.1   Mobility Parameters Test

In these experiments, all the angular velocities of the driving motors are set to be the same, then the data of maximum velocity and acceleration time is got.

Fig. 16. The exprimental prototypes of chassis

Table 3. The experimental data of mobility parameters

Program	Maximum velocity [m/s]	Acceleration time [s]
Three-wheel A	0.68	1.5
Three-wheel B	0.60	1.1
Four-wheel C	0.62	1.2
Four-wheel D	0.83	1.4

5.2   Stability Parameters Test

Experiment methods: Make all the chassis schemes travel in the same direction for 10 meters, then measure the deviation that chassis deviate from the moving direction to compare the moving stability.

Fig. 17. The deviation from moving direction of chassis

Table 4. The experimental data of stability parameters

Program	Deviation of mass center [m]
Three-wheel A	0.083
Three-wheel B	0.042
Four-wheel C	0.012
Four-wheel D	0.120

6   Conclusions

6.1   The Comparison Result of Mobility Performance

According to the simulation data in Tables 1, 2 and experimental data in 3, there are:
  (1)When the number of wheels are the same, the chassis program (A)/(D) has greater speed and shorter acceleration time than the other one, obviously their mobility are better; (2)When the layout are oblique arranged, the four-wheel scheme (D) has a greater speed and a shorter acceleration time than the three-wheel program (A), so the four-wheel program D has better mobility.

6.2   The Comparison Result of Stability Performance

According to the simulating data in Tables 1, 2 and experiment data in table 4, there are:

(1)When the number of wheels that on the chassis are the same, we can find out that: the   four-wheel program(D) moving stability is better than program(C) in theory,but program(C) has better stability than (D) in experiment, this is because some other factors are ignored during theorical analyzing. The three-wheel program (A) is better than program (B); (2)When the number of wheels are different , the four-wheel chassis has better moving stability than the three-wheel program, and the program (C) has the best stability in the four scenarios .

6.3   Expectation

In this paper, Only the mobility and stability performance of four Omni-directional chassis schemes are studied. However, when we choose the chassis proposal, we must consider the obstacle climbing ability and anti-slip performance. Hence, the climbing ability and anti-slip performance of the chassis are expected to be researched in the future.

References

1. Wei, Z.: Robot server Smart Pal. Robotic Technology and Application (2007)
2. Takahashi, M., Suzuki, T.: A Mobile Robot for Transport Applications in Hospital Domain with Safe Human Detection Algorithm. In: International Conference on Robotics and Biomimetics (2009)
3. Guo-rong, Y., Hai-bin, Z.: A new kind of wheel-model all-directional moving mechanism. Journal of Harbin Institute of Technology (2001)
4. Chao, Z.: Research on the design and control of a robot Omni-directional platform. Master's thesis. HE HAI university (2007)
5. Chun-tao, L., Qi-xin, C.: Anisotropy of 4-wheeled Omni-directional mobile robots. CAAI Transactions on Intelligent Systems (2007)
6. Ashmore, M., Barnes, N.: Omni-drive robot motion on curved paths: the fastest path between two points is not a straight-line. In: Proc. Australian Joint Conference on Artificial Intelligence, Canberra, Australia (2002)
7. Ashmore, M., Barnes, N.: Omni-directional robot motion on curved paths: The fastest Path between two points is not a straight line. In: Proc. Australian Joint Conference on Artificial Intelligence, vol. 12, pp. 225–236 (2002)
8. Lei, W., Zeng-qi, S.: Research on Structural Design of Soccer Robot. Electro-Mechanical Engineering (2004)
9. Meehnaieal Dnymaies. Using ADAMS view 34–36 (1998)
10. Li, J., Xing, J.-w.: ADAMS application tutorial, pp. 98–99. Beijing institute of technology press, Beijing (2002)

A Novel Distributed Tuned Mass Damper Design Approach

Fan Yang[1], Ramin Sedaghati[2], and Esmailzadeh Esmailzadeh[3]

[1] South China University of Technology,
School of Automation Science & Engineering, Guangzhou, P.R. China
Xmyf@hotmail.com
[2] Concordia University, Department of Mechanical and Industrial Engineering,
Montréal, Canada
Sedagha@encs.concordia.ca
[3] Faculty of Engineering and Applied Science,
University of Ontario Institute of Technology, Oshawa, Canada
Ezadeh@uoit.ca

Abstract. The Distributed Tuned Mass Damper system, which is defined as the multiple Tuned Mass Damper design based on one specific vibration mode of the main structure, is investigated in this study. As those for single TMD design cases, the challenge work in this area is to attain the best vibration suppression performance through an optimally designed DTMD system. In the traditional DTMD or TMD design, the general approach is to focus on the attached spring(s) and damper(s). In this study, a novel DTMD design methodology will be proposed, in which the design parameters are the attached masses in the DTMD system under assumed constant spring(s) and damper(s). The presented method provides a simple and straight-forward way to design the DTMD system, and may provide a more cost-efficient approach in manufacturing, installation and also maintenance than the traditional design. The numerical examples will be presented to illustrate the validity and effectiveness of the proposed DTMD design approach.

1 Introduction

The Tuned Mass Damper (TMD) is one of the most promising and effective passive vibration suppression devices. The optimal design theory of TMD systems for an undamped Single Degree-of-Freedom (SDOF) primary structure under harmonic loading was firstly developed by Den Hartog [1]. Since then, many optimal design methods of TMD systems have been developed to suppress the structural vibration induced by various types of excitation sources [2-7].

Based on the working principle of an optimally designed TMD system, one could easily realize that its vibration suppression performance is very sensitive to the off-tuning of the related tuned natural frequency [6 and 7], which practically means that small deviations of the stiffness for a TMD system from its optimum value will lead to significant attenuation of the vibration suppression effectiveness.

C.-Y. Su, S. Rakheja, H. Liu (Eds.): ICIRA 2012, Part III, LNAI 7508, pp. 268–276, 2012.
© Springer-Verlag Berlin Heidelberg 2012

To overcome the above issue and also improve the vibration suppression performance, Xu and Igusa [8 and 9] introduced the multiple TMDs system, as that shown in Fig. 1. In this paper, to distinguish it from the multiple TMDs design based on multiple modes of the main structures, the multiple TMDs design based on one specific mode [8 and 9], as illustrated in Fig. 1, is named as the Distributed Tuned Mass Damper (DTMD) system.

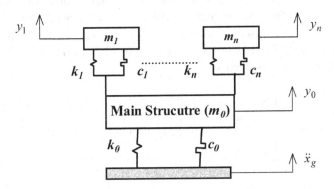

Fig. 1. Schematic of a Distributed Tuned Mass Damper (DTMD) design

Based on the DTMD design schematic illustrated in Fig. 1, one can easily realize that the design principle of a DTMD system is to tune the natural frequencies of a set of small TMD systems distributed around the designed mode of the primary structures. Therefore, to attain the best vibration suppression performance, the masses, stiffness and damping coefficients of the attached DTMD system should also be determined through a design optimization procedure.

In the design of the DTMD and/or TMD systems, the general approach is to focus on the attached spring(s) and damper(s), as the research papers presented by Xu and Igusa [8 and 9], and Yang *et al* [10]. Considering the cost of manufacturing, installation, and maintenance, this paper will present a simple and straightforward DTMD design approach with high efficiency, in which the spring(s) and damper(s) will be pre-defined based on the classic optimal TMD design, and the optimization procedure is to attain the values of each attached masses. Illustrated examples will be presented to verify the validity and effectiveness of the developed approach through the comparisons of structural dynamic responses and those presented in available literatures.

2   Formulations

The schematic of a DTMD design problem has been illustrated in Fig. 1, in which $\ddot{x}_g$ represents the acceleration of base-excitation; y_0 and y_i are the relative (relative to the base) displacement of the main structure and the ith TMD in the DTMD system, respectively; m_0 and m_i represent the mass of the main structure and the ith attached TMD in the DTMD system, respectively; k_0, c_0, k_i and c_i represent the stiffness and damping coefficient of the main structure and the ith attached TMD in the DTMD system, respectively. The equation of motion in a general form for the DTMD design problem shown in Fig. 1 can be expressed as:

$$[M]\{\ddot{q}\} + [C]\{\dot{q}\} + [K]\{q\} = [M][E_s]\ddot{x}_g \tag{1}$$

where $[M]$, $[C]$ and $[K]$ are the structural mass, damping and stiffness matrices, respectively; $[E_s]$ is the direction matrix related to base acceleration ($\ddot{x}_g$); $\{q\}$, $\{\dot{q}\}$ and $\{\ddot{q}\}$ are the displacement, velocity and acceleration vectors, respectively. Let us assume total n small TMDs will be utilized to establish a DTMD system, thus the above parameters can be defined as:

$$[M]_{(n+1)\times(n+1)} = \begin{bmatrix} m_0 & 0 & \cdots & 0 \\ 0 & m_1 & \cdots & 0 \\ \vdots & \vdots & \ddots & \vdots \\ 0 & 0 & \cdots & m_n \end{bmatrix}, \quad [E_s]_{(n+1)\times 1} = -\begin{Bmatrix} 1 \\ 1 \\ \vdots \\ 1 \end{Bmatrix}, \quad \{q\} = \begin{Bmatrix} y_0 \\ y_1 \\ \vdots \\ y_n \end{Bmatrix}$$

$$[K] = \begin{bmatrix} k_0 + k_1 + \cdots + k_n & -k_1 & \cdots & -k_n \\ -k_1 & k_1 & 0 & 0 \\ \vdots & & 0 & \ddots & \vdots \\ -k_n & & 0 & \cdots & k_n \end{bmatrix}, \tag{2}$$

$$[C] = \begin{bmatrix} c_0 + c_1 + \cdots + c_n & -c_1 & \cdots & -c_n \\ -c_1 & c_1 & 0 & 0 \\ \vdots & & 0 & \ddots & \vdots \\ -c_n & & 0 & \cdots & c_n \end{bmatrix}$$

Now, based on the established equation of motion, the design procedures proposed in this study can be summarized as:

Step 1: Defining the initial masses (m_{i0}) for the DTMD system, and then based on these initial masses to evaluate the variables k_i and c_i using the classic TMD design approach, such as the work presented by Den Hartog [1] for harmonic excitation, as:

$$f_i = \frac{1}{1 + \mu_i} \quad \text{and} \quad \xi_i = \sqrt{\frac{3\mu_i}{8(1 + \mu_i)}} \tag{3}$$

where μ_i, f_i and ξ_i represent the mass ratio, frequency ratio and damping factor of the ith attached small TMD, respectively, which can be defined as:

$$\mu_i = \frac{m_i}{m_0}, \quad f_i = \frac{\omega_i}{\omega_0} = \frac{\sqrt{k_i/m_i}}{\sqrt{k_0/m_0}} \quad \text{and} \quad \xi_i = \frac{c_i}{2\sqrt{k_i m_i}} \tag{4}$$

where ω_i and ω_0 represent the natural frequency of the ith attached TMD and the main structure, respectively. Therefore, under the given mass (m_{i0}) for each small TMD in the DTMD system, one can easily utilize Eqs. (3) and (4) to determine the parameters k_i and c_i.

Step 2: Defining the masses of DTMD system as:

$$m_i = m_{i0} + \Delta m_i \tag{5}$$

where Δm_i represents the changing of the attached mass of the ith small TMD consisting of the DTMD system, and is considered as design variable; m_i is the variable constructing the mass matrix $[M]$ in Eqs. (1) and (2).

As the effectiveness of the spring and damper are both directly related to the relative displacement and velocity between the main structure and the small masses of the attached DTMD system, one can define the following transfer function to be convenient for the optimization procedure:

$$\{q\} = \begin{Bmatrix} y_0 \\ y_1 \\ \vdots \\ y_n \end{Bmatrix} = \begin{bmatrix} 1 & 0 & 0 & 0 \\ 1 & 1 & 0 & 0 \\ \vdots & 0 & 1 & 0 \\ 1 & 0 & 0 & 1 \end{bmatrix} \begin{Bmatrix} y_0 \\ y_1 - y_0 \\ \vdots \\ y_n - y_0 \end{Bmatrix} = [T_s]\{p\} \tag{6}$$

Obviously, in vector $\{p\}$ of Eq. (6) the first variable represents the displacement of the main structure, and other variables represent the relative displacement between the main structure and the attached small masses of the DTMD system. Substituting Eq. (6) to Eq. (1) and then transferring Eq. (1) to the state-space form, yields:

$$\{\dot{x}\} = [A]\{x\} + [E]\{\ddot{x}_g\} \tag{7}$$

where $\{x\}$ is the state vector $\{p, \dot{p}\}^T$, and

$$[A] = \begin{bmatrix} [0] & [I] \\ -[T_s]^{-1}[M]^{-1}[K][T_s] & -[T_s]^{-1}[M]^{-1}[C][T_s] \end{bmatrix}, \text{ and } [E] = \begin{bmatrix} [0] \\ [T_s[^{-1}[E_s] \end{bmatrix} \tag{8}$$

As the absolute acceleration of the structural response can be easily measured, the output vector in this study is defined as the absolute acceleration of the main structure. Based on Eqs. (7) and (8), the absolute acceleration (z) of the main structure can be obtained through:

$$z = [P_1]\left(-[T_s]^{-1}[M]^{-1}[K][T_s] \quad -[T_s]^{-1}[M]^{-1}[C][T_s] \right)\{x\} = [C_1]\{x\} \tag{9}$$

where matrix $[P_1]$ is the direction matrix utilized to pick up the variables related to the main structure from vector $\{p\}$, and can be defined as:

$$[P_1] = \begin{bmatrix} 1 & \overbrace{0 \quad \cdots \quad 0}^{n} \end{bmatrix}$$ (10)

Using Eqs. (7)-(10), the transfer function between output absolute acceleration (z) of the main system and ground acceleration ($\ddot{x}_g$) can now be established as:

$$[G_{z\ddot{x}_g}] = [C_1](s[I] - [A])^{-1}[E]$$ (11)

Base on Eq. (11), the H_2 norm of the transfer function will then be obtained as:

$$\|H\|_2^2 = \frac{1}{2\pi} \int_{-\infty}^{+\infty} trace\left[\mathbf{G}'_{z\ddot{x}_g}(j\omega)\mathbf{G}_{z\ddot{x}_g}(j\omega)\right]d\omega$$ (12)

Here, it should be noted that the matrices [A] and [C_1] are both related to the design variable Δm_i.

Step 3: Base on Steps 1 and 2, the developed optimization problem in this case can be expressed as:

Find:	*optimal mass changing Δm_i*	
To minimize:	*the H_2 norm of transfer function $\lfloor G_{z\ddot{x}_g} \rfloor$*	(13)
Subjected to:	$-m_{i0} < \Delta m_i < m_{i0}$;	

Here, it should also be noted that the constrains defined in Eq. (13) can provide effective bandwidth for the tuned frequency range, and avoid the minus mass situation, which is impractical.

It should be emphasized that although the objective function adopted in this study is the H_2 norm of the transfer function, based on the transfer function in the state-space form provided in Eqs. (7) - (9), one can easily attain the magnitude of the transfer function, Dynamic Magnitude Factor (DMF), variance or RMS of the response. Therefore, one can easily select different optimization criterions based on practical applications, and then it can be found that the developed optimization approaches for the DTMD design are straight forward and powerful.

3   Illustrated Examples

To validate the developed optimization design approach for the DTMD system, illustrated examples will be provided in this section. An optimal DTMD system composed of 5 small TMDs will be investigated in detailed.

Here, the DTMD system is assumed to be composed of 5 small TMDs ($n=5$), and the total initial mass ($\sum_{i=1}^{n} m_{i0}$) of the DTMD system is assumed to be 1% of the mass of the main structure ($m_0=1000g$), and is uniformly distributed ($m_{i0}=0.01m_0/n$). Therefore, the initial stiffness and damping factors can be obtained through Eqs. (3)

and (4). All pre-defined parameters have been summarized in Table 1. In Table 1, m_0, k_0, c_0 and ω_0 represent the mass, stiffness, damping coefficient and natural frequency of the main structure, respectively.

Table 1. Defining structural parameters and initial parameters for the DTMD system

$m_0\,(g)$	$k_0\,(n/m)$	$c_0(ns/m)$	$\omega_0(rad/s)$	$\sum m_{i0}\,(g)$	n	$m_{i0}\,(g)$	$k_i\,(n/m)$	$c_i\,(ns/m)$
1000	1.2×10^5	438.178	10.95	10	5	2	239.0429	1.1964

3.1 Optimization

The optimization problem has been established in Eq. (13). The optimum parameters of the DTMD system with 5 TMDs and input (initial) total mass ratio equal to 1% have been obtained and summarized in Table 2. Moreover, to compare the result with that design based on the spring and damper of the DTMD system [10], Table 2 summarizes the results proposed by Yang *et al* [10]. Here, it should be noted that the final total mass ratio, obtained through the methodology proposed in this study, is slightly different from their relative initial mass ratio.

Table 2. Optimum results for DTMD design under total mass ratio equal to 1% the mass of main structure

Methodology	Initial and optimum	DTMD system				
		1	2	3	4	5
Ref. [10]	k_{Ti}	273.6004	253.671	222.6816	273.3039	207.5967
	c_{Ti}	0.6849	0.7316	0.6363	0.8003	0.6545
Design Approach in this study	$m_{i0}\,(g)$	2	2	2	2	2
	$\Delta m_i\,(g)$	-0.1998	-0.0958	0.0228	0.1482	0.3032
	$m_i\,(g)$	1.8002	1.9042	2.0228	2.1482	2.3032

To compare the vibration suppression performance of the designed DTMD systems to that for single optimal TMD design, one TMD with mass 10(g), which is equal to the total initial mass of the DTMD system, has also been investigated. The optimization procedure for the single TMD design can also been expressed as that shown in Eq. (13) or follow the methodology provided in Refs. [6 and 7]. The results for optimal single TMD have been attained and summarized in Table 3.

Table 3. Optimal single TMD parameters

n	$m(g)$	$k\,(n/m)$	$c\,(ns/m)$	f_{TMD}	ξ_{TMD}
1	10	1179.9216	10.8221	0.9916	0.0498

To illustrate the effectiveness of the developed DTMD systems, Fig. 2 compares the structural frequency domain responses for uncontrolled structure, structure with optimal DTMD based on design approach proposed in this study, given in Table 2, structure with optimal single TMD system given in Table 3, and those presented in Ref. [10].

From Fig. 2, one can easily find that: (1) the DTMD design approaches can provide superior vibration suppression performance comparing with that for single TMD design; (2) unlike that for single TMD, the effectiveness of the DTMD system can cover a small frequency range (bandwidth), and provide smooth performance in this bandwidth, especially for the DTMD design approach proposed in this study; (3) the DTMD design method provided in this study can provide superior vibration performance comparing with those presented in Ref. [10].

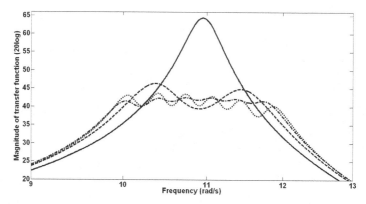

Fig. 2. Structural frequency response comparison. Solid, dashed, dashed-dotted and dotted lines represent the uncontrolled structure, structure with optimal single TMD in Table 3, structure with optimal DTMD in Table 2, and those presented in Ref. [10], respectively.

3.2   The Effect of the Total Mass of the DTMD System

This section will investigate the effect of the total mass of the DTMD system to the vibration suppression performance. Here, the number of the TMDs in the DTMD system is still 5, and the total (initial) mass ratio of the DTMD system has been changed to 2%, 5% and 10%, respectively.

Following the optimal design approaches established in Section 2, the optimal DTMD systems based on total (initial) mass ratio equal to 2%, 5% and 10% have been attained, and the results have been summarized in Table 4.

Table 4. The optimal DTMD system with total mass (initial) ratio equal to 2%, 5% and 10%, respectively

Mass Ratio(Initial)	DTMD system (g)				
	1	2	3	4	5
2%	3.485	3.746	4.077	4.433	4.895
5%	8.266	9.106	10.419	11.878	13.985
10%	15.895	17.772	21.601	26.052	33.222

Fig. 3 compares the structural frequency responses for structure with the optimal DTMD systems based on the optimal listed in Tables 2 and 4 for mass ratio equal to 1%, 2%, 5% and 10%, respectively. Here, it should also be noted that the final total mass ratio for different cases is slightly different from their relative initial mass ratio.

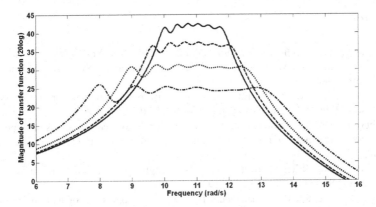

Fig. 3. Structural frequency response comparison. Solid, dashed, dotted and dashed-dotted lines represent structure with optimal DTMD design with 5 small TMDs under total mass ratio equal to 1.01786%, 2.0636%, 5.3654% and 11.4542%, respectively.

From Fig. 3, one can find that the effectiveness of the DTMD system can be improved with the increase of the total mass of the attached DTMD system.

4   Conclusion

In this study a novel DTMD design approach is developed to meet the requirement of practical application, in which the stiffness and damping factors of the DTMD system are all constant, and the design variables are each attached masses of the DTMD system. The developed optimization procedures provide a simple, clear and straight forward way to effectively attain the optimum parameters of the DTMD system. Based on the developed methodology, one can easily extend the study to multiple DOF main structures or continuous structures.

Illustrated examples have also been provided to verify the validity of the developed DTMD design methodology. The results show that, the optimal DTMD systems can suppress the structural response effectively in a frequency bandwidth around tuned frequency, and provide better vibration suppression performance than that for single TMD under the same (close) mass (total) ratio.

Comparing the results illustrated in this study with those proposed in Ref. [10], one can easily make the conclusion that the optimal DTMD design approach proposed in this study is better than that shown in Ref. [10], as it can provide the superior vibration suppression for almost similar total mass of the DTMD system. Moreover, manufacturing, installation and maintenance issues are simpler than that obtained based on the design approach proposed in Ref. [10].

Acknowledgement. Support from the Fundamental Research Funds for the Central Universities, SCUT (No: 2012ZZ0109) and Natural Sciences and Engineering Research Council of Canada (NSERC) are gratefully acknowledged.

References

1. Den Hartog, J.P.: Mechanical Vibrations. McGraw-Hill, New York (1956)
2. Crandall, S.H., Mark, W.D.: Random Vibration in Mechanical Systems. Academic Press, New York (1963)
3. Warburton, G.B., Ayorinde, E.O.: Optimum absorber parameters for simple systems. Earthquake Engineering and Structural Dynamics 8, 197–217 (1980)
4. Warburton, G.B.: Optimum absorber parameters for various combinations of response and excitation parameters. Earthquake Engineering and Structural Dynamics 10, 381–401 (1982)
5. Rana, R., Soong, T.T.: Parametric study and simplified design of tuned mass dampers. Engineering Structures 20, 193–204 (1998)
6. Yang, F., Sedaghati, R., Esmailzadeh, E.: Vibration suppression of non-uniform curved beam under random loading using optimal Tuned Mass Damper. Journal of Vibration and Control 15(2), 233–261 (2009)
7. Yang, F., Sedaghati, R., Esmailzadeh, E.: Optimal vibration suppression of Timoshenko beam with Tuned-Mass-Damper using finite element method. Journal of Vibration and Acoustics 131(3), 031006-1–031006-8 (2009)
8. Xu, K., Igusa, T.: Dynamic characteristics of multiple substructures with closely spaced frequencies. Earthquake Engineering and Structural Dynamics 21(12), 1059–1070 (1992)
9. Igusa, T., Xu, K.: Vibration control using multiple tuned mass dampers. Journal of Sound and Vibration 175(4), 491–503 (1994)
10. Yang, F., Sedaghati, R., Esmailzadeh, E.: Vibration Suppression Using Distributed Tuned Mass Damper Technology. In: Proceedings of the ASME 2010 International Design Engineering Technical Conferences & Computers and Information in Engineering Conference, DETC, 2010–28738 (2010)

The Basic Component of Computational Intelligence for AX-12 Robotic Arm Manipulator

Tadeusz Szkodny*

Silesian University of Technology, Institute of Automatic Control,
Akademicka 16 St. 44-100 Gliwice, Poland
Tadeusz.Szkodny@polsl.pl

Abstract. In this paper an essential component of the future of computer intelligence of the manipulator is presented. This component is the solution algorithm of inverse kinematics problem for AX-12 Robotic Arm with four degree of freedom (DOF) manipulator. This algorithm will be implemented into the controller of these manipulators and it will allow to control these manipulators by using the vision information, which specifies required location of the end-effector. This required location makes it possible for the end-effector to approach a manipulation object (observed by cameras) and pick it up, without the necessity of preliminary leading the manipulator to the object. Currently, the information obtained from the camera is sending via Internet to the user. User is remote controlling via the Internet the movement of manipulator, by means of joystick. These manipulators have are five links joined by revolute joint. First the location of end-effector in relation to the base of the manipulator was described. Next the analytical formulas for joint variables (dependent on these location) were presented. These formulas have take in account the multiple solutions for singular configurations of these manipulators.

Keywords: Robot Intelligence, Kinematics, Manipulators, Mechanical System.

1 Introduction

AX-12 Robotic Arm controller manufactured by Crust Crawler from the U.S., yet are unable to control in Cartesian space. The paper [1] describes a manual remote control system via the Internet-based on the Service-oriented architectures (SOA). This system also allows monitoring of the four-link manipulators, with the force effector, laser and vision system based on high-resolution camera GoPro Hero HD and frame grabber. Management of multimedia devices, and intercepting the video stream is realized using libraries DirectShow.NET. Infrastructure for remote management, authentication, streaming media and servo control is based on Windows Communication Foundation (WCF). Manual control uses three-axis joystick compatible with DirectX library. The paper [1] summarizes the experiences and problems associated with the use of WCF in robotics.

---

* Author have used the western naming convention, with given names preceding surnames.

C.-Y. Su, S. Rakheja, H. Liu (Eds.): ICIRA 2012, Part III, LNAI 7508, pp. 277–288, 2012.

With the algorithm solving the inverse kinematics presented in this article will be possible to control the manipulator in Cartesian space, using the vision information environment obtained by cameras. The algorithm takes into account the singular configurations of the manipulator and the limitations of the workspace. With cameras manipulator will be able to reach observed manipulation objects without the necessity of preliminary leading the manipulator to the object. The implemented algorithm coupled with the cameras and laser sensors will form the basis for designing the own driver software, regardless of the manufacturer of these manipulators. The development of this software will enable the creation of computer intelligence of these manipulators.

In the second chapter a description of the manipulator's kinematic structure is presented, followed by the forward kinematics equations. The solutions for inverse kinematics problem are presented in chapters 3 and 4. The fifth chapter contains the example of the inverse kinematic problem solutions, obtained by means of the *KinodwrAX12* program. Sixth chapter summarize the paper.

2   The Forward Kinematics Problem

Fig.1 illustrates a AX-12 Robotic Arm manipulator. Fig.2 illustrates a manipulator kinematics schema with a co-ordinate systems (frames) associated with links according to a Denavit-Hartenberg notation [2-8]. The base link 0 is fixed to ground and the other links 1-4 are movable. The last link with number 4 will be called an end-effector. The gripper, or other tool, is attached to this link. The neighbouring links are connected by revolute joint. The $x_5y_5z_5$ frame is associated with the gripper. Position and orientation of the links and tool are described by homogenous transform matrices. Matrix A_i describes the position and orientation of the i-th link frame in relation to i-1-st. T_4 is a matrix, that describes the position and orientation of the end-effector frame in relation to the base link. Matrix E describes the gripper frame in relation to the end-effector frame. Matrix X describes the position and orientation of the gripper frame in relation to the base link. Matrix A_i is described by (1) [4,7,8,9].

$$A_i = Rot(z,\Theta_i)Trans(0,0,\lambda_i)Trans(l_i,0,0)Rot(x,\alpha_i) , \qquad (1)$$

where Θ_i, λ_i, l_i, α_i are Denavit-Hartenberg parameters. Values of these parameters are shown in Table 1.

Table 1. Denavit-Hartenberg Parameters

Link	l_i [mm]	λ_i [mm]	α_i [°]	Θ_i [°]
1st	55.1	92.1	90	0 ÷ 360
2nd	173	0	0	0 ÷ 90
3rd	20	0	90	0 ÷ 180
4th	0	68	0	-180 ÷ 180

Fig. 1. AX-12 Robotic Arm manipulator

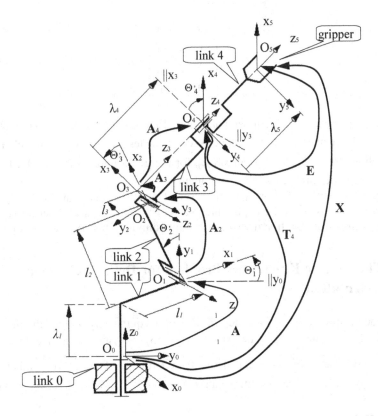

Fig. 2. Kinematic scheme of the AX-12 Robotic Arm manipulator, Denavit-Hartenberg parameters, joint variables and link frames

For further description of the kinematics Θ_i joint variables will be used. The variables $\Theta_1' = \Theta_1 - 90°$, $\Theta_2' = \Theta_2 - 90°$, $\Theta_3' = \Theta_3$ and $\Theta_4' = \Theta_4$. For notation simplicity following denotations will be used: $S_i = \sin \Theta_i'$, $C_i = \cos \Theta_i'$, $S_{ij} = \sin \Theta_{ij}'$, $C_{ij} = \cos \Theta_{ij}'$, $\Theta_{ij}' = \Theta_i' + \Theta_j'$.

The matrix $\mathbf{X}$ is described by Eq. (2).

$$\mathbf{X} = \mathbf{A_1 A_2 A_3 A_4 E} =$$

$$= \begin{bmatrix} S_1 S_{23} C_4 + C_1 S_4 & -S_1 S_{23} S_4 + C_1 C_4 & -S_1 C_{23} & -(\lambda_4 + \lambda_5) S_1 C_{23} + l_3 S_1 S_{23} + l_2 S_1 S_2 - l_1 S_1 \\ -C_1 S_{23} C_4 + S_1 S_4 & C_1 S_{23} S_4 + S_1 C_4 & C_1 C_{23} & (\lambda_4 + \lambda_5) C_1 C_{23} - l_3 C_1 S_{23} - l_2 C_1 S_2 + l_1 C_1 \\ C_{23} C_4 & -C_{23} S_4 & S_{23} & (\lambda_4 + \lambda_5) S_{23} + l_3 C_{23} + l_2 C_2 + \lambda_1 \\ 0 & 0 & 0 & 1 \end{bmatrix}. \quad (2)$$

The matrix $\mathbf{E}$ has form (3)

$$\mathbf{E} = \begin{bmatrix} 1 & 0 & 0 & 0 \\ 0 & 1 & 0 & 0 \\ 0 & 0 & 1 & \lambda_5 \\ 0 & 0 & 0 & 1 \end{bmatrix}, \quad (3)$$

where $\lambda_5 = 120mm$ is the gripper parameter. Equation (2) allows to compute the position and orientation of the gripper's co-ordinates system $x_5 y_5 z_5$ in relation to the base link's co-ordinates system $x_0 y_0 z_0$, for the given joint variables Θ_i'. It is the forward kinematics problem of the manipulator.

The position extended workspace is a set of position coordinates of the gripper frame origin relative to the base, possible to achieve. The analytical description of this subspace results from the first three rows of four column of matrix X in the Eq. (2).

3   The Inverse Kinematics Problem for Defined Gripper Orientation

The defined gripper orientation is described by a unequivocally defined the first three columns of the matrix $\mathbf{X}_{req}$, described by Eq.(5). Solving of inverse kinematics problem in this case consists in calculating the coordinates $\Theta_1' \div \Theta_4'$ from this matrix. In those calculations we use the matrix method [2-5,7-11] based on equations $(1) \div (3)$.

$$\mathbf{X}_{req} = \begin{bmatrix} a_x & b_x & c_x & d_x \\ a_y & b_y & c_y & d_y \\ a_z & b_z & c_z & d_z \\ 0 & 0 & 0 & 1 \end{bmatrix}. \tag{4}$$

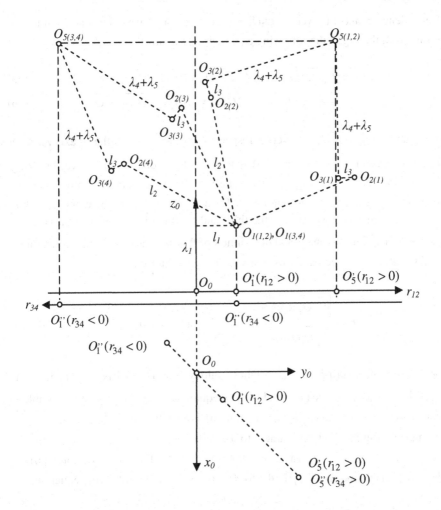

Fig. 3. The origins of the manipulator's frames. Numbers in indexes parentheses represent numbers of configuration. $r12$ is the coordinate r for configurations 1 and 2, r_{34} - coordinate r for configurations 3 and 4.

The AX-12 Manipulator Robotic Arm has four DOF. Therefore the manipulator has a subspace of position and orientation [7-9,11]. One of the necessary conditions to achieve the position and orientation of the gripper frame $x_5y_5z_5$ relative to the base frame $x_0y_0z_0$, described by the matrix $\mathbf{X}_{req}$, is the belonging of the matrix elements to the manipulator's subspace. An elements of the matrix $\mathbf{X}_{req}$ will be belong to this subspace if the versor of axis z_5 will be lie on the extension of the vector $\overrightarrow{O_3O_5}$. From the manipulator kinematic structure result that vector $\overrightarrow{O_3O_5}$ depends on the coordinates of the vector $\vec{d}$, describing the location of the origin gripper O_5.

Dependence connecting vector $\overrightarrow{O_3O_5}$ with the vector $\vec{d}$ we determine from Fig. 3. It results from the Fig. 3 the following equations and relations:

$$\vec{d} = \overrightarrow{O_0O_5} = \lambda_1\vec{k}_0 + l_1\vec{1}_r + \overrightarrow{O_1O_2} + \overrightarrow{O_2O_3} + \overrightarrow{O_3O_5}, \tag{5a}$$

$$O_1O_2 = l_2, \; O_2O_3 = l_3, \; O_3O_5 = \lambda_4 + \lambda_5, \; \overrightarrow{O_2O_3} \perp \overrightarrow{O_3O_5}. \tag{5b}$$

In equation (5a) $\vec{1}_r$ and $\vec{k}_0$ are versor respectively of axis r and the of axis z_0. After taking into account dependences (5b) it is possible to determine the vector $\overrightarrow{O_3O_5}$ from equation (5a). From Fig. 3 results the possibility of obtaining four solutions, corresponding to the four configurations, for a given vector $\vec{d}$. Vectors $\vec{c}$ and $\vec{d}$ describe the elements, respectively the third and fourth columns of the matrix $\mathbf{X}_{req}$, in the form (4). Thus, an analytical description of this subspace is the key equation (7) [7-10], resulting from the parallelism of vectors $\overrightarrow{O_3O_5}$ and $\vec{c}$.

$$arctg \frac{\left|\vec{c} \times \overrightarrow{O_3O_5(\vec{d})}\right|}{\vec{c} \cdot \overrightarrow{O_3O_5(\vec{d})}} = 0 \quad i \quad \vec{c} \cdot \overrightarrow{O_3O_5(\vec{d})} > 0. \tag{6}$$

If the position of the gripper frame origin (resulting from the matrix $\mathbf{X}_{req}$) belongs to the position extended workspace and the key equation is satisfied (6), it is possible to calculate the joint variables. Key equation (6) is satisfied only for vectors $\overrightarrow{O_3O_5}$, resulting from Fig.3, which are parallel to the versor $\vec{c}$.

Computing Θ_1. The joint variable $-90° \leq \Theta_1 \leq 270°$. From comparison matrix $\mathbf{X}$ in the form (2) and matrix $\mathbf{X}_{req}$ in the form (4), we obtain the following equation:

$$C_1d_x + S_1d_y = 0.$$

This equation has the solutions depend on sums $d_x^2 + d_y^2$ and $c_x^2 + c_y^2$.

For $d_x^2 + d_y^2 > 0$

$$\Theta_1' = \begin{cases} \Theta_1^* & for \quad d_y > 0, \\ \Theta_1^* + 180° & for \quad d_y < 0, \\ \Theta_1^* \ or \ \Theta_1^* + 360° & for \quad d_y = 0 \ i \ d_x < 0, \end{cases}$$

$$\Theta_1^* = arctg \frac{-d_x}{d_y}. \tag{7a}$$

For $d_x^2 + d_y^2 = 0$ and $c_x^2 + c_y^2 > 0$ we replace the equation $C_1 d_x + S_1 d_y = 0$ by the equation $C_1 c_x + S_1 c_y = 0$. It allows to obtain the solution (7b).

$$\Theta_1' = \begin{cases} \Theta_1^* & for \quad c_y > 0, \\ \Theta_1^* + 180° & for \quad c_y < 0, \\ \Theta_1^* \ or \ \Theta_1^* + 360° & for \quad c_y = 0 \ and \ c_x < 0, \end{cases}$$

$$\Theta_1^* = arctg \frac{-c_x}{c_y}. \tag{7b}$$

For $d_x^2 + d_y^2 = 0$ and $c_x^2 + c_y^2 = 0$ the variable Θ_1' has infinite number of solutions. In this case, we can obtain a finite number of solutions only for the sum or difference $\Theta_1' \pm \Theta_4'$. It is a singular configuration. More detail, this case will be considered below, in calculating the coordinates Θ_4'.

Computing Θ_2' *and* Θ_3'. The variable Θ_2' belongs to the range $[-135°, 45°]$, the variable Θ_3' - to the range $[0°, 180°]$. To the calculation of these angles we use the coordinates (r, z_0) of points $O_{1(i)}$, $O_{2(i)}$, $O_{3(i)}$ and $O_{5(i)}$ from Fig. 3, illustrated in Fig. 4, where i is the number of configuration satisfying the key equation (7). From Fig. 4 results the following relationships:

$$S_{2i} = \sin \Theta_2' = \frac{l_1 - r_{O2i}}{l_2}, \quad C_{2i} = \cos \Theta_2' = \frac{z_{O2i} - \lambda_1}{l_2}.$$

Hence we obtain formula (8) for the variable Θ_2':

$$\Theta_{2i}' = \begin{cases} \Theta_{2i}^* & for \quad C_{2i} \geq 0, \\ \Theta_{2i}^* - 180° & for \quad C_{2i} < 0, \end{cases}$$

$$\Theta_{2i}^* = arctg \frac{S_{2i}}{C_{2i}}. \tag{8}$$

Following system of equations for $S_{23i} = \sin(\Theta'_{2i} + \Theta'_{3i})$ and $C_{23i} = \cos(\Theta'_{2i} + \Theta'_{3i})$ results from the Fig. 4:

$$l_3 C_{23i} + (\lambda_4 + \lambda_5) S_{23i} = d_z - z_{02i} = k_1,$$
$$-l_3 S_{23i} + (\lambda_4 + \lambda_5) C_{23i} = r_5 - r_{02i} = k_2.$$

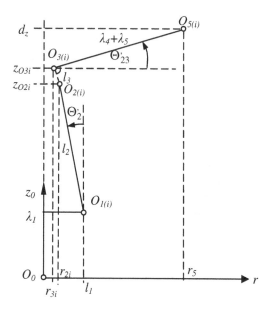

Fig. 4. The variables Θ'_2 and Θ'_{23}

After substituting the dependences $S_{23i} = S_{2i} C_{3i} + C_{2i} S_{3i}$ and $C_{23i} = C_{2i} C_{3i} - S_{2i} S_{3i}$ in this system equations, and solution it, we obtain:

$$S_{3i} = \frac{k_1[-l_3 S_{2i} + (\lambda_4 + \lambda_5) C_{2i}] - k_2[l_3 C_{2i} + (\lambda_4 + \lambda_5) S_{2i}]}{l_3^2 + (\lambda_4 + \lambda_5)^2},$$

$$C_{3i} = \frac{k_2[-l_3 S_{2i} + (\lambda_4 + \lambda_5) C_{2i}] + k_1[l_3 C_{2i} + (\lambda_4 + \lambda_5) S_{2i}]}{l_3^2 + (\lambda_4 + \lambda_5)^2}.$$

Thus

$$\Theta'_{3i} = \begin{cases} \Theta^*_{3i} & for \quad C_{3i} \geq 0, \\ \Theta^*_{3i} + 180° & for \quad C_{3i} < 0, \end{cases}$$

$$\Theta_{3i}^* = arctg \frac{S_{3i}}{C_{3i}}.$$ (9)

Computing Θ_4'. The variables Θ_4' changes in the range $[-360°, 0°]$. From comparison the matrix $\mathbf{X}$ in the form (2) and matrix $\mathbf{X}_{req}$ in the form (4), we obtain the following equations:

$$sign(S_4) = -sign(C_{23i}) \cdot sign(b_z), \quad sign(C_4) = sign(C_{23i}) \cdot sign(a_z).$$

Let's remember that i-is the number of configurations satisfying the key equation (6). Way of calculation of variable Θ_4' depends on the sum $a_z^2 + b_z^2$ of the elements of matrix $\mathbf{X}_{req}$ described by Eq. (4).

For $a_z^2 + b_z^2 > 0 \quad (\equiv C_{23i} \neq 0)$

$$\Theta_4' = \begin{cases} \Theta_4^* & for \quad sign(S_4) < 0 \quad and \quad sign(C_4) \geq 0, \\ \Theta_4^* - 180° & for \quad sign(C_4) < 0, \\ \Theta_4^* - 360° & for \quad sign(S_4) > 0 \quad and \quad sign(C_4) > 0, \\ 0° \ or - 360° & for \quad sign(S_4) = 0 \quad and \quad sign(C_4) > 0, \end{cases}$$

$$\Theta_4^* = arctg \frac{-b_z}{a_z}.$$ (10)

For $a_z^2 + b_z^2 = 0 \quad (\equiv C_{23i} = 0)$ x_5-axis versor $\vec{a}$ and y_5-axis versor $\vec{b}$ are parallel to the plane $x_0 y_0$, and z_5-axis versor $\vec{c}$ is perpendicular to this plane. Thus $c_x^2 + c_y^2 = 0$ i $c_z = \pm 1$. Such a case appeared in the calculation of the variable Θ_1' from the formula (7b). In the commentary to this formula for such a case, we found that we can obtain only a finite number of solutions for the sum or difference $\Theta_1' \pm \Theta_4'$. In this case, from the comparison of matrix $\mathbf{X}$ in the form (2) and matrix $\mathbf{X}_{req}$ in the form (4), we obtain the following equations:

$$b_x = \cos\Theta_{14}' = C_{14}, \ b_y = \sin\Theta_{14}' = S_{14}, \ \Theta_{14}' = \Theta_1' + sign(c_z)\Theta_4'.$$

From these equations results

$$\Theta_{14}^* = arctg \frac{b_y}{b_x}.$$

For the $c_z = 1$, we calculate $\Theta_{14}' = \Theta_1' + \Theta_4' \in [-450°, 270°]$ from the formula (11a).

$$\Theta_{14} = \begin{cases} \Theta_{14}^* + 180° & or & \Theta_{14}^* - 180° & for\ sign(C_{14}) < 0, \\ \Theta_{14}^* & or & \Theta_4^* - 360° & for\ sign(C_{14}) > 0, \\ -450°\ or -270° & or -90° & or\ 90°\ or\ 270° & for\ sign(C_{14}) = 0. \end{cases} \quad (11a)$$

For $c_z = -1$, we calculate $\Theta_{14} = \Theta_1' - \Theta_4' \in [-90°, 630°]$ from the formula (11b).

$$\Theta_{14}' = \begin{cases} \Theta_{14}^* + 180° & or & \Theta_{14}^* + 540° & for\ sign(C_{14}) < 0, \\ \Theta_{14}^* & or & \Theta_4^* + 360° & for\ sign(C_{14}) > 0, \\ -90°\ or\ 90° & or\ 270° & or\ 450°\ or\ 630° & for\ sign(C_{14}) = 0. \end{cases} \quad (11b)$$

4   The Inverse Kinematics Problem for Undefined Gripper Orientation

For undefined of the gripper desired orientation only vector $\vec{d} = \overrightarrow{O_0 O_5}$, corresponding to the fourth column of the matrix $\mathbf{X}_{req}$ in the form (4), is uniquely defined. Other first three columns of this matrix can take any value. Now the calculation of coordinates do not need to check the key equation (6), because the orientation is undefined. Each of the four manipulator configurations resulting from Fig.3 belongs to the subspace of position and orientation of the manipulator. For each configuration we can assign versor $\vec{c}$ parallel to the vector $\overrightarrow{O_3 O_5}$.

For $d_x^2 + d_y^2 > 0$ the variable Θ_1 we calculate from the formula (7a). This variable has infinite number of solutions for $d_x^2 + d_y^2 = 0$. For the calculation of the variables Θ_{2i}' and Θ_{3i}' we use the formulas (8) and (9). From an analysis of the form (2) of the matrix $\mathbf{X}$ result that variable Θ_4' affects only the orientation of the gripper frame. Therefore this variable has infinitely numbers of solutions for undefined orientation of gripper. This results from the formulas (10) and (11), in which are only elements of the first three columns of the matrix $\mathbf{X}_{req}$, which can take any value.

5   Example of Calculation

We will present an example of solutions of link variables of manipulator AX-12 Robotic Arm, using *KinodwrAX12* program. This program allows the user to define the orientation of the gripper as the unambiguous or any. After the declaration of this orientation as unambiguous defined, program allows the user to enter a position coordinates d_{xreq}, d_{yreq}, d_{zreq}, and orientation Φ_{req}, Θ_{req}, Ψ_{req}. For these coordinates the matrix $\mathbf{X}_{reqd} = Trans(d_{xreqd}, d_{yreqd}, d_{zreqd})\ Rot(z, \Phi_{req})$

$Rot(y, \Theta_{req})$ $Rot(z, \Psi_{req})$ is calculated. This program also allows the user define a matrix $\mathbf{X}_{req}$ by means of the link variables $\Theta_{1req} \div \Theta_{4req}$. The second way is convenient for testing the correctness of the solutions of the inverse kinematics problem.

For orientation declared as any the user entering only the coordinates of the position d_{xreq}, d_{yreq}, d_{zreq}.

After calculate the matrix $\mathbf{X}_{req}$, the program checks if required position belongs to position extended workspace. Next for unambiguous defined orientation of gripper the program checks if the key equation (6) is satisfied. If the checks are positive, the program calculates all possible sets of solutions $(\Theta_1', \Theta_2', \Theta_3', \Theta_4')$ from the range of their variability, using the formulas presented in this work. Otherwise, the program gives the user a message indicating the failure to satisfy the conditions tested and stops.

Below are presented an example of calculations. In this example, the gripper orientation was declared as any and the position coordinates $d_{xreq} = -78.5\ mm$, $d_{yreq} = 0\ mm$, $d_{zreq} = 405.1\ mm$. The program calculated the six following solutions $(\Theta_1', \Theta_2', \Theta_3')$: $(-90°, 44.0°, 44.0°)$, $(-90°, 2.2°, 123.9°)$, $(90°, 27.1°, 24.1°)$, $(90°, -35.7°, 143.8°)$, $(270°, 44.0°, 44.0°)$, $(270°, 2.2°, 123.9°)$.   Moreover, the program reported that the variable Θ_4' can take any value. This means that each of these solutions corresponds to an infinite number of solutions $(\Theta_1', \Theta_2', \Theta_3', \Theta_4')$. This program calculated the elements d_x, d_y and d_z of the fourth column of the matrix $\mathbf{X}$, described by equation (2), for these solutions. Also, the differences $d_x - d_{xreq}$, $d_y - d_{yreq}$ and $d_z - d_{zreq}$ were calculated. The calculation shows that the calculated coordinates are different from the required at most 0.04 mm.

6   Summary

Algorithm for solving the inverse kinematics problem presented in this article allowed to write the *KinodwrAX12* program, that is computing the link variables of AX-12 Robotic Arm manipulator. This program is the basis for the development of software which, after implementation into the controller, allows to:

- robot motion control to manipulation objects, observed by the camera without the necessity of preliminary leading the manipulator to the object,
- avoid the need for remote serving via the Internet of link variables by using the joystick as before,
- remote serving via Internet of gripper position and orientation, for example, by using a joystick (in the teleoperator system [12]), which previously served the link variables.

In the context of the above possibilities of the future software, the *KinodwrAX12* program is an essential component of future computer intelligence of this manipulator. After creating a knowledge base, together with the appropriate software, the manipulator will be able to do the appropriate action automatically, based on vision information about the state of the cameras environment, For example, after fixing the laser to the fourth link, integrating it with the driver and the creation of medical knowledge base concerning exposure of human skin invaded by the cancer, the manipulator will be able automatically to approach the laser to the proper distance from the affected area of skin and effectively irradiated.

References

1. Mikulski, M.A., Szkodny, T.: Remote Control and Monitoring of AX-12 Robotic Arm Based on Windows Communication Foundation. In: Czachórski, T., Kozielski, S., Stańczyk, U. (eds.) Man-Machine Interactions 2. AISC, vol. 103, pp. 77–83. Springer, Heidelberg (2011)
2. Jezierski, E.: Dynamics and Control of Robots, ch. 2. WNT, Warsaw (2006) (in Polish)
3. Kozłowski, K., Dutkiewicz, P.: Modeling and Control of Robots, ch. 1. PWN, Warsaw (2003) (in Polish)
4. Paul, R.P.: Robot Manipulators: Mathematics, Programming and Control, ch. 2. The MIT Press, Cambridge (1983)
5. Szkodny, T.: Modeling and Simulation of Industrial Robot Manipulator Motion, ch. 2. Silesian University of Technology Publ. Company, Gliwice (2004) (in Polish)
6. Szkodny, T.: Basic Component of Computational Intelligence for IRB-1400 Robots. In: Cyran, K.A., Kozielski, S., Peters, J.F., Stańczyk, U., Wakulicz-Deja, A. (eds.) Man-Machine Interactions. AISC, vol. 59, pp. 637–646. Springer, Heidelberg (2009)
7. Szkodny, T.: Kinematics of Industrial Robots, Poland, ch. 2,3,4. Silesian University of Technology Publ. Company, Gliwice, Poland (2009) (in Polish)
8. Szkodny, T.: Foundation of Robotics Problems Set, ch. 2. Silesian University of Technology Publ. Company, Gliwice, Poland (2010) (in Polish)
9. Szkodny, T.: Foundation of Robotics, Poland, ch. 3, 4. Silesian University of Technology Publ. Company, Gliwice, Poland (2011)
10. Szkodny, T.: The Basic Component of Computational Intelligence for KUKA KR C3 Robot. In: Jeschke, S., Liu, H., Schilberg, D. (eds.) ICIRA 2011, Part I. LNCS (LNAI), vol. 7101, pp. 44–52. Springer, Heidelberg (2011)
11. Craig, J.J.: Introduction to robotics, ch. 4. Addison-Weseley Publ. Comp., New York (1989)
12. Baczyński, M.: Transformation of the mechanical impedance of the object to the teleoperator server. The doctoral dissertation. Technical University of Łódź. Łódź, ch.1 (2010) (in Polish)

Guiding Sampling-Based Motion Planning by Forward and Backward Discrete Search

Erion Plaku

Dept. of Electrical Engineering and Computer Science
Catholic University of America, Washington DC 20064
plaku@cua.edu

Abstract. This paper shows how to effectively compute collision-free and dynamically-feasible robot motion trajectories from an initial state to a goal region by combining sampling-based motion planning over the continuous state space with forward and backward discrete search over a workspace decomposition. Backward discrete search is used to estimate the cost of reaching the goal from each workspace region. Forward discrete search provides discrete plans, i.e., sequences of neighboring regions to reach the goal starting from low-cost regions. Sampling-based motion planning uses the discrete plans as a guide to expand a tree of collision-free and dynamically-feasible motion trajectories toward the goal. The proposed approach, as shown by the experiments, offers significant computational speedups over related work in solving high-dimensional motion-planning problems with dynamics.

1 Introduction

The deployment of robots in exploration, navigation, search-and-rescue missions requires the capability to efficiently plan motions that enable the robots to reach desired goal regions while avoiding collisions. In order to follow the planned motions in the physical world, it is essential to take into account the underlying motion dynamics during planning. Motion planning with dynamics, however, poses significant computational challenges. In addition to collision avoidance, the planned motions need to satisfy differential constraints imposed by the dynamics on position, orientation, velocity, acceleration, and curvature. As an illustration, such differential constraints ensure, for example, that wheels on a car-like robot do not slide sideways but instead roll in the direction they are pointing.

Among the various approaches proposed over the years, sampling-based motion planning has had significant success in motion planning with dynamics [1,2]. The underlying idea is to treat the problem of computing a collision-free and dynamically-feasible motion trajectory from an initial state to a goal region as a search problem over the continuous state space of feasible robot motions. The search starts at the initial state and is incrementally expanded as a tree whose branches correspond to collision-free and dynamically-feasible trajectories. Such trajectories are obtained by sampling input controls and simulating the motion

C.-Y. Su, S. Rakheja, H. Liu (Eds.): ICIRA 2012, Part III, LNAI 7508, pp. 289–298, 2012.

dynamics forward in time for several steps or until a collision is detected. The search terminates successfully when a tree branch reaches the goal region.

The computational efficiency of sampling-based motion planners depends on their ability to effectively guide the search toward the goal. Successful approaches, such as Rapidly-exploring Random Tree (RRT) [3] and others [4–11], have relied on nearest neighbors, distance metrics, probability distributions, and other factors to guide the search, as surveyed in [1, 2]. To further improve the computational efficiency in motion planning with dynamics, recent work by the author [12] has proposed to guide sampling-based motion planning by using discrete search over a workspace decomposition. The discrete search provides sampling-based motion planning with sequences of workspace regions along which to expand the search toward the goal, while sampling-based motion planning feeds back information gathered during exploration to further improve the discrete search. Experimental results have shown significant computational speedups over RRT and other state-of-the-art sampling-based motion planners [12].

This paper builds upon the success of combining sampling-based motion planning with discrete search. In distinction from earlier work [12], the proposed approach uses both forward and backward discrete search to guide sampling-based motion planning. The workspace on which the robot operates is triangulated into a number of regions. The physical adjacency of the workspace regions is captured by the edges of a graph whose vertices correspond to workspace regions. Backward discrete search on the decomposition graph is used to estimate the cost of reaching the goal from each region. The cost estimates are used to construct a probability distribution that is more likely to expand the search from low-cost regions. Forward discrete search is then employed to compute a discrete plan to reach the goal starting from a region selected according to the above probability distribution. Such discrete plans guide the sampling-based motion planner to expand the search rapidly towards the goal. This coupling of sampling-based motion planning with forward and backward discrete search, as shown by the experiments, offers significant computational speedups over related work in solving high-dimensional motion-planning problems with dynamics.

2   Problem Specification

A motion-planning problem with dynamics is specified by a tuple

$$P = (S, U, f, \text{VALID}, s_{init}, \text{GOAL}), \text{ where}$$

- S is the state space consisting of a finite set of variables that describe the state of the robot;
- U is a control space consisting of a finite set of input variables that can be applied to the robot;
- $f : S \times U \to \dot{S}$ defines the equations of motion as a set of differential equations which describe the differential constraints imposed by the dynamics;
- VALID $: S \to \{\texttt{true}, \texttt{false}\}$ specifies constraints which states should satisfy, e.g., collision avoidance, bounds on steering angle, velocity, turning radius;

- $s_{init} \in \mathcal{S}$ is the initial state;
- GOAL : $S \to \{\texttt{true}, \texttt{false}\}$ is the motion-planning goal, i.e., GOAL$(s) = \texttt{true}$ iff s satisfies the motion-planning goal.

A dynamically-feasible trajectory $\zeta : [0, T] \to \mathcal{S}$ starting at $s \in \mathcal{S}$ is obtained by computing a control function $\tilde{u} : [0, T] \to \mathcal{U}$ and propagating the dynamics forward in time through numerical integration of $\dot{\zeta}(h) = f(\zeta(h), \tilde{u}(h))$, i.e.,

$$\zeta(t) = s + \int_0^t f(\zeta(h), \tilde{u}(h)) \, dh.$$

The objective of motion-planning with dynamics is then to compute a control function $\tilde{u} : [0, T] \to U$ such that the dynamically-feasible trajectory $\zeta : [0, T] \to S$ resulting from applying $\tilde{u}$ to the initial state $s_{init} \in S$ reaches the goal, i.e., GOAL$(\zeta(T)) = \texttt{true}$, while avoiding collisions with obstacles and satisfying all state constraints, i.e., VALID$(\zeta(t)) = \texttt{true}, \forall t \in [0, T]$.

Fig. 1. Workspaces used in the experiments. Obstacles are in blue. Goal region is in red. The robot is in green and is shown in an initial state. Triangulations are in gray.

Example: Snake-Like Robot Model. To facilitate presentation, this section provides examples of the snake-like robot model and the workspaces used in the experiments. The workspaces in which the robot operates, as in related motion-planning work [1–3, 12], are populated with polygonal obstacles. The goal is also specified as a polygonal region, denoted r_{goal}, which the robot should reach while avoiding collisions. As shown in Fig. 1, these workspaces provide challenging environments, as the snake-like robot has to wiggle its way through various narrow passages in order to reach the goal.

The snake-like robot, as shown in Fig. 1, consists of several links attached to each other. The continuous state

$$s = (x, y, \theta_0, v, \psi, \theta_1, \theta_2, \ldots, \theta_N),$$

consists of the position $(x, y) \in \mathbb{R}^2$ ($|x| \leq 30, |y| \leq 25$), orientation $\theta_0 \in [-\pi, \pi)$, velocity v ($|v| \leq 2$), and steering-wheel angle ψ ($|\psi| \leq 1 rad$) of the head link, and the orientation θ_i ($\theta_i \in [-\pi, \pi), 1 \leq i \leq N$) of each trailer link, where N is the number of trailers. The robot is controlled by setting the acceleration a ($|a| \leq 1$) and the rotational velocity ω ($|\omega| \leq 1 rad/s$) of the steering-wheel angle. The differential equations of motions $f : S \times U \to \dot{S}$ are modeled as a car pulling trailers (adapted from [2, pp. 731]), and are specified as

$$\dot{x} = v \cos(\theta_0) \quad \dot{y} = v \sin(\theta_0) \quad \dot{\theta}_0 = v \tan(\psi) \quad \dot{v} = a \quad \dot{\psi} = \omega$$

$$\dot{\theta}_i = \tfrac{v}{d}(\sin(\theta_{i-1}) - \sin(\theta_0)) \prod_{j=1}^{i-1} \cos(\theta_{j-1} - \theta_j),$$

where $1 \leq i \leq N$ and $d = 0.05$ is the hitch length. A continuous state s is considered valid iff the robot does not collide with the obstacles and the robot does not self intersect, i.e., non-consecutive links do not collide with each other.

By increasing the number of trailer links, the snake-like robot provides challenging test cases for high-dimensional motion-planning problems with dynamics. In the experiments in this paper, the number of trailer links is varied from 5 to 15 yielding problems with 10 to 20 DOFs.

3   Method

Sampling-based motion planning uses a tree data structure $\mathcal{T}$ as the basis for conducting the search in the continuous space S. Each vertex $v \in \mathcal{T}$ is associated with a collision-free continuous state, denoted as $state(v)$. Each edge $(v', v'') \in \mathcal{T}$ is associated with a collision-free and dynamically-feasible trajectory, denoted as $traj(v', v'')$, which connects $state(v')$ to $state(v'')$. Initially, $\mathcal{T}$ contains only its root vertex v_1, where $state(v_1)$ corresponds to the initial state s_{init}. As the search progresses, $\mathcal{T}$ is extended by adding new vertices and new collision-free and dynamically-feasible trajectories. As described in Section 3.5, these collision-free and dynamically-feasible trajectories are obtained by sampling control inputs and propagating forward for several steps the motion dynamics of the robot, and stopping the propagation if a collision is found. The tree search terminates successfully if a new vertex v that satisfies the motion-planning goal is added to $\mathcal{T}$, i.e., GOAL($state(v)$) = **true**. The solution trajectory is then given by $traj(\mathcal{T}, v)$, which is obtained by concatenating the collision-free and dynamically-feasible trajectories associated with the tree edges connecting v_1 to v.

To effectively obtain a collision-free and dynamically-feasible trajectory that enables the robot to reach the goal, the proposed approach uses both forward and discrete search to guide sampling-based motion planning. Pseudocode is given in Algo 1. Descriptions of the main steps of the algorithm follow.

Algorithm 1. MOTIONPLANNING(S, U, f, VALID, $s_{init}, r_{goal}, t_{max}$)

1: $G = (R, E) \leftarrow$ create adjacency graph based on workspace triangulation
2: $(cost(r_1), \ldots, cost(r_n)) \leftarrow$ BACKWARDDISCRETESEARCH(G, r_{goal})
3: $\mathcal{T} \leftarrow$ CREATETREE(s_{init})
4: **while** TIME() $< t_{max}$ **and** SOLVED() = **false do**
5:     $r_{from} \leftarrow$ SELECTREGIONBASEDONCOST(Γ), $\Gamma = \{r : r \in R \land |vertices(\mathcal{T}, r)| > 0\}$
6:     $\sigma \leftarrow$ FORWARDDISCRETESEARCH(G, r_{from}, r_{goal})
7:     **for** several times **do**
8:         $\sigma_{nonempty} \leftarrow \emptyset$; add $\leftarrow$ **true**
9:         **for** $i = |\sigma|$ down to 1 **and** add = **true do**
10:           $r \leftarrow \sigma(i)$
11:           **if** $|vertices(\mathcal{T}, r)| > 0$ **then**
12:             $\sigma_{nonempty}.pushback(r)$
13:             **if** RANDREAL(0,1) $< p$ **then** add $\leftarrow$ **false**
14:         **for** several times **do** $\diamond$ *expand $\mathcal{T}$ along the regions in $\sigma_{nonempty}$*
15:           $r \leftarrow$ SELECTREGION($\sigma_{nonempty}$)
16:           $v \leftarrow$ SELECTVERTEX($vertices(\mathcal{T}, r)$)
17:           $u \leftarrow$ SAMPLECONTROLINPUT()
18:           **for** several steps **do** $\diamond$ *extend $\mathcal{T}$ from vertex v by applying control u*
19:             $dt \leftarrow$ STEP($state(v), u$); $s_{new} \leftarrow$ INTEGRATEMOTIONEQS($f, state(v), u, dt$)
20:             **if** VALID(s_{new}) = **false then** break for loop of extend $\mathcal{T}$
21:             $r_{new} \leftarrow$ LOCATEREGION(s_{new})i
22:             $v_{new} \leftarrow$ ADDNEWVERTEX($\mathcal{T}, s_{new}, u, dt, r_{new}, v$)
23:             $vertices(\mathcal{T}, r_{new}).pushback(v_{new})$
24:             **if** $r_{new} = r_{goal}$ **then return** $traj(\mathcal{T}, v_{new})$
25:             **if** $r_{new} \notin \sigma_{nonempty}$ **then** $\sigma_{nonempty}.pushback(r_{new})$
26:             $v \leftarrow v_{new}$

3.1 Workspace Decomposition

Each workspace is triangulated using the Triangle package [13]. The triangulation excludes the obstacles and the goal region r_{goal}, treating them as holes inside the workspace bounding box [13]. Fig. 1 provides provides some examples.

The triangles $t_1, \ldots, t_m$ and the goal region r_{goal} give rise to an adjacency region graph $G = (R, E)$ (Algo. 1:1), where

- $R = \{t_1, \ldots, t_m, r_{goal}\}$ denotes the regions of the decomposition and
- $E = \{(r_i, r_j) : r_i, r_j \in R$ are physically adjacent$\}$ denotes the edges.

Note that regions r_i and r_j are physically adjacent if they share part of their boundaries, i.e., r_i and r_j have a common vertex or a common edge.

In addition to the region graph $G = (R, E)$, the approach also uses a function LOCATEREGION : $\mathbb{R}^2 \to R$, which maps a point $(x, y) \in \mathbb{R}^2$ to the corresponding region $r \in R$. The function LOCATEREGION can be implemented to run in polylogarithmic time [14].

3.2   Backward Discrete Search to Estimate Region Costs

Each region $r \in R$ in the workspace decomposition is associated with a cost, denoted as $cost(r)$, which estimates the difficulty of reaching the goal region r_{goal} from r. In this work, $cost(r)$ is defined as the length of the shortest path in the graph $G = (R, E)$ to reach r_{goal}. The cost of an edge $(r', r'') \in E$ is computed as the Euclidean distance between the centroids of regions r' and r''.

A* shortest-path discrete search is then used to compute the costs for each region by running the search backwards, starting at r_{goal} and terminating when its priority queue becomes empty (Algo 1:2). A* is guided by the admissible heuristic function HEURISTIC(r), which returns the Euclidean distance between the centroid of regions r and r_{goal}. When A* removes a region r from its priority queue it means that the shortest path from r_{goal} to r has been found; in that case, $cost(r)$ is set to the length of this shortest path.

3.3   Region Selection Based on Cost Estimates

At each iteration, a region r_{from} is selected from which to expand the search tree $\mathcal{T}$. To facilitate the selection, tree vertices are grouped according to their associated regions, i.e.,

$$vertices(\mathcal{T}, r) = \{v : v \in \mathcal{T} \land region(v) = r\},$$

where $region(v)$ denotes the region associated with vertex v. More specifically, $region(v)$ is computed as LOCATEREGION(x, y), where (x, y) denotes the position component of the state $state(v)$.

Let Γ denote all the regions that have been reached by $\mathcal{T}$, i.e.,

$$\Gamma = \{r : r \in R \land |vertices(\mathcal{T}, r)| > 0\}.$$

The region r_{from} is selected from Γ according to the probability distribution

$$prob(r) = \frac{1}{1 + cost^2(r)} \Big/ \sum_{r' \in R} \frac{1}{1 + cost^2(r')}.$$

Note that this selection scheme gives preference to low-cost regions, since such regions are connected by short discrete paths to the goal. Such selection provides a greedy component to sampling-based motion planning as it aims to expand the search tree from the selected region toward the goal. To balance greedy with methodical search, in order to avoid getting stuck, the scheme also allows for the selection of high-cost regions (although less frequently). Such selections enable the sampling-based motion planner to expand the search along new directions.

From an implementation perspective, the region selection can be made to run in logarithmic time, i.e., $O(\log(|\Gamma|))$, by arranging the regions in Γ as leaf nodes in a balanced binary tree. Each node B in the binary tree contains the sum of the costs of its children B_{left} and B_{right}. To select a region with $prob(r)$, a number w is generated uniformly at random from 0 to c, where c is the cost at the top of the binary tree. The selection moves recursively either to the left or to the right subtree until it reaches a leaf node, i.e.,

$$\text{SELECT}(B, w) = \begin{cases} region(B), & \text{if } B \text{ is a leaf node} \\ \text{SELECT}(B_{left}, w), & \text{if } w < cost(B_{left}) \\ \text{SELECT}(B_{right}, w - cost(B_{left})), & \text{otherwise.} \end{cases}$$

3.4   Forward Discrete Search to Compute Discrete Plans

After selecting a region r_{from} from which to expand the search, forward discrete search is employed to compute a discrete plan σ, which consists of a sequence of neighboring regions that connects r_{from} to r_{goal} (Algo. 1:6). To provide sampling-based motion planning with greedy guides towards the goal, the discrete plan σ is computed, with probability q, as the shortest path using the A* algorithm. To guide the sampling-based motion planner toward new regions, which provide alternative routes that may prevent the tree expansion from getting stuck, the discrete plan is computed as a random path with probability $1 - q$. A randomized version of depth-first-search, which visits the out-going vertices in a random order is used for the computation of random paths. The combination of shortest paths and random paths from r_{from} to r_{goal} provides a balance between greedily and methodically guiding the sampling-based motion planner.

3.5   Sampling-Based Motion Planning to Expand the Search Tree

After a discrete plan σ is computed, sampling-based motion planning is invoked to expand the search tree $\mathcal{T}$ from r_{from} to r_{goal} along the regions associated with the discrete plan σ. The tree expansion consists of adding several collision-free and dynamically-feasible trajectories from vertices associated with regions in σ. Note that $\mathcal{T}$ can be expanded only from those regions $r \in \sigma$ that have been reached by $\mathcal{T}$, i.e., $|vertices(\mathcal{T}, r)| > 0$. For this reason, σ is scanned backwards and r is added to $\sigma_{nonempty}$ if $|vertices(\mathcal{T}, r)| > 0$. To ensure that $\sigma_{nonempty}$ is not too long, the scanning stops after each addition with probability p (set to 0.15 in the experiments) (Algo 1:9-13). In this way, non-empty regions that are close to the goal are added to $\sigma_{nonempty}$.

Expanding $\mathcal{T}$ from regions in $\sigma_{nonempty}$ has the potential of further advancing the search toward the goal. At each iteration, a region r and a vertex v are selected uniformly at random from $\sigma_{nonempty}$ and $vertices(\mathcal{T}, r)$, respectively (Algo. 1:15-16). A control input u is sampled uniformly at random (Algo. 1:17).

Note that other selection and sampling strategies are possible, as discussed in [1,2]. Random selections and sampling are commonly used in motion planning and are shown to work well for the problems studied in this work. A collision-free and dynamically-feasible trajectory is obtained by applying the control input u to $state(v)$ and integrating the motion dynamics forward in time for several steps or until a collision is found. To ensure accuracy, as advocated in the literature, this paper uses Runge-Kutta methods with an adaptive integration step (Algo 1:19-20). Intermediate collision-free states are added as new vertices to the tree. Each new vertex v_{new} is associated with the corresponding region r_{new} (Algo 1:21). r_{new} is added to $\sigma_{nonempty}$ if not already there (Algo 1:23-24). Such additions enable the sampling-based motion planner to expand the search toward new regions. The search terminates successfully if a new vertex v_{new} reaches the goal region, i.e., $r_{new} = r_{goal}$ (Algo 1:24). The solution is given by $traj(\mathcal{T}, v_{new})$, which is obtained by concatenating the collision-free and dynamically-feasible trajectories associated with the tree edges connecting its root to v_{new}.

4   Experiments and Results

Experimental validation is provided by comparing the proposed approach to related work. As described in Section 2 and shown in Fig. 1, different workspaces and a high-dimensional snake-like robot model are used in the experimental comparisons. By increasing the number of links, the snake-like robot provides challenging test cases. In the experiments, the number of links is varied from 5 to 15 yielding problems with 5 to 20 DOFs. The running time for each problem instance is obtained as the average of thirty different runs. Experiments are run on an Intel Core 2 Duo machine (CPU: P8600 at 2.40GHz, RAM: 8GB) using Ubuntu 11.10. Code is compiled with GNU g++-4.6.1

The approach is first compared to RRT [3], which is one of the most successful sampling-based motion planners. At each iteration, RRT extends the tree from the nearest vertex to a randomly sampled state. The RRT implementation, as advocated in the literature [1, 2], uses the connect version, which extends each trajectory until it reaches the randomly sampled state or finds a collision. In addition, goal bias is also used to guide the search toward the goal. Efficient data structures are used for the nearest neighbors computations [15].

As results in Fig. 2 show, RRT is able to solve all problem instances. The running time of RRT, however, increases rapidly as a function of the dimensionality of the problem. In contrast, the proposed approach is shown to be significantly faster than RRT. As it has been noted noted in [1,2,5,6,12,16], when dealing with high-dimensional problems with dynamics, the tree exploration in RRT and many other sampling-based motion planners slows down significantly. By using forward and backward discrete search to guide sampling-based motion planning, the proposed approach is able to effectively advance the search toward the goal.

The approach is also compared to Syclop [12], which introduced the idea of using discrete search to guide sampling-based motion planning. Results in Fig. 2 show that the new approach considerably improves over Syclop [12]. By

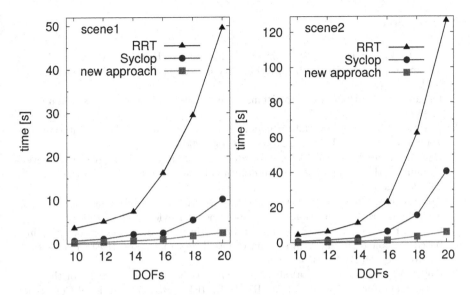

Fig. 2. Comparison of the proposed motion-planning approach to RRT [3] and Syclop [12]. Results are shown over the two scenes (Fig. 1) when varying the number of DOFs of the snake-like robot from 10 to 20. For each problem instance, the plots show the average running time, which is obtained over thirty different runs.

relying on backward and forward discrete search to guide sampling-based motion planning, the new approach is able to explore new directions while rapidly advancing the search toward the goal. The computational advantages become more pronounced as the difficulty of the problems is increased.

5   Discussion

To effectively compute a collision-free and dynamically-feasible robot motion trajectory from an initial state to a goal region, this paper combined sampling-based motion planning over the continuous state space with forward and backward discrete search over a workspace decomposition. The approach leveraged from sampling-based motion planning the idea of searching for a solution trajectory by selectively sampling and exploring the continuous space of feasible robot motions. Backward discrete search provided sampling-based motion planning with cost estimates in order to determine the regions from which to expand the search toward the goal. Forward discrete search provided discrete plans which suggested sequences of regions along which to expand the search in order to reach the goal. This combination of sampling-based motion planning with forward and backward discrete search, as shown by the experiments, offered significant computational speedups over related work in solving high-dimensional motion-planning problems with dynamics.

References

1. Choset, H., Lynch, K.M., Hutchinson, S., Kantor, G., Burgard, W., Kavraki, L.E., Thrun, S.: Principles of Robot Motion: Theory, Algorithms, and Implementations. MIT Press (2005)
2. LaValle, S.M.: Planning Algorithms. Cambridge University Press, Cambridge (2006)
3. LaValle, S.M., Kuffner, J.J.: Randomized kinodynamic planning. International Journal of Robotics Research 20(5), 378–400 (2001)
4. Hsu, D., Kindel, R., Latombe, J.C., Rock, S.: Randomized kinodynamic motion planning with moving obstacles. International Journal of Robotics Research 21(3), 233–255 (2002)
5. Tsianos, K.I., Sucan, I.A., Kavraki, L.E.: Sampling-based robot motion planning: Towards realistic applications. Computer Science Review 1, 2–11 (2007)
6. Cheng, P., Frazzoli, E., LaValle, S.: Improving the performance of sampling-based motion planning with symmetry-based gap reduction. IEEE Transactions on Robotics 24(2), 488–494 (2008)
7. Jaillet, L., Yershova, A., LaValle, S.M., Simeon, T.: Adaptive tuning of the sampling domain for dynamic-domain RRTs. In: IEEE/RSJ International Conference on Intelligent Robots and Systems, Edmonton, Canada, pp. 4086–4091 (2005)
8. Jaillet, L., Cortes, J., Simeon, T.: Transition-based RRT for path planning in continuous cost spaces. In: IEEE/RSJ International Conference on Intelligent Robots and Systems, Nice, France, pp. 2145–2150 (2008)
9. Dalibard, S., Laumond, J.P.: Control of probabilistic diffusion in motion planning. In: International Workshop on Algorithmic Foundations of Robotics, Guanajuato, Mexico, pp. 467–481 (2008)
10. Berenson, D., Srinivasa, S., Ferguson, D., Romea, A.C., Kuffner, J.: Manipulation planning with workspace goal regions. In: IEEE International Conference on Robotics and Automation, Kobe, Japan, pp. 618–624 (2009)
11. Gonzalez-Banos, H.H., Hsu, D., Latombe, J.C.: Motion planning: Recent developments. In: Autonomous Mobile Robots: Sensing, Control, Decision-Making and Applications. CRC Press (2006)
12. Plaku, E., Kavraki, L.E., Vardi, M.Y.: Motion planning with dynamics by a synergistic combination of layers of planning. IEEE Transactions on Robotics 26(3), 469–482 (2010)
13. Shewchuk, J.R.: Delaunay refinement algorithms for triangular mesh generation. Computational Geometry: Theory and Applications 22(1-3), 21–74 (2002)
14. de Berg, M., Cheong, O., van Kreveld, M., Overmars, M.H.: Computational Geometry: Algorithms and Applications, 3rd edn. Springer (2008)
15. Brin, S.: Near neighbor search in large metric spaces. In: International Conference on Very Large Data Bases, pp. 574–584 (1995)
16. Ladd, A.M., Kavraki, L.E.: Motion planning in the presence of drift, underactuation and discrete system changes. In: Robotics: Science and Systems, Boston, MA, pp. 233–241 (2005)

Kinematic Modeling of a Heavy-Duty Forging Manipulator

Wenhua Ding, Hua Deng, and Jianming Hu

School of Mechanical and Electrical Engineering,
Central South University, Changsha, 410083, China
dwh00@163.com,
Hdeng@csu.edu.cn,
hujianming200722@163.com

Abstract. In this paper, a number of kinematics problems of a heavy-duty forging manipulator are studied. The closed-form inverse and forward kinematic equations are established. Secondly, based on hierarchical modeling idea, velocity and acceleration analytical equation are deduced. Finally, all the kinematic equations are validated on a virtual prototype with the ADAMS software package. An interesting result is found that there exits only a weak coupling between main motions of the manipulator, which is very valuable for the decoupling controller design of the manipulator in further study. The researches in this paper aim at motion planning and automation for the heavy-duty manipulator in an integrated open-die forging centre.

Keywords: Kinematic modeling, forging manipulator, multi-closed loop mechanism, hierarchical modeling.

1 Introduction

Forging manipulator, whose main task is to hold and manipulate the work piece during heavy forging, is indispensable to improve manufacturing ability, forging quality, safety, efficiency and so on. A forging manipulator generally consists of a gripper carrier that is connected to a truck frame through one or more closed-loop kinematic chains together so as to improve its payload capacity. The gripper carrier can be moved horizontally, vertically and rotationally in a plane, which are three main motions of a forging manipulator in forging processes. Therefore, a forging manipulator is a complicated 3-degree-of-freedom (DOF) planar mechanism generally. From the viewpoint of achieving the necessary DOF, there exist many different kinds of mechanism structures for a forging manipulator. However, at present, two typical mechanisms of forging manipulator, which are parallel-link mechanism and swing-link mechanism respectively, have been widely applied in forging processes [1, 2, and 3], and other researchers [1] and [2] had proved that the forging manipulator with parallel links is chosen as a better one for many good kinematics properties. Therefore, the parallel-link forging manipulator should be given a more detail and systematic analysis for the automatic programmed forging plan.

C.-Y. Su, S. Rakheja, H. Liu (Eds.): ICIRA 2012, Part III, LNAI 7508, pp. 299–310, 2012.
© Springer-Verlag Berlin Heidelberg 2012

The forging manipulator is a complex multi-closed-chain mechanism, i.e. we refer to the mechanism as "parallel robots" in the robotics literatures. It is well known that a parallel manipulator has been paid more and more attention recently because of its advantages of a low weight/load ratio, high rigidity, high accuracy and so on [4]. As parallel mechanisms are characterized by complex kinematics relations, thus deducing the multi-closed-chain kinematic equations still remains an active topic research [5, 6]. The problems such as the velocity and acceleration of the mechanism are very important in any mechanism kinematics. The velocity and acceleration of robot's end-effector could reflect the capability. Moreover, Jacobian and Hessian matrices play an important role in evaluating a manipulator's performance and its parameter optimum design [7, 8, 9]. However, the calculation of the Jacobian and Hessian matrices of complex mechanical system like forging manipulators and other similar spatial parallel manipulators is very complex due to the geometry constraints caused by the multi-closed loop topology [10].

In this work, analytic equations of the inverse and forward kinematics are derived. Based on hierarchical modeling idea, the Jacobian and Hessian Matrices are deduced. Velocity and acceleration analytic formulations are developed, which can be used for the motion planning of and performance optimization of the heavy-duty manipulator in an integrated open-die forging centre.

2   Structure Description and Coordinate Systems

The schematic diagrams of the overall forging manipulator system are shown in Figs.1 and 2, respectively. The forging manipulator consists of a truck frame and an on-board multi-loop mechanism. The research presented in this paper is part of a wider research study on an intelligent forging center developed by the authors' laboratory. This paper focuses on the kinematic modeling the on-board multi-loop mechanism, which is the major motion mechanism, shown in Fig. 2. The whole construction enables movements of the gripper in two directions (Y–and Z–axes) and its rotation about the axis norm to the $O–YZ$ planes, which achieve lifting, pitching and horizontal buffering motions of the gripper and are driven by three pair of linear hydraulic actuators assembled on the truck frame respectively. Thus, the forging manipulator is a 3-DOF planar multi-closed loop mechanism.

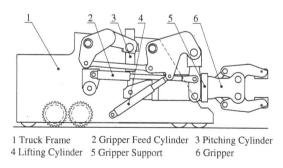

1 Truck Frame   2 Gripper Feed Cylinder 3 Pitching Cylinder
4 Lifting Cylinder   5 Gripper Support   6 Gripper

Fig. 1. Schematic of the forging manipulator

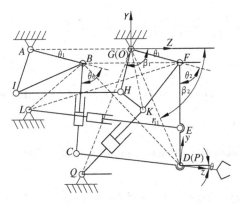

Fig. 2. Geometric representation of major motion mechanism

To facilitate the analysis, as shown in Fig.2, a based coordinate system $O-YZ$ is assign at the point G of the truck frame with Z-axis along the vector from point A to B on the frame, and a moving coordinate system $P-yz$ is fixed at the point D of the gripper with z-axis along the vector form point C to D. The detail structure parameters of the links are shown in Table 1 and other geometry parameters are shown in Fig.2.

Table 1. Primary geometry parameters of the forging manipulator's mechanism

Parameter	Value	Parameter	Value
GF、AB	l_1	GK	l_6
FD	l_2	$\angle KGF$	ϕ_5
AG、HI、CD	l_3	QK	d_1
FE	l_4	LE	d_2
GH、AI	l_5	BC	d_3

3   Position Analysis of Mechanism

3.1   Inverse Kinematics

Inverse kinematics is that the inputs $[d_1 \quad d_2 \quad d_3]^T$ of three pair of linear actuators are solved when the structure parameters and position of the gripper $[y \quad z \quad \theta]^T$ are given. Quadrangle $AIHG$ is a parallelogram. From Fig.2, coordinates of points B, C, D, E and F in the base coordinate system $O-YZ$ can be expressed as

$$B = [-l_1 \sin\theta_1 \quad -l_3 + l_1 \cos\theta_1]^T \tag{1}$$

$$C = [y + l_3 \sin\theta \quad z - l_3 \cos\theta]^T \tag{2}$$

$$D(P) = [y \quad z]^T \tag{3}$$

$$F = [-l_1 \sin\theta_1 \quad l_1 \cos\theta_1]^T \tag{4}$$

$$E = \frac{(F + \lambda D)}{1 + \lambda} = \left[\frac{-l_1 \sin\theta_1 + \lambda y}{1 + \lambda} \quad \frac{l_1 \cos\theta_1 + \lambda z}{1 + \lambda} \right]^{\mathrm{T}} \tag{5}$$

where $\gamma_2 = \theta_2 + \theta_6$, $\gamma_1 = \theta_1 + \theta_2$, $\lambda = \dfrac{FE}{ED} = \dfrac{l_4}{l_2 - l_4}$.

In the reference frame $O - YZ$, the points Q and L be written as

$$Q = \begin{bmatrix} y_Q & z_Q \end{bmatrix}^{\mathrm{T}} \quad \text{and} \quad L = \begin{bmatrix} y_L & z_L \end{bmatrix}^{\mathrm{T}} \tag{6}$$

Then, the inverse kinematic problem can be solved writing following constraint equation

$$\begin{cases} d_1 = |QK| = \left[(y_Q + l_6 \sin(\theta_1 + \phi_5))^2 + (z_Q - l_6 \cos(\theta_1 + \phi_5))^2 \right]^{1/2} \\ d_2 = |LE| = \left[\left(y_L - \dfrac{-l_1 \sin\theta_1 + \lambda y}{1 + \lambda} \right)^2 + \left(z_L - \dfrac{l_1 \cos\theta_1 + \lambda z}{1 + \lambda} \right)^2 \right]^{1/2} \\ d_3 = |CB| = \left[(y + l_3 \sin\theta + l_1 \sin\theta_1)^2 + (z - l_3 \cos\theta + l_3 - l_1 \cos\theta_1)^2 \right]^{1/2} \end{cases} \tag{7}$$

By observation of Fig.2, angle θ_1 can be expressed as

$$\theta_1 = \beta_2 - \angle DGF \tag{8}$$

where $\beta_2 = \cos^{-1}\left(z / |DG| \right)$, using the cosine law for triangle $\triangle DGF$ in Fig.2, angle $\angle DGF$ are

$$\angle DGF = \cos^{-1}\left(\frac{|DG|^2 + l_1^2 - l_2^2}{2 l_1 |DG|^2} \right) \tag{9}$$

where $|DG| = \left[y^2 + z^2 \right]^{1/2}$

Two solutions exist for angles $\angle DGF$ from Eq. (9). Therefore, there are two inverse kinematic solutions. However, in real situations, motion ranges of three pair of linear actuators are limited, which only a solution is suited.

3.2   Forward Kinematics

Given a set of actuated inputs $\begin{bmatrix} d_1 & d_2 & d_3 \end{bmatrix}^{\mathrm{T}}$, the position of the gripper $\begin{bmatrix} y & z & \theta \end{bmatrix}^{\mathrm{T}}$ can be obtained by the forward kinematic analysis. By observation of Fig.2, the position of the gripper can be obtained directly as

$$\theta = -\tan^{-1}\left(\frac{y_P - y_C}{z_P - z_C} \right) = -\arctan^{-1}\left(\frac{-l_2 \sin\gamma_1 + d_3 \sin\gamma_2}{l_2 \cos\gamma_1 + l_3 - d_3 \cos\gamma_2} \right) \tag{10}$$

$$\begin{bmatrix} y & z \end{bmatrix}^{\mathrm{T}} = D(P) = \begin{bmatrix} -l_1 \sin\theta_1 - l_2 \sin\gamma_1 & l_1 \cos\theta_1 + l_2 \cos\gamma_1 \end{bmatrix}^{\mathrm{T}} \tag{11}$$

where $\gamma_2 = \theta_2 + \theta_6$, $\gamma_1 = \theta_1 + \theta_2$.

Eqs. (10) and (11) is the forward kinematic solutions. However, the parameters θ_1 、 γ_1 、 γ_2 in the Eqs. (10) and (11) are unknown. In order to complete the forward position problem, the unknown parameters must be represented by $[y \quad z \quad \theta]^T$.

From triangle $\triangle QGK$ in Fig.2, using the cosine law, $\angle QGK$ can be obtained:

$$\angle QGK = \cos^{-1}\left(\frac{|QG|^2 + l_6^2 - d_1^2}{2l_6|QG|}\right) \tag{12}$$

$$\theta_1 = \beta_1 - \angle QGK - \phi_5 \tag{13}$$

where $|QG| = \left[y_Q^2 + z_Q^2\right]^{1/2}$

Similarly, from triangles $\triangle BFL$ and $\triangle LFE$ in Fig.2, the following equations can be obtained:

$$\angle BFL = \cos^{-1}\left(\frac{l_3^2 + |FL|^2 - |LB|^2}{2l_3|FL|}\right) \tag{14}$$

$$\angle LFE = \cos^{-1}\left(\frac{|FL|^2 + l_4^2 - d_2^2}{2l_4|FL|}\right) \tag{15}$$

$$\gamma_1 = \pi - \angle BFL - \angle LFE \tag{16}$$

where $|FL| = \left[(-l_1\sin\theta_1 - y_L)^2 + (l_1\cos\theta_1 - z_L)^2\right]^{1/2}$, $|LB| = \left[(y_L + l_1\sin\theta_1)^2 + (z_L - l_1\cos\theta_1 + l_3)^2\right]^{1/2}$

Two solutions exist for angle $\angle BFL$ and $\angle LFE$ from Eqs. (14) and (15). However, recalling that these angles refer to the inside angles of a triangle, they must lie within the range $0° \leq \angle BFL, \angle LFE \leq 180°$ for which only one solution may be obtained from Eq. (16).

From triangles $\triangle CBD$ and $\triangle DBF$ in Fig.2, angle γ_2 can be derived as follows

$$\angle CBD = \cos^{-1}\left(\frac{d_3^2 + |DB|^2 - l_3^2}{2d_3|DB|}\right) \tag{17}$$

$$\angle DBF = \cos^{-1}\left(\frac{|DB|^2 + l_3^2 - l_2^2}{2l_3|DB|}\right) \tag{18}$$

$$\gamma_2 = \angle CBD + \angle DBF \tag{19}$$

where $|DB| = \left[(l_2\sin\gamma_1)^2 + (l_2\cos\gamma_1 + l_3)^2\right]^{1/2}$, likewise, $\angle CBD$ and $\angle DBF$ are within the range $0° \leq \angle CBD, \angle DBF \leq 180°$

Form equations $(10)-(19)$, the direct position problem of the mechanism can be achieved.

4   Velocity and Acceleration Analysis of the Manipulator

4.1   Hierarchical Modeling Approach of Jacobian

Output velocity of the end-effector for a robot can be represented as follows

$$\dot{p} = J\dot{q} \tag{20}$$

where $\dot{q}$ is the velocity vector of the actuated pairs, $\dot{p}$ is the output velocity vector of the end-effector. J is the forward kinematic Jacobian matrix. Thus, velocity analysis of a manipulator is to solve matrix J. However, directly deriving Jacobian matrix is very difficult, even impossible for many multi-closed loop mechanisms due to the complex geometry constraints. Hierarchical or modular modeling method is introduced to calculated Jacobian matrix J [11, 12].

If there exists a group vectors about passive joints $q_1 = [\theta_{11} \ \ \theta_{12} \ \ \cdots \ \ \theta_{1i}]^{\mathrm{T}}$ 、 $q_2 = [\theta_{21} \ \ \theta_{22} \ \ \cdots \ \ \theta_{2i}]^{\mathrm{T}} \cdots q_n = [\theta_{k1} \ \ \theta_{k2} \ \ \cdots \ \ \theta_{ki}]^{\mathrm{T}}$, where θ_{ki} is some variables from the passive joints, and if the vectors also meets the following recurrence relations.

$$\dot{q}_1 = J_1\dot{q} , \ \ \dot{q}_2 = J_2\dot{q}_1 , \ \ \cdots \ \ \dot{q}_n = J_n\dot{q}_{n-1} , \ \ \dot{p} = J_{n+1}\dot{q}_n \tag{21}$$

According to Eq.(21), the following expression can be obtained recursively

$$\dot{p} = J_1 J_2 J_n J_{n+1}\dot{q} \tag{22}$$

Comparing Eq.(20) and Eq.(22), the Jacobian matrix can be expressed as follows

$$J = J_1 J_2 J_n J_{n+1} \tag{23}$$

Remark: the Jacobian matrix J is a function about the group vectors $q_1 , q_2 \cdots q_n$ and the vector of the actuated pairs q, which is not from differentiating forward or inverse kinematic equations with respect to time directly. Therefore, to some extent, deriving Jacobian matrix J will be much easier based on the method. Similarly, the Hessian matrix also can be solved based on the hierarchical modeling approach.

4.2   Velocity Analysis

For the forging manipulator, the actuated input vector is $\dot{q} = \begin{bmatrix} \dot{d}_1 & \dot{d}_2 & \dot{d}_3 \end{bmatrix}^{\mathrm{T}}$, which is the input vector of three linear hydraulic actuators, corresponding to the output vector of the gripper is $\dot{p} = \begin{bmatrix} \dot{y} & \dot{z} & \dot{\theta} \end{bmatrix}^{\mathrm{T}}$

Differentiating Eq. (11) with respect to time, lead to

$$\begin{bmatrix} \dot{y} \\ \dot{z} \end{bmatrix} = \begin{bmatrix} -l_1\cos\theta_1 & -l_2\cos\gamma_1 \\ -l_1\sin\theta_1 & -l_2\sin\gamma_1 \end{bmatrix} \begin{bmatrix} \dot{\theta}_1 \\ \dot{\gamma}_1 \end{bmatrix} \tag{24}$$

According Fig.2, the length of vector CB can be also expressed as

$$d_3 = |CB| = \left[(-l_2\sin\gamma_1 + l_3\sin\theta)^2 + (l_2\cos\gamma_1 - l_3\cos\theta + l_3)^2 \right]^{1/2} \tag{25}$$

Differentiating Eq. (25) with respect to time, lead to

$$\dot{\theta} = \begin{bmatrix} p_{32} & p_{33} \end{bmatrix} \begin{bmatrix} \dot{\gamma}_1 & \dot{d}_3 \end{bmatrix}^{\mathrm{T}}$$

(26)

where $p_{32} = g_1/g_2$, $p_{33} = g_3/g_2$

$g_1 = l_2 l_3 \cos \gamma_1 \sin \theta - l_2 l_3 \sin \gamma_1 \cos \theta + l_2 l_3 \sin \gamma_1$

$g_2 = l_2 l_3 \cos \gamma_1 \sin \theta - l_2 l_3 \sin \gamma_1 \cos \theta + l_3^2 \sin \theta$

$g_3 = \left[(-l_2 \sin \gamma_1 + l_3 \sin \theta)^2 + (l_2 \cos \gamma_1 - l_3 \cos \theta + l_3)^2 \right]^{1/2}$

Combining Eq. (24) and (26), the following equations can be obtain as

$$\begin{bmatrix} \dot{y} \\ \dot{z} \\ \dot{\theta} \end{bmatrix} = P \begin{bmatrix} \dot{\theta}_1 \\ \dot{\gamma}_1 \\ \dot{d}_3 \end{bmatrix} = \begin{bmatrix} p_{11} & p_{12} & p_{13} \\ p_{21} & p_{22} & p_{23} \\ p_{31} & p_{32} & p_{33} \end{bmatrix} \begin{bmatrix} \dot{\theta}_1 \\ \dot{\gamma}_1 \\ \dot{d}_3 \end{bmatrix}$$

(27)

where $p_{11} = -l_1 \cos \theta_1$; $p_{12} = -l_2 \cos \gamma_1$; $p_{13} = 0$; $p_{21} = -l_1 \sin \theta_1$; $p_{22} = -l_2 \sin \gamma_1$; $p_{23} = 0$;

In order to solve $\dot{p}$, the passive joints $\dot{\theta}_1$ and $\dot{\gamma}_1$ in the equations (27) must be represented by $\dot{d}_1, \dot{d}_2$. According to Fig.2, vector **LE** can be also written as

$$d_2 = |LE| = \left[(y_L + l_1 \sin \theta_1 + l_4 \sin \gamma_1)^2 + (z_L - l_1 \cos \theta_1 - l_4 \cos \gamma_1)^2 \right]^{1/2}$$

(28)

Taking the derivative of Eq. (28) and the 1st formulation of Eq. (7) with respect to time leads to

$$\begin{bmatrix} \dot{d}_1 \\ \dot{d}_2 \end{bmatrix} = F \begin{bmatrix} \dot{\theta}_1 \\ \dot{\gamma}_1 \end{bmatrix} = \begin{bmatrix} f_{11} & f_{12} \\ f_{21} & f_{22} \end{bmatrix} \begin{bmatrix} \dot{\theta}_1 \\ \dot{\gamma}_1 \end{bmatrix}$$

(29)

where $f_{11} = h_1/h_2$; $f_{12} = 0$; $f_{21} = h_3/h_4$; $f_{22} = h_5/h_4$; $h_1 = l_6 \left(y_Q \cos(\theta_1 + \phi_5) + z_Q l_6 \sin(\theta_1 + \phi_5) \right)$

$h_2 = \left[(y_Q + l_6 \sin(\theta_1 + \phi_5))^2 + (z_Q - l_6 \cos(\theta_1 + \phi_5))^2 \right]^{1/2}$

$h_3 = (y_L + l_1 \sin \theta_1 + l_4 \sin \gamma_1) l_1 \cos \theta_1 + (z_L - l_1 \cos \theta_1 - l_4 \cos \gamma_1) l_1 \sin \theta_1$

$h_4 = \left[(y_L + l_1 \sin \theta_1 + l_4 \sin \gamma_1)^2 + (z_L - l_1 \cos \theta_1 - l_4 \cos \gamma_1)^2 \right]^{1/2}$

$h_5 = (y_L + l_1 \sin \theta_1 + l_4 \sin \gamma_1) l_4 \cos \gamma_1 + (z_L - l_1 \cos \theta_1 - l_4 \cos \gamma_1) l_4 \sin \gamma_1$

When the mechanism is away from singularities, the reverse form of the Eq. (29) is as follows

$$\begin{bmatrix} \dot{\theta}_1 \\ \dot{\gamma}_1 \end{bmatrix} = F^{-1} \begin{bmatrix} \dot{d}_1 \\ \dot{d}_2 \end{bmatrix} = \begin{bmatrix} l_{11} & l_{12} \\ l_{21} & l_{22} \end{bmatrix} \begin{bmatrix} \dot{d}_1 \\ \dot{d}_2 \end{bmatrix}$$

(30)

where $l_{11} = h_2/h_1$; $l_{12} = 0$; $l_{22} = -h_3 h_2/h_1 h_5$; $l_{22} = h_4/h_5$

Substituting Eq. (30) into Eq. (27), the forward velocity analysis of the mechanism is represents as

$$\begin{bmatrix} \dot{y} \\ \dot{z} \\ \dot{\theta} \end{bmatrix} = J \begin{bmatrix} \dot{d}_1 \\ \dot{d}_2 \\ \dot{d}_3 \end{bmatrix} = \begin{bmatrix} j_{11} & j_{12} & j_{13} \\ j_{21} & j_{22} & j_{23} \\ j_{31} & j_{32} & j_{33} \end{bmatrix} \begin{bmatrix} \dot{d}_1 \\ \dot{d}_2 \\ \dot{d}_3 \end{bmatrix} \tag{31}$$

where $j_{11} = p_{11}l_{11} + p_{12}l_{21}$; $j_{12} = p_{11}l_{12} + p_{12}l_{22}$; $j_{13} = p_{13}$; $j_{21} = p_{21}l_{11} + p_{22}l_{21}$;

$j_{22} = p_{21}l_{12} + p_{22}l_{22}$; $j_{23} = p_{23}$; $j_{31} = p_{31}l_{11} + p_{32}l_{21}$; $j_{32} = p_{31}l_{12} + p_{32}l_{22}$; $j_{33} = p_{23}$

Therefore, Jacobian matrix of the complicated mechanism can be obtained easily by the hierarchical approach. Likewise, the method also can be used to solve the Hessian matrix of acceleration equations in the following section.

4.3   Acceleration Analysis

Differentiating Eq. (20) with respect to time, the forward acceleration equation is

$$\ddot{p} = J\ddot{q} + \dot{q}^{\mathrm{T}} H \dot{q} \tag{32}$$

where $\ddot{d} = \begin{bmatrix} \ddot{d}_1 & \ddot{d}_2 & \ddot{d}_3 \end{bmatrix}^{\mathrm{T}}$ denotes the acceleration vector of three pair of actuators; $\ddot{q} = \begin{bmatrix} \ddot{y} & \ddot{z} & \ddot{\theta} \end{bmatrix}^{\mathrm{T}}$ denotes the acceleration vector of the gripper; $H \in R^{3 \times 3 \times 3}$ denotes the Hessian matrix, which is a three-dimensional tensor which has three layers and each layer is a 3×3 matrix. [13]

Similarly, differentiating the velocity Eq. (27) with respect to time, the following equations can be obtained

$$\begin{bmatrix} \ddot{y} \\ \ddot{z} \\ \ddot{\theta} \end{bmatrix} = P \begin{bmatrix} \ddot{\theta}_1 \\ \ddot{\gamma}_1 \\ \ddot{d}_3 \end{bmatrix} + \begin{bmatrix} \dot{\theta}_1 & \dot{\gamma}_1 & \dot{d}_3 \end{bmatrix} \begin{bmatrix} \begin{pmatrix} l_1 \sin\theta_1 \\ 0 \\ 0 \end{pmatrix} & \begin{pmatrix} 0 \\ l_2 \sin\gamma_1 \\ 0 \end{pmatrix} & \begin{pmatrix} 0 \\ 0 \\ 0 \end{pmatrix} \\ \begin{pmatrix} -l_1 \cos\theta_1 \\ 0 \\ 0 \end{pmatrix} & \begin{pmatrix} 0 \\ -l_2 \cos\gamma_1 \\ 0 \end{pmatrix} & \begin{pmatrix} 0 \\ 0 \\ 0 \end{pmatrix} \\ \begin{pmatrix} 0 \\ 0 \\ 0 \end{pmatrix} & \begin{pmatrix} 0 \\ \dfrac{p_{32}(g_2 f_1 - g_1 f_3) + (g_2 f_2 - g_1 f_4)}{g_2^2} \\ \dfrac{p_{33}(g_2 f_1 - g_1 f_3)}{g_2^2} \end{pmatrix} & \begin{pmatrix} 0 \\ \dfrac{-g_3 f_4 - p_{32} g_3 f_3}{g_2^2} \\ \dfrac{f_5 - p_{33} g_3 f_3}{g_2^2} \end{pmatrix} \end{bmatrix} \begin{bmatrix} \dot{\theta}_1 \\ \dot{\gamma}_1 \\ \dot{d}_3 \end{bmatrix} \tag{33}$$

where $f_1 = l_2 l_3 \cos(-\theta + \gamma_1)$; $f_2 = -l_2 l_3 \cos(-\theta + \gamma_1) + l_1 l_3 \cos\gamma_1$; $f_3 = l_2 l_3 \cos(-\theta + \gamma_1) + l_3^2 \cos\theta$; $f_4 = -l_2 l_3 \cos(-\theta + \gamma_1)$; $f_5 = l_3 \left(l_3 \sin\theta - l_2 \sin(-\theta + \gamma_1) \right)$

To eliminate the passive variables $\ddot{\theta}_1$ and $\ddot{\gamma}_1$, the follow equations will be derived from differentiating Eq. (29) with respect to time.

$$\begin{bmatrix} \ddot{\theta}_1 \\ \ddot{\gamma}_1 \end{bmatrix} = F^{-1} \begin{bmatrix} \ddot{d}_1 \\ \ddot{d}_2 \end{bmatrix} - \begin{bmatrix} \dot{\theta}_1 & \dot{\gamma}_1 \end{bmatrix} F^{-1} * \begin{bmatrix} \begin{pmatrix} k_{111} \\ 0 \\ k_{211} \\ k_{212} \end{pmatrix} & \begin{pmatrix} 0 \\ 0 \\ k_{221} \\ k_{222} \end{pmatrix} \end{bmatrix} \begin{bmatrix} \dot{\theta}_1 \\ \dot{\gamma}_1 \end{bmatrix} \tag{34}$$

where $k_{111} = \left(-y_Q d_1 l_6 \sin(\theta_1 + \phi_5) + z_Q d_1 l_6 \cos(\theta_1 + \phi_5) - f_{1,1} h_1\right)/d_1^2$

$k_{211} = \left(-d_2 y_L l_1 \sin\theta_1 + d_2 z_L l_1 \cos\theta_1 - d_2 l_1 l_4 \cos(\gamma_1 - \theta_1) - h_3 f_{2,1}\right)/d_2^2$

$k_{212} = \left(d_2 l_1 l_4 \cos(\gamma_2 - \theta_1) - h_3 f_{2,2}\right)/d_2^2$; $k_{221} = \left(l_1 l_4 d_2 \cos(\theta_1 - \theta_2) - h_5 f_{2,1}\right)/d_2^2$

$k_{222} = \left(-y_L l_4 d_2 \sin\theta_2 + z_L l_4 d_2 \cos\theta_2 - l_1 l_4 d_2 \cos(\theta_1 - \theta_2) - h_5 f_{2,2}\right)/d_2^2$

The sign "*" denotes a generalized scalar product [13, 14]. The generalized scalar product of two matrices $X \in \Re^{m \times n}$ and $Y \in \Re^{n' \times n \times n'}$ have been defined as follows

$$[X * Y]_{k::} = \sum_{l=1}^{n} X_{k:l} Y_{l:} \in \Re^{n \times n} \qquad k = 1, 2, ..., m \qquad (35)$$

where $X * Y \in \Re^{m \times n}$, $X_{k:l}$ denotes the element on the kth row and l^{th} column of the matrix X. Substituting Eq. (34) and (30) into (33), the following acceleration equation can be derived as

$$\begin{bmatrix} \ddot{y} & \ddot{z} & \ddot{\theta} \end{bmatrix}^T = [J] \begin{bmatrix} \ddot{d}_1 & \ddot{d}_2 & \ddot{d}_3 \end{bmatrix}^T + \begin{bmatrix} \ddot{d}_1 & \ddot{d}_2 & \ddot{d}_3 \end{bmatrix} [H] \begin{bmatrix} \ddot{d}_1 & \ddot{d}_2 & \ddot{d}_3 \end{bmatrix}^T \qquad (36)$$

5   Validation and Analysis of Kinematic Model

5.1   Validation of Kinematic Model

The virtual prototype provides a better test bed to validate model via computer technology [15], such as ADAMS and Matlab, for it is a huge cost for a laboratory to afford the development of a heavy-duty forging manipulator physical prototype. In this study, ADAMS software is used to validate the kinemaitc model firstly.

Table 2. Kinematic parameters of the forging manipulator's mechanism

Parameter	Value	Parameter	Value
l_1	1.750m	$Q(y_Q \quad z_Q)$	(-2.865m, -1.505m)
l_2	1.800m	$L(y_Q \quad z_Q)$	(-1.280m, -2.444m)
l_3	2.757m	ϕ_5	0.9250rad
l_4	1.100m	d_1	2.600m(Initial Value)
l_5	0.827m	d_2	4.150m(Initial Value)
l_6	1.356m	d_3	1.5000m(Initial Value)

In ADAMS, a virtual prototype for the forging manipulator with kinematic parameters described in Table 2 has been created. Let the displacements of three pair of linear actuators are $d_1 = 300\sin(2\pi t)$mm , $d_2 = 100\sin(\pi t)$mm mm, $d_3 = 200\sin(3\pi t)$mm , respectively. The acceleration of end-effector from kinematic model is shown in Fig.4, and that in Fig.5 is form ADAMS simulation. (The unit of angle acceleration A_θ is rad/s^2 and others are mm/s^2) According to Fig.4 and Fig.5, the kinemaitc problem is validated.

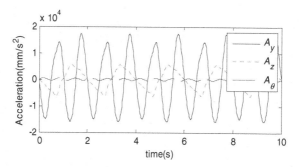

Fig. 3. The acceleration of end-effector from kinematic model

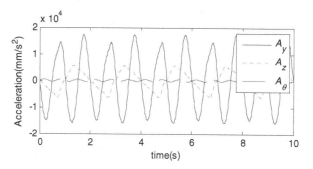

Fig. 4. The acceleration of end-effector from ADAMS simulation

5.2   Kinematic Analysis of the Forging Manipulator

When $d_1 = 300\sin(2\pi t)$mm , $d_2 = 0$ and $d_3 = 0$, velocities of the end-effector are shown in Fig. 6, and When $d_1 = 300\sin(2\pi t)$mm , $d_2 = 0$ and $d_3 = 0$, velocities of the end-effector are illustrated in Fig. 7. From the two figures, it can be concluded that there exits only a weak coupling between the actuators. When pitching cylinders drive alone, the conclusion is same also. The conclusion is very valuable for the decoupling controller design of the manipulator in further study.

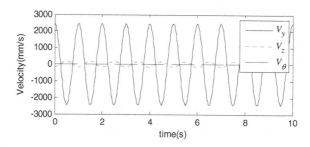

Fig. 5. Alone motion of lifting cylinders and others locked

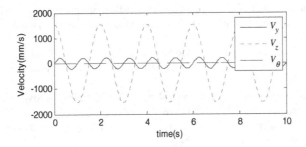

Fig. 6. Alone motion of buffering cylinders and others locked

6 Conclusions

In this paper, kinematic analytic model of a forging manipulator is given in detail. Jacobian and Hessian matrices are solved based on hierarchical modeling approach. The system's Jacobian and Hessian matrices of the forging manipulator can be easily solved by utilizing some passive joints variables. An interesting result is found that there exits only a weak coupling between three motions, which is very valuable for decoupling controller design of the manipulator. In order to realized the development of an Intelligent Open Die Forging System, dynamic simulation and control of the system will be further studied systematically.

References

1. Ren, Y., Lu, C., Han, Q.: Simulated comparison on kinematics properties of two typical mechanisms of forging manipulator. In: 4th International Conference on Metronics and Information Technology, Japan, pp. 942–947 (2007)
2. Xu, Y., Zhao, Y.: Comparative analysis of two typical Mechanisms of forging manipulator. In: 2010 International Conference on Mechanic Automation and Control Engineering (MACE), China, pp. 2314–2317 (2010)
3. Tong, X., Gao, F., Zhang, Y.: Research on decoupling performance of major-motion mechanism for forging manipulators. Journal of Mechanical Engineering 46(11), 14–20 (2010) (in Chinese)
4. Wenger, P., Gosselin, C., Maille, B.: A comparative study of serial and parallel mechanism topologies for machine tools. In: PKM 1999, Italy, pp. 23–32 (1999)
5. Tsai, M.S., Shiau, T.N., Tsai, Y.J.: Direct kinematic analysis of a 3-PRS parallel mechanism. Mechanism and Machine Theory 38(1), 71–83 (2003)
6. Piccin, O., Bayle, B., Maurin, B.: Kinematic modeling of a 5-DOF parallel mechanism for semi-spherical workspace. Mechanism and Machine Theory 44(8), 1485–1496 (2009)
7. Gosselin, C., Angeles, J.: The optimum kinematic design of a spherical three-degree-of-freedom parallel manipulator. ASME Journal of Mechanisms, Transmissions, and Automation in Design 111(2), 202–207 (1989)
8. Li, H.B., Liu, S., Guo, X.J.: Performance analysis for 3-RR (RR) R parallel mechanism based on Hessian matrix. In: 2nd IEEE/ASME International Conference on Mechatronic and Embedded Systems and Applications, Beijing, pp. 1–4 (2006)

9. Liu, X.J., Jin, Z.L., Gao, F.: Optimum design of 3-DOF spherical parallel manipulator with respect to the conditioning and stiffness. Mechanism and Machine Theory 35(9), 1257–1267 (2000)

10. Chen, G., Wang, H., Zhao, K.: Modular calculation of the Jacobian matrix and its application to the performance analyses of a forging robot. Advanced Robotics 23(10), 1261–1279 (2009)

11. Eberhard, P., Schiehlen, W.: Hierarchical modeling in multibody dynamics. Archive of Applied Mechanics 68(3), 237–246 (1998)

12. Kubler, R., Schiehlen, W.: Modular simulation in multibody system dynamics. Multibody System Dynamics 4(2), 107–127 (2000)

13. Zhu, S.J., Huang, Z., Ding, H.F.: Forward/reverse velocity and acceleration analysis for a class of lower-mobility parallel mechanisms. Journal of Mechanical Design 129, 390 (2007)

14. Huang, Z., Fang, Y.F., Kong, L.F.: Theory and control of parallel robotic mechanisms. Press of Mechanical Engineering, Beijing (1997) (In Chinese)

15. Li, Y.M., Xu, Q.S.: Dynamic modeling and robust control of a 3-PRC translational parallel kinematic machine. Robotics and Computer Integrated Manufacturing 25, 630–640 (2009)

Simultaneous Localization and Map Building for Wheeled Robot with Colored Measurement Noise

Yi Yingmin, Liu Ding, Xin Jing, and Yang Yanxi

Faculty of Automation and Information Engineering, Xi'an University of Technology,
Xi'an,710048, China

Abstract. For colored measurement noise model, paper presents a Simultaneous Localization and Mapping (SLAM) algorithm for wheeled robot with colored measurement noise. Colored measurement noise model is converted into white measurement noise model by recombining the process model and the measurement model for wheeled robot. In order to make the process noise and the measurement noise irrelevant each other, the process model is re-defined. Estimating state and building a map are conducted in accordance with the virtual process model and the virtual measurement model. In data association step, part observed landmarks are processed as redundant landmarks. Some indicators of the filter are used to evaluate the performance the algorithm. The simulation results show that the proposed algorithm is consistent and robust.

Keywords: colored measurement noise; wheeled robots; SLAM; consistency and robustness of algorithm.

1 Introduction

Mobile robot Self-positioning and navigation must be based on the reliable awareness of environmental information. However, the sensor's own is limited that a variety of sensors measuring information is susceptible to noise interference. There are different degrees of uncertainty. The uncertainty of the measurement information will inevitably lead to uncertainty for system model. The traditional approach is to use Gaussian white noise model to characterize the measurement information. However, in practice, this noise model is often gotten by the approximated model.

In robot SLAM problems, the measurement sensors such as vision sensors, laser sensors and sonar sensors are commonly used. Vision sensor is used to get the image information of environment through the camera. The relative distance and angle can be calculated with the image information and the spatial relationship of robot body. Vision-based SLAM algorithm is divided into three categories. First, the stereo vision SLAM algorithms are one category. The measurement information from such methods is related to the outcome of camera calibration. The physical parameters of camera and the precision of image processing algorithms may lead to colored noise from the measurements of three-dimensional visual. The omni-vision SLAM algorithms are second category. The images from these algorithms have a great distortion. Precision of

C.-Y. Su, S. Rakheja, H. Liu (Eds.): ICIRA 2012, Part III, LNAI 7508, pp. 311–320, 2012.

image correction and physical parameters of the camera can cause the measurement of colored noise. The monocular vision SLAM algorithms are third category. The measurement information from such methods is related to the physical camera optical center and the focal length of the calibration. Due to limitations from manufacturing processes and image processing algorithms, the visual measurement model cannot to be approximated as the Gaussian white noise model.In the measurement systems with laser sensors and direction sensors, the laser sensor center and the direction sensors center are assumed coincidence. In practice, however, the measurement is colored noise because the centers can not be overlap. In robot SLAM system with ultrasonic sensors, the sensors are often installed around the robot body. In algorithm model, there is always assumed that all ultrasonic sensors are located in the same radiation center. The measurement is colored noise because the mechanical installation assembly can not meet in actual. In these problems, the actual colored noise model is approximated with the Gaussian white noise model for robot simultaneous localization and map building. The error accumulated over time cause the system to diverge eventually.

2   State Space and System Model

The described SLAM system state is formed by the robot's pose and the observed coordinates of the landmarks in the static environments. The joint state vector at the k moment is shown as:

$$x_k = \left[x_{vk}, y_{vk}, \phi_{vk}, x_1, y_1, \cdots, x_N, y_N\right]^T = \begin{bmatrix} x_{vk} \\ n \end{bmatrix} \tag{1}$$

In (1), $x_{vk}, y_{vk}, \phi_{vk}$ stand for the position and heading of the robot in two-dimensional space respectively. The map is static. Notice that the map parameters $n = \left[x_1, y_1, \cdots, x_N, y_N\right]^T$ do not have a time subscript as they are modeled as stationary. The robot's movement model is rolling motion constraints (i.e., assuming zero wheel slip).

$$\mathbf{x}_k = f_v(\mathbf{x}_{vk-1}, \mathbf{u}_k) = \begin{bmatrix} x_{vk-1} + V_k \Delta T \cos(\varphi_{vk-1} + \gamma_k) \\ y_{vk-1} + V_k \Delta T \sin(\varphi_{vk-1} + \gamma_k) \\ \varphi_{vk-1} + \frac{V_k \Delta T}{B} \sin(\gamma_k) \end{bmatrix} \tag{2}$$

In (2), the time interval between $k-1$ and k is ΔT, the velocity v_k and the steering angle G_k are constants and they consist of the controlled vector $u_k = \left[v_k, \gamma_k\right]^T$, The wheelbase between the front and rear axles is B.

The observation model is given by

$$z_{ik} = h_i(\mathbf{x}_k) = \begin{bmatrix} \sqrt{(x_i - x_{vk})^2 + (y_i - y_{vk})^2} \\ \arctan \frac{y_i - y_{vk}}{x_i - x_{vk}} - \varphi_{vk} \end{bmatrix} \tag{3}$$

The measurement noise is written in the form

$$v_k = \Phi_{k-1} v_{k-1} + \xi_{k-1}$$

In (3), Φ_{k-1} is transition matrix, where ξ_k is a vector of temporally uncorrelated measurement errors with zero mean and variance R.

3   The Robot SLAM Algorithm under Colored Measurement Noise

The main idea of the algorithms is as follow: the virtual measurement models with Gaussian white noise is constructed by the colored measurement models. To meet the process noise and the measurement noise irrelevant each other, a virtual process model is re-constructed by the original process model. The robot state estimation and map building are conducted in accordance with the virtual process model and the virtual measurement model.

3.1   Whitening Colored Measurement Model

In the EKF-SLAM Algorithm, the measurement model is filtering estimation process under the white noise. Equation (3) is reconstructed for the colored noise model is transformed white noise measurement model.

$$
\begin{aligned}
z_{k-1}^* &= z_k - \Phi_{k-1} z_{k-1} \\
&= (H_k F_{k-1} - \Phi_{k-1} H_{k-1}) x_{k-1} + H_k \Gamma_{k-1} \omega_{k-1} + \xi_{k-1} \\
&= H_{k-1}^* x_{k-1} + v_{k-1}^*
\end{aligned}
\tag{4}
$$

Here, $H_k = \frac{\partial h}{\partial x_k}\big|_{\hat{x}_{k|k-1}}$, $F_k = \frac{\partial f}{\partial x_k}\big|_{\hat{x}_{k-1|k-1}}$, $\Gamma_k = \frac{\partial f}{\partial w_k}\big|_{\hat{x}_{k-1|k-1}}$, v_{k-1}^* are white noises. As the virtual measurement noise and the process noise are related, the process model must be decorrelated by the extended Kalman filter. Equation (4) is brought into the process model to construct the virtual process model.

$$
\begin{aligned}
x_{k+1} &= F_k x_k + \Gamma_k \omega_k + J_k (z_k^* - H_k^* x_k - v_k^*) \\
&= (F_k - J_k H_k^*) x_k + J_k z_k^* + (\Gamma_k \omega_k - J_k v_k^*) \\
&= F_k^* x_k + u_k^* + \omega_k^*
\end{aligned}
\tag{5}
$$

Here, J_k is the undetermined coefficient matrix, ω_k is zero mean white noise variance, u_k^* is the virtual control vector. J_k should meet the virtual process noise and measurement noise is not related. The expectation is as

$$E[\omega_k^* (v_k^*)^T] = 0 \tag{6}$$

J_k is solved by equation (6).

$$J_k = \Gamma_k Q_k \Gamma_k^T H_{k+1}^T (H_{k+1} \Gamma_k Q_k \Gamma_k^T H_{k+1}^T + R_k)^{-1} \tag{7}$$

Equation (7) is brought into equation (5). Then the virtual process model is constructed.

3.2   Robot SLAM Algorithm Under Colored Measurement Noise

The CON-SLAM algorithm is recursive process: the state vector prediction, measurement covariance prediction, data association, the virtual measurement update and map building.

3.2.1   State Vector Prediction

$$x_{k|k-1} = F_{k-1}^* x_{k-1} \tag{8}$$

3.2.2   Measurement

The measured data of the robot is gotten by calculating measurement model equation (3).

3.2.3   Covariance Forecast

From (7) calculated according to equation (5) to derive predicted covariance.

$$P_{k|k-1} = F_k^* P_{k-1|k-1} (F_k^*)^T + J_k H_k^* P_{k-1|k-1} (J_k H_k^*)^T + \Gamma_k Q \Gamma_k^T \tag{9}$$

3.2.4   Data Association

Algorithm to obtain the map is two-dimensional maps of the data associated with the use of Singer's other nearest neighbor methods [6]. Associated with the measurement data z associated with the measurement z_k and decomposition of the new feature point measurements z_{nk}. For equation (4) of the virtual measurement model, measurement occurred during such a situation may occur: the moment $k-m$ the robot observed feature points in the circle, the point in time k is not observed, but in time $k+m$ the point observed. To meet the virtual measurement model (4) of the associated requirements, decomposition of the associated measurement z_k z_{ko} and $z_{k,k-1}$ then

$$z_k = \begin{bmatrix} z_{ko} & z_{k,k-1} & z_{nk} \end{bmatrix}^T$$

Where z_{ko} is outdated measurements, the measurement of the actual measurement of the total small proportion in the literature [7] shows that this part can be seen as redundant measurements discarded.

3.2.5 Virtual Measurement
The virtual measurement is performed according to virtual model of measurement equation (4).

3.2.6 Update
Update step of the associated data to be updated.

$$x_{k|k} = x_{k|k-1} + W_k (z_k^* - H_k^* \hat{x}_{k|k-1})$$

$$P_{k|k} = P_{k|k-1} - W_k H_k^* P_{k|k-1}$$

$$S_k = H_k^* P_{k|k-1} (H_k^*)^T + R_k$$

$$W_k = P_{k|k-1} (H^*)^T S_k^{-1}$$

(10)

3.2.7 Mapping
The new feature points can be measured to build to the map.

$$x_k^{new} = h^{-1}(z_{nk}, x_{vk})$$

$$x_k = \begin{bmatrix} x_k & x_k^{new} \end{bmatrix}^T$$

(11)

4   Simulation and Analysis

Robot SLAM simulation is performed in the environment 60m*70m, 54 feature points randomly distributed in the environment. Equation (2) model is used in experimental simulation, the robot's speed $V = 3m/s$, $T = 0.025s$. The nearest neighbor data association method is used, the maximum correlation distance $4m$, identified as new features associated with the minimum distance point $25m$.

4.1   The Consistency of Simulation Algorithm

Data association algorithm is used to test the impact of consistency of filtering estimate. Robot closure and non-closure motion simulation is performed.

a. Non-Closure Motion Simulation
Non-closed path of robot experiments were carried out in two experimental conditions MonteCarlo simulation 50 times, Experiment 1: colored measurement noise $v_k = \begin{bmatrix} 0.02 \\ 0.02 \end{bmatrix} + \xi_k$, Experiment 2: colored measurement noise $v_k = \begin{bmatrix} 0.04 \\ 0.04 \end{bmatrix} + \xi_k$.

50 robot pose NEES mean curve is shown in Figure 1 (a). Feature points for the characterization of all the features, take sides in the center of the two feature points (-37.3,38.2) and (13.6, -23), 50 MonteCarlo simulation of two feature points of the joint state NEES mean curve is shown in Figure 1 (b).

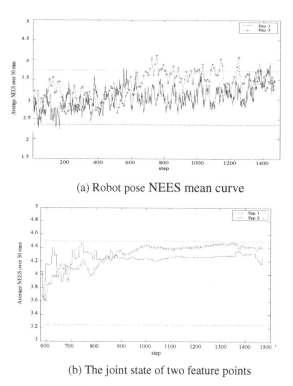

(a) Robot pose NEES mean curve

(b) The joint state of two feature points

Fig. 1. The mean non-closed path of the NEES

Figure 1 (a) and (b) shows the robot position and orientation of the NEES obey the χ^2 distribution mean, Experiment 2 measured the noise means 2 times the experimental one, but two curves are still [2.36,3.72] between; two feature points of the curve of the joint state of NEES mean increase in the mean measurement noise case is still close to 4. The literature [8] estimated that the algorithm is theoretical consistency can be estimated.

b. Closure Motion Simulation

Closed path of the robot experiment shown in Figure 2. Respectively in the two experimental conditions MonteCarlo simulation 50 times, Experiment 3: In accordance with the terms of a closed experimental path experiments; Experiment 4: According to

Experiment 2 Experimental conditions for closing the path. Robot's pose the NEES mean curve shown in Figure 3 (a). 50 MonteCarlo simulation of the two feature points of the joint state of NEES mean curve shown in Figure 3 (b).

Figure 3 (a) and (b) shows the experimental mean of four measurements for the experimental noise, three 2-fold, but the two experimental conditions, the robot position and orientation of the NEES mean curves are in [2.36,3.72], between two feature points of the joint state of NEES mean curve in the vicinity of 4. Comparing

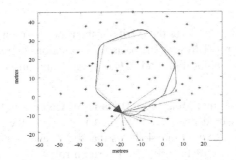

Fig. 2. Robot motion path closed

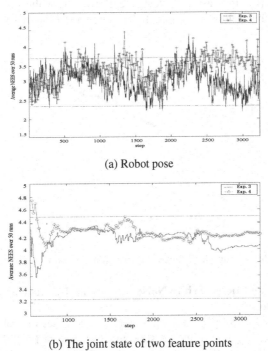

(a) Robot pose

(b) The joint state of two feature points

Fig. 3. Mean closed path of the NEES

Figure 1 (a) and Figure 3 (a), although the closed path of the χ^2 distribution curve than non-closed path of the χ^2 distribution curve volatility increases, but the curve is basically in [2.36,3.72], between the literature [8] estimation theory can that the algorithm is consistent estimate.

4.2   Under the Conditions of Colored Noise, the Simulation Analysis of Several Algorithms

CON-SLAM algorithm to evaluate the merits of the robot position and orientation of the root mean square error (RMS) as the basis for evaluation. Were used EKF-SLAM algorithm, Fast-SLAM algorithm and CON-SLAM algorithm 200 MonteCarlo simulation.

a. Experimental Conditions: Measuring Distance of Color, Angle of White Noise
    Figure 4 is the measured distance of colored noise case, the robot position and orientation of the RMS curve. Figure 4 shows that the mean is relatively small in the colored noise case, the use of Fast-SLAM algorithm robot pose and the RMS curve increases monotonically diverge. Using EKF-SLAM algorithm and CON-SLAM algorithm robot pose the RMS curves converge, but in the first 800 steps starting bifurcation, indicating the accumulation of errors caused by colored noise EKF-SLAM algorithm error increases; curve lies entirely within the proposed algorithm EKF-SLAM algorithm below, show that the proposed algorithm has better positioning accuracy.

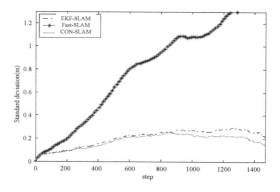

Fig. 4. Measuring the distance of the robot pose colored noise RMS

b. Experimental Conditions: White Noise Measuring Distance and Angle for the Case of Colored Noise
    Figure 5 is a measuring point for the colored noise case, the robot position and orientation of the RMS curve. Figure 5 shows that the use of EKF-SLAM algorithm and the Fast-SLAM algorithm robot pose the RMS curves are monotonically increasing and divergent. CON-SLAM algorithm using the robot pose convergence of the RMS curve, indicating that the proposed algorithm has better robustness.

c. Experimental Conditions: Measuring Distance and Angles for the Case of Colored Noise
    Figure 6 is the measured distance and angles for the case of colored noise, the RMS curve of robot pose. Figure 6 shows that the use of EKF-SLAM algorithm and

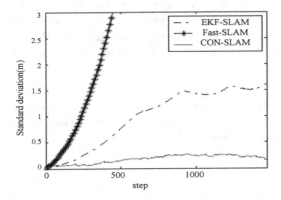

Fig. 5. Measuring the angle of the robot pose colored noise RMS

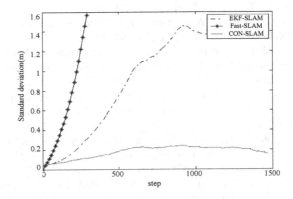

Fig. 6. The distance and angle are colored RMS noise of the robot pose

the Fast-SLAM algorithm robot pose the RMS slope of the curve greater than in Figure 5, and divergence. CON-SLAM algorithm using the robot pose convergence of the RMS curve, indicating that the proposed algorithm has better robustness.

In the simulation experiment, the measurement noise as colored noise, EKF-SLAM algorithm and the Fast-SLAM algorithm is still under Gaussian white noise model for the robot simultaneous localization and map building, this model because of the color measurement is approximately Gaussian white noise model leads to SLAM algorithm divergence. The use of CON-SLAM algorithm, the robot pose convergence of the RMS, indicating that the proposed algorithm for colored noise measurement robustness.

5   Conclusion

This paper presents a colored measurement noise for the next robot simultaneous localization and map building algorithm. The process by constructing a virtual model and the measurement model, the colored noise model into the white noise model.

Robot SLAM algorithm in accordance with the virtual process model and measurement model for simultaneous localization and map building. Simulation results verify the data associated with the consistency of redundant processing is filtered estimates. With the EKF-SLAM algorithm and Fast-SLAM algorithm, the proposed method is robust.

Acknowledgments. This work was supported by the science research programs of education department of Shaanxi Province (11JK0899) and the National Science Foundation of China under Grant 61075044.

References

1. Gehrig, S.K., Stein, F.J.: Dead reckoning and cartography using stereo vision for an autonomous car. In: Proceedings of the IEEE International Conference on Intelligent Robots and Systems, pp. 1507–1512. IEEE, Piscataway (1999)
2. Xu, J.-y., Wang, J.-c., Chen, W.-d.: Omni-vision-Based Simultaneous Localization and Mapping of Mobile Robots. Robots 30(4), 289–297 (2008)
3. Davison, A.J.: Real-time simultaneous localization and mapping with a single camera. In: Proc. Proceedings of the Ninth IEEE International Conference on Computer Vision, Nice, pp. 1403–1410 (2003)
4. Leung, C., Huang, S., Dissanayake, G.: Active SLAM in structured environments. In: 2008 IEEE International Conference on Robotics and Automation, Pasadena, CA, USA, pp. 1989–1903 (2008)
5. He, F., Fang, Y., Wang, Y., Ban, T.: Practical feature-based simultaneous localization and mapping using sonar data. In: Proceedings of the 27th Chinese Control Conference, Kunming, Yunnan, China, pp. 421–425 (2008)
6. Singer, R.A., Sea, R.G.: A new filter for optimal tracking in dense multi-target environment. In: Proceedings of the Ninth Allerton Conference Circuit and System Theory, pp. 201–211. Univ.of Illinois, Urbana-Champaign (1971)
7. Dissanayake, G., Durrant-Whyte, H., Bailey, T.: A computationally efficient solution to the simultaneous localisation and map building (SLAM) problem. In: IEEE International Conference on Robotics and Automation, vol. 2, pp. 1009–1014 (2000)
8. Bar-Shalom, Y., Li, X.R., Kirubarajan, T.: Estimation with applications to tracking and navigation, pp. 234–235. John Wiley and Sons (2001)

A Comparison of Different Metaheuristic Algorithms for Optimizing Blended PTP Movements for Industrial Robots

Sven Severin[1] and Juergen Rossmann[2]

[1] RIF e.V. Department Robot Technology, Joseph-von-Fraunhofer-Str. 20,
44227 Dortmund, Germany
sven.severin@rt.rif-ev.de
[2] Institute for Man-Machine Interaction, RWTH Aachen University, Ahornstr. 55,
52074 Aachen, Germany
rossmann@mmi.rwth-aachen.de

Abstract. The optimization of robot paths is important to reduce cycle times in industrial production processes. Even small time savings will accumulate and thus reduce production costs. This paper shows a method to automate the optimization of blended PTP movements for industrial robots and compares the performance of three metaheuristics.

Keywords: Industrial robot, PTP movement, optimization, metaheuristics.

1 Introduction

A robot position can be described as a vector of robot-joint values. A synchronous PTP movement drives the robot joints in a way such that acceleration and deceleration times for all joints are equal. The movement distance and the motor specification of each joint determine which joint is the slowest. The speed and acceleration of all other joints is determined by the slowest joint. PTP movement is by definition the fastest possible movement between two positions.

In case a PTP movement would lead to a collision between the robot and its environment, additional positions are necessary to circumvent the collision. Each stop at such an intermediate position increases the cycle time of the movement. This can be regarded unnecessary since the intermediate positions do not have to be reached exactly. The blend parameter as shown in **Fig. 1** will force the robot to leave its path before it reaches the intermediate position. The robot preserves its momentum and uses it to move to the next position. The loss of time is thus reduced. The challenge is to find the optimal location of such an intermediate position, minimizing the duration of the movement while avoiding collisions with the environment.

Fig. 1 illustrates a robot moving along a PTP trajectory. On the left side no blending occurs, on the right side the position P_I is blended. The blend parameter b describes the position on the trajectory from point P_S to the intermediate point P_I,

C.-Y. Su, S. Rakheja, H. Liu (Eds.): ICIRA 2012, Part III, LNAI 7508, pp. 321–330, 2012.
© Springer-Verlag Berlin Heidelberg 2012

where the trajectory is modified and blended into the movement to point P_T. Parameter b can be specified as the percentage of the distance the slowest axis has to travel.

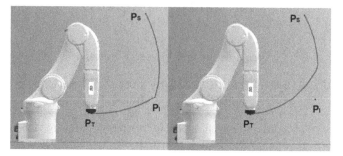

Fig. 1. PTP motion without and with blending

To describe this optimization problem, we need a kinematic device that is capable of executing PTP motions, as well as a start and a target position for the movement. In addition to that, a description of the surrounding geometry that prevents the robot from moving directly from the start position to the end position without any collisions has to be provided. In this paper we compare different metaheuristic algorithms. To solve this optimization problem we develop a fitness function and give a set of application scenarios to test the different algorithms. Additionally, we provide a criterion to compare the results of the algorithms on different scenarios.

2   State of the Art

Many offline programming systems for industrial robots include modules to plan and/or optimize robot trajectories for different applications like polishing, brushing, milling, cutting, gluing, water jet cutting or laser welding. All these modules need the knowledge of a process expert to specify the robot motion and are not fitted to optimize a general movement. The path planning system GLEAM [1] uses genetic algorithms to produce paths for industrial robots. Although it is theoretically qualified to generate optimized PTP movements, the focus of GLEAM is on the planning of collision free paths, not on the optimization of single movements. In [2], a method is shown that uses genetic algorithms to generate a trajectory for an industrial robot to follow a given path. Although it shows the superiority of genetic algorithms over hill-climbing and random search, the author demonstrates his method only on a kinematic device with three degrees of freedom. Tangpattanakul and Artrit [3] demonstrate how to use the harmony search algorithm to optimize a given path according to the movement duration. This method does not consider a standard movement type like PTP and therefore needs a special control unit for the robot. So, currently, there exists no method to help robot programmers to optimize PTP movements for industrial robots in real world application scenarios.

3   Test Scenarios

To test the optimization, we have developed several scenarios. Each scenario consists of a robot, a start position, a target position, and obstacles that prevent the robot from moving directly between the two positions. The goal for the optimization algorithm is to find the fastest trajectory from the start position to the target position without colliding with the obstacles. The scenario design takes into account the most common use cases of PTP movements in robot applications.

The scenarios include predominant industrial robot types. These are the standard six-axis kinematic, a palletizer and a SCARA. They are assigned different roles: pick-and-place, handling, or machine-to-machine transfer. Several difficulties were added in the form of narrow operating space, big gripper geometries and configuration changes during the movement.

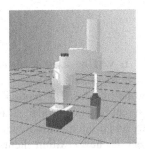

Fig. 2. Scenarios A and B with special robot types

Fig. 2 depicts scenario A containing a SCARA, optimized for pick-and-place tasks and scenario B containing a palletizing robot. In both cases, the task is to move the work piece across the obstacle to a target position without collisions.

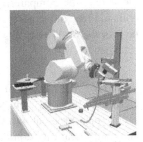

Fig. 3. Machine-to-machine transfer (left) and handling tasks in scenario D and E (right)

Scenario C that is shown on the left in **Fig. 3** is an example of machine-to-machine transfer. Scenario D (**Fig. 3** middle) features a robot within a very narrow operating space. The task is to transfer a work piece from the magazine and put it onto the lower cylinder. Scenario E (**Fig. 3** right) shows a table mounted workstation. The task of moving the work piece from the magazine to the tray requires a configuration change during the movement.

4   Solution Approach

Every possible solution to the optimization problem is given by a sequence of intermediate positions and associated blend parameters. A solution may be written as a solution vector, where the length of the vector depends on the type of robot and the number of intermediate positions. A solution vector for a kinematic device with n degrees of freedom and p intermediate positions is given by $sol = ((g_{1,1}, g_{2,1}, \ldots, g_{n,1}, b_1), \ldots, (g_{1,p}, g_{2,p}, \ldots, g_{n,p}, b_p))$. Where $g_{i,j}$ are the value of joint j at position i and b_i blend parameters. The performance of such a solution depends on three factors:

— The movement has to be free of collisions.
— The required movement time should be minimal.
— There should be no unnecessary movements.

4.1   Fitness Function

The fitness function is a mapping $F: \overrightarrow{sol} \rightarrow \mathbb{R}_+$. It will be used to determine the performance of a given solution and compare it to other solutions. In order to calculate a fitness function, we need to quantify the blended PTP motion. Thus, we actually have to interpolate the PTP motion like a real robot controller. It is assumed that any algorithm used for interpolation depends on an interpolation interval (IPO). Changes in speed may only occur between intervals, never within them. The IPO cycle for industrial robots ranges from approximately 1ms to 12ms.

It is sufficient for the fitness function to check whether a collision occurs or not. Time, duration, position, or involved bodies in a collision are not necessary to be known for performance evaluation. The movement's duration t_{sol} can be taken as the movement time of the slowest joint. The usefulness of a movement cannot be directly measured but compared between two solutions. Hence, if the durations of two collision free movements are equal, the one with more overall motion is considered to be less useful. We define the overall motion of all axes as:

$$w = \sum_N \sum_I |g_{n,i} - g_{n,i-1}| \tag{1}$$

Where N is the number of joints, I the number of interpolation steps, and $g_{n,i}$ the n-th element of the joint value vector for interpolation step i.

The measurement will be used as the base value for the fitness function. Collisions and unnecessary motion can be added as penalty times and extend the duration of the movement. Each trajectory containing a collision should be rated worse than any collision-free trajectory. If two solutions result in movements of equal duration, the one with less unnecessary motion should be rated better. To achieve this, we make use of the fact that the difference in duration between two solutions is either 0 ms or at least one IPO cycle. The measured, accumulated travelling distance of all axes w will be mapped on an interval [0, IPO). To achieve this, an upper bound for w has to be found. Then, the penalty for colliding trajectories is equal to the maximum duration of a movement for a given problem. The fitness function will thus evaluate to smaller values for better performance.

The maximum movement time for a trajectory depends on the kinematic structure and the number of intermediate positions. With g_- as minimum joint value vector, g_+ as maximum joint value vector, and n_{IP} as number of intermediate positions, the maximum time t_{kin} and motion w_{kin} between g_- and g_+ can be derived from the interpolation between these positions. These have to be multiplied by the desired number of intermediate positions.

$$t_{max} = t_{kin} \cdot (n_{IP} + 1) \tag{2}$$

$$w_{max} = w_{kin} \cdot (n_{IP} + 1) \tag{3}$$

These values are only valid for a specific optimization problem and cannot be compared to fitness values for different problems (different robots, start positions, or target positions). The duration t_{sol} and combined motion w_{sol} of an actual solution are incorporated into the fitness function as follows:

$$F_i = \begin{cases} t_{sol} + \frac{w_{sol}}{w_{max}} \cdot IPO & \text{, if not colliding} \\ 2t_{max} - (t_{sol} + \frac{w_{sol}}{w_{max}} \cdot IPO) & \text{, coll. and } i \in 2Z \\ t_{max} + (t_{sol} + \frac{w_{sol}}{w_{max}} \cdot IPO) & \text{, coll. and } i \in 2Z + 1 \end{cases} \tag{4}$$

The different treatment for odd and even solution indices i is used to reflect two alternative optimization strategies when the solution trajectory leads to a collision. For collisions occurring at the end effector of the robot, it is in generally necessary to elongate the trajectory to find a way around the obstacle. Thus, even indices search for longer path durations. In cases were the collision occurs e.g. at the shoulder of the robot, a shorter path could lead to collision avoidance. Therefore, the odd solution indices will be better rated for longer durations.

4.2   Parameterization

A complete factorial experimental design as specified in [4] was constructed to configure the metaheuristics. The determined values for all parameters are given at the end of the description of each metaheuristic.

5   Metaheuristics

For the given problem, swarm-based algorithms seem to be qualified best because they are able to search efficiently through a large and complex configuration space. Therefore, focus of this paper is on the comparison of particle swarm optimization, firefly algorithms and harmony search.

All these algorithms have in common that a solution is represented by a swarm member. In case of particle swarm and firefly algorithms, the solution is represented by the position of the particle. This position may be adapted during each iteration, depending on rules defined by the algorithm. The newly found solutions will then be evaluated by the fitness function. The number of elements in the swarm will be denoted as n.

5.1   Particle Swarm Optimization

The particle swarm optimization [5] was inspired by the behavior of birds in a swarm. The swarm elements, called particles, keep track of their own velocity and change it, according to their own best and global best position. An inertia factor ensures that particles do not jump too fast towards a global minimum. The formula to compute the velocity of a particle for the current iteration is given as:

$$v_{i,d}^{t+1} = w^t \cdot v_{i,d}^t + c_1 \cdot rand \cdot (x^*_{i,d} - x_{i,d}^t) + c_2 \cdot rand \cdot (g^*_d - x_{i,d}^t) \tag{5}$$

Where $v_{i,d}^t$ is the element d of the velocity of particle i at iteration t, w^t is the inertia factor at iteration t, c_1 and c_2 are constants to determine the influence of the own best x^*_i and global best position g^*, and x_i^t is the particles own position at iteration t. The function $rand$ generates a random number within [0, 1]. The inertial weight w^t has to be evaluated in every iteration:

$$w^t = \begin{cases} W_{max} - (W_{max} - W_{min}) \cdot (\frac{I}{W_I \cdot I_{max}}) & , I < W_I \cdot I_{max} \\ W_{min} & , else \end{cases} \tag{6}$$

The optimal parameterization determined for our use case is $n = 100$, $I_{max} = 200$, $W_{max} = 0.9$, $W_{min} = 0.444$, $W_I = 150$, $c_1 = c_2 = 2$.

5.2   Firefly Algorithm

The firefly algorithm [6] is similar to the particle swarm optimization. The individual swarm elements, here called fireflies, have no global knowledge about the best position, but gather information about fireflies in optical range. So, in theory, the algorithm should be able to locate more than one minimum in the fitness function by clustering particles around them. In each step, every firefly x_i has to be tested against every other firefly x_j. If the fitness of firefly x_j is better than the fitness of firefly x_i, x_i will move towards x_j as in the following formula described.

$$x_i = x_i + \beta_0^{-\gamma \cdot r^2} \cdot (x_j - x_i) + \alpha \left(rand - \frac{1}{2} \right) \tag{7}$$

The distance between the fireflies is r, the parameters β_0 and γ determine how the distance limits the influence on the position. The parameter α is a multiplier for the random value.

The optimal parameterization determined for our use case is $n = 32$, $\alpha = 1$, $\beta_0 = 0.5$, $\gamma = 10^{-5}$. The maximum number of Iterations $I_{max} = 625$ is chosen to concur to the maximum number of function evaluations used in the particle swarm optimization parameterization.

5.3   Alternative Versions of the Firefly Algorithm

The last expression in the position update function of the firefly algorithm indicates potential for further optimization. Some authors suggested alternatives to the strict random addition.

The adaptive firefly algorithm of Farahani et. al. [7] uses a factor W_{itr} which adapts α to the current iteration. The value for W_{itr} is given by the following formula:

$$W_{itr} = X + \frac{(itr_{max}-itr)^n}{itr_{max}^n}(Y - X) \tag{8}$$

Where X is the minimum and Y the maximum factor, itr_{max} the maximum number of iterations and itr the current iteration index.

The chaotic firefly algorithm of Coelho et. al. [8] uses chaotic sequences to randomize the length of the random step. The value $\alpha(t)$, generated by the following formulas, is used instead of $\alpha(rand - 0.5)$:

$$\gamma(t) = \mu 1 \cdot \gamma(t-1) \cdot [1-\gamma(t-1)] \tag{9}$$

$$\alpha(t) = \mu 2 \cdot \gamma(t-1) \cdot [1-\alpha(t-1)] \tag{10}$$

A version called Lévy-flight firefly algorithm is described in [9]. Here, length of the random step is not uniformly distributed but Lévy-distributed. This generates a large amount of small steps (like the expression $\alpha(rand - 0.5)$), breached by a number of outliers that helps to escape local minima.

5.4   Harmony Search

The harmony search algorithm [10] was inspired by the same approach a musician follows when composing a song. The algorithm uses a memory to store and recall found solutions and combines or changes them. Better solutions will replace the worst solution in memory. Initially, the memory has to be populated with a number of solutions. Three probability values decide in which way a solution will be altered. A new solution is generated at each iteration. For every element e in the solution vector, a new probability r is generated. If r is bigger than r_accept, the element e will be randomly set. If not, e will be set to the corresponding value of a random solution resident in the memory. If r is bigger than r_pa, the value read from memory will be altered by a random amount controlled by the factor pa.

The optimal parameterization determined for our use case is $n = 30$, $r_{accept} = 0.95$, $r_{pa} = 0.3$, $pa = 1000$.

6   Comparison

In the following sections, we will present a criterion that allows us to compare the algorithms performance and discuss the results.

6.1   Criteria

A criterion is necessary to measure the success of an optimization. Because the fitness value depends on the kinematic structure and the scenario, it is inadequate as quantification. Thus, we introduce a measure called the *utilization of the optimization potential*. This implies the necessity of two guesses. The minimum potential F_0 is a fitness value of what can be easily achieved. The maximum value F_{100} describes suitable results. In the present case, the minimum values are manually optimized solutions for all the test cases. The maximum values were calculated from the first automated parameterization tests and chosen from 280 individual results per scenario.

Table 1. Optimization potential

Scenario	F_0	F_{100}
A	0.936100	0.820793
B	1.631200	1.211195
C	1.730500	1.200411
D	1.161200	0.670972
E	0.916100	0.771133

Table 1 shows the manually obtained fitness value (F_0) and the maximum (F_{100}) fitness values. The potential utilization of any given fitness value for one of these scenarios can be calculated as:

$$P = 1 - \frac{(F - F_{100})}{(F_0 - F_{100})} \tag{11}$$

Where P is the utilized potential and F is the fitness value of the solution. All results were obtained by simulating the corresponding solutions in the simulation system CIROS [11].

6.2   Comparison by Scenario

The results in **Table 2** show the utilization of the optimization potential for all reviewed metaheuristics and variants. The results were averaged over 25 runs per scenario.

The usage of a firefly algorithms variant tends to perform better only in some of the given scenarios. A small improvement was achieved, but involved worse results in other scenarios. Only the adaptive variant was able to produce similar results as the standard firefly algorithm in all scenarios.

While the combined results for particle swarm optimization and standard firefly algorithm are roughly equal, the particle swarm optimization is inferior to firefly in scenario D. The results for harmony search are in most scenarios just below the values for the other metaheuristics, but are especially low for scenario D. Closer inspection of scenario D points out that the difficulty to achieve good results seems to be due to the very narrow collision free maneuvering space which the robot may use.

Table 2. Utilized potential for the firefly algorithm

Scenario	Particle Swarm	Firefly Standard	Firefly Adaptive	Firefly Chaotic	Firefly Lévy	Harmony Search
A	96,03%	95.05%	94,70%	96,34%	96,36%	95,67%
B	99,51%	99.14%	99,04%	99,51%	99,52%	98,75%
C	95,73%	98.70%	96,95%	98,84%	98,86%	92,48%
D	86,05%	92.26%	94,30%	80,41%	88,57%	51,91%
E	93,38%	93.10%	93,10%	88,96%	93,10%	93,10%
Mean	94,14%	95.65%	95,61%	92,81%	95,28%	86,38%

6.3   Comparison by Algorithm

As seen in the comparison by scenario, the tested variants of the firefly algorithm are no improvement over the standard algorithm. Therefore, the variants will not be considered in the following comparison.

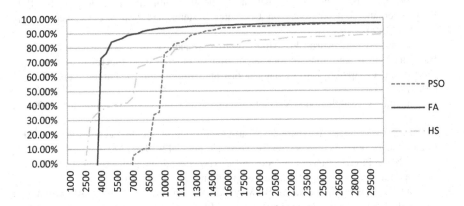

Fig. 4. Comparison of algorithms

Fig. 4 shows a comparison of the reviewed algorithms. The x-axis indicates the number of function evaluations that are necessary to achieve a result as set on the y-axis. The dotted line shows the performance of the particle swarm algorithm, the continuous line shows the performance of the firefly algorithm, and the dot-and-dashed line shows the performance of the harmony search. The firefly algorithm outperforms all other algorithms. Although the harmony search reached a 30% optimization after 2500 function evaluations, it is quickly outperformed by the particle swarm optimization algorithm and the firefly algorithm. Note that the firefly algorithm always needs fewer function evaluations than the particle swarm optimizer. The harmony search failed to exceed the 90% threshold even after 30000 function evaluations and reached approximately 89.5%.

7   Conclusion

All reviewed algorithms are capable of optimizing the examined problem. Especially the firefly algorithm needs less than 15000 function evaluations to utilize up to 95% of the existing optimization potential. The firefly algorithm was able to optimize all scenarios to at least 90%, which indicates a good general applicability. Additional modifications for the firefly algorithm were studied. None of these modifications has led to a significantly higher performance in all scenarios at the same time.

The impact of the automated optimization can be illustrated by an example. The robots movement in the machine-to-machine transfer scenario C took 1.76s in the manually optimized version. After optimizing the movement with the standard firefly algorithm it took 1.5s, which is ~15 % less.

References

1. Blume, C., Jakob, W.: GLEAM - General Learning Evolutionary Algorithm and Method. KIT Scientific Publishing, Karlsruhe (2009)
2. Davidor, Y.: Robot programming with a genetic algorithm. In: Proceedings of the 1990 IEEE International Conference on Computer Systems and Software Engineering, pp. 186–191 (1990)
3. Tangpattanakul, P., Artrit, P.: Minimum-time trajectory of robot manipulator using Harmony Search algorithm. In: 6th International Conference on Electrical Engineering / Electronics, Computer, Telecommunications and Information Technology, pp. 354–357 (2009)
4. Kleppmann, W.: Taschenbuch Versuchsplanung. Carl Hanser Verlag, München (2003) (in German)
5. Kennedy, J., Eberhart, R.: Particle Swarm Optimization. In: Proceedings of the IEEE International Conference on Neural Networks IV, pp. 1942–1948 (2003)
6. Yang, X.S.: Firefly Algorithm, Stochastic Test Functions and Design Optimisation. International Journal on Bio-Inspired Computation 2(2), 78–84 (2010)
7. Farahani, S., Abshouri, A., Nasiri, B., Meybodi, M.: An Improved Firefly Algorithm with Directed Movement. In: Proceedings of 4th IEEE International Conference on Computer Science and Information Technology, Chengdu, pp. 248–251 (2011)
8. Coelho, L., Bernert, D., Mariani, V.: A Chaotic Firefly Algorithm Applied To Reliability-.Redundancy Optimization. In: IEEE Congress on Evolutionary Computation (CEC), pp. 517–521 (2011)
9. Yang, X.S.: Firefly Algorithm, Levy Flights and Global Optimization. In: Bramer, M., Ellis, R., Petridis, M. (eds.) Research and Development in Intelligent Systems XXVI, pp. 209–218. Springer, London (2010)
10. Geem, Z.W., Kim, J.H., Loganathan, G.V.: A New Heuristic Optimization Algorithm: Harmony Search. SIMULATION 76, 60–68 (2001)
11. Roßmann, J., Wischnewski, R., Stern, O.: A Comprehensive 3-D Simulation System for the Virtual Production. In: Proceedings of the 8th International Industrial Simulation Conference (ISC), Budapest, pp. 109–116 (2010)

Stable Gait Planning for Biped Robot's Lower Limb Based on Natural ZMP Trajectories

Guanlun Wu, Xiaohui Xiao, Lu Liu, Wei Luo, Xiaobin Ye, and Yang Yang

School of Power and Mechanical Engineering, Wuhan University
430072 Wuhan, Hubei, China

Abstract. This paper generates the walking trajectory reference with the method of natural Zero Moment Point (ZMP) criterion and Linear Inverted Pendulum Model (LIPM), and then proposes an approach to adjust the ZMP reference according to the gait parameters. The reference equations of the center of mass (CoM) of the biped robot are coupled with the interpolation function of the ankle joint. Assuming the height of biped robot hip is constantly during a step, the simulation shows that the height of CoM varies less than 2.6%, which can be further reduced via adjusting the gait height of the swing foot. Finally, using Natural ZMP-based reference and considering the legs mass, the kinematics simulation of a biped prototype is performed in MATLAB. The results show that the CoM trajectory is stable, and the variation of CoM trajectory compared to its reference is less than 0.6%.

Keywords: biped robot, LIPM, natural ZMP, gait planning, simulation.

1   Introduction

Compared to other types of mobile robot, biped robot has better obstacle avoidance property with less energy comsumption, especially in complex terrain. The biped robot is a multi-DOF (degree of freedom) system with nonlinear strong-coupling and non-holonomic constraints, leading to challenge in walking control [1][2][3][4].

Stable walking is the basis of the biped robot application. Many methods for stable walking plan have being put forward, including joint interpolation method and gait stability criterion based on ZMP criterion. S. Ali proposed a gait planning with the method of joint interpolation [8]. N. Mir-Nasiri and H. Siswoyo Jo achieve the gait planning for a 4-DOF biped robot with the similar method [9]. M.Vukobratovic is the first one to propose ZMP criterion in dynamic equilibrium principle of biped robot [5][6]. Among these ZMP-based walking planning strategies, a significant one is the combination of LIPM and ZMP. When ZMP trajectory is kept inside the support graphic of foot, the biped walking is stable [7]. As for the LIPM, when a reasonable trajectory is generated, the equations of CoM can be solved to satisfy traditional gait stability criterion based on ZMP.

According to the planned ZMP trajectory, Choi,Y. et. al solved the ZMP trajectory equation of the LIPM, further derived the time-domain equation of CoM under single

C.-Y. Su, S. Rakheja, H. Liu (Eds.): ICIRA 2012, Part III, LNAI 7508, pp. 331–341, 2012.

support phase (SSP)[11]. Okan Kurt, firstly, based on the proposed method of natural ZMP trajectory in [11], which has benefits in stability and energy efficiency due to humanoid naturalness. After obtain the ZMP equations and CoM equations of the SSP, they added double support phase (DSP) referenced Lanczos Sigma Factor's method and introduced a parameter DSP to optimize the gait planning [10]. However with the introduced DSP, the original shape of the reference CoM curve of SSP is affected.

The traditional stability criterion based on ZMP is adopted in this paper. The coupling of reference CoM curve under DSP and interpolation function of ankle joint is achieved by adjusting concerning parameters. Moreover, considering the mass of lower limb, we make the simulated CoM of a prototype model matched with the reference CoM. Since the gait planning is satisfied with the traditional gait stability criterion based on ZMP, the stable walking is guaranteed.

2   Reference Generation with Natural ZMP Trajectory

Set x and y as the walking and lateral direction, while z the gravity direction. The equations of ZMP are derived as follows [10]:

$$p_x = \frac{\sum_{i=1}^{n} m_i (\ddot{z}_i - g_z) x_i - \sum_{i=1}^{n} m_i (\ddot{x}_i - g_x) z_i}{\sum_{i=1}^{n} m_i (\ddot{z}_i - g_z)}$$

$$p_y = \frac{\sum_{i=1}^{n} m_i (\ddot{z}_i - g_z) y_i - \sum_{i=1}^{n} m_i (\ddot{y}_i - g_x) z_i}{\sum_{i=1}^{n} m_i (\ddot{z}_i - g_z)} \tag{1}$$

where, p_x, p_y are coordinates of the ZMP trajectory; x_i, z_i are coordinates of the CoM of each part of the robot; g_x, g_z are the gravity values in x-direction and z-direction.

The gait planning is divided into two stages as SSP and DSP. Suppose a step motion starts from SSP, first generate the CoM reference based on traditional gait stability criterion. Then Lanczos Sigma Factor is introduced to insert the CoM trajectory of DSP into that of two adjacent SSPs.

By analyzing human walking, the natural ZMP trajectory is generated as shown in Fig.1[10]. In SSP, the ZMP trajectory moves from the heel to the toes of support foot, while another foot called swing foot moves forwards and touches the ground. Hereto, the SSP shifts to the DSP, the ZMP trajectory moves from the toes of support foot to the heel of swing foot, which is the beginning of next SSP.

The ZMP trajectory in natural humanoid walking is not a simple line as above. Moreover, the change of ZMP trajectory with time is not taken into consideration in Fig 1. It is assumed that the changes of the ZMP trajectory in both SSP and DSP are equal. The change of x coordination with time in SSP is shown in Fig. 2, while a

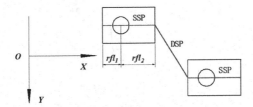

Fig. 1. Natural ZMP trajectory of a walking period

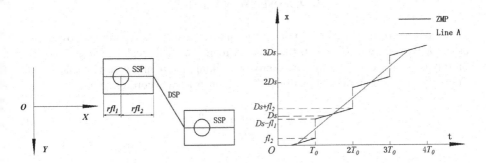

Fig. 2. ZMP trajectory in a walk period   **Fig. 3.** Natural ZMP Trajectory in SSP

DSP-SSP walking period is shown in Fig. 3, where Ds is a foot step, and T_0 is a time sustains from a SSP. The X-direction movement of ZMP trajectory during T_0 is a foot step $fl_1 + fl_2$. In Fig. 1, the symbol of real foot length is $rfl_1 + rfl_2$, while in Fig. 2, the symbol is $fl_1 + fl_2$. At first, $fl_i = rfl_i$, $i=1,2$, then the fl is changed to fit with rfl.

When $t = k \cdot T_0$ (k is an integer), the ZMP trajectory shifts from one foot to another, at the same time, p_x increases by $D_s - fl_1 - fl_2$.

The foot consists of two parts, which is general and in accordance with the physical prototype adopted in the paper. However in the following calculation process, $fl_1 = fl_2$ is defined. If $fl_1 \neq fl_2$, the integral process is tedious. The position of fl_1, fl_2 can be distinguished by the parallel translation of the curve in y-direction.

Assuming that the mechanism is a linear inverted pendulum model (LIPM) with a COM($[c_x, c_y, c_z]$), and the mass of two legs are neglected. In case of energy waste due to the height changes of COM, c_z is set to a constant. c_z is substituted into (1):

$$p_x = c_x - \frac{1}{\omega_n^2}\ddot{c}_x, \quad p_y = c_y - \frac{1}{\omega_n^2}\ddot{c}_y \tag{2}$$

where, $\omega_n^2 = \dfrac{g}{z_c}$.

Equation (2) is arranged:

$$\ddot{c}_x = \omega_n^2 c_x - \omega_n^2 p_x, \quad \ddot{c}_y = \omega_n^2 c_y - \omega_n^2 p_y \tag{3}$$

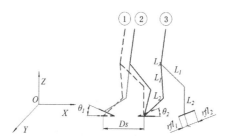

Fig. 4. A DSP-SSP Walking Period

To reduce errors caused by ignoring legs' mass, the follows regards the lower limb as a bar-type system, of which the CoM is regarded as the calculated CoM of the prototype model. Considering periodicity of walking, the p_x and p_y are expanded with Fourier Series. The periodic function $p_x^{ad}(t)$ is constructed according to p_x.

$$p_x^{ad}(t) = p_x(t) - \frac{D_s}{T_0}(t - \frac{T_0}{2}) \tag{4}$$

where, $\frac{D_s}{T_0}(t - \frac{T_0}{2})$ is the line A shown in Fig 2. $p_x^{ad}(t)$ is an odd function with period T_0. Given the Fourier Series form of p_x, $c_x(t)$ can be derived by (3) and (4) :

$$C_x(t) = \frac{D_s}{T_0}(t - \frac{T_0}{2}) + \sum_{n=1}^{\infty}\left[a_n \cos(\frac{n\pi}{T_0}t) + b_n \sin(\frac{n\pi}{T_0}t) \right] \tag{5}$$

Substitute (3), (4) into (2), then:

$$p_x^{ad}(t) = \sum_{n=1}^{\infty}\left[a_n(1 + \frac{n^2\pi^2}{T_0^2\omega_n^2})\cos(\frac{n\pi}{T_0}t) + b_n(1 + \frac{n^2\pi^2}{T_0^2\omega_n^2})\sin(\frac{n\pi}{T_0}t) \right] \tag{6}$$

Where, $a_n = 0, b_n(1 + \frac{n^2\pi^2}{T_0^2\omega_n^2}) = \frac{2}{T_0}\int_0^{T_0} p_x^{ad}(t)\sin(\frac{n\pi}{T_0}t)d \tag{7}$

First, substitute (4) into (7), set $fl_1=fl_2=fl$, then

$$b_n = \frac{(D_s - 2fl)T_0^2\omega_n^2}{n\pi(T_0^2\omega_n^2 + n^2\pi^2)} \tag{8}$$

Substitute (8) into (5) and (4), get the equations of ZMP and CoM in x-direction:

$$P_x(t) = \frac{D_s}{T_0}(t - \frac{T_0}{2}) + \sum_{n=1}^{\infty}\left[\frac{(D_s - 2fl)(1 + \cos n\pi)}{n\pi}\sin(\frac{n\pi}{T_0}t) \right] \tag{9}$$

$$C_x(t) = \frac{D_s}{T_0}(t - \frac{T_0}{2}) + \sum_{n=1}^{\infty}\left[\frac{(D_s - 2fl)(1 + \cos n\pi)T_0^2\omega_n^2}{n\pi(T_0^2\omega_n^2 + n^2\pi^2)}\sin(\frac{n\pi}{T_0}t)\right] \qquad (10)$$

Considering the prototype parameters adopted in this paper, parameters is set as:

$Ds = 0.6\ m$; $fl = 0.1235\ m$; $T_0 = 1.5\ m$; $Z_c = 0.5\ m$;

Generate the ZMP trajectory - $P_x(t)$ and the CoM trajectory - $C_x(t)$ in Fig. 5(a). With the same method, the equations of ZMP and CoM in Y-Direction can be obtained:

$$p_y(t) = \sum_{n=1}^{\infty}\left[\frac{2A(1 - \cos n\pi)}{n\pi}\sin(\frac{n\pi}{T_0}t)\right] \qquad (11)$$

$$C_y(t) = \sum_{n=1}^{\infty}\left[\frac{2AT_0^2\omega_n^2(1 - \cos n\pi)}{n\pi(T_0^2\omega_n^2 + n^2\pi^2)}\sin(\frac{n\pi}{T_0}t)\right] \qquad (12)$$

The $P_y(t)$ and $C_y(t)$ curves are shown in Fig. 5(b).

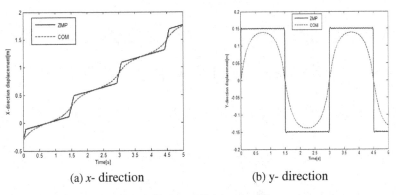

(a) x- direction   (b) y- direction

Fig. 5. ZMP and CoM trajectories

In order to insert the ZMP trajectory of the DSP into the SSP, the Fourier Transform based on Lanczos Sigma Factor - sinc() is introduced :

$$P_x(t) = \frac{D_s}{T_0}(t - \frac{T_0}{2}) + \sum_{n=1}^{\infty}[\frac{(D_s - 2fl)(1 + \cos n\pi)}{n\pi}\sin c(\frac{n\pi}{DSP})\sin(\frac{n\pi}{T_0}t)] \qquad (13)$$

$$C_x(t) = \frac{D_s}{T_0}(t - \frac{T_0}{2}) + \sum_{n=1}^{\infty}[\frac{(D_s - 2fl)(1 + \cos n\pi)T_0^2\omega_n^2}{n\pi(T_0^2\omega_n^2 + n^2\pi^2)}\sin c(\frac{n\pi}{DSP})\sin(\frac{n\pi}{T_0}t)] \qquad (14)$$

With a smaller *DSP*, the time that it inserts into the SSP is longer. When *DSP* increases, the curve approaches to the SSP curve. Because *DSP* changes the reference shape, the parameters must be adjusted in order that the time and the displacement of both SSP and DSP are accord with the foot length *rfl* of the physical prototype.

3   CoM Parameters Adjustment Based on Natural ZMP Trajectory

The shape of ZMP curve in Fig. 6 is determined by T_0, *fl* and *DSP*.
T_0 is a time sustains from a SSP before the introduction of parameter *DSP*. And it becomes the sum time of the T_{SSP} and the T_{DSP} after that:

$$T_{DSP} + T_{SSP} = T_0 \qquad (15)$$

fl : In a period T_0, the forward displacement S of the ZMP trajectory during SSP decreases as the introduction of *DSP*. Thus the value of *fl* is raised to increase S.
DSP: After derivate of (13), $p_x^{'}(t)$ can be found as follows:

$$p_x^{'}(t) = \frac{D_S}{T_0} + \sum_{n=1}^{\infty} \left[\frac{(D_S - 2fl)(1 + \cos n\pi)}{T_0} \sin c(\frac{n\pi}{DSP}) \cos(\frac{n\pi}{T_0}t) \right] \qquad (16)$$

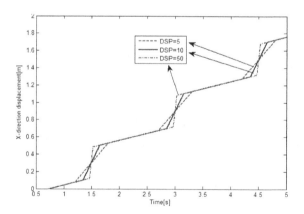

Fig. 6. Shape Influence of ZMP Caused by DSP

The switch of the DSP and the SSP is accomplished at the point of the slope jumping of a ZMP trajectory. When the abscissa of these points is determined and combined with Equation 15, the T_{DSP}, T_{SSP} and S can be settled. The desired T_{DSP}, T_{SSP} and S are obtained through the adjustment of T_0, *fl* and *DSP*. Set

$$\frac{t}{T_0} = \frac{1}{DSP} \qquad (17)$$

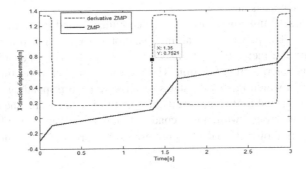

Fig. 7. ZMP trajectory in *x* direction and its derivate

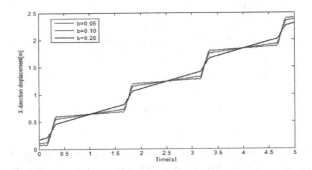

Fig. 8. Influence of ZMP trajectory (13) in *x* direction Caused by f1

The value of *t*, which represents the abscissa of the first jumping point in Fig. 7, can be solved. Given the periodicity of the curve, the other jumping points can be solved.

If *DSP*=10 and T_0=1.5, *t*=0.15 can be solved, that is, the abscissa of the second jumping point is *t'*=T_0-*t*=1.35, which is well matched with the results in Fig. 7.

Even though the algorithm above has not been proved strictly, it provides quantitative results of the changes of the curve shape after the introduction of *DSP*, in addition, the results can be confirmed by simple measurement.

4   Gait Planning

The posture and all joint coordinates of the biped robot can be obtained when the gait planning based on the given ZMP and the CoM is determined.

The model includes five rods: two thighs L_1, two legs L_2, and L_3 which connects two hip joints. This model includes six joints: two ankle joints, two knee joints, two hip joints, in which there is only one hip knee used because the model is plane. The *x* and *y* coordinates of the hip, knee and ankle joint is set as (x_h, z_h), (x_{k1}, z_{k1}) and $(x_{k2},$

z_{k2}), (x_{a1}, z_{a1}) and (x_{a2}, z_{a2}), respectively. Assume the mass of the hip joint bar is 4 time of the thigh and leg mass m.

The model has 12 unknown variables: 10 coordinates, and two joint angles (θ_1, θ_2 shown in Fig. 2). The paper makes an interpolation of (x_{a1}, z_{a1}), and then adjusts the ZMP curve with the method stated in section 3. Thus the T_{DSP}, T_{SSP} and S are well coupled with the interpolation function. The walking period of lower limb is planned (shown in Fig. 9), which includes 6 states. Each state is corresponding to the system time that from 0 second to the relevant point. The third state ensures the separation of swing foot and the ground while the second state moves forward to the forth state. T_d represents the period of DSP, and T_c–T_d represents the period of SSP. Thus, T_0=T_c.

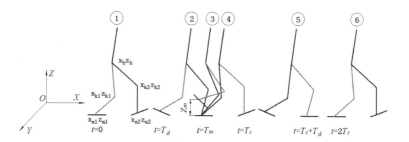

Fig. 9. A Walking Period

The interpolation function Pchip() provided by MATLAB is adopted to obtain the three equations $\theta(t)$, $x_a(t)$, $z_a(t)$. Since the walking process is periodic. In addition, the trajectories of two legs are same but different in phase. Therefore the X and Z coordinates of another leg can be obtained. Due to the constant of the four rods of the legs, following equations can be obtained

$$
\begin{aligned}
(x_h - x_{k1})^2 + (z_h - z_{k1})^2 &= L_1^2 \\
(x_h - x_{k2})^2 + (z_h - z_{k2})^2 &= L_1^2 \\
(x_{k1} - x_{a1})^2 + (z_{k1} - z_{a1})^2 &= L_2^2 \\
(x_{k2} - x_{a2})^2 + (z_{k2} - z_{a2})^2 &= L_2^2
\end{aligned}
\tag{18}
$$

The CoM coordinate (COM_x, COM_z) of the frame model is expressed by using the coordinates of joints, and then set COM_x as in Equation (14). Ten coordinates are unknown and nine equations are built by now.

The CoM and ZMP equations are based on the assumption that c_z is a constant set in section 2, so COM_z=c_z. In order to reduce the amount of calculation, in this paper, z_h is regarded as a constant. In this way, the CoM of the model in Z-Direction is variable, whereas, this error can be ignored. Moreover, the error can be reduced by adjusting the highest position of swing foot in Fig. 9.

5   Simulation Tests with a Biped Robot Prototype

The numerical simulation of the model (shown in Section 4) is performed. Set simulation time as 3 seconds, and define the start of DSP as the initial attitude, as the first state shown in Fig. 9. The result can be seen in Fig. 10:

(1)When the highest position of swing foot is Z=0.16m, the variation of the CoM in height is less than 2.6%.

(2)The simulation result of knee joint is reasonable, the CoM and the ankle joint are coupled well.

Then, the prototype (shown in Fig. 11) is abstracted as a bar system to valid the proposed method in this paper. The simulation result is shown in Fig 12. When the model moves forwards, it swings at the same time.

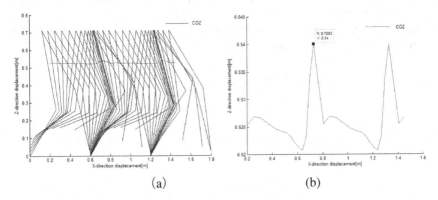

(a)   (b)

Fig. 10. Walking simulation and CoM trajectory of the five bar planar model

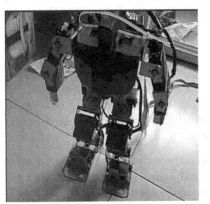

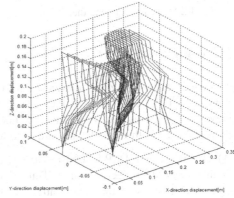

Fig. 11. Physical Prototype   **Fig. 12.** 3D Simulation of Physical Prototype in 3D

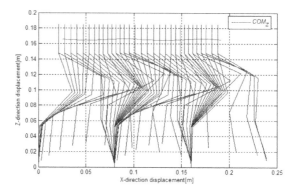

Fig. 13. Projection of the prototype model in X-Z Plane and the simulated CoM trajectory

The projection of the model in X-Z plane under walking process is shown in Fig. 13, the CoM error in Z-Direction is less than 0.6%.

Compared the time function of the CoM in X-direction to the theoretical result solved in formula (14), they are well matched, which can be seen in Fig. 14.

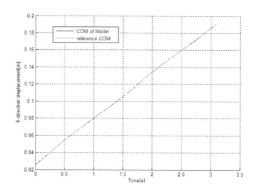

Fig. 14. Measure result and theoretical result of the physical prototype in X-direction

6   Conclusions

In this paper, humanoid ZMP reference trajectories with Fourier series approximation techniques for the solution of LIPM dynamics equations are employed in order to achieve naturalness in the walk planning. Focusing on result of this experiment, the walk is stable and other conclusions are as follows:

1) The time of the DSP is adjusted through quantitatively turning *DSP* parameters to realize the ZMP trajectory curve. Thus, the CoM equations of the biped robot are coupled effectively with the interpolation function of the ankle joints.

2) The height of hip z_h is assumed as a constant to simplify the calculation, while the height of the CoM in the simulation of biped walking mechanism varies less than

2.6%. Moreover, as for a biped walking mechanism, the height error can be further reduced via reduce the maximum height of swing foot (z_m).

3) The method proposed in this paper is applied to a biped robot prototype, and a 3D bar-type model is built. The simulation result shows that the CoM trajectory is stable. The error compared to the theoretical CoM is less than 0.6%.

References

1. Yamaguchi, J.-I., Takanishi, A., Kato, I.: Development of a biped walking robot compensating for three-axis moment by trunk motion. In: IEEE International Conference on Intelligent Robots and Systems, pp. 561–566. IEEE Press (1993)
2. Sakagami, Y., Watanabe, R., Aoyama, C., Shinichi, M., Higaki, N., Fujimura, K.: The intelligent ASIMO: System overview and Integration. In: IEEE International Conference on Intelligent Robots and Systems, pp. 2478–2483. IEEE Press, Switzerland (2002)
3. Zhu, C., Yoshihito, T., Luo, X., Atsuo, K.: Biped Walking with Variable ZMP, Frictional Constraint, and Inverted Pendulum Model. In: IEEE International Conference on Robotics and Biomimetics, China, pp. 425–430 (2004)
4. Raibert, M.H.: Legged Robots that Balance. MIT Press, Cambridge (1986)
5. Vukobratovic, M., Frank, A.A., Jricic, D.: On The Stability of Biped Locomotion. In: IEEE Transactions on Biomedical Engineering, BME 17-1, 25–36 (1970)
6. Vukobratovic, M., Brovac, B.: Zero-Moment Point-Thirty five years of its life. J. Humanoid Robotics 1, 157–173 (2004)
7. Zhu, M., Li, M., Wang, J., Lin, Y.: Static Gait Analysis and Planning of Biped Robot. In: 7th IEEE Conference on Intelligent Information Hiding and Multimedia Signal Processing, pp. 113–116. IEEE Press (2011)
8. Ali, S., Alghooneh, A.M., Takhmar, M.: A.:Stable Trajectory Planning, Dynamics Modeling and fuzzy Regulated Sliding Mode control of a Biped Robot. In: 7th IEEE-RAS International Conference on Humanoid Robots, pp. 471–476. IEEE Press (2007)
9. Mir-Nasiri, N., Siswoyo Jo, H.: Joint Space Legs Trajectory Planning for Optimal Hip-Mass Carry Walk of 4-DOF Parallelogram Bipedal Robot. In: IEEE International Conference on Mechatronics and Automation, pp. 616–621. IEEE Press (2010)
10. Kurt, O., Erbatur, K.: Biped robot reference Generation with Natural ZMP Trajectories. In: IEEE International Workshop on Advanced Motion Control, pp. 403–410. IEEE Press (2006)
11. Choi, Y., You, B.J., Oh, S.R.: On the Stability of Indirect ZMP Controller for Biped Robot Systems. In: IEEE International Conference on Intelligent Robots and Systems, pp. 1966–1971. IEEE Press, Japan (2004)

Numerical and Analytical Methods for Synthesis of Central Pattern Generators

Yonghui Hu[1,3], Wei Zhao[2], Jianhong Liang[3], and Tianmiao Wang[3]

[1] School of Control and Computer Engineering, North China Electric Power University, Beijing 102206, P. R. China
[2] IBM Research-China, Beijing 100193, P.R. China
[3] School of Mechanical Engineering and Automation, Beihang University, Beijing 100191, P.R. China
huyhui@gmail.com

Abstract. This paper presents numerical and analytical methods for synthesis of a CPG network to acquire desired locomotor patterns. The CPG network is modeled as a chain of coupled Hopf oscillators with a coupling scheme that eliminates the influence of afferent signals on amplitude of the oscillator. The numerical method converts the related CPG parameters into dynamical systems that evolve as part of the CPG network dynamics. The frequency, amplitude and phase relations of teaching signals can be encoded by the CPG network with the proposed learning rules. For direct specification of the phase relations, the expression that defines the dependence of phase difference on coupling weights is analytically derived. The ability of the numerical methods to learn instructed locomotor pattern is proved with simulations. The effectiveness of the analytical method is also validated by the numerical results.

Keywords: Central pattern generators, Synthesis method, Learning.

1   Introduction

Animals are capable of move in complex and unstructured environments with ease and grace. Understanding how such locomotion is controlled by the central nervous system (CNS) forms a main challenge for modern neuroscience. An important concept regarding the neural basis of rhythmic locomotor activity is central pattern generators (CPGs), i.e. neuronal circuits capable of producing coordinated patterns of rhythmic activity without any rhythmic inputs from sensory feedback or from higher control centers [1]. CPGs are found in both invertebrate and vertebrate animals, and they underlie the production of most rhythmic motor behaviors, such as walking, running, swimming and flying. The rhythmic patterns, endogenously produced by CPGs, can be modulated by simple descending signals from the brain. Sensory feedback can also alter the motor patterns in order to cope with environmental perturbations.

Inspired by neurobiological findings on the mechanisms for locomotor rhythm generation, the concept of CPG is exploited to control biomimetic robots, whose

C.-Y. Su, S. Rakheja, H. Liu (Eds.): ICIRA 2012, Part III, LNAI 7508, pp. 342–351, 2012.
© Springer-Verlag Berlin Heidelberg 2012

locomotion is characterized by coordinated rhythmic movement of multiple joints. The CPG-based locomotion controller is usually implemented as a system of coupled nonlinear oscillators that exhibit limit cycle behaviors. With this approach, the gaits can be generated online and complicated trajectory planning can be avoided. The couplings between oscillators ensure synchronization and phase coordination between joints. Smooth transition between different gaits can be realized with simple control parameters. Moreover, CPGs can readily integrate sensory feedback signals for adaptation to environmental changes.

In order to understand how patterned rhythmic activities are generated by CPGs, many theoretical analysis methods have been developed in the literature, such as perturbation theory and averaging [2], Malkin Theorem for weakly connected oscillators [3], contraction analysis [4], and multivariable harmonic balance method [5]. These methods can provide essential insights into the dynamical behavior of CPGs, but they are not adequate for the synthesis problem, i.e. find parameters of the CPG network to achieve prescribed oscillation profiles. In most robotics research involving CPGs, the locomotor controllers are tailor-made in terms of CPG model type, coupling topology and sensory feedback pathways, in order to accomplish some specific task. It is difficult for many CPG models to acquire explicit control over characteristic quantities of the oscillation profile, such as frequency, amplitude and especially phase relations. A well-established synthesis methodology for CPG is still missing, and approaches like hand-coding, search and optimization have been extensively exploited [1], [7]. Exploration in the multidimensional parameter space of CPG generally requires considerable trial and error efforts for hand-coding methods and tedious and time-consuming computation for search and optimization algorithms.

In this paper, numerical and analytical methods for synthesis of CPGs which are modeled as a chain of Hopf oscillators are presented. When designing a CPG-based controller, the desired locomotor patterns may be given by teaching signals or by explicit specification of the oscillation frequency, amplitude and phase relations. The proposed methods apply to these two situations respectively, and achieve the same results for a given locomotor pattern. The frequency and amplitude of Hopf oscillator are defined by model parameters, while the phase relations are determined by inter-oscillator couplings. The numerical method converts the related CPG parameters into dynamical systems that evolve as part of the CPG network dynamics. The appropriate parameter set that reproduces the profile of the teaching signals can be obtained in a supervised learning manner. With the analytical methods, expressions that define the dependence of phase relations on coupling strengths are derived, which facilitates the selection of coupling weights for the desired phase relations.

The remaining sections of this paper are organized as follows. Section 2 presents the model of CPG network with a novel coupling scheme. The numerical and analytical synthesis methods are described in Section 3. Numerical verifications of the proposed methods are given in Section 4. Finally, we conclude the paper in Section 5.

2 Model of CPG Network

The CPG network is based on Hopf oscillator that generates harmonic oscillation and has explicit parameters for setting frequency and amplitude. The dynamics of Hopf oscillator is governed by the following nonlinear differential equations

$$\begin{cases} \dot{u} = (\rho - r^2)u - \omega v \\ \dot{v} = (\rho - r^2)v + \omega u \end{cases} \tag{1}$$

where $r = \sqrt{u^2 + v^2}$, u and v are state variables in Cartesian space, $\rho > 0$ controls the amplitude of the oscillation, and ω specifies the intrinsic frequency of the oscillator (in rad s^{-1}). The Hopf oscillator has a stable harmonic limit cycle, and the steady state solution of the system can be written as $u_\infty(t) = \sqrt{\rho}cos(\omega t + \phi_0)$ and $v_\infty(t) = \sqrt{\rho}sin(\omega t + \phi_0)$, where ϕ_0 is determined by the initial condition. The analytical solution of the oscillator facilitates parameter specification for a desired oscillation behavior.

One CPG unit is responsible for the control of one joint in a robotic mechanism. To produce coordinated oscillatory signals for gait generation, the oscillators should be connected together with appropriate coupling scheme. The coupling term is most often implemented as an additive perturbation on the nonlinear oscillator, which can influence the phase dynamics of the oscillator. Thus inter-joint coordination can be achieved in such a way that one oscillator perturbs another in order to realize frequency synchronization and to maintain a stable phase difference between them. However, the oscillation amplitude of the perturbed oscillator will also be modified, which makes it hard to specify parameter for a desired oscillation amplitude. In order to eliminate this undesirable side effect, we allow the afferent signal p to be transformed before it acts on the state variables of the oscillator [6]. The perturbed oscillator can be described by

$$\begin{cases} \dot{u} = (\rho - r^2)u - \omega v + \dfrac{pv^2}{r} \\ \dot{v} = (\rho - r^2)v + \omega u - \dfrac{puv}{r} \end{cases} \tag{2}$$

The phase relations among a network of CPGs can be achieved by feeding weighted states u and v of one oscillator to the other, as illustrated by the following equations

$$\begin{cases} \dot{u}_i = (\rho_i - r_i^2)u_i - \omega_i v_i + \sum\limits_{j} \dfrac{(a_{i,j}u_j + b_{i,j}v_j)v_i^2}{r_i} \\ \dot{v}_i = (\rho_i - r_i^2)v_i + \omega_i u_i - \sum\limits_{j} \dfrac{(a_{i,j}u_j + b_{i,j}v_j)u_i v_i}{r_i} \end{cases} \tag{3}$$

where $a_{i,j}$ and $b_{i,j}$ denote the connection weights between the ith and the jth oscillator. The phase difference between the coupled oscillators is determined by the connecting weights $a_{i,j}$ and $b_{i,j}$. In this paper, we consider CPG network with chain topology and nearest-neighbor descending couplings. Thus each oscillator can only be affected by its adjoining frontal oscillator. With this setting, the coupling weight $a_{i,j}$ and $b_{i,j}$ that don't satisfy $i = j + 1$ will be set as zero. Fig. 1 shows the structure of the CPG network.

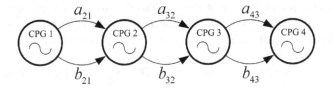

Fig. 1. Structure of CPG network

3   Synthesis Methods for CPG

3.1   Numerical Method

The numerical synthesis method can acquire the appropriate CPG parameters when the desired locomotor pattern is given in the form of teaching signals. By converting the parameters controlling frequency, amplitude and phase relations into new state variables with their own dynamics, the waveforms of the teaching signals and their phase relations can be encoded by the CPG network in a simple and efficient way. The learning is embedded into the dynamics of the oscillator, and no external optimization or preprocessing of the teaching signal is required.

The CPG controller generates harmonic outputs, thus only teaching signals with almost sinusoidal waveform can be learned. During learning, the teaching signal for each CPG unit is received by the oscillator as an additive perturbation. Then the network of CPG, with coupling between adjacent oscillators and additive inputs of the periodic teaching signals, can be described by the following equations

$$\begin{cases} \dot{u}_i = (\rho_i - r_i^2)u_i - \omega_i v_i + \dfrac{a_{i,i-1}u_{i-1}v_i^2}{r_i} + \dfrac{b_{i,i-1}v_{i-1}v_i^2}{r_i} + \dfrac{\epsilon T_i v_i^2}{r_i} \\ \dot{v}_i = (\rho_i - r_i^2)v_i + \omega_i u_i - \dfrac{a_{i,i-1}u_{i-1}u_i v_i}{r_i} - \dfrac{b_{i,i-1}v_{i-1}u_i v_i}{r_i} - \dfrac{\epsilon T_i u_i v_i}{r_i} \end{cases} \tag{4}$$

where T_i is the teaching signal for the ith oscillator, $\epsilon > 0$ is an adaptation constant. Let $u = r\cos\phi$ and $v = r\sin\phi$, equation (4) can be transformed into polar coordinates

$$\begin{cases} \dot{r}_i = (\rho_i - r_i^2)r_i \\ \dot{\phi}_i = \omega_i - a_{i,i-1}r_{i-1}\cos\phi_{i-1}\sin\phi_i - b_{i,i-1}r_{i-1}\sin\phi_{i-1}\sin\phi_i - \epsilon T_i \sin\phi_i \end{cases} \tag{5}$$

The phase space representation shows clearly how the behavior of the limit cycle system is influenced by external perturbations. In the following, we derive the learning rules of frequency, coupling weight and amplitude from a geometric point of view.

Learning Frequency. In phase plane representation, a periodic perturbation can result in an average acceleration or deceleration of the rotating phase point. The effects of external perturbation on activity of the oscillator can be used to tune the intrinsic frequency of the oscillator. The adaptation mechanism for frequency is designed following the approach presented in refs. [8] and [7]. Therefore, according to equation (5) the learning rule of frequency can be given by

$$\dot{\omega}_i = -a_{i,i-1}r_{i-1}cos\phi_{i-1}sin\phi_i - b_{i,i-1}r_{i-1}sin\phi_{i-1}sin\phi_i - \epsilon T_i sin\phi_i \qquad (6)$$

The intrinsic frequency changes according to the total effect of the input signals. It is reasonable to require the teaching signals for the CPG network to have the same frequency. Therefore, the right side of equation (6) contains only one frequency component and after learning all oscillators will run at the same frequency.

Learning Coupling Weight. The coupling between a pair of oscillators is a composite signal coming from the two state variables of the forcing oscillator, each alone producing some phase lag on the forced oscillator. By adjusting the relative strengths of components of the signal, a range of phase difference between oscillators can be attained. We formulate the learning rule of coupling weights using the time-averaged effects of the input signals on phase dynamics of the oscillator. With the correlation-based learning law, the coupling weight should be enforced when the signal from the forcing oscillator and the teaching signal push the phase point in the same direction, and be weakened otherwise. The learning rule that modulates the coupling weights to produce the phase difference specified by the teaching signals takes the following form

$$\dot{a}_{i,i-1} = \gamma \int_{t-\tau_i}^{t} r_{i-1}cos\phi_{i-1}sin\phi_i dt \int_{t-\tau_i}^{t} T_i sin\phi_i dt \qquad (7)$$

$$\dot{b}_{i,i-1} = \gamma \int_{t-\tau_i}^{t} r_{i-1}sin\phi_{i-1}sin\phi_i dt \int_{t-\tau_i}^{t} T_i sin\phi_i dt \qquad (8)$$

where γ is a positive constant controlling the learning rate, and $\tau_i = 2\pi/\omega_i$ is the oscillation period of the ith oscillator, indicating that the time-averaged effects are evaluated over an oscillatory cycle of the oscillator.

Learning Amplitude. The learning rule of coupling weights can ensure in-phase synchronization between the teaching signal and the CPG output which equals the state variable u. The adaptation law of amplitude is based on the correlation between the CPG output and its difference with the teaching signal, which is given by the following equation

$$\dot{\rho}_i = \eta(T_i - r_i cos\phi_i)r_i cos\phi_i \qquad (9)$$

where η is a positive constant that determines the rate of learning. The adaptation of amplitude starts when the CPG output and the teaching signal become in phase. The evolution law increases the amplitude when the CPG output and the error signal are correlated, and decreases the amplitude when uncorrelated.

The amplitude converges to the maximum value of the teaching signal, in which case the waveform of the CPG output matches the waveform of the teaching signal.

We have formulated the learning rules of intrinsic frequency, coupling weight and amplitude for a network of Hopf oscillators in polar coordinates. By transforming the learning rules into Cartesian coordinates, we obtain the model of the adaptive CPG with six state variables, which are summarized by the following equations

$$
\begin{cases}
\dot{u}_i = (\rho_i - r_i^2)u_i - \omega_i v_i + \dfrac{a_{i,i-1}u_{i-1}v_i^2}{r_i} + \dfrac{b_{i,i-1}v_{i-1}v_i^2}{r_i} + \dfrac{\epsilon T_i v_i^2}{r_i} \\[2mm]
\dot{v}_i = (\rho_i - r_i^2)v_i + \omega_i u_i - \dfrac{a_{i,i-1}u_{i-1}u_i v_i}{r_i} - \dfrac{b_{i,i-1}v_{i-1}u_i v_i}{r_i} - \dfrac{\epsilon T_i u_i v_i}{r_i} \\[2mm]
\dot{\omega}_i = -\dfrac{a_{i,i-1}u_{i-1}v_i}{r_i} - \dfrac{b_{i,i-1}v_{i-1}v_i}{r_i} - \dfrac{\epsilon T_i v_i}{r_i} \\[2mm]
\dot{a}_{i,i-1} = \gamma \int_{t-\tau_i}^{t} \dfrac{u_{i-1}v_i}{r_i}dt \int_{t-\tau_i}^{t} \dfrac{T_i v_i}{r_i}dt \\[2mm]
\dot{b}_{i,i-1} = \gamma \int_{t-\tau_i}^{t} \dfrac{v_{i-1}v_i}{r_i}dt \int_{t-\tau_i}^{t} \dfrac{T_i v_i}{r_i}dt \\[2mm]
\dot{\rho}_i = \eta(T_i - u_i)u_i
\end{cases}
\tag{10}
$$

3.2 Analytical Method

In case the characteristic quantities of the oscillation profile are given, the CPG parameters can be tuned with analytical method. The explicit parameters for frequency and amplitude allow direct specification of the corresponding oscillation characteristics. Of primary importance is the derivation of dependence of phase difference on coupling weights. Here the method presented in ref. [10] will be adopted to obtain such a relation.

In the CPG network, each oscillator except the one at the rostral end of the chain is influenced by descending couplings. We denote the intersegmental phase difference, i.e. the difference in phase between adjacent oscillators, as $\phi_i^d = \phi_{i+1} - \phi_i$. Without perturbations from teaching signals, the derivative of phase difference can be obtained from equation (5) and described by

$$
\begin{aligned}
\dot{\phi}_i^d = {} & \omega_{i+1} - \omega_i - a_{i+1,i}r_i cos\phi_i sin\phi_{i+1} - b_{i+1,i}r_i sin\phi_i sin\phi_{i+1} \\
& + a_{i,i-1}r_{i-1}cos\phi_{i-1}sin\phi_i + b_{i,i-1}r_{i-1}sin\phi_{i-1}sin\phi_i
\end{aligned}
\tag{11}
$$

Due to intersegmental couplings, the oscillators are synchronized with constant phase relations after some transient period of phase adjustment. Therefore, after the steady phase locked state is reached at t_0, we have

$$
\lim_{t \to \infty} \int_{t_0}^{t} \dot{\phi}_i^d dt = 0
\tag{12}
$$

This integration can be carried out implicitly by integration over ϕ_{i+1} in steady state. It is assumed that steady state is reached when $\phi_{i+1} = \Theta_0$ and the phase locking is maintained thereafter. The integration can be rewritten as

$$
\dot{\phi}_i^{d,res} = \lim_{\Theta \to \infty} \int_{\Theta_0}^{\Theta} \dot{\phi}_i^d d\phi_{i+1} = 0
\tag{13}
$$

Substitution of equation (11) into (13) yields

$$
\begin{aligned}
0 &= \int_0^{2\pi} (\omega_{i+1} - \omega_i - a_{i+1,i} r_i \cos\phi_i \sin\phi_{i+1} - b_{i+1,i} r_i \sin\phi_i \sin\phi_{i+1} \\
&\quad + a_{i,i-1} r_{i-1} \cos\phi_{i-1} \sin\phi_i + b_{i,i-1} r_{i-1} \sin\phi_{i-1} \sin\phi_i) d\phi_{i+1} \\
&= \int_0^{2\pi} \{ \underbrace{\omega_{i+1} - \omega_i}_{\omega_i^d} \\
&\quad - \frac{a_{i+1,i} r_i}{2} [\underbrace{\sin(\phi_i^d)}_{const} + \underbrace{\sin(2\phi_{i+1} - \phi_i^d)}_{periodic,\ zero\ mean}] - \frac{b_{i+1,i} r_i}{2} [\underbrace{\cos(\phi_i^d)}_{const} - \underbrace{\cos(2\phi_{i+1} - \phi_i^d)}_{periodic,\ zero\ mean}] \\
&\quad + \frac{a_{i,i-1} r_{i-1}}{2} [\underbrace{\sin(\phi_{i-1}^d)}_{const} + \underbrace{\sin(2\phi_i - \phi_{i-1}^d)}_{periodic,\ zero\ mean}] + \frac{b_{i,i-1} r_{i-1}}{2} [\underbrace{\cos(\phi_{i-1}^d)}_{const} - \underbrace{\cos(2\phi_i - \phi_{i-1}^d)}_{periodic,\ zero\ mean}] \} d\phi_{i+1} \\
&= 2\pi\omega_i^d - \pi a_{i+1,i} r_i \sin(\phi_i^d) - \pi b_{i+1,i} r_i \cos(\phi_i^d) + \pi a_{i,i-1} r_{i-1} \sin(\phi_{i-1}^d) + \pi b_{i,i-1} r_{i-1} \cos(\phi_{i-1}^d)
\end{aligned}
\tag{14}
$$

The oscillators within a CPG network should have the same intrinsic frequency, thus we have $\omega_i^d = 0$. For $i = 1$, the last two terms in equation (14) don't exist. Therefore, we have the following equation that defines the relation between the phase difference and coupling weights for the first two oscillators

$$
a_{2,1} sin(\phi_1^d) + b_{2,1} cos(\phi_1^d) = 0 \tag{15}
$$

Substitute equation (15) into (14), we can obtain iteratively the general relation

$$
a_{i+1,i} sin(\phi_i^d) + b_{i+1,i} cos(\phi_i^d) = 0 \tag{16}
$$

Through a simple transformation, we obtain

$$
tan(\phi_i^d) = -\frac{b_{i+1,i}}{a_{i+1,i}} \tag{17}
$$

It is obvious that the phase difference is determined by the relative strength of coupling weights. Once the desired phase difference is given, the coupling weights can be chosen by following the above relation.

4   Numerical Simulations

To examine the effectiveness of the proposed methods, we use sinusoidal signals that can be described explicitly as the teaching signals. For the above CPG network, it suffices to consider a pair of oscillators with couplings from one to the other. The sinusoidal teaching signals are described by the following equations:

$$
T_1(t) = 1.2 sin(2t - 0.2) \tag{18}
$$

$$
T_2(t) = 1.6 sin(2t - 1.2) \tag{19}
$$

Fig. 2 shows the evolution of intrinsic frequency, coupling weight and amplitude during learning. With the proposed learning rule, the intrinsic frequencies of both oscillators gradually adapt to the frequency of the teaching signals. But the intrinsic frequencies oscillate around rather than converge to the desired frequency. The amplitudes of the oscillations are related to the learning rate. The faster the oscillator learns, the larger the adaptation error will be. To attain the correct frequency of the teaching signal, we employ a first-order low-pass filter $\tau_f \dot{\bar{\omega}} = -\bar{\omega} + \omega$ to attenuate the oscillation, where τ_f is a time constant. When the learning stops, $\bar{\omega}$ is used as the intrinsic frequency of the oscillator.

The convergence values of coupling weights are determined not only by the phase difference between oscillators, but also their initial values and the initial phase difference. We investigate the evolution of coupling weights with several pairs of initial values and the same initial phase difference. Table 1 shows the initial and convergence values of coupling weights, with the phase difference specified by equation (18) and (19). It illustrates that different combinations of coupling weights can produce the same phase difference. But the ratios of a_{21} and b_{21} are almost the same, which follows that the relative strength of coupling weights is what really matters to the phase difference. In addition, the dependence of convergence values of coupling weights on initial phase difference between oscillators is examined. As shown in Table 2, with the same initial values of coupling weights and different initial phase differences, several combinations of coupling weights are obtained, while their relative strength remains almost fixed. Moreover, the phase difference between the teaching signals is -1 rad. With equation (17) obtained from the analytical method, the ratio of coupling weights should be 0.6421, which illustrates that small adaptation errors exist for the numerical method. Nevertheless, the effectiveness of the numerical and analytical synthesis methods can be mutually proved.

Table 1. Convergence values of coupling weights with different initial values and the same initial phase difference

initial values		convergence values		ratio of
a_{21}	b_{21}	a_{21}	b_{21}	convergence values
0.8	0.05	0.096500	0.145116	0.664985
0.2	0.04	0.065210	0.098047	0.665089
0.1	0.1	0.062226	0.093560	0.665092
0.01	0.15	0.068786	0.103429	0.665055

Table 2. Convergence values of coupling weights with the same initial values and different initial phase difference. The initial coupling weights are $a_{21} = 0.1$, $b_{21} = 0.1$.

initial values of state variables				convergence values		ratio of
u_1	v_1	u_2	v_2	a_{21}	b_{21}	convergence values
-0.1	0.1	-0.1	0.1	0.062226	0.093560	0.665092
-0.1	0.1	0.1	-0.1	0.089473	0.134544	0.665009
-0.1	0.1	-0.1	-0.1	0.109308	0.164408	0.664858
-0.1	0.1	0.1	0.1	0.109779	0.165133	0.664791

Before the oscillator and its teaching signal become in phase, the amplitude decreases quickly. To avoid negative value of the amplitude that will cause failure

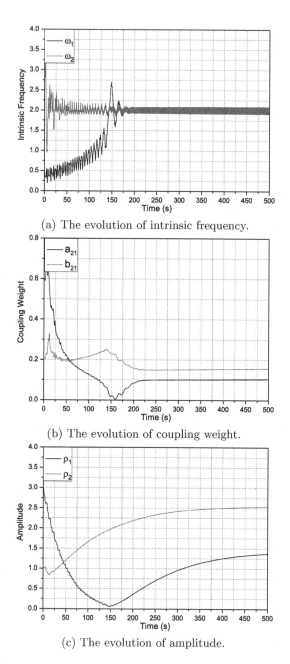

(a) The evolution of intrinsic frequency.

(b) The evolution of coupling weight.

(c) The evolution of amplitude.

Fig. 2. The evolution of intrinsic frequency, coupling weight and amplitude during learning

of the learning, small learning rate should be used. Once in-phase synchronization is achieved, the amplitude starts to adapt to the desired value.

5 Conclusions

In this contribution, we presented numerical and analytical methods for synthesis of a CPG network which was modeled as a chain of coupled Hopf oscillators. For desired locomotor patterns given in the form of teaching signals, we formulated the learning rules of frequency, amplitude and coupling weight with phase plane representation of the oscillator. The expression that defines the dependence of phase difference on coupling weights was analytically derived for explicit specification of the phase relations. The effectiveness of the proposed methods was validated through numerical simulations.

Acknowledgments. This work was supported by National Natural Science Foundation of China under Grant 61105108.

References

1. Ijspeert, A.J.: Central Pattern Generators for Locomotion Control in Animals and Robots: A Review. Neural Netw. 21, 642–653 (2008)
2. Guckenheimer, J., Holmes, P.: Nonlinear Oscillations, Dynamical Systems, and Bifurcations of Vector Fields. Springer, New York (1983)
3. Hoppensteadt, F.C., Izhikevich, E.M.: Weakly Connected Neural Networks. Springer, New York (1997)
4. Pham, Q.C., Slotine, J.J.: Stable Concurrent Synchronization in Dynamic System Networks. Neural Netw. 20, 62–77 (2007)
5. Iwasaki, T.: Multivariable Harmonic Balance for Central Pattern Generators. Automatica 44, 3061–3069 (2008)
6. Hu, Y., Tian, W., Liang, J., Wang, T.: Learning Fish-like Swimming with A CPG-based Locomotion Controller. In: IEEE/RSJ Int. Conf. Intelligent Robots and Systems, pp. 1863–1868. IEEE Press, New York (2011)
7. Buchli, J., Righetti, L., Ijspeert, A.J.: Engineering Entrainment and Adaptation in Limit Cycle Systems: From Biological Inspiration to Applications in Robotics. Biol. Cybern. 95, 645–664 (2006)
8. Righetti, L., Buchli, J., Ijspeert, A.J.: Dynamic Hebbian Learning in Adaptive Frequency Oscillators. Physica D 216, 269–281 (2006)
9. Buchli, J., Iida, F., Ijspeert, A.J.: Finding Resonance: Adaptive Frequency Oscillators for Dynamic Legged Locomotion. In: IEEE/RSJ Int. Conf. Intelligent Robots and Systems, pp. 3903–3909. IEEE Press, New York (2006)
10. Buchli, J., Ijspeert, A.J.: Distributed Central Pattern Generator Model for Robotics Application Based on Phase Sensitivity Analysis. Lect. Notes Comput. Sc. 3141, 333–349 (2004)

Trajectory Planning for Omni-Directional Mobile Robot Based on Bezier Curve, Trigonometric Function and Polynomial

Chaobin Chen, Haichen Qin, and Zhouping Yin

State Key Laboratory of Digital Manufacturing Equipment and Technology,
Huazhong University of Science and Technology,
Luoyu Road 1037, 430074 Wuhan, China
ccbhahao@163.com

Abstract. This paper proposes a systematic trajectory planning algorithm for omni-directional mobile robot, which consists of three parts: path planning, line velocity planning and posture planning. Third-order Bezier curve is applied to the path planning algorithm and proved to be feasible by analysis of radius of curvature. Further more, the method that constructing a complex path by splicing multi-segment Bezier curves turns out to be effective. Then trigonometric function is utilized in the line velocity planning algorithm. The results demonstrate effectiveness and rationality of the algorithm. Lastly, based on trigonometric function and polynomial, a posture planning algorithm for omni-directional mobile robot is designed to plan the posture, angular velocity and angular acceleration. Results show that it can guarantee the continuity of the angular acceleration with excellent effect. On the basis of the case study on a complex path, it is concluded that the trajectory planning algorithm has good adaptability.

Keywords: Trajectory Planning, Omni-Directional Mobile Robot, Bezier Curve, Path Planning.

1 Introduction

In recent years, mobile robots have been widely applied in various fields, and relevant researches have made lots of achievements. Under holonomic constraints [1], omni-directional mobile robot has three degrees of freedom in the horizontal motion plane [2]. So it is much more flexible than ordinary non-omni-directional mobile robot, which makes it especially suitable for working in tight space [3].

In the research on omni-directional mobile robot, trajectory planning is a critical field. For most mobile robots, trajectory planning aims to find out the optimized trajectory with respect to a given objective function [4]. Up till now, there are many research methods about this issue. In the research on three-wheeled omni-directional vehicle, Kuo-Yang Tu advanced a trajectory planning method based on kinematic constraints and linear dynamics. According to the method, velocity, acceleration, angular velocity and angular acceleration were planned, via 3 cases: two intersecting lines, a straight line and a circle [5]. In Hongjun Kim and Byung-Kook Kim's

C.-Y. Su, S. Rakheja, H. Liu (Eds.): ICIRA 2012, Part III, LNAI 7508, pp. 352–364, 2012.
© Springer-Verlag Berlin Heidelberg 2012

research on three-wheeled omni-directional mobile robot, the energy consumption is taken into account. They established the minimum-energy translational trajectory planning algorithm to achieve an optimal trajectory [6]. By designing the velocity and acceleration filters, Hashemi, E., Jadidi, M.G. and Babarsad, O.B. built up a dynamic model for four-wheeled omni-directional mobile robot, and utilized artificial intelligence and machine vision package in positioning and path planning [7]. Hongxia Zhang and Kyung Seok Byun applied trapezoidal acceleration profile to velocity planning and acceleration planning. Thus they achieved the real time path planning for three-wheeled omni-directional mobile robot [8].

Since proposed, Bezier curve has been widely used in computer graphics and animation [9]. With advantages such as symmetry and first-order continuous, in recent years it has been applied to trajectory planning for mobile robots. Gregor Klančar and Igor Škrjanc worked on collision-avoidance problem based on Bernstein-Bezier path tracking for multiple robots with known constraints [10], using a two-wheeled differentially driven robot. Khatib, M., Jaouni, H., Chatila, R. and Laumond, J.P. applied Bezier polynomials to a smoothing method, and made the original path more reasonable to meet the kinematic constraints [11]. Jung-Hoon Hwang, Arkin, R.C. and Dong-Soo Kwon utilized Bezier curve in creating a smooth trajectory, which was applied to online trajectory generation for supervisory control [12]. As for path planning for the automatic guided vehicle (AGV), Petrinec, K. and Kovačić, Z. proposed a method that combined Bezier curve and spline functions [13]. To sum up, most studies on the application of Bezier curve in trajectory planning are in connection with nonholonomic mobile robots.

This paper is organized as follows: Section 2 begins by describing the Bezier curve and its mathematical expression. In section 3, a path planning algorithm for the omni-directional mobile robot based on third-order Bezier curve is proposed. Section 4 discusses a trigonometric velocity planning algorithm. Section 5 focuses on the posture planning based on polynomial and trigonometric function. Using the above-mentioned theories, a complicated trajectory is planned for an omni-directional mobile robot in section 6. Finally, section 7 provides a brief conclusion of this paper.

2   Bezier Curve

Bezier curve was invented in 1962 by the French engineer Pierre Bezier for designing automobile bodies [9]. Different from other curves, Bezier curve doesn't go through data points that define it, which are known as control points. With fewer turning points, Bezier curve is much smoother than other spline curves on the same order [14].

Given position vectors of n+1 points in a certain space as $P_i(i = 0,1, ... , n)$, Bezier curve can be defined as

$$P(u) = \sum_{i=0}^{n} P_i Bin(u), \quad u \in [0,1] \tag{1}$$

Where u is a parameter. n is the order of Bezier curve, and i is the summation index. $P_i(i = 0,1, ... , n)$ constitute the Bezier characteristic polygon. $Bin(u)$ is the Bernstein function, given by

$$Bin(u) = C_n^i u^i (1-u)^{n-i} = \frac{n!}{i!(n-i)!} u^i (1-u)^{n-i}, (i = 0,1, \cdots n) \qquad (2)$$

Especially, $0^0 = 1$, $0! = 1$.

Given four control points (x_0, y_0), (x_1, y_1), (x_2, y_2), (x_3, y_3), a third-order Bezier curve can be expressed as

$$\begin{cases} x = x_0(1-u)^3 + 3x_1(1-u)^2 u + 3x_2(1-u)u^2 + x_3 u^3 \\ y = y_0(1-u)^3 + 3y_1(1-u)^2 u + 3y_2(1-u)u^2 + y_3 u^3 \end{cases} \quad u \in [0,1] \qquad (3)$$

Bezier curve is generated as u changes from 0 to 1.

For instance, when the coordinate is defined in cm, given control points (1, 2), (2, 4), (5, 2), (6, 3), we can get the Bezier curve shown in Fig. 1.

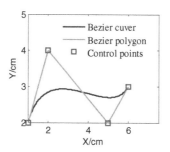

Fig. 1. A Bezier curve

3   Path Planning Based on Third-Order Bezier Curve

This section discusses how to apply third-order Bezier curve to path planning for omni-directional mobile robots.

From Eq. (3), we can see that, to construct a third-order Bezier curve, these four control points must be determined: a start point, an end point and two intermediate points. However, generally in practice, we should construct third-order Bezier curves between adjacent points when information of a series of points is given. It means that only the information of the start point and the end point is known. Thus before path planning, we need to construct two intermediate points according to some criteria.

Now, we can make use of the information of the start point and the end point, especially the directions of the velocity vectors. With the information of the start point and the end point known, the third-order Bezier curve should satisfy the following conditions as

$$\begin{cases} f(x_s) = y_s \\ df(x_s)/dx = tan(\alpha_s) \end{cases} \qquad (4)$$

$$\begin{cases} f(x_g) = y_g \\ df(x_g)/dx = tan(\alpha_g) \end{cases} \qquad (5)$$

Where $f(x)$ is the mathematical expression of this Bezier curve. (x_s, y_s) and (x_g, y_g) are the coordinates of the start point and the end point, whose velocity directions are α_s and α_g.

Eqs. (4) and (5) restrict the third-order Bezier curve. For Bezier curve, the tangent directions of the start point and the end point are respectively the same as the first and the last edge of the characteristic polygon [15]. Therefore, to satisfy the above constraints, the missing intermediate coordinates must meet the following conditions:

$$\begin{cases} (y_2 - y_s) \cdot cos(\alpha_s) = (x_2 - x_s) \cdot sin(\alpha_s) \\ (y_g - y_3) \cdot cos(\alpha_g) = (x_g - x_3) \cdot sin(\alpha_g) \end{cases} \tag{6}$$

Where (x_2, y_2) and (x_3, y_3) are the coordinates of the intermediate points.

According to Eq. (6), the intermediate points can be expressed as follows:

$$\begin{cases} y_2 = y_s + \lambda_1 sin(\alpha_s) \\ x_2 = x_s + \lambda_1 cos(\alpha_s) \end{cases} \tag{7}$$

$$\begin{cases} y_3 = y_g - \lambda_2 sin(\alpha_g) \\ x_3 = x_g - \lambda_2 cos(\alpha_g) \end{cases} \tag{8}$$

Where λ_1 and λ_2 are positive, which represent the influence of the velocity directions of the start point and the end point. The greater λ_1 and λ_2 are, the greater the influence is. Actually, in order to make the omni-directional mobile robots adjust the velocity direction as soon as possible, λ_1 tends to be smaller, but λ_2 tends to be greater, on the premise that the mechanical requirements are fulfilled.

λ_1 and λ_2 should correlate to the distance between the start point (x_s, y_s) and the end point (x_g, y_g). Assuming this correlation is proportional, λ_1 and λ_2 can be

$$\begin{cases} \lambda_1 = D_1 \sqrt{(x_s - x_g)^2 + (y_s - y_g)^2} \\ \lambda_2 = D_2 \sqrt{(x_s - x_g)^2 + (y_s - y_g)^2} \end{cases} \tag{9}$$

Where D_1 and D_2 are scale factors which are greater than 0.

According to Eq. (9), we can obtain λ_1 and λ_2, and substitute them into Eqs. (7) and (8). Then the coordinates of intermediate points are available.

Thus, the Bezier curve that connects P_s and P_g can be expressed as follows:

$$\begin{cases} x = x_s(1-u)^3 + 3x_2(1-u)^2u + 3x_3(1-u)u^2 + x_gu^3 \\ y = y_s(1-u)^3 + 3y_2(1-u)^2u + 3y_3(1-u)u^2 + y_gu^3 \end{cases} \quad u \in [0,1] \tag{10}$$

Where (x_2, y_2) and (x_3, y_3) are determined by Eqs. (7), (8) and (9).

For instance, when the coordinate is defined in cm, with $(x_s, y_s) = (2, 4)$, $(x_g, y_g) = (4, 6)$, $\alpha_s = 60°$, $\alpha_g = 120°$ and $D_1 = D_2 = 1/4$, we can obtain the third-order Bezier curve that links the start point and the end point, based on Eqs. (7) ~ (10). The output is clearly shown in Fig. 2.

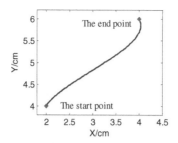

Fig. 2. Result of path planning

Additionally, the tangential direction and radius of curvature can be calculated as

$$\alpha = atan(dy/dx) \tag{11}$$

$$r = 1/((d^2y \cdot dx - dy \cdot d^2x) * (dx \cdot dx + dy \cdot dy)^{-1.5}) \tag{12}$$

Where α is the velocity direction, and r is the radius of curvature.

Taking the path in Fig. 2 as an example, we can obtain the velocity direction curve and the radius of curvature curve which are shown in Fig. 3.

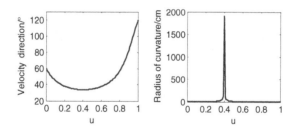

(a) Velocity direction   (b) Radius of curvature

Fig. 3. Velocity direction curve and radius of curvature curve

By the method above, we can generate n Bezier curves between n+1 control points, and splice them together. It is interesting that they are still first-order continuous. Eventually we can obtain a complete path planning algorithm for omni-directional mobile robot based on third-order Bezier curve. For example, when the coordinate is defined in cm, some information is in the following table.

Table 1. Information of three control points

Control point	Coordinates/cm	Velocity direction
point A	(2, 5)	30°
point B	(6, 9)	60°
point C	(16, 7)	45°

With $D_1 = D_2 = 1/4$, the outcome is shown below.

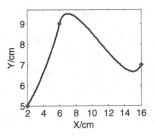

Fig. 4. A simple path

4   Line Velocity Planning Based on Trigonometric Function

Taking dynamics and smoothness running into account, the trajectory of the omni-directional mobile robots should be second-order derivative, so that it can avoid impact and improve kinematics performance.

Suppose the path is a Bezier curve, while the start velocity is v_s, and the end velocity is v_g, the robot has to meet the following constraints:

1) Continuous acceleration ;
2) The integral of velocity with respect to time (ie, distance) should equal the length of the previously planned Bezier curve.

In view of the first constraint, let acceleration and time meet the law of sine curve as follows:

$$a(t) = Asin(\varphi t) \tag{13}$$

Where $a(t)$ is the acceleration function, A is the maximum acceleration, φ is an undetermined parameter.

Integrating Eq. (13) on both sides, we can get the relationship between velocity and time as follows:

$$v(t) = -A/\varphi \cdot cos(\varphi t) + B \tag{14}$$

Where $v(t)$ is the velocity function, and B is an undetermined parameter. As a result of $v(0) = -A/\varphi + B = v_s$, there is:

$$A = \varphi(B - v_s) \tag{15}$$

When t=0, distance equals zero. Integrating Eq. (14) on both sides, we will obtain the relationship between distance $S(t)$ and time as follows:

$$S(t) = -A/\varphi^2 \cdot sin(\varphi t) + Bt \tag{16}$$

Sum up Eqs. (13), (14) and (16) as follows:

$$\begin{cases} a(t) = A sin(\varphi t) \\ v(t) = -A/\varphi \cdot cos(\varphi t) + B \\ S(t) = -A/\varphi^2 \cdot sin(\varphi t) + Bt \end{cases} \tag{17}$$

In the equations above, A, φ and B need to be determined. T stands for the time that the robot spends on the whole path. In order to make acceleration continuous at intersections of adjacent Bezier curves, the easiest way is to let the acceleration equal zero at each start point and end point, that is, $A sin(\varphi T) = 0$. Because $A \neq 0$, $sin(\varphi T) = 0$.

And $v(T) = -A/\varphi \cdot cos(\varphi T) + B = v_g$. Substituting Eq. (15) into it, there is:

$$(v_s - B) \cdot cos(\varphi T) + B = v_g \tag{18}$$

As $sin(\varphi T) = 0$, $cos(\varphi T) = \pm 1$. When $cos(\varphi T) = 1$, Eq.(18) is not permanent tenability. So $cos(\varphi T) = -1$. Substituting it into Eq. (18), the result is given by:

$$B = (v_g + v_s)/2 \tag{19}$$

Now let's come to the second constraint. The length of the Bezier curve can be obtained by calculus. Dividing the control variable u into n equal parts, we can get n +1 points on the Bezier curve. Connect adjacent points with straight-line and then calculate the length of each section. Finally, adding up the length of all sections, we can approximate get the length of the Bezier curve. The greater n is, the closer the result will approach the theoretical value. When n is great enough, the error is so small that the outcome can be regarded as approximations to the theoretical value. Length of the path (S) is obtained by calculus as follows:

$$S = -A/\varphi^2 \cdot sin(\varphi T) + BT = (v_g + v_s)T/2 \tag{20}$$

Solving the equation above, T can be defined as

$$T = 2S/(v_g + v_s) \tag{21}$$

As $sin(\varphi T) = sin(2S\varphi/(v_g + v_s)) = 0$, we can transform it into another expression: $2S\varphi/(v_g + v_s) = \pi$, which also can be written as

$$\varphi = \pi(v_g + v_s)/(2S) \tag{22}$$

Substituting Eq. (22) into Eq. (15), the maximum acceleration is defined by

$$A = \pi(v_g^2 - v_s^2)/(4S) \tag{23}$$

Substituting Eqs. (19), (21), (22) and (23) into Eq. (17), we can get three equations which meet the above-mentioned constraints as follows:

$$\begin{cases} a(t) = \pi(v_g^2 - v_s^2)/(4S) \cdot sin(\pi t(v_g + v_s)/(2S)) \\ v(t) = (v_s - v_g)/2 \cdot cos(\pi t(v_g + v_s)/(2S)) + (v_g + v_s)/2 \\ S(t) = S(v_s - v_g)/(\pi(v_g + v_s)) \cdot sin(\pi t(v_g + v_s)/(2S)) + (v_g + v_s)t/2 \end{cases} \tag{24}$$

Therefore, given the coordinates, velocity and velocity directions of two points, firstly we can plan the path and obtain its length S. Then substituting S into Eq. (24), we can figure out how distance, velocity and acceleration vary with time. Connecting all of adjacent Bezier curves, we can get the entire result of line velocity planning.

Taking the path in Fig. 4 as an example, Table 2 gives the information of the points.

Table 2. Information of the 3 control points

Control point	Coordinates/cm	Velocity/(cm/s)	Velocity direction
point A	(2, 5)	10	30°
point B	(6, 9)	20	60°
point C	(16, 7)	30	45°

The relationship between the acceleration and time is illustrated below.

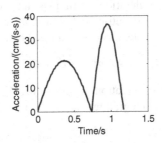

Fig. 5. The relationship between the acceleration and time

Fig. 5 clearly shows that the acceleration is continuous.
The velocity curve and the distance curve are shown in Fig. 6.

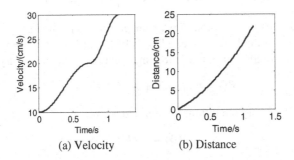

(a) Velocity   (b) Distance

Fig. 6. The velocity curve and the distance curve

Fig. 5 and **Fig. 6** illustrate that the line velocity planning algorithm based on trigonometric function is entirely reasonable.

5   Posture Planning

Compared with ordinary two-wheeled mobile robot, a prominent advantage of the omni-directional mobile robot is that it can achieve flexible posture adjustment (namely rotating movement) and rapid translation at the same time. The flexibility allows it to perform complex work better.

In order to control the posture, it must be planed reasonably. Next, a posture planning algorithm for the omni-directional mobile robot will be discussed.

Generally in posture planning, the posture and expected angular velocity at the start and end points (i.e., θ_s, θ_g, ω_s, ω_g in turn) are known. We should design a reasonable law of posture variation, making the posture and angular velocity at the start and end points equal the set value, with the angular acceleration continuous. At the same time, another implicit restriction must be met, that is, the time spent during the posture planning must equal the time T that has been identified in line velocity planning.

In order to make angular acceleration continuous, let it equal zero at the start and end points. Considering trigonometric function and quadratic polynomial, the relationship between angular acceleration and time can be designed as follows:

$$\beta(t) = Msint + Nt^2 + Ct \tag{25}$$

Where $\beta(t)$ is the angular acceleration function, M, N and C are undetermined parameters, t stands for time. Integrating Eq. (25) on both sides, the expression of angular velocity is given by

$$\omega(t) = -Mcost + \frac{1}{3}Nt^3 + \frac{1}{2}Ct^2 + E \tag{26}$$

Where $\omega(t)$ is the angular velocity function and E is an undetermined parameter. Integrating Eq. (26) on both sides, angle (i.e., posture) is given by

$$\theta(t) = -Msint + \frac{1}{12}Nt^4 + \frac{1}{6}Ct^3 + Et + F \tag{27}$$

Where $\theta(t)$ is the posture function. F is an undetermined parameter.

Now let's come to the boundary conditions of Eqs. (25) ~ (27). For Eq. (25), it's obvious that $\beta(0)=0$. Similarly, the following equation is also necessary.

$$\beta(T) = MsinT + NT^2 + CT = 0 \tag{28}$$

For Eq. (26), the boundary conditions are defined as

$$\omega(0) = -M + E = \omega_s \tag{29}$$

$$\omega(T) = -McosT + \frac{1}{3}NT^3 + \frac{1}{2}CT^2 + E = \omega_g \tag{30}$$

For Eq. (27), the posture of the start and end points can be defined as

$$\theta(0) = F = \theta_s \tag{31}$$

$$\theta(T) = -MsinT + \frac{1}{12}NT^4 + \frac{1}{6}CT^3 + ET + F = \theta_g \qquad (32)$$

Therefore, we can get the simultaneous equations below.

$$\begin{cases} MsinT + NT^2 + CT = 0 \\ -M + E = \omega_s \\ -McosT + \frac{1}{3}NT^3 + \frac{1}{2}CT^2 + E = \omega_g \\ F = \theta_s \\ -MsinT + \frac{1}{12}NT^4 + \frac{1}{6}CT^3 + ET + F = \theta_g \end{cases} \qquad (33)$$

Obviously, we can obtain the unique solution. The outcome is shown below.

$$\begin{cases} M = (\theta_g - \theta_s - 0.5T(\omega_s + \omega_g))/(0.5T - sinT + T^2 sinT/12 + 0.5TcosT) \\ C = 6(\omega_g - \omega_s - M(1 - cosT) + MTsinT/3)/T^2 \\ N = (-MsinT - CT)/T^2 \\ E = M + \omega_s \\ F = \theta_s \end{cases} \qquad (34)$$

Substituting ω_s, ω_g, θ_s, θ_g and T into Eq. (34), we can obtain M, C, N, E and F in turn. Then substituting these parameters into Eqs. (25)~(27), we can achieve the posture planning for the omni-directional mobile robot.

Still take the path in Fig. 4 as an example. With other information unchanged, posture at point A equals 0°, and its angular velocity is 0°/s; posture at point B equals 10°, and its angular velocity is 20°/ s; posture at point C equals 20°, and its angular velocity is 0°/s. We can obtain the outcome of posture planning as follows:

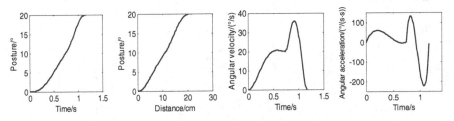

Fig. 7. Results of posture planning

From the results in Fig. 7, it's clear that the posture curve and the angular velocity curve are relatively smooth when the robot moves from point A to point C.

6   A Case Study for Omni-Directional Mobile Robot

After systematically introducing the trajectory planning algorithm for omni-directional mobile robot, in this section, we will apply it to practical operation and test its effect. The expected information of control points is given in the following table.

Table 3. Information of control points

Number	Coordinates/cm	Velocity/(cm/s)	Velocity direction	Posture	Palstance /(°/s)
1	(326, 50)	0	18°	30°	0
2	(650, 150)	200	14.9313°	30°	0
3	(987.5, 240)	165	14.9313°	60°	0
4	(1090, 350)	140	90°	60°	0
5	(1000, 425)	110	180°	60°	0
6	(900, 425)	90	180°	60°	0
7	(800, 400)	0	−143.2394°	60°	0

According to the information in Table 3, we can carry out the trajectory planning. With $D_1 = D_2 = 1/3$, the result of path planning is clearly shown in Fig. 8.

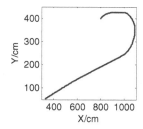

Fig. 8. The result of path planning

It can be seen from Fig. 8 that the whole path is relatively smooth. Some other results are as follows:

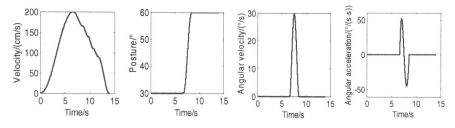

Fig. 9. Some other results

These results suggest that even though the path is very complicated, this trajectory planning algorithm still has a good effect. Therefore, the algorithm has been applied to the 10th ABU Asia-Pacific Robot Contest which was held in Bangkok in 2011.

7   Conclusion

The trajectory planning algorithm for omni-directional mobile robot which is presented in this paper consists of three parts: path planning which is based on third-order Bezier curve, line velocity planning which is based on trigonometric function, posture planning which is based on polynomial and trigonometric function. These parts are closely linked, step by step. Each part carries out detailed theoretical analysis and effect validation. Finally, using the algorithm, a more complicated trajectory is planned, and the results show that the algorithm has good adaptability to work in complex environment. The algorithm applies to not only competition robots, but also industrial and household omni-directional mobile robots. The trajectory planning under dynamic environment is not taken into account in this paper, and this will be emphasis in our future research.

References

1. Liu, Y., Wu, X., Zim Zhu, J., Lew, J.: Omni-Directional Mobile Robot Controller Design by Trajectory Linearization. In: Proceedings of the American Control Conference, pp. 3423–3428. IEEE Press, New Jersey (2003)
2. Treesatayapun, C.: A Discrete-Time Stable Controller for an Omni-Directional Mobile Robot Based on an Approximated Model. Control Engineering Practice 19, 194–203 (2011)
3. Zhao, D., Yi, J., Deng, X.: Structure and Kinematic Analysis of Omni-Directional Mobile Robots. Robot 25, 394–398 (2003)
4. Kim, K.-B., Kim, B.-K.: Minimum-Time Trajectory for Three-Wheeled Omnidirectional Mobile Robots Following a Bounded-Curvature Path with a Referenced Heading Profile. IEEE Transactions on Robotics 27, 800–808 (2011)
5. Tu, K.-Y.: A Linear Optimal Tracker Designed for Omnidirectional Vehicle Dynamics Linearized Based on Kinematic Equations. Robotica 28, 1033–1043 (2010)
6. Kim, H., Kim, B.-K.: Minimum-Energy Translational Trajectory Planning for Battery-Powered Three-Wheeled Omni-Directional Mobile Robots. In: Proceedings of the International Conference on Control, Automation, Robotics and Vision, pp. 1730–1735. IEEE Press, New Jersey (2008)
7. Hashemi, E., Jadidi, M.G., Babarsad, O.B.: Trajectory Planning Optimization with Dynamic Modeling of Four Wheeled Omni-Directional Mobile Robots. In: Proceedings of the IEEE International Symposium on Computational Intelligence in Robotics and Automation, pp. 272–277. IEEE Press, New Jersey (2009)
8. Zhang, H., Byun, K.S.: Real Time Path Planning Using Trapezoidal Acceleration Profile for Omnidirectional Mobile Robot. In: Proceedings of the International Conference on Control, Automation and Systems, pp. 830–833. IEEE Press, New Jersey (2008)
9. Choi, J.-w., Elkaim, G.H.: Bezier Curve for Trajectory Guidance. In: Proceedings of the World Congress on Engineering and Computer Science, pp. 625–630. International Association of Engineers, Hong Kong (2008)
10. Klančar, G., Škrjanc, I.: A Case Study of the Collision-Avoidance Problem Based on Bernstein-Bezier Path Tracking for Multiple Robots with Known Constraints. Journal of Intelligent and Robotic Systems 60, 317–337 (2010)
11. Khatib, M., Jaouni, H., Chatila, R., Laumond, J.P.: Dynamic Path Modication for Car-Like Nonholonomic Mobile Robots. In: Proceedings of the IEEE International Conference on Robotics and Automation, pp. 2920–2925. IEEE Press, New Jersey (1997)

12. Hwang, J.-H., Arkin, R.C., Kwon, D.-S.: Mobile Robots at Your Fingertip: Bezier Curve On-line Trajectory Generation for Supervisory Control. In: Proceedings of the IEEE International Conference on Intelligent Robots and Systems, pp. 1444–1449. IEEE Press, New Jersey (2003)

13. Petrinec, K., Kovačić, Z.: The Application of Spline Functions and Bezier Curves to AGV Path Planning. In: Proceedings of the IEEE ISIE Conference, pp. 1453–1458. IEEE Press, New Jersey (2005)

14. Jolly, K.G., Kumar, R.S., Vijayakumar, R.: A Bezier Curve Based Path Planning in a Multi-Agent Robot Soccer System without Violating the Acceleration Limits. Robotics and Autonomous Systems 57, 23–33 (2009)

15. Wang, X., Shang, J.: Concrete Application of Triple Bezier Curve Jointing Model in Method of Curve-Rization to Broken-Lined Contours. Science of Surveying and Mapping 36, 192–194 (2011)

A Low-Cost, Practical Localization System for Agricultural Vehicles

Gustavo Freitas, Ji Zhang, Bradley Hamner,
Marcel Bergerman, and George Kantor

Electrical Eng. Dept., Federal University of Rio de Janeiro, Brazil
Field Robotics Center, Robotics Institute, Carnegie Mellon University, Pittsburgh, US
gfreitas@coep.ufrj.br, zhangji@andrew.cmu.edu, bradley.hamner@gmail.com,
marcel@cmu.edu, kantor@ri.cmu.edu
http://cascrop.com/

Abstract. This paper addresses the refactoring of an agricultural vehicle localization system and its deployment and field-testing in apple orchards. The system enables affordable precision agriculture in tree fruit production by providing the vehicle's position in the orchard without the use of expensive differential GPS. The localization methodology depends only on the wheel and steering encoders and the laser rangefinder already on the vehicle for row following, thus adding zero hardware cost to the overall setup. It employs an Extended Kalman Filter to integrate the information from the sensors, with the pose being predicted via encoder odometry and updated via point and line features detections. The objective of this paper is to describe the complete refactoring of the initial proof-of-concept localization system, with the goal of making it robust, modular and reusable. Field test results indicate that the final system has sufficient accuracy for deployment of autonomous vehicles in tree fruit orchards.

Keywords: Autonomous Agricultural Vehicles, GPS-Free Localization, Extended Kalman Filter.

1 Introduction

Specialty crops are defined in US as fruits, vegetables, tree nuts, dried fruits and nursery crops, including floriculture. In 2007 they accounted for almost 17% of the US agricultural market, or US$50 billion, with fruit and tree nut production alone generating about 13% of all farm cash receipts [6]. Within specialty crops, tree fruit production is particularly challenged by the large cost of labor and its seasonal needs-for example, seven times more apple orchard workers are needed in the state of Washington during harvest season than during the winter pruning season. Today, there is a real opportunity to introduce automation solutions into tree fruit production to lower labor costs, smooth out labor requirements, and increase production efficiency. This opportunity is compounded by the introduction, in the past twenty years, of high-density "fruit wall" planting architectures.

C.-Y. Su, S. Rakheja, H. Liu (Eds.): ICIRA 2012, Part III, LNAI 7508, pp. 365–375, 2012.

Autonomous vehicles driving down along these rows of structured trees can mow and spray, as well as carry workers pruning, thinning, performing tree maintenance, and harvesting. Figure 1 shows two of the four vehicles we developed and deployed since 2008. Together, they logged a combined 350 km in research and commercial apple orchards in several US states. The vehicle on the left, Laurel, is a development platform where we test new row following and turning and localization methods and algorithms before integrating them on the other vehicles. It is equipped with wheel and steering encoders, laser range finders, cameras, and a differential GPS receiver used to generate ground truth for driving and localization experiments. The vehicle on the right, Cascade, is a barebones version with only the encoders and the laser. Cascade and its "twin" Allegheny are equipped with a scissors lift from where workers prune, thin, tie trees to wires, place pheromone dispensers, etc. They are used on a weekly basis by Extension educators and growers in time trials comparing the performance of workers on the platform versus workers on ladders.

Fig. 1. (Left) Autonomous orchard vehicle "Laurel." This experimental vehicle is equipped with encoders, laser rangefinder, cameras, and a differential GPS receiver for ground truth. (Right) "Cascade" in use by workers at Allan Bros. Orchards, in Prosser, WA, to thin green fruit. Time trials show that work on the top half of the trees, when conducted from the autonomous platform, can be more than twice as efficient than from ladders.

Vehicle localization is key to introduction of autonomous vehicles in tree fruit orchards, for various reasons. First, it enables precision agriculture applications similar to those performed today in field crops (corn, wheat, soy, etc.). For example, with a vehicle that knows how much fertilizer or herbicide each tree received, growers can correlate future yield with past maintenance records, and thus be able to manage production at a much finer scale. Second, it enables practices that are prohibitively costly today, such as counting and sizing fruit on the tree and creating yield maps. Last, but not least, accurate vehicle localization may increases accuracy of row following. While our vehicles' row following performance is satisfactory, the current navigation system employs a pure-pursuit approach [1] and does not rely on the vehicle's pose inside the orchard. This information could improve the navigation reliability and safety.

In four years of work developing autonomous orchard vehicles for the apple industry, we concluded that a key requirement is to be able to localize the vehicle within a half-meter of its true position. Such sub-metric accuracy can be obtained with differential GPS receivers, but their cost is unrealistic when compared to the target cost of the vehicle itself. Standard GPS is cheap, but may provide position errors of up to 20 m, or the equivalent to four of five rows of trees. Besides, GPS signals get degraded under the heavy canopies adopted by some growers.

The original localization system [3,4] is a proof-of-concept implementation designed to validate the hardware and the extended Kalman filter (EKF) algorithm. It presented the accuracy necessary for operations in a variety of typical orchards. This paper describes the refactoring of the localization software in a way that makes it robust, modular and reusable. Our approach is to list the main shortcomings of the initial implementation and demonstrate, via actual experimental results, how they were addressed in the refactored software. The new system was validated over 5 km of driving in orchards in Pennsylvania and Washington.

The paper is structured as follows. Section 2 presents in more detail the autonomous orchard vehicle used in this work. Section 3 presents the localization system from a functional perspective. Section 4 discusses the original implementation and the results it affords. Section 5 presents the refactored software, and Section 6 presents the experimental results obtained. Section 7 presents an analysis of the results and a discussion on future work.

2   Autonomous Orchard Vehicle

The base vehicle used in this work is Laurel (Figure 1, left). It is based on the Toro MDE eWorkman electric utility vehicle, retrofitted to function either in manual or drive-by-wire mode. Laurel is a research vehicle, where we implement and test orchard navigation technologies before they are ported to others. It is important to note that, while Laurel is equipped with a high-accuracy Applanix POS 220 LV GPS-assisted inertial navigation system, we do not use it for the localization estimation proposed here. The Applanix data is used only during the EKF setup, including the process of mapping the orchard block where we operate. It also provides ground truth so we can assess the performance of the localization system. The presence of the Applanix does not constitute an operation limitation, as explained in Section 7.

The relevant sensors for this work are: steering and wheel encoders with linear resolution of 2.33×10^{-5} m/tick and angular resolution of $0.38°$/tick; one SICK LMS 291 laser rangefinder with $180°$ field-of-view, $1°$ resolution, and maximum scanning range of 80 m; and a SICK LMS 111 laser rangefinder with $270°$ field-of-view, $0.5°$ resolution, and maximum scanning range of 30 m. The onboard computer is a rugged, waterproof, industrial unit with an Intel Core 2

Duo 1.6 GHz CPU with 4GB DDR2 DRAM from Small PC. The localization software runs on Ubuntu Linux, with the message passing provided by the Robot Operating System (ROS).

3   Localization Methodology

The localization system estimates the position of the vehicle in the orchard using an Extended Kalman Filter. The orchard terrain is assumed to be locally flat, and the pose is defined as $x = [x_r, y_r, \theta_r]^T$, where x_r, y_r represent the vehicle's planar position and θ_r its orientation with respect to an initial predefined configuration.

In the prediction step, the EKF uses the wheel and steering encoders to estimate the vehicle's pose. In the update step, it uses point and line features from the environment, obtained from laser data, to correct the initially estimated value. The system's simplified functional architecture is illustrated in Figure 2.

The proposed solution assumes the vehicle starts in a known initial position and orientation with respect to a previously-built reference map that contains the tree rows' ending positions. The current procedure used to create the map

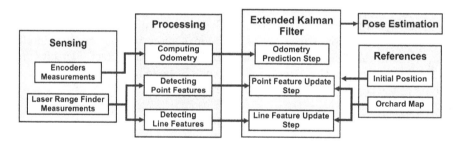

Fig. 2. Functional architecture of the localization system. The Extended Kalman Filter uses data from encoders and laser rangefinder to estimate the vehicle's pose. The software uses as reference the initial position and an orchard map obtained off-line.

Fig. 3. (Left) Apple orchard with reflective tape installed on the row ends for mapping purposes. (Right) The resulting orchard map, used for vehicle localization.

consists on driving the vehicle around the orchard and combining the measurements from the Applanix and lower laser to obtain the position of landmark reflective tape placed on the row ends (Figure 3).

4 Original Localization Estimation System

All of the orchard vehicle's software runs on Willow Garage's ROS, an open source framework for robotic system development, which in turn runs on Ubuntu Linux [5]. ROS is a useful tool because it provides a structured communication layer above Linux. A particularly useful ROS feature is the recording of messages in "bag" files. With them, it is possible to playback the messages to recreate past experiments, which is specially important during software implementation and debugging.

Each software module is implemented as a ROS node. The nodes exchange information by subscribing and publishing messages to ROS topics. The localization node subscribes to the sensor topics, receiving input measurements to run the EKF. After processing the information, the node publishes the pose estimation into another topic.

The localization node begins operation by loading the orchard map. It then acquires the vehicle position and subscribes to different sensor topics. After initialization, the node enters a polling mode running at 100 Hz. At every cycle, it checks for new measurement messages. As they arrive, it calls the respective EKF steps - prediction for encoder measurements and update for point and line features. The odometry messages are published at 45 Hz, laser measurements

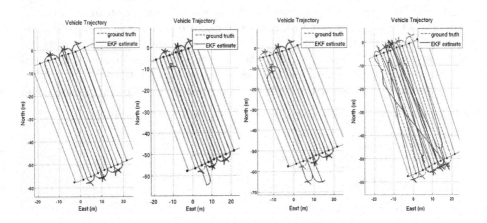

Fig. 4. Original localization system results using playback data. The left image shows a good result where the system achieved the necessary sub-metric accuracy. The other images contain results with progressive faults, with playback data yielding different results every time it is processed off-line. The errors are a result of the manner with which ROS handles messages.

for landmark detection at 75 Hz and line feature detections at 15 Hz. The localization node publishes a new pose message at each polling cycle that invokes the Kalman filter.

To evaluate the performance of the original localization system, we used playback data from bag files recorded during experiments conducted in September 2010 in our half-acre experimental nursery. This is a block with eight tree rows 54 m long and 3.5 m wide. The original implementation is able to reach the required sub-metric accuracy, as presented on the left in Figure 4.

The original software, however, is not always consistent, presenting different results when processing off-line the same playback data (Figure 4, center and right). The different results are caused by problems related to the ROS messaging mechanism, which may lose messages or process them out of chronological order. Despite achieving the accuracy required for the task we are pursuing, the original localization system implementation is not robust to ROS's asynchronous messaging scheme.

5   Refactored Localization Estimation System

Once the localization approach was validated, we set out to refactor the code so as to deal with the ROS message passing inefficiencies and also to make it modular and reusable in future projects. The refactored localization system implements the EKF through object-oriented software written in C++.

In the new version, the localization software is still implemented as a ROS node. As before, it begins operation loading the orchard map, acquiring the vehicle's position and subscribing to different sensor topics.

The difference is after initialization, when the new localization software operates similarly to an interruption-based system, in comparison to the original program. This is implemented using the command *ros::spinOnce()* inside a while loop running at 1 KHz. Whenever the node receives a ROS message, it calls the correspondent EKF step. As before, the odometry messages trigger the prediction step, and the point and line features activate the update step.

The software main algorithm is briefly described in the following pseudo-code:

```
global applanixDataMsg, encoderDataMsg, pointFeatureDataMsg, lineFeatureDataMsg;

void treatRosApplanix(applanixDataMsg);
void treatRosEncoder(encoderDataMsg);
void treatRosPointFeat(pointFeatDataMsg);
void treatRosLineFeat(lineFeatDataMsg);

int main () {

  poseEstimation = [x, y, theta];

  loadMap();
  getInitialPosition(applanixDataMsg);

  ros::Subscriber applanixDataSubscriber => treatRosApplanix(applanixDataMsg);
  ros::Subscriber encoderDataSubscriber => treatRosEncoder(encoderDataMsg);
  ros::Subscriber pointFeatDataSubscriber => treatRosPointFeature(pointFeatDataMsg);
  ros::Subscriber lineFeatDataSubscriber => treatRosLineFeature(lineFeatDataMsg);
  ros::Publisher poseEstimationDataPublisher => poseEstimationDataMsg;
```

```
while(true){
ros::spinOnce();
loop_rate.sleep(1KHz);

if encoderDataMsg
 odometryPredictionStep(encoderDataMsg, poseEstimation);

if pointFeatureDataMsg
 pointFeatUpdateStep(pointFeatDataMsg, poseEstimation);

if lineFeatureDataMsg
 lineFeatUpdateStep(lineFeatDataMsg, poseEstimation);

poseEstimationDataPublisher(poseEstimation);
}
}
```

Considering the frequencies at which each component of the localization system runs (see Section 4), we expected it would be capable of processing all sensor measurements. During debugging procedures, however, we identified that the node loses 5% of the odometry and line feature messages. The problem is aggravated for landmark detection, with 50% of the messages not being processed. We also noticed that the localization software does not receive the different sensor messages in chronological order.

These problems were reported to the ROS mailing list (see http://bit.ly/LggVu7). In response, we were informed by Willow Garage that the time when messages buffers are serviced can vary greatly, independently from the frequency of the main node. They also confirmed that when receiving messages from different sources, ROS does not guarantee the order in which they will be received and processed.

To solve the problems, we used vectors to store messages coming from different sensors. An algorithm looks into the vectors and selects which message should be sent to the localization node. The code does not lose measurements, and also selects the messages in chronological order before calling the EKF steps.

During the software refactoring, the code was divided into auxiliary functions and files, increasing its modularity, and better documented. The final software retains the accuracy of the original one and is simpler, clearer, easier to understand, and easier to adapt to other applications.

Figure 5 presents the result obtained with the refactored software when processing the same playback data in Figure 4. After the refactoring, the localization system presents consistent results and yields the exact same results every time it is processed off-line.

Because of the line feature corrections, the maximum crosstrack error is about 0.5 m. The small errors are caused by the line detection process. The line feature parameters corresponding to the tree rows are estimated by a particle filter [2]. Due to the canopy shape, the parameters are constantly changing. When the vehicle drives in straight line, the dead reckoning longtrack error accumulates due to small errors propagation. The maximum longtrack error of 0.55 m corresponds to 1% of the row length, compatible with the expected wheel slippage deviation. The error is corrected at the row ending, when the vehicle identifies a landmark.

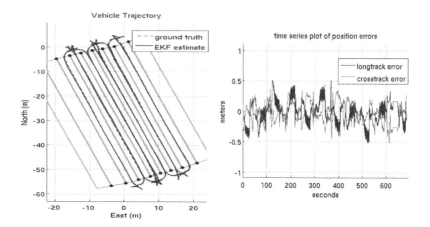

Fig. 5. Trajectory and position error obtained by the refactored localization software processing playback data acquired during field tests

Figure 6 presents the distribution of errors for the experiment in Figure 5. The crosstrack error is within 30 cm of the ground truth for more than 95% of the time. The 3σ (99.7% of final value) interval is 0.45 m. The longtrack error is also lower than 0.5 m during almost the entire operation, except at a few isolated locations. The position estimate is within 30 cm of ground truth for more than 90% of the time. The 3σ (99.7% of the steady state) interval is 0.5 m.

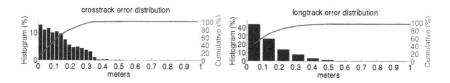

Fig. 6. Crosstrack and longtrack error distributions obtained with the refactored localization software. The maximum crosstrack error is about 0.5 m and the localization estimate is within 30 cm of ground truth for more than 95% of the time. The longtrack error is also within 30 cm of ground truth for more than 90% of the time.

6   Experiments in Apple Orchards

To assess the performance of the refactored localization system, we conducted several field tests at Washington State University's Sunrise Orchard in Rock Island, WA, and Ridgetop Orchards in Fishertown, PA. At both locations we drove the vehicle manually inside the tree rows, with the goal of verifying the localization system's robustness and functionality over long-term operations in real crops.

Figure 7 presents two representative results at Sunrise; Table 1 summarizes three of them. The vehicle traveled a total of 5,924 m in blocks 9A, 9B and 9C, and its position was estimated with sub-metric precision. The mean errors range from 0.17 to 0.23 m, and all the 3σ distances are less than 1 m. The good results are in part due to the flat, dry terrain, which don't generate much wheel slippage, and short tree rows, which brings the landmarks into view more quickly, reducing odometry-associated errors. All were obtained on-line as the vehicle drove in between rows.

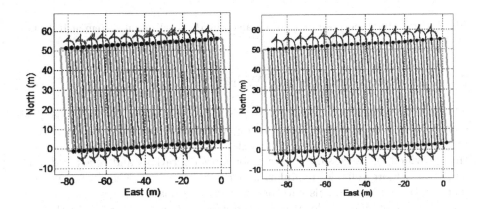

Fig. 7. Trajectory obtained by the localization system at Sunrise Orchard's blocks 9A and 9B. The estimated position is plotted in blue, and the Applanix ground truth data is plotted in red.

Table 1. Summary of experiments conducted at Sunrise

Test site	Block 9A	Block 9B	Block 9C (*)
Total distance [m]	1898	2136	1893
Mean longtrack error [m]	0.22	0.19	0.21
Mean crosstrack error [m]	0.23	0.17	0.22
3σ longtrack error [m]	0.91	0.65	0.98
3σ crosstrack error [m]	0.76	0.51	0.72

(*) Not shown in Figure 7.

Figure 8 presents the results obtained at Ridgetop Orchards. This is a much more challenging environment, with rows that are 300 m long and very steep (up to 12.5° of inclination). At Ridgetop we traversed four rows. When the robot is driving inside the rows, there is no correction for the longtrack error and the encoder odometry drifting accumulates. The maximum long track error is about 2 m when the vehicle is going downhill and up to 6 m when going uphill, again compatible with wheel odometry.

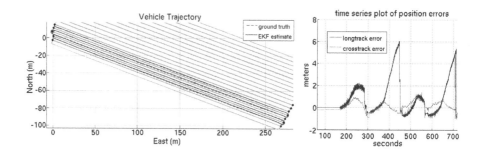

Fig. 8. Trajectory and position error obtained by the localization system at Ridgetop Orchards

7   Conclusion and Future Work

The localization system described in this paper is part of the larger goal of demonstrating the feasibility of operating autonomous orchard vehicles in commercial tree fruit production environments year-round. We started with a system that provided the necessary accuracy for most operations and refactored it to end with a more reliable, modular, and reusable version. The documentation includes three user manuals with detailed instructions on how to generate the orchard map, execute the localization software, and analyze the results. Fifteen experimental data sets are included in the documentation for development and test of future improvements

Experiments conducted in apple orchards showed that the new localization system presents satisfactory results, obtaining sub-metric precision in locations with relatively flat terrain. It does not meet the required accuracy, however, when operating in very long or very steep rows. The former cause EKF updates to take too long to kick in, leading to odometry drift; the latter causes wheel slippage that confound the odometry. In the worst case, when driving uphill on a very long and steep row, the localization error reached 6 m, or 2% of the traveled linear distance.

One possible solution to improve accuracy consists on computing odometry using cameras, because visual odometry is not affected by wheel slippage. We have begun work in this direction and expected to enhance the localization system accuracy by one order of magnitude.

The localization methodology was tested with data from two laser rangefinders, one detecting point and the other detecting line features. In an actual field deployment, only one laser rangefinder would have to provide data to both the navigation and localization. Also, Laurel is the only vehicle using the Applanix high-accuracy localization system. The others rely only on the system presented here to obtain position estimation. The vehicles do not have GPS, requiring alternative solutions to obtain the initial position and also the orchard map.

For initialization purposes, the vehicle can start the operation in a known position. Regarding the mapping requirement, one procedure already in use consists on placing a low-cost GPS receiver at each landmark, or even only the four corners of the block, for about one hour, and correcting the position data with RTK post-processing data from the USGS. In the future, the mapping procedure may even be eliminated entirely and replaced with a simultaneous localization and mapping (SLAM)-type method.

Acknowledgments. We would like to thank all members of the Comprehensive Automation for Specialty Crops. We also thank the crew from Sunrise and Ridgetop orchards were we tested the APM and the localization system.

This work is supported by the US Department of Agriculture under the Specialty Crop Research Initiative, award number 2008-51180-04876. Gustavo Freitas is funded by a grant from the Brazilian National Council for Research and Development (CNPq).

References

1. Coulter, R.: Implementation of the pure pursuit path tracking algorithm. DTIC Document, Tech. Rep. (1992)
2. Hamner, B., Bergerman, M., Singh, S.: Autonomous orchard vehicles for specialty crops production. In: ASABE Annual International Meeting, Louisville, Kentucky (2011)
3. Libby, J., Kantor, G.: Accurate GPS-free positioning of utility vehicles for specialty agriculture. In: ASABE Annual International Meeting, Pittsburgh, PA (2010)
4. Libby, J., Kantor, G.: Deployment of a point and line feature localization system for an outdoor agriculture vehicle. In: IEEE Int. Conf. on Robotics and Automation, Shangai (May 2011)
5. Quigley, M., Gerkey, B., Conley, K., Faust, J., Foote, T., Leibs, J., Berger, E., Wheeler, R., Ng, A.: ROS: an open-source robot operating system. In: ICRA Workshop on Open Source Software (2009)
6. Singh, S., Bergerman, M., Cannons, J., Grocholsky, B.P., Hamner, B., Holguin, G., Hull, L., Jones, V., Kantor, G.A., Koselka, H., Li, G., Owen, J., Park, J., Shi, W., Teza, J.: Comprehensive Automaton for Specialty Crops: Year 1 results and lessons learned. Journal of Intelligent Service Robotics (July 2010)

Static Gait Control for Quadruped Robot

Nie Hua, Sun Ronglei, Hong Xiaofeng, and Huang Xi

State Key Lab of Digital Manufacturing Equipment and Technology,
Huazhong University of Science & Technology,
Wuhan 430074, China
niehua21@163.com

Abstract. This paper presents a motion planning algorithm of static walking gait for a quadruped robot. First, the kinematics and dynamics equations of quadruped are built which can be used to research legged locomotion. Based on kinematics equations, foot trajectory is proposed with some optimization methods. Then the problem of redundant freedom in the joint angle is solved through dynamic optimization. Finally, the quadruped robot walking is realized by MATLAB calculation and ADAMS simulation.

Keywords: kinematic structure, dynamics, trajectory planning, adams simulation.

1 Introduction

Walking robots were developed in the 1960s, many studies have been carried out on walking robots in recent years. Walking robots have an advantage over wheeled robots in walking on uneven terrain which is divided into biped robot, quadruped robot and multi-legged robot. Taking the robot structure and ground adaptability into account, quadruped robot was chosen for our research. At present, bigdog robot has a good environment adaptability and anti-jamming capability which was developed by Boston Dynamics under DARPA Learning Locomotion program, and it will has a good prospect of application in the military field[1] [2].

Our research is based on a quadruped robot model likes bigdog robot. There are two key problems that waiting for us to solve. The first is to design a foot trajectory when robot's walking. In the text, we design a trajectory based on the robot stability, and it has been applied in our simulation. The second question is the redundancy of joint angle. The key to solve the problem is to find a constraint, and we solve it through the optimization of joint torque [3] [4].

This paper is organized as follows: the robot structure and kinematic analysis are addressed in Section 2. Trajectory planning and redundancy of joint angle are described in Section 3 and Section 4. Experimental result and concluding remarks are presented in Section 5 and Section6, respectively.

C.-Y. Su, S. Rakheja, H. Liu (Eds.): ICIRA 2012, Part III, LNAI 7508, pp. 376–384, 2012.

2   Kinematic Model

The quadruped robot structure is shown in Fig.1. Each leg has four DOF(degrees of freedom) joints, the first joint moves in lateral direction and the three joints does in frontal direction.

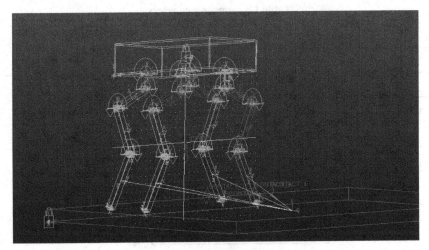

Fig. 1. Link structure

The main aim of this study is to implement a static gait with the quadruped robot, which assumes that the vertical projection of the COG(center of gravity) remains always inside the stability polygon during all phases of movements. In order to increase the robot stability, the quadruped robot's duty factor is taken as 5/6 and is shown in Fig 2[5]. Here we use FR,FL,BL,BR instead of robot's right front leg, left front leg, left behind leg, right behind leg.

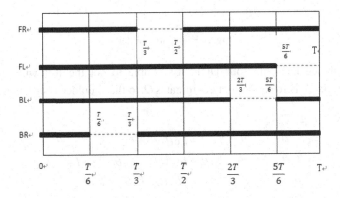

Fig. 2. Sequence diagram of static walking gait

In front, some basic information about the quadruped robot are introduced. Next, the kinematic equations of single leg will be built. Kinematic structure of the robot is shown in Fig 3 where $O_0, O_1, O_2, O_3, O_4, O_5$ denote the coordinates assigned at each joins according D-H(Denavit-Hartenberg) convention. The parameters of D-H model are in table 1[6].

Table 1. kinematic parameters

i	α_{i-1}	a_{i-1}	d_i	θ_i
1	0	0	0	θ_1
2	90	l_1	0	θ_2
3	0	l_2	0	θ_3
4	0	l_3	0	θ_4
5	0	l_4	0	0

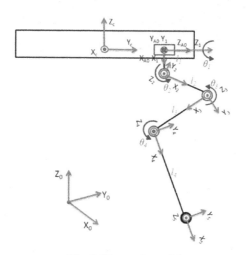

Fig. 3. Kinematic model

Since each leg has only four DOF, it's simple to get the following coordinate transformation, ^0_5T is from the foot coordinates O_5 to the shoulder coordinates O_0.

$$^0_5T = {}^0_1T \, {}^1_2T \, {}^2_3T \, {}^3_4T \, {}^4_5T =$$

$$\begin{bmatrix} c\theta_1 c\theta_{234} & -c\theta_1 s\theta_{234} & s\theta_1 & l_1 c\theta_1 + l_2 c\theta_1 c\theta_2 + l_3 c\theta_1 c\theta_{23} + l_4 c\theta_1 c\theta_{234} \\ s\theta_1 c\theta_{234} & -s\theta_1 s\theta_{234} & -c\theta_1 & l_1 s\theta_1 + l_2 s\theta_1 c\theta_2 + l_3 s\theta_1 c\theta_{23} + l_4 s\theta_1 c\theta_{234} \\ s\theta_{234} & c\theta_{234} & 0 & l_2 s\theta_2 + l_3 s\theta_{23} + l_4 s\theta_{234} \\ 0 & 0 & 0 & 1 \end{bmatrix} . \quad (1)$$

It is easily to get the inverse kinematics equation through transformation matrix, and it will be discussed in part four.

3   Foot Trajectory Planning

The foot trajectory of the walking robot is determined by two factors. First, the foot trajectory shape should be similar to the trajectory of the animal. Second, it can't produce a great impact when the robot foot lands on the ground.

In the Fig 2, it shows a leg will take only T/6 to complete its own motion, so here, T_l is taken as T/6 for short.

In order to have a high stability, the foot trajectory must meet these requirements that the leg trajectory should be continuous and its velocity and acceleration must be zero, when it starts to lift leg and land on the floor. Foot trajectory must be a 5 order equations, its Y orientation is defined as:

$$Y(t) = a_0 + a_1 t + a_2 t^2 + a_3 t^3 + a_4 t^4 + a_5 t^5 . \tag{2}$$

It must meet the following requirements:

$$\text{Position}: \begin{cases} Y(0) = Y_0 \\ Y(T_l) = Y_0 + \Delta Y \end{cases}$$

$$\text{Velocity}: \begin{cases} \dot{Y}(0) = 0 \\ \dot{Y}(T) = 0 \end{cases} . \tag{3}$$

$$\text{Acceleration}: \begin{cases} \ddot{Y}(0) = 0 \\ \ddot{Y}(T) = 0 \end{cases}$$

Then $Y(t)$ is (Y_0 is the start position while ΔY is the distance it moves):

$$Y(t) = Y_0 + \frac{10\Delta Y}{T_l^3} t^3 - \frac{15\Delta Y}{T_l^4} t^4 + \frac{6\Delta Y}{T_l^5} t^5 \ (0 \le t \le T_l) . \tag{4}$$

The same as Y, we can get Z (Z_0 is the start height while ΔZ is the height it moves):

$$Z(t) = \begin{cases} Z_0 + \dfrac{10\Delta Z}{\left(\frac{T_l}{2}\right)^3} t^3 - \dfrac{15\Delta Z}{\left(\frac{T_l}{2}\right)^4} t^4 + \dfrac{6\Delta Z}{\left(\frac{T_l}{2}\right)^5} t^5 \left(0 \le t \le \frac{T_l}{2}\right) \\[4mm] Z_0 + \Delta Z - \dfrac{10\Delta Z}{\left(\frac{T_l}{2}\right)^3}\left(t - \frac{T_l}{2}\right)^3 + \dfrac{15\Delta Z}{\left(\frac{T_l}{2}\right)^4}\left(t - \frac{T_l}{2}\right)^4 - \dfrac{6\Delta Z}{\left(\frac{T}{2}\right)^5}\left(t - \frac{T_l}{2}\right)^5 \left(\frac{T_l}{2} \le t \le T_l\right) \end{cases} \tag{5}$$

The following are the Y and Z direction displacement, velocity and acceleration curves.

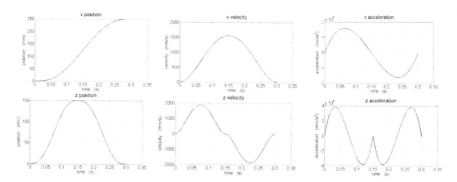

Fig. 4. Curves of the planning trajectory

There are also other methods to plan the trajectory of quadruped robot, like Sinusoidal Trajectory, Cubic Trajectory and so on. None of these trajectories take the acceleration into account, and it will be proved that the trajectory we proposed is better through adams simulation. The experimental data in fig.5 describe the vertical displacement of the robot center which can be used to measure the stability of the quadruped robot. It's easily to find that the fluctuation of the robot center's vertical displacement is very little.

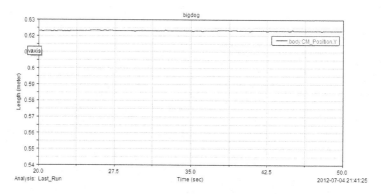

Fig. 5. Position fluctuations of the quadruped robot's center in a cycle

4   Control of Joint Angle

The aim of this part is to solve the redundancy of joint angle. The method we use is optimal torque of the joint angle. So the first task is to solve the torque of the joint angle. The quadruped robot model is already shown in fig 3. Each leg consists of four links. The torque of each joint will be calculated through Lagrange Equation [7] [8].

The Lagrange Equation is:

$$L = E_K - E_P.$$

$$(6)$$

The dynamic equation of the system is (T_i is the joint torque of the θ_i. i=2,3,4,5):

$$T_i = \frac{d}{dt}\frac{\partial L}{\partial \dot{\theta}_i} - \frac{\partial L}{\partial \theta_i}. \tag{7}$$

The centroid of each link is assumed to be the center of it. And the mass is assumed uniformity distributed. The torque of each link is calculated below:

For the first link, the equation is:

$$\begin{cases} P_1 = -\frac{1}{2}m_1 g l_1 \cos\theta_1 \\ K_1 = \frac{1}{8}m_1 l_1^2 \dot{\theta}_1^2 + \frac{1}{2}I_{zz1}\dot{\theta}_1^2 \end{cases} \tag{8}$$

It's easy to obtain $K_2, K_3, K_4, P_2, P_3, P_4$. Then T_1, T_2, T_3, T_4, will be worked out through equation (7)and(8), and it is expressed in a matrix:

$$T = \begin{bmatrix} T_1 \\ T_2 \\ T_3 \\ T_4 \end{bmatrix}, q = \begin{bmatrix} \theta_1 \\ \theta_2 \\ \theta_3 \\ \theta_4 \end{bmatrix} \tag{9}$$

$$T = D(q)\ddot{q} + h(q,\dot{q}) + G(q)$$

As the result is very complex, it won't be written here in detail. In the equation, $D(q)$ is the inertia matrix of the robot; $h(q,\dot{q})$ is centrifugal force and coriolis force vector and $G(q)$ is the gravity vector.

Now, I'd like to talk about the redundancy of the joint angle. Three kinematic equations are built through using the kinematic model in part two and the spatial position relationship of joint angle. ${}^0X_5, {}^0Y_5, {}^0Z_5$ donate the spatial coordinate of the point O_5 which is in the coordinates O_0.

$$\begin{cases} {}^0Y_5 = -L_2 \cdot \sin\theta_2 - L_3 \cdot \sin(\theta_3 - \theta_2) - L_4 \cdot \sin(\theta_4 - \theta_3 + \theta_2) \\ {}^0Z_5 = \left[L_1 - L_2\cos\theta_2 + L_3\cos(\theta_3 - \theta_2) - L_4\cos(\theta_4 - \theta_3 + \theta_2)\right] \cdot \cos\theta_1 \\ {}^0X_5 = {}^0Z_5 \cdot \tan\theta_1 \end{cases} \tag{10}$$

It is obvious that there are four unknown variables in the three equations, so we can't solve these equations. In order to solve this problem, another restricted condition must be given. Now attention is paid to the torque of the joint angle, which is very important in robot walking. The value of the four joints torque can't be too large, as the motor can't withstand a large load. Another important requirement is that the angle between the fourth link and the plane must meet requirement of friction cone. So if we know the angle (φ_5) between the fourth link and the plane, the kinematic equations will be solved. Now the torque of each joint is calculated when a series of φ_5 value is selected, and the result is in fig.6.

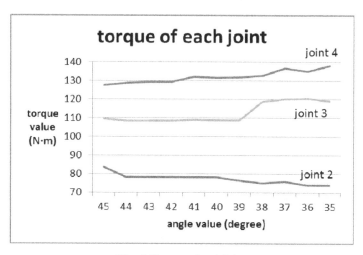

Fig. 6. Torque of each joint

Refer to the figure above, the torque of each joint won't be too large, when φ_5 is chosen between 42 and 44 degrees. With the constraint of the angle of φ_5, the kinematic equations will be solved. The result is:

$$
\begin{cases}
\theta_1 = \tan^{-1} \dfrac{{}^0X_5}{{}^0Z_5} \\[2mm]
\theta_2 = \dfrac{3}{2}\pi - \sin^{-1}\left(\dfrac{A^2 + B^2 + L_3^2 - L_4^2}{2 \cdot L_3 \cdot \sqrt{A^2 + B^2}} \right) + \tan^{-1} \dfrac{B}{A} \\[2mm]
\theta_3 = \cos^{-1}\left[\dfrac{L_3^2 + L_4^2 - \left(A^2 + B^2\right)}{2 \cdot L_3 \cdot L_4} \right] \\[2mm]
\theta_4 = 2\pi - \varphi_5 - \cos^{-1}\left[\dfrac{L_3^2 + L_4^2 - \left(A^2 + B^2\right)}{2 \cdot L_3 \cdot L_4} \right] - \tan^{-1} \dfrac{B}{A} + \sin^{-1}\left(\dfrac{A^2 + B^2 + L_3^2 - L_4^2}{2 \cdot L_3 \cdot \sqrt{A^2 + B^2}} \right)
\end{cases}
\tag{11}
$$

Where A and B are :

$$
\begin{aligned}
A &= \sqrt{{}^0Z_5{}^2 + {}^0X_5{}^2} - L_1 - L_4 \cdot \sin \varphi_5 \\
B &= {}^0Y_5 - L_4 \cdot \cos \varphi_5
\end{aligned}
\tag{12}
$$

5   Adams Simulation

Through the above analysis, we solve some problems encountered in the robot walking. Then walking simulation is done in adams. Combined simulation is divided into two steps. First, building a quadruped robot model in adams, and it is done in part two. Then, the corresponding control model should be built by Simulink which can be used to drive the model in adams. Finally, static gait walking of the quadruped robot is realized. As we know, the static gait is divided into six steps, which are lifting RB(right behind) leg, RF(right front) leg, shifting body to right, lifting LB leg, LF leg and shifting body to left. They are shown from (1) to (6) in fig.7.

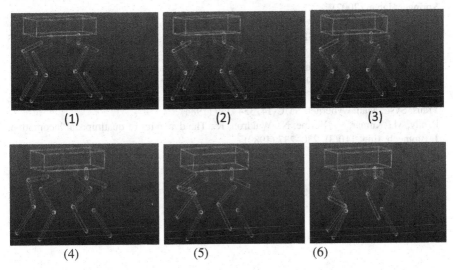

Fig. 7. Adams simulation

6   Conclusion

In this paper, we propose a new trajectory of robot leg, which is proved that it's better than other trajectories. Next, we find a good way to solve the redundancy of the joint angle. Last, we realize the quadruped robot's walking through admas simulation experiment.

Currently, our research mainly concentrated in even plane. The next step, we will achieve the quadruped walking on hollow and rough plane, and it needs a higher stability requirements. Next step, we will study the robot dynamic stability and contact force distribution to achieve quadruped walking under various environments.

Acknowledgments. This work was supported by the National Science Fund for '863' Hi-Tech Research and Development Program of China(Grant No.2011AA040701), National   Natural Science Foundation of China(Grant No. 50875100).

References

1. Raibert, M., Blankespoor, K., Nelson, G., Playter, R.: the BigDog Team: Bigdog, the rough-terrain quadraped robot. In: Proc. 17th World Congress of the International Federation of Automatic Control, pp. 10 822–10 825 (2008)

2. Wooden, D., Malchano, M., Blankespoor, K., Howard, A., Rizzi, A., Raibert, M.: Autonomous Navigation for BigDog. In: Proc. of the IEEE Internation
3. Sakakibara, Y., Kan, K., Hosoda, Y., Hattori, M., Fujie, M.: Foot trajectory for a quadruped walking machine. In: IEEE Int. Workshop Intelligent Robots and Systems, pp. 315–322 (1990)
4. Kiguchi, K., Kusumoto, Y., Watanabe, K., Izumi, K., Fukuda, T.: Energy-Optimal Gait Analysis of Quadruped Robots. In: Artificial Life and Robotics, vol. 6, pp. 120–125. Springer, Japan (2002)
5. Hugel, V., Blazevic, P.: Towards efficient implementation of quadruped gaits with duty factor of 0.75. In: Proc. IEEE Int. Conf. on Robotics and Automation, vol. 3, pp. 2360–2365 (1999)
6. Yi, S.: Reliable Gait Planning and Control for Miniaturized Quadruped Robot Pet. Mechatronics 20(4), 485–495 (2010)
7. Raibert, M., Wimberly, F.: Tabular control of balance in a dynamic legged system. IEEE Trans. Syst., Man, Cybernet. SMC-14, 334–339 (1984)
8. Pandy, M., Kumar, V., Berme, N., Waldron, K.: The dynamics of quadrupedal locomotion. J. Biomech. Eng. 110(3), 230–237 (1989)

Accurate Correction of Robot Trajectories Generated by Teaching Using 3D Vision by Laser Triangulation

Alberto Tellaeche, Ramón Arana, and Iñaki Maurtua

IK4 – Tekniker. Avda. Otaola 20, 20600 Eibar, Spain
{atellaeche,rarana,imaurtua}@tekniker.es

Abstract. Normal utilization of robot manipulators of anthropomorphic type does not reach beyond the reiteration of preprogrammed trajectories. While static robot programs may be sufficient for high volume manufacturers, they are not adequate in one-off or small-batch manufacturing, where programs must be adapted and modified in a dynamic way to fulfill the changing requirements in this type of production. Among the different techniques for robot programming, teaching is one of the fastest when changes have to be applied in complex trajectories. The main drawback of this technique is that a lot of time is lost defining the robot points very precisely. The objective of the work presented in this paper is to facilitate robot programming by combining teaching programming techniques and a 3D machine vision based accurate trajectory following.

Keywords: Teaching robot programming, 3D vision, laser triangulation, trajectory correction.

1 Introduction

There are multiple manufacturing processes where robots play (or might play) an important role. It is well known their use in welding, deburring and other un-safe or risky operations. Despite the intrinsic usefulness of robot manipulators of anthropomorphic type, their normal utilization is a repetition of established trajectories.

Nowadays, one of the main bounds for the growth and widespread of robotized cells in the context of small and medium enterprises is the complexity in the programming of robots. In the industry, the training level required for that kind of operation represents one of the biggest obstacles in order to prefer other automation solutions, intrinsically easier to setup.

This is particularly true for SMEs that cannot afford for big investments required for robot introduction and use, and cannot make expensive efforts in personnel robot training.

The objective of this work is to integrate a 3D visual servoing approach to adjust the rough trajectories generated by teaching robot programming using a Manual Guidance Device (MGD) and to allow accurate end-effector positioning by automatic correction of Tool Central Point (TCP) path. As a result, it will be possible to program

C.-Y. Su, S. Rakheja, H. Liu (Eds.): ICIRA 2012, Part III, LNAI 7508, pp. 385–394, 2012.
© Springer-Verlag Berlin Heidelberg 2012

robotic applications in an easy and fast way, focusing the attention on the process (laser cladding, deburring, etc) regardless programmatic problems.

2   State of the Art and Related Work

The common robot programming techniques, namely offline programming and lead-through programming with teach pendant, lead to several problems for SME applications. A highly skilled operator is necessary and the teaching takes a long time.

With teaching techniques, several programming approximations are referred, such as Programming by Demonstration, Programming by Example, Walk-Through Approach, Computer Assisted Teach and Play, or Programming by Manual Guidance. Also, Virtual Reality plays an important role in robot teaching techniques.

Programming by Demonstration is an intuitive programming method that can be done using the manual guidance of the robot. The operator moves the robot by applying forces to the robot tip, or other parts of the robot. The robot moves with deactivated actuators or with active/passive compliance. Using this programming method the operator has not to program directly in an explicit way, but the robot program is composed of the result of an interaction between the robot and the human. The robot is moved to each desired position, the controller records the internal joint coordinates corresponding to that position. This information is collected to process a program composed by a sequence of vectors with joint coordinates and some activation signals for external equipment such as the gripper aperture. When the program is executed, the robot moves through the specified sequence of joint coordinates, reproducing the indicated signals. In [1] the programming of industrial robots with the methods of 'Programming by Manual Guidance' is described.

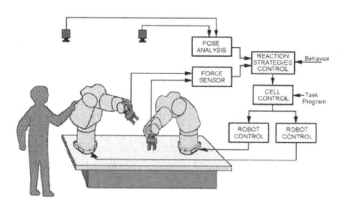

Fig. 1. Typical system configuration for programming by manual guidance [1]

In [2] a programming system for welding in shipyards is described. Robots can be programmed in a very fast pace by a 'Walk-Through Approach', a custom man-machine interface is implemented and the welding parameters are optimized by the system.

A further programming system called 'Computer-Assisted Teach and Play' is implemented for the whole arm manipulator (Barrett Technology Inc.) by Leeser et al. [3]. The operator can get help from the system by virtual surfaces, a gravity compensation for the arm and also for the tool and the payload are integrated.

Another interesting application, the insertion of pistons in a motor block is presented by Albu-Schaeffer et al. for 'Programming by Manual Guidance' [4]. The Light-Weight Arm developed at DLR can be guided manually on the desired trajectory.

Recently an innovative control strategy has been developed by Grunwald et al. [5]. The strategy is applied to a lightweight robot with a distributed system of sensors. In this case, it is possible to program the robot in an intuitive way.

Asada and Izumi [6] developed a method to generate a program for hybrid position/force control using a back-drivable robot guided by the human operator's hand directly.

In [7] an approach for real-time robot programming by human demonstration for 6D force controlled actions has been done. A human operator uses a joystick to guide a robot with a force sensor to execute a task including continuous contact between a manipulated object and an unmodeled environment.

Sato et al. present an alternative method of robot programming that does not need the use of force/torque sensors [8]. This implementation has been done on a high-speed parallel robot to carry out fast and complicated tasks.

Virtual reality is another approach to robot teaching. In [9], Takahashi et al. the authors propose a robot teaching interface which uses virtual reality. Takahashi et al. also propose robot teaching methods using VPL Data Gloves in a virtual workspace [10].

In [11] Kawasaki et al. Explain a virtual robot teaching system, consisting of human demonstration and motion-intention analysis in a virtual reality environment.

Finally, in [12] it is presented a new development method for event-driven robot teaching in a virtual environment.

3   Experiment Definition

This research has as main objective the development of a rapid robot programming system, combining teaching techniques for definition of robot points with a 3D system composed of a SICK Ranger E55 camera and a Class 2 red laser line.

The teaching points will be defined manually as approximate points by which the final trajectory will have to pass through. In this approach there is no need to define all the points of the trajectory, because the points will be recorded by the robot in real time and also will be corrected by the data obtained from the calibrated 3D image.

Based on the needs of the experiment, a prototype board has been constructed in Aluminum. This prototype has different trajectories defined, such as: straight line, curve, etc. The track defined in the prototype has a width of 60 mm and a depth of 7 mm, with a central nerve of 10 mm. Detail of this board can be observed in fig.2

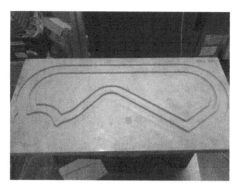

Fig. 2. Detail of the prototype board with different trajectories

3.1   Robot Position Tracking

For this research a NM45 robot from COMAU Robotics has been used. The points defining the trajectory in a rough way have been defined using the provided COMAU MGD.

Once the trajectory has been defined, parallel to trajectory program, the robot executes a parallel task to register the TCP positions in a text file. These positions are recorded whenever an increment of 0.5 mm is detected in the Euclidean distance from the previous recorded point or when an increment of 1° is detected in the α angle (rotation of the camera). The registered points have the following formal definition:

$$< x, y, z, \alpha, \beta, \gamma > .$$ (1)

The robot also synchronizes the recording of each point with a 3D line scan of the camera by a trigger pulse.

Every 500 pulses, the file containing the 500 coordinates and the 1536 * 500 pixel 3D image acquired are processed for trajectory correction. In parallel, the next capture of points is being performed.

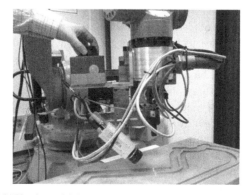

Fig. 3. COMAU robot with laser triangulation system scanning the prototype

3.2   3D Image Acquisition

For 3D visual trajectory correction, a laser triangulation system has been used. This system is composed by a SICK Ranger E55 Camera and a Class 2, red laser line. The camera has a 1536 * 512 pixel sensor and is capable of obtaining up to 35K profiles per second.

3D vision by means of laser triangulation has been widely used in industrial applications, like surface control or coordinate extraction. Works related to this can be found in [13] and [14].

There are four main principles for mounting the camera and the laser line in laser triangulation systems. These are:

1. *Ordinary setup*: The camera is mounted right above the object – perpendicular to the direction of movement – and the laser is illuminating the object from the side. This geometry gives the highest resolution when measuring range, but also results in miss-register – that is, a high range value in a profile corresponds to a different y coordinate than a low range value.

2. *Reversed ordinary setup*: As the ordinary setup, but the placement of the laser and the camera has been switched so that the lighting is placed above the object. When measuring range, the reversed ordinary geometry does not result in miss-register, but gives slightly lower resolution than the ordinary geometry.

3. *Specular:* The Ranger and the lighting are mounted on opposite sides of the normal. Specular geometries are useful for measuring dark or matte objects.

4. *Look-away:* The Ranger and the lighting are mounted on the same side of the normal. This geometry can be useful for avoiding unwanted reflexes but requires more light than the other methods and gives lower resolution.

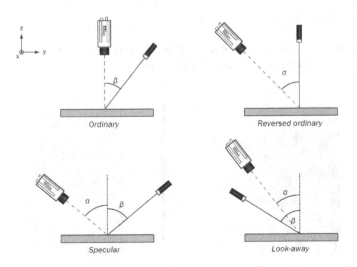

Fig. 4. Four different setup for laser triangulation

Fig. 4 shows a schematic representation of the geometrical setup for laser triangulation. According to [15], the *reversed ordinary setup* provides a good height resolution avoiding miss-register problems. The height resolution can be expressed as follows:

$$\Delta Z \approx \Delta X / \sin(\alpha). \tag{2}$$

The Ranger E55 camera internally calibrates the 3D images obtained, giving the d and z coordinates in real world mm. d is the Euclidean distance from the target (borders) to the center of the camera sensor, and z the point height. Also, during system set up, the center of the sensor of the Ranger E55 camera has been adjusted and calibrated to coincide with the robot Tool Center Point (TCP).

Using the 3D calibrated images acquired with the recorded coordinate points of the robot it is possible to correct the rough trajectory recorded by teaching, obtaining the very accurate path necessary in many robotic applications.

4   Trajectory Correction and Adjustment

Prior to robot movement, the user must select what type of edge must be adjusted in the subsequent operation. Attending to the shape of the track constructed in the prototype, options are: left border of the track, left border or the central nerve, right border of the central nerve, right border of the track. This setup will be used in the image processing to detect the correct border. Also, the reference z coordinate must be adjusted, to place in the height range where the camera provides correctly calibrated measures.

4.1   Image Processing

As explained in previous sections every 500 recorded points, two images are obtained from the ranger camera, d calibration and z calibration.

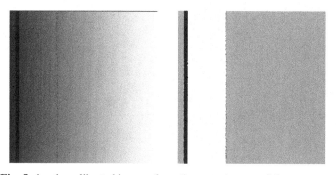

Fig. 5. d and z calibrated images from the central nerve of the prototype

After performing image filtering for noise reduction, the line profiles composing the 3D z calibrated image are processed, calculating the derivate signal for each one. With the derivative signal, it is possible to detect in a very precise manner the level transitions (borders) present in the line profile. When there is a high to low transition, corresponding to the left track border or to the right border of the central nerve, a minimum peak appears in that point in the derivative signal. On the other hand, when there is a low to high transition corresponding to left border of the central nerve, or to right track border, a maximum appears in the derivative signal. The rest of the values in the derivative signal tend to 0.

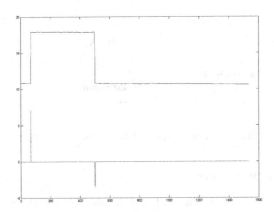

Fig. 6. line profile (above) and its derivative (below)

Taking into account the maximums and minimums present in the derivative signal and their relative position, it is possible to estimate the pixel in the line profile where a certain border is. Using that pixel value, the z calibrated value is obtained from the z calibrated image, and the d calibrated value is obtained from the d calibrated image. These values are converted to robot coordinates in the format presented in (1). This conversion is:

$$x = d \cos(\alpha) . \tag{3}$$

$$y = d \, \text{sen}(\alpha) . \tag{4}$$

4.2   Estimation of the Trajectory from the 3D Image.

By the process explained in the previous section, it is possible to estimate the real points of the border under inspection and thus, obtain the trajectory. Although the image is processed to avoid errors due to noise or lack of data in certain points, it has been implemented a restriction in the position of the points in the trajectory, taking into account the previous (x,y) positions of the two previous correct points obtained.

Let (x_0, y_0) and (x_1, y_1) be the two previous correct points calculated in the trajectory. The maximum increment in x and y coordinates is defined by a maximum Euclidean distance of 0.5 mm between two consecutive points.

$$(x_{2max}, y_{2max}) = (x_1 + \Delta x_{max}, y_1 + \Delta y_{max}). \tag{5}$$

If $x_2 > x_1 + \Delta x_{max}$ or $y_2 > y_1 + \Delta y_{max}$, then (x_2, y_2) is estimated as follows:

$$y_2 = y_1 + \Delta y_{max} \quad . \tag{6}$$

$$x_2 = (x_1 - x_0)(y_2 - y_0)/(y_1 - y_0) + x_0. \tag{7}$$

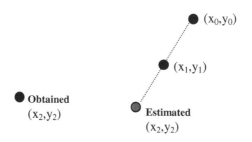

Fig. 7. Graphical representation of point estimation

4.3   Final Trajectory Correction

The center of the sensor of the Ranger E55 coincides with the robot TCP. Thus, the x_c and y_c point coordinates of the border detected in the 3D image correspond to the Δx and Δy final corrections of each point recorded by the robot.

Given a recorded point of the robot:

$$X_r = < x_r, y_r, z_r, \alpha_r, \beta_r, \gamma_r > \quad . \tag{8}$$

and the coordinates of the border obtained from the camera:

$$X_c = < x_c, y_c, z_c, \alpha_c, \beta_c, \gamma_c > \quad . \tag{9}$$

The final correction is:

$$X_r - X_c = < x_r - x_c, y_r - y_c, z_r, \alpha_r, \beta_r, \gamma_r > \quad . \tag{10}$$

The α angle variation is implicitly taken into account in (3) and (4), so it is not necessary to change the recorded value from the robot. z coordinate is calibrated and the real height value of the point of the trajectory being followed is obtained from the camera.

5   Experimental Results

To assess the performance of the correction method proposed, several tests have been carried out, using three different types of trajectories and the four different borders in the prototype.

The three trajectories used for validation are: straight, curve and combined straight-curve trajectories.

The borders are: left border of the track, left border or the central nerve, right border of the central nerve and right border of the track.

Table 1 shows the results obtained. The precision of the trajectory corrected is expressed in terms of mean and standard deviation of the accumulated error in trajectory estimation. These measurements are expressed in mm.

Table 1. Results obtained for trajectory estimation

		Predefined Trajectories		
		Straight	Curve	Straight-Curve
left border of the	Mean	0.020	0.078	0.065
track	Std. Dev	0.041	0.1	0.071
left border or the	Mean	0.013	0.068	0.057
c. nerve	Std. Dev	0.043	0.091	0.077
right border of the	Mean	0.012	0.063	0.060
c. nerve	Std. Dev	0.039	0.087	0.071
right border of the	Mean	0.014	0.072	0.051
track	Std. Dev	0.037	0.102	0.069

Analyzing the results obtained, it can clearly be seen that the system has a better performance in correcting straight trajectories. This is caused because in curve trajectories, there are more variables that can increment the overall error. While in straight trajectories all the inaccuracies depend purely on linear movements, in curve trajectories, apart from these linear movements, there are also flange rotations. However, the errors obtained can be assumed in the majority of robotic applications.

6   Conclusions and Future Work

With this research, it has been developed a new system for quick robot programming. The rough trajectory generated with teaching points in the COMAU robot, can afterwards be precisely corrected with the calibrated data obtained from the 3D images provided by the Ranger E55 camera.

The work done until now corrects the trajectories but does not take into account the robot tool orientation (β and γ angles). Tool correction and orientation will be the next steps for this research to obtain total robot trajectory correction.

Acknowledgments. This work has been carried out under the experiment "EASYPRO – Accurate Manual Guided robot programming". EASYPRO experiment belongs to the ECHORD platform, an EU-funded project within the Seventh Framework Program.

In the EASYPRO experiment, the consortium is composed by an Spanish research center, Tekniker-IK4, and two Italian companies, CNR-ITIA (Research center) and COMAU Robotics.

References

1. Frigola, M., Poyatos, J., Casals, A., Amat, J.: Improving Robot Programming Flexibility through Physical Human - Robot Interaction. In: IROS Workshop on Robot Programming by Demonstration, Las Vegas (October 2003)
2. Ang, H., Lin, W., Lim, S.-Y.: A Walk-Through Programmed Robot for Welding in Shipyards. Industrial Robots 26(5) (1999)
3. Leeser, K., Donoghue, J., Townsend, W.: Computer-Assisted Teach and Play: Novel User-Friendly Robot Teach Mode Using Gravity Compensation and Backdrivability. In: Proceedings of S ME Fifth World Conference on Robotics Research, Cambridge, USA (1994)
4. Albu-Schaffer, A., Hirzinger, G.: Cartesian Impedance Control Techniques for Torque Controlled Light-Weight Robots. In: Proceedings of the 2002 IEEE International Conference on Robotics and Automation, Washington DC (May 2002)
5. Grunwald, G., Schreiber, G., Albu-Schaffer, A., Hirzinger, G.: Programming by touch: The different way of Human-Robot Interaction. IEEE Transactions on Industrial Electronics 50(4) (2003)
6. Asada, H., Izumi, S.: Direct Teaching and Automatic Program Generation for the Hybrid Control of Robot Manipulators. In: IEEE International Conference on Robotics and Automation, Raleigh (1987)
7. Bruyninckx, H., De Schutter, J.: Specification of force controlled actions in the task frame formalism — a synthesis. IEEE Trans. on Robotics and Automation 12(4), 581–589
8. Sato, D., Shitashimizu, T., Uchyama, M.: Task Teaching to a Force Controlled High Speed Parallel Robot. In: Proceedings of IEEE International Conference on Robotics & Automation, Taipei, Taiwan (2003)
9. Takahashi, T., Ogata, H.: Robotic assembly operation based on task-level teaching in virtual reality. In: Proceedings of IEEE International Conference on Robotics & Automation, Nice, France (1992)
10. Takahashi, T., Sakai, T.: Teaching robot´s movement in virtual reality. In: IEEE/RJS International Workshop on Intelligent Robots and Systems. Proceedings 'Intelligence for Mechanical Systems' IROS, Osaka, Japan (1991)
11. Kawasaki, H., Furukawa, T., Ueki, S., Mouri, T.: Virtual Robot Teaching Based on Motion Analysis and Hand Manipulability for Multi-fingered Robot. Journal of Advanced Mechanical Design, Systems, and Manufacturing 3(1), 1–12 (2009)
12. Cui, M., Dong, Z., Tian, Y.: Simulation and execution of event-driven robot teaching in a virtual environment. In: Fifth World Congress on Intelligent Control and Automation, WCICA, Hangzhou (2004)
13. Leopold, J., Gunther, H., Leopold, R.: New developments in fast 3D-surface quality control. Measurement 33(2), 179–187 (2003)
14. Picón, A., Bereciartua, M.A., Gutiérrez, J.A., Pérez, J.: Machine vision in quality control. Development of 3D robotized laser-scanner. Dyna. 84(9), 733–742 (2010)
15. Boehnke, K.E.: Hierarchical Object Localization for Robotic Bin Picking. Ph.D. dissertation. Faculty of Electronics and Telecommunications. Politehnica University of Timisoara (September 2008)

Improved Method of Robot Trajectory in IBVS Based on an Efficient Second-Order Minimization Technique

Jie Zhang, Ding Liu, Yanxi Yang, and Gang Zheng

School of Automation and Information Engineering ,
Xi'an University of Technology, Xi'an 710048, China
zhangjlive@163.com

Abstract. In image-based visual servoing, image space trajectories are desired, while those in Cartesian space are always distorted. In order to improve the 3D robot trajectory, this paper suggests a new servoing method based on an Efficient Second-order Minimization technique and the idea of interpolation intermediate image features. In this algorithm, each robot displacement is determined with image features and corresponding Jacobians at present, initial and desired pose; error signals decrease with uniform speed in the whole operation process since the proposed algorithm divides the servoing task into multi-subtasks. Finally, the algorithm is verified through simulations.

Keywords: image-based visual servoing, 3D robot trajectory, feedback control law, efficient second-order minimization technique, interpolating strategy.

1 Introduction

In terms of the definition of feedback signal, visual servoing can be divided into two broad groups, i.e. position-based visual servoing (PBVS) and image-based visual servoing (IBVS) [1]. In PBVS, robot trajectory is always desired, but system performance is sensitive to external disturbances and calibration error; while the latter performs better in robustness and feasibility, but robot trajectory is always distorted. Accordingly, it's worthwhile planning 3D trajectory in IBVS. Ideally, the desired 3D trajectory, a straight one connecting the initial and desired robot position, is expected.

In IBVS, two main factors, Image features and control law, can affect the system performance. Image features with better property can effectively improve system behaviors, such as image moments [2-4], cylindrical coordinates [5], spherical projection features [6], etc. Some progress has been made in the system performance by advancing control law, e.g. Jacobian Pseudo-inverse Control method (JPC) [7] obtained from the first-order Taylor series. In order to get higher convergence rate, literature [8] suggests two Efficient Second-order Minimization (EMS) techniques based on the second-order Taylor series. Literature [10] presents an extended ESM control strategy, but without concrete parameter selection rules. O. Tahri and Y. Mezouar introduced tension conversion matrix T to improve ESM algorithm [11], and tested its advantages via experiments [9]. But this algorithm uses homogeneous

C.-Y. Su, S. Rakheja, H. Liu (Eds.): ICIRA 2012, Part III, LNAI 7508, pp. 395–405, 2012.

transformation matrix from current to desired robot poses to determine T, which is difficult to realize in practice. Being similar to JPC, EMS is also an approximation to the nonlinear relationship between image space and Cartesian space [9].

Literatures [12-14] introduce series of image features in servoing process so as to improve robot trajectories. Based on this thinking, we produce a series of intermediate feature points using an ESM algorithm - Pseudo-inverse of Mean of Jacobian method (PMJ) [8], and suggest a new servoing strategy. Analytically, our suggested algorithm is an improvement of traditional algorithms, i.e. JPC and PMJ, which can better approximate to the non-linear projection from Cartesian space to feature space.

The remainder of this paper is organized as follows. Part II describes the principle of JPC and PMJ algorithms. Part III introduces the ESM Based Median Interpolation technique, points out its disadvantages, and then gives the simpler ESM Based Sequence Interpolating technique. Part IV describes a new servoing strategy based on Sequence Interpolation. Part V illustrates simulation results to validate the advantage of our suggested algorithm. Part VI is the conclusion.

2   Visual Servoing Strategy Based on the Second-Order Minimization Technique

Given the 3D robot pose vector, system state, $x \in R^m$, and image feature vector, system output, $s(x) \in R^n$ with $n \geq m$, the servoing task is to remove the robot from its initial pose x_1 to the desired one x_2 in terms of system output $s(x)$. The control problem consists in finding a feedback law in such a way that the output $s(x_1)$ reaches its expected value $s(x_2)$.

2.1   Jacobian Pseudo-Inverse Control Method (JPC)

The servoing task above can be viewed as a Nonlinear Least Squares (NLS) minimization. Considering its special structure, the first-order Taylor series of $s(x)$ about x_1, evaluated at x_2

$$s(x_2) = s(x_1) - J(x_1)\Delta x + O_s(\Delta x^2) \qquad (1)$$

where $\Delta x = x_1 - x_2$. Furthermore, we can obtain:

$$\Delta s \approx -J(x_1)\Delta x \qquad (2)$$

where $\Delta s = s(x_2) - s(x_1)$. Consequently, for the robot control problem above, supposing that $J(x_1)$ is full rank, we get:

$$T = -\lambda J(x_1)^+ \Delta s \qquad (3)$$

where $J^+ = (J^T J)^{-1} J^T$ represents the pseudo-inverse of J, λ is the proportion. Thus, the robot can be controlled using the value derived from equation (3) iteratively until the image feature reaches its expected value $s(x_2)$. This method, with the current image Jacobian in IBVS, has relative low convergence rate [8].

2.2   Pseudo-Inverse of the Mean of Jacobians Method (PMJ)

ESM represents two efficient servoing methods; the representative algorithm – PMJ is introduced here. In considering the second order Taylor series of $s(x)$ [8]:

$$s(x_2) = s(x_1) + J(x_1)(x_2 - x_1) + \frac{1}{2}M(x_1, x_2 - x_1)(x_2 - x_1) + O_s(\Delta x^3) \quad (4)$$

and in using the first-order Taylor series of $J(x)$,

$$J(x_2) = J(x_1) + M(x_1, x_2 - x_1) + O_J(\Delta x^2) \quad (5)$$

the following equation can be obtained:

$$\Delta s = -\frac{1}{2}(J(x_1) + J(x_2))\Delta x + O_{PMJ}(\Delta x^3) \quad (6)$$

where $O_{PMJ}(\Delta x^3) = O_s(\Delta x^3) - O_J(\Delta x^2)\Delta x$ is the total remainder being cubic in Δx [8]. Then, the robot displacement can be computed by,

$$T = -\lambda\left[(J(x_1) + J(x_2))/2\right]^+ \cdot \Delta s \quad (7)$$

This algorithm is to use mean of Jacobians at current and expected features to get quadratic convergence rate at linear calculation quantity [8], and achieve better 3D robot trajectory than JPC method. Literatures [15-22] apply PMJ algorithm in different servoing systems to improve the system performances effectively.

3   Producing Intermediate Image Features in Servoing Process Based on ESM Algorithm

Likening JPC, PMJ is also an approximation to the nonlinear relation from the Cartesian space to image space; its performance will decrease at large initial deviation [11]. This paper adopts the thinking of interpolating strategy and the principle of ESM to produce a series of intermediate image features, so as to divide the servoing task into multi sub-tasks with smaller deviations to give full play to IBVS at small displacement.

3.1   ESM Based Median Interpolation Technique (ESM-MI)

In order to release the degradation of PMJ advantage at large initial deviation, we assume that there are two robots carrying out the servoing task from initial pose x_1

and desired pose x_2 simultaneously. Ideally, they can reach median point x_0 of the line segment connecting x_1 and x_2. This is about equal to dividing the servoing task into two sub-tasks with smaller initial deviation. ESM-MI method is presented based on this thinking to interpolate a median $s(x_0)$ between initial $s(x_1)$ and expected $s(x_2)$ of image features, whereby making the corresponding state x_0 located at the middle point of the desired trajectory, i.e. the line segment connecting initial x_1 and the desired x_2 of the robot pose. The second-order Taylor series of $s(x)$ about x_1 and x_2, evaluated at x_0

$$s(x_0) = s(x_1) + J(x_1)(x_0 - x_1) + \frac{1}{2}M(x_1, x_0 - x_1)(x_0 - x_1) \tag{8}$$

$$s(x_0) = s(x_2) + J(x_2)(x_0 - x_2) + \frac{1}{2}M(x_2, x_0 - x_2)(x_0 - x_2) \tag{9}$$

where $M(x_1, x_0 - x_1) = \left[\partial J(x_1)/\partial x(1) \cdot (x_0 - x_1), \cdots, \partial J(x_1)/\partial x(6) \cdot (x_0 - x_1)\right]_{n \times 6}$, reference [23] for more details. In terms of the principle of formula (5), we can obtain

$$M(x_2, x_1 - x_2) = 2 \cdot M(x_2, x_0 - x_2) = J(x_1) - J(x_2) \tag{10}$$

$$M(x_1, x_2 - x_1) = 2 \cdot M(x_1, x_0 - x_1) = J(x_2) - J(x_1) \tag{11}$$

substituting them into formulas (8) and (9), we can have:

$$(x_0 - x_1) = T_1 \cdot \left[s(x_0) - s(x_1)\right] \tag{12}$$

$$(x_0 - x_2) = T_2 \cdot \left[s(x_0) - s(x_2)\right] \tag{13}$$

where
$$T_1 = \left[\frac{3}{4}J(x_1) + \frac{1}{4}J(x_2)\right]^+ \tag{14}$$
$$T_2 = \left[\frac{1}{4}J(x_1) + \frac{3}{4}J(x_2)\right]^+$$

Given that x_0 is the middle point of the desired trajectory, $(x_0 - x_1) = -(x_0 - x_2)$. Furthermore, we can get:

$$s(x_0) = (T_1 + T_2)^+ \cdot \left[T_1 \cdot s(x_1) + T_2 \cdot s(x_2)\right] \tag{15}$$

It can be seen that in order to obtain the middle point $s(x_0)$, the image features, $s(x_1)$ and $s(x_2)$, as well as the corresponding Jacobians, $J(x_1)$ and $J(x_2)$, are required. Two median points can further be produced on the 2 sub-tasks divided by

$s(x_0)$ between $s(x_1)$ and $s(x_2)$. The above operations are carried out in successions until there are enough intermediate image features.

The aim of ESM-MI is to divide the large initial deviation into several small ones so as to give full play to IBVS at small displacements. The comparison among ESM-MI, PMJ and JPC is made in considering a simple example. Suppose the (2×1) polar coordinate vector $s(\mathbf{x}) = (r, \theta)$ is measurement of system state $\mathbf{x} = (x, y)$, coordinates of points. JPC and PMJ are used to complete the control tasks, while ESM-MI is used to produce intermediate feature trajectory. Fig. 1 shows the comparison trajectories with $\mathbf{x}_1 = (0.2, 0.95)$ and $\mathbf{x}_2 = (0.4, 0.1)$, where dashed lines are isolines. Simulation results show that PMJ performs better than JPC, while the intermediate feature trajectory produced by ESM-MI is mostly close to the desired trajectory. Several other simulations with different beginning and ending states are carried out with similar results obtained.

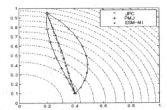

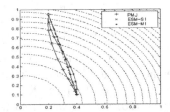

Fig. 1. Comparison among JPC, PMJ and ESM-MI

Fig. 2. Comparison among PMJ, ESM-MI and ESM-SI

3.2   ESM Based Sequential Interpolation Technique (ESM-SI)

Each operation of ESM-MI above can only obtain one median point between initial and terminal features. If more middle features are expected, it must be used in multilevel recursive operation, so that the algorithm is difficult to realize, and needs a large quantity of calculation with solution of Jacobians at each intermediate points. Aiming at the disadvantage of ESM-MI, we further suggest a simple sequential interpolation algorithm, ESM-SI. Again, the desired trajectory, i.e. a line segment connecting initial and desired states, is expected.

The principle of ESM-SI is interpolating $n-1$ features $s(x_p)$ between initial $s(x_1)$ and the expected $s(x_{n+1})$, so as to make the corresponding system states x_p, $p = 2, \cdots, n$ locate at and equi-divide the desired trajectory. The concrete algorithm is given as follows:

Evaluate the second-order Taylor series of $s(x)$ about x_1 and x_{n+1} at any middle points $s(x_p)$, $p = 2, \cdots, n$ (refer to formulas (8) (9)). Considering x_p equi-divide the desired trajectory, we can obtain:

$$s(x_p) - s(x_1) = \left[J(x_1) + \frac{1}{2}M\left(x_1, \frac{p-1}{n}(x_{n+1} - x_1)\right) \right] \cdot \left[\frac{p-1}{n}(x_{n+1} - x_1) \right] \quad (16)$$

$$s\left(x_p\right) - s\left(x_{n+1}\right) = \left[J\left(x_{n+1}\right) + \frac{1}{2}M\left(x_{n+1}, \frac{n+1-p}{n}\left(x_1 - x_{n+1}\right)\right)\right] \cdot \left[\frac{n+1-p}{n}\left(x_1 - x_{n+1}\right)\right] \quad (17)$$

substituting the conclusions of equations (10) (11) into formulas above, we get,

$$\left(x_{n+1} - x_1\right) = T_1 \cdot \left[s\left(x_p\right) - s\left(x_1\right)\right] \tag{18}$$

$$\left(x_1 - x_{n+1}\right) = T_2 \cdot \left[s\left(x_p\right) - s\left(x_{n+1}\right)\right] \tag{19}$$

in considering $\left(x_1 - x_{n+1}\right) = -\left(x_{n+1} - x_1\right)$, we can have,

$$s\left(x_p\right) = \left(T_1 + T_2\right)^+ \cdot \left[T_1 \cdot s\left(x_1\right) + T_2 \cdot s\left(x_{n+1}\right)\right] \tag{20}$$

where
$$T_1 = \frac{n}{p-1} \cdot \left[J\left(x_1\right) + \frac{1}{2} \cdot \frac{p-1}{n}\left(J\left(x_{n+1}\right) - J\left(x_1\right)\right)\right]^+$$

$$T_2 = \frac{n}{n+1-p} \cdot \left[J\left(x_{n+1}\right) + \frac{1}{2} \cdot \frac{n+1-p}{n}\left(J\left(x_1\right) - J\left(x_{n+1}\right)\right)\right]^+ \tag{21}$$

We have noted that equations (15) and (20) are the same in structure, only with different T_1 and T_2 values. It is worth putting forward that when $p = n/2$ in equation (20), i.e. x_p is located at the right middle of the desired trajectory, equation (15) and (20) are equivalent, so that ESM-SI is the extension of ESM-MI, while ESM-MI is just a special case of ESM-SI.

Table 1. Comparison between ESM-MI and ESM-SI

Sampling points	2	6	9	13	16	20	23	27	31
ESM-MI x	0.3942	0.3711	0.3539	0.3312	0.3139	0.288	0.2678	0.2408	0.2137
ESM-SI x	0.4003	0.3913	0.3754	0.3452	0.3178	0.2789	0.2506	0.2192	0.2014
Error x	0.0061	0.0202	0.0215	0.0140	0.0039	0.0091	0.0172	0.0216	0.0123
ESM-MI y	0.1266	0.2331	0.3132	0.4212	0.5022	0.6082	0.6873	0.7924	0.8975
ESM-SI y	0.1277	0.2377	0.3188	0.425	0.5033	0.6065	0.6837	0.7879	0.895
Error y	0.0011	0.0046	0.0056	0.0038	0.0011	0.0017	0.0036	0.0045	0.0025

As to the control example in part 3.1, we use both ESM-MI and ESM-SI to produce 31 intermediate points. Table I gives 9 sampling points data in comparison. The first and second lines represent x-axial coordinates of system state produced by ESM-MI and ESM-SI respectively. The third line is error of the first and second lines. The fourth and fifth lines represent y-axial coordinates of system state produced by ESM-MI and ESM-SI respectively. The sixth line is error of the fourth and fifth lines.

Simulation data indicate that errors of corresponding intermediate points produced by the two interpolation techniques are very small, while simulation results (Fig. 2) show that the trajectory produced by ESM-SI is less close to the desired trajectory than that by ESM-MI, but still makes a big improvement in comparison with that by PMJ. Besides, ESM-SI can produce any number of intermediate feature points in succession only with the knowledge of the features and Jacobians at initial and desired states. Accordingly, ESM-SI is easier to implement than ESM-MI, with small quantity of calculations.

4   Application of ESM-SI in Image-Based Visual Servoing

To use ESM-SI in IBVS systems, we have to carry out a comparatively tedious process that firstly produce enough neighboring intermediate points, and then with each point as the expected feature by order in steps until the servoing task is fulfilled. Here, a simple application strategy of using ESM-SI in IBVS is given.

Suppose that current robot pose is x_l, the intermediate feature in the next step produced by ESM-SI, namely the current expected feature, is $s(x_m)$. We use the control rate of equation (3) with proportion $\lambda = 1$, which means the robot is expected to have one-step movement to make $s(x_l)$ reach $s(x_m)$. This hypothesis is rational so long as enough intermediate points are produced. Then, the current robot displacement is:

$$T = -J\left(x_l\right)^{+}\left[s\left(x_l\right) - s\left(x_m\right)\right] \tag{22}$$

Furthermore, according to equation (20), we have

$$T = -J\left(x_l\right)^{+} \cdot \left\{s\left(x_l\right) - T_{s1} \cdot s\left(x_1\right) - T_{s2} \cdot s\left(x_{n+1}\right)\right\} \tag{23}$$

where $T_{s1} = \left(T_{1m} + T_{2m}\right)^{+} T_{1m}$, $T_{s2} = \left(T_{1m} + T_{2m}\right)^{+} T_{2m}$, here T_{1m} and T_{2m} representing T_1 and T_2 values at point x_m (formula (21)), $m = 2, \cdots, n+1$.

Accordingly, the application of ESM-SI in IBVS needn't calculating intermediate image features first. As long as servoing steps are well set up, the robot displacement at each step can be directly obtained by formula (23), being similar to JPC and PMJ. We call this servoing strategy Equal-Step-Visual-Servoing (ESVS).

ESVS necessitates image features and Jacobians at initial, current and expected points, which is more complicated than the existing algorithms, i.e. JPC and PMJ. However, it can be known analytically that this combination is more approximate to the nonlinear relationship between image space and Cartesian space via guaranteeing that each robot displacement is carried out within a very small range.

5   Simulation Experiments

As far as an eye-in-hand PUMA 560 visual servoing simulation system [24] is concerned, coordinates of points, image moments and cylindrical coordinates are selected as features to fulfill servoing tasks so as to test the advantages of ESVS.

5.1   Visual Servoing Based on Coordinates of Points

As for an object composed of 2 points, coordinates of the 2 points are selected as image features. JPC, PMJ and ESVS are used to fulfill the servoing task with $s(x_1) = [390, 76, 367, 206]^T$, $s(x_2) = [350, 256, 162, 256]^T$. Suppose that the object is always parallel to the camera plane in the whole servoing process, robot rotation around x and y axes is not considered and the 4-th and 5-th columns of Jacobian are neglected [1]. Simulation results are indicated in fig. 3 and fig. 4. Fig. 3 shows trajectories of the 2 objective points in image space; Fig. 4 shows distances of corresponding sampling points from real 3D robot trajectories to the desired one.

It can be seen from the simulation results that JPC can obtain better trajectories in image space, while 3D robot trajectory is distorted greatly. PMJ improves trajectory in Cartesian space at the expenses of that in image space. ESVS has done the harmony between image space and Cartesian spaces; in comparison with PMJ, trajectories in both spaces have been improved.

Both error signals of JPC and PMJ decrease exponentially due to the proportional control law, while that of ESVS is even in the whole servoing process for the equal subtasks divided by the intermediate points. The convergence speed is slow in comparison with JPC and PMJ, but trajectory in Cartesian space is the best, i.e. closest to the desired trajectory. In addition, peaks of the three curves in fig. 4 appear at different sample points, while not at different 3D robot pose, merely.

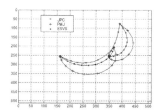

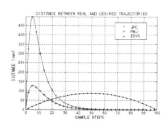

Fig. 3. Trajectories of JPC, PMJ, and ESVS in image space

Fig. 4. Distances between real and desired 3D trajectories of JPC, PMJ, and ESVS

5.2   Visual Servoing Based on Image Moments

Image moment vector $\left[x_g, y_g, a, \alpha \right]^T$ [4] is selected as features to fulfill 4-DOF operation of $\left[T_x, T_y, T_z, W_z \right]^T$ with respect to a rhombus object. Simulation results, with $s(x_1) = [134, 134, 15713, -0.523]^T$ and $s(x_2) = [256, 256, 11720, 0]^T$, as shown in fig. 5 and fig. 6 are similar with those based on coordinates of points. In Cartesian space, the deviation of trajectory by JPC is the largest while that by ESVS is smallest from the expected one.

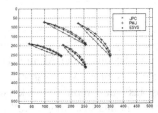

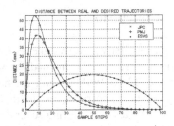

Fig. 5. Trajectories of JPC, PMJ, and ESVS in image space

Fig. 6. Distances between real and desired 3D trajectories of JPC, PMJ, and ESVS

5.3   Visual Servoing Based on Cylindrical Coordinates

Cylindrical coordinates are used in literature [5] to improve the system performance. Here, we use ESVS to improve the distorted trajectory produced by cylindrical coordinates at a 2-DOF servoing task. In servoing procedure, only the previous two columns of Jacobian are considered. Simulation results, with $s(x_1) = [288.499, 0.785]^T$ and $s(x_2) = [72.138, -0.805]^T$, are shown in fig. 7 and fig. 8.

Simulation results are different from those in previous two groups, while the trajectory produced by ESVS is still nearest to the expected one in Cartesian space.

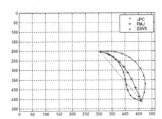

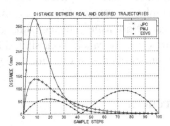

Fig. 7. Trajectories of JPC, PMJ, and ESVS in image space

Fig. 8. Distances between real and desired 3D trajectories of JPC, PMJ, and ESVS

ESVS performs best in all three groups above, but fails to complete the tasks when initial deviations are too large in simulations, and this maybe caused by the singularity in calculating intermediate features. Furthermore, we found via simulations that robot trajectories are better with slower convergence speed if more intermediate points are set up; while they are less smooth with faster convergence if less intermediate points are produced. ESVS can always complete servoing tasks at any number of intermediate points set, accordingly a compromise must be found between convergence speed and 3D trajectory. Furthermore, it can be predicated that when ESVS is used in the real robot experimental system, the results obtained will be found in agreement with those of simulations described above, since the robot displacement at each step is calculated through the algorithm if only the robot has enough executive capacity.

6   Conclusions

This paper firstly reviews the traditional control strategy in IBVS, i.e. Jacobian Pseudo-inverse Control method, as well as an Efficient Second-order Minimization technique, PMJ. With an aim at the degradation problem of ESM at large initial deviation, this paper suggest to divide the servoing task into multi subtasks with smaller deviates via inserting several intermediate feature points so as to give full play to IBVS at small displacement. The intermediate feature points produced by ESM-MI can nearly approach the desired trajectory of system state, but is complicated with a large quantity of calculations. ESM-SI is easier to realize, whose state trajectory is inferior to that of ESM-MI slightly, but still superior to PMJ. This paper further applies ESM-SI to IBVS system and suggests a new control strategy, ESVS. Finally, the advantages of newly suggested method - ESVS, compared with JPC and PMJ, are tested through three simulation servoing systems with different feature selections.

Jacobian matrix is a linear approximation to the relationship between image space and Cartesian space so that it is only valid at small initial deviation. When the initial deviation is large, 3D robot trajectory will deviate from the expected one. PMJ introduces Jacobian at expected pose into the control law, so that robot trajectory is somewhat improved. ESVS is able to guarantee that each step of robot movement is carried out within a small displacement via dividing the servoing task into multi sub-tasks, so that 3D trajectory is much better.

ESVS is more complex than JPC and PMJ in structure, but theoretical analysis and simulation results show that this combination can more approximate to the nonlinear relationship between image space and Cartesian space and obtain better robot trajectories. Much work should be further done on analysis of singularity when the system initial deviation is too large for ESVS to fulfill the task.

References

1. Chaumette, F., Hutchinson, S.: Visual Servo Control, Part I: Basic Approaches. IEEE Robotics and Automation Magazine 13(4), 82–90 (2006)
2. Chaumette, F.: Image moments: a general and useful set of features for visual servoing. IEEE Transactions on Robotics 20(4), 713–723 (2004)
3. Tahri, O., Chaumette, F.: Point-based and region-based image moments for visual servoing of planar objects. IEEE Transactions on Robotics 21(6), 1116–1127 (2005)
4. Tahri, O., Mezouar, Y., Chaumette, F., Corke, P.: Decoupled Image-Based Visual Servoing for Cameras Obeying the Unified Projection Model. IEEE Transactions on Robotics 26(4), 684–697 (2010)
5. Iwatsuki, M., Okiyama, N.: A New Formulation of Vision Servoing Based on Cylindrical Coordinate System. IEEE Transactions on Robotics 21(2), 266–273 (2005)
6. Fomena, R.T., Chaumette, F.: Visual servoing from spheres using a spherical projection model. In: IEEE Conference on Robotics and Automation, pp. 2080–2085. IEEE Press, Roma (2007)
7. Espiau, B., Chaumette, F., Rives, P.: A new approach to visual servoing in robotics. IEEE Transactions on Robotics and Automation 8(3), 313–326 (1992)

8. Malis, E.: Improving vision-based control using efficient second-order minimization techniques. In: IEEE Conference on Robotics and Automation, pp. 1843–1848. IEEE Press, New Orleans (2004)

9. Tahri, O., Mezouar, Y.: On visual servoing based on efficient second order minimization. Robotics and Autonomous Systems 58, 712–719 (2010)

10. Marey, M., Chaumette, F.: Analysis of classical and new visual servoing control laws. In: IEEE Conference on Robotics and Automation, pp. 3244–3249. IEEE Press, Pasadena (2008)

11. Tahri, O., Mezouar, Y.: On the Efficient Second Order Minimization and Image-Based Visual Servoing. In: IEEE Conference on Robotics and Automation, pp. 3213–3218. IEEE Press, Pasadena (2008)

12. Hashimoto, K., Noritsugu, T.: Enlargement of Stable Region in Visual Servo. In: IEEE Conference on Decision and Control, pp. 3927–3932. IEEE Press, Sydney (2000)

13. Mezouar, Y., Chaumette, F.: Design and Tracking of Desirable Trajectories in the Image Space by Integrating Mechanical and Visibility Constraints. In: IEEE Conference on Robotics and Automation, pp. 731–736. IEEE Press, Seoul (2001)

14. Park, J.S., Chung, M.J.: Path Planning With Uncalibrated Stereo Rig for Image-Based Visual Servoing Under Large Pose Discrepancy. IEEE Transactions on Robotics and Automation 19(2), 250–258 (2003)

15. Benhimane, S., Malis, E.: Real-time image-based tracking of planes using efficient second-order minimization. In: IEEE/RSJ Conference on Intelligent Robots and Systems, pp. 943–948. IEEE/RSJ Press, Sendai (2004)

16. Benhimane, S., Malis, E.: Integration of euclidean constraints in template-based visual tracking of piecewise-planar scenes. In: IEEE/RSJ Conference on Intelligent Robots and Systems, pp. 1218–1223. IEEE/RSJ Press, Beijing (2006)

17. Bourger, F., Doignon, C., Zanne, P., de Mathelin, M.: A model-free vision-based robot control for minimally invasive surgery using esm tracking and pixels color selection. In: IEEE Conference on Robotics and Automation, pp. 3579–3584. IEEE Press, Roma (2007)

18. Abdul Hafez, A.H., Cervera, E., Jawahar, C.V.: Optimizing image and camera trajectories in robot vision control using on-line boosting. In: IEEE/RSJ Conference on Intelligent Robots and Systems, pp. 352–357. IEEE/RSJ Press, San Diego (2007)

19. Silveira, G., Malis, E., Rives, P.: An Efficient Direct Approach to Visual SLAM. IEEE Transactions on Robotics 24(5), 969–979 (2008)

20. Mei, C., Benhimane, S., Malis, E., Rives, P.: Efficient Homography-Based Tracking and 3-D Reconstruction for Single-Viewpoint Sensors. IEEE Transactions on Robotics 24(6), 1352–1364 (2008)

21. Mansard, N., Remazeilles, A., Chaumette, F.: Continuity of Varying-Feature-Set Control Laws. IEEE Transactions on Automatic Control 54(11), 2493–2505 (2009)

22. Malis, E., Mezouar, Y., Rives, P.: Robustness of Image-Based Visual Servoing With a Calibrated Camera in the Presence of Uncertainties in the Three-Dimensional Structure. IEEE Transactions on Robotics 26(1), 112–120 (2010)

23. Wetter, W.J.: Matrix Calculus Operations and Taylor Expansions. Society for Industrial and Applied Mathematics 15(2), 352–369 (1973)

24. Corke, P.I.: Robotics TOOLBOX for MATLAB (Release 7). Manufacturing Science and Technology Pullenvale. 4069, AUSTRALIA (2002)

Tactile Sensors Based Object Recognition and 6D Pose Estimation

Achint Aggarwal and Peter Kampmann

DFKI Gmbh, Robotics Innovation Center (RIC),
Robert Hooke Str. 5, D-28359 Bremen, Germany
{achint.aggarwal,peter.kampmann}@dfki.de
http://www.dfki.de/robotics

Abstract. For robots working in real world environments, especially in the underwater area, it is necessary to achieve robust recognition and 6D pose estimation of freely standing movable objects using tactile sensors. Until now this problem remains unsolved due to the limited capability of the available tactile sensors. However, in our research group we have developed a highly reliable tactile sensor system, with high spatial and force resolution [2]. Such a sensor system enables us to achieve robust recognition and 6D localization of static objects as well as freely standing movable objects in high noise conditions which can be expected underwater. In this paper we will present our approaches and simulation based results.

Keywords: Haptic object recognition, 6D pose estimation, freely standing movable objects, high measurement noise, underwater applications.

1 Introduction and Related Work

Research efforts in tactile sensing based object recognition have been limited, due to the sparse availability of such sensors. Further, most of the work is based on past generations of tactile sensors which had extremely limited force and spatial resolution. Thus, the practical problem of **"Recognition and 6D Pose Estimation of a freely standing movable object using tactile sensors on a robotic hand"** still remains unsolved. Recently, a highly reliable tactile sensor system with high spatial and force resolution has been realized [2] in our research group, that is even suitable for deep sea exploration [1]. This changing paradigm in technology has enabled a revision in the perspective of algorithms used for haptic object recognition. We have now reached a position where we can robustly evaluate highly informative local surface features on an object using locally dense point clouds collected from touch. Hence, feature matching algorithms, that have been successfully demonstrated in range sensing applications, can be used for object recognition and 6D localization using tactile sensors.

The basic problem with tactile sensors, in contrast to vision and range sensors where extensive environment information is obtained in a single click or scan, is that tactile sensors only yield local information of the environment. An object has to be explored gradually to retrieve object surface information. If the

C.-Y. Su, S. Rakheja, H. Liu (Eds.): ICIRA 2012, Part III, LNAI 7508, pp. 406–416, 2012.
© Springer-Verlag Berlin Heidelberg 2012

object is static, approaches like [13] can be used to fuse the data collected over multiple contacts. However, for practical scenarios, a freely standing object is liable to move nondeterministically from its initial position during the course of exploration. Thus, the most challenging problem is to usefully combine the information collected during successive touches to correctly recognize and localize the object.

Some researchers like [8] and [9] have concentrated on the reconstruction of the complete shape of unknown objects using tactile sensors. This involves the complete exploration of the object surface using an exploration strategy, and definition of the object shape using geometric models like superquadrics. This has been limited to static objects, objects with relatively simple shapes, and is an over-kill for the common practical scenario where a known object needs to be recognized quickly using minimal tactile data.

There are, however, several other techniques in the range sensing literature that can be effectively applied to the haptic object recognition domain if the contact information from tactile sensors is modeled as point clouds. [11] provide an excellent review of such techniques.

The most noticeable attempts to recognize and localize movable objects have been cited recently in [6] and [5]. [6] clearly highlight the shortcomings of the past generation hardware for 6D object localization. Using a force sensing probe as a tactile sensor, the 6D localization of an object could take several weeks! They present Bayesian methods for fast and efficient 6D localization of simple shaped objects with planar faces using only a single tactile probe. [5] use high resolution grids of tactile sensors to localize objects in 3 dimensions (allowing only planar motion) using sequential state estimation. Some machine learning approaches like [4] have been used to identify objects in the haptic space (using finger geometry and tactile data) itself without building a complete 3D representation of the object.

There are three main contributions of this paper. Firstly, we present the adaptation and results of the feature matching approach of [10] for object recognition and localization using tactile sensors. We also discuss a strategy for object exploration using our gripper. Secondly, we present the application of the Monte Carlo technique for sequential use of tactile data for robust recognition and 6D pose estimation for static objects. This method is shown to deal with objects of complex shapes and is robust to a large positional and tactile noise. Thirdly, we present the extension of this Monte Carlo approach for recognition and 6D pose estimation of freely standing movable objects. The results in this paper are limited to simulation only, although we have already planned to test these on the real system.

We introduce our hardware and software architecture in Section 2. Section 3 deals with our object exploration strategy and the basic feature matching based object identification method. Section 4 explains the Monte Carlo based algorithm and its results for static objects and Section 5 deals with movable objects. Section 6 lists the conclusions and gives directions for future work.

2   Hardware and Software Architecture

2.1   Hardware

The robotic system which will be used to evaluate the object exploration strategies is a three-fingered gripper system which has been designed to work underwater in depths of up to 6000 meters. The kinematic chains are similar to a 3 fingered BarrettHand. Each of the fingers has two limbs which are equipped with a variety of force sensing modalities. A detailed description of the gripper system and its actuation mechanisms can be found in [1] and [3]. Especially important in terms of object recognition is the sensory system which serves as input to the high-level object exploration algorithms. Figure 1 shows the proposed sensor setup of our gripper system.

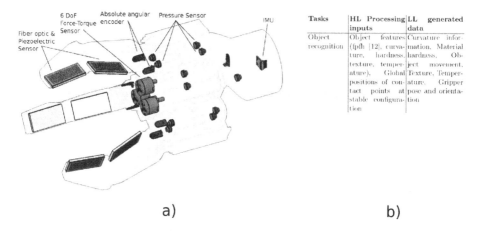

Fig. 1. The sensor system of the gripper (a) and the Data Interface between High-Level and Low-Level Data Processing (b)

Selecting appropriate measurement principles which allow sensing different modalities under water is a challenging task due to the fact that most force and pressure sensors are being compressed by the resulting force of the water column. The selected measuring principles have been either known from the literature to be working in deep-sea or have been tested at out institute [1] in a pressure chamber at 600 bar which corresponds to the force acting from a water column at 6000 meters depth.

2.2   High and Low Level Software

Compared to other gripper systems, this manipulator is equipped with a huge amount of sensor elements. As the complete system will consist of up to 2100 single sensor elements, transmitting the data that is sensed becomes a challenge for the preprocessing electronics that is integrated into the gripper system.

A classic centralistic architecture that transmits all the collected data to a single processing unit is not feasible as the necessary processing load demands for high-end processing units which add problems like heating, power consumption and size to the system integration. This is why a decentralized processing architecture is chosen which enables local preprocessing and fusion of the sensor data. This has the advantage of lower processing load on high-level processing units and also reduces communication load on the communication lines.

Figure 1 shows how the interface between high-level data processing and the low-level data preprocessing can be realized in terms of object recognition algorithms. As can be seen, many of the desired features for the high-level tasks can be directly generated on the low-level processing layer. Additional behaviors like ensuring a stable grasp or others which reduce data transmission by calculating the expected sensory feedback as well as starting data transmission in a context aware manner support the minimization of centralized processing power and low throughput on communication lines in the system.

3 Object Exploration and Database Matching

3.1 Exploration Strategy

Our Object Exploration Strategy for data collection is divided into two parts. The *Coarse Exploration* strategy is responsible for the motion planning of the 7dof manipulator to which the gripper is attached (see Figure 4). At a given time step, the maximum unexplored region on the object surface is considered as the next exploration direction. This is determined by the widest open cone strategy similar to [7] and shown in Figure 2. The vertex of the cone is at the centroid of the current explored object pointcloud. The axis of the cone defines the next exploration direction. Secondly, the *Fine Exploration* strategy is responsible for maximizing the exploration of the object from a fixed wrist position using all the degrees of freedom of the gripper. Actions like *Close Fingers To Maximize Contact Area* and *Rotate Fingers And Touch* are used for fine exploration.

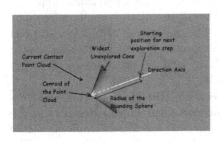

Fig. 2. Widest Unexplored Cone based coarse exploration strategy

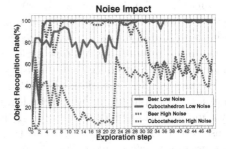

Fig. 3. Impact of noise on object recognition

Measurement Noise: We add a realistic amount of white Gaussian noise to the measurements from each tactile sensor element using the spatial resolution of the elements in the grid. The spatial dimensions of one tactile element are $2mmX2mm$ and the maximum compression is 4mm [1]. Assuming a 50% force resolution noise, the covariance matrix to model the uncertainty as Gaussian white noise is chosen as $Q = diag(2mm, 2mm, 2mm)$ similar to [13]. In addition to this, we also add a high position error of 5mm in each of the x-y-and-z coordinate axes at each tactile sensor grid.

Results: This exploration strategy has been tested in simulation and works well for the exploration of static objects, even for objects of complex shapes. For static objects, the information collected from each exploration step can be transformed to the global frame using the forward kinematics of the robot, and simply added together to form the global object map. The results of exploring the first four objects of Figure 4 using our gripper are shown in Figure 5. The global maps of the explored objects are illustrated at regular intervals. The horizontal axes illustrate the *Coarse Exploration* steps (marked by CE) and the *Fine Exploration* steps (F). It is clear that the global object maps after a few *Coarse Exploration* steps reflect the complete shapes of the objects. The noise causes the resulting object maps to be distorted with respect to the actual object.

3.2   Feature Matching Based Object Recognition

For most of the common robotic applications it is practical to maintain a database of known objects which can be queried in real time with tactile sensing inputs for object identification. However, to maintain generality, the algorithm should be scalable with respect to the number of objects in the database. Thus, our feature matching algorithm is similar to the Batch RANSAC method presented in [10]. This algorithm combines feature-based model indexing (for initial pruning of large databases) and geometric constraint based alignment (RANSAC using only the pruned database) for efficient 3D object recognition from a large model database. At any stage of object exploration, the algorithm matches the corresponding input contact pointcloud (Figure 5) with the database to generate object recognition and pose estimation hypotheses for that particular step.

Our object database consists of 20 objects (Figure 4) with similar sizes such that they can be grasped with our gripper. The objects are completely scanned using a simulated laser scanner, filtered with a voxel grid to eliminate overlapping points and the resulting XYZ pointclouds[1] are saved in the database. Features of these are also saved in feature pointclouds.

We use the 33-dimensional Fast Point Feature Histogram (FPFH) [12] feature for our application with a search radius of 1.0 cm which is lesser than the maximum continuous contact patch radius that we can expect from our tactile sensors pads. However, any other feature can be used with our algorithm. The algorithm is briefly explained below.

---

[1] A pointcloud is a collection of points of similar types. XYZ pointclouds contain points defined by their x, y and z locations. Feature pointclouds consist of points containing the value of a feature.

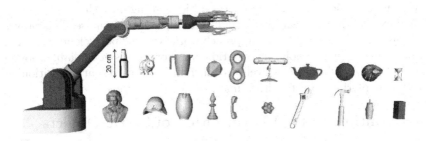

Fig. 4. Equally scaled models of the 7dof WAM manipulator with our gripper and the 20 database Objects

Sampling and Database Pruning: A triplet of points is randomly selected from the input XYZ pointcloud such that the points are spaced away from each other and do not lie on the edges of the input patches. The features for these three points are calculated. Next, the database is pruned by estimating the closest matching W features for each triplet point.

RANSAC Based Recognition: RANSAC between the triplet and pruned database is used for generating R object and pose hypotheses weighed with the quality of match. Triplet sampling and RANSAC based verification is repeated N times to yield $N * R$ weighed hypotheses. The hypothesis with the maximum weight is returned as the recognized object with the 6D pose.

Results: We evaluated the effectiveness of this feature based Batch RANSAC object recognition algorithm on a database of 20 objects (Figure 4) using inputs from the tactile sensors collected with our exploration strategy (including large noise) as explained in Section 3.1. The parameters used are: W=1000, N=20, R=2000. The results are shown in Figure 5 for the first four objects of Figure 4. The data is averaged over 50 complete cycles of exploration. At each exploration step, object recognition rate represents the percentage of times the correct object was identified and is shown by continuous red curves w.r.t. the left vertical axis. The pose estimation error[2] is shown by the red dotted curves w.r.t the right vertical axis. For clarity, the state of the explored object maps are also illustrated at regular intervals along the exploration step axes. It can be seen that the object recognition rate varies between 10 and 100% depending on the object and the state of exploration. Mostly the object recognition rate is low in the beginning of exploration but increases with greater surface of the object being explored. However, sometimes the performance degrades after a considerable part of the object is explored (particularly for cuboctahedron). This is due to the large noise that accumulates over time and leads to incorrect local feature estimation. We can confirm this by our experiments using lesser noise. Figure 3 clearly shows the

---

[2] Pose estimation error is the average distance between points of the database object pointcloud at the actual object position and the closest points of another similar cloud at the estimated pose.

improvements in object recognition for two objects using only the tactile sensel noise, and excluding the tactile grid's high spatial positioning noise. This proves that although the Batch RANSAC approach works well for pointcloud matching with range sensors (where noise distribution is uniform) it is not reliable enough for our applications where noise levels are much higher due to spatial positioning errors while exploring objects with a manipulator and gripper.

4 Recognition and 6D Localization of Static Objects

The success of the Batch RANSAC approach depends on the selection of the correct object matches in the first feature based pruning approach and then on finding the correct sample matches during RANSAC. Thus, even if the database is pruned correctly, unless we comprehensively test all possible object and 6D pose hypotheses, there is a possibility of the correct object and pose not being detected. Also, even if the correct object and pose is detected successfully at one instance during the course of exploration, it does not have any influence on the correct hypothesis being selected again at a subsequent exploration step. This explains the moderate and unstable object recognition rates even after a large part of the object has been explored.

In this section we use a Monte Carlo approach that is built upon the Batch RANSAC approach but enables us to perform robust object recognition and pose estimation after only a few exploration steps. This is achieved by keeping track of the top hypotheses from Batch RANSAC outputs at every exploration step, and successively evolving them with new measurements updates from each exploration step. These hypotheses represent the most promising parts of the search space and thus we divert more computational power to these regions. With every new measurement update, ICP is used to finely correct the old object poses using the new updated object map. The algorithm is explained below.

Initialization: Using the initial XYZ pointcloud, the Batch RANSAC algorithm generates an initial State $S_0 = \{s_0, s_1, ..., s_m\}$, consisting of weighed object and pose hypotheses $s_i = \{obj_i, x_i, y_i, z_i, \alpha_i, \beta_i, \gamma_i, wt_i\}$ where obj represents the object that the hypothesis points to, $\{x_i, y_i, z_i, \alpha_i, \beta_i, \gamma_i\}$ represents the 6D pose and wt_i represents the belief in the hypothesis.

Measurement Update: In this step we utilize the fact that there is a higher probability of the correct solution lying in the vicinity of the previous hypotheses than any other random place in the 6D space. Since these hypotheses were determined from old partial measurements, there is some chance of their poses being partially incorrect. Thus, the new measurement is used to finely correct the previous pose hypotheses using ICP with the new updated object map. Only the top $\Phi\%$ of hypotheses in state S_t are evolved to form a state S_t' by this pose correction and the rest are rejected. The new quality of matches are also computed and the hypotheses are sorted in decreasing weights.

Generating New Hypotheses Using Batch RANSAC: Using the updated object map, the Batch RANSAC algorithm generates a new set of hypotheses S_t^{new}. The top ranked hypotheses in S_t^{new} are combined with S_t' to form the new state S_{t+1} such that total size does not exceed N_{max}.

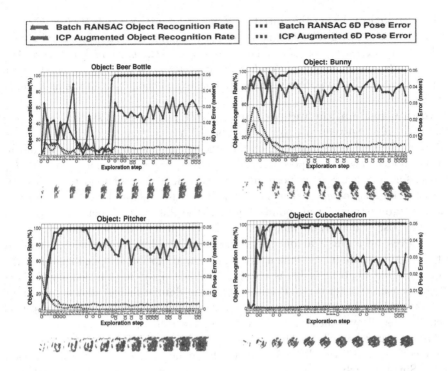

Fig. 5. Static object recognition and pose estimation comparisons between simple Batch RANSAC and Monte Carlo based approaches

Object Recognition and Pose Estimation: At a given step t, the hypothesis $s_{t,i} \in S_t$ with the maximum weight represents the recognized object $obj_{t,i}$ and 6D pose $\{x_{t,i}, y_{t,i}, z_{t,i}, \alpha_{t,i}, \beta_{t,i}, \gamma_{t,i}\}$.

Results: The same tactile sensor contact measurements as Section 3.2 were used for evaluating the performance. We used the following values of the parameters: W=1000, N=20, R=2000 for Batch RANSAC and $\Phi = 20\%$ and $N_{max} = 100$ for the Monte Carlo algorithm. The results for the same four database objects as before are shown by the green curves in Figure 5. It can be clearly seen that we consistently achieve 100% recognition rates for all objects after only a few exploration steps. For some objects this represents over two times improvement. The pose estimation error also tends to zero after a few exploration steps which denotes the convergence to the correct pose. These results have also been evaluated under high noise conditions mentioned in Section 3.1.

5   Recognition and 6D Localization of Movable Objects

This section deals with the extension of the Monte Carlo approach for recognition and pose estimation of freely standing objects that can move when touched with a gripper while exploration. The methodology is explained below.

Initialization: Using the initial XYZ pointcloud, the Batch RANSAC algorithm generates an initial State $S_0 = \{s_0, s_1, ..., s_m\}$, consisting of weighed object and pose hypotheses $s_i = \{obj_i, x_i, y_i, z_i, \alpha_i, \beta_i, \gamma_i, wt_i, xyzcloud_i\}$ as before. We also save the object map $xyzcloud_i$ separately for each hypothesis. In the first step of creation of a hypothesis, this map consists of the points in the first step's input pointcloud.

Motion Estimation and Measurement Update: For a state S_t at step t, $\forall s_{t,i} \in S_t$, ICP between the $obj_{t,i}$'s database XYZ pointcloud at the hypothesis pose and the new measurement cloud M_t yields an estimate of the motion of the object and the new object pose $\{x'_{t,i}, y'_{t,i}, z'_{t,i}, \alpha'_{t,i}, \beta'_{t,i}, \gamma'_{t,i}\}$. The map $xyzcloud_{t,i}$ is transformed to this new pose, and measurement M_t is added to it to form the new map $xyzcloud'_{t,i}$. The new weight wt'_i is evaluated by the inverse of the average distance of all points between the database object pointcloud at the new pose and the new map $xyzcloud'_{t,i}$. To utilize the fact that the object only moves by a small amount in every step, the hypotheses with a motion estimate greater than twice the maximum allowed motion are penalized. In such a case the old hypothesis $s_{t,i}$ is also retained but again with a penalty. This is to compensate for wrong ICP results and the double factor allows pose error correction. Finally the hypotheses are sorted in decreasing weights. Thus, this step evolves all hypotheses in a state S_t to a state S'_t.

Generating new hypotheses using Batch RANSAC: Using the measurement M_t, the Batch RANSAC algorithm generates a new set of hypotheses S_t^{new}. Since a newly generated hypothesis is only created from the current partial measurement, it is down-weighed as compared old hypotheses which have evolved over several measurements. The top ranked $\Phi\%$ hypotheses in S_t^{new} are combined with the top ranked hypotheses of S'_t to form the new state S_{t+1} such that total size does not exceed N_{max}.

Object Recognition and Pose Estimation: At a given step, the hypothesis with the maximum weight represents the recognized object and its 6D pose.

Results: We used the same 20 object database as before. Of the two most prominent approaches for movable object localization, [6] models object motion with a Gaussian noise of 2cm translational and 10 degrees angular standard deviations. In [5] the object moves in the range of [10, 10] mm in both the x- and y-directions and the entire range of rotations in the xy plane. We used three different values of object transformations. First, the object was moved at each exploration step by a transformation sampled uniformly at random from the range [-10, 10] mm in each of x, y and z-directions (max $\sqrt{1^2 + 1^2 + 1^2} = \sqrt{3}$cm), and range [-5,5] degrees about each of the three orientation axes. The second case was for [-20,20]mm ($\sqrt{12}$cm) and [-5,5] degrees and the third with [-30,30]mm ($\sqrt{27}$cm) and [-5,5] degrees. This object motion was used to transform the tactile sensor measurements collected at different stages of object exploration in the static object case (without concatenating inputs at each step). Thus the inputs are sparse contact positions similar to the measurements at the first exploration step of Figure 5. We used W=500, N=20, R=2000 for Batch RANSAC and $\Phi = 80\%$ and $N_{max} = 100$ for the Monte Carlo algorithm. We averaged the re-

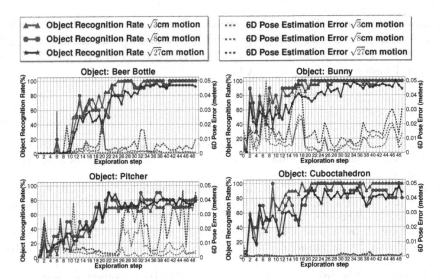

Fig. 6. Movable Object Recognition and 6D Localization results for 3 different levels of allowed movement of the objects

sults over 20 complete exploration runs for each object for each value of allowed motion. The results for the first four database objects are shown in Figure 6. The object recognition rates increase constantly with increasing number of measurements and we attain a maximum value between 80 and 100% for all cases. The pose estimation error increases with the amount of allowed motion which is understandable. There are instances where the localization error suddenly increases like in the case of bunny and pitcher. This is because some measurements may not be sufficient for estimating the correct object motion and can thus, cause the ICP to return incorrect object motions. However, this error quickly stabilizes with future measurements. For allowed motion of $\sqrt{3}$cm we were able to localize objects with an error less than 5mm. We got higher bounds for other cases which were still below the maximum object motion limit. Overall, we achieved satisfactory results for recognition and 6D localization using sparse partial contact clouds in this difficult scenario where an object moves nondeterministically.

6 Conclusion and Future Work

We achieved robust and accurate object recognition and 6D pose estimation of complex objects using our high resolution tactile sensors even under high noise conditions. We successfully demonstrated the ability to recognize and localize these objects even if they are allowed to move while being explored. In future, will test our approaches with actual hardware in indoor as well as underwater environments. We will also utilize multi-modal tactile sensor information like object hardness and texture for faster recognition.

Acknowledgments. The results presented in this paper are based on technologies, developed in the SeeGrip project which is funded by the German Federal Ministry of Economics and Technology (BMWi) according to a resolution of the German Bundestag, grant no. 03SX291.

References

1. Kampmann, P., Kirchner, F.: Towards a fine-manipulation system with tactile feedback for deep-sea environments. J. Robotics and Autonomous Systems (to appear)
2. Kampmann, P., Kirchner, F.: A Tactile Sensing System for Underwater Manipulation. In: 7th ACM/IEEE International Conference on Human-Robot Interaction, Boston, United States (2012)
3. Lemburg, J., Kampmann, P., Kirchner, F.: A small-scale actuator with passive-compliance for a fine-manipulation deep-sea manipulator. In: OCEANS 2011, Kona, Hawaii (2011)
4. Gorges, N., Navarro, S.E., Göger, D., Wörn, H.: Haptic object recognition using passive joints and haptic key features. In: IEEE International Conference on Robotics and Automation, ICRA (2010)
5. Pezzementi, Z., Reyda, C., Hager, G.D.: Object mapping, recognition, and localization from tactile geometry. In: IEEE International Conference on Robotics and Automation, ICRA (2011)
6. Petrovskaya, A., Khatib, O.: Global Localization of Objects via Touch. IEEE Transactions on Robotics 27, 569–585 (2011)
7. Mazzini, F., Kettler, D., Guerrero, J., Dubowsky, S.: Tactile Robotic Mapping of Unknown Surfaces, With Application to Oil Wells. IEEE Transactions on Instrumentation and Measurement 60, 420–429 (2011)
8. Allen, P.K., Roberts, K.S.: Haptic Object Recognition Using a Multi-Fingered Dextrous Hand. In: IEEE Intl Conf on Robotics and Automation (1989)
9. Bierbaum, A., Gubarev, I., Dillmann, R.: Robust Shape Recovery for Sparse Contact Location and Normal Data from Haptic Exploration. In: IEEE/RSJ International Conference on Intelligent Robots and Systems, IROS (2008)
10. Shan, Y., Matei, B., Sawhney, H.S., Kumar, R., Huber, D., Hebert, M.: Linear Model Hashing and Batch RANSAC for Rapid and Accurate Object Recognition. In: IEEE International Conference on Computer Vision and Pattern Recognition (2004)
11. Mian, A.S., Bennamoun, M., Owens, R.: Automatic correspondence for 3D modeling: an extensive review. International Journal of Shape Modeling 11, 253 (2005)
12. Rusu, R.B., Blodow, N., Beetz, M.: Fast Point Feature Histograms (FPFH) for 3D registration. In: IEEE International Conference on Robotics and Automation, ICRA (2009)
13. Meier, M., Schöpfer, M., Haschke, R., Ritter, H.: A Probabilistic Approach to Tactile Shape Reconstruction. IEEE Transactions on Robotics 27, 630–635 (2011)

Graph-Based Detection of Objects with Regular Regions

Cunzhao Shi, Chunheng Wang, Baihua Xiao, and Yang Zhang

State Key Laboratory of Management and Control for Complex Systems,
Institute of Automation, Chinese Academy of Sciences
Beijing, 100190, China

Abstract. Most objects with regular regions could be detected as Maximally Stable Extremal Regions (MSER) [20]. In this paper, We formulate object detection as a bi-label (object and non-object regions) segmentation problem, and propose a graph-based object detection method using edge-enhanced MSER. Specifically, we focus on detecting text in natural images, which is a special kind of object. First, edge-enhanced MSERs are detected as basic letter components; non-text MSERs are then efficiently eliminated by minimizing the cost function which combines both region-based and context-relevant information; and finally, mean-shift clustering is used to group text components into regions. The proposed method is naturally context-relevant, scale-insensitive and readily to be applied on detecting other objects. Experimental results on the ICDAR 2011 competition dataset show that the proposed approach outperforms state-of-the-art methods both in recall and precision.

Keywords: Object, text, detection, MSER, graph, cost function.

1 Introduction

In order to automatically understand the content of the image, detecting interested object in images is receiving more and more attention. Text, as a special kind of object, could provide exact and unique information about the content, detecting, extracting and recognizing text in images and videos is receiving increasing attention in the recent years. Since text detection is the premise for the later stages and is critical to the overall system performance, a large number of approaches have been proposed to address this problem as surveyed in [9] [11] [17]. Most of the existing text detection methods could be roughly classified into two categories: region-based and connected component (CC) based.

Based on the assumption that text has distinct textural features compared with the background, region-based methods apply various approaches such as Fast Fourier Transform or wavelet decomposition to extract textural features from each local region which are then fed into a classifier to estimate whether the region is text or not [16] [10] [5].

As opposed to region-based method, CC-based methods first use various approaches to get the initial CCs, then heuristic rules or classifiers are used

C.-Y. Su, S. Rakheja, H. Liu (Eds.): ICIRA 2012, Part III, LNAI 7508, pp. 417–426, 2012.
© Springer-Verlag Berlin Heidelberg 2012

to remove nontext CCs, and finally the candidate CCs are grouped into lines [13] [8] [15] [4].

Although some of the existing methods have achieved good performance, there is still room for improvement. For region-based methods, a large number of training set of text and non-text samples are necessary to train a suited classifier and it is especially difficult to make sure the non-text samples are representative. Moreover, as region-based methods need to scan the image at different scales, the speed is relatively slow. On the other hand, for CC-based methods, it is quite difficult to design a fast and also reliable CC analyzer to eliminate false positives without losing the text components.

To overcome the above problems, we consider text as a special kind of object with regular stable region, and propose a graph-based object detection methods using MSER as basic components. As shown by Kimmel et al. [20], MSER tend to be regular regions, such as text regions. Thus, first, we use edge-enhanced MSERs [6] [4] detected in the original image as basic CCs; then, an irregular graph is constructed whose nodes are the MSERs; next, non-text MSERs are eliminated by minimizing the cost function via graph cut algorithm ; and finally, the candidate components are grouped into lines by mean-shift clustering [18] and the false positives are removed by a trained classifier. The proposed method is naturally scale-insensitive, context relevant and readily to be applied on detecting other objects. Experimental results on ICDAR 2011 text localization competition dataset [14] report promising performance.

The rest of this paper is organized as follows. Section 2 details the proposed method. Experiments and results are presented in Section 3 and conclusions are drawn in Section 4.

2   The Proposed Approach

The flowchart of the proposed method is shown in Fig. 1. First, two kinds of edge-enhanced MSERs, dark-on-white and white-on-dark, are detected. Then, a graph whose nodes are the MSERs are constructed. Next, carefully designed unary and pairwise cost functions are defined for the graph and non-object MSERs are removed by minimizing the cost function via max-flow/min-cut algorithm [2]. Since we focus on detecting text in this paper, mean-shift clustering are used to group candidate text CCs to text lines and a classifier is used to remove the non-text blocks. Finally, results from both kinds of the MSERs are merged.

2.1   Edge-enhanced MSER Detection in the Original Images

Due to the robustness against view point, scale, and lighting changes, MSER has been identified as one of the best region detectors [12]. Actually, the detected MSER tend to be regular and uniform regions [20] as shown in Fig. 2. Since text is a special kind of object and usually has distinct contrast to its background and relatively uniform intensity or color, MSER is a natural choice for text detection. However, MSER is sensitive to image blur. To cope with the blurred images,

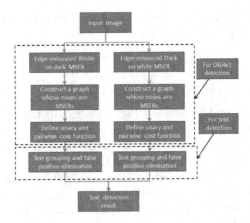

Fig. 1. The flowchart of the algorithm

we use edge-enhanced MSER detection method proposed by Chen et al. [4] as the basic CCs. The edge-enhanced MSER provide an improved representation of the text where individual letters are separated, which is beneficial for the following MSER labeling process. The two kinds of MSERs, white areas on dark background and the dark areas on white background, are handled separately to eliminate their mutual influence. Geometric rules are used to eliminate obvious non-text regions. The following process is applicable for both kinds of MSERs. Some of the detected MSERs are shown in Fig. 2. As we can see, objects as well as some background are detected as MSERs.

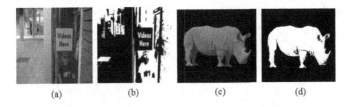

| (a) | (b) | (c) | (d) |

Fig. 2. MSER detection result: (a) and (c) are original images; (c) and (d) are detected MSERs

2.2 Constructing the Graph to Label MSERs As Text or Non-text Areas

In addition to object areas, a lot of unwanted areas are also detected as MSERs. We need to remove the non-object MSERS while also preserving the object ones. To this end, we construct a graph for these MSERs. An undirected graph $G = (V, E)$ is composed of nodes (vertices V) and undirected edges (E) that connect these nodes. As shown in Fig. 3, each MSER corresponds to a node in the undirected graph and the neighboring nodes for each node are those ones that satisfy the criterion defined below:

$$dist(x_i, x_j) < 2 \times min[max(w_i, h_i), max(w_j, h_j)]$$
$$\&\& \ min(w_i, w_j)/max(w_i, w_j) > 0.4 \tag{1}$$
$$\&\& \ min(h_i, h_j)/max(h_i, h_j) > 0.4,$$

where $dist(x_i, x_j)$, w, and h represent the Euclidean distance between two component centroids, the width and height of component's bounding box respectively. There are also two terminals, the background and the foreground terminals linking to each node. Each edge in the graph is assigned a nonnegative weight as the cost of cutting the edge. Thus, the MSER labeling problem could be formulated as a segmentation problem by labeling the object candidates as 1 (foreground) and non-object areas as 0 (background). Concretely, let P be all the nodes in the graph and N be a set of pairs $\{p, q\}$ of the neighboring nodes in P. $L = \{L_1, L_2, ..., L_p, ...\}$ is a binary vector whose components L_p specify the label of node p in P. Each L_p could be either 1 (foreground) or 0 (background). The cost function for each segmentation L is defined as [1]:

$$E(L) = \sum_{p \in P} R_p(L_p) + \lambda \sum_{\{p,q\} \in N} B_{\{p,q\}} * \delta(L_p, L_q), \tag{2}$$

where

$$\delta(L_p, L_q) = \begin{cases} 1 \ if \ L_p \neq L_q \\ 0 \ otherwise \end{cases} . \tag{3}$$

The coefficient λ is a trade-off factor between the region cost R and the boundary cost B. Thus, the target of the labeling problem is to find a segmentation L^* that minimizes the cost function as shown in (4). In the following sections, we will give details about the unary and pairwise cost functions.

$$L^* = \arg\min_{L}(E(L)). \tag{4}$$

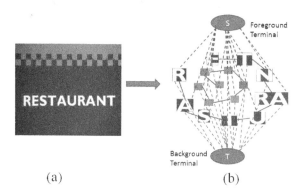

(a)   (b)

Fig. 3. Illustration of MSER labeling via graph cut: (a) original image; and (b) the construction of the graph

2.3 Defining the Cost Function

The Unary Cost Function. Unary cost function measures the individual penalties for labeling node p as foreground (object component) or background (non-object component) and each node has two cost weights $U_p(1)$ and $U_p(0)$,

Fig. 4. The symmetric structures of characters

corresponding to linking cost to foreground and background respectively. If the possibility of the MSER being object candidates is very high, say, close to 1, the cost weight $U_p(1)$ should be small and $U_p(0)$ should be large. Thus, we train a classifier to estimate the possibility of the MSER being object. Here we focus on a special kind of object, text. From our observation, we find text regions have the following three characteristics: 1) most characters have intrinsic low-rank textures [19] such as symmetric structures, regular shapes or parallel edges as shown in Fig. 4; 2) characters have rich edges; and 3) most characters tend to have gradients of various orientations. In order to reflect the above characteristics, we use the lowest rank, the edge density and the gradient of 8 directions as the features. As the characters in scene images might have various deformations, to compute the lowest rank, we rotate the character from minus 30 degrees to 30 degrees and the rank of each image is computed. We choose the minimum one as the lowest rank feature. All the ranks are divided by the smaller one of the width and height for normalization. In Fig. 5, the rank of the original image is 0.6388, while the rank of the rotation image of 5 degrees is 0.5634 which is chosen as the feature for the rank.

We collect the training samples from ICDAR 2011 competition training dataset [14]. All the training samples are normalized with a height of 24 while remaining the ratio of the width and the height. We choose Random Forests [3] as the region-based classifier due to its fast speed and relatively better generalization performance. As text usually has several letters and the context information is important, in addition to the classification result of the current node, the results of the neighboring nodes also contribute to the unary cost as defined below:

$$U_p(1) = -ln(\lambda S_c + (1 - \lambda)A_n), \tag{5}$$

$$U_p(0) = -ln(-\lambda(1 - S_c) + (1 - \lambda)(1 - A_n)). \tag{6}$$

where S_c, A_n and λ are the classification result of the current MSER, the average classification result of the neighboring MSER and the trade-off parameter respectively. In the experiment, λ is set to 0.7 by cross-validation.

The Pairwise Cost Function. The pairwise cost reflects penalties for discontinuity between neighboring components. It could be defined as a decreasing

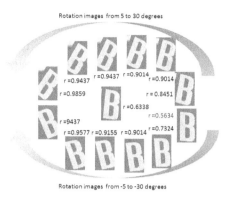

Fig. 5. Illustration of the computation of low rank feature

function of the distance between the neighboring nodes p and q, which means if the features of p and q are similar, the penalty for assigning different labels to the neighboring nodes should be large and vice versa. Color distance and shape distance are used to define the pairwise cost function:

$$B_{\{p,q\}} = exp(-\frac{\alpha \times Dis_c + \beta \times Dis_s}{2 \times \sigma^2}), \tag{7}$$

where

$$Dis_c = abs(color_p - color_q), \tag{8}$$

and

$$Dis_s = max\{\frac{abs(H_p - H_q)}{min(H_p, H_q)}, \frac{abs(W_p - W_q)}{min(W_p, W_q)}\}. \tag{9}$$

Dis_c and Dis_s represent the color and shape distance between two neighboring areas. H and W are the height and width of the area respectively. This function means that if the color and shape of the two neighboring areas are similar, the cost of labeling different labels is large and vice versa.

Minimizing Cost Function to Get the Labeling Result. Given the graph whose nodes are the MSERs as well as the two terminals, the cost of labeling each node as foreground or background could be calculated and it could be minimized by finding the minimum cut of the graph. Considering the high speed and relatively satisfactory performance, the max-flow/min-cut algorithm [2] is used to optimize the cost function to get a binary image whose object candidates are white and non-text areas are black. Some of the MSERs before and after labeling are shown in Fig. 6. As we can see, most of the non-text areas are removed while the text candidates are also well preserved, making the following text grouping much easier.

If we need to detect other objects, cost function that is suitable to the specific object could be defined and non-object areas could be removed using the same framework proposed in this section.

Fig. 6. MSERs before and after labeling: (a) before; and (b) after

2.4   Text Grouping by Mean-shift Clustering

As most of text appears in a liner form and letters in the same text usually have similar height, width and color, we extract several features from each text candidate component and use mean-shift clustering [18] to cluster them into text lines. We use the row index of the centroid, the height, the ratio of the width and the height and the average color of the MSER as the features.

2.5   Eliminating False Positives

To eliminate the false positive, the text blocks are normalized with height of 16 pixels, and a trained classifier is used to classify the sub-image of size 16×16 scanned with step of 8 pixels from the normalized text block. The confidence of the whole text block is the average result of each scanned window.

3   Experiments and Results

In order to evaluate the proposed algorithm, we use the challenging ICDAR 2011 text localization competition dataset [14] as the benchmark dataset. We use the same measures as in the competition [14], recall, precision and f-measures which are defined as follows:

$$Precision = \sum_{r_e \in E} m(r_e, T)/|E|, \qquad (10)$$

$$Recall = \sum_{r_t \in T} m(r_t, E)/|T|, \qquad (11)$$

$$f = 1/(\alpha/p + \alpha/R), \qquad (12)$$

where $m(r, R)$ is the best match for a rectangle r in a set of rectangles R, E, T are the estimated and ground truth rectangles respectively, and α is set to 0.5 to give equal weights to precision and recall.

3.1   Evaluation of the MSER Labeling Method

Since the MSER labeling process which eliminates most of the non-text MSERs is essential to the final text detection result, we compare the proposed MSER labeling by graph cut algorithm (MSERGC) with two other methods, MSER labeling simply by MSER classification (MSERC) and MSER without labeling (NMSERL). The comparison results are shown in Table 1. As we can see, without the MSER labeling process, not only does the precision drop a lot due to the non-text MSERs, the recall also decreases several percents because the non-text MSERs disturb the text grouping process, making the text areas submerged in the non-text areas. Furthermore, the proposed MSER labeling algorithm also outperforms the MSERC method, suggesting the effectiveness of the proposed MSER labeling process which considers both region-based and the context-relevant information.

Table 1. Comparison results of MSER labeling methods (%)

Algorithm	Recall	Precision	F
NMSENL	49.9	56.9	53.17
MSERLC	57.5	75.8	65.39
MSERLGC	62.8	83.21	71.58

3.2   Comparison Results with other Methods

The result of our method and the results from the competition [14] are shown in Table 2. The result demonstrates that the proposed method performs better both in recall and precision. The experiments are implemented on a PC with Intel(R) Core(TM)2 Duo CPU 2.33GHZ using Matlab, and the speed is relatively fast, taking 1.5 seconds on average for image with size 640×480 and 4.5 seconds for those with size 1280×960. Some of the text detection results are shown in Fig. 7. As we can see, the proposed method can detect text of various illuminations, sizes and deformations.

Table 2. Results of different text detection algorithms (%)

Algorithm	Recall	Precision	F
Our method	62.8	83.21	71.58
Kims Method	62.47	82.98	71.28
Yis Method	58.09	67.22	62.32
TH-TextLoc System	57.68	66.97	61.98
Neumanns Method	52.54	68.93	59.63
TDM IACS	53.52	63.52	58.09
LIP6-Retin	50.07	62.97	55.78
KAIST AIPR System	44.57	59.67	51.03
ECNU-CCG Method	38.32	35.01	36.59
Text Hunter	25.96	50.05	34.19

Fig. 7. Some examples of detection results

4 Conclusions

In this paper, we present a graph-based object detection method using edge-enhanced MSER as basic components. Specifically, we focus on a special kind of object, text. The text detection method integrates region-based classification result into a CC-based framework and achieves promising result on IC-DAR 2011 competition dataset. Low-rank and gradient based region features and context information contribute to the cost function which is minimized via max-flow/min-cut algorithm [2] so that non-text MSERs are efficiently removed, making the text grouping much easier. Although the proposed method reports encouraging performance, it still needs further improvement. Some detected text lines are incorrectly filtered during the last stage, making the recall decrease several percents. In the future, more effective false positive elimination methods needs to be further researched so that we could improve the recall as well as the precision. Furthermore, since the proposed method could be easily applied on detecting other objects by changing the cost function, we would try to detect other objects using the same framework.

Acknowledgments. This work is supported in part by the National Natural Science Foundation of China under Grant No. 60933010 and No. 60835001.

References

1. Boykov, Y., Jolly, M.: Interactive graph cuts for optimal boundary & region segmentation of objects in nd images. In: 8th IEEE International Conference on Computer Vision, vol. 1, pp. 105–112. IEEE (2001)
2. Boykov, Y., Kolmogorov, V.: An experimental comparison of min-cut/max-flow algorithms for energy minimization in vision. IEEE Transactions on Pattern Analysis and Machine Intelligence 26(9), 1124–1137 (2004)
3. Breiman, L.: Random forests. Machine learning 45(1), 5–32 (2001)
4. Chen, H., Tsai, S., Schroth, G., Chen, D., Grzeszczuk, R., Girod, B.: Robust text detection in natural images with edge-enhanced maximally stable extremal regions. In: International Conference on Image Processing, pp. 2609–2612 (2011)
5. Chen, X., Yuille, A.: Detecting and reading text in natural scenes. In: IEEE Computer Society Conference on Computer Vision and Pattern Recognition, vol. 2, pp. II–366. IEEE (2004)
6. Chum, J., Urban, M., Pajdla, T.: Robust wide baseline stereo from maximally stable extremal regions. In: British Machine Vision Conference, vol. 72 (2002)

7. Dalal, N., Triggs, B.: Histograms of oriented gradients for human detection. In: IEEE Computer Society Conference on Computer Vision and Pattern Recognition, vol. 1, pp. 886–893 (2005)

8. Epshtein, B., Ofek, E., Wexler, Y.: Detecting text in natural scenes with stroke width transform. In: 2010 IEEE Conference on Computer Vision and Pattern Recognition (CVPR), pp. 2963–2970 (2010)

9. Jung, K., In Kim, K., Jain, A.K.: Text information extraction in images and video: a survey. Pattern recognition 37(5), 977–997 (2004)

10. Lee, C., Jung, K., Kim, H.: Automatic text detection and removal in video sequences. Pattern Recognition Letters 24(15), 2607–2623 (2003)

11. Liang, J., Doermann, D., Li, H.: Camera-based analysis of text and documents: a survey. International Journal on Document Analysis and Recognition 7(2), 84–104 (2005)

12. Mikolajczyk, K., Tuytelaars, T., Schmid, C., Zisserman, A., Matas, J., Schaffalitzky, F., Kadir, T., Gool, L.: A comparison of affine region detectors. International Journal of Computer Vision 65(1), 43–72 (2005)

13. Pan, Y., Hou, X., Liu, C.: A hybrid approach to detect and localize texts in natural scene images. IEEE Transactions on Image Processing (99), 1–1 (2011)

14. Shahab, A., Shafait, F., Dengel, A.: Icdar 2011 robust reading competition challenge 2: Reading text in scene images. In: 2011 International Conference on Document Analysis and Recognition (ICDAR), pp. 1491–1496. IEEE (2011)

15. Shivakumara, P., Phan, T., Tan, C.: A laplacian approach to multi-oriented text detection in video. IEEE Transactions on Pattern Analysis and Machine Intelligence 33(2), 412–419 (2011)

16. Ye, Q., Huang, Q., Gao, W., Zhao, D.: Fast and robust text detection in images and video frames. Image and Vision Computing 23(6), 565–576 (2005)

17. Zhang, J., Kasturi, R.: Extraction of text objects in video documents: Recent progress. In: 8th IAPR International Workshop on Document Analysis Systems, DAS 2008, pp. 5–17. IEEE (2008)

18. Fukunaga, K., Hostetler, L.: The estimation of the gradient of density function, with applications in pattern recognition. IEEE Transactions on Information Theory 21(1), 32–40 (1975)

19. Zhang, Z., Liang, X., Ganesh, A., Ma, Y.: Tilt: transform invariant low-rank textures. In: Computer Vision–ACCV 2010, pp. 314–328 (2011)

20. Kimmel, R., Zhang, C., Bronstein, A.M., Bronstein, M.M.: Are MSER features really interesting? IEEE Transactions on Pattern Analysis and Machine Intelligence (2011)

Semantic Interpretation of Novelty in Images Using Histograms of Oriented Gradients

Nicolas Alt*, Werner Maier, Qing Rao, and Eckehard Steinbach

Institute for Media Technology
Technische Universität München
80333 München, Germany
http://www.lmt.ei.tum.de/

Abstract. An approach for the semantic interpretation of image-based novelty in real-world environments is presented. We measure novelty using the concept of pixel-based surprise, which quantifies how much a new observation changes the robot's current probabilistic appearance model of the environment. The corresponding surprise maps are utilized as prior information to reduce the search space of a "Histograms of Oriented Gradients" object detector. Specifically, detection windows are scored and selected using surprise values. Several object classes are simultaneously searched for and learned from a low number of manually taken reference images. Experiments are performed on a human-size robot in a cluttered household environment. Compared to object detection based on a search of the complete image, a 35-fold speed-up is observed. Additionally, the detection performance increases significantly.

Keywords: object class detection, novelty detection, visual attention.

1 Introduction

Class-level object detection in natural images is an important task for many robotics applications. It is crucial for an intelligent robot to understand the semantics of its environment for problems such as action planning, navigation or grasping. Additionally, robotic systems need to perform these tasks rapidly, reliably and sometimes with limited computing power.

The variability of appearance within one object class is typically large and difficult to model. For instance, mugs, while following a general "shape idea", come with many different shapes and textures, yet they must all be classified as the same object class. Inner and outer gradients have been shown to be good cues for the object class detection problem. One popular approach is "Histograms of Oriented Gradients" (HOG) [1], which we use in our work. Several extensions have been proposed for HOG, such as pairing of spatially separated features in

---

* This work has been supported, in part, within the DFG excellence initiative research cluster *Cognition for Technical Systems – CoTeSys*, see also www.cotesys.org.

C.-Y. Su, S. Rakheja, H. Liu (Eds.): ICIRA 2012, Part III, LNAI 7508, pp. 427–436, 2012.

[2]. Another popular method for object detection is the Viola-Jones detector, which uses Haar-like features [3].

In many robotic applications a fast and reliable detection of new, appearing or changing objects is of interest. Static scene content, on the other hand, often does not demand immediate action. For instance, humans would expect from a domestic robot to detect changes quickly and react accordingly, possibly even to pre-plan trajectories for a future object-related task. Another example is a clean-up robot which needs to detect objects in a room that are in a wrong or unexpected place. Depending on the object class, a corresponding action would be triggered – such as grasping the object and moving it to a class-specific designated storage location. In this work, we use surprise detection [4,5] as a scene change detector in mobile robotic applications and integrate it as prior information into the object detection process. Novelty is detected using a probabilistic model of the robot's environment which allows for a realistic prediction of its appearance, based on the robot's past perception. This allows us to limit the search space of the object class detector and hence reduce the computational complexity and the robot's reaction time.

Our contribution in this paper is the rapid semantic interpretation of novel scene content. We show how object detection based on HOG can be improved both in speed and robustness when a prior about scene change is introduced. The prior reduces the search space adaptively, depending on the surprising scene content. In this work, surprise maps are used as a prior, but the approach is also applicable to other detectors for local change, attention or saliency. Additionally, we describe a training method which builds a large sample database from a low number of natural object pictures.

The remainder of the paper is structured as follows: In the following section, we review related work and introduce existing methods which we adopt in our approach. Sec. 3 explains the proposed method for semantic interpretation. Before we conclude this work, we present experiments for a household robot scenario in Sec. 4.

2   Related Work

HOG was originally proposed by Dalal and Triggs [1] for pedestrian detection, but showed good performance as a versatile object class detector. In short, the descriptor is calculated on a gradient image which is subdivided into a dense grid of uniformly spaced cells of size 8×8. Local contrast normalization is applied to a group of cells. Within a cell, each pixel votes for one of nine gradient orientation bins, weighted with the respective gradient magnitude. An object covers multiple cells (e.g. in a 128×64 window), yielding a descriptor which is a concatenation of all corresponding histograms. During detection, the window is sliding over the test image in steps of 8 pixels and the obtained descriptor is classified into object or non-object using a support vector machine (SVM) classifier [6]. In order to be able to detect objects at different scales, the process is typically applied on a multi-resolution (scale-space) representation of the image.

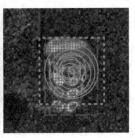

Fig. 1. One of the frames from the experiments with corresponding surprise map (cropped). Scene change was triggered by adding a new object, the white mug. The overlapping windows of high surprise values (red) do not cover the entire object, but are still connected to one region (surrounded by dashed red line). The HOG detection window with the highest score $\mathcal{S}_W$ is outlined with a green dashed line. More windows with highest scores are indicated by green circles, which show center locations and scales.

Due to the high number of detection windows and the large feature size, HOG detection can be time-consuming, especially when combined with a non-linear classifier. Several methods have been suggested to reduce both the number of detection windows and the size of the feature vector for one window. The former can be tackled by selecting windows sparsely in the image around feature points, as discussed in a recent study in the context of action recognition [7]. Our approach for window selection takes advantage of an additional "out-of-band" side channel, the surprise detection, and selects densely spaced windows within a limited image region. Therefore the two approaches are complementary. The authors of [7] note that sparse sampling generally reduces the detection performance. Our approach does not suffer from this problem, as we retain dense sampling in a local region. In addition, it is a common approach to reduce the size of feature vectors with feature selection techniques. For instance, the most relevant features can be identified during the SVM learning process, see [8].

The detection of surprising scene content is a major cue for attentional control. A computational model for measuring the surprise level of visual stimuli is presented in [9]. This approach is based on statistical models of the firing rates of neurons in the early visual cortex. A new visual stimulus which changes the prior models inferred over time leads to elevated surprise values. A method for surprise detection from the field of robotics is proposed in [10]. New landmarks are detected along a mobile robot's path by identifying new local image features in a probabilistic approach. In contrast to the feature-based environment representation in [10], a realistic appearance representation is used for surprise detection as a prior model of the environment in [5]. This representation is appropriate for modeling objects with complex appearance like glasses. Together with the extension towards illumination invariance in [11], a robot is able to robustly detect novelty in an observation and to distinguish relevant changes from irrelevant changes, e.g. caused by varying lighting conditions.

3   Semantic Interpretation of Novelty

The proposed approach consists of an offline stage where detectors are trained for pre-defined object classes. Then, during the detection phase, we search for novelty in the scene caused by new objects using surprise maps. These maps are calculated from the current camera image and an internal scene model. HOG detection is applied to the camera image in regions with a high surprise score, using the previously learned models.

3.1   Object Model Training

For offline training of a detector, a large number of positive and negative sample images is required. As there is no suitable image database for all object classes used, we generate our own object database: Around 20 reference pictures are taken from different viewpoints of one or several objects for each class shown in Fig. 2. The viewpoint range covers about 140° around the vertical axis of the object and 3 different heights. Thanks to a blue background it is possible to generate a mask and to automatically extract the foreground object. Model properties (M_*) are extracted from all masks of one class, namely the mean and standard deviation of the masks' areas, widths, heights and centroids.

Fig. 2. Object classes used in the experiments

The low number of manually generated reference pictures is augmented to a large set of positive training samples as follows: The foreground object in the reference picture is extracted, scaled down and transformed with a homography that is obtained by randomly moving the corners of the bounding box by $\frac{1}{8}$ of the object size. Next, noise and a random brightness shift is added. Like that, over-specific SVM models can be avoided. Finally, the object is pasted onto a random background image, keeping a margin of at least 8 pixels around the object. The size of the training image is pre-defined for each class and at least 64 pixels in width and height. This process is repeated for each reference picture with arbitrary background images until 1200 samples are generated. As negative samples, we take 12000 images from an object-free background database. These parameters are chosen similar to those of [1].

For each positive and negative sample, the HOG descriptor is calculated as outlined in Sec. 2. The descriptor elements are used as features for training an

SVM model using *libsvm* [12]. Optimal kernel parameters (C, γ) are found by exhaustive search and cross-validation. First, a linear kernel is used, as suggested by [1] because of speed considerations. Second, we also work with a radial basis function (*rbf*) kernel, which allows for non-linear separation boundaries, but also requires much more computational time. Runtime can be considerably reduced when only using a subset of the features space. Therefore, we select the best features according to the F-score [8], which is a simple yet effective approach to measure how well a feature discriminates between positive and negative samples. The feature size for a typical HOG window is in the range of 3000 – 6000. As discussed in Sec. 4, we found that a reasonable runtime below 1s can be obtained with a feature dimension of 512, which still allows for a good detection performance.

3.2 Surprise Detection

The detection of novelty (or changes in the scene) in this work is based on a probabilistic representation of the environment's appearance which is inferred from images captured by a moving camera [5]. This representation is inspired by image-based scene representations [13] used in computer graphics as realistic models of the complex appearance of real-world environments. Similar to image-based scene models the luminance and chrominance of the environment are represented at dense reference viewpoints. While image-based representations provide a static model of the scene, this representation accounts for the uncertainty which arises from inconsistent color values captured in dynamic parts of the environment over time. To this end, the luminance and chrominance at a viewpoint are modeled by probability distributions. For the interpolation of the probabilistic priors at intermediate views, a depth map is stored for each reference view as well as its pose.

Surprise, as proposed in [5], quantifies how much the luminance and chrominance in a newly captured image change these prior distributions. We refer to the surprise associated with a captured image as *surprise map*. As shown in [5], surprise detection is more tolerant to small modeling errors (pose inaccuracies, erroneous depth estimates) than change detection based on the difference image between a new camera image and a virtual image rendered from an image-based environment representation.

3.3 Object Class Detection

Surprise Preprocessing. In general, the surprise map does not show the exact shape of the object, so it cannot be directly used for object detection. For instance, in case of a similar appearance of object and background, it may exhibit gaps, see Fig. 1. Similarly, there may be artifacts caused by shadows or scene changes not directly caused by the object. Additionally, small movement in the scene or an inaccurate pose estimation results in artifacts along edges.

To mitigate these effects, preprocessing is applied to the surprise maps. Spurious pixels or edges are removed by image dilation. Then, similar to the cell partitioning in HOG, the surprise map is subdivided into overlapping quadratic windows of size 8×8 spaced 4 pixels apart. Surprise values are summed up in each window, yielding a *surprise energy* $\mathcal{E}$. The summation is efficiently implemented using integral images [3]. Using surprise energy increases the stability against remaining spurious elements and simplifies the identification of regions with high surprise values: We identify surprise regions by connecting neighboring windows with $\mathcal{E} \geq \theta$. Due to the windowing, the threshold is rather uncritical – here, $\theta = \frac{1}{4}\mathcal{E}_{max}$ is used. Ideally, there is only a single region which corresponds to the new object. If additional regions are mistakenly detected, the performance degrades only slightly.

HOG Detection. A scale-space representation of the input image is required to detect objects at different sizes or levels of detail. It is generated by repeatedly down-sizing the input image by a certain scale factor. Like that, objects that appear at the same or a larger size as during training or larger can be detected. It is beneficial to apply training at the smallest possible scale to keep the descriptor dimension low. We use 16 levels in the scale-space with a scale factor of 1.05, resulting in a "zoom-out" factor of 2.2.

HOG detection windows in classic approaches cover the entire search space (x-y-scale) densely in an overlapping fashion. We propose to score each window on how well it fits to the prior given by the surprise region(s), assuming that the deviations between the window's and the prior's centroid position $(\delta x, \delta y)$ and scaling $(s = \sqrt{M_{area}/\text{surprise area}})$ follow a normal distribution:

$$\mathcal{S}_W = e^{-\frac{\delta x^2}{2\sigma_x^2}} \cdot e^{-\frac{\delta y^2}{2\sigma_y^2}} \cdot e^{-\frac{(s-1)^2}{2\sigma_s^2}}$$

The σ-values denote how much deviation is acceptable or expected and depend on the model properties $(M_\star, \text{Sec. 3.1})$ as follows: $\sigma_x = \frac{1}{2}M_{width} + M_{\sigma,x}$, σ_y respectively and $\sigma_s = 2\sqrt{1 + M_{\sigma,area}/M_{area}} - 1$ (as the uncertainty in scale is largest). Only windows in proximity to surprise regions need to be evaluated.

In this work, we test at least the 100 best windows and all windows with $\mathcal{S}_W > 0.9^3$. However, the window scores allow for several window selection strategies, depending on system design and constrains:

– For best detection performance, all windows down to a certain score are tested. The number of windows and thus the computation time will vary, depending both on object properties as well as the surprise prior.
– Real-time systems test as many windows as possible in a given time frame. Scoring makes sure that the system focuses on the most likely windows.
– For systems with low computational power, the number of detection windows is chosen very low. Together with a simple change detection, such as background subtraction, this allows for fast object class detection in simple environments on such low-end systems.

HOG-based object detection is performed on the camera image within the identified windows. The size of a detection window and thus the dimensionality of the HOG features is defined during training on a per-class basis. For each window, one HOG descriptor is extracted as outlined in Sec. 2 and classified by all SVMs trained in Sec. 3.1. The classifiers yield binary decisions (object/non-object) and a probability score. For each object class, the positive result with the highest probability $\mathcal{S}_{Dp}$ is kept. True positives are usually confirmed by windows neighboring in scale and location, so additionally, the number of decisions with $p > 0.5$ is counted and normalized to $[0; 1]$, yielding $\mathcal{S}_{D\#}$.

4 Experiments and Results

Experimental Setup. The proposed detector is tested under real-world conditions with a human-size robot operating in a cluttered household environment which consists of several textured static objects placed on a table, see Fig. 1. As a preparative step, an environment model is learned (Sec. 3.2) which serves as the basis for surprise map generation: An unexpected change of the environment triggers surprise in the respective region. The acquisition of an environment model could be performed simultaneously with detection, but we decided to separate the process for a clearer analysis. Next, the robot drives around the table recording an image sequence while a human successively adds and removes objects of the classes depicted in Fig. 2. The groundtruth class is known for each frame by manual labeling.

Fig. 3. Some of the ca. 1400 testing images used in the experiments. The generality of the detector is verified by using different poses and instances for an object class, as shown here for mugs and horses.

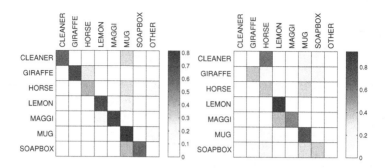

Fig. 4. Left: Confusion matrix of the proposed detector with an *rbf-512* kernel for a threshold value of 0.5. Rows correspond to the groundtruth class, while columns show the detected class. Right: The standard HOG detector generally shows a lower detection performance, especially for the classes *cleaner, horse* and *soapbox*. Note that some of the objects used in our experiments have similar shape features and are thus hard to distinguish.

Detection Results. The detection scores $(\mathcal{S}_{Dp}, \mathcal{S}_{D\#})$ obtained for each object class in each frame are combined by a weighted sum with weights $(0.7, 0.3)$ and analyzed as follows: In a first step, a single object class is detected per image by choosing the best score above a certain threshold, see Fig. 3. If there is no detector above the threshold, the detection result is empty ("other"). This results in the confusion matrix depicted in Fig. 4, which shows the rate of detection for the entire test sequence. Rows correspond to groundtruth classes, while columns stand for the detected class. The diagonal is clearly dominant for all classes, which means that the correct object class is detected with a high confidence after only one or a few observations.

Second, Fig. 5 shows the detection-rate over the number of false positives per image (FPPI). In [1] the false positive rate is given per window, which is not feasible here as the number of windows per image is variable. For a window size of 64×128 and an image of 640×480 in the scale-space introduced above, there are 23500 windows per image. Each detector with a score larger than a threshold θ is counted as a positive, which is why the FPPI rate may be larger than 1. Using the groundtruth class, these positive detections are either classified as true positives or false positives. Sweeping θ from 0 to 1 yields the depicted plots.

The proposed detector requires on average 0.6s per image and object with a linear kernel and 0.7s with an *rbf-512* kernel (512 features) in single-threaded mode on a modern 3.4GHz CPU. Surprise maps are calculated in parallel on a mid-range GPU which requires about 0.1s per frame. Compared to HOG detection on the entire image with *rbf-512*, a 35-fold speed-up is observed. Search space reduction also improves detection performance significantly (e.g. by 0.4@FPPI=0.5 for *soapbox*), as the chance to catch false positives is lowered. The acceleration is contributed to a reduction of the search space to only 250 windows on average. Overall, the performance of the *rbf-512* kernel is slightly better than that of the linear one. Only for some objects, such as *horse* in Fig. 5,

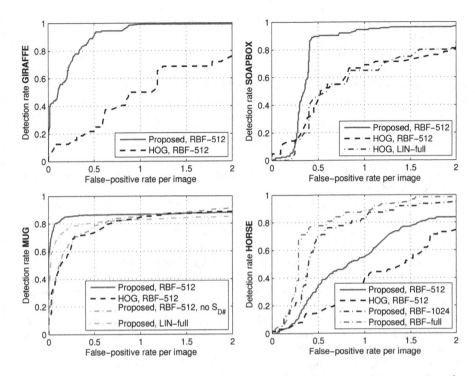

Fig. 5. Detection performance of 4 classes, depicted as the true positive rate over the average number of false positives per image. All plots show the proposed rapid detector with an *rbf-512* kernel (red), which always outperforms the standard HOG detector (black, dashed) due to the integration of the surprise prior. Additionally, examples are given for the influence of some parameters in the three latter plots: With full image search, linear and *rbf-512* kernel perform similarly (*soapbox*). Performance is lower with a linear kernel or when the score $S_{D\#}$ is ignored (*mug*). Larger *rbf*-kernels improve the performance of the rather weak *horse* detector considerably.

a substantial performance gain is seen with the *rbf-1024* kernel that requires a runtime of 1.2s.

5   Conclusion

In this work, we present an object class detector based on HOG that integrates a pixel-based novelty detector for surprising scene content as prior information. This enables rapid interpretation of scene change on a semantic level. Detection runtime and false-positive rate are significantly reduced due to the integration of the prior and the resulting reduction of the search space. A large training set is generated artificially from a small number of object pictures. Still, the classifier generalizes well for other instances of the same object class and for pose variation. The proposed system is targeted for mobile robots, which operate in unstructured environments and need to react quickly and reliably on changes they observe.

In future work, a cascade structure for early rejection of unlikely classes could be implemented in order to keep runtime feasible for a larger number classes. A further speed-up could be achieved by applying a hierarchical search strategy to the selected detection windows.

References

1. Dalal, N., Triggs, B.: Histograms of oriented gradients for human detection. In: Proc. CVPR, San Diego, CA, USA (June 2005)
2. Watanabe, T., Ito, S., Yokoi, K.: Co-occurrence Histograms of Oriented Gradients for Pedestrian Detection. In: Wada, T., Huang, F., Lin, S. (eds.) PSIVT 2009. LNCS, vol. 5414, pp. 37–47. Springer, Heidelberg (2009)
3. Viola, P., Jones, M.: Rapid object detection using a boosted cascade of simple features. In: Proc. CVPR, Kauai, Hawaii, USA (December 2001)
4. Maier, W., Mair, E., Burschka, D., Steinbach, E.: Visual homing and surprise detection for cognitive mobile robots using image-based environment representations. In: Proc. ICRA, Kobe, Japan (May 2009)
5. Maier, W., Steinbach, E.: A probabilistic appearance representation and its application to surprise detection in cognitive robots. IEEE Trans. on Autonomous Mental Development 2(4), 267–281 (2010)
6. Cortes, C., Vapnik, V.: Support-vector networks. Machine Learning 20(3), 273–297 (1995)
7. Wang, H., Ullah, M.M., Klaser, A., Laptev, I., Schmid, C.: Evaluation of local spatio-temporal features for action recognition. In: BMVC, London, United Kingdom (September 2009)
8. Chen, Y., Lin, C.: Combining SVMs with Various Feature Selection Strategies. In: Feature Extraction. STUDFUZZ, vol. 207, pp. 315–324. Springer, Heidelberg (2006)
9. Itti, L., Baldi, P.: Bayesian surprise attracts human attention. Vision Research 49(10), 1295–1306 (2009)
10. Ranganathan, A., Dellaert, F.: Bayesian surprise and landmark detection. In: Proc. ICRA, Kobe, Japan (May 2009)
11. Maier, W., Eschey, M., Steinbach, E.: Image-based object detection under varying illumination in environments with specular surfaces. In: Proc. ICIP, Brussels, Belguim (September 2011)
12. Chang, C., Lin, C.: LIBSVM: a library for support vector machines. ACM Transactions on Intelligent Systems and Technology 2(3) (2011)
13. Shum, H., Chan, S., Kang, S.: Image-Based Rendering. Springer, New York (2007)

Far-Field Terrain Perception Using Max-Margin Markov Networks

Jun Tu[1,*], Chengliang Liu[1], Mingjun Wang[2], Liang Gong[1], and Yanming Li[1]

[1] Shanghai Jiaotong University, Shanghai, China
{roke,chlliu,gongliang_mi,ymli}@sjtu.edu.cn
[2] Ningbo University of Technology, Ningbo, China
{mjwang1104}@126.com

Abstract. Far-field terrain perception plays an important role in performing outdoor robot navigation, such as earlier recognition of obstacles, efficient path planning. Stereo vision is an effective tool to detect obstacles in the near-field, but it cannot provide reliable information in the far-field, which may lead to suboptimal trajectories. This can be settled through the use of machine learning to accomplish near-to-far learning, in which near-field terrain appearance features and stereo readings are used to train models able to predict far-field terrain. In this paper, we propose a near-to-far learning method using Max-Margin Markov Networks (M3N) to enhance long-range terrain perception for autonomous mobile robots. The method not only includes appearance features as its prediction basis, but also uses spatial relationships between adjacent parts. The experiment results show that our method outperforms other existing approaches.

Keywords: robot navigation, stereo vision, machine learning, Max Margin Markov Networks.

1 Introduction

Autonomous robot navigation in unstructured outdoor environments is a challenging area of active research. The navigation task requires identifying traversable paths that allow the robot to reach a goal while avoiding obstacles. General approaches to accomplish the task use ranging sensors such as stereo vision or radar to recover the 3-D shape of the terrain. A variety of features of the terrain such as slopes or discontinuities are then analyzed to determine traversable regions [1-4]. However, ranging sensors such as stereo visions are limited because of nearsightness and could only give reliable obstacle detection to a range of approximately 5 meters [5]. Navigating solely on short-range perception can lead to wrong identification of the labels of terrain in the far field, inefficient path following due to nearsightedness [6].

---

[*] Corresponding author.

C.-Y. Su, S. Rakheja, H. Liu (Eds.): ICIRA 2012, Part III, LNAI 7508, pp. 437–447, 2012.
© Springer-Verlag Berlin Heidelberg 2012

To solve the problem of nearsightness, near-to-far-learning-based, long-range perception approaches are developed, which collect both appearances and stereo information from the near-field regions as inputs for training appearance-based models and then applies these models in the far field in order to predict safe terrain and obstacles far from the robot where stereo readings are unavailable [7-10]. Dahlkamp, H., *et al.* [7] used a pose estimation system with sensor information from a laser range finder to identify a nearby superpixel of drivable surface at first. Then they constructed appearance-based models by using this superpixel to find the drivable surface outward into the far range. Bajracharya, M., *et al.* [8] proposed a system which is composed of two learning algorithms: a short-range, geometry-based local terrain classifier that learns from very few proprioceptive examples; and a long-range, image-based classifier that learns from geometry-based classification and continuously generalizes geometry to the appearance. Happold, M., *et al.* [9] proposed a method for classifying the traversability of terrain by combining unsupervised learning of color models that predict scene geometry with supervised learning of the relationship between geometric features and the traversability. In their work, a neural network is trained offline on hand-labeled geometric features computed from the stereo data. An online process learns the relationship between color and geometry, enabling the robot to assess the traversability of far regions with little range information by estimating the geometry from the color of the scene and passing this to the neural network. Procopio, M.J., *et al.* [10] proposed a near-to-far learning approach through the use of classifier ensembles that allow terrain models trained on data seen at different points in time to be preserved and referenced later.

Fig. 1. A challenging navigating scene

Almost all the appearance-based methods assume that the near-field mapping from the appearance to traversability is the same as the far-field mapping. However, there exists mapping deviation which is shown in Fig. 1. Fig. 1 is a navigating scene taken from the natural datasets made by the DARPA LAGR (Learning Applied to Ground Vehicle) program [6]. We see that the tops of the hay bales looks very like the shadows. It illustrates that in a challenging navigating scene, terrain regions with different class labels may appear very similar to each other due to varying lighting condition and complex terrain geometry. We called this phenomenon mapping deviation which can easily confuse the vision system of robots.

Support vector machines (SVM) are popularly used in near-to-far terrain classification [8]. In pattern recognition, support vector machines (SVM) have been proved impressive successes on a broad range of tasks, including image classification, document categorization and so on. A great success of SVM is its ability to allow the classifier to exploit a very high-dimensional feature space by using kernels. Strong generalization guarantee is an important attribute of SVM, which is derived from the margin-maximizing properties of the learning algorithm. However, SVMs cannot help us to label a set of inter-related instances. So SVMs cannot solve mapping deviation. To deal with mapping deviation, structured classification may be a better way. Therefore, the probabilistic graphical models such as hidden Markov model (HMM) [11] or conditional random field (CRF) [12-14] can be used. The advantage of the probabilistic approaches is that they can exploit the correlations between the different labels, often resulting in significant improvements in accuracy for inter-related instances. Though the probabilistic approaches have this advantage, they do not usually achieve the same level of generalization accuracy as SVM. Moreover, they are not associated with generalization bounds comparable to those of margin-based classifiers. In 2004, Taskar, B. *et al.* [15] proposed maximum margin Markov networks (M3N), which unify the frameworks of the probabilistic graphical models and SVM, and combine the advantages of both. In M3N, a log-linear Markov network is defined over a set of label variables; this network allows us to represent the correlations between these label variables. Therefore, in this paper, we apply the M3N in our study.

The remainder of this paper is as follows. We present a brief review of the algorithm of the M3N in Section 2. In Section 3, generation of samples for M3N is given including image segmentation, visual word construction and feature determination. In Section 4, we provide the experimental results and our discussion. Finally, we make conclusion in Section 5.

2   Max Margin Markov Networks

Given instance $S = \{(x^{(i)}, y^{(i)} = t(x^{(i)}))\}_{i=1}^{m}$ drawn from a fixed distribution $D_{X \times Y}$, where $Y = Y_1 \times ... \times Y_l$ with $Y_i = \{y_1, ..., y_k\}$, considering multi-label classification. The M3N uses a CRF to parameterize in a factored way the conditional distribution $P(y \mid x)$ shown in Eq. (1)

$$P(y \mid x) \propto \exp(w^T F(x, y)) \tag{1}$$

The corresponding classifier is

$$h_w(x) = \arg\max_{y} w^T F(x, y) \tag{2}$$

In structured classification, $F(x, y)$ is defined as a sum of features

$$F_k(x, y) = \sum_{(i, j) \in E} F_k(x, y_i, y_j) \tag{3}$$

Features may often be defined as $F_k(x, y_i, y_j) = p_k(y_i, y_j)\phi^{ij}(x)$, where $p_k(y_i, y_j)$ is a selector function and $\phi^{ij}(x)$ is a kernel function.

Follow the work in [15], the margin used in M3N is the difference between the values of the discriminant for the true label with the value of the best runner up. So, the max-margin framework for M3N thus becomes:

$$\begin{aligned}
&\operatorname*{minimise}_{w, \xi} && \frac{1}{2}\|w\|^2 + C\sum_{x \in S} \xi_x \\
&\text{subject to} && w^T \Delta F_x(y) \geq \Delta t_x(y) - \xi_x, \quad \forall x \in S, \; \forall y
\end{aligned} \tag{4}$$

where $\Delta F_x(y) = F(x, y^P) - F(x, y)$, and $\Delta t_x(y) \triangleq \sum_{i=1}^{n} I\{y_i \neq y_i^P\}$, the number of individual errors, is defined as the loss function. ξ_x is the slack variable.

The dual formulation of Eq. (4) with variables $\alpha_x(y)$ is

$$\begin{aligned}
&\text{maximize} && \sum_{x, y} \alpha_x(y)\Delta t_x(y) - \frac{1}{2}\left\|\sum_{x, y} \alpha_x(y)\Delta F_x(y)\right\|^2 \\
&\text{subject to} && \sum_{y} \alpha_x(y) = C, \forall x; \; \alpha_x(y) \geq 0, \; \forall x, y
\end{aligned} \tag{5}$$

Then the marginal variables are defined as follows

$$\begin{aligned}
\mu_x(y_i, y_j) &= \sum_{y \sim [y_i, y_j]} \alpha_x(y), \quad \forall (i, j) \in E, \forall y_i, y_j, \; \forall x \\
\mu_x(y_i) &= \sum_{y \sim [y_i]} \alpha_x(y), \quad\quad \forall i, \forall y_i, \; \forall x
\end{aligned} \tag{6}$$

Finally, the Quadratic Programming (QP) for M3N is

$$\begin{aligned}
&\text{maximize} && \sum_{x} \sum_{i, y_i} \mu_x(y_i)\Delta t_x(y_i) - \\
&&& \frac{1}{2} \sum_{x, x'} \sum_{\substack{(i, j) \\ y_i, y_j}} \sum_{\substack{(g, h) \\ y_g, y_h}} \mu_x(y_i, y_j)\mu_{x'}(y_g, y_h)f_x(y_i, y_j)^T f_{x'}(y_g, y_h) \\
&\text{subject to} && \sum_{y_i} \mu_x(y_i, y_j) = \mu_x(y_j); \\
&&& \sum_{y_i} \mu_x(y_i) = C; \quad \mu_x(y_i, y_j) \geq 0
\end{aligned} \tag{7}$$

The variables w can be computed as follows

$$w = \sum_x \sum_{i=1}^{l} \sum_{y_i, y_{i+1}} \mu_x(y_i, y_{i+1}) \Delta F_x(y_i, y_{i+1})$$ (8)

To solve the M3N optimization problem in Eq. (7), Sequential Minimal Optimization (SMO) [16], one of the fastest algorithms for large scale problems when training SVM, is used. However, due to lack of space, we do not give the detail information here. Readers may refer to [15] and [17].

3   Sample Generation

3.1   Image Segmentation

Most near-to-far approaches [8-10] incorporate patch-level operation. However, a patch may include various terrain class., which is not suitable for classification. So, we segment the image into various superpixels, following the work of [18]. A superpixel is a set of neighboring pixels. Fig. 2 shows the superpixel representation of an image. In our implementation, we only use cliques with two vertices for M3N application. See in Fig. 2, two adjacent superpixels forms a clique, like CA and AB.

Fig. 2. Superpixel representation

Each superpixel produces one appearance feature vector. Each element of the feature vector is an appearance feature. In our implementation, 2D normalized color histogram, computed using $r = R / (R + G + B)$ and $g = G / (R + G + B)$ with 16×16 bins, is selected as the appearance features. The use of the r-g color space over the raw RGB color space offers more lighting independence and a smaller feature length, and the histogram captures a basic notion of texture [9].

Readers may refer to [12] for the generation of training samples and testing samples.

3.2   Visual Word Construction

As the appearance features are sensitive to noise [19], we do visual vocabulary construction to assign a word to each superpixel. This relates to the state-of-the-art bag of words [20]. Usually, K-means [21] is employed to cluster the image features to create words. Each cluster got by K-means is recognized as a word. All words form a dictionary. However, K-means requires us to predetermine the cluster number K. We use the method proposed by Ray, S., et al. [22] to automatically determine the number of clusters.

Fig. 3 shows the result of visual word construction for the image in Fig. 2. Each color represents a visual word.

Fig. 3. Result of visual word construction

3.3   Features for M3N

To do M3N for image classification, we need to determine the features, i.e. F_k for M3N. It is known that F_k consists of a selector function $p_k(y_i, y_j)$ and a kernel function $\phi^{ij}(x)$. In our implementation, the popular Gaussian kernels are employed. Then, we need to define the selector function for each feature. Because we use M3N to label inter-related samples, the features used should be composed of individual features that describe the compatibility of a superpixel to a particular label and interaction features that describe the relationship between neighboring nodes. Before giving the definition of the selector functions, we denote several events as follows:

A1: the label of the current node is 0 (GROUND)
A2: the label of the current node is 1 (OBSTACLES)
A3: the label of the other node of the edge is 0
A4: the label of the other node of the edge is 1

B1: the word of the current node is $'c_i'$

B2: the word of the other node of the edge is $'c_j'$

Eq. (9) gives the selector functions of individual features; Eq. (10) gives the selector functions of interaction features.

$$p_1^{ind} = I(\text{if B1, then A1}) \quad \forall i$$

$$p_2^{ind} = I(\text{if B1, then A2}) \quad \forall i \tag{9}$$

$$p_1^{int} = I(\text{if B1 and B2, then A1 and A3}) \quad \forall i,j$$

$$p_2^{int} = I(\text{if B1 and B2, then A1 and A4}) \quad \forall i,j$$

$$p_3^{int} = I(\text{if B1 and B2, then A2 and A3}) \quad \forall i,j \tag{10}$$

$$p_4^{int} = I(\text{if B1 and B2, then A2 and A4}) \quad \forall i,j$$

where $I(\bullet)$ is an indicator function.

4 Experiment

4.1 Datasets

The datasets used in this paper are taken from logged field tests conducted by DARPA evaluators [23]. Overall, three scenarios are considered. Each scenario is associated with two distinct image sequences, each representing a different lighting condition. Each dataset consists of a 100-frame hand-labeled image sequence. Each image was manually labeled, with each pixel being placed into one of three classes: Obstacle, Groundplane, or Unknown. If it was difficult for a human to tell what a certain area of an image was, then that region was labeled as Unknown. Each frame in the datasets has a MAT file. Each MAT file has the raw RGB image as well as the disparity information. Also included in the MAT file is an integer "mask" of the image indicating a pixel-wise labeling: 0 means ground plane, 1 means obstacle, and 2 means "this pixel was not labeled by a human. Unlabeled areas may be regions for which the terrain class was hard to tell or they may be "don't care" (e.g., sky).

4.2 Baseline Algorithm

The baseline algorithm we used is the SMINE algorithm (single model per image, nonensemble) described in [10]. SMINE can be used with any underlying classification algorithm in long-range terrain perception. We use the nonensemble method SMINE because we only want to know whether M3N could outperform the traditional SVM used in [9].

4.3   Performance Metrics

Precision and recall are used as the performance metrics in out experiment. Eq. (11) and Eq. (12) gives the definition of precision and recall.

$$Precision = \frac{\text{Number of pixels correctly identified as Label A}}{\text{total number of pixels identified as label A}} \times 100\% \tag{11}$$

$$Recall = \frac{\text{Number of pixels correctly identified as Label A}}{\text{total number of pixels with Label A}} \times 100\% \tag{12}$$

4.4   Results and Discussion

The parameter of our method is the width σ of the Gaussian kernel. According to our experiments, it is found that when σ is below 0.01, our method performs the best. So, in this paper, we set σ to 0.005.

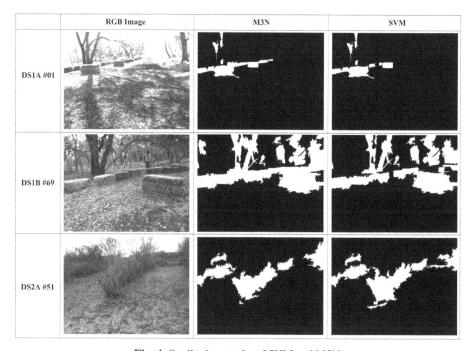

Fig. 4. Qualitative results of SVM and M3N

In Fig. 4, we compare the qualitative results of SVM with those of M3N. The left columns show the original RGB images (DS1A #01, DS1B #69 and DS2A #51), the mid columns are the labeling results of M3N, and the right columns are the result of SVM. White regions of the classification results indicate the ground and black regions correspond to obstacles. From Fig. 4, we observe that M3N achieves better results. It is seen that SVM sometimes confuses obstacles with the ground. For examples, in DS1A #01, the stacks in the far-field region have the similar appearance of the shadows in the near-field region. So, SVM labels the stacks as the ground. This will bring about pseudo paths which will guide the robot toward the obstacles until the stereo vision finds that it is a wrong decision. However, M3N can correctly label the stacks as obstacles. This is because M3N learns that the dark regions below the bright ground in the image are traversable and those similar ones above the bright ground are obstacles.

Table 1 gives the quantitative results of SVM and M3N over the six datasets. From Table 1, it is clear that M3N generally outperforms SVM under various combinations of performance metrics and terrain classes. For example, consider the obstacle recall of both algorithms on all datasets, the increased percentages of M3N compared with SVM are 9.7, 7.5, 5.2, 10.3, 1.9 and 5.0 respectively. Such an increase is of great significance for the long-range perception of mobile robots. Another finding is related to the robustness of classifications. Consider the results of DS2A and DS2B, which are logged from the same scenario but in a different day and lighting condition. The difference between obstacle recalls of M3N on DS2A and DS2B is 13.5 while that of SVM is 18.6. In other words, the performance of SVM, based on appearance only, is relatively subject to detailed lighting conditions, compared with M3N. So it can be said that M3N is more robust than SVM with respect to lighting conditions.

Table 1. Quantitative results of SVM and M3N

Datasets	Recall(%)				Precision(%)			
	ground		obstacle		ground		obstacle	
	SVM	M3N	SVM	M3N	SVM	M3N	SVM	M3N
DS1A	94.5	96.9	52.8	62.5	92.8	94.9	63.3	71.2
DS1B	93.4	96.7	56.2	63.7	81.5	86.5	87.2	93.7
DS2A	92.5	94.4	72.3	77.5	86.2	89.2	92.5	95.3
DS2B	97.8	98.3	53.7	64.0	68.5	74.9	95.1	96.4
DS3A	92.4	94.3	91.5	93.4	90.1	93.0	95.6	96.5
DS3B	91.2	93.2	77.2	82.2	83.3	88.6	90.1	92.9

5   Conclusion

In this paper, we apply Max Margin Markov Networks (M3N) to do near-to-far terrain classification. First, the incoming image is segmented into various superpixels. Next, we do clustering to assign a word to each superpixel. Then we put forward the conception of individual features and interaction features and use M3N to do classification. Experimental results show that M3N outperforms traditional used SVM in long-range perception.

In the future, we plan to enhance our M3N with other contexts such as temporal contexts, e.g., the temporal relationship between the current frame and the next. And we will use some ensemble algorithm to enhance M3N.

Acknowledgement. This work is supported by the Agriculture Science Technology Achievement Transformation Fund of Ministry of Science and Technology of the People's Republic of China (No. 2011GB23800022), National Project of Scientific and Technical Supporting Programs of China (No. 2011BAD20B04), and the Natural Science Foundation of Zhejiang Province (Q12F030004).

Reference

1. Matthies, L.: Stereo vision for planetary rovers: Stochastic modelling to near real-time implementation. International Journal of Computer Vision 8(1), 71–91 (1992)
2. Pagnot, R., Grandjean, P.: Fast cross-country navigation on fair terrains. In: IEEE International Conference on Robotics and Automation, vol. 3, pp. 2593–2259 (1995)
3. Singh, S., Simmons, R., Smith, T., Stentz, A., Verma, V., Yahja, A., Schwehr, K.: Recent progress in local and global traversability for planetary rovers. In: IEEE International Conference on Robotics and Automation, vol. 2, pp. 1194–1200 (2000)
4. Rieder, A., Southall, B.: Stereo perception on an off-road vehicle. In: Proc. IEEE Intelligent Vehicle Symposium, vol. 1, pp. 221–226 (2002)
5. Ollis, M., Huang, W.H., Happold, M., Stancil, B.A.: Image-based path planning for outdoor mobile robots. In: IEEE International Conference on Robotics and Automation, pp. 2723–2728 (2008)
6. Jackel, L.D., Krotkov, E., Perschbacher, M., Pippine, J., Sullivan, C.: The DARPA LAGR program: Goals, challenges, methodology, and phase I results. Journal of Field Robotics 23(11-12), 945–973 (2006)
7. Dahlkamp, H., Kaehler, A., Stavens, D., Thrun, S., Bradski, G.: Self-supervised monocular road detection in desert terrain. In: Robotics: Science & Systems (2006)
8. Bajracharya, M., Howard, A., Mathies, L.H., Tang, B., Turmon, M.: Autonomous off-road navigation with end-to-end learning for the LAGR program. Journal of Field Robotics 26(1), 3–25 (2009)
9. Happold, M., Ollis, M., Johnson, N.: Enhancing supervised terrain classification with predictive unsupervised learning. In: Robotics: Science and Systems (2006)
10. Procopio, M.J., Mulligan, J., Grudic, G.: Learning terrain segmentation with classifier ensembles for autonomous robot navigation in unstructured environments. Journal of Field Robotics 26(2), 145–175 (2009)
11. Rabiner, L.R.: A Tutorial on Hidden Markov Models and Selected Applications in Speech Recognition. Proceedings of IEEE 77, 257–286 (1989)
12. Wang, M.J., Zhou, J., Tu, J., Liu, C.L.: Learning Long-range Terrain Perception for Autonomous Mobile Robots. International Journal of Advanced Robotic Systems 7(1), 55–66 (2010)
13. Wang, M.J., Zhou, J., Tu, J., Liu, C.L.: Large-scale conditional random field for natural outdoor scene labeling. Optical Engineering 48(10), 102705(10) (2009)

14. Lafferty, J., McCallum, A., Pereira, F.: Conditional random fields: Probabilistic models for segmenting and labeling sequence data. In: Proc. ICM, vol. 01 (2001)
15. Taskar, B., Guestrin, C., Koller, D.: Max-margin Markov Networks. In: Advances in Neural Information Processing System (2004)
16. Platt, J.C.: Sequential Minimal Optimization: A Fast Algorithm for Training Support Vector Machines. Technical Report MSR-TR-98-14, Microsoft Research, Redmond, Washington (1998)
17. Spengler, A.: Maximum margin Markov networks for XML tag relabelling. Master's thesis, University of Karlsruhe (2005)
18. Felzenszwalb, P., Huttenlocher, D.: Efficient graph-based image segmentation. International Journal of Computer Vision 59(2), 167–181 (2004)
19. Filliat, D.: A visual bag of words method for interactive qualitative localization and mapping. In: Proceedings of the International Conference on Robotics and Automation (ICRA), Rome, Italy (2007)
20. Csurka, G., Dance, C., Fan, L., Williamowski, J., Bray, C.: Visual categorization with bags of keypoints. In: ECCV 2004 Workshop on Statistical Learning in Computer Vision, pp. 59–74 (2004)
21. MacQueen, J.B.: Some Methods for classification and Analysis of Multivariate Observations. In: Proceedings of 5th Berkeley Symposium on Mathematical Statistics and Probability, pp. 281–297. University of California Press (1967)
22. Ray, S., Turi, R.H.: Determination of Number of Clusters in K-Means Clustering and Application in Colour Image Segmentation. In: Proceedings of the 4th International Conference on Advances in Pattern Recognition and Digital Techniques (ICAPRDT 1999), Calcutta, India, pp. 137–143 (1999)
23. Procopio, M.J.: Hand-labeled DARPA LAGR data sets, http://ml.cs.cororado.edu/~procopio/labeledlagrdata/

An Adaptive Trajectory Prediction Method for Ping-Pong Robots

Yifeng Zhang, Rong Xiong*, Yongsheng Zhao, and Jian Chu

State Key Laboratory of Industrial Control Technology, Zhejiang University,
Hangzhou, China
rxiong@iipc.zju.edu.cn

Abstract. Trajectory prediction is a key issue to a ping-pong robot,
many algorithms have been developed. To get more robust and accuracy prediction under different serving conditions, this paper presents a
new prediction method. The proposed method establishes two equivalent
forms of the dynamic model of flying ball, where the discrete form for
state estimation and the continuous form for trajectory prediction. The
two forms share the same parameters' value. According to force analysis,
It is found that the model parameters are deeply related to ball's state
(position, velocity) . So we train the model parameters offline respect
to ball's state, instead of setting them to a constant value. This enables
the model to be adapted accordingly online. Experimental results show
the effectiveness and accuracy of the proposed method for the ball with
different velocities.

Keywords: ping-pong robot, trajectory prediction, adaptive.

1 Introduction

Ping-Pong robot as a classic real-time 'eye-hand' platform is now attracting more
and more researchers. Compared with other sports, the ping-pong ball is moving
fast and the distance/time of flying is very short. To leave enough time for the
robot to act, it is very essential to predict the ball's trajectory effectively and
accurately. Trajectory prediction also has very important significance in many
other applications such as target tracking, space intercept.

Many algorithms have been proposed to predict flight trajectory. R.L. Andersson[2] gave the moving equation based on three significant forces in ball's flight:
gravity, air drag, and the Magnus Effect. But the spin is hardly perceptible and
the author hasn't given the resolution. Z. Zhang et al[14] and Y. Wang et al[12]
gave a more detailed analysis on the aerodynamic model of ball's flight, and gave
the estimated values of forces impacted on. But to simplify the calculation, only
gravity and air drag were applied in their predicting algorithm. Y. Zhang et al[13]
used a model that also considers only gravity and air drag, and the air drag was
simplified to be one-order respected to velocity. They built a linear equation to

---

* Corresponding author.

C.-Y. Su, S. Rakheja, H. Liu (Eds.): ICIRA 2012, Part III, LNAI 7508, pp. 448–459, 2012.
© Springer-Verlag Berlin Heidelberg 2012

describe flight trajectory, then a kalman filter with constant parameters was used to estimate ball's state. F. Miyazaki et al[7][8] built three input-output maps to determine the flight trajectory and paddle hitting command to return the ball to a desired point, the input value is the ball's state, which was calculated by fitting a first-order polynomial in horizontal direction and a second-order polynomial in vertical direction, thus no physical model was used. The spinning influence of objects with sphere shape has also been discussed. A. Nakashima et al[10] and R. Cross[4][5] analyzed the spinning influence of a tennis ball when flying and bouncing. Y. Huang et al[6] analyzed the ping-pong ball's flight model with spinning, and deduced the spinning velocity by observing the offset of the ball's flight trajectory, but it depends on very accurate perceptions and works only when the ball is spinning heavily. By now it is still a very challenge task to predict ball's trajectory accurately under different serving conditions.

This paper focuses on online prediction of ball trajectory. There are two key processes have to be dealt with: estimate current ball's state and predict following flight trajectory. Most of existing implements estimated ball's state by fitting polynomial[7][8][12][14] or by a kalman filter[9][13], and predicted trajectory with discrete model[3][6][12][14] or trained results[7][8][13]. We handle these two processes using a same dynamic model. The model is built through force analysis and have discrete and continuous forms. The discrete form is for state estimation based on discrete position caught by stereo-vision system, and the continuous form is for trajectory prediction. The two forms are equivalent and share the same parameters. Instead of simplifying model parameters to be a constant value, we train the relationships between parameters and ball's state offline, then the parameters can adapt with ball's state online. The vision system is working in 120 fps (frame per second) and the experimental results show the validity and effectiveness of the method proposed.

In the following of this paper, Section 2 gives the frame of adaptive prediction process and defines some importance events in ball's flight. Section 3 describes the two forms of dynamic models based on force analysis. Section 4 describes the whole process of filter and trajectory prediction. In Section 5, the experiments are provided to verify the effectiveness of the proposed method. Finally, a conclusion is given in Section 6.

2   Adaptive Prediction Policies

2.1   The Frame of Adaptive Prediction Process

The frame of adaptive prediction process is shown in Fig. 1. The force impacted on a flying ball and the dynamic model of ball's flight is analyzed first. Then two equivalent forms of flight model are established accordingly, the discrete one is used to estimate current ball's state and the continuous one is used to predict flight trajectory. These two form models share the same model parameters. According to force analysis, the model parameters are deeply related to ball's state. A neural network is applied to train the relationships between model parameters and ball's state. Thus the model parameters can be adapted online, both for estimation and prediction.

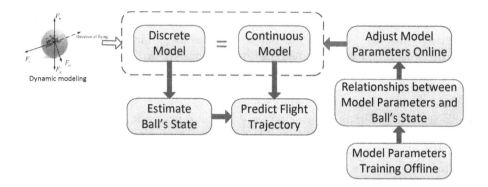

Fig. 1. The frame of model adaption process

2.2   Definition of Ball Events in One Stroke

To make the following explanation clear, we define some "ball events", as shown in Fig. 2. Ball is flying from opponent's court to robot's court. Virtual plane is a standard measurement plane for parameters offline training and online adapting. That means wherever ball is, it have to trace back/forward to the point when it passes through virtual plane to adapt the model. Hit plane is where the robot hits the ball.

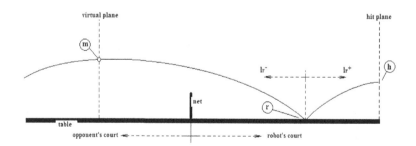

Fig. 2. Definition of ball events

There are three important events in one stroke, and the ball' state on these events is also recorded as following:

- Event (v): ball is passing through the virtual plane with state (S_v, V_v).
- Event (r): ball is bouncing on the table with state (S_r, V_r^-, V_r^+).
- Event (h): ball is hit back by robot with state (S_h, V_h).

S is ball's position and V is velocity, V_r^-, V_r^+ are velocities before and after bounce. The flight trajectory can be split into two parts based on event (r). Donate l_r^- is trajectory before bouncing and l_r^+ is trajectory after bouncing.

3 Models of Ball's Flight

3.1 Dynamic Model of Flying Ball

The ball flying in the air is a typical aerodynamic problem, based on the analysis of fluid mechanics. There are four main forces impacted on the ball: gravity F_g, buoyancy F_b, air drag F_r, and Magnus force F_m. Fig. 3 shows the direction of each force, and the detailed calculation can be refer to literature[14].

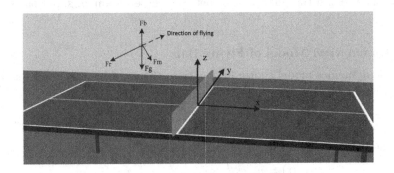

Fig. 3. Force analysis of flying ball

The world coordinate is also defined in Fig. 3. It is reasonable to assume that the movements along x y z are independent with each other, and the dynamics of the movements along x and y are same. So only the dynamics of movements along x and z are discussed here.

Donate a_x and a_z are respectively the accelerations of ping-pong ball along axis x and z. According to the force analysis above, the dynamic model along axis x and axis z are

$$ma_x = -F_{rx} + F_{mx} = -\frac{1}{2}k\rho_a A v_x{}^2 + \frac{1}{2}k\rho_a Al\omega v_x \tag{1}$$

$$ma_z = -F_{rz} - F_{mz} + F_b - F_g = -\frac{1}{2}k\rho_a A v_z{}^2 - \frac{1}{2}k\rho_a Al\omega v_z + \rho_a V g - mg \tag{2}$$

v_x and v_z are respectively the velocities of ball along axis x and z, m is the quality of ball, g is acceleration due to gravity, k is the resistance coefficient, ρ_a is the air density, l is the lift coefficient, ω is the angular velocity, A is the cross-sectional area, V is the volume of ball. Denote

$$K_x = f(v_x) = \frac{1}{2}k\rho_a A v_x - \frac{1}{2}k\rho_a Al\omega \tag{3}$$

$$K_z = f(v_z) = \frac{1}{2}k\rho_a A v_z + \frac{1}{2}k\rho_a A l\omega \qquad (4)$$

$$F_v = constant = -\rho_a V g + mg \qquad (5)$$

Thus (1) and (2) can be simplified as follows.

$$ma_x = -K_x v_x \qquad (6)$$

$$ma_z = -K_z v_z - F_v \qquad (7)$$

K_x and K_z are variables strongly related to ball's state. And though the parameters m, g, ρ_a, k, l are constant and can be known by data-sheet in advance, but their values are varied in some range and are inaccurate. For example, the value range of ρ_a is usually $1.21 \sim 1.27(kg/m^3)$. So it will significantly influence the precision of prediction if K_x and K_z were set to a constant value. In this paper, we will try to train the relationships between these parameters and ball's state later.

3.2   Kinematical Model of Flying Ball

With the dynamics model shown in equations (6) and (7), we can get the kinematical model of flying ping-pong ball. Denote

$$p_x = -\frac{K_x}{m}, \quad p_z = -\frac{K_z}{m}, \quad q_z = -\frac{F_v}{m}, \qquad (8)$$

The continuous kinematical model can be presented as

$$v_x(t) = v_{x_0} e^{p_x t} \qquad (9)$$

$$v_z(t) = v_{z_0} e^{p_z t} + \frac{q_z}{p_z}(e^{p_x t} - 1) \qquad (10)$$

$$s_x(t) = s_{x_0} + \frac{v_{x_0}}{p_x}(e^{p_x t} - 1) \qquad (11)$$

$$s_z(t) = s_{z_0} + \frac{v_{z_0} + \frac{q_z}{p_z}}{p_z}(e^{p_z t} - 1) - \frac{q_z}{p_z}t \qquad (12)$$

(s_x, s_y, s_z) is the position of the flying ball, $(v_{x_0}, v_{y_0}, v_{z_0})$ and $(s_{x_0}, s_{y_0}, s_{z_0})$ are the initial velocities and positions of the trace.

Considering the perception of vision system is periodical and discrete, there should also be a discrete model to estimate ball's state. With the assuming that the acceleration and the velocity between two sample times is constant, and let the discrete velocity be the position distance.

$$s(i + 1) = s(i) + v(i) \qquad (13)$$

The discrete kinematical model can be presented as

$$v_x(i + 1) = v_x(i)p'_x \qquad (14)$$

$$v_z(i + 1) = v_z(i)p'_z + \frac{q_z}{p_z}(p'_z - 1) \qquad (15)$$

$$s_x(i + 1) = s_x(i) + v_x(i) \qquad (16)$$

$$s_z(i + 1) = s_z(i) + v_{zx}(i) \qquad (17)$$

where

$$p'_x = e^{p_x \Delta t}, \quad p'_z = e^{p_z \Delta t} \tag{18}$$

Δt is the sample period and is known in advance.

These two forms of kinematical model are equivalent and their parameters can be transformed to each other easily. Once we have trained the set of parameters of one model form, the parameters of the other model form are also trained spontaneously.

3.3 Bouncing Model

A significant feature of ping-pong game is that the ball will collide with the table and bounce up before the player hits it. Such a collision involves the degradation of energy which results in the change of velocity, and it will change the flight trajectory of ball dramatically. According to the law of conservation of energy

$$\frac{1}{2}mv^{+2} = \eta^2 \frac{1}{2}mv^{-2} \tag{19}$$

Here η is the coefficient of energy degradation, v^- and v^+ are respectively the velocities before and after collision. We assume that the values of η are varied in x and z axis, thus

$$v_x^+ = \eta_x v_x^-, v_z^+ = \eta_z v_z^-, \tag{20}$$

η_x and η_z are universal in both continuous and discrete model forms. Their values are variable and will be trained later.

4   Training Model Parameters

As discussed in Section 2.2, the entire flight process can be split into three parts based on event(r): flying before bouncing, bouncing, and flying after bouncing. Assuming that parameters of all models are the same in axis x, y, and trajectory l_r^- and l_r^+ share the same flying model but with different parameters. There are eight parameters in all:

- (p_x, p_z, q_z): flying model parameters of l_r^-.
- $(p_{x_2}, p_{z_2}, q_{z_2})$: flying model parameters of l_r^+.
- (η_x, η_z): bouncing model parameters.

To train the model parameters, we have collected 1107 trajectories recorded by high-speed vision system, with various initial positions and velocities served by human and a server machine. For each trajectory, ball's states on event points $(S_v, V_v, S_r, V_r^-, V_r^+, S_h, V_h)$ were fitted through a kalman smoother. Then all the model parameters for this trajectory can be calculated based on these key values using (9) to (12).

Based on (3) and (4), model parameters K_x and K_z are functions of ball velocity and spinning velocity. Since the spinning velocity is hardly perceptible, only relationships between parameters and velocity will be trained. We assume that the ball flight is a Markov process, the model parameters are constant in different points of the same flight trajectory, and are determined by ball's state when it pass through the virtual plane. We collect a large number of parameter pairs: $(V_m - p_x, p_z, q_z)$, $(V_r^- - \eta_x, \eta_z)$, $(V_r^+ - p_{x_2}, p_{z_2}, q_{z_2})$, then all the parameters can be trained by AI learning method. The result of neural network training was shown in Fig. 4.

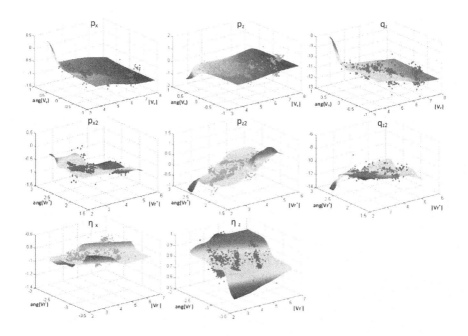

Fig. 4. Model parameters training results by neural network

Fig. 4 illustrates the relationships between model parameters and the input values, and all the model parameters can be determined by (S_v, V_v) through following steps:

1. Get (p_x, p_z, q_z) based on (S_v, V_v) and training result.
2. Predict V_r^- based on $(S_v, V_v, p_x, p_z, q_z)$.
3. Get (η_x, η_z) based on V_r^- and training result.
4. Calculate V_r^+ based on (V_r^-, η_x, η_z).
5. Get $(p_{x_2}, p_{z_2}, q_{z_2})$ based on V_r^+ and training result.

5   Trajectory Prediction

5.1   Estimation of Ball's State

As discussed in section2, the perception is discrete and periodical. A kalman filter is used to estimate the ball state on every sample time. Based on the discrete kinematical model, the state function is presented as follows:

$$\begin{bmatrix} s_x(i+1) \\ v_x(i+1) \end{bmatrix} = \begin{bmatrix} 1 & 1 \\ 0 & p'_x \end{bmatrix} \begin{bmatrix} s_x(i) \\ v_x(i) \end{bmatrix} + W_x(i) \tag{21}$$

$$\begin{bmatrix} s_z(i+1) \\ v_z(i+1) \end{bmatrix} = \begin{bmatrix} 1 & 1 \\ 0 & p'_z \end{bmatrix} \begin{bmatrix} s_z(i) \\ v_z(i) \end{bmatrix} + \begin{bmatrix} 0 \\ \frac{q_z}{p_z}(p'_z - 1) \end{bmatrix} + W_z(i) \tag{22}$$

The observation functions are same in different axis and can be presented as:

$$\check{s}(i) = \begin{bmatrix} 1 & 0 \end{bmatrix} \begin{bmatrix} s(i) \\ v(i) \end{bmatrix} + R(i) \tag{23}$$

$\check{s}$ is the raw ball position caught by vision system on each sample time, W_x, W_z are the process noise and R is the observation noise, their values are set in advance based on the analysis of kinematical model process and perception accuracy of vision system.

5.2   Prediction of Ball Flight Trajectory

Once the ball's state of current ball is obtained, the following trajectory can be calculated easily by (9) to (12). Compared with discrete model, the continuous model can provide the entire information of following flight and more accurate bouncing process. There are two key steps in the predict process: adapting model parameters and modifying ball's state when bouncing. The model parameters are updated each time when vision system catches new ball position. To adapt new model parameters, the ball's state should be predicted to or backtracked to the measurement virtual plane to get (S_v, V_v). The steps to calculate model parameters based on (S_v, V_v) are discussed in Section 3.4 and the adapting process is an iterative process to get a set of optimized parameters for current flight.

The collision position on axis z is known as the radius of ping-pong ball. Thus according to

$$s_z(t_{col}) = r = s_0 + \frac{v_0 + \frac{q_z}{p_z}}{p_z}(e^{p_z t_{col}} - 1) - \frac{q_z}{p_z} t_{col} \tag{24}$$

The time of collision t_{col} can be calculated. With the flying model and bouncing model, the bouncing process can be resolved accordingly and the flight after bouncing can also be calculated with new flying model parameters (p_{x2}, p_{z2}, q_{z2}).

6   Experimental Results

Experiments are conducted to verify the models and prediction method proposed. Two PointGrey Grasshopper cameras working in 120fps and 640*480 pixels are used to catch 3D ball position, the maximal error of static localization is 0.9cm. The method proposed works effectively and the time cost is only related to bouncing times, normally less than 0.002ms on PC.

Table 1. Model parameters of two methods used in Fig. 5

K_m	K_{r_x}	K_{r_y}	K_{r_z}	b_x	b_y	b_z	g
\multicolumn{8}{c}{Model parameters of method in [14]}
0.160	0.503	0.752	-0.813	0.107	-0.011	0.322	11.200

p_x	p_z	q_z	p_{x2}	p_{z2}	q_{z2}	η_x	η_z
\multicolumn{8}{c}{Model parameters of method proposed}
0.657	0.218	10.540	0.789	0.311	10.535	0.736	-0.912

Table 2. Error analysis in Fig. 5

		\multicolumn{2}{c}{Method in [14]}	Method proposed without adapting parameters	
		x	y	x	y
prediction error on bouncing point	/mm	x	y	x	y
	average	4.26	10.73	4.29	11.81
	variance	6.11	13.83	6.21	16.39
prediction error on hitting point	/mm	x	y	x	y
	average	48.00	19.90	9.61	13.07
	variance	52.97	27.42	12.00	18.51

Fig. 5 compares the prediction errors on bouncing point and hitting point with the method in [14], which estimates ball's state by fitting polynomial and predicts trajectory using a two-order air drag discrete model. Ball is served with similar initial positions and velocities, the parameters of both methods are fixed to a constant value optimized to this trajectory set, which is given in Table 1. The prediction is executed when ball passing through the virtual plane. These two methods both work well on prediction of bouncing point. But on hitting point, the method proposed works much better because it considers the model change caused by bouncing process. The error analysis is shown in Table 2.

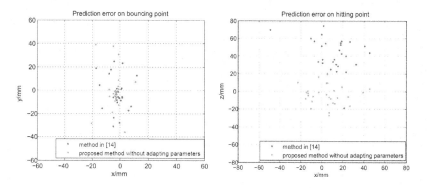

Fig. 5. Prediction errors on bouncing point and hitting point with similar (s_0, v_0)

Table 3. Model parameters of each sample period in Fig. 6

sample period	3	4	5	6
(p_x, p_z, q_z)	0.819,0.169,11.123	0.664,0.245,10.559	0.669,0.260,10.595	0.670,0.262,10.604
$(p_{x_2}, p_{z_2}, q_{z_2})$	0.665,0.330,10.400	0.507,0.149,10.465	0.513,0.144,10.506	0.514,0.143,10.505
η_x, η_z	0.764,-0.903	0.746,-0.920	0.746,-0.919	0.746,-0.918

Table 4. Error analysis in Fig. 7

	Method in [14]		Method proposed without adapting parameters		Method proposed with adapting parameters	
/mm	x	y	x	y	x	y
average	8.72	39.23	6.46	46.82	4.49	9.91
variance	10.34	56.01	11.17	71.78	5.71	12.79

Fig. 6 demonstrates another important feature of the method proposed, parameters are adapted during prediction. The green trajectory is the predicted results of each future sample time, compared with the white trajectory observed and fitted posterior. The prediction process is enabled since the 3rd sample period, using model parameters given in advance. Table 3 list the model parameters of each sample period. Model parameters are adapted since the 4th sample period and dramatically improve the precision of prediction.

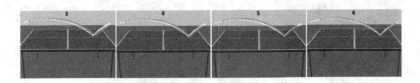

Fig. 6. Prediction results on different sample periods

Fig. 7 compares the prediction errors on bouncing point under different serving conditions, of method proposed with and without adapting model parameters, and the method in [14]. Ball is severed with various initial velocities ($4.37 - 8.32 m/s$), and various initial angles ($3.24 - 20.92\,^\circ$). The prediction is executed when ball passing through the virtual plane. Table 4 shows the error analysis of these three methods. While initial velocity changes, both the method in [14] and the method proposed without adapting parameters works unsatisfactorily. That means fixed parameters would not meet this situation, especially for the model proposed which greatly simplifies the flying model. But while model parameters adapted, the prediction accuracy improved dramatically and fully meets the rally task.

We applied the proposed method to two humanoid ping-pong robots Wu and Kong, and the results suggest that when the hitting point is in robot's valid

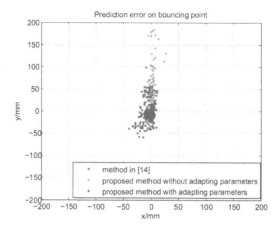

Fig. 7. Prediction errors on bouncing point with varied (s_0, v_0)

movement area, the probability of successfully returning the ball is about 100%. The best record is 88 turns (176 strokes) rally with each other and 145 turns with a human. Fig. 8 shows a scene of robots playing with each other and with human, full video are reachable on the website http:www.youtube.com/watch? v=t_qN3dgYGqE .

Fig. 8. The ping-pong robots Wu and Kong play with each other and with human

7   Conclusion

In this paper, we have discussed a new approach to describe and to predict ball's trajectory. The whole trajectory is split into three parts, and is modeled both in continuous and discrete form, which makes the parameters adapting realizable. The effectiveness and accuracy of this method under various serving conditions is validated by experiments. And it works very well on ping-pong robots to rally with each other and with human.

Acknowledgment. This work was supported by the National Nature Science Foundation of China (Grants No. NSFC: 61075078), and the Key Project of the National 863 plan (Grants No.2008AA042602).

References

1. Acosta, L., Rodrigo, J.J., Mendez, J.A., Marichal, G.N., Sigut, M.: Ping-Pong player prototype. IEEE Robotics & Automation Magazine 10, 44–52 (2003)
2. Andersson, R.L.: Understanding and applying a robot ping-pong player's expert controller. In: IEEE International Conference on Robotics and Automation, vol. 3, pp. 1284–1289 (1989)
3. Chen, X., Tian, Y., Huang, Q., Zhang, W., Yu, Z.: Dynamic model based ball trajectory prediction for a robot ping-pong player. In: IEEE International Conference on Robotics and Biomimetics (ROBIO), pp. 603–608 (2010)
4. Cross, R.: Bounce of a spinning ball near normal incidence. American Journal of Physics 73, 914–920 (2005)
5. Cross, R.: Measurement of horizontal coefficient of restitution for a superball and a tennis ball. American Journal of Physics 70, 482–489 (2001)
6. Huang, Y., Xu, D., Tan, M., Su, H.: Trajectory Prediction of Spinning Ball for Ping-Pong Player Robot. In: IEEE/RSJ International Conference on Intelligent Robots and Systems (IROS), pp. 3434–3439 (2011)
7. Matsushima, M., Hashimoto, T., Takeuchi, M., Miyazaki, F.: A learning approach to robotic table tennis. IEEE Transactions on Robotics 21, 767–771 (2005)
8. Matsushima, M., Hashimoto, T., Miyazaki, F.: Learning to the robot table tennis task - ball control & rally with a human. In: IEEE International Conference on Systems, Man and Cybernetics, vol. 3, pp. 2962–2969 (2003)
9. Mulling, K., Kober, J., Peters, J.: A Biomimetic Approach to Robot Table Tennis. In: IEEE/RSJ International Conference on Intelligent Robots and Systems (IROS), pp. 1921–1926 (2010)
10. Nakashima, A., Ogawa, Y., Kobayashi, Y., Hayakawa, Y.: Modeling of Rebound Phenomenon of a Rigid Ball with Friction and Elastic Effects. In: American Control Conference (ACC), pp. 1410–1415 (2010)
11. Wang, Z., Lampert, M.K., Scholkopf, B., Peters, J.: Learning anticipation policies for robot table tennis. In: IEEE/RSJ International Conference on Intelligent Robots and Systems (IROS), pp. 332–337 (2011)
12. Wang, Y., Sun, L., Liu, J., Yang, Q., Zhou, L., He, S.: A novel trajectory prediction approach for table-tennis robot based on nonlinear output feedback observer. In: IEEE International Conference on Robotics and Biomimetics (ROBIO), pp. 1136–1141 (2010)
13. Zhang, Y., Wei, W., Yu, D., Zhong, C.: A tracking and predicting scheme for ping pong robot. Journal of Zhejiang University-SCIENCE C (Computer & Electronics) 12, 110–115 (2011)
14. Zhang, Z., Xu, D., Tan, M.: Visual Measurement and Prediction of Ball Trajectory for Table Tennis Robot. IEEE Transactions on Instrument and Meansurement 59, 3195–3205 (2010)

A New Method of Stereo Localization
Using Dual-PTZ-Cameras

Jing Xin, Xiaomin Ma, Yi Deng, Ding Liu, and Han Liu

School of Information & Automation, Xi'an University of Technology, 710048, China
{xinj}@xaut.edu.cn

Abstract. To improve the localization accuracy and robustness of the moving 3D-target under the nature scenes, we propose a new target localization method through combining MSER (Maximally Stable Extremal Region) detector with SIFT (Scale Invariant Feature Transform) descriptor into the dual-PTZ-cameras stereo vision system. Firstly, stereo vision rectification is performed on the right-and-left images captured from the dual-PTZ-cameras with different focal lengths using designed Look-up-table(LUT)and BP neural network. Secondly, more high quality affine invariant features are extracted from the rectified images to perform initial matching using affine invariant feature detector and descriptor. Thirdly, erroneous correspondences is detected by RANSAC. Then, robust features matching under the multi-view-point and multi-focal-length is achieved. The localization experimental results of the moving 3-D target in a complex environment show that the proposed method has good localization accuracy and robustness.

Keywords: PTZ cameras, stereo vision correction, MSER detector, SIFT descriptors, 3D target localization.

1 Introduction

The intelligent video surveillance system has been widely used in banking, electricity, transportation, military, etc. It can perform the fast and accurate target localization without human intervention, and give the alarm or provoke other actions in abnormal situation. Most of video surveillance systems adopt monocular or bino-cular static stereo system, but it would not capture enough effective image informa-tion for the moving 3D-target, which will limit its applications. To solve this problem, some stereo system using PTZ (Pan /Tilt /Zoom) cameras are proposed[1]. Compared to the static stereo system, the two PTZ active stereo system can obtain the global and high-resolution images simultaneously by changing the viewpoint and focal length of the PTZ camera. However, robust and accurate feature extraction and stereo matching become more difficult for the dual PTZ active stereo system.

At present, the SIFT[2] algorithm, which is proposed firstly in 1999 and refined in 2004 by Lowe, is usually used for the local features detection and description. It mainly contains two steps. Firstly, a DOG (Difference of Gaussian) detector is used to extract features in the images, secondly, a 128-valued SIFT descriptor is generated to

C.-Y. Su, S. Rakheja, H. Liu (Eds.): ICIRA 2012, Part III, LNAI 7508, pp. 460–472, 2012.

describe the features. The algorithm has good distinctiveness and robustness. It is invariant to the change of the illumination, image noise, rotation, scaling, and small changes of the viewpoint. However, the features detected by DOG detector are not affine invariant. To solve this problem, a new algorithm which combined MSER[3] with SIFT descriptor was presented by Samir in 2011[4], it could extract more high quality affine invariant features. Based on this affine invariant features detector and descriptor, we proposed a new high-precision target localization method using dual PTZ cameras stereo vision system.

The remaining part of this paper is organized as follows. The basic principle of the target localization based on stereo vision is briefly introduced in section 2. The details of our algorithm are described in section 3, where we proposed a robust target localization method using dual PTZ cameras. Some experimental results and analysis are given in Section 4. Section 5 will conclude the paper by discussing the proposed approach and give some improvement issues for the further research.

2   Principle of the Stereo Localization

Consider a stereo vision system with two pinhole cameras shown in Fig. 1.

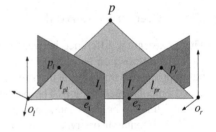

Fig. 1. Schematic diagram of stereo vision system

Suppose a 3D space point P of target is projected into the 2D image plane point $P_l(P_r)$ given by the intersection of image plane $I_l(I_r)$ with the line containing P and optical center $O_l(O_r)$ of the right-and-left cameras. The points P, P_l, P_r, O_l, O_r are all on a single plane. The line between point O_l and point O_r is called as the baseline. The intersection of baseline with image plane, e_1 and e_2 are called as epipole. The conjugate point of P_l in the right image is constrained to lie on a line called the epipolar line (i.e. l_{pr}).The purpose of target localization based on stereo vision system is to get 3-D information of feature points on the target. The whole localization procedure can be described briefly as follow:

Step1: Obtain the camera intrinsic parameters of each camera by camera calibration.

Step2: Find the image coordinates of P_l and P_r by feature extraction and stereo matching.

Step3: Calculate the disparity d of 3D point P between image plane of the right-and-left cameras I_l and I_r by SSD algorithm described in section 3.3.

Step4: Calculate the coordinates $(x_w, y_w, z_w)^T$ of 3D point P in the world reference frame using Eq. (1)

$$z_w = f_r \frac{B}{d}, x_w = \frac{x_l z_w}{f_r}, y_w = \frac{y_l z_w}{f_r} \tag{1}$$

where f_r is the focal length of right camera, B denotes the baseline distance, (x_l, y_l) is the image coordinates of 3D point P in the left camera image, i.e. P_l.

3   Principle of the MSER-SIFT Based Dual-PTZ-Cameras Stereo Localization

According to the principle of target localization using stereo vision and the property of PTZ camera, the whole dual-PTZ-camera stereo localization procedure can be divided into four steps:1) camera calibration;2) stereo vision correction;3) feature extraction and stereo matching;4) localization; Among them, step 2) and 3) are the key points in the process of target localization. In this paper, we proposed a new localization method based on the dual-PTZ-cameras stereo vision system.

3.1   Stereo Vision Correction

There exist great difference between image pairs captured from dual-PTZ-cameras for the different position and focal length of each PTZ camera. Therefore, images should be preprocessed firstly by using stereo vision rectification(or correction) which is also called epipolar rectification. The purpose of the stereo vision rectification is to make epipolar lines to be horizontal and parallel through projection transformation, i.e. there is only horizontal disparity, and improve the speed and accuracy of stereo matching.

Given a pair of stereo images and assume that the cameras are calibrated, i.e. the intrinsic parameter matrix A and extrinsic parameter matrix R, t are known. Then the unrectified perspective projection matrix $\tilde{P}_{OL}$ and $\tilde{P}_{OR}$ of each image are given by Eq.(2)

$$\tilde{P} = A[R, t] \tag{2}$$

After applied projective transformation for each image, the two image planes are coplanar and parallel to the baseline. The new rectified perspective projection matrices $\tilde{P}_{NL}$ and $\tilde{P}_{NR}$ can be factorized   from Eq.(3)

$$\tilde{P}_{NL} = A[R, -RC_L], \quad \tilde{P}_{NR} = A[R, -RC_R] \tag{3}$$

To keep 3D geometry identical, the new optical centers C_L and C_R must remain at the same position as the old optical centers O_l and O_r in space, i.e., $C_L = O_l$, $C_R = O_r$. The rotation matrix R will be specified by Eq.(4)

$$R = \begin{bmatrix} r_1 & r_2 & r_3 \end{bmatrix}^T \tag{4}$$

where, vector r_1, r_2 and r_3 are the X, Y, and Z axes, respectively, of the camera reference frame, expressed in world coordinates. They can be obtained as following

(a) The new X axis parallel to the baseline $C_L C_R$, r_1 is given by

$$r_1 = \frac{C_L - C_R}{\| C_L - C_R \|} \tag{5}$$

(b) The new Y axis orthogonal to X and k, r_2 is given by $r_2 = k \times r_1$, where, k is an unit vector of the old Z axis, "$\times$"means cross product operator.

(c) The new Z axis orthogonal to XY, r_3 is given by $r_3 = r_1 \times r_2$

Hence, the relationship between rectified and unrectified image plane can be described as

$$\tilde{m}_{NL} = \lambda P_{NL} P_{OL}^{-1} \tilde{m}_{OL}, \quad \tilde{m}_{NR} = \lambda P_{NR} P_{OR}^{-1} \tilde{m}_{OR} \tag{6}$$

$\tilde{m}_{OL}$ and $\tilde{m}_{OR}$ are a pair of unrectified corresponding points , $\tilde{m}_{NL}$ and $\tilde{m}_{NR}$ are rectified points, λ is an arbitrary factor of proportionality. The transformation $T = P_{NR} P_{OR}^{-1}$ is defined as rectification matrix and applied to the original left image to generate the rectified image. Note that the rectified process is under the condition that the intrinsic and extrinsic parameters matrix are known. But the position and focal length of cameras are variable in the PTZ stereo vision system, i.e. the intrinsic and extrinsic parameters matrix are changeable, So this algorithm is time-consuming and therefore it is not possible to compute the rectification transforms in real time. Here we introduce LUT (look-up-table) and BP network rectification model to solve this problem.

a. Construction of the LUT Offline

LUT is a look-up-table, the equal focal length of right-and-left cameras is the precondition of its offline construction. An LUT contains projective matrices corresponding to various image pairs captured at predefined pan and tilt angles .The process to construct the LUT are divided into four steps :

step1: Sample the different pan and tilt angles for the whole ranges of dual PTZ cameras into n_1 equal intervals as $(p_l^i, t_l^i)_{i=1:1:n_1}$ and $(p_r^i, t_r^i)_{i=1:1:n_1}$

step2: Capture images $(I_l^{i,j})_{i=1:1:n_1}^{j=1:1:n_1}$ and $(I_r^{i,j})_{i=1:1:n_1}^{j=1:1:n_1}$ corresponding to $(p_l^i, t_l^j)_{i=1:1:n_1}^{j=1:1:n_1}$ and $(p_r^i, t_r^j)_{i=1:1:n_1}^{j=1:1:n_1}$

steps3: Computer the possible $k(k > n_1 \times n_1)$ pairs of projective matrices for the different combination of these stereo images.

step4: Store all (p_l, t_l, p_r, t_r) and corresponding pairs of projective matrices into LUT.

Thus, the construction of the LUT is finished offline. The constructed LUT will be used as sample set of BP rectification model.

b BP Rectification Model

Once the LUT is constructed, a BP network model with 4-input-24-output is used for image rectification. Different combination of the pan and tilt angles (p_l, t_l, p_r, t_r) are used as the input of BP network, the corresponding two 3×4 respective projective matrices of (p_l, t_l, p_r, t_r) are used as output. After the BP rectification model is well-trained. The rectified projective matrices for any arbitrary orientation of both PTZ cameras to given unrectified image pairs can be found by this BP model . Thus, the real-time stereo rectification can be achieved.

c Zoom Compensation

Note that the LUT is constructed under the condition that the right-and-left cameras have equal focal length, but in order to obtain panoramic images and close-rang images, the focal length of the two PTZ cameras can actually be different. So the LUT data cannot be directly adopted, in this case, compensation of unequal zoom settings is needed before stereo matching is performed. Here we use a focal-ratio-based methodology [6,7] to solve this problem. It contains two steps as following

step1: Image shrinking

Image shrinking is used to compensate the effect of different focal lengths between stereo images. Firstly, we compute the focal ratio $R = f_d / f_s$,where, f_d and f_s are the focal lengths of the dual PTZ cameras respectively. Secondly, if $R > 1$, then we shrink the image I_d by R times into I_d' .if $R < 1$, then we shrink the image I_s by $1/R$ times into I_s'. If $R = 1$, we do not shrink any image.

step2: Zero padding

Here we assume that $R > 1$. Firstly, we find the smaller image in size between I_s and I_d' . Secondly, If $I_s > I_d'$, we add zero padding of size $w_d' \times v_1$ on the left and right side of I_d' , and zero padding of size $u_1 \times h_s$ on the above and below side, where u_1 and v_1 can be given as

$$u_1 = \frac{|w_s - w_d'|}{2} \quad \text{and} \quad v_1 = \frac{|h_s - h_d'|}{2}$$

If $I_s < I_d'$, we add zero padding of size $w_s \times v_2$ on the left and right side, and zero padding of size $u_2 \times h_d'$ on the above and below side of image I_s , where u_2 and v_2 can be given as

$$u_2 = \frac{|w_d' - w_s|}{2} \quad \text{and} \quad v_2 = \frac{|h_d' - h_s|}{2}$$

Otherwise, zero padding is not required .The pair of images obtained by the above mentioned operations can directly use the data of LUT and BP rectification model to rectify images in real-time.

3.2   Feature Extraction and Stereo Matching

Feature extraction involves feature detection and feature description. In other words, the detection component of the feature extraction obtains features, and the descriptor information will be used to match these distinct feature points in other image plane. After feature extraction, the image points are divided into different subsets which are usually edges, corners, blobs, etc. Stereo matching is an important part of a stereo vision system. Given one point in an image, the essence of stereo matching is to find the corresponding point in the other image, consequently, making the two points being the projection of the same 3-D point. Stereo matching method can basically be divided into three categories: the area-based matching method, the feature-based matching method and the phase-based matching method. Many important theory researches and practical applications of the computer vision, such as 3-D reconstruction, surveillance, motion analysis and target localization etc, are making under the assumption that the problem of stereo matching has been solved. In this paper, we use the new stereo matching method based on combining MSER detector[3] with SIFT descriptor[2] (henceforth MSER-SIFT). The main idea of the MSER-SIFT method is to chose the MSER by detecting the stability of connected components which are extracted from a certain image using a proper threshold, then describe the gradient direction of the detected MSERs by using SIFT descriptor.

The whole feature extraction and stereo matching algorithm can be divided into four steps: Extract MSERs, Fitting elliptical regions, Generate SIFT descriptor, Perform MSER matching.

Step1: Extract MSERs, MSERs include maximal regions (MSER+) and minimal regions (MSER-), possessing the property of affine invariance, stability and multi-scale detection. MSERs can be extracted without the need of image smooth process and the MSERs mainly exist in nested forms. Taking MSER+ extraction as an example, we increase the threshold Δ gradually from 0 to 255 (the extraction of MSER- is to reduce the threshold Δ gradually from 255 to 0) and compare with the intensity of each pixel, marking the pixels those above or equal the threshold, the are defined as connection regions which are composed with the adjacent marked points. In the process of continuously increasing threshold, the sizes of some extremal regions are invariable, thus such regions are known as MSER+.

Specifically, imagine an image I(x), $x \in \Lambda$ is a real function of a limited set Λ. For the sake of simplicity, we define $\Lambda=[1, 2, \ldots, N]^n$, n is a arbitrarily positive integral , the elements of Λ are called pixels. S(x) of the image I(x) is the set of pixels that have intensity not greater than I(x), i.e.

$$S(x)=\{y \in \Lambda:I(y) \leq I(x)\} \tag{7}$$

A path $(x_1, \ldots, x_n)$ is a continuous sequence of pixels (i.e. such that x_i amd x_{i+1} are 4-way or 8-way neighbors for $i = 1, \ldots, n-1$). A connected component C is a subset of the set Λ, the connected component is maximal if any other connected component C' containing C is equal to C. An extremal region R is a maximal connected component of a level set S(x). R(I) is the set of all extremal regions of image I, Let I(R) of the extremal region R be the maximum image value attained in the region R, i.e.

$$I(R) = \sup_{x \in R} I(x) \qquad (8)$$

$\Delta > 0$. R+Δ is the smallest extremal region containing R

$$R_{+\Delta} = \arg\min \left\{ \begin{array}{l} |Q| : Q \in R(I), Q \supset R \\ I(Q) \geq I(R) + \Delta \end{array} \right\} \qquad (9)$$

Similarly, R–Δ is the biggest extremal region containing R

$$R_{-\Delta} = \arg\max \left\{ \begin{array}{l} |Q| : Q \in R(I), Q \supset R \\ I(Q) \leq I(R) - \Delta \end{array} \right\} \qquad (10)$$

Considering regional variation

$$\rho(R; \Delta) = \frac{|R_{+\Delta}| - |R_{-\Delta}|}{|R|} \qquad (11)$$

The region R is maximally stable if it is a minimum for the area variation

Step2. Fitting elliptical regions, MSERs present the irregular shape. In order to describe MSERs with SIFT descriptor easily, The method of fitting ellipse[8] is used to normalize MSERs. Fitting elliptical regions amount to compute the first and second order moments of each maximally stable extremal region R, i.e.

$$\mu(R) = \frac{1}{|R|} \sum_{X \in R} X \qquad \sum(R) = \frac{1}{|R|} \sum_{X \in R} (X - \mu)(X - \mu)^T \qquad (12)$$

Where X is a vector or coordinates (x,y) of any point in R. R is the irregular area, | R | is the number of pixels in R. Covariance matrix is acquired by Eq.(13)

$$U = \begin{bmatrix} D(x) & Cov(x, y) \\ Cov(x, y) & D(y) \end{bmatrix} \qquad (13)$$

$D(x)$ and $D(y)$ are respectively the horizontal and vertical coordinates variance of all point in the region, $Cov(x, y)$ is the covariance of the horizontal and vertical coordinates. The amplitude and direction of the fitting ellipse's long axis and short axis depend on the eigenvector and eigenvalue of the covariance matrix. The normalized local features have strictly affine invariance.

Step3.   Generate SIFT Descriptor
SIFT descriptor is a local feature description algorithm proposed by David G. Lowe in 2004, it is based on scale space and is invariant to image translation, scaling and rotation. After the detected MSER is affine normalized, the SIFT descriptor is generated to describe MSER. In order to guarantee rotation invariance, axis should be rotated to the main direction of the key point (i.e. the centroid of MSER) and a 16×16 window centered in the key point is defined A gradient orientation histogram of 8 bins is calculated for each of the 4×4 array and 16 seeds are formed. Thus the

description of MSER elliptical region using a 128-valued feature vector is generated, i.e. each MSER elliptical region corresponds to a SIFT descriptor feature vector.

Step4. Perform MSER Matching

The Euclidean distance between feature vectors of MSERs is used as the criterion of stereo matching. Here, we assume that x, y are two n-dimension vectors, which represent two feature regions to be matched. The ratio defines as:

$$d(x,y) = \| x - y \| = \left[\sum_{i=1}^{n} (x_i - y_i)^2 \right]^{\frac{1}{2}} \tag{14}$$

Set an appropriate threshold, and the match is considered to be successful when $d(x,y)$ is less than the threshold. Finally, we use RANSAC (Random Sample Consensus) to detect the erroneous correspondences and realize the feature extraction and stereo matching under the proposed algorithm.

3.3 Localization

The required disparity value is the one that minimizes the SSD (sum of square differentces)[9]

$$d_0(x,y) = \min_d C(x,y,|d|) \tag{15}$$

where,

$$C(x,y,d) = \frac{\sum_{(\xi,\eta)} [J_l(x+\xi, y+\eta) - J_r(x+d+\xi, y+\eta)]}{\sqrt{\sum_{(\xi,\eta)} J_l(x+\xi, y+\eta)^2 \sum_{(\xi,\eta)} J_r(x+\xi, y+\eta)^2}}$$

SSD is defined as

$$D(x,y,d) = \sum_{(\xi,\eta)} [J_l(x+\xi, y+\eta) - J_r(x+d+\xi, y+\eta)] \tag{16}$$

where $\xi \in [-n, n]$ and $\eta \in [-m,m]$ define a window centred in (x, y), while d_0 is the disparity. Once the disparity d_0 is computed, the 3-D coordinates of the target in real environment are computed by Eq.(1)

4   Simulation and Experimental Results

In order to achieve the accurate localization of the moving 3-D target under a complex environment with variable view and focal, and demonstrate the validity of the proposed target localization method, we construct the dual-PTZ-cameras stereo vision system and conduct several experiments. Experiment set of the dual-PTZ-cameras stereo vision system is shown in fig.2.The system is composed of two PTZ cameras(MV-VS078FC-L).The highest resolution of image is 1024×768 in pixels, unit pixel size is $4.65\mu m \times 4.65\mu m$ and the baseline is 260 mm.

4.1   Calibration Results

Here we use Zhang's method[10] to calibrate the camera parameters. This method is a 2-D model plane based calibration method, which lies between traditional camera calibration method and self-calibration method and widely used in computer vision. Calibration board used in the experiment is shown in Fig.4 , where, the size of each grid is 21mm×21mm.

In the calibration experiment, when the zoom level is 3 (or 4), we select six different pan and tilt angles in each direction by sampling with a step size of 3.0 degree for both PTZ cameras to cover entire experimental outdoor environment. In this way, a total of 98 images have been captured by each camera. Calibration results are shown in Table I.

Fig. 2. Experiment Set

Where fx and fy are the equivalent focal lengths along x axis and y axis, (u_0,v_0) are the coordinates of the principal points. Then, LUT and BP rectification model are constructed according to the calibration results

Fig.3. Calibration Board

Table 1. Internal parameters of cameras

zoom level	Left/right cameras	fx	fy	u_0	v_0
3	Left	1687.36	1692.51	519.062	566.115
	Right	1931.4	1935.28	540.313	550.754
4	Left	2811.94	2917.38	1624.5	663.877
	Right	2579.87	2486.07	326.844	1121

4.2   Rectification Results

Several images of moving 3-D target are captured when the position and focal length of PTZ cameras are changeable, then we use the LUT data and BP model to rectify images. There are two rectification experiments and relative results, the right pictures in Fig.4 and Fig.6 plot the epipolar lines (*red lines*) corresponding to the points (*green "+"*) marked in the left pictures. We can see that the epipolar lines are convergent before rectification, this greatly affect the rapidity and accuracy of stereo matching. After rectification, the epipolar lines corresponding to the points (green "+") are parallel and horizontal, this is conducive to enhancing the rapidity and accuracy.

Experiment 1: The Rectification Under the Same Focal Length

Images of moving 3-D target are captured in the condition of the same focal length. Fig.4 shows the result when the zoom level of focal length is 4 and position parameters of the dual PTZ cameras are $p_l = 6°, t_l = 6°, p_r = 10°, t_r = 10°$, here $R=1$.

Fig. 4. The original stereo pair (*left*) and rectified pair(*right*). ($R=1$)

Experiment 2: The Rectification Under the Different Focal Lengths

Fig.4 shows the result when the zoom levels of dual PTZ cameras are 5 and 4, parameters of cameras position are $p_l = 2°, t_l = 2°, p_r = 4°, t_r = 4°$, here $R>1$, so zoom compensation is needed before rectification and the process is shown in Fig.5

Fig. 5. The process of zoom compensation

Fig. 6. The original stereo images (top) and rectified images (bottom) ($R>1$)

4.3   Matching Results

Experiment 3: Feature Extraction and Stereo Matching of Static Targets

In order to make performance comparison between SIFT and MSER-SIFT, several images of the static targets are captured from different fields of view, among them, six stereo pairs are randomly selected for feature extraction and stereo matching. Fig.7 is one of the matched stereo images. The blue line in Fig. 7(a) and the yellow line in Fig.7 (b) represent the matching line, yellow ellipses in Fig. 7(b) represent MSERs. It can be seen that MSER-SIFT can extract more accurate feature points and have higher correct matching ratio which is the key point and directly influencing factor of high-precision localization.

Matching results are shown in table 2, It can be seen that the correct matching rate of MSER-SIFT is higher than SIFT alone which demonstrates the feasibility and high efficiency of MSER-SIFT.

(a) SIFT alone   (b) MSER-SIFT

Fig. 7. Results of feature extraction and matching

Table 2. Matching results of the two algorithms

Test pair	SIFT				MSER-SIFT			
	#total matches	#false Matches	false matching rate	time complexity	#total matches	#false matches	false matching rate	time complexity
1	104	5	4.8%	2.459s	12	0	`0	9.032s
2	45	2	4.4%	2.14s	11	0	0	8.781s
3	24	1	4.2%	1.862s	9	0	0	7.218s
4	73	3	4.1%	2.378	13	1	7.7%	9.078s
5	50	3	6%	2.281s	14	0	0	10.297s
6	10	1	10%	1.75s	11	0	0	8.513s
	average false rate : 5.58% average time complexity : 2.15s				average false rate : 1.28% average time complexity : 8.83s			

Experiment 4: Feature Extraction and Stereo Matching of Moving 3-D Target

In order to further validate the effectiveness of MSER-SIFT, several stereo images of moving 3-D target are captured under the variable position and focal length of PTZ cameras. Fig. 8 (a) shows the matching results of rectified image pairs when focal lengths of right-and-left cameras are same. Fig. 8 (b) shows the matching results of rectified image pairs when focal lengths of right-and-left cameras are different.

The experiment results show that MSER-SIFT can still realize the totally matching of the corresponding MSERs, and the disparity exists only in horizontal direction which could greatly improve the rapidity and accuracy of target localization.

4.4   Localization Results

The experimental results are obtained from three different pairs of images of moving 3-D target captured in the condition that the position and focal length of PTZ cameras are variable. Firstly, these images are used for stereo vision rectification and stereo

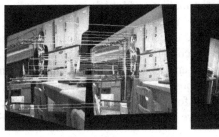 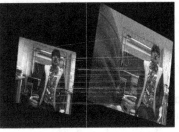

(a) $R=1$ (b) $R>1$

Fig. 8. Results of feature extraction and matching

Table 3. The localization result of moving 3-D target

Group number	Left image coordinates /pixel		experimental value /mm			measure value /mm	relative error
	x	y	Zw	Xw	Yw	Zw'	E*
NO.1	273	634	5591.4	788.7	1831.6	5630	0.7%
	300	645	6063.0	939.7	2020.5	5980	1.4%
	313	629	5591.4	904.2	1817.1	5510	1.5%
NO.2	370	507	2516.1	481.0	659.1	2480	1.4%
	393	530	2676.7	543.5	732.9	2630	1.7%
	427	533	2780.3	613.4	765.6	2760	0.7%
NO.3	469	838	3458.6	628.6	1123.1	3480	0.6%
	617	745	3354.8	802.1	968.5	3320	1.0%
	734	732	3388.7	963.8	961.2	3410	0.6%

Note: $relative\ error = \dfrac{|\ measure\ value - experimental\ value\ |}{measure\ value} \times 100\%$

matching. Secondly, three correct matching points are randomly selected from each pair. Finally, the localization results are obtained according to SSD algorithm and Eq.(1) .Table III shows the localization results. It can be seen that the relative errors are between 0.6% and 1.7% which are computed by experimental value and measure value of nine object points, Experimental results show that the proposed target localization method has high localization accuracy.

5 Conclusion

We proposed a new stereo localization method based on MSER-SIFT using dual-PTZ-camera stereo system. SIFT descriptor is invariant to image translation, scaling and rotation. MSER detector has significant affine invariance. MSER-SIFT which use the complementarities on the spatial distribution and invariance presented in different cases has greatly enhanced the robustness and correct matching rate. Finally, through several localization experiments, fully and effectively point information of moving 3-D target have been obtained and used to compute their 3-D coordinates, and after the comparison between experimental value and measure value, the localization experimental results have shown that the proposed method could achieve high precision localization and has a broad foreground for its application. In the future we plan to combine FAST9 algorithm[11] to improve the time complexity of MSER-SIFT.

Acknowledgement. This work was supported in part by the Shaanxi Provincial Natural Science Foundation of China under Grant 2009JQ8011 and Educational Commission of Shaanxi Province of China under Grant 2010JK737;by the National Science Foundation of China under Grants 61174101.

References

1. Kumar, S., Micheloni, C., Piciarelli, C.: Stereo Localization Using Dual PTZ Cameras. In: Jiang, X., Petkov, N. (eds.) CAIP 2009. LNCS, vol. 5702, pp. 1061–1069. Springer, Heidelberg (2009)
2. Lowe, D.G.: Distinctive Image Features from Scale-Invariant Keypoints. International Journal of Computer Vision 60(2), 91–110 (2004)
3. Matas, J., Chum, O., Urban, M., et al.: Robust Wide-base Line Stereo from Maximally Stable Extremal Regions. Image and Vision Computing 22(10), 761–767 (2004)
4. Samir, B.V.R., Na, S.I., Kalia, R.: Image Matching with SIFT descriptor on Affine Normalized MSERs. In: 17th Korea-Japan Joint Workshop on Korea-Japan Joint Workshop on Frontiers of Computer Vision, pp. 1–4 (2011)
5. Lin, G.Y., Zhang, W.G.: An Effective Robust Rectified Method for Stereo Vision. Journal of Image Graphic 11(2), 203–209 (2006)
6. Kumar, S., Micheloni, C., Piciarelli, C., Foresti, G.L.: Stereo Rectification of Uncalibrated and Heterogeneous images. Pattern Recognition Letters 31(11), 1445–1452 (2010)
7. Kumar, S., Micheloni, C., Piciarelli, C., Foresti, G.L.: Stereo Localization based on Network's Uncalibrated Camera Pairs. In: 6th IEEE International Conference on Advanced Video and Signal Based Surveillance, pp. 502–507 (2009)
8. Forssen, P., Lowe, D.: Shape Descriptors for Maximally Stable Extremal Regions. In: 11th International Conference on Computer Vision, pp. 59–73 (2007)
9. Zhou, W.H., Du, X., Ye, X.Q.: Binocular Stereo Vision System Based on FPGA. Journal of Image Graphic 10(9), 1166–1170 (2005)
10. Zhang, Z.Y.: A Flexible New Technique for Camera Calibration. IEEE Trans on PAMI 22(11), 374–376 (2000)
11. Rosten, E., Drummond, T.W.: Machine Learning for High-Speed Corner Detection. In: Leonardis, A., Bischof, H., Pinz, A. (eds.) ECCV 2006. LNCS, vol. 3951, pp. 430–443. Springer, Heidelberg (2006)

Monocular Depth from Motion
Using a New Closed-Form Solution

Mohamed Hasan and Mohamed Abdellatif

Mechatronics and Robotics Engineering Department
Egypt-Japan University of Science and Technology
{mohamed.hasan,mohamed.abdellatif}@ejust.edu.eg

Abstract. Monocular depth has been found using estimation, closed-form solution and learning techniques. Estimation and closed-form solution compute the depth from motion, while learning techniques calculate the depth using a single image with a depth map as a supervisor. This paper presents a new closed form solution for monocular depth from motion. The proposed method builds on the notation that an interest point in an image of a static scene has a static world location. Camera pose and calibration parameters are used as constraints to provide the depth solution. The proposed method is verified through real experiments on indoor mobile robot platform. The effect of uncertainty in the solution variables is studied and the results are benchmarked to groundtruth.

Keywords: monocular depth, real-time depth from motion.

1 Introduction

Depth calculation is necessary for several applications in computer vision and robotics, such as navigation, obstacle avoidance, visual simultaneous localization and mapping. Traditionally, stereo vision has been used to compute depth through the epipolar geometry. Alternatively, monocular depth is the depth computed from the images captured by a single camera [1]. Computing monocular depth has been introduced through estimation, closed-form solution and learning techniques.

Estimation and closed-form solution techniques compute the depth from the motion of the observing camera. This requires tracking of a number of interest points through the captured monocular sequence of images. Estimation techniques mainly employ Kalman filters to iteratively estimate depth and geometrical structure of the scene [2-7]. However, closed-form solutions impose the geometrical constraints of motion to reduce the number of unknowns and determine the depth in real time [8]. On the other hand, supervised learning has been used to find depth from a single image with a groundtruth depth map acting as a teacher [9-10].

For the applications of mobile robots, depth recovery from visual information is necessary for navigation. The estimation techniques of depth from motion take a number of iterations until settled to a depth value and thus affecting the accuracy of robotic missions like obstacle avoidance, localization and mapping. On contrary,

C.-Y. Su, S. Rakheja, H. Liu (Eds.): ICIRA 2012, Part III, LNAI 7508, pp. 473–483, 2012.

closed-form solutions can compute the depth in real time and thus enable safe navigation of mobile robots. The closed-form solutions depend on several constraints to simplify the depth calculations such as the planar robot motion, the geometrical constraints and the known camera calibration parameters [8, 11]. Murphey *et al* have used the geometrical constraints to find depth from motion using a closed form solution [8]. However, they neglected the camera calibration parameters and the camera rotation information as well.

In this paper, a new closed-form solution for depth from motion is presented. The proposed solution recovers the depth of a static point in real time without the need of iterative estimation. Both the camera pose and the calibration parameters information have been used to compute the depth. The new depth solution builds on the notation that any interest point existing in an image of a static scene, has a static location in world. This constraint has been used to calculate the depth of an image point from just two monocular views of that point. The proposed solution differs from the traditional triangulation methods [12] because it only needs matching for one image point. The paper is organized as follows. The closed-form solution is introduced in the next section. The results of experiments on indoor mobile robot are presented in section 3 along with uncertainty analysis. Discussion of the results and the limitations of the proposed method are given in section 4. Finally, conclusions are drawn in section 5.

2   Closed-Form Solution

The proposed method works under the following assumptions:

- The camera is calibrated.
- The observed features are static.
- The robot pose is known.

The calibrated camera is assumed to move and a sequence of monocular images is captured. Consider a static point feature $p_i^w = (X \quad Y \quad Z)^T$ represented in world coordinates. The camera observes p_i^w twice from two different world positions: r_1^{wc}, r_2^{wc} as shown in Fig. 1. The distances between the camera and p_i^w in the two observations are denoted as h_1^c and h_2^c which are represented in the camera coordinates. Transformation from camera to world coordinates is performed by the rotation matrices: R_1^{wc}, R_2^{wc} which are functions of the camera pitch angles: θ_1, θ_2. The pitch angle is the rotation of the planar robot around the vertical axis Y^c. The projections of p_i^w on the image plane are $(u_1, \ v_1)$ in the first image and $(u_2, \ v_2)$ in the other image.

The intrinsic parameters of the camera are given from prior camera calibration. Standard pinhole camera model- without lens distortion- [1] has been used along with these intrinsic parameters. The distance between the camera and an observed point is composed of three Euclidean components; $h^c = (h_x \quad h_y \quad h_z)^T$. Thus, the pixel coordinates of the observed point are given by the camera model:

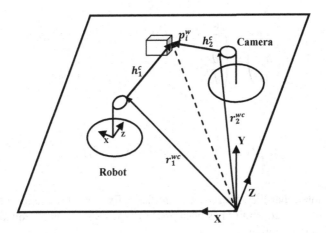

Fig. 1. The mobile robot with the onboard camera observing a feature from two different positions

$$\begin{pmatrix} u \\ v \end{pmatrix} = \begin{pmatrix} u_0 - \dfrac{f}{d}\dfrac{h_x}{h_z} \\ v_0 - \dfrac{f}{d}\dfrac{h_y}{h_z} \end{pmatrix} \tag{1}$$

where u_0, v_0 are the camera center in pixels, f is the focal length and d is the pixel size.

The world location of the point feature can be determined given the location of the camera and the distance from this location to the point. This may be written for the two different observations as:

$$p_i^w = r_1^{wc} + R_1^{wc} h_1^c \tag{2}$$

$$p_i^w = r_2^{wc} + R_2^{wc} h_2^c \tag{3}$$

where:

$$r_i^{wc} = \begin{pmatrix} x_i \\ y_i \\ z_i \end{pmatrix}, \quad R_i^{wc} = \begin{pmatrix} \cos\theta_i & 0 & \sin\theta_i \\ 0 & 1 & 0 \\ -\sin\theta_i & 0 & \cos\theta_i \end{pmatrix} \tag{4}$$

From (1)

$$h_i^c = \begin{pmatrix} h_{xi} \\ h_{yi} \\ h_{zi} \end{pmatrix} = \begin{pmatrix} \dfrac{d}{f}(u_0 - u_i)h_{zi} \\ \dfrac{d}{f}(v_0 - v_i)h_{zi} \\ h_{zi} \end{pmatrix} = h_{zi}\begin{pmatrix} a_i \\ b_i \\ 1 \end{pmatrix} \tag{5}$$

where

$$a_i = \frac{d}{f}(u_0 - u_i), \qquad b_i = \frac{d}{f}(v_0 - v_i) \tag{6}$$

and $i=1, 2$ in (4-6).

It can be noted that the observed feature has a fixed world location regardless of camera motion. This constraint has been used to provide solution by equating (2), (3), using (4-6) and rearranging:

$$\begin{pmatrix} a_1 \cos\theta_1 + \sin\theta_1 & -a_2\cos\theta_2 - \sin\theta_2 \\ b_1 & -b_2 \\ -a_1\sin\theta_1 + \cos\theta_1 & -a_1\sin\theta_1 + \cos\theta_1 \end{pmatrix}\begin{pmatrix} h_{z1} \\ h_{z2} \end{pmatrix} = $$
$$\begin{pmatrix} x_2 - x_1 \\ y_2 - y_1 \\ z_2 - z_1 \end{pmatrix} \tag{7}$$

or equivalently:

$$A\,h_z = B \tag{8}$$

where $h_z = (h_{z1} \quad h_{z2})^T$.

The depth of the feature can now be calculated from (8):

$$h_z = (A^T A)^{-1} A^T B \tag{9}$$

This completes the solution of the depth of the point.

3   Experiments and Results

The proposed depth solution has been verified using an indoor mobile robot platform (Robotino). Camera is fixed on the planar mobile robot as shown in Fig. 1. The robot is translated laterally facing a scene in our lab space while capturing a sequence of monocular images. This robot motion is repeated at three different distances from the scene (d_1, d_2, d_3) resulting in three different scales for each image. In each group of images, distinctive features are detected in the first image and their pixel measurements are recorded. These features are then tracked through the images sequence in each group and the matched measurements are recorded for each feature. The image coordinates of the feature in the first image and its match in the other image during motion are now known. Also the location and orientation of the camera while capturing both images can be acquired from robot odometry. These data along with camera intrinsic parameters provide a depth solution as given in (9).

The three robot lateral paths start at d_1=3.48m, d_2=2.64m and d_3=1.44m from the nearest point in the scene, respectively. The distance between the nearest and the farthest points in the scene is 1.6m. Twenty five images have been captured during each robot motion for about 92 cm at equidistant points. Thus, three groups of monocular images of a static scene at three different scales are provided. In each group of images, a number of distinctive features is tracked through the sequence and matches for every point are recorded.

3.1   Manual Matching

In the first experiment, features have been selected and tracked in a manual mode to evaluate the proposed method. For example, the fourth frame from each group of images is shown with the selected points in Fig. 2.

The measurements of the selected features in the first frame are used as (u_1, v_1), while the matched location of the feature in every subsequent image is (u_2, v_2) as in section 2. Depth is calculated using these measurements through (5-7) at every image. The calculated depth of each feature at every frame is used in (2) to calculate the world location of the feature. The Z-coordinate of the feature location (depth coordinate) is compared to the measured groundtruth of feature and the error is found. The errors in depth calculations for some of the features in the first group are described in Table 1 Results are shown for the calculations at five different lateral positions.

The effect of the observing distance between camera and feature has been studied for three features in the three groups of measurements. The first feature appears with the feature numbers 6, 3 and 1 in the three groups respectively. The other two features numbers are (8, 4, 2) and (9, 5, 3) respectively. Results of errors in depth calculations are shown in Fig. 3.

The proposed method of depth solution is affected by the uncertainty in points matching (u, v), robot pose (x, z, θ) and camera calibration (d/f). These effects have been studied for the third feature in Fig.3 at the third distance, since this has the minimalist error. The solution parameters associated with this case of minimum error have been selected as reference values. Perturbations have then been made around these reference values and the error in the resulting depth is shown. The error in depth is normalized by the groundtruth depth of the feature. The effects of uncertainty in matching the features through the image sequence have been studied for a range of ±5 pixels. The errors in horizontal matching (u-image coordinate) and vertical matching (v-image coordinate) are shown in Fig.4. The effect of errors in camera calibration parameters; the ratio (d/f) is shown in Fig. 5. Finally, the effect of error in robot pose

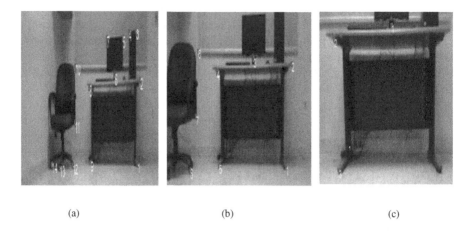

(a) (b) (c)

Fig. 2. The fourth frame in the the monocular sequence of the captured scene in the three groups at different distances (a) d_1= 4m. (b) d_2=2.8. (c) d_3=1.6m

Table 1. Depth errors for features in the first group matched manually

P	Z (m)	Error (m) at different frames					Mean error (m)	% Mean error
		5	10	15	20	25		
1	4.44	-0.004	0.013	-0.017	-0.029	-0.026	-0.012	-0. 270
2	4.33	0.498	-0.074	-0.094	-0.105	0.217	0.088	2.032
3	4.42	-0.026	-0.214	-0.301	-0.112	-0.160	-0.163	-3.687
4	4.42	0.147	-0.056	-0.048	0.023	-0.007	0.011	0.248
5	4.65	0.277	-0.105	-0.150	-0.068	-0.09	-0.028	-0.602
6	4.68	0.462	-0.021	-0.043	-0.065	-0.010	0.064	1.367
7	4.65	0.320	0.093	-0.002	0.025	0.009	0.089	1.913

has been studied through testing error in the robot lateral position, forward position and heading angle (θ) as shown in Fig. 6. The errors in robot pose and calibration parameters are normalized by their original non-noisy value.

3.2 Automatic Matching

The evaluation technique used in section 3.1 has been repeated but with automatic matching of the features through the sequence. The first seven features displayed in Fig. 2 (a) with their depth results in Table 1, are now tracked through the images of the first group. A fixed-size template has been extracted from the first image centered on each feature's image location. This template has been used as the descriptor for the feature and has been tracked using Fast template matching [13].

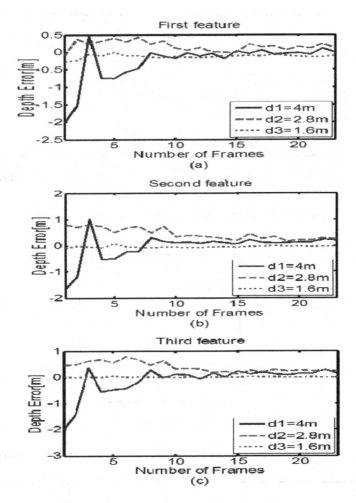

Fig. 3. Depth errors for three features evaluated at the three capturing distances: d_1, d_2, d_3

Fast template matching method implements Normalized Cross Correlation, NCC in frequency domain using pre-computed tables containing the integral of the image and image square over the search window. The normalized form of cross correlation is necessary to overcome the problem that image and templates are not the same size. More important, NCC deals with the variation in the intensity of both the image and templates. Fast Fourier transform is adopted to switch to the frequency domain. Transform computations are efficiently performed using summed-area tables containing the integral of the image (running sum) and image square over the search area.

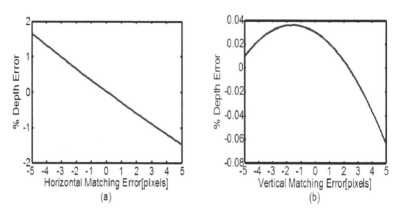

Fig. 4. The effect of error in matching on the depth calculations

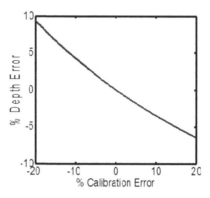

Fig. 5. The effect of error in camera calibration parameters (d/f) on depth calculations

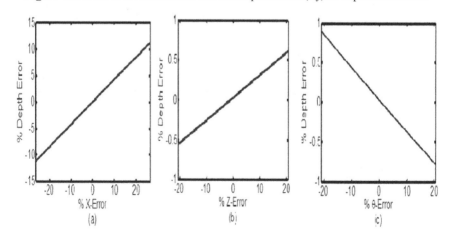

Fig. 6. The effect of error in robot pose on the depth calculations

Every five frames, a matching score is calculated between the templates and the image in order. The image point having the peak of the matching score is compared to an empirically defined threshold (0.85). If the matching score passes the threshold, then this image point is the match of the feature. The results of matching the features are shown in Fig. 7 for three frames in the sequence.

The first three features have not been tracked well through all images. The results of depth calculations of all features are given in Table 2. The effect of matching error is apparent in the large error in the depth of the first three features. The maximum mean error of depth of the other features is 7.60 cm which is 1.63 % of the true depth.

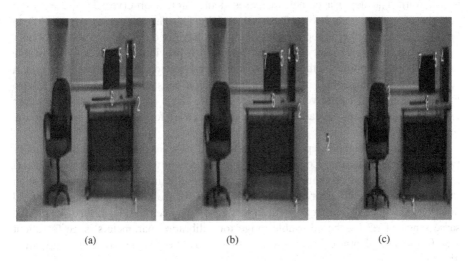

| (a) | (b) | (c) |

Fig. 7. Fast template matching results for the first group of images: (a) 5th frame (b) 15th frame (c) 25th fame. The first three features have large error in matching.

Table 2. Results of depth calculations using automatic matching. The first three features have large error in matching and hence in depth.

P	Z (m)	Error (m) at different frames					Mean error (m)	% Mean error
		5	10	15	20	25		
1	4.44	0.370	0.340	0.354	0.455	-24.58	-4.612	-103
2	4.33	0.682	0.187	0.261	-5.225	-5.510	-1.921	-44.3
3	4.42	-0.098	-0.284	-0.260	-6.846	-7.907	-3.079	-69.6
4	4.42	0.185	-0.138	-0.064	0.100	0.0456	0.025	0.565
5	4.65	0.383	-0.087	-0.103	-0.082	-0.063	0.009	0.193
6	4.68	0.211	-0.167	-0.140	-0.038	-0.088	-0.044	-0.949
7	4.65	0.496	-0.039	-0.051	-0.026	0.004	0.076	1.634

4   Discussion

The error in depth calculations using the proposed method has not exceeded 3.7% in case of manual matching; while with robust automatic matching the depth in error has been below 1.7%. The proposed method depends on observing a feature at two different world positions. The amount of lateral translation between these two positions of observation has great effect on the depth result. It is shown in Table 2 that the amount of translation should not be less than about 20 cm (distance between five images). The mean of the depth error for each feature is shown to be in the range from 1 cm to 16 cm. Fig.3 shows that the depth error is degraded at the tenth frame (40 cm translation). The depth accuracy increases if the camera observes the feature from near distances as already known from stereo vision [1]. These accuracy conditions can be considered suitable for applications like visual navigation of indoor mobile robots.

The effects of uncertainty described in Fig. 4-6 provide the ranges of allowable errors for the proposed method. Due to the lateral motion of the robot observing a static scene, the horizontal image coordinate has a considerable change as clear in Fig.4 (a) compared to the vertical change in (b). These results show that the depth error don't exceed ±2 % (about ±8 cm in this case) for ± 5 pixels in horizontal matching error.

The proposed method depends on the amount of translation between the robot's two observing positions. Consequently, Fig. 5 (a) shows that the error in lateral motion has greater effect than that of the forward motion in (b) or rotational motion in (c). To keep the depth error inside a range of ±2 %, the allowable range for lateral position error is ±5 % (about ±4 cm in this case). To keep the depth error inside the same range of ±2 %, the allowable range for calibration parameters is ±6 % (about 1.8e-004). The depth calculations are thus sensitive to the error in calibration parameters.

5   Conclusions

A new closed-form solution for depth from motion has been introduced. The proposed method makes use of the constraint that the world location of an image point is fixed regardless of motion. The method assumes that the pose and the calibration parameters of the camera are known. Experimental results on an indoor planar mobile robot have been presented to verify the solution. From the discussion given in the previous section, some conclusions can be given about the validity of the proposed method:

- The error in the depth solution with automatic points matching is below 1.7%.
- The error in points matching should be within a range of ± 5 pixels.
- The amount of translation between the camera observing locations should not be less than 20 cm.
- The error of the camera position should not exceed ±5 % of the true position.

Acknowledgement. The first author is supported by a scholarship from the Ministry of Higher Education, Government of Egypt which is gratefully acknowledged.

References

[1] Szeliski, R.: Computer Vision: Algorithms and Applications. Springer, London (2011)

[2] Franke, U., Rabe, C., Badino, H., Gehrig, S.K.: 6D-Vision: Fusion of Stereo and Motion for Robust Environment Perception. In: Kropatsch, W.G., Sablatnig, R., Hanbury, A. (eds.) DAGM 2005. LNCS, vol. 3663, pp. 216–223. Springer, Heidelberg (2005)

[3] Hung, Y., Ho, H.: A Kalman Filter Approach to Direct Depth Estimation Incorporating Surface Structure. IEEE Trans. on Pattern Analysis and Machine Intelligence Pami 21(6), 570–575 (1999)

[4] Szeliski, R.: Bayesian modeling ofuncertainty inlow-level vision. Int. J. of Computer Vision 5(3), 271–301 (1990)

[5] Franke, U., Rabe, C.: Kalman filter based depth from motion with fast convergence. In: IEEE Symp. on Intelligent Vehicles, pp. 181–186 (2005)

[6] Matthies, L., Kanade, T., Szeliski, R.: Kalman filter-based algorithms for estimating depth from image sequences. Int. J. of Computer Vision 3(3), 209–236 (1989)

[7] Civera, J., Davison, A., Montiel, J.: Inverse Depth Parametrization for Monocular SLAM. IEEE Trans. on Robotics 24(5), 932–945 (2008)

[8] Murphey, Y., Chen, J., Crossman, J., Zhang, J., Richardson, P., Sieh, L.: DepthFinder, A Real-time Depth Detection System for Aided Driving. In: IEEE Symp. on Intelligent Vehicles, pp. 122–127 (2000)

[9] Saxena, A., Chung, S., Ng, A.: 3-D Depth Reconstruction from a Single Still Image. Int. J. of Computer Vision 76(1), 53–69 (2008)

[10] Michels, J., Saxena, A., Ng, A.: High Speed Obstacle Avoidance using Monocular Vision and Reinforcement learning. In: Int. Conf. on Machine Learning, pp. 593–600 (2005)

[11] Ortin, D., Montiel, J.: Indoor robot motion based on monocular images. J. Robotica 19(3), 331–342 (2001)

[12] Hartley, R., Zisserman, A.: Multiple View Geometry in Computer Vision, 2nd edn. Cambridge University Press (2004)

[13] Lewis, J.: Fast Template Matching. In: Vision Interface 1995, Canadian Image Processing and Pattern Recognition Society, pp. 120-123 (1995)

Fast Template Matching of Objects for Visual SLAM

Mohamed Hasan and Mohamed Abdellatif

Mechatronics and Robotics Engineering Department
Egypt-Japan University of Science and Technology
{mohamed.hasan,mohamed.abdellatif}@ejust.edu.eg

Abstract. The majority of visual SLAM techniques utilize interest points as landmarks. Therefore, they suffer from two main problems; scalability and data association reliability. Recently, there has been increasing interest in using higher level object description to reduce the number of tracked features and improve the data association among frames. In this paper, a simple visual mono SLAM algorithm is presented utilizing objects as landmarks and uses fast template matching to track predefined templates of these objects in an indoor environment. The results are described for real experiments with an indoor mobile robot platform. The performance of the proposed technique is evaluated and compared to recent methods.

Keywords: Visual SLAM, mobile robots, objects tracking.

1 Introduction

Simultaneous localization and mapping, SLAM is an important problem for several robotics applications which is reviewed in [1]. Ultrasonic sensors and laser range finders were the main sensors used classically for SLAM systems. Visual SLAM, VSLAM has recently been used due to the rich information gain and the affordable cost of the camera as the only sensor [2]. Interest points have been used commonly as the landmarks in VSLAM research [3].

The VSLAM problem has been solved in real time using points features [4]. However, using point features has two main problems. Firstly, the number of interest points is very large in each image (e.g. around 500 SIFT keypoints [5]) causing the scalability problem of SLAM [1]. This problem motivated other researchers to use grouped features like Lines and higher level structures [6]. Moreover, a map of interest points can be considered as a means for localization rather than an output in itself [7]. This means that the mapping problem in such systems has not been solved well as done with localization.

Using objects as landmarks introduces a natural solution for the problems of point features. Objects are salient features in the scene and humans may depend on them in navigation. Objects are considered as a collection of many salient points packed together and using a suitable object representation, can solve the problem of scalability. Moreover, generating a map of objects is intuitive and provides a meaningful map that may be useful for a variety of mobile robot applications.

C.-Y. Su, S. Rakheja, H. Liu (Eds.): ICIRA 2012, Part III, LNAI 7508, pp. 484–493, 2012.

Using objects for VSALM rather than points is not new approach in itself since it has been used in, e.g. [5] and [8]. Castle *et al* presented a combination of mono SLAM with object recognition for scene augmentation using a wearable camera [5]. A database of objects has been constructed beforehand using single views of planar objects. Objects have been detected using appearance models learned from SIFT features. However, parallel computations and high storage space are required. Moreover, a calibration rig is used to resolve the depth/speed scaling ambiguity inherent in mono SLAM. In [8] an indoor mobile robot detects objects using both SIFT descriptors and contours of objects with the help of other image analysis in parallel. His work has the advantage of autonomous object detection at the expense of complex parallel computations to overcome the slow processing of SIFT features.

In this work, an alternative visual mono SLAM algorithm is presented that adopts objects as landmarks to overcome the problems of point features and provide an intuitive map representation. The appearance of predefined templates of objects is tracked by fast template matching without using the slow SIFT algorithm or contours extraction. Inverse depth parameterization is used to overcome structuring of the environment by a calibrating rig. The VSLAM system is solved in the traditional Extended Kalman Filter EKF framework. Results are described for an indoor mobile robot and compared with related work of [5], [8] and [10].

This paper is arranged as follows. The next section introduces the robot motion, the measurement and the inverse depth models. In section 3, the proposed algorithm is presented together with the traditional EKF predict-update cycle. The algorithm shows the object tracking method; how to detect objects, add them to the map and the data association. Fast template matching technique is described in section 4. The results of implementing the proposed algorithm using an indoor mobile robot are shown and discussed in section 5. Finally, conclusions are given in section 6.

2   The SLAM Model

The VSLAM problem is solved here using the traditional EKF filter in the common prediction and update stages. Inverse depth parameterization [9] is selected to express depth from objects to camera. The constant angular and linear velocity model of [10] is used to describe the robot motion. The robot state is defined as:

$$x_v = (r^{WC} \quad q^{WC} \quad v^W \quad \omega^W)^T \tag{1}$$

where r^{WC} is the position vector of the camera in world coordinates, q^{WC} is quaternion describing the orientation, v^W is linear velocity and ω^W is angular velocity. The motion model of the camera/robot controls the prediction step of the EKF and is given by:

$$f_v = \begin{pmatrix} r_{k+1}^{WC} \\ q_{k+1}^{WC} \\ v_{k+1}^{W} \\ \omega_{k+1}^{W} \end{pmatrix} = \begin{pmatrix} r_k^{WC} + \left(v_k^W + V^W\right)\Delta t \\ q_k^{WC} \times q((\omega_k^W + \Omega^W)\Delta t) \\ v_k^W + V^W \\ \omega_k^W + \Omega^W \end{pmatrix} \tag{2}$$

Inverse depth parameterization expresses any 3D scene feature point as shown in Fig. 1 using the following state:

$$f_i = (x_i \quad y_i \quad z_i \quad \theta_i \quad \phi_i \quad \rho_i)^T \tag{3}$$

where x_i, y_i, z_i denote the camera center when the ith point was first observed, θ_i and ϕ_i are the azimuth and elevation angles respectively and ρ_i is the inverse depth of the point.

The full state vector comprises the camera/robot state and the entire n map features:

$$X = (x_v^T, f_1^T, \dots, f_n^T)^T \tag{4}$$

Note that the points $f_1^T, \dots, f_n^T$ can serve as suitable representations for the object landmarks numbered from 1 to n, and this will be detailed in section 4. The measurement prediction in the EKF is controlled by the measurement model which is shown in Fig. 1 and given as:

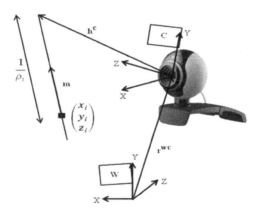

Fig. 1. Inverse depth parameterization and measurement model

$$h^C = R^{CW}\left(\begin{pmatrix} x_i \\ y_i \\ z_i \end{pmatrix} + \frac{1}{\rho_i}\, m(\theta_i, \phi_i) - r^{WC}\right) \tag{5}$$

$$m(\theta_i, \phi_i) = (cos\phi_i \, sin\theta_i \quad -sin\phi_i \quad cos\phi_i \, cos\theta_i) \qquad (6)$$

The model is completed by using the pinhole camera model and the standard two-parameter distortion model as detailed in [10].

3   The VSLAM Algorithm

The proposed algorithm is described in Fig. 2. A database of templates of the probable objects in the environment is given to the robot beforehand. New features are added to the full state vector and hence the map in the object recognition stage. This is performed by searching the current image for new templates other than those currently stored in the map. The template search checks if the current image matches any of the templates that have not been added yet using a fast and robust template matching method.

The EKF prediction estimates the robot state after motion using the motion model of (2). This updates only the robot state vector x_v since motion doesn't affect the features state. Measurement prediction finds if the currently stored features are

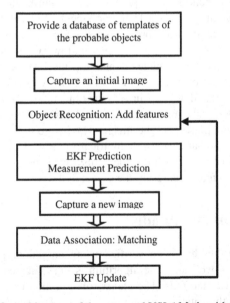

Fig. 2. Architecture of the proposed VSLAM algorithm

predicted to still appear in the new image after the robot motion and estimates their new predicted locations. This prediction exploits the measurement model of (5).

A new image is now captured and template matching stage performs the important part of data association in SLAM. Data association means here to find if the new image matches any of the stored templates that have been predicted to still appear in the scene. This is performed also by the fast template matching technique which outputs the matched location of the predicted features. The difference between the matched and the predicted locations of features is called the innovation term. This term is used to update both the robot and the map states in the last stage of EKF update. It is important to note that all previous calculations are referenced to the first camera frame.

4   Fast Template Matching

The common detection and description techniques used with point features should be modified to suit the objects landmarks. There are several ways to represent the appearance features of objects: probability densities of object appearance, active appearance models, multi view appearance models and templates [11]. An advantage of a template is that it carries both spatial and appearance information. On the other hand, templates are not invariant to rotation or scale changes. Thus, they are only suitable for tracking objects whose appearance doesn't vary considerably during motion. This is the case for indoor mobile robot that moves with medium translational and rotational speed. Therefore, we adopt template matching for its simplicity and we use the fast template matching technique for speed requirements.

Fast template matching method [12] implements Normalized Cross Correlation, NCC in frequency domain using precomputed tables containing the integral of the image and image square over the search window. Computations are efficiently performed using summed- area tables containing the integral of the image (running sum) and image square over the search area. As previously stated, fast template matching is adopted to: add new features in the object recognition stage and match the stored features in the data association stage. In both cases, a matching score is calculated between templates and the image. The image point having the peak of the matching score is compared to an empirically defined threshold (0.85). If the matching score passes the threshold, then this image point is at the center of the template and it is selected to represent the object in the map.

5   Experiments and Results

The proposed algorithm has been verified using an indoor mobile robot platform (Robotino) carrying a webcam. The algorithm is implemented in MATLAB making use of the code of [10] and [13]. The planar robot motion is in the XZ-plane and the pitch angle denotes the rotation around the Y-axis. The results are benchmarked as follows: the output of the EKF computations is first transformed from the first camera frame of reference to the world frame, and then the error between the world and groundtruth data is calculated. Let $r_{C_k}^{C_1}$ denotes the location of the camera (robot) across the camera frames and referenced to the first frame. The robot trajectory is aligned with the world frame $r_{C_k}^{W}$, by using the following transformation:

$$r_{C_k}^W = s\, R_{C_1}^W r_{C_k}^{C_1} + t_{C_1}^W \tag{7}$$

The translation term in (7) $t_{C_1}^W$ is given by the groundtruth data of the initial position of the robot.

Pseudo inverse optimization is used to find the scale (s) and rotation ($R_{C_1}^W$) that minimize the error between the groundtruth data (r_g^W) and the aligned trajectory as described by (8).

$$s\, R_{C_1}^W = \left(r_g^W - t_{C_1}^W\right) r_{C_k}^{C_1\,T} \, (r_{C_k}^{C_1} r_{C_k}^{C_1\,T})^{-1} \tag{8}$$

The value of $\left(s\, R_{C_1}^W\right)$ obtained from (8) is used in (7) to find $r_{C_k}^W$ and then calculate the error ($r_{C_k}^W - r_g^W$).

The templates of five objects are given to the robot beforehand, and then the robot is driven on a suitable path. The given templates are images of five naturally existing objects in the lab (PC monitor-poster-DC motor kit-power supply-oscilloscope) as shown in Fig. 3.

In the experiment, the robot moves along a line of 280 cm distance at our lab space capturing images sequentially. The robot path is measured using robot onboard odometry to provide the groundtruth. The path is checked manually by a scale with point markers at the ground. Odometry readings can be trusted in this experiment since the path of the robot is segmented in short (4 cm) steps.

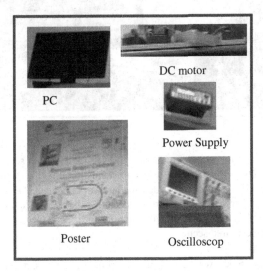

Fig. 3. Database of the objects templates

Fig. 4 (a) shows the captured scene in the left and the XZ plane of robot motion in the right where the triangle represents the robot and the '+' marks show the estimated feature location. The added features are shown in the captured scene by the box around the detected template. The two arrows in the right indicate that the two detected features have initially infinite depth uncertainty. The generated map associated with this captured scene is shown in Fig. 4 (b). The XY projection of the map is shown as a panoramic picture of the video sequence relative to the first camera frame.

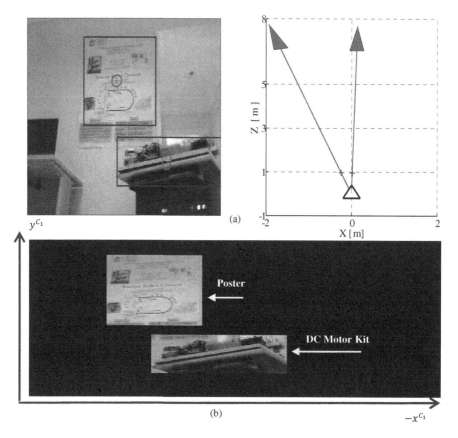

Fig. 4. Snapshot from the algorithm output. (a) Left: the captured scene with boxes enclosing the detected objects. Ellipses show the uncertainty around the feature location. Red '+' represents the center of the object added to the map and green '+' is its match. Right: the triangle represents the robot and the arrows mean that the added features have initially infinite depth uncertainty. (b) Panorama picture showing the XY projection of the map of objects associated with the captured scene.

Similarly, Fig. 5 shows the captured scene in a subsequent frame. The arrows disappeared and shrinking ellipses describe now the decreasing depth uncertainty as shown in the right subplot of Fig. 5 (a). Again, the XY projection of the map is shown in Fig. 5 (b) with the three currently stored objects. When the DC motor kit object exits the scene, it still appears in the map referenced to the first camera frame.

The localization results are given in Fig. 6 showing the error in position (X, Z) and in orientation (Pitch angle) of the robot. The error ranges in Fig. 6 are comparable to those of [8] and [10] -for a similar experiment with 60 camera frames- as shown in Table 1.

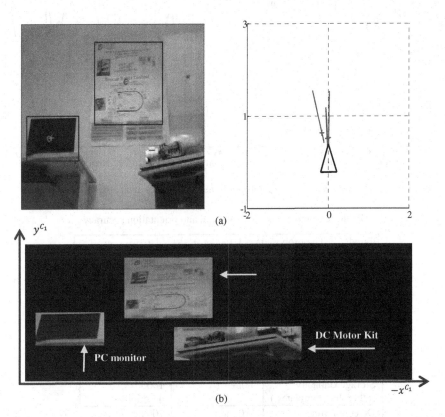

(a)

(b)

Fig. 5. Snapshot from the algorithm output. (a) Left: the captured scene with boxes enclosing the detected objects. Ellipses show the uncertainty around the feature location. Right: the triangle represents the robot and shrinking ellipses denote decreasing depth uncertainty. (b) Panorama picture showing the XY projection of the map of all currently stored objects. Note that the dc motor kit appears here although it is not completely visible.

The storage capacity and timing for this experiment are compared to the similar five-objects experiment of [5] and summarized in Table 2. Only the templates of objects are stored as entries in the database, whereas in [5] additional 2000 descriptors are needed for each object. Hence, the proposed algorithm requires less storage capacity and detection time as can be observed in Table 2. The proposed method is simpler than both [5] and [8] since it doesn't require parallel computations for image processing or SIFT points extraction. Using inverse depth parameterization overcomes the need to structure the environment by a calibrating rig. One disadvantage of the proposed method is the need for predefined templates, which will be considered for future work.

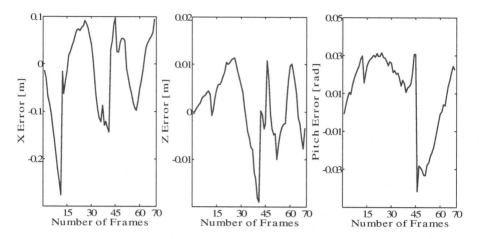

Fig. 6. Localization errors along the robot translation (X, Z) and rotation angle (Pitch)

Table 1. Comparison of the motion and orientation accuracy

Bounds of error	The proposed Method	Lee *et al* [8]	Civera *et al* [10]
X(m)	- 0.15 – 0.10	0.10 – 0.18	-0.05 – 0.10
Z(m)	- 0.02 – 0.01	0.10 – 0.30	-0.02 – 0.10
θ(rad)	- 0.03 – 0.03	0.08 – 0.47	-0.03 – 0.08

Table 2. Comparison of the storage capacity and timing

	The proposed Method	Castle *et al* [5]
Storage Capacity (other than templates)	none	10000 descriptors
Detection time	170 ms	700 ms
Matching time	315 ms	45 ms

6   Conclusions

Scalability is a major problem of the state of the art VSLAM systems due to the dependency on huge number of interest points. Data association of interest points is also difficult due to the existence of inliers. Moreover, a map of point features may not be suitable interpretation for some robotic applications. Objects are used in this study since they are salient landmarks that can be used to reduce the number of features and hence solve the scalability problem. Reduction of the number of features is useful to enable long missions without high storage requirements. A simple visual mono SLAM algorithm is presented that adopts objects as landmarks and uses fast template matching to track their appearance. Experimental results show that objects can be used as visual landmarks to reduce the number of tracked features and improve the data association without reducing the SLAM accuracy. The proposed method is simple since it does not require complex parallel computations or high storage capacity.

Acknowledgement. The first author is supported by a scholarship from the Ministry of Higher Education, Government of Egypt which is gratefully acknowledged.

References

1. Durrant-Whyte, H., Bailey, T.: Simultaneous Localization and Mapping: Part I. IEEE Robotics and Automation Magazine 13(2), 99–110 (2006)
2. Davison, A.: SLAM with a Single Camera. CML Workshop at ICRA (2002)
3. Mikolajczyk, K., Schmid, C.: A Performance Evaluation of Local Descriptors. IEEE Transactions on Pattern Analysis and Machine Intelligence 27(10), 1615–1630 (2005)
4. Davison, A., Reid, I., Molton, N., Stasse, O.: MonoSLAM: Real-Time Single Camera SLAM. IEEE Transactions on Pattern Analysis and Machine intelligence 29(6), 1052–1067 (2007)
5. Castle, R., Klein, G., Murray, D.: Combining monoSLAM with object recognition for scene augmentation using a wearable camera. Journal of Image and Vision Computing 28(11), 1548–1556 (2010)
6. Jeong, W., Lee, K.: Visual SLAM with Line and Corner Features. In: IEEE/RSJ International Conference on Intelligent Robots and Systems, pp. 2570–2575 (2006)
7. Davison, A.: Real-Time Simultaneous Localization and Mapping with a single camera. In: IEEE International Conference onComputer Vision, vol. 2, pp. 1403–1410 (2003)
8. Lee, Y., Song, J.: Autonomous selection, registration, and recognition of objects for visual SLAM in indoor environments. In: ICCAS International Conference on Control, Automation and Systems, pp. 668–673 (2007)
9. Civera, J., Davison, A., Montiel, J.: Inverse Depth Parametrization for Monocular SLAM. IEEE Transactions on Robotics 24(5), 932–945 (2008)
10. Civera, J., Grasa, Ó., Davison, A., Montiel, J.: 1-Point RANSAC for EKF Filtering: Application to Real-Time Structure from Motion and Visual Odometry. Journal of Field Robotics 27(5), 609–631 (2010)
11. Yilmaz, A., Javed, O., Shah, M.: Object tracking: A survey. ACM Computing Surveys 38(4) (2006)
12. Lewis, J.: Fast TemplateMatching. In: Vision Interface 1995, Canadian Image Processing and Pattern Recognition Society, pp. 120–123 (1995)
13. Kroon, D.:
   http://www.mathworks.com/matlabcentral/fileexchange/24925-fastrobust-template-matching (accessed at September 1, 2011)

Body Pixel Classification by Neural Network

Hazar Chaabani[1,2], Wassim Filali[3], Thierry Simon[1,4], and Frederic Lerasle[3]

[1] Lrpmip-Université de Toulouse : UTM-IUT Toulouse 2 Figeac,
Avenue de Nayrac, 46100 Figeac, France
[2] LARODEC, Université de Tunis, ISG de Tunis
41 Rue de la Liberté, Cité Bouchoucha 2000 Le Bardo, Tunisie
[3] CNRS, LAAS, 7 avenue du Colonel Roche, F-31400 Toulouse, France
[4] Université de Toulouse; INSA, UPS, Mines Albi, ISAE; ICA
(Institut Clément Ader); Campus Jarlard, F-81013 Albi, France

Abstract. Body pixel classification is a multiclass pixel by pixel image segmentation problem that aims to classify each image pixel to its correspondent human body part. In this article we initially adopted for this problem a Multilayer Perceptron neural network (MLP) classifier using back propagation algorithm to learn network weights and biases. Then confidence intervals based on *diffMax* criterion are computed in order to make classification more certain. This criterion is computed by the difference between the first and second maximum value of MLP output vector.

A 92 % correct classification rate was achieved after applying confidence classification. The classification result will be integrated as an input to a human posture recognition system.

Keywords: neural network, human posture, classification confidence.

1 Introduction

Human pose estimation is a very challenging domain that consists of configuring an articulated body from images in terms of joint positions [1]. We propose to describe the use of a multi-layer perceptron in the first step of human posture recognition process inspired by the work of Shotton et al. [3] which concerns body pixel classification. The application uses a synthetic silhouette on which the areas of the body are identified. The silhouette is built by considering an indoor scene observed from several points of view. The scene evolves dynamically modified by the nonrectilinear trajectory of a moving person, this assumption considers that each sensor sees all the parts of the body in the same way. A local index topologically characterizing each pixel of the silhouette is calculated. This index must be calculable by an algorithm implemented in hardware to be computed at video rate, it is the element of input for the neural network which its method of classification is most easily implemented on hardware. The outputs of the network are the parts of the body, these outputs will be used in their relative position to determine the posture, this part is not treated in this article. The aim of this application is that in the event of interpreted posture as an emergency

C.-Y. Su, S. Rakheja, H. Liu (Eds.): ICIRA 2012, Part III, LNAI 7508, pp. 494–502, 2012.
© Springer-Verlag Berlin Heidelberg 2012

then a mobile platform can carry assistance. To ensure a good interpretation, it is necessary that classification is certified. We propose to qualify the classification of the pixels by exploiting output vector to define a confidence on the result.

Paper is structured in four parts, the first briefly presents the index used to characterize the pixels of the silhouette, the second describes the network used and the organization of the database for the training, the third specifies the strategy of computation of the classification confidence, the fourth presents the results.

2   Local Index

The silhouette consists of the pixels covering the body detected by the difference of the image in the presence of the person and the fixed background in absence of anybody. Several background subtraction techniques, that allow to detect foreground objects in a frame sequence, exist in the literature. Most of them used the motion information [2](see [4] for a review). In the case of real data, various body parts are manually labelled. This long procedure is often replaced by a generation of a synthetic silhouette with an automatic labelling which we exploited in our application. This technique makes it possible to test the generalization ability of the neural networks in the case of presentation of real data.

Before proceeding with classification, image content is described using global or local descriptor. A global descriptor is a global features based vector computed on the whole image [5]. Local descriptors [6] are calculated on the base of interest points or image zones. This latters are preferred to global descriptors since they are more flexible and more robust [8].

The local index descriptor is calculated to leave the (x, y) position of a pixel in the silhouette by looking at the presence of close pixels in six directions and at various distances. The distances are adjusted according to a scale factor depending on the size of the silhouette. The directions are selected in order to ensure invariance in rotation and covering a disc surrounding the pixel with an angle of $60°$.

Each pixel of the silhouette is been affected to a vector whose components are binary values *0, 1* respectively depending on the absence and presence of close pixels (*Fig. 1*). The number of distances depends on the method of posture determination. This parameter will be selected according to the performance and time computing. In our case, 7 distances were retained to construct a vector with 42 components, input of our network. This index is a SIFT resulting from the work of Mortensen et al. [7]. We verified that the dimension of the vector was not reducible by traditional methods PCA or LDA.

3   Database and Training

To train the network, we use a multi view image data set. Totally we have 5 views to be used. Each view consists of a 408 synthetically generated images

Fig. 1. Pixel descriptor

characterizing a walk sequence. On average, each 640x480 image is represented by 18000 foreground body pixels (*Fig. 2*). This data organization allows a OneView learning by training a specific network for each sensor. However, these networks still useful only when located person moves in one direction.

Another way of data rearrangement can be carried out by organizing data per frame gathering the images of the five views at the instant t. To adopt this flexible strategy that consists of configuring a network able to label a picture from any view, it becomes necessary to sort data and filter doubles in order to eliminate redundancy.

Whatever the organization mode used, the data set is randomly splitted into train, validation and test sets with three different proportions of ratio 60, 20 and 20. In order to speed the learning process and deal with memory space constraint, for each training image, only m pixels are randomly selected to train the network. Adding to that, we proceed with a sequential training of the network by initializing weights and biases of the ith session with those stored in the i-1 session where i varies from 1 to n, where n is the number of training images divided by the number of images per session.

4   Confidence Computing

In several object recognition applications, to not classify an object is much better than classifying it with uncertainty. So to optimize recognition, a criterion based confidence intervals for either well-classified pixels (WCP) and misclassified pixels (MCP) are calculated. This criterion, which we call *diffMax*, is the difference between the first and the second maximum value of each pixel output vector since in most confusion situations, increasingly small differences were detected (*Fig. 3*).

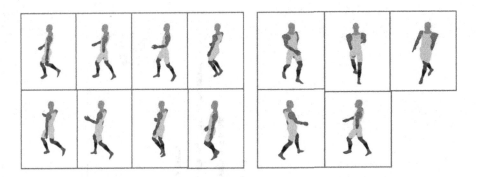

Fig. 2. A sample of used images : on the right silhouettes from five views at the same instant and different silhouettes from one view on the left

To find the model that fits data, an empirically method is used to be oriented toward symmetric or asymmetric distributions. Then, we apply the Chi-squared (chi2) goodness-of-fit test to select the best theoretical distribution. However, this test is developed to handle small samples counting miles of examples [9]. Subsequently such test cannot operate with large samples since it is difficult to represent millions of observations with a 2 or 3-parameter model. That is why the best distribution is the one that minimize the distance:

$$d = \sum_{i=1}^{n} \left(\frac{(p_i^* - p_i)^2}{p_i} \right)$$

where p_i is the empirical frequency and p_i^* the theoretical estimated frequency.

After estimating mode and standard deviation parameters, switch the diffMax criterion, we attribute to each pixel the following classification decision (*Fig. 4*):

- (0) pixel is classified but without confidence.
- (1) pixel is classified with confidence.
- (2) pixel is not classified with confidence.

According to the disposition of confidence intervals of WCP and MCP, we can distinguish two situations the first one when confidence intervals are well separated and subsequently there is no confusion and the second otherwise.

5   Results

The two classification approaches were applied to the data set described in section 3 with the following parameters: m=10000; n=16.
The network structure is a full connected three-layer feed forward perceptron with the following characteristics (*Fig. 5*):

- A 42 elements input vector describing each image pixel using local descriptor.
- A 30 elements hidden vector founded empirically according to network performance.

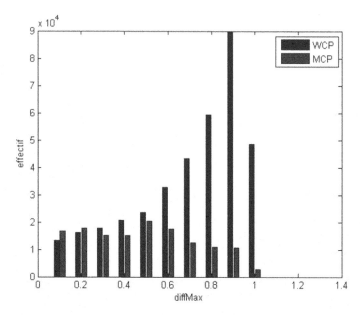

Fig. 3. The histogram shows the number of WCP and MCP for each diffMax bin

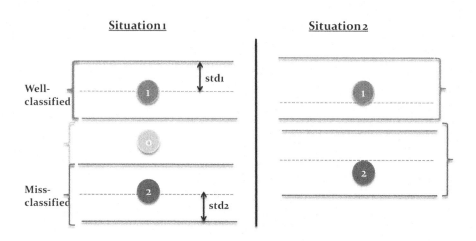

Fig. 4. Confidence intervals disposition

– 8 output nodes describing body part classes (head, shoulder, arm, hand, leg, foot, elbow and torso).

According to *Fig. 7,8*, 74 % average classification accuracy was achieved under the OneView approach against only 69.6 % under the AllView approach.

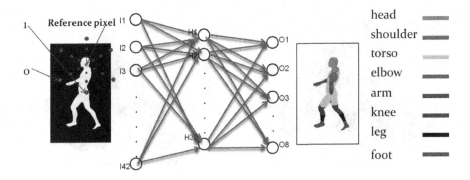

Fig. 5. Network architecture

Fig. 6 shows an example of classification visualization where head is the most recognized part. Shoulder, elbow and left arm are confused with torso part. Elbow, torso and leg parts are recognized by the OneView approach better than the AllView approach.

The second part of this work consists of pixel classification using confidence intervals. As can be seen in *Fig. 9*, the diffMax criterion takes small values in the set of misclassified pixels compared with well-classified ones. To choose the theoretical distribution that adjusts empirical data, first, parameters of different candidate distributions for each body part class are estimated using maximum-likelihood estimation. Then, a distance between theoretical and empirical data is calculated since adjustment tests like chi2 cannot be used when samples are too large. The chosen distribution is the one that minimizes this distance.

Computing the distance d, for each of the Normal, Rayleigh, Gamma and Wei-bull distributions, has given the different choices shown in *Table 1*, where W_i and M_i denote respectively well-classified and miss-classified pixels of the ith class, i=1:8. The selected distribution is the one that minimizes the error d.

Final decision given by *Table 2* shows that 50 % of classes of WCP respectively MCP follow the Gamma respectively the Rayleigh distribution.

Fig. 6. Classification result visualization from left to right: target classification, OneView classification, AllVue classification

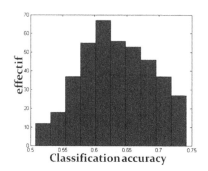

Classification accuracy

Fig. 7. OneView approach correct classification rate Histogram

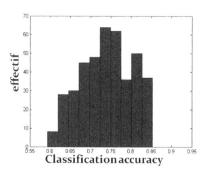

Classification accuracy

Fig. 8. AllView approach correct classification rate Histogram

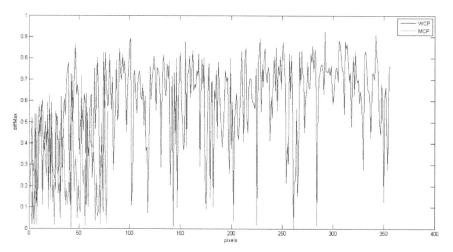

Fig. 9. Visualization of diffMax values for WCP and MCP

Table 1. Per class distribution choice

distribution	W_1	W_2	W_3	W_4	W_5	W_6	W_7	W_8	M_1	M_2	M_3	M_4	M_5	M_6	M_7	M_8
normal			×		×							×				
rayleigh	×								×	×			×		×	
gamma		×	×				×	×			×			×		×
wei-bull				×												

Table 2. Final distribution choice

	Normal	Rayleigh	Gamma	Weibull
WCP	25 %	12.5 %	50 %	12.5 %
MCP	12.5 %	50 %	37.5 %	0 %

Table 3. Confidence intervals per class

class	LBW	UBW	LBM	UBM	% of WCP	% of MCP
1	0.50	1.04	0.10	0.59	0.97	0.51
2	0.31	0.98	0.13	0.77	0.92	0.62
3	0.19	0.91	0.06	0.65	0.92	0.61
4	0.20	0.77	0.10	0.62	0.92	0.60
5	0.35	0.99	0.07	0.66	0.92	0.60
6	0.26	0.92	0.09	0.67	0.92	0.60
7	0.35	0.95	0.09	0.59	0.92	0.60
8	0.20	0.90	0.08	0.60	0.92	0.60

As shown in *Table 3*, for all body classes the two confidence intervals are mixed. This means that we are in the second situation (*Fig. 4*). Subsequently, the confidence level for a classification is fixed to the upper bound of the misclassified confidence interval(UBM) which is approximately equal to 0.64.

After classifying pixels switch confidence level, the percentage of well-classified pixels that we previously decide to classify with confidence is on average equal to 92.6 %, with 97 % for the head part, and the percentage of wrongly classified pixels that we previously decide not to classify with confidence is equal to 60 % with 51 % for the head part.

Fig. 10. From left to right: Target classification, neural network classification, confidence classification using mean and confidence classification using mode

Since data distributions are not symmetric, using mean to compute confidence interval eliminate a significant proportion of pixels even so they are well-classified (*Fig. 10*). However, using mode, we have almost the same recognition rate but keeping more well-classified pixels.

The main confidence level allowed to remove confusion regions such as body parts borders and arm-torso partial occlusion. This latter is a well-known segmentation problem that was evoked by many researchers as in [10].

6 Conclusion

In this paper, we have adopted a multilayer perceptron learner to body pixels classification problem. Confidence intervals are subsequently calculated on the basis of the diffMax criterion in order to maintain maximum certainty. The correct classification rate of pixels having a diffMax value upper to the confidence boundary is equal to 92 %. This automatic pixel-by-pixel classification is just the first step in a pose estimation process.

In the future work, we will focus on classifying voxel data images and human pose estimation. The proposed diffMax criterion can be used in other classification problems where certainty is required to make critical decisions.

References

[1] Rosales, R., SclaroffInferring, S.: Body Pose without Tracking Body Parts. In: Proceedings of the IEEE Computer Vision and Pattern Recognition (2000)

[2] Lacassagne, L., Manzanera, A.: Motion Detection: Fast and robust algorithms for embedded systems. In: Proceedings of the 16th IEEE International Conference on Image Processing (2009)

[3] Shotton, J., Fitzgibbon, A., Cook, M., Sharp, T., Finocchio, M., Moore, R., Kipman, A., Blake, A.: Real-Time Human Pose Recognition in Parts from Single Depth Images. In: Proceedings of the IEEE Computer Vision and Pattern Recognition Conference, pp. 1297–1304 (2011)

[4] Piccardi, M.: Background Subtraction Techniques:a review. In: Proceedings of the International Conference on Systems, Man and Cybernetics, pp. 3199–3104 (2004)

[5] Belongie, S., Malik, J., Puzicha, J.: Shape matching and object recognition using shape contexts. IEEE Transactions on Pattern Analysis and Machine Intelligence 24, 509–522 (2002)

[6] Calonder, M., Lepetit, V., Strecha, C., Fua, P.: BRIEF: Binary Robust Independent Elementary Features. In: Daniilidis, K., Maragos, P., Paragios, N. (eds.) ECCV 2010, Part IV. LNCS, vol. 6314, pp. 778–792. Springer, Heidelberg (2010)

[7] Mortensen, E.N., Deng, H., Shapiro, L.: A SIFT descriptor with global context. In: Computer Vision and Pattern Recognition (2005)

[8] Amsaleg, L., Gros, P., Mezhoud, R.: Mise en base d'images indexées par des descripteurs locaux: problèmes et perspectives. In: Research report No. 1316. Institut de Recherche en Informatique et Systèmes Aléatoires, Rennes, France (2000)

[9] Hamburg, M., Young, P.: Statistical analysis for decision making, 6th edn., Edition Technip. (1993) ISBN: 0-03-096914-X

[10] Porle, R.R., Chekima, A., Wong, F., Sainarayanan, G.: Wavelet-based skin segmentation for detecting occluded arms in human body pose modelling system. In: Proceedings of the International Conference on Intelligent and Advanced Systems, pp. 764–769 (2007)

Robust Recognition against Illumination Variations Based on SIFT

Farzan Nowruzi, Mohammad Ali Balafar, and Saeid Pashazadeh

Department of Information Technology
Faculty of Electrical and Computer Engineering
University of Tabriz, Tabriz, East Azerbaijan, Iran
farzan87@gmail.com,
{balafarila,pashazadeh}@tabrizu.ac.ir

Abstract. Feature matching is one of the basic approaches to many of computer vision applications, such as *object recognition*. Dealing with illumination variations is an open problem in this field. In this paper we present an approach to make a more robust algorithm against real world illumination changes and variations in direction of the light source on our object of interest, by using a set of training images for sampling these variations from their *SIFT* keypoints. A comprehensive *keypoint descriptor* based on the variations of illumination in training data is acquired to have a high recognition rate against real 3D illumination changes. This large number of keypoints is simplified to achieve a smaller number of robust keypoints and significantly faster matching phase.

Keywords: Object Recognition, SIFT, Keypoint Descriptor, Sampled Training.

1 Introduction

Scale Invariant Feature Transform (SIFT) is a method that tries to match an image of an object, in a real-time performance by extracting its distinctive invariant features and comparing them with the queried image's features. SIFT was first introduced and then expanded by Lowe [12][3]. Using features to represent images of objects is an important objective in the field of data compression and mobile applications.

SIFT transforms an image of object to a collection of local feature vectors (SIFT keypoint descriptors) which they are invariant to scaling, rotation and translation of image and are partially invariant against affine and orientation and also, they are tolerant against image noise. In addition, these features are unaffected by nearby clutter or partial occlusion. It tries to find potential keypoints by smoothing and down sampling the input image and subtracting adjacent levels to create a pyramid of Difference-of-Gaussian. Then, it looks for minima and maxima points in scale space. After finding stable keypoints, the gradient orientation histogram is computed to find dominant orientations. Once

C.-Y. Su, S. Rakheja, H. Liu (Eds.): ICIRA 2012, Part III, LNAI 7508, pp. 503–511, 2012.

a keypoint orientation has been selected, the feature descriptor vector is computed. To match computed features of an image to the features of an object in database, nearest neighbor algorithm is utilized [13].

However, the algorithm itself is robust against small illumination changes, but large changes in illumination conditions, or let's say changes in direction of light, specially on 3-Dimensional objects will cause dramatic decrease in recognition performance of algorithm [4]. Some of algorithms perform normalization steps like histogram equalization, Gamma correction and logarithmic transformations [20], wavelet illumination normalization [21]. Some other uses an other types of representation like self quotient image with Logarithmic Total Variation (LTV) smoothing [8], wavelet based facial structure representation [9] and the combination of histogram equalization and homomorphic filtering presented in [10]. Chen et al. [18] have used Wiener filter approach to extract illumination invariant features from images which outperform previous state-of-the-art algorithms, both in recognition performance and computational efficiency. These are some of different approaches to compensate the effect of illumination variations on subject of interest. SIFT is relying on texture features of an image. Therefore, satisfactory results could not be achieved using methods that cause dramatic changes on texture features, in combination with SIFT.

We tried to put forward another simple solution to make a fast algorithm to work on a large databases, providing robust recognition for such variations. This is achieved by combining extracted features under various illumination changes and producing a comprehensive keypoint descriptor file. Produced file will have a large number of keypoints which will require more time to match them. So, we propose a simplifying step to select a small number of robust features.

2   Related Works

Mikolajczyk and Schmid [5] have shown that SIFT descriptor is superior to other descriptors such as the distribution-based shape context, the geometric histogram descriptor which is very similar to SIFT by implementing the same idea, the derivative-based complex filters, and the moment invariants.

There is a number of SIFT derivations and extensions. Some examples that have been developed include Principal Components Analysis-SIFT (PCA-SIFT) [14] and Speeded-Up Robust Features (SURF) [6] which claim to provide more robustness and distinctiveness with scaled-down complexity to have faster matching stages. SIFT and its derivations have been applied for a wide range of applications in scene recognition and detection, image registration, stereo camera calibration, robot localization, motion tracking, 3D modeling and reconstruction.

PCA-SIFT, instead of smoothed weighted histograms, utilizes PCA to normalize gradients. PCA is a standard technique for dimensionality reduction. The keypoints SIFT produces has a high dimensionality (128 element for a feature vector as Lowes default [12][3]) therefore it is suitable to project them into a low dimensional feature space to extract dominant features. This results a smaller feature vector to be used in the same matching step. Consequently, having smaller features will also require smaller storage and faster matching speed.

SURF has a slightly different approach to detect features than SIFT. It is a scale and rotation invariant detector which is based on integral images for image convolutions that causes filtering to be done in almost constant time. This is done by using a Hessian matrix-based measure for the detector, and a distribution-based descriptor. The Laplacian-based indexing strategy makes the matching step faster without any loss in terms of performance. SURF also produces fewer keypoints than SIFT.

Although SIFT is slow due to the number of features and the size of it's keypoints, and has low invariance against illumination changes, but it has a high stability in most of other situations. SURF is the fastest between these two algorithms while having an overall recognition performance close to SIFT but it is not much stable against rotation and illumination changes. Finally, PCA-SIFT performs better on variations occur in rotation and illumination [4]. In this paper, we will focus on effects of illumination to provide more robust feature descriptors to overcome this weakness of SIFT compared to SURF and PCA-SIFT.

Methods described are depending on costly descriptors for detection of interest points and matching them. Recently, as a new alternative, Oriented fast and Rotated BRIEF (ORB) [15] is introduced. ORB is based on oriented BRIEF [2] and is a very fast binary descriptor. It is also invariant to rotation and noise. It has been showed that in two orders of magnitude, ORB is faster than SIFT, while maintaining a recognition performance close to it in some situations.

Javanmard and Mahmoudi presented MGS-SIFT [19] which is very similar to the method presented by Nowruzi and Habibi [1]. MGS-SIFT tries to evaluate 3D illumination changes on a 2D image using alpha transform to produce multiple features in different illuminations. Since SIFT has some robustness to illumination variations, this algorithm could achieve a small increase in recognition performance compared to the method presented in [1], which uses real world images. Given the additional overload and the growing size of descriptor, these algorithms will be much slower in descriptor generation and matching steps.

3   Algorithm

To make SIFT more robust against illumination changes, we have created our own approach based on the simple idea on biological perception. How much more a human sees an object/scene in different conditions he/she becomes more familiar with its characteristics. As a result, he/she can recognize them faster and more precisely. During this process robust features of objects are captured in different conditions. We are trying to make an algorithm to find those important features by using SIFT to gather them from objects. More features we collect more easily we will be able to identify the distinctive features of the object in different conditions.

3.1 SIFT

The proposed algorithm involves SIFT and an additional matching step. We would alter some parts in keypoint generation step for training purpose and generate a comprehensive descriptor, to select the most robust features in image.

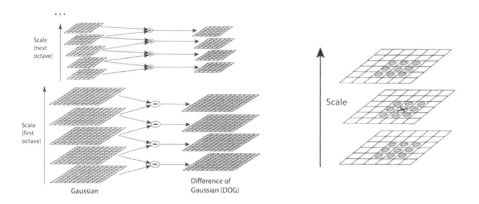

Fig. 1. Process of finding initial *candidate keypoints* [3]. Left: *Difference-of-Gasussians* calculated by finding difference between two adjacent Gaussian smoothed images with different σ values. Right: Candidate keypoint selection by *extrema point* detection from adjacent points in same, upper and lower scales.

In the first step, we are trying to identify the interest points of SIFT which are invariant against scale, rotation variations. Scale-space is a framework for having a one-parameter family of smoothed images of our original image. Lindeberg [7] showed that Gaussian function is the only kernel to be used as smoothing kernel for scale space analysis. After convolving with Gaussian kernel and producing scale-space images, they are grouped in an octave. Using a bi-linear interpolation, scale-space images are down sampled to create next level of the pyramid. Detection of extrema points in scale-space is done by subtracting adjacent blurred images in each octave, called Difference-of-Gaussian (DoG) function. Each point in DoG are compared to 26 neighbors of its. This neighborhood consists of points in lower, same and upper scales. If the point was a minima or maxima in its neighborhood, it is selected as potential keypoint location. Scale-space extrema detection produces too many keypoint candidates. A large number of pixels are eliminated in the first few matches.

After finding these candidate keypoints, a fit to nearby data is performed to achieve location, scale, and ratio of principal curvatures. This process rejects low contrast feature locations but is not sufficient enough to acquire all stable keypoints. The noise sensitive points or the points which are poorly localized along an edge should be removed too.

In third step, to achieve robustness against image rotation, each keypoint is assigned with one or more orientations based on local image gradients. At each keypoint, gradient orientations of a window around the keypoint form the orientation histogram which contains 36 bins to cover 360 degree range of rotations, is computed. This process has been performed in a scale invariant manner by selecting Gaussian smoothed image with respect to the scale of keypoint. Gradient magnitude of samples and a Gaussian weighted circular window are used for weighting the samples before being added to histogram for illumination robustness. In addition to dominant direction of local gradients, any other local maxima within 80 percents of the dominant direction are also kept. In case of existing multiple peaks of similar magnitude in the histogram, new keypoints are created at different orientations for the same location and scale. A few points selected to have multiple orientations which significantly improve the stability of matching. For every image we calculate a descriptor file based on 128 attributes represented in a file along with 4 fields for location information.

3.2   Illumination Sampling

We add a new attribute v to keypoint descriptors k in training phase. The purpose of this new attribute is to calculate the matching times of corresponding keypoints in different training examples for the same object of interest. This process leads us to find most salient key points. In matching step, we will increase match times of each of matched keypoints. Keypoint files in each subset is matched to all other in the same subset. The keypoints with highest votes from large number of keypoints are selected. These keypoints are the most robust keypoints for each subset and are used as representative of each subset for matching the input image to whole database. The number of representative keypoints in our model is bound to be 100 keypoints per each subset. This is small enough to have a fast search step with a high accuracy. Finally, representative keypoints from each subset are gathered together to make *illumination sampled keypoints (IS-SIFT)* for each subject.

```
for each Subject
  for each Subset
    for each DescriptorFile
      for each Descriptor
        v = times that k in a DescriptorFile
            matched in other DescriptorFiles
        v added as last column of vector k
      end
    end
    all DescriptorFiles concatinated and sorted with respect to v
    and only top m Descriptors selected as Subset representative
  end
  selected Descriptors concatinated to form FS
end
```

SIFT is robust against changes in illumination that doesnt change gradient orientations and only affects gradient magnitudes. A change in light source position will affect both magnitude and orientations. Taking benefit of this quality of SIFT, we divide our database to 5 similar groups of images having acceptable amounts of illumination variations to maintain similarity of images in the same subset. We perform our training step distinctively for each of these subsets. Each of the produced keypoints are added together to make a final keypoint file for each subject. The number of keypoints in this file is in between 400 to 500. In our model each subset consists of 12.8 images per subset in average. The average number of keypoints for each image in each subset is approximatly 100. Given these values, we represent each subset with only 6.25% to 7.81% of keypoints. High recognition speed is achieved by this huge amount of decrease in the number of keypoints.

3.3   Matching Phase

Matching is done using nearest neighbor algorithm with the distance set to 0.6 as a standard in SIFT. First, a dot product between each keypoint of first image to second image is calculated. Then, after taking *acos* of the dot product, we find the first and second best matches. If the first best match was smaller than 0.6 times of second best match then it is selected as the final match.

Finally, we will have a number of matched images. We start to sort matched images by their number of matched keypoints and their similarity score. Similarity score is defined as the mean distance between matched keypoints of two images. Lower distance represents a closer matching, consequently, a better result. Number of matched keypoints for query image and each of images in database is counted. The images which have matched keypoints at least more than half of the best matching image are selected as candidate results. Among the images which have the same number of matched keypoints, images are sorted based on the values of mean distance of matching. Images having smaller values of mean distance of matching come first. The image represented by the first row most probably is the exact face that we are looking for.

$$similarity = \tfrac{1}{n} \sum acos(k_{matched} \cdot FS_{matched})$$

$$(n = number\ of\ matched\ keyoints)$$

(1)

In cases of vital recognition applications, the selected candidate images can be verified again by matching with comprehensive keypoints of the same subjects identified by algorithm. Also, a value denoting the accuracy of the match based on the number of matched keypoints and the mean distance of the first and second best matches can be used as a measure of confidence to show validity of result. In most cases after matching we will have only one matched image but in some cases few matches are possible. Utilizing this technique we will only add a small amount of extra burden to the system which still preserves to have a high performance compared to whole database matching.

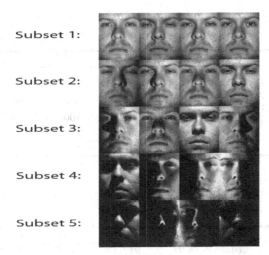

Fig. 2. Sample imgaes of Extended Yale B database. Each subset is generated with respect to variations in light source angles.

4 Experiments

We have tested this algorithm using extended Yale B database [11]. This database consists of 64 frontal greyscale image of 39 different subjects with same pose and expression in different illumination conditions in a resolution of 168 × 92 pixels. Ambient lights is set to be off which makes process even more challenging. This database is the most challenging database because of large changes in light source angle and ambient lighting condition, that is set to be off. We have created 5 subsets for each subject as proposed by previous works [18][10], which is based on the angles of light source applied on subjects.

Images in Subset 1 have a light source angle smaller than 12 degrees from optical axis, Subset 2 has angles between 20 and 25 degrees, Subset 3 consists of images having angles of 35 to 50 degrees, Subset 4 to have 66 to 77 degrees and subset 5 to include all remaining images.

We have tried to match each image of different subjects in a subset to our generated robust keypoints for that subset distinctively. Results show that our algorithm works better on subsets having smaller variations in the angle of light source which have higher similarity to each other.

Table 1 presents the comparison of our algorithm to other state-of-the-art algorithms using ideal images [18]. Frontal lighting images are considered as ideal images.

Average results of 64 different lighting conditions for each algorithm is presented in Table 2. Our algorithm uses a slightly different approach from previous models and produces same results.

The computational speed was one of other concerns in our research. Whole program is implemented in C++ using OpenCV library running on a 2.0 Ghz

Table 1. Recognition percentages for different algorithms using ideal images on Extended Yale B face database

Subset	SQI [16]	LTV [8]	TT [17]	NDF [18]	IS-SIFT
1	89.87	88.72	93.98	100	99.99
2	100	100	100	100	100
3	80.55	80.14	93.61	100	99.97
4	80.78	78.11	98.25	100	99.96
5	77.11	80.3	99.03	100	99.91
Average	84.23	84.48	97.33	100	99.97

Table 2. Average recognition percentages using all 64 images of Extended Yale B face database

Subset	SQI [16]	LTV [8]	TT [17]	NDF [18]	IS-SIFT
1	79.70	74.97	91.92	97.15	99.99
2	77.59	77.01	89.02	94.96	100
3	67.20	71.59	86.25	94.42	99.97
4	72.68	78.96	90.89	96.47	99.96
5	72.96	86.93	93.80	98.54	99.91
Average	73.25	78.91	90.41	96.43	99.97

Core 2 Duo system. We have achieved an average 673.92 ms per image for recognition between 39 subjects of 192 x 168 pixels resolution. Verification average per image is 17.6 ms. With respect to the speed comparison provided at [18], TT and NDF appear to be faster and than our method while running on a slightly faster machine.

5   Conclusion

We presented a new approach to provide high recognition accuracy with fast processing times by creating comprehensive keypoint for all images in each subset. Then, we use matching technique to simplify and select a previously determined number of keypoints. Our method lowers the cost of recognition on large databases to an acceptable range. A higher recognition performance will result in a better online learning.

The future work involves the investigation of the effects of online learning on recognition rates, merging and simplifying final robust keypoint files to achieve higher computation speeds while maintaining recognition performance.

References

1. Nowruzi, F., Habibi Zad Navin, A.: Object Detection Using SIFT for @Home Robots, Bachelors degree final project (2010)

2. Calonder, M., Lepetit, V., Strecha, C., Fua, P.: BRIEF: Binary Robust Independent Elementary Features. In: Daniilidis, K., Maragos, P., Paragios, N. (eds.) ECCV 2010, Part IV. LNCS, vol. 6314, pp. 778–792. Springer, Heidelberg (2010)
3. Lowe, D.G.: Distinctive Image Features from Scale-Invariant Keypoints. International Journal of Computer Vision 60, 91–110 (2004)
4. Juan, L., Gwun, O.: A Comparison of SIFT, PCA-SIFT and SURF. International Journal of Image Processing 3, 187–245 (2009)
5. Mikolajczyk, K., Schmid, C.: A performance evaluation of local descriptors. IEEE Transactions on Pattern Analysis and Machine Intelligence 27, 1615–1630 (2005)
6. Bay, H., Ess, A., Tuytelaars, T., Van Gool, L.: Speeded-Up Robust Features (SURF). J. Computer Vision and Image Understanding 10, 346–359 (2008)
7. Lindeberg, T.: Scale-space theory: A basic tool for analysing structures at different scales. J. Applied Statistics 21, 224–270 (1994)
8. Chen, T., Zhou, X.S., Huang, T.S.: Total variation models for variable lighting face recognition. IEEE Transactions on Pattern Analysis and Machine Intelligence 28, 1519–1524 (2006)
9. Zhang, T.P., Tang, Y.Y., Fang, B., Shang, Z.W., Liu, X.Y.: Face recognition under varying illumination using gradientfaces. Transactions on Image Process 18(11), 2599–2606 (2009)
10. Fan, C.N., Zhang, F.Y.: Homomorphic filtering based illumination normalization method for face recognition. Pattern Recognition Letters 32(10), 1468–1479 (2011)
11. Lee, K., Ho, J., Kriegman, D.: Acquiring linear sub-spaces for face recognition under variable lighting. IEEE Transactions on Pattern Analysis and Machine Intelligence 27(5), 684–698 (2005)
12. Lowe, D.G.: Object Recognition from Local Scale-Invariant Features. In: IEEE International Conference on Computer Vision, pp. 1150–1157 (1999)
13. Beis, J., Lowe, D.G.: Shape indexing using approximate nearest-neighbour search in high-dimensional spaces. In: Conference on Computer Vision and Pattern Recognition, pp. 1000–1006 (1997)
14. Ke, Y., Sukthankar, R.: PCA-SIFT: a more distinctive representation for local image descriptors. In: Conference on Computer Vision and Pattern Recognition, pp. 506–513 (2004)
15. Rublee, E., Rabaud, V., Konolige, K., Bradski, G.: ORB: An efficient alternative to SIFT or SURF. In: International Conference on Computer Vision, pp. 2564–2571 (2011)
16. Wang, H., Li, S., Wang, Y.: Face recognition under vary- ing lighting conditions using self quotient image. In: Sixth IEEE International Conference on Automatic Face and Gesture Recognition Proceedings, pp. 819–824 (2004)
17. Tan, X., Triggs, B.: Enhanced local texture feature sets for face recognition under difficult lighting conditions. IEEE TIP 19(2), 1635–1650 (2010)
18. Chen, L.H., Yang, Y.H., Chen, C.S., Cheng, M.Y.: Illumination invariant feature extraction based on natural images statistics - Taking face images as an example. In: CVPR (2011)
19. Javanmard, R., Mahmoudi, F.: MGS-SIFT: A New Illumination Invariant Feature Based on SIFT. In: Proc. IEEE Conf. on 3th International Conference on Machine Vision (2010)
20. Savvides, M., Kumar, V.: Illumination Normalization Using Logarithm Transforms for Face Authentication. In: Kittler, J., Nixon, M.S. (eds.) AVBPA 2003. LNCS, vol. 2688, pp. 549–556. Springer, Heidelberg (2003)
21. Du, S., Ward, R.: Wavelet-based illumination normalization for face recognition. In: IEEE International Conference of Image Process, vol. 2 (2005)

Robust Real-Time Stereo Edge Matching by Confidence-Based Refinement

Jonas Witt and Uwe Weltin

IZT at the Hamburg University of Technology,
Eißendorfer Straße 40, 21073 Hamburg, Germany
{jonas.witt,weltin}@tuhh.de

Abstract. Edges are important features for tasks like object detection and vision-based navigation. In this paper, a novel real-time capable stereo edge refinement technique is presented. It propagates confidence and consistency along the detected edges, which reduces false matches significantly. Unmatched pixels are safely recovered by interpolation. We also investigate suitable support regions for edge-based matching. In the proposed solution, depth discontinuities are specifically accounted for. All approaches are extensively tested with the Middlebury benchmark datasets[1] and compared to a sparse and several popular dense stereo algorithms.

Keywords: Robotic vision, edge-based, real-time, sparse stereo.

1 Introduction

Dense stereo correspondence algorithms have been thoroughly studied in the last decades. Many different approaches with individual performance characteristics exist [12]. However, for robotic applications like object detection and navigation, dense information is often not required. Point-based systems currently are most common, but fail in sparsely textured cases. Edge-based systems can fill the gap as shown e.g. by Tomono [13] and Chandraker et al [3] with their SLAM systems. In [5] an object detection system was presented, which uses only edges with depth information.

Matching edge-segments across two views poses different challenges than dense matching. Many edges lie on object borders, which can be a problem for correlation based algorithms if the matching window is not carefully chosen. Horizontal segments are particularly difficult. Also, since the matching is only sparse, one can not gain confidence in disparities over homogeneous surfaces. On the other hand the search space is significantly simplified due to the restriction of disparities to edge loci, resulting in less computational effort. Thus, an evaluation of the performance of sparse versus dense methods that are sparsified to edge locations is interesting.

---

[1] Thanks to Daniel Scharstein and Richard Szeliski for maintaining their vision homepage http://vision.middlebury.edu/stereo/ and providing many benchmark datasets.

C.-Y. Su, S. Rakheja, H. Liu (Eds.): ICIRA 2012, Part III, LNAI 7508, pp. 512–522, 2012.
© Springer-Verlag Berlin Heidelberg 2012

Previous papers present very different approaches to the problem of matching edges in two or three views. Different algorithms for straight lines have been proposed by [9], [8] and [1], the latter of which was also extended to parametric curves in [11]. A more recent publication proposes a multi-scale phase based algorithm with a probabilistic model for matching [14]. Here, we discuss a correlation-based approach which uses winner-takes-all (WTA) matching and an efficient confidence-based refinement technique which enforces smooth disparities along edges.

2   Stereo Edge Matching

For sparse edge matching one can not simply apply well known refinement techniques like median filtering or other local consensus-based methods due to sparsity. Also, edges often lie on object borders which specifically needs to be accounted for, as we will examine in section 2.2. On the other hand, edges in most cases are more distinctive than an ordinary pixel on a smooth surface in the case of dense matching. And we can still gain matching confidence by incorporating knowledge about adjacent edge pixels.

The common steps involved for stereo matching are preprocessing, cost aggregation, matching and refinement. Since we are interested in real-time capable algorithms for navigation purposes we investigate simple winner-takes-all matching with a more sophisticated but fast refinement step to significantly improve the matching performance. The preprocessing step basically consists of gaussian filtering and Canny edge detection [2] with subpixel refinement as proposed in [4]. While still matching at the pixel level we gain subpixel accurate disparities for vertical and diagonal edges with minimal additional computations.

2.1   Matching Cost

Many different matching cost functions, similarity measures and transforms exist for the purpose of stereo matching [12]. Common matching costs for real-time stereo matching are the squared intensity difference and the absolute intensity difference. Both measures can be truncated to improve robustness in the face of outliers. Several tests on the Middlebury stereo sets and with a stereo camera in an office environment resulted in the truncated sum of absolute differences (SAD) being selected as the measure of choice in our case. Additionally we subtract the mean intensity difference $\mu(\mathbf{x}, d)$ to improve matching of mildly shiny objects with specular reflections and also to cope with different camera sensor sensitivities. We also truncate this value at $t_\mu = 10$ to not match uniform surfaces with arbitrary intensity differences. The matching cost $m(\mathbf{x}, d)$ at location $\mathbf{x}$ with the support region Γ and disparity $\mathbf{d} = (d, 0)^T$ accordingly is:

$$\mu(\mathbf{x}, d) = max\left(min\left(\frac{1}{|\Gamma|}\sum_{\mathbf{s}\in\Gamma} I_L(\mathbf{x}+\mathbf{s}) - I_R(\mathbf{x}+\mathbf{s}-\mathbf{d}),\ t_\mu\right),\ -t_\mu\right) \quad (1)$$

$$m(\mathbf{x}, d) = \frac{1}{|\Gamma|}\sum_{\mathbf{s}\in\Gamma} min\left(I_L(\mathbf{x}+\mathbf{s}) - I_R(\mathbf{x}+\mathbf{s}-\mathbf{d}) - \mu(\mathbf{x}, d),\ t_{trunc}\right) \quad (2)$$

The term $\frac{1}{|\Gamma|}$ normalizes the matching score by dividing by the number of pixels in the support region Γ. The truncation parameter was empirically adjusted and finally set to $t_{trunc} = 30$. Different matching windows are investigated in the following section.

2.2 Cost Aggregation

For the aggregation of the matching costs, using simple symmetric support regions as often used in real-time dense matching is not useful. This is due to the nature of edges, since they are intensity gradients which divide homogeneous intensity surfaces. These intensity gradients can occur on textured planar surfaces but also at depth discontinuities as a result of overlapping surfaces of different intensity. Accordingly, many edge pixels lie on object borders which have an intensity that is usually a mixture of both surface intensities. In effect the edge pixel intensity depends on the subpixel location $\alpha \in [0, 1]$ of the edge and both surface intensities I_1 and I_2:

$$I_{edge} = (1 - \alpha)I_1 + \alpha I_2 \quad (3)$$

which results in an arbitrary value $I_{edge} \in [I_1, I_2]$ which depends on the orientation and position of the camera. Basically this is true for every pixel, but by definition edge pixels mark the locations where this effect has the biggest impact on pixel intensities. Accordingly, edge pixels themselves are not very suitable for including them in an intensity based matching score. Figure 1 shows block matching on an edge segment. Here, 20% of the pixels in the support region belong to the edge which can have a significant influence on the overall matching cost. Making the support region larger reduces this effect, but also decreases the ability to match small objects.

The common occurence of depth discontinuities at edge locations also has to be specifically incorporated into the design of the support region. Consider again the edge depicted in figure 1. If the region to the left of the edge belongs to a foreground object and the region to the right to the background, the actually matching pixels of the background will be shifted by the difference in disparities, which is three in this case. This can be accounted for, as described in [6], but at a computational cost. Shiftable filters as evaluated in [12] are a more efficient possibility. For the use in edges they need to be adapted, though. With simple block matching we may end up with less than 50% of the pixels in the support region being suitable matching candidates on object borders. If an object border even extends in depth direction, we can even expect disparity offsets on the same

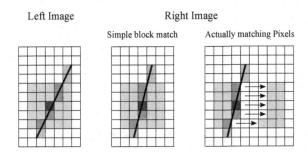

Fig. 1. Block matching with a 5x5 window. The window overlaps the edge which is problematic if the edge belongs to a depth discontinuity.

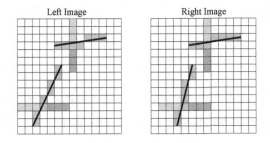

Fig. 2. Shifted pixel-block matching windows for two edges with different angles. The pixel-blocks do not include the edge pixel itself (here 3x1 pixel-blocks are matched).

object within the support region (an example of this are the two top rows of the support region in figure 1).

For these reasons we propose simplified shifted pixel-blocks which do not suffer of any of these problems and almost introduce no computational overhead. These shifted pixel-blocks are matched on either side of a candidate edge pixel, as shown in figure 2. Only edges that differ by no more than α_{match} in orientation in the left and right image are considered. The actual edge pixel is not included in the pixel-block, due to their intrinsic unsuitability for intensity-based matching. Depending on the edge orientation, left and right or top and bottom pixel-blocks are matched. This helps in disambiguating horizontal edge disparities. In either case only the minimum matching cost is taken. If an edge lies on an object border, the foreground disparity is retrieved and the consistency of the support region is preserved. Increasing the width of the support regions (e.g. from one to three or more pixels) makes the individual matches more robust, however in combination with the adjacent edge pixels this essentially yields no additional information, since support regions of edge pixels overlap in this case. Figure 3 shows the performance of several different support regions. For the combined support region (11x11 + 11x11 Block) the minimum cost of the three is taken.

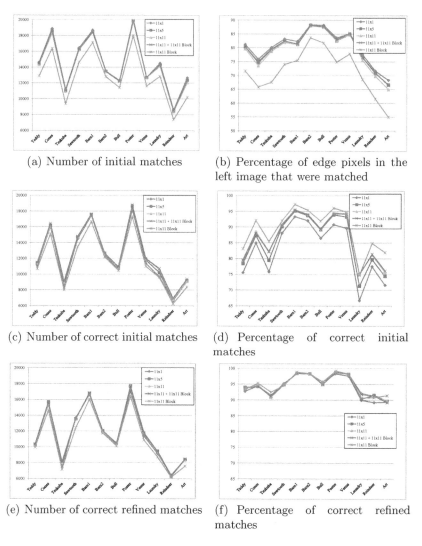

(a) Number of initial matches

(b) Percentage of edge pixels in the left image that were matched

(c) Number of correct initial matches

(d) Percentage of correct initial matches

(e) Number of correct refined matches

(f) Percentage of correct refined matches

Fig. 3. Comparison of the influence of several different support regions on matching performance. Shifted pixel blocks (11x1, 11x5, 11x11), a simple block match (11x11 Block) and a combined variant (11x11 + 11x11 Block) are tried. Initial matches are straight WTA-matches while refined matches refer to the technique in section 2.3.

Finally, if the resulting matching score is below the threshold th_{match}, it is considered valid. Despite being quite fast, the results with pure winner-takes-all (WTA) matching are not yet overwhelming, as can be seen by the percentage of correct matches in figure 3(d). It is visible, that the size of the support region has a considerable influence on the quality of the initial matches.

In figures 3(e) and 3(f) the results of the refinement algorithm that is introduced in the next section are shown. What is specifically interesting is that the dependency on the support region from figure 3(d) has lessened significantly, which is due to the incorporation of edge connectivity information. Effectively, adjacent edge pixels build one big virtual support region along the edge, when disparity smoothness is enforced.

It is also visible that the total number of correct matches for unshifted block matching (*11×11 Block*) is the lowest (see figure 3(e)). While this seems insignificant, the missing disparities often lie on object borders which are very interesting for robotic vision tasks. Another observation is, that the matching of an unshifted pixel block does not seem to yield much additional information, since the results of the *11×11* shifted support window and the combined *11×11 + 11×11 Block* window are basically indistinguishable. The best robustness/performance trade-off seems to be the *11×5* and in most cases even the *11×1* window.

2.3 Confidence-Based Refinement

In this section we will introduce the novel refinement algorithm that enforces consistency and smoothness among the disparities of edge segments. The improvement over the initial WTA matches stems from the fact that many individual edge points are ambiguous, which leads to isolated and unsmooth disparities, if they are matched independently. The discriminative power of a whole edge segment in contrast is much higher. However, since common edge detectors do not yield perfect edges that do not cross object borders or produce other "glitches" it is not trivial to take full advantage of the connectivity information.

In order to refine our initial disparities we first need to rank the reliability of the found matches. We do this with the ratio of the best match $m_{1st}(\mathbf{x})$ and the second best match $m_{1st}(\mathbf{x})$ at a location $\mathbf{x}$:

$$C(\mathbf{x}) = \begin{cases} 3, \, if \, \, m_{2nd}(\mathbf{x})/m_{1st}(\mathbf{x}) > 2 \\ 2, \, if \, \, m_{2nd}(\mathbf{x})/m_{1st}(\mathbf{x}) > 1.5 \\ 1, \, m_{1st}(\mathbf{x}) < th_{match} \\ 0, \, no \, match \, found \end{cases} \tag{4}$$

If the second best match has more than a doubled matching score, we know that our best match is probably the right one. We reward this with the highest confidence. A confidence value of one is usually assigned to ambiguous matches like horizontal edges or repetetive patterns. If no valid match is found the confidence is zero.

Edge connectivity can be enforced by a simple consistency check: if an edge is traversed in the left image, the corresponding pixels in the right image have to be connected. This can be checked for the edge pixels $\mathbf{x}_1 = (x_1, y_1, d_1)^T$ and $\mathbf{x}_2 = (x_2, y_2, d_2)^T$ that are adjacent in the left image. The disparities are consistent if $|(x_1 - d_1) - (x_2 - d_2)| \leq 1$, meaning that the distance in x-direction of the corresponding edge pixels in the right image is less than or equal to one. In the following pseudo-code listing this check is referred to by the isConsistent(...)

```
function insertNeighbour(p, edge, curConf)
  if visited(p)
    return false;
  add p to edge;
  if NOT isConsistent(p, parent(p)):        // pixels inconsistent!
    curConf := 0;
    refinedDisparity(p) := UNKNOWN;         // don't trust this disparity
  else if curConf >= minFixConf:
    refinedDisp(p) = initialDisp(p);        // confident disparity!
  else    // pixels are consistent but not enough confidence yet
    curConf += confidence(p);               // build up confidence
    refinedDisp(p) := −initialDisp(p);      // save disparity with neg. sign
    if curConf >= minFixConf:
      for all previous invalid pixels:
        change sign of negative disparities
        linearly interpolate UNKNOWN disparities
  return true;

function followEdge(p, parentEdge, curConf)
  edge := new Edge;
  link edge to parentEdge;
  curNeighbours := p;
  while sizeOf(curNeighbours) > 0:
    if sizeOf(curNeighbours) > 1:           // spawn child edges
      for each neighbour n of curNeighbours:
        childEdge := followEdge(n, edge, curConf);
        link edge to childEdge;
      break;
    if NOT insertNeighbour(curNeighbours[0], edge, curConf):
      break;
    curNeighbours = neighbours(curNeighbours[0]);
  return edge;

function refineDisparities()
  for each matched pixel p:    // search for confident start points
    if confidence(p) == 3:
      for each neighbour n of p:
        if confidence(n) >= 2 AND
           confidence(nextNeighbour(n)) >= 2 AND
           isConsistent(p, n) AND
           isConsistent(n, nextNeighbour(n)):
          e = followEdge(n1, 0, minFixConf);  // good confidence!
          if length(e) > 1:
            add e to edges;
  return edges;
```

Listing 1. Pseudo-code of the confidence-based refinement algorithm.

function call. The function **neighbours(p)** searches the 8-connected neighbour-hood of the pixel for adjacent edge pixels. It disregards the direction of its parent pixel, so we exclusively move forward along the edge.

The underlying idea of the refinement algorithm is to propagate a confidence level along the edge (named **curConf** in listing 1). First, groups of three adjacent and consistent high-confidence edge pixels are searched for as starting point. Then, starting with maximum confidence, the edge is traversed, checking each pixel for consistency with its predecessor. If an unmatched pixel or an inconsistency is encountered, the confidence is dropped to zero. With each consistent pixel-pair the confidence value recovers until it is greater than the tuning parameter `minFixConf`. Then, the algorithm tries to recover the intermediate disparities. For inconsistent or unmatched pixels, linear interpolation between the enclosing confident disparities is performed. This way it is possible to keep the total number of matches high and at the same time boost the percentage of correct matches.

3 Experimental Results

In the following, we benchmark the proposed edge matching by confidence-based refinement (EMCBR) with the middlebury database. Figure 5 shows the disparity errors of EMCBR with a 11×5 matching window to the previously used selection of 12 image sets, the quantitative results of which were shown in figure 3(e) and 3(f). The parameterization was empirically investigated and set as follows: $\alpha_{match} = \pi/16$, $th_{match} = 12$, $minFixConf = 8$. To yield suitable sparse ground truth, the middlebury ground truth images were dilated with a 3×3 structuring element to always yield foreground disparities on object borders. Subsequently the images were sparsified by masking with the edge locations.

A comparison with probabilistic phase-based sparse stereo (PPBSS, [14]) and several popular dense methods is given in table 1 and visually in figure 4. The results of scanline optimization (SO), dynamic programming (DP) and graph cuts (GC) refer to [12], while semiglobal matching (SemiGlob) refers to [6], AD-Census (ADCensus, currently ranked first in the middlebury benchmark) to [10] and graph cuts with occlusions (GC+occl) to [7]. Thus, a diverse mix of scanline-based algorithms to complex global optimization techniques is compared.

Table 1. Edge matching performance comparison of sparse (EMCBR and PPBSS) and dense algorithms that have been sparsified to edge loci

	Tsukuba		Teddy		Cones		Venus		Sawtooth	
	Matches	Errors	Matches	Errors	Matches	Errors	Matches	Errors	Matches	Errors
EMCBR	8550	8.8%	10514	5.3%	16147	5.3%	11816	2.0%	13117	5.4%
PPBSS	2089	17.0%	-	-	-	-	1163	6.0%	2938	5.0%
DP	13775	14.6%	17192	11.1%	23590	12.6%	14601	6.7%	19393	6.0%
SO	13778	16.9%	17709	20.8%	24489	19.3%	14770	8.2%	19598	7.1%
SemiGlob	13765	8.6%	18001	10.6%	24868	9.0%	14930	1.5%	-	-
GC	13801	9.0%	17696	17.4%	24399	15.0%	14737	2.9%	19560	4.9%
GC+occl	13803	6.3%	17995	15.8%	24868	11.6%	14929	1.7%	19777	0.8%
ADCensus	13900	20.8%	18001	6.9%	24868	6.8%	14930	0.4%	-	-

The most obvious difference between the matching results of the sparse and the dense methods is the number of matches. This stems from inconsistently detected edges in the left and right images. For example the upper bound for correctly matched pixels in the Tsukuba image set without gap filling is 8529

520   J. Witt and U. Weltin

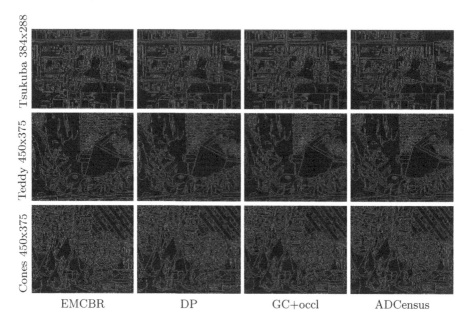

Tsukuba 384x288 Teddy 450x375 Cones 450x375

EMCBR   DP   GC+occl   ADCensus

Fig. 4. Comparison of EMCBR to sparsified popular dense algorithms. Green pixels depict disparity errors ≤ 1, red pixels are errors > 1 and white pixels correspond to unmatched pixels. The dense methods usually match almost all edge pixels.

matches. This number is calculated by taking the ground truth disparities at edge loci in the left image and checking if an edge with an edge angle difference smaller than α_{match} exists at the corresponding location in the right image. Since the dense algorithms do not restrict their disparity search to edge loci, this is the main reason for the difference in match counts. However, this is nonrelevant for the applications of sparse methods. It is much more important to extract consistent edge segments on sparsely textured objects. The middlebury stereo sets can be regarded as a stress test for edge-based stereo matchers since they are highly textured, leading to many inconsistently detected edges. Nevertheless, EMCBR performs great in terms of error percentages, especially if one takes into account that (except for DP and SO) very sophisticated dense algorithms are compared which take at least seconds to execute on a modern CPU. Except for some long horizontal edge segments as in Tsukuba, the algorithm efficiently and reliably finds the correct disparities, while being much less of a computational burden.

The experiments were run on an Intel i7-2640M CPU (2.8 GHz) using both cores. For a maximum diparity of 64, the compuation times of EMCBR per image set were between 20ms and 45ms with the *11×5* support region including preprocessing and refinement. Cost aggregation and matching takes about 10ms to 15ms and about the same amount of time is spent on refinement.

Fig. 5. Middlebury benchmark disparity results of EMCBR with a *11×5* shifted pixel-block support region. Green pixels depict disparity errors ≤ 1, red pixels are errors > 1 and white pixels correspond to unmatched pixels. The test images in the left column are Teddy (450×375), Sawtooth (434×380), Barn1 (432×381), Bull (433×381), Venus (434×383) and Poster (435×383). The images in right colomn are Cones (450×375), Tsukuba (384×288), Barn2 (430×381), Reindeer (447×370), Laundry (447×370) and Art (463×370).

4 Discussion and Future Work

In this paper we presented a robust and real-time capable stereo edge refinement technique and investigated the consideration of depth discontinuities at the matching location. We showed that good results are possible with sparse matching, producing better error rates than most dense algorithms while being computationally less demanding.

The refinement algorithm enforces consistent disparities along edges and is able to reliably interpolate missing ones. The main remaining source for errors and unmatched edges is the quality of the edge detector. Often, object edges are distorted or disrupted by adjacent surfaces of similar intensity. This is especially true for highly textured objects. This situation can be improved by more costly edge detectors that take color, edge biases and scale-space into account. Unfortunately, sophisticated edge detectors would have a severe impact on the execution time. However, in further research with edge-based SLAM and real world indoor scenes the algorithm already showed good performance with the current edge detector.

References

1. Ayache, N., Faverjon, B.: Efficient registration of stereo images by matching graph descriptions of edge segments. IJCV 1(2), 107–131 (1987)
2. Canny, J.: A Computational Approach to Edge Detection. PAMI 8(6), 679–698 (1986)
3. Chandraker, M., Lim, J., Kriegman, D.: Moving in stereo: Efficient structure and motion using lines. In: Proc. of ICCV, pp. 1741–1748. IEEE (2009)
4. Devernay, F.: A Non-Maxima Suppression Method for Edge Detection with Sub-Pixel Accuracy. Tech. rep., INRIA (1995)
5. Helmer, S., Lowe, D.: Using stereo for object recognition. In: Proc. of ICRA, pp. 3121–3127. IEEE (2010)
6. Hirschmüller, H., Innocent, P.R., Garibaldi, J.: Real-Time Correlation-Based Stereo Vision with Reduced Border Errors. IJCV 47(1), 229–246 (2002)
7. Kolmogorov, V., Zabih, R.: Computing visual correspondence with occlusions using graph cuts. In: Proc. of ICCV, vol. 2(1), pp. 508–515 (2001)
8. Li, Z.N.: Stereo correspondence based on line matching in Hough space using dynamic programming. TSMC 24(1), 144–152 (1994)
9. Medioni, G., Nevatia, R.: Segment-based stereo matching. Computer Vision, Graphics, and Image Processing 31(1), 2–18 (1985)
10. Mei, X., Sun, X., Zhou, M., Jiao, S., Wang, H., Zhang, X.: On building an accurate stereo matching system on graphics hardware. In: ICCV Workshops, pp. 467–474. IEEE (2011)
11. Robert, L., Faugeras, O.D.: Curve-based stereo: Figural continuity and curvature. In: Proc. of CVPR, pp. 57–62. IEEE (1991)
12. Scharstein, D., Szeliski, R.: A taxonomy and evaluation of dense two-frame stereo correspondence algorithms. IJCV 47(1), 7–42 (2002)
13. Tomono, M.: Robust 3D SLAM with a stereo camera based on an edge-point ICP algorithm. In: Proc. of ICRA, pp. 4306–4311. IEEE (2009)
14. Ulusoy, I., Halici, U., Hancock, E.: Probabilistic phase based sparse stereo. In: Proc. of ICPR, vol. 4, pp. 84–87. IEEE (2004)

A Symbol Identifier Based Recognition and Relative Positioning Approach Suitable for Multi-robot Systems

Hanbo Qian[1], Wenbo Yuan[2], Xilong Liu[2], Zhiqiang Cao[2],
Chao Zhou[2], and Min Tan[2]

[1] The Center of Coordination&Support of SASTIND, Beijing 100081, China
[2] State Key Laboratory of Management and Control for Complex Systems,
Institute of Automation, Chinese Academy of Sciences, Beijing 100190, China
{hanbo.qian,wenbo.yuan,xilong.liu,
zhiqiang.cao,chao.zhou,min.tan}@ia.ac.cn

Abstract. In this paper, a symbol identifier based recognition and relative positioning approach suitable for multi-robot systems is proposed. The symbol identifier is composed of central area and peripheral area, and there exists radial spokes in central area. The recognition approach utilizes some features including luminance feature of center point, luminance difference between center point and its ambient region, the number and distribution of spokes as well as the shape of peripheral area to filter the points in the image. Finally, the resulting pixel points set to characterize the center points of symbol identifiers is generated. On this basis, the positions of these center points relative to the camera are then calculated. The proposed approach is verified by the experiments.

Keywords: symbol identifier, recognition and relative positioning, radial spokes.

1   Introduction

Multi-robot system has become a research hotspot of robotics[1]-[2] and it has a wide variety of potential applications in industry, military, aerospace and service fields. In order to fully display the group performance of multi-robot systems, the abilities of mutual recognition and relative positioning among robots become important, especially for heterogeneous robotic system with different identities corresponding to different abilities. In nature, the higher organisms including humans complete the recognition and posture estimation of teammates mainly through vision. Currently, in multi-robot systems domain, the vision plays an import role in mutual recognition and relative positioning among robots.

Mutual recognition among robots belongs to the domain of object recognition. Based on D. Marr's vision theory[3], the visual information is described by using the three-dimensional representation and many effective object recognition approaches are developed[4]-[6]. However, it is difficult to apply many mature approaches

C.-Y. Su, S. Rakheja, H. Liu (Eds.): ICIRA 2012, Part III, LNAI 7508, pp. 523–531, 2012.

directly to multi-robot cooperative system in unknown complex environments, which is due to the influence from environmental complexity and real-time demand, etc. The robot vision system needs enough adaptability to cope with the environment variations, and multiple different targets should be distinguished. In addition, the computational complexity of algorithms must satisfy the real-time requirement.

At present, it is widely used to equip the robot with artificial identifier. The Color coded identifier is one of the most common selections, for example, in soccer robot system[7]. Reference [8] adopts a two-color cylindrical color coded identifier for robot identity recognition. However, the usage of color coded identifier is limited by its disadvantages. Firstly, the color is influenced significantly by light conditions. For slight light changes, some means such as spherical coordinate transform[9] and HSI color space transformation[10] etc are used for correction. When the light conditions change greatly, it is difficult to satisfy the demand, which makes the color coded identifier based approach be suitable for the structured environments. The quality of recognition may be improved by artificial calibration in advance, which leads to a tedious process. Secondly, this method needs an enough large zone of color coded identifier in the image, which has a negative impact on recognition distance. In addition, due to using color feature as the basis of recognition, the information contained is limited and the discrimination degree is relatively low. On one hand, this may result in a higher error recognition rate. On the other hand, it is hard to mark a huge number of multiple targets.

Using shape feature as the basis of recognition is an effective way to overcome the shortages brought by color coded identifier. The bar code is a typical example. The QR code[11] developed by Denso company is used for object recognition in [12]. The peripheral identification is added for the improvement of recognition speed as well as recognition distance. Inspired by the QR code, reference [13] has designed a label with a combination of shape and color features. Compared with the QR code, although it contains less information, the recognition distance is enlarged due to less demanding of details in image space. A radial symbol identifier is designed in [14]. This identifier possesses the invariance of visual angle and distance, and the cascade classifiers are constructed to filter the points in image without the need of image preprocessing, which improve the recognition performance. However, the richness of symbol is limited due to its central symmetry as well as the usage of the number of spokes as difference among different symbols. In addition, it is unable to acquire the distance information by a single symbol identifier.

In this paper, a general symbol identifier is designed for the purpose of the richness and recognition adaptability. The corresponding recognition and positioning approach is proposed, which satisfies the requirements in complex and unknown environment.

The rest of the paper is organized as follows. In Section 2, the symbol identifier is designed and the recognition approach is given. Section 3 presents the relative positioning based on peripheral information of symbol identifier. The experiments are demonstrated in section 4 and section 5 concludes the paper.

2   The Symbol Identifier and Its Recognition Approach

2.1   The Design of Symbol Identifier

The symbol identifier to be developed should contain identity information with positioning information implied. Fig. 1 provides a general symbol identifier, which is divided into central area and peripheral area. The following characteristics are included.

i) The central area is divided into four parts, named I, II, and III, IV, respectively (see Fig. 2). Each part has a certain amount of spokes (usually it is no more than 4) emitted from the center point. These spokes may be ray or curve, and all of them are gradually away from the center point.

ii) The peripheral area is outside of central area. It may be a circle with its center being the center point of symbol identifier, and it is also an arc region formed by top zone and bottom zone of the symbol identifier. Each zone is formed by two concentric circular arcs.

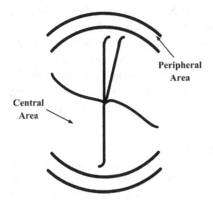

Fig. 1. The symbol identifier

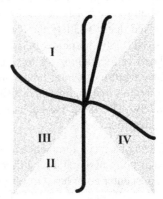

Fig. 2. The four parts division of center area

The number of spokes in each part may be 0, 1, 2, 3 or 4, therefore, the combination of four parts may produce $5^4 = 625$ different symbols. Even we remove some invalid cases such as there is not a radial spoke in all part, it still exists a substantial quantity of symbols. By the ordered combination of the spokes, the useful information of robot including the motion mode, resource and identity may be shown systematically. The symbol identifier is characterized by shape instead of color, which will lead to a good discrimination degree and the adaptability to light is enhanced. It should be noted that the spokes may be black or saturated colors, such as saturated red, saturated blue, etc. The circle or arc region in peripheral area may also have saturated color. The saturated color refers to the color that two color components of R, G and B are 0, while another is larger (usually it is more than 125). In order to express conveniently, the nonzero color component of saturated color is called principal component while the other two color components are called vice component. For example, the three color components of typical saturated red are 255, 0 and 0. There are at least two color components with larger difference among different saturated colors as well as the pure white and pure black color. The larger contrast is helpful to improve the stability and robustness of recognition. In addition, the symbol identifier with saturated color may express more meaning and have a better discrimination degree. The error recognition rate may also be reduced based on the feature of color difference. However, it requires more storage space and it will cost more computing resource.

2.2   Symbol Identifier Recognition

The recognition of symbol identifier may be transformed into the search of center point of each symbol in the image, and the corresponding eigenvector of spokes distribution is acquired. Then the meaning of symbol identifier may be obtained by inquiring the eigenvector library constructed in advance. In order to improve the real-time recognition, a series of classifiers are constructed and cascaded to classify the pixel points in the image into several categories, such as center point of non-symbol, center point of symbol 1, ..., center point of symbol S. For any classifier, if the point to be judged doesn't satisfy the feature of center point of each symbol, the point will be removed. Only the points passing the judgment of a classifier will be sent to the next classifier for judging. In this paper, the classifiers are designed on the basis of luminance feature of center point, luminance difference between center point and its ambient region, the number and distribution of spokes, the shape of peripheral area, respectively. The point passing all judgments is identified as a center point of a symbol identifier.

1)   Filtering based on luminance feature of center point
The center point of symbol identifier is the intersection of multiple spokes. For black spokes, the center point has a lower gray value and belongs to the low brightness area. Similarly, for saturated color spokes, the center point has a dark saturated color, which will lower the principal component. Therefore, the points in the image are filtered firstly by setting a threshold T_1, and the point whose gray value or principal component is greater than T_1 will be removed.

2)   Filtering based on luminance difference between center point and its ambient region
Due to radial characteristics of symbol identifier, from spatial distribution perspective, the farther away from the center point, the sparser the sopkes become. Therefore, within the symbol identifier scope in the image, the average value of gray values (black spokes) or saturated color vice components (saturated color spokes) in circular ring whose center is center point of symbol identifier is significantly greater than the corresponding value of center point. In addition, the average value increases gradually with the increasing of the ring's radius. Therefore, take the point to be judged as the center and obtain the corresponding average value $f(R_p)$ of the ring with the increasing radius R_p. The points with the differences between $f(R_p)$ and the corresponding value of center point is less than T_2 will be removed, where T_2 is a

threshold. In addition, the judgment condition $f(R_p) > f(R_q)(R_p > R_q)$ is also utilized for further filtering.

3) Filtering based on the number and distribution of spokes

Similar to four parts division of center area for symbol identifier, we obtain the up, down, left and right parts around the point to be judged as well as the number of spokes in each part. As illustrated in Fig. 3, a series of arcs for spokes detection are constructed, and we calculate the significant ups and downs number P of gray value or corresponding vice component for the points in each arc, which is given as follows.

$$P = \sum_{i=1}^{K} c(i), \; c(i) = \begin{cases} 0 & g(i) - g(i-1) \neq 1 \\ 1 & g(i) - g(i-1) = 1 \end{cases} (i = 2,3,...,K), \; c(1) = \begin{cases} 0 & g(1) - g(K) \neq 1 \\ 1 & g(1) - g(K) = 1 \end{cases} \quad (1)$$

$$g(i) = \begin{cases} 0 & f_R^i(u_m, v_n) < avr - T_3 \\ 1 & f_R^i(u_m, v_n) \geq avr - T_3 \end{cases} (i = 1, 2,...,K). \quad (2)$$

where $c(i)$ reflects the significant ups and downs of gray value or corresponding vice components for the points in an arc for spokes detection; K is the number of all pixel points in the arc for spokes detection; $f_R^i(u_m, v_n)$ is the value of gray value or corresponding vice components for i^{th} pixel point (u_m, v_n) in the arc for spokes detection; avr is the average value of gray values or corresponding vice components of all pixel points in the arc for spokes detection; T_3 is a given threshold. If the ups and downs number for each arc for spokes detection in each part of point to be judged are not equal or more than 4, it means that the point will be removed, or else, the ups and downs number of each part of the point is registered as the spokes number of corresponding part.

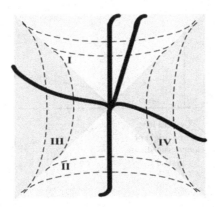

Fig. 3. The arcs constructed for spokes detection in each part

4) Filtering based on the shape of peripheral area

The last filtering is based on the shape of peripheral area. From center point of symbol identifier, two rays are emitted upward and downward with the angle of 180°. The gray value or corresponding vice components for pixel points in these two rays will have two significant ups and downs in peripheral area, which provides an important filtering criterion. Therefore, for the point to be judged, two rays R_u and R_d are emitted correspondingly, and the point satisfying the following conditions will be kept.

c_1) There exists two ups and downs that exceed T_4, where T_4 is a threshold, and the ratio of the distance d_f between these two ups and downs to the distance d_s between first ups and downs and original searching point is within a fixed range;

c_2) $0.85 < S_f/S_s < 1.18$, where S_f, S_s are searching steps to second ups and downs for the rays R_u and R_d, respectively.

Finally, the resulting pixel points set Γ_{rp} is generated to characterize the center points of symbol identifiers, and an eigenvector $T_{spoke} = (t_1, t_2, t_3, t_4)$ for every point in Γ_{rp} is also given and it reflects the number and distribution of spokes. Meanwhile, we obtain two endpoints' coordinates (u_1, v_1), (u_2, v_2) of diameter d in vertical direction in the image for estimation of relative positions.

3   Relative Positioning with Monocular Camera Based on Peripheral Information of Symbol Identifier

The camera is placed horizontally, namely the camera's optical axis is horizontal. Normally, the target's posture would not change in pitch direction and we may think the diameter in vertical direction of the circle where peripheral area's arcs locate is always perpendicular to optical axis of the camera. Based on (u_1, v_1), (u_2, v_2) as well as the length l_A of actual outer diameter d_A of symbol identifier, the space position of center point relative to the camera may be calculated.

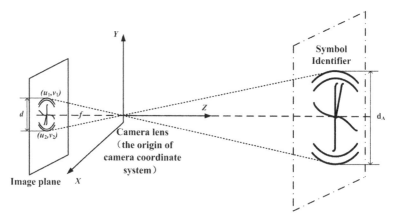

Fig. 4. The positioning based on peripheral information of symbol identifier

As shown in Fig. 4, we establish the camera coordinate system whose origin point is camera lens and Z axis is lens axis. Therefore, we have

$$
\frac{l_d}{f} = \frac{l_A}{z}
$$

$$
\frac{x_1}{u_1} = \frac{x_2}{u_2} = \frac{y_1}{v_1} = \frac{y_2}{v_2} = \frac{z}{f} \quad .
$$

$$
l_d = \sqrt{(u_2 - u_1)^2 + (v_2 - v_1)^2}
$$

(3)

where (x_1, y_1, z), (x_2, y_2, z) are space coordinates of two endpoints of outer diameter d_A, respectively; f is the focal length in pixels of the camera. The center position of symbol identifier may be given by $((x_1+x_2)/2, (y_1+y_2)/2, z)$.

4   The Experiments

The experiments are conducted for verifying the proposed approach. The symbol identifier adopted with outer diameter of 15cm is shown in Fig. 5(a). The recognition result is given in Fig. 5(b), which is displayed in a red circle.

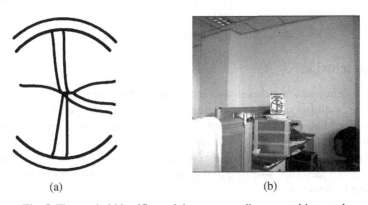

(a)   (b)

Fig. 5. The symbol identifier and the corresponding recognition result

In order to testify the adaptability to light conditions, we conduct the following experiment and the results are depicted in Fig. 6. Fig. 6(a) and 6(b) give the recognition results with brighter illumination and darker illumination, respectively. It is seen that the proposed recognition approach may cope with the environmental change to some extent.

Fig. 7 gives the positioning result for a moving target. The actual path of center point of symbol identifier is expressed by the line and measurement positions are displayed with "+", which shows the feasibility of the proposed approach.

(a) brighter illumination   (b) darker illumination

Fig. 6. The adaptability experiment to light conditions

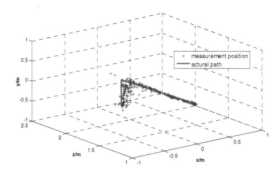

Fig. 7. The positioning result for a moving target

5   Conclusion

In order to improve the richness and recognition adaptability of symbol identifiers suitable for multi-robot systems, a novel symbol identifier is designed and the corresponding relative positioning approach is also presented. The proposed approach has a better environmental adaptability without calibration. In the future, the positioning accuracy will be considered to be further improved by kalman filter etc. and the symbol identifier will be equipped with actual mobile robots for recognition and relative positioning.

Acknowledgments. This work is supported in part by the National Natural Science Foundation of China under Grants 61175111, 60805038, and in part by the National High Technology Research and Development Program of China (863 Program) under Grant 2011AA041001.

References

1. Ren, W., Sorensen, N.: Distributed coordination architecture for multi-robot formation control. Robotics and Autonomous Systems 56(4), 324–333 (2008)
2. Bicchi, A., Fagiolini, A., Pallottino, L.: Towards a Society of Robots. IEEE Robotics & Automation Magazine 17(4), 26–36 (2010)

3. Marr, D.: Vision: A Computational Investigation into the Human Representation and Processing of Visual Information. W.H. Freeman, San Francisco (1982)
4. Kuno, Y., Okamato, Y., Okada, S.: Robot Vision Using a Feature Search Strategy Generated from a 3-D Object Model. IEEE Transactions on Pattern Analysis and Machine Intelligence 13(10), 1085–1097 (1991)
5. Vaidyanathan, A.G., Whitcomb, J.A.: Adaptive image analysis for object recognition Part I- Entropic Object Location. In: Proceedings of the IEEE International Conference on Systems, Man and Cybernetics, pp. 1888–1891 (1995)
6. Xia, G.H., Xing, Z.Y.: A New Algorithm for Target Recognition and Tracking for Robot Vision System. In: 2007 IEEE International Conference on Control and Automation, pp. 1004–1008 (2007)
7. Tang, H.B., Wang, L., Sun, Z.Q.: Accurate and Stable Vision in Robot Soccer. In: 8th International Conference on Control, Automation, Robotics and Vision, pp. 2314–2319 (2004)
8. Zhang, W.W., Wang, J., Cao, Z.Q., Yuan, Y., Zhou, C.: A Local Interaction Based Multi-robot Hunting Approach with Sensing and Modest Communication. In: Xie, M., Xiong, Y., Xiong, C., Liu, H., Hu, Z. (eds.) ICIRA 2009. LNCS (LNAI), vol. 5928, pp. 90–99. Springer, Heidelberg (2009)
9. Hyams, J., Powell, M., Murphy, R.: Position estimation and cooperative navigation of micro-rovers using color segmentation. Autonomous Robots 9, 7–16 (2000)
10. Ren, H., Zhong, Q.B.: A New Image Segmentation Method Based on HSI Color Space for Biped Soccer Robot. In: Proceedings of IEEE International Symposium on IT in Medicine and Education, pp. 1058–1061 (2008)
11. Zhang, C.H., Zhang, D., Zhao, S.X.: Bar code technology and application. Tsinghua University Press (2003) (in Chinese)
12. Xue, H.T., Tian, G.H., Li, X.L., Lu, F.: Application of the QR Code for various object identification and manipulation. Journal of Shandong University (Engineering Science) 37(6), 25–30 (2007) (in Chinese)
13. Yang, F.F., Meng, Z.D.: Label Recognition of Service Robot in Family Environment. Computer & Digital Engineering 36(11), 116–119 (2008) (in Chinese)
14. Liu, X.L., Qian, H.B., Cao, Z.Q., Tan, M.: Visual recognition method based on symbol features. Journal of Huazhong University of Science and Technology (Natural Science Edition) 39(sup. II), 120–123 (2011) (in Chinese)

New Stereovision Self-calibration Method and Its Application in Vision Guided Approaching

Huawei Wang and Ying Sun

East China Research Institute of Electronic Engineering, Hefei, 230088, P.R. China
{whw1981128,sywhwlucky}@126.com

Abstract. A simple and flexible self-calibration method is proposed for an active stereovision platform. It calibrates the parameters implicitly including the intrinsic and extrinsic ones of the visual system with a series of relative positions formed by translational motions of a selected point on the end-effector of a manipulator. A new visual measurement model based on the calibrated parameters is presented to obtain the relative position of an object with a rectangle mark. Then a position-based visual control system with end-effector closed loop is employed for vision guided approaching with the manipulator. Experiments are provided to validate the proposed self-calibration and measurement methods.

Keywords: self-calibration, visual measurement, stereovision, approaching.

1 Introduction

Camera calibration is considered to be a fundamental task for computer vision and Its applications, and the existed methodologies can be divided into two categories such as traditional calibration and self-calibration.

The traditional methods [1][2][3] usually calibrate the intrinsic and extrinsic parameters of stationary cameras with 3D or 2D references placed at several positions, and could obtain more accurate parameters with high-precision references. However, the traditional methods are inconvenient because of the special calibration reference not always available in practice. Meanwhile it is a tedious task to frequently recalibrate the dynamically changing visual parameters for active vision system.

Self-calibration methods are proposed to obtain more flexibility by using a sequence of camera or scene motions. Pure-rotation-based self-calibration methods [4][5][6][7][8] are received considerable attentions due to their algorithmic simplicity. Some of other works paid attention to translation-based self-calibration methods [9][10][11][12]. Up to now, the existed self-calibration methods calibrate the intrinsic and extrinsic parameters of cameras separately, and their procedures are complex.

The motivation of this work is to present a more simple and flexible self-calibration method using general translations of a single point for an active

C.-Y. Su, S. Rakheja, H. Liu (Eds.): ICIRA 2012, Part III, LNAI 7508, pp. 532–541, 2012.
© Springer-Verlag Berlin Heidelberg 2012

stereovision platform, and develop a visual measurement and control system for approaching. Experiments are provided to validate the proposed self-calibration method and its application in visual guided approaching and grasping.

2 Self-calibration for an Active Stereovision

An active stereovision platform with two cameras freely yawing around their axes is designed for an indoor service robot to track objects at the places near or far [13] in the environment. The cameras are well adjusted so that their yawing axes are parallel and their optical axes are coplanar.

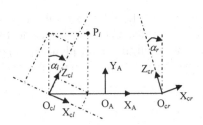

Fig. 1. Active stereovision and frame assignment

For the cameras, as shown in Fig.1, their frame is assigned at the optical centers, Z-axes are selected to the directions from the cameras to scene along the optical axes, X-axes are assigned to the horizontal imaging directions, Y-axes are assigned to the vertical imaging directions. The system frame A is assigned at the midpoint of the line linking optical centers O_{cl} and O_{cr}. Its X-axis X_A is selected to the direction from O_{cl} to O_{cr}, its Y-axis Y_A is defined as the direction perpendicular to X_A and coplanar with Z_{cl} and Z_{cr}, its Z-axis Z_A is assigned to the direction parallel to Y_{cl} and Y_{cr}.

2.1 Self-calibration Method Based on Relative Positions

The lenses used in the visual system are of long focal length, whose distortion is negligible and not considered here. According to the pinhole model of cameras, For any point p_i (x_i, y_i, z_i) in the system frame A, the relationship between its coordinates in the system frame and images' coordinates can be expressed as

$$\begin{cases} (u_{ih} - \widetilde{u}_h)[x_i - \frac{(-1)^h d}{2}]\frac{t\alpha_h}{k_{xh}} + (u_{ih} - \widetilde{u}_h)\frac{y_i}{k_{xh}} - [x_i - \frac{(-1)^h d}{2}) + y_i t\alpha_h = 0 \\ (v_{ih} - \widetilde{v}_h)[x_i - \frac{(-1)^h d}{2}]\frac{t\alpha_h}{k_{yh}} + (v_{ih} - \widetilde{v}_h)\frac{y_i}{k_{yh}} + \frac{1}{c\alpha_h}z_i = 0 \end{cases} \quad (1)$$

where $h = 1, 2$ represents the right and the left cameras, respectively. α_h denotes the yawing angles of the cameras with respect to the axis Y_A. d is the distance between the optical points. (u_{ih}, v_{ih}) and $(\widetilde{u}_h, \widetilde{v}_h)$ are the image coordinates of p_i and the principal points, respectively. k_{xh} and k_{yh} denote the normalized focal lengths of the cameras. $c\alpha = \cos\alpha$, $s\alpha = \sin\alpha$, $t\alpha_h = \tan\alpha_h$.

For two points such as initial position $p_0=(x_0, y_0, z_0)$ and i-th sampling position $p_i=(x_i, y_i, z_i)$ in the system frame A, (1) is satisfied if they are in the common view field of the cameras. With the subtraction of those equation and the simplification, (2) is deduced.

$$
\begin{cases}
\Delta x_i - \dfrac{t\alpha_h}{k_{xh}}u_{ih}\Delta x_i + \dfrac{\tilde{u}_h t\alpha_h}{k_{xh}}\Delta x_i - t\alpha_h \Delta y_i - \dfrac{1}{k_{xh}}u_{ih}\Delta y_i + \dfrac{\tilde{u}_h}{k_{xh}}\Delta y_i \\
\quad - \dfrac{t\alpha_h(x_0-(-1)^h d/2)+y_0}{k_{xh}}\Delta u_{ih} = 0 \\[2mm]
\dfrac{t\alpha_h}{k_{yh}}v_{ih}\Delta x_i - \dfrac{\tilde{v}_h t\alpha_h}{k_{yh}}\Delta x_i + \dfrac{1}{k_{yh}}v_{ih}\Delta y_i - \dfrac{\tilde{v}_h}{k_{yh}}\Delta y_i + \dfrac{1}{c\alpha_h}\Delta z_i \\
\quad + \dfrac{t\alpha_h(x_0-(-1)^h d/2)+y_0}{k_{yh}}\Delta v_{ih} = 0
\end{cases}
\tag{2}
$$

where $(\Delta x_i, \Delta y_i, \Delta z_i)$ represents the relative position of p_i with respect to p_0. $(\Delta u_{ih}, \Delta v_{ih})$ determined by (3) denotes the displacement of image coordinates between projections of p_i and p_0 on the image planes. p_0 and p_i are unknown, but $(\Delta x_i, \Delta y_i, \Delta z_i)$ can be read from the manipulator's controller in the procedure of self-calibration.

$$
\Delta u_{ih} = u_{ih} - u_{0h}, \quad \Delta v_{ih} = v_{ih} - v_{0h}
\tag{3}
$$

Generally $(k_{xh} \approx k_{yh}) = k_h$ is satisfied for industrial cameras. Based on (2),

$$
\begin{cases}
\Delta x_i - \dfrac{t\alpha_h}{k_h}u_{ih}\Delta x_i + \dfrac{\tilde{u}_h t\alpha_h}{k_h}\Delta x_i + \left(\dfrac{\tilde{u}_h}{k_h} - t\alpha_h\right)\Delta y_i \\
\quad - \dfrac{1}{k_h}u_{ih}\Delta y_i - \dfrac{t\alpha_h(x_0-(-1)^h d/2)+y_0}{k_h}\Delta u_{ih} = 0 \\[2mm]
\dfrac{t\alpha_h}{k_h}v_{ih}\Delta x_i - \dfrac{\tilde{v}_h t\alpha_h}{k_h}\Delta x_i + \dfrac{1}{k_h}v_{ih}\Delta y_i - \dfrac{\tilde{v}_h}{k_h}\Delta y_i + \dfrac{1}{c\alpha_h}\Delta z_i \\
\quad + \dfrac{t\alpha_h(x_0-(-1)^h d/2)+y_0}{k_h}\Delta v_{ih} = 0
\end{cases}
\tag{4}
$$

Define parameter vectors M_h, the above equation (4) could be expressed as

$$
\begin{cases}
m_{h1}u_{ih}\Delta x_i - m_{h2}\Delta x_i + m_{h4}\Delta y_i + m_{h6}u_{ih}\Delta y_i + m_{h7}\Delta u_{ih} = \Delta x_i \\
m_{h1}v_{ih}\Delta x_i - m_{h3}\Delta x_i - m_{h5}\Delta y_i + m_{h6}v_{ih}\Delta y_i + m_{h7}\Delta v_{ih} = -\dfrac{\Delta z_i}{c\alpha_h}
\end{cases}
\tag{5}
$$

with

$$
\begin{aligned}
M_h &= [m_{h1}\ m_{h2}\ m_{h3}\ m_{h4}\ m_{h5}\ m_{h6}\ m_{h7}] \\
&= \left[\dfrac{t\alpha_h}{k_h}\ \dfrac{\tilde{u}_h t\alpha_h}{k_h}\ \dfrac{\tilde{v}_h t\alpha_h}{k_h}\ t\alpha_h - \dfrac{\tilde{u}_h}{k_h}\ \dfrac{\tilde{v}_h}{k_h}\ \dfrac{1}{k_h}\ \dfrac{t\alpha_h(x_0-(-1)^h d/2)+y_0}{k_h}\right]
\end{aligned}
\tag{6}
$$

As shown in (5), the parameter vectors M_h are desirable to link the i-th point p_i to the initial point p_0 in terms of their relative position and image coordinates in the left and the right cameras. Therefore the visual system calibration is to determine the parameter vectors combining the intrinsic and extrinsic parameters of the active stereovision platform.

2.2   Solve Parameter Vectors with Iterative Method

For each point p_i, 2 equations in (5) are satisfied for each camera. So the unknown 7 parameters in M_h can be solved with at least four points except the initial point. The least square and iteration methods are employed to solve the parameter vectors M_1 and M_2 with n points, $n \geqslant 4$. Of course, more points are helpful to improve the estimated accuracy of the parameters.

Initial Value. The initial value of parameter vectors can be calculated with neglecting the coefficients $\frac{1}{c\alpha_1}$ and $\frac{1}{c\alpha_2}$. According to (5), we have

$$
\begin{bmatrix} A_1 \\ \vdots \\ A_n \end{bmatrix} \begin{bmatrix} M_1^0 \\ M_2^0 \end{bmatrix} = \begin{bmatrix} b_1^0 \\ \vdots \\ b_n^0 \end{bmatrix}
\tag{7}
$$

$$
A_i = \begin{bmatrix}
u_{i1}\Delta x_i & -\Delta x_i & 0 & \Delta y_i & 0 & u_{i1}\Delta y_i & \Delta u_{i1} \\
v_{i1}\Delta x_i & 0 & -\Delta x_i & 0 & -\Delta y_i & v_{i1}\Delta y_i & \Delta v_{i1} \\
u_{i2}\Delta x_i & -\Delta x_i & 0 & \Delta y_i & 0 & u_{i2}\Delta y_i & \Delta u_{i2} \\
v_{i2}\Delta x_i & 0 & -\Delta x_i & 0 & -\Delta y_i & v_{i2}\Delta y_i & \Delta v_{i2}
\end{bmatrix}
\tag{8}
$$

$$
b_i^0 = [\Delta x_i \quad -\Delta z_i \quad \Delta x_i \quad -\Delta z_i \quad]^T
\tag{9}
$$

Using the least square algorithm, the initial parameter vectors can be determined as

$$
\begin{bmatrix} M_1^0 \\ M_2^0 \end{bmatrix} = \left(\begin{bmatrix} A_1 \\ \vdots \\ A_n \end{bmatrix}^T \begin{bmatrix} A_1 \\ \vdots \\ A_n \end{bmatrix} \right)^{-1} \begin{bmatrix} A_1 \\ \vdots \\ A_n \end{bmatrix}^T \begin{bmatrix} b_1^0 \\ \vdots \\ b_n^0 \end{bmatrix}
\tag{10}
$$

Then the corresponding value of yawing angles of the two cameras can be calculated as

$$
\alpha_h^0 = \arctan \frac{M_{h1}^0}{M_{h6}^0}
\tag{11}
$$

Iteration. Taking into consideration of the coefficients $\frac{1}{c\alpha_1}$ and $\frac{1}{c\alpha_2}$, in the k-th iterative step, the vector b_i^k is determined as

$$
b_i^k = \left[\Delta x_i \quad -\frac{\Delta z_i}{c\alpha_1^{k-1}} \quad \Delta x_i \quad -\frac{\Delta z_i}{c\alpha_2^{k-1}} \right]^T
\tag{12}
$$

$$
\alpha_h^{k-1} = \arctan \frac{M_{h1}^{k-1}}{M_{h6}^{k-1}}
\tag{13}
$$

Then the parameter vectors in the k-th step can be calculated with the least square method similar to (10). When the yawing angles meet with the constraint described in (14), the iteration would be ended and the parameter vectors M_h^k are considered as the optimal result. Here ε is the given tolerance.

$$
\|\alpha_h^k - \alpha_h^{k-1}\| \leq \varepsilon
\tag{14}
$$

3   Visual Measurement Model

Based on the calibrated parameter vectors, a visual measurement system is developed to obtain the relative position and the pose of an object with its geometric information.

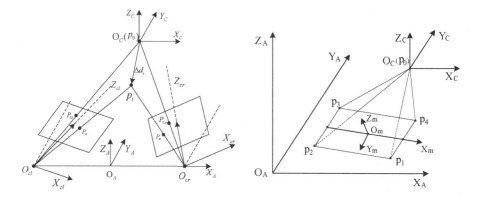

Fig. 2. Relative position measurement   **Fig. 3.** Orientation measurement

3.1   Relative Position Measurement

In the visual measurement system, a reference frame is employed to express points' positions. The reference frame is assigned at the initial point p_0 sampled in the procedure of self-calibration and has the same orientation as the vision system frame A. The active visual measurement system just calculates the position in the reference frame rather than that in the vision system frame. According to (5), we have

$$\begin{cases} (m_{h1}u_{ih} - m_{h2} - 1)\Delta x_i + (m_{h4} + m_{h6}u_{ih})\Delta y_i = -m_{h7}\Delta u_{ih} \\ (m_{h1}v_{ih} - m_{h3})\Delta x_i + (m_{h6}v_{ih} - m_{h5})\Delta y_i + \frac{\Delta z_i}{c\alpha_h} = -m_{h7}\Delta v_{ih} \end{cases} \tag{15}$$

In (15), the image coordinates of p_i in the cameras can be obtained with image processing technology. With the calibrated parameter vectors, the position of p_i in the reference frame can be easily calculated through (16) using the least square algorithm.

$$\Delta d_i = (C^T C)^{-1} C^T b \tag{16}$$

with

$$C = \begin{bmatrix} m_{11}u_{i1} - m_{12} - 1 & m_{14} + m_{16}u_{i1} & 0 \\ m_{11}v_{i1} - m_{13} & m_{16}v_{i1} - m_{15} & \frac{1}{c\alpha_1} \\ m_{21}u_{i2} - m_{22} - 1 & m_{24} + m_{26}u_{i2} & 0 \\ m_{21}v_{i2} - m_{23} & m_{26}v_{i2} - m_{25} & \frac{1}{c\alpha_2} \end{bmatrix} \tag{17}$$

$$b = \begin{bmatrix} -m_{17}\Delta u_{i1} & -m_{17}\Delta v_{i1} & -m_{27}\Delta u_{i2} & -m_{27}\Delta v_{i2} \end{bmatrix}^T \tag{18}$$

where $\Delta d_i = (\Delta x_i, \Delta y_i, \Delta z_i)$ represent the position of point p_i in the reference frame.

3.2   Orientation Measurement

To measure the orientation of a rectangle in the vision system frame, an objective frame is assigned to its centroid. As shown in Fig.3, its X-axis, X_m, is defined to be parallel with edge p_1p_2 from p_2 to p_1. Its Z-axis, Z_m, is set to be perpendicular to the plane. Its Y-axis, Y_m, is determined by $Y_m = Z_m \times X_m$.

The relative position of four corners in the reference frame could be calculated with (16). Then the position vector $\overrightarrow{p_ip_j}$ from p_i to p_j can be defined as

$$\overrightarrow{p_ip_j} = \Delta d_j - \Delta d_i \tag{19}$$

where Δd_i and Δd_j denote the relative positions of points p_i and p_j.

Then the orientation matrix R of the object in the vision system frame A could be calculated as

$$R = \begin{bmatrix} n & o & a \end{bmatrix} \tag{20}$$

with

$$\begin{cases} n = \frac{\overrightarrow{p_2p_1}+\overrightarrow{p_3p_4}}{\|\overrightarrow{p_2p_1}+\overrightarrow{p_3p_4}\|} \\ \tilde{o} = \frac{\overrightarrow{p_4p_1}+\overrightarrow{p_3p_2}}{\|\overrightarrow{p_4p_1}+\overrightarrow{p_3p_2}\|} \\ a = n \times \tilde{o} \\ o = a \times n \end{cases} \tag{21}$$

The last equation is used to ensure that the vectors n, o and a are orthogonal.

4   Visual Control System for Approaching

In the vision guided approaching, two attached rectangular marks are employed to recognize the gripper and the object, and their poses are considered as the poses of the gripper and the object respectively. So their relative positions and orientations can be calculated with (12) and (16). Then the position and orientation disparity δt and δR between them is acquired as

$$\begin{cases} \delta t = \Delta d_o - \Delta d_g \\ \delta R = [r_{ij}]_{3\times3} = R_oR_g^{-1} \end{cases} \tag{22}$$

where Δd_o and Δd_g denote the relative positions while R_o and R_g represent the orientation matrix of the object and the gripper respectively.

A scheme of position based visual control system [14] is illustrated as Fig.4 for approaching and grasping. The position and orientation disparity between the

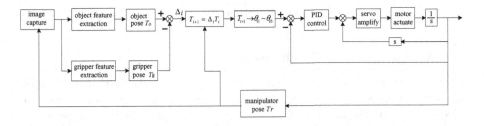

Fig. 4. Visual control system employed for approaching

gripper and the object in the vision system frame can be acquired to calculate the displacement of the end-effector in the manipulator base frame. Together with the current transformation matrix T_r, the objective transformation matrix in the next cycle can be obtained for the manipulator. It is used to generate the six objective angle positions and increments in joint space with inverse kinematics solution algorithm. For joint angle position control, inner speed and outer position closed loops are adopted for each joint, and PID control law is employed in the visual guided approaching procedure.

5 Experiments

An experiment system was designed as given in Fig.5. It consisted of a stereovision platform with two cameras, a manipulator UP6, a gripper as end-effector and an industrial computer equipped with image capture card. Two rectangular marks with red and green color were used to identify the gripper and the object respectively. In the experiments, the stereovision platform was located at the left of the manipulator UP6 to capture the images of workshop scene. Its orientation was well adjusted so that its X_A-axis and Y_A-axis were the inverse directions of the X-axis and Y-axis of the manipulator base frame.

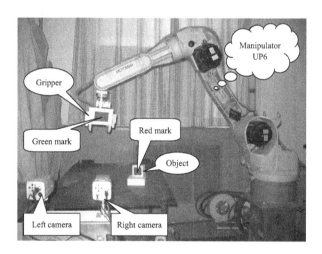

Fig. 5. Experiment system

5.1 Visual System Self-calibration

When the manipulator was at initial pose, the centroid of the mark on its gripper was selected as initial point p_0. With the gripper translating many steps, the selected point on the mark would form a series of points. For the i-th point, its image coordinates (u_{ih}, v_{ih}), $(\Delta u_{ih}, \Delta v_{ih})$ could be obtained by feature extraction. While its relative position to p_0 in the manipulator base frame could be read from the manipulator controller and transformed to the relative position $(\Delta x, \Delta y, \Delta z)$ in the vision system frame.

With the proposed self-calibration method, the parameter vectors for the visual system were obtained and listed in (23). The iteration was converged in two steps and its cost was less than 3ms.

$$\begin{cases} M_1 = [0.000240, 0.0706, 0.0551, -0.301, 0.372, 0.0015, 1.854] \\ M_2 = [-0.000152, -0.0541, -0.0230, 0.413, 0.342, 0.00140, 1.797] \end{cases} \quad (23)$$

5.2 Visual Measurement

An experiment was conducted to compare the measured relative positions and the actual ones of the rectangular mark's centroid. The relative position resulted from the manipulator controller and obtained by the visual measurement system were considered as actual ones and measured ones.

The experimental results and the errors of the measured ones are illustrated as Fig.6 and Fig.7, respectively. It can be seen that the errors in X_A- and Z_A-axes are very small with no more than 2 mm, while the errors in Y_A- axis is about 8 mm at its maximum. However, it is acceptable for the relative position in Y_A-axis that represents the depth information of the visual system and sensitive to errors. The good coincidence between them verifies the validity of the proposed stereovision self-calibration and measurement methods.

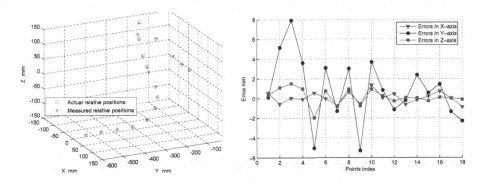

Fig. 6. The actual and measured relative positions

Fig. 7. Error of measured relative position with respect to the actual in 3-axes

5.3 Visual Guided Approaching and Grasping

The experiment is conducted to validate the application of the proposed system in vision guided approaching and grasping. Meanwhile a comparative approaching experiment was also conducted with stereovision system pre-calibrated with traditional method [3] in the same conditions such as the localizations of the object and the starting state of the gripper. In order to avoid the crash of the gripper to the object, a path point was set at the position above the object, according to the measured position and orientation of the object.

For the two methods, the approaching trajectories of the end-effector in the manipulator base frame are illustrated as Fig.8, and the final states ready for grasping are listed in table 1. For the visual system calibrated by the two methods, in spite of different trajectories, the final states of the gripper had a good accordance in terms of position and orientation. The whole procedure of approaching the object about 1000 mm away cost about 30s.

The experimental results show that the proposed visual system with self-calibration has as good performance as the visual system with traditional calibration and stereovision method for the application in vision guided approaching and grasping.

Table 1. Comparison of Final Position and Pose

Methods	x (mm)	y (mm)	z (mm)	θ_x (rad)	θ_y (rad)	θ_z (rad)
Traditional method	1228.093	-28.557	-54.115	3.114366	-0.033336	-1.174781
Proposed method	1228.657	-33.800	-52.780	3.120300	-0.038223	-1.167451

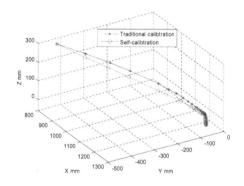

Fig. 8. Approaching Trajectories with the proposed and pre-calibrated visual system

6   Conclusion

In this paper, a new self-calibration method is proposed for an active stereovision platform, and a new active visual system is developed for approaching and grasping. For the designed stereovision platform with two motion-independent cameras, the proposed self-calibration method uses a single point undergoing a series of (at least 4) translation motions to obtain its parameter vectors combining the intrinsic and extrinsic parameters. With the reference point, the designed visual measurement system can obtain the relative position of any point as well as the orientation of an object with its geometric information. Then a position-based visual control system is employed for approaching and grasping. Finally, two groups of experiments are provided to verify the proposed methods. One group is to compare the actual and measured relative positions. The other group is to compare the developed visual system with the pre-calibrated visual system, which verifies the proposed self-calibration method and the designed visual system for approaching and grasping.

References

1. Faugeras, O.D., Toscani, G.: The Calibration Problem for Stereo. In: IEEE international Conference on Computer Vision and Pattern Recognition, pp. 15–20. IEEE Press, Florida (1986)
2. Tsai, R.Y., Lenz, R.K.: A New Technique for Fully Autonomous and Efficient 3D Robotics Hand/eye Calibration. IEEE Transactions on Robotics and Automation 5(3), 345–358 (1989)
3. Zhang, Z.: A Flexible New Technique for Camera Calibration. IEEE Transactions on Pattern Analysis and Machine Intelligence 22(11), 1330–1334 (2000)
4. Hartley, R.I.: Self-calibration from Multiple Views with a Rotating Camera. In: 3rd European Conference on Computer Vision, Stocklholm, pp. 471–478 (1994)
5. Quan, L.: Self-calibration of an Affine Camera from Multiple Views. International Journal of Computer Vision 19(1), 95–105 (1996)
6. Kim, H., Hong, K.S.: A Practical Self-calibration Method of Rotating and Zooming Cameras. In: 15th International Conference on Pattern Recognition, Barcelona, pp. 354–357 (2000)
7. Agapito, L., Hayman, E., Reid, I.: Self-Calibration of Rotating and Zooming Cameras. International Journal of Computer Vision 45(2), 107–127 (2001)
8. Ji, Q., Dai, S.: Self-calibration of a Rotating Camera with a Translational Offset. IEEE Transactions on Robotics and Automation 20(1), 1–14 (2004)
9. Maybank, S.J., Faugeras, O.D.: A Theory of Self-calibration of a Moving Camera. International Journal of Computer vision 8(2), 123–151 (1992)
10. Ma, S.D.: A Self Calibration Technique for Active Stereo Vision System. IEEE Transaction on Robotics and Automaton 12(1), 114–120 (1996)
11. Malm, H., Heyden, A.: Extensions of Plane-based Calibration to the Case of Translational Motion in a Robot Vision Setting. IEEE Transactions on Robotics 22(2), 322–333 (2006)
12. Menudet, J.F., Becker, J.M., Fournel, T., Mennessier, C.: Planebased Camera Self-calibration by Mmetric Rectification of Images. Image and Vision Computing 26(7), 913–934 (2008)
13. Xu, D., Li, Y.F., Tan, M., Shen, Y.: A New Active Visual System for Humanoid Robots. IEEE Transactions on Systems, Man, and Cybernetics-part B: Cybernetics 38(2), 320–330 (2008)
14. Chaumette, F., Hutchinson, S.: Visual Servo Control, Part I: Basic Approaches. IEEE Robotics and Automation 13(4), 82–90 (2006)

A Real-Time On-Board Orthogonal SLAM
for an Indoor UAV

Mirco Alpen, Klaus Frick, and Joachim Horn

Helmut-Schmidt-University / University of the Federal Armed Forces Hamburg,
Department of Electrical Engineering, Institute for Control Engineering,
P.O. Box 700822, D-22008 Hamburg, Germany

Abstract. Over the last years we developed a real-time on-board orthogonal SLAM (simultaneous localization and mapping) algorithm for an indoor UAV based on successfully implemented techniques for ground robots. The algorithm delivers a 2D floor plan of the investigated area. The robot is able to act with full autonomy in an unknown indoor environment because all essential computations are done on-board.

The focus of this paper is on two key features in the topic of SLAM algorithms. The first one is the computation of the robot's movement and especially of the robot's rotation between two scans and the measurement of the robots orientation in an indoor environment in general. In this paper we present a very simple method based on angle histograms. The second one is the loop-closing problem. We present some results that will show that the loop-closing is possible with our very simple approach of SLAM algorithm. Finally, it comprises the results of an autonomous indoor flight of the industrial quadrotor AR100B® of the AirRobot® company equipped with a self-constructed functional group. In contrast to our former paper [1], all essential computations including the SLAM algorithm are done in real-time and on-board.

1 Introduction

To act with full autonomy in an unknown environment a mobile robot must have two key features. At first it must be able to build a map and localize itself in it and secondly the robot needs a navigation strategy. The first point is known as SLAM problem and is of increasing interest in recent years. Solutions to this problem have been proposed in several forms and can be divided into two main groups. The first group includes algorithms based on landmarks like Fast-SLAM [2] for example. The other group contains algorithms needing no information about the environment. Therefore algorithms of this group, like DP-SLAM [3] for example, are suitable to get full autonomy of mobile robots. A general survey of the SLAM history is given by Durrent-Whyte and Bailey [4, 5].

To enable a small flight robot to operate in an unknown indoor environment, often a ground station for the calculation of the SLAM algorithm is needed [6]. Due to this, these robots cannot act with full autonomy. In our work we focus on unknown indoor environments. Therefore the orthogonal SLAM [7] presented

C.-Y. Su, S. Rakheja, H. Liu (Eds.): ICIRA 2012, Part III, LNAI 7508, pp. 542–551, 2012.

for the first time in 2006 is a useful way to build a floor plan with a low memory requirement. We assume that the environment can be represented by lines that are parallel or orthogonal. In our version of the orthogonal SLAM algorithm presented in 2010 [8] only one step of iteration is needed to integrate a new scan into the global map. This allows an evaluation of the computing time without worst case assumptions and a clear statement for the real-time behavior of the complete system. The used SLAM algorithm is briefly discussed in section 3.

In general, the mapping of an indoor environment by a flying object is a 3D problem. With the assumption that the robot only acts with a constant altitude in a structured indoor environment like corridors, it can be reduced to a 2D problem.

The measurement of the robot's orientation in an indoor environment is a key issue of our SLAM approach and not that easy. Due to the ferromagnetic materials, working with magnetometer causes lots of problems. Furthermore a GPS signal cannot be ensured. In several applications of indoor UAV an IMU (inertial measurement unit) is used to compute the robot's orientation. To ensure appropriate accuracy of this method, a sample rate around 100 Hz is needed. As said before, we use an industrial quadrotor for our experiments and that's why we are not able to get the needed information with the attended sample rate. Therefore we compute the robot's orientation based on the data of the laser range finder just by evaluating the angular histograms. This method is based on the cross correlation approach presented in [9] and is discussed in section 4.

If a robot explores an indoor environment the probability of reaching a position which was passed before is quite high. The task of deciding whether or not a vehicle has, after an excursion of arbitrary length, returned to a previously visited area is known as loop-closing problem. Reliable loop-closing is both essential and hard [10]. In section 5 we present a result showing that the loop-closing is possible with our very simple approach of SLAM algorithm.

Combining all parts of our work, section 6 of this paper shows the result of a full autonomous flight of an industrial quadrotor equipped with the functional group named intelligent control and measurement unit (ICAM) presented in the following section 2.

2   Introductive System Description

The AR100B® quadrotor is by default equipped with an inertial measurement unit (IMU), compass, GPS, and a camera. The payload of this aerial vehicle is around 0.4kg and the diameter is about 1m [11]. The definition of axes and angles in the body-fixed reference frame is shown in figure 1(a).

Because of the robot's varying orientation represented by the state Ψ we need to establish the earth coordinate system. Body-fixed coordinates are denoted as (x_R, y_R, z_R), earth coordinates as (x_E, y_E, z_E).

We replaced the robot's camera by our ICAM which is shown in figure 1(b). It is composed of a Hokuyo® laser range finder with an effective reach of 30m and two 16bit Infineon® microcontrollers.

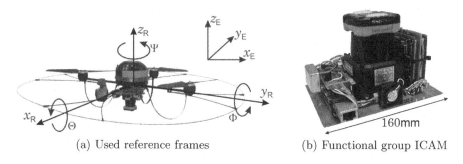

(a) Used reference frames   (b) Functional group ICAM

Fig. 1. The industrial quadrotor and the functional group ICAM

All needed controllers and other time-critical functions are implemented on these microcontrollers. One is used for the autonomous flight with a sampling rate of 5Hz and the other is used for the SLAM algorithm. This algorithm works with a sampling rate of 1Hz. For indoor environments this frequency turns out as a reasonable compromise between accuracy and the amount of data. The 270 degree laser range finder will be used with an angle resolution of 1 degree.

Optionally the ICAM comprises a WLAN module or a wired connection to enable monitoring on a ground station without interruptions. The weight of this functional group shown in figure 1(b) is 0.45kg and the power consumption is approximately 10W.

One of the microcontrollers is connected with the quadrotor via RS232 to receive the current states of the robot (altitude, orientation) and transmit the corresponding actuating variables. To ensure safety and enable a manual operated mode at any time a hand held transmitter is embedded in the transmission line of the actuating variables.

3   SLAM Algorithm

The used SLAM algorithm was presented in detail in 2010 [8]. Thus, it is only discussed briefly in this section. The basic idea is shown in figure 2.

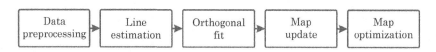

Fig. 2. Basic flowchart of SLAM algorithm

One can see that our algorithm comprises five steps. Within the first step named 'Data preprocessing' erroneous measurements of the laser range finder are excluded and the scan values are transformed into the earth coordinates regarding the robot's orientation Ψ. The way how we estimate the orientation is described in the following section 4. During the second step lines are estimated based on the split and merge algorithm presented in [12]. These lines are checked for orthogonality within the third step. Extracted lines that are slightly non-orthogonal are changed to orthogonal. All other lines are neglected and will not be part of the global map.

The fourth part of the SLAM algorithm is the most important one. The extracted lines of the current scan have to be integrated in the global map. To integrate the new lines successfully one has to estimate the robot's movement accurately. In our case this is done by just one step of iteration. As mentioned before the data processing is done considering the robot's orientation Ψ. Therefore the orthogonal lines are all parallel to one of the axes of the earth coordinates x_E or y_E fixed on the first scan and the calculation of the robot's movement can be divided in these two directions.

In the last part of the algorithm named 'Map optimization' double lines are merged to reduce the total number of lines in the global map. With this step the computing time of the following map update and the memory requirements are reduced.

4 Estimating the Robot's Orientation

Estimating the robot's orientation in an indoor environment differs from the outdoor approaches. As mentioned in section 1, using a magnometer or a GPS might cause lot of problems. Therefore some indoor approaches have been developed over the last years. The first of these techniques needs an a priori map of the environment like the approach of Cox [13]. A few years later an approach based on a cross correlation was presented [9]. In this case, the key assumption was a predominant rectangular structure of the environment. As can be seen in section 3, we are dealing with an orthogonal SLAM which is based on the same assumption. Therefore it seems obvious to use this cross correlation approach. As known from the literature and from the formulas themselves, there is a closed relation between the cross correlation

$$r_{x_1 x_2}(\tau) = \int_{-\infty}^{\infty} x_1(t)x_2(t + \tau)dt \tag{1}$$

and the convolution of two signals

$$y(t) = x_1(t) * x_2(t) = \int_{-\infty}^{\infty} x_1(\tau)x_2(\tau - t)d\tau. \tag{2}$$

The two differences between these functions are the integration variables and the algebraic sign in the second term of integration. Due to the positive algebraic sign there is no mirroring of the second function $x_2(t)$ regarding to the y-axes. One attribute of the convolution is that the Dirac function $\delta(t)$ is the neutral element as can be seen in equation (3):

$$x(t) * \delta(t) = x(t) \tag{3}$$

Assuming that we are dealing with a non-shifted Dirac function $\delta(t)$, the mirroring regarding to the y-axes has no effect. Thus, the attribute of the convolution shown in equation (3) can be adopted to the cross correlation.

If we assume a rectangular structure we can define an ideal angular histogram with four maxima for the whole 360 degree cycle. Reducing the interval to a band around one of these maxima, we are dealing with a non-shifted Dirac function. Thus, the maximum of the current angular histogram leads directly to the robot's orientation in relation to the referance given by the Dirac function.

To show the functionality of the described method we give an example which is close to application on the flight platform later on. To save computation time for the real time application, the robots orientation is computed based on 50 scan values. The whole set in our application consists of 270 values.

Figure 3(a) shows the test scenario in our laboratory. The laser range finder is placed in the origin of the given plot and is marked with the grey filled circle. The grey lines on the left hand side represents the current environment in the earth coordinates (x_E, y_E) and the black dots represent the current scan transformed in body fixed coordinates (x_R, y_R). As can be seen, there is a small rotation between the current scan and the reference.

As defined in [9] the angular histogram is computed from the current scan values as follows. The scan values are interpreted as vectors. In this case, the vector difference between two consecutive vectors can be calculated. The results of these calculations are summarized in a distribution of the occurred angles. This statistical distribution is called angular histogram. For this small example the result is given in figure 3(b).

To reduce noise in the given histogram we adopt the advice from [9]. The histogram printed in black was computed by getting the vector difference between one vector and its 10th successor.

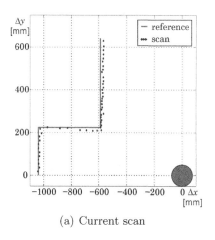
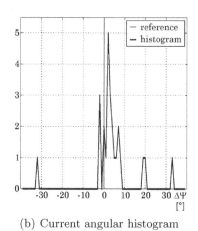

(a) Current scan   (b) Current angular histogram

Fig. 3. Example scan and the current angular histogram

The angular histogram in figure 3(b) shows a maximum at $\Delta\Psi = 2$. The grey line in the middle of the plot at $\Delta\Psi = 0$ marks the reference histogram. The difference between the maximum and the reference gives the information about the robot's orientation.

Regarding the computed rotation of $\Delta\Psi = 2$ the current scan can be transformed from the body fixed grid (x_R, y_R) into the earth coordinates (x_E, y_E). The result is given in figure 4.

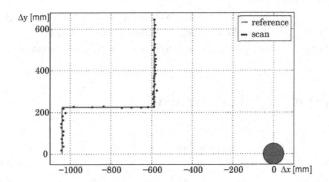

Fig. 4. Current scan regarding the computed orientation

One can see that after the transformation the congruence between the reference and the current scan values is nearly excellent. The only inaccuracy that remains is the measurement noise of the laser range finder.

The last part of this section deals with the accuracy of the described method. In our case we are dealing with a resolution of 1 degree. Due to the measurement noise of the laser range finder a higher angle resolution does not make sense. Therefore we have a worst case quantisation noise of ±0.5 degree.

To get information about the accuracy of the given method we have made a long term measurement. During this measurement the orientation of the laser range finder was −14.5 degree regarding to the reference angle. Thus, the worst case quantisation noise is taken into account. The result of 1000 measurements is given in figure 5.

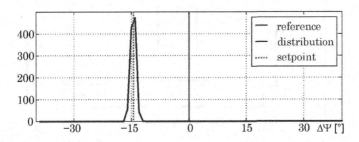

Fig. 5. Distribution of the measured angles $\Delta\Psi$

The figure shows the distribution of the 1000 measurements. The reference is marked with the grey line at 0 degree and the dashed line marks the real orientation at −14.5 degree. As mentioned before, we reduced the search space for the current orientation to ±45 degree in relation to the reference. Thus, figure 5 shows the distribution of the measurement results over the whole search space.

As can be seen the accuracy is within ±1.5 degree. In relation to the full circle with 360 degree, this leads to an error below 1%. Thus, this method to estimate the robots orientation is quite successful and it is used for control and the SLAM algorithm in the following experiments.

There are two possibilities to cover the full circle. On the one hand, the reference can be changed if the robot does a 90 degree turn. On the other hand the arising angles can be mapped into the current search space between −45 and 45 degree.

5   Validation by Flight Simulation

In this section we present a result of a preparatory experiment with a ground robot. We call it flight simulation because the flight robot was replaced by a ground robot. Thus, we have a simulation of a flight with a constant altitude. All calculations during this experiment were done on the ICAM presented in section 2. The generated actuating variables by the control algorithms were interpreted by the ground robot. Due to the vibration during the robots movement, some occurring disturbances during a real flight were reproduced as well. With these experiments we want to show that the SLAM algorithm and the robot's navigation using the method presented in section 4 works well and that the loop closing problem can be solved with this kind of algorithm, too.

The grey line in figure 6 shows the small test environment that was set up in our laboratory. It has a rectangular structure and a squared area in the middle. Due to this area it is ensured that the robot has to move around to get all features of the scenario. Furthermore the loop closing problem is included.

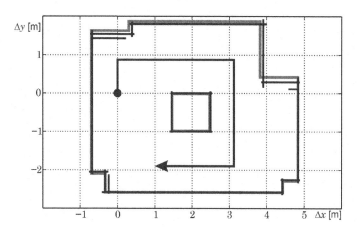

Fig. 6. Result of the SLAM algorithm in a small scenario

The black dot at the origin marks the robot's starting point. From there it moved along the black arrow in parallel to the given structure. In the respective corners of the environment, the robots does a 90 degree turn on the spot. During this turn, the reference angle for the angular histogram is changed. This change of the reference angle enables the robots to move through complex structures.

The bold black lines represent the result of the given experiment. Figure 6 shows that the SLAM algorithm using the presented method of computing the robot's orientation worked well. Furthermore it can be seen that the loop closing problem is solved, too. During its way through the scenario, the SLAM algorithm works stable and the resulting map is well-arranged and has a quite good scaling. Thus this result show great promise for a successful experiment with the flight robot which is described in the following section.

6   Experimental Results

Here we come to the result of a completely autonomous flight of the AR100B® equipped with the ICAM described in section 2. As can be seen in figure 7 a test environment was built up in a sports hall at our university. Canvases were used to give a structure to the inner part of the hall. The resulting scenario was formed like the capital letter 'L'. We choose this location and this kind of environment to ensure adequate space in each direction.

This scenario is a preliminary experiment for the loop closing. The loop closing problem itself is not part of the presented experiment.

Fig. 7. The flight robot during the experiment

During the experiment, the robot had to move with a constant velocity and altitude in a constant distance to its leading wall on the left hand side. If the robot recognized a corner it did a 90 degree turn on the spot similar to the experiment presented in section 5. The reference angle for the robot's orientation is changed in the same way.

The test environment for the flight experiment can be seen in figure 8. The previously mentioned capital 'L' is upside down and marked with the grey lines.

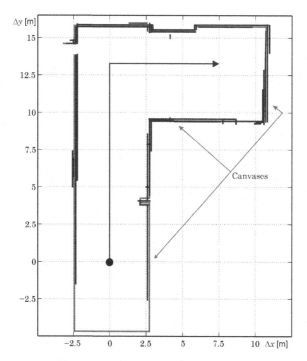

Fig. 8. Result of an autonomous flight

The robot's path during the experiment is marked with the black arrow. The black dot at the origin of figure 8 represents the starting point and the bold black lines gives the result of the on-board real-time SLAM algorithm. Every feature of the environment can be recognized in the resulting map. One can see the door in the upper right corner of the map as well as the column on the right hand wall.

The scaling of the map is quite good. To come to a full loop-closing experiment with the flight robot, we have to do some work on the hardware to ensure a complete data monitoring. With such corresponding improvements we expect a positive progress in such an experiment based on the presented results.

7   Conclusion

The focus of this paper was on two key features in the topic of SLAM algorithm. At first we showed the computation of the robot's rotation between two scans and the measurement of the robot's orientation in an indoor environment in general. We used a very simple method based on angle histograms which was founded on the well-known cross correlation method. The results of the validating experiment showed that this method works very sufficient and with a quite good accuracy.

In the next step the presented method of estimating the robot's orientation was integrated in our previously presented real-time on-board orthogonal SLAM algorithm for an indoor UAV. This algorithm merges a new scan into the global map without any iteration. Due to this it is very suitable for real-time applications.

The algorithm delivers a 2D floor plan of the investigated area. All essential computations are done on two microcontrollers which are mounted on the industrial quadrotor AR100B®. Based on a small test environment, we showed that the loop closing problem can be solved with this comparatively simple method as well.

The final experiment shows that the robot is able to map an unknown indoor environment with full autonomy. With some hardware improvements we expect a positive progress based on the presented results.

References

1. Alpen, M., Frick, K., Horn, J.: On the Way to a Real-Time On-Board Orthogonal SLAM for an Indoor UAV. In: Jeschke, S., Liu, H., Schilberg, D. (eds.) ICIRA 2011, Part I. LNCS (LNAI), vol. 7101, pp. 1–11. Springer, Heidelberg (2011)
2. Montemerlo, M., Thrun, S., Koller, D., Wegbreit, B.: FastSLAM: factored solution on the simultaneous localization and mapping problem. In: AAAI, Mobile Robot Competition and Exhibition, Edmonton, Canada (2002)
3. Eliazar, A., Parr, R.: DP-SLAM: fast, robust simultaneous localization and mapping without predetermind landmarks. In: 18th Int. Joint Conf. on Artificial Intelligence (IJCAI), pp. 1135–1142. Morgan-Kaufmann Publishers, Acapulco (2003)
4. Durrant-Whyte, H., Bailey, T.: Simultaneous localization and mapping (SLAM): Part I The essential algorithms. IEEE Robotics and Automation Magazine 13(2) (2006)
5. Bailey, T., Durrant-Whyte, H.: Simultaneous localization and mapping (SLAM): Part II State of the art. IEEE Robotics and Automation Magazine 13(3) (2006)
6. Grzonka, S., Grisetti, G., Burgard, W.: Towards a navigation system for autonomous indoor flying. In: International Conference of Robotics and Automation (ICRA), Kobe, Japan (2009)
7. Nguyen, V., Harati, A., Martinelli, A., Seigwart, R.: Orthogonal SLAM - a step toward lightweight indoor autonomous navigation. In: IEEE/RSJ International Conference on Intelligent Robots and Systems (IROS), Beijing, China (2006)
8. Alpen, M., Willrodt, C., Frick, K., Horn, J.: On-board SLAM for indoor UAV using a laser range finder. In: SPIE Defence, Security and Sensing, Orlando, USA (2010)
9. Wei, G., Wetzler, C., von Puttkamer, E.: Keeping Track of Position and Orientation of Moving Indoor Systems by Correlation of Range-Finder Scans. In: International Conference on Intelligant Robots and Systems (ICRA), Munich, Germany (1994)
10. Newman, P., Ho, K.: SLAM-Loop Closing with Visually Salient Features. In: IEEE International Conference on Robotics and Automation (ICRA), Barcelona, Spain (2005)
11. Wiggerich, B.: Operating Instructions AR100B. Airrobot, Arnsberg (2008)
12. Choi, Y.-H., Lee, T.-K., Oh, S.-Y.: A line feature based SLAM with low grade range sensors using geometric constrains and active exploration for mobile robot. Springer, Autonomous Robots 24(1) (January 2008)
13. Cox, I.J.: Blanche - An experiment in guidance and navigation of an autonomous robot vehicle. IEEE Transactions on Robotics and Automation 7(2) (April 1991)
14. Alpen, M., Frick, K., Horn, J.: Nonlinear modeling and position control of an industrial quadrotor with on-board attitude control. In: IEEE International Conference on Control and Automation (ICCA), Christchurch, New Zealand (2009)
15. Meister, O.: Integrierte Navigationssysteme: Sensordatenfusion, GPS und Inertiale Navigation. Oldenbourg, Munich, Germany (2007)

An Infrastructure-Free Indoor Navigation System for Blind People*

Diansheng Chen, Wei Feng, Qiteng Zhao, Muhua Hu, and Tianmiao Wang

Robotic Institute, Beihang University, Beijing 100191, China
chends@163.com

Abstract. Numbers of indoor navigation systems have been proposed by using different sensing technologies. However, there is still lack of research on blind people focused indoor navigation system. This study aims to develop a high accurate indoor navigation system for blind people to meet this demand. The proposed system is based on inertial measurement unit, which is infrastructure-free and robust. The kinematic characteristics of walking have been investigated. The step frequency detection algorithm and the step length estimation method are developed. Moreover, an effective positioning correction algorithm has been proposed to improve locating accuracy. The experiments showed that this indoor navigation system have a high positioning accuracy, and capable to provide navigation service for blind people in indoor environment.

Keywords: Blind People, Indoor Navigation, Inertial System, Feature Recognition.

1 Introduction

Blind and low vision people are increasing 1 million to 2 million per year, this estimate indicates that the total number of blind people will achieve 100 million in 2020, not include low vision people [1]. The defect in vision constrains the activity scope of blind and low vision people, which slows the improvement of life quality in this rapid developing society.

As the development of Location Based Service (LBS) recently, navigation system for outdoor environment is relative mature, which is ready to provide navigation service for blind people. However, indoor navigation technology still has enough potential to be improved.

A number of different indoor navigation techniques have been developed, which can be divided by types of sensing data. Image matching [2] [3] and laser ranging [4] locating techniques are based on the optical signal. Ultrasound ranging locating technique is based on the sound signal [5]. Also, radio frequency based locating technique can be used for indoor navigation, for instance, RFID technique [3] [6] and

---

* This work was supported by the National High Technology Research and Development Program of China (863 Program) (No. 2008AA040207).

C.-Y. Su, S. Rakheja, H. Liu (Eds.): ICIRA 2012, Part III, LNAI 7508, pp. 552–561, 2012.
© Springer-Verlag Berlin Heidelberg 2012

Pseudolite techniques [7-9]. However, most of above techniques are infrastructure-dependent, which means that different kinds of sensors need to be pre-implemented into the environment. Some image matching locating system can achieve infrastructure-free navigation, but it is still hard to be applied in complex environments. When the inertial measurement unit (IMU) became more accurate and affordable recently, the inertial navigation systems (INS) are becoming a more suitable choice for indoor navigation. It is infrastructure-free, low-cost and more robust. Several researches have been conducted in following four aspects in this field:

- Step Frequency Detection

Accelerator is the most common sensor to detect step. For recognizing the kinematic pattern while walking, the step frequency can be measured [10] [11]. Besides, Toth et al. [12] introduced a new type step counter, a set of four micro-switches are implanted into the insole to detect forces. While a timer synchronized with GPS system to measure the step frequency.

- Step Length Estimation

Step length is distance between two heels when walking, which varies in different situations and hard to directly measure. Weinberg et al. [13] proposed the relationship between step length and body vertical acceleration in 2002. Beauregard et al. [14] further investigate this relationship with Artificial Neural Network (ANN), using GPS measured step length as the ideal output to train ANN model. In 2011, Shin et al. [15] investigated the linear relationship between step length and step frequency and body vertical acceleration by statistical methods.

- Walking Direction Detection

Walking direction can be detected by electronic compasses and gyroscopes. Because electronic compasses are vulnerable to electromagnetic interference, most researches adopted the combination solution (electronic compasses plus gyroscopes) to detect walking direction [16-19].

- Position Correction

As the characteristic of inertial navigation systems (INS), cumulated error exists and increases as time goes by. Zero velocity updating (ZUPT) is suitable technique to decrease cumulated error, especially for walking position correction, because there is a zero velocity moment in every step when feet grapping ground. Zhou et al. [20] proposed a new zero velocity moment detecting method. It used shoe-embedded low-power radars to detect the phase difference to identify the zero velocity moment. Besides, other indoor locating techniques were used to improve the positioning accuracy. Kourogi et al. [21], Girard et al. [5] and Ruiz et al. [6] adopted image matching, ultrasound ranging and RFID techniques to aid positioning respectively.

Generally speaking, designing an effective indoor navigation system is still a challenging task. Moreover, most of previous researches in this field are focus on healthy users. For blind people, the navigation system requires a more accurate positioning algorithm and a different user interface design. This paper is motivated by this research gap and proposed to address the demand of indoor navigation for blind people.

2   System Design

2.1   System Overview

The indoor navigation system contains two main modules: one is the sensing module for sampling kinematic data, and the other one is data processing module for preforming navigation algorithm and background monitoring. Based on the requirements of system function, a high accurate inertial navigation system (INS) – "iFLY" System designed by Beihang University [22] was selected as the sensing module in this research. Besides, a laptop or a PDA is used as the data processing module receiving sensing data by wireless communication. This hardware configuration is set up for navigation algorithm research. Hence, it could be simplified to a more compact embedded system in the future. Fig. 1 shows the hardware configuration of the indoor navigation system.

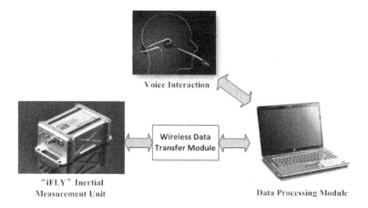

Fig. 1. Hardware Configuration

2.2   Navigation Algorithm

Basically, navigation algorithm consists two main parts, which are positioning process and orientation process. Positioning process is in charge of estimating the current location based on multiple inertial inputs. Orientation process is designed for generating ideal path from current position to the destination. Thus, these two sub-processes answer the following two questions:

1. Where am I in this building?
2. How can I reach my destination?

Continually asking and answering these two questions is the core process of the navigation system. The main procedures of the navigation system are demonstrated in Fig. 2. To obtain the current position of users, inertial data is sampled by INS, and then calculate three key parameters in pedestrian navigation, which are walking direction, step frequency and step length. The initial current position is calculated by this formula:

$$\overrightarrow{\text{relativePosition}} = \int_0^t \text{stepLength} * \text{stepFrequency} * \overrightarrow{\text{stepDirection}} * dt \qquad (1)$$

Position correction is performed after initial locating to improve the positioning accuracy. In this paper, an effective position correction algorithm, named "Directional Step Serial Matching", is proposed. To obtain the orientation guidance, current position and destination are compared to generate walking path. Then, the orientation guidance could be provided based on current position. In following parts, four key procedures in this indoor navigation system, includes step frequency detection, step length estimation, walking direction detection and position correction, are detailed illustrated.

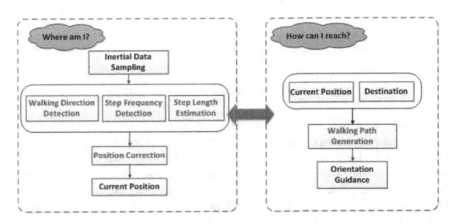

Fig. 2. Processes in Navigation System

Step Frequency Detection

For step frequency detection, an acceleration time window based algorithm has been adopted. The characteristics of every step cycle can be concluded in following two points:

1. The vertical acceleration (z axis) changes dramatically in a short time.
2. The interval time between two steps is relative stable.

Thus, the step frequency detection algorithm is designed according to these characteristics. The acceleration dynamic and the detection algorithm are illustrated in Fig. 3.

As shown in Fig. 3 the "Detecting" phase in the figure is the detecting time window for acceleration monitoring. The "Timeout" phase presents the minimum interval time between steps, in which phase the sampled data are not processed. The "T" is the threshold for acceleration change, which caused by the forces between feet and supporting ground.

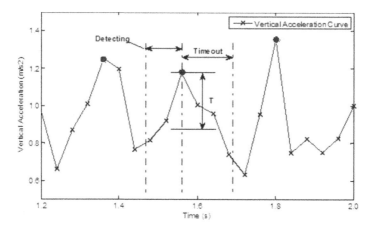

Fig. 3. Vertical acceleration dynamic while walking

The process of the step detection algorithm is as following steps. Firstly, the vertical acceleration (perpendicular to the ground) is collected in detecting phase, the time window in this phase is around 150ms. Secondly, if the maximum acceleration change exceeds threshold (T), which is around 0.5g, a step is detected. Otherwise, another detecting phase started. Lastly, if a new step detected, the timeout phase starts, which is around 200ms. In this phase, no acceleration data is analyzed to reduce false detection. When the timeout phase ends, the detecting phase starts automatically.

Step Length Estimation

According to previous researches in this field, step length can be calculated directly by acceleration integration or estimated by other dynamic parameters. Because the accuracy of directly calculation is relative low and depending on the hardware specifications, the second route is selected to estimate the step length in this research.

Intensive experiments of walking had been performed, and the result showed that the step length increases with the step frequency. Fig. 4 shows the quantitative analysis of the relationship between step length and step frequency. Numerical matching is applied to obtain the relationship equation:

$$stepLength = a + b * stepTimeInterval + c * stepTimeInterval^2 \qquad (2)$$

In above equation, a, b, c are the parameters vary from different users, these parameters can be determined by calibration process before the first usage for a new user.

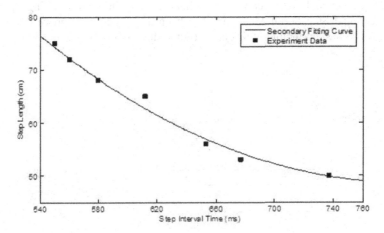

Fig. 4. Relationship between step length (cm) and step interval time (ms). In this case, the parameters a, b and c are 328.68, -0.71 and 0.00045 respectively.

Walking Direction Detection

The step direction is calculated by the sample data from "iFLY" system. Because the sensors are attached on the waist of users, the step direction can be obtained by Euler angles of "iFLY" system. The axis direction is shown in Fig. 5.

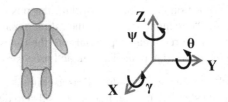

Fig. 5. Wear Direction of "iFLY" system

The Euler angles are calculated by angular velocity integration in 3 dimensions. The calculation equations are as follow:

$$\begin{bmatrix} \gamma \\ \theta \\ \psi \end{bmatrix} = \int_0^t \begin{bmatrix} \dot{\gamma} \\ \dot{\theta} \\ \dot{\psi} \end{bmatrix} dt = \int_0^t \frac{1}{\cos\theta} \begin{bmatrix} -\sin\gamma\sin\theta & \cos\theta & -\cos\gamma\sin\theta \\ \cos\gamma\cos\theta & 0 & \sin\gamma\cos\theta \\ \sin\gamma & 0 & \cos\gamma \end{bmatrix} \begin{bmatrix} \omega_x \\ \omega_y \\ \omega_z \end{bmatrix} dt \qquad (3)$$

In above equations, ω_x, ω_y, ω_z are the angular velocities in 3 dimensions, ψ, θ, γ are Yaw, Pitch and Roll angles. In current wear pattern, the Yaw angle indicated the relative step direction.

Position Correction

As the step direction is function of time, the error is cumulated as time goes by. In long-distance positioning case, the data from inertial sensor system could contain relative big error, and even become not applicable. Thus, in our positioning algorithm, the "Directional Step Serial Matching" has been developed to improve the position accuracy. The basic principle of this algorithm is shown in Fig. 6.

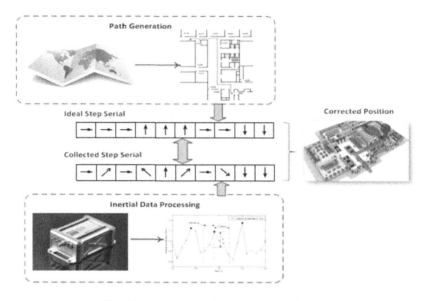

Fig. 6. Directional Step Serial Matching algorithm

In this position correction algorithm, the positioning process and path generation process are "communicate" with the "directional step serials" to estimate the best positions. The directional step serials are the time-based serial with step directions to identify the pedestrian path. The detailed process of this algorithm is as following:

1. Sample inertial data includes 3D accelerations and angular velocities.
2. Calculate step length, step frequency and step direction.
3. Generate collected directional step serial based on above three parameters.
4. Generate ideal directional step serial based on walking path.
5. Compare collected and ideal step serials for position correction.
6. Estimate the best current position.

For step serial matching, the ideal directional step serial is defined as α_i, the corresponding ideal position serial is defined as P_i, while the collected directional step serial is defined as β_j, which i and j are the step number in the serial. A matching window with N step directions is created for evaluating matching error. Thus, the matching error inside the window is:

$$\varphi_i = \sqrt{\frac{\sum_i^{i-N}(\alpha_i - \beta_i)^2}{N}} \tag{4}$$

For every detected step, the matching window moves along the ideal step serial in a defined range for the best fit position. In the equation, m represents the best position number in corresponding position serial. Thus, the best estimated position for step i is P_{i+m}.

$$m = \min(\varphi_j), \forall j \in (-N, N) \tag{5}$$

3   Experiments and Results

3.1   Experiment Design

Five healthy individuals, including four males and one female, aged 23-27 years were invited to perform indoor navigation experimentations. The average height and weight of the volunteers were 170.2 cm and 65.6 kg, respectively. The experiment site is on the third floor in the New Main Building of Beihang University. The volunteers were asked to wear eyeshades to imitate blind walking. Over twenty different paths are selected to test the system performance. One typical walking path is demonstrated in this part (Fig. 8). The whole distance is around 48 m, while the total step number is from 68 steps to 85 steps for different volunteers.

3.2   Experiment Results

As the positioning error is the main contributor of the overall navigation error, all the position errors of each step are measured for performance evaluation. The summary of the positioning error is illustrated in Table 1.

Table 1. Positioning Error

	Distance from the true position (m)				
	μ	σ	Max	Min	Ending
Initial Positioning	1.02	0.42	4.71	0.05	4.62
Step Serial Matching Positioning	0.23	0.08	0.98	0.05	0.15

As Table 1 shown, the step serial matching algorithm significant improves the positioning accuracy. Especially in long-distance navigation, the step serial matching algorithm could control and decrease the cumulated error of inertial navigation system. Fig. 8 can demonstrate this improvement more concrete. The green point is the start point; the orange point is the destination. The green line is the ideal walking path, and the black line with small arrows is the tracking path.

(a)   (b)

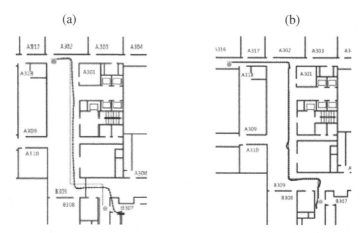

Fig. 8. Navigation performance: (a) Navigation without step serial matching. (b) Navigation with step serial matching.

4   Conclusion

In conclusion, this study aims to develop an infrastructure-free indoor navigation system for blind people with high positioning accuracy. Through analysis of the kinetics characteristics of walking, the step frequency detection algorithm is developed; the step length estimation method was investigated. Moreover, an effective positioning correction algorithm – "Directional Step Serial Matching" is proposed to improve the locating accuracy. The result of initial experiments showed that this indoor navigation system have a high positioning accuracy, and capable to provide navigation service for blind people in indoor environment.

References

1. Wang, C.: Market Analysis of Audio Book,
   http://blog.sciencenet.cn/home.php?
   mod=space&uid=51004&do=blog&id=379745
2. Fang, L., Antsaklis, J.P., Montestruque, L.A., McMickell, M.B., Lemmon, M., Sun, Y., Fang, H., Koutroulis, I., Haenggi, M., Xie, M., Xie, X.: Design of a Wireless Assisted Pedestrian Dead Reckoning System-The NavMote Experience. IEEE Transactions on Instrumentation and Measurement 54(6), 2342–2358 (2005)
3. Kourogi, M., Sakata, N., Okuma, T., Kurata, T.: Indoor/Outdoor Pedestrian Navigation with an Embedded GPS/RFID/Self-contained Sensor System. In: Pan, Z., Cheok, D.A.D., Haller, M., Lau, R., Saito, H., Liang, R. (eds.) ICAT 2006. LNCS, vol. 4282, pp. 1310–1321. Springer, Heidelberg (2006)
4. Grejner-Brzezinska, D.A., Toth, C.K., Moafipoor, S.: Performance Assessment of a Multi-Sensor Personal Navigator Supported by an Adaptive Knowledge Based System. In: ISPRS Archives, XXXVII (B5), Beijing, pp. 857–867 (2008)
5. Girard, G., Côté, S., Zlatanova, S., Barette, Y., St-Pierre, J., Van Oosterom, P.: Indoor Pedestrian Navigation Using Foot-Mounted IMU and Portable Ultrasound Range Sensors. Sensors 11(8), 7606–7624 (2011)

6. Ruiz, A.R.J., Granja, F.S., Honorato, J.C.P., Rosas, J.I.G.: Pedestrian indoor navigation by aiding a foot-mounted IMU with RFID signal strength measurements. In: 2010 International Conference on IEEE Indoor Positioning and Indoor Navigation (IPIN), p. 1 (2010)

7. Barnes, J., Rizos, C., Wang, J., Small, D., Voigt, G., Gambale, N.: Locata: A New Positioning Technology for High Precision Indoor and Outdoor Positioning. In: Proceedings, ION GNSS, Portland, OR, CD ROM, pp. 1119–1128 (2003)

8. Barnes, J., Rizos, C., Wang, J., Small, D., Voigt, G., Gambale, N.: High Precision Indoor and Outdoor Positioning using LocataNet. In: Proceedings of Int. Symp. On GPS/GNSS, Tokyo, Japan, CD ROM, pp. 9–18 (2003)

9. Kee, C., Jun, H., Yun, D., Kim, B., Kim, Y., Parkinson, B., Lenganstein, T., Pullen, S., Lee, J.: Development of Indoor Navigation System using Asynchronous Pseudolite. In: Proceedings of the 13th International Technical Meeting of the Satellite Division of the Institute of Navigation, ION GPS, Salt Lake City, Utah, pp. 1038–1045 (2000)

10. Hausdorff, J.M., Ladin, Z., Wei, J.Y.: Footswitch System for Measurement of the Temporal Parameters of Gait. Journal of Biomechanics 28, 347–351 (1995)

11. Ladetto, Q., Merminod, B., Terrier, P., Schutz, Y.: On Foot Navigation: When GPS Alone is not Enough. In: Proceedings of ION Global Navigation Satellite System, GNSS, Genova, Italy, pp. 443–449 (1999)

12. Toth, C.K., Grejner-Brzezinska, D.A., Moafipoor, S.: Pedestrian Tracking and Navigation using Neural Networks and Fuzzy Logic. In: Proceedings of the IEEE International Symposium on Intelligent Signal Processing, Alcala De Henares, Madrid, Spain, CD ROM, pp. 657–662 (2007)

13. Weinberg, H.: Using the ADXL202 in Pedometer and Personal Navigation Applications. Application Note, AN-602, ANALOG DEVICES (2002)

14. Beauregard, S., Haas, H.: Pedestrian dead reckoning: A basis for personal positioning. In: Proceedings of the 3rd Workshop on Positioning, Navigation and Communication (WPNC 2006), p. 27 (2006)

15. Shin, S.H., Park, C.G.: Adaptive step length estimation algorithm using optimal parameters and movement status awareness. Medical Engineering & Physics 33, 1064–1071 (2011)

16. Hoff, B., Azuma, R.: Autocalibration of an Electronic Compass in an Outdoor Augmented Reality System. In: Proceedings of IEEE and ACM International Symposium on Augmented Reality, Munich, Germany, pp. 159–164 (2000)

17. Retscher, G.: Multi-Sensor Systems for Pedestrian Navigation. In: Proceedings of the ION GNSS Symposium, Long Beach, CA, CD ROM, pp. 1076–1088 (2004)

18. Hu, X., Liu, Y., Wang, Y., Hu, Y., Yan, D.: Autocalibration of an Electronic Compass for Augmented Reality. In: Proceedings of the 4th IEEE/ACM International Symposium on Mixed and Augmented Reality, Vienna, Austria, pp. 182–183 (2005)

19. Elkaim, G.H., Foster, C.C.: MetaSensor: Development of a Low-Cost, High Quality Attitude Heading Reference System. In: Proceedings of the ION GNSS Meeting, Fort Worth, Texas, pp. 1124–1135 (2006)

20. Zhou, C., Downey, J., Stancil, D., Mukherjee, T.: A Low-Power Shoe-Embedded Radar for Aiding Pedestrian Inertial Navigation. IEEE Transactions on Microwave Theory and Techniques 58(10), 2521–2528 (2010)

21. Kourogi, M., Ishikawa, T., Kameda, Y., Ishikawa, J., Aoki, K., Kurata, T.: Pedestrian dead reckoning and its applications. In: Proceedings of "Let's Go Out" Workshop in Conjunction with ISMAR (2009)

22. Beijing Borch Technology Group, http://www.iflyuas.com/default_en.asp

Q-Tree: Automatic Construction of Hierarchical State Representation for Reinforcement Learning

Tao Mao, Zhao Cheng, and Laura E. Ray

Dartmouth Collge, Thayer School of Engineering
14 Engineering Drive, NH 03755, USA
{tao.mao,zhao.cheng.th,laura.e.ray}@dartmouth.edu

Abstract. A primary challenge of agent-based reinforcement learning in complex and uncertain environments is escalating computational complexity with the number of the states. Hierarchical, or tree-based, state representation provides a promising approach to complexity reduction through clustering and sequencing of similar states. We introduce the Q-Tree algorithm to utilize the data history of state transition information to automatically construct such a representation and to obtain a series of linear separations between state clusters to facilitate learning. Empirical results for the canonical PuddleWorld problem are provided to validate the proposed algorithm; extensions of the PuddleWorld problem obtained by adding random noise dimensions are solved by the Q-Tree algorithm, while traditional tabular Q-learning cannot accommodate random state elements within the same number of learning trials. The results show that the Q-Tree algorithm can reject state dimensions that do not aid learning by analyzing weights of all linear classifiers for a hierarchical state representation.

Keywords: Reinforcement learning, hierarchical state representation, intelligent agent.

1 Introduction

Current solutions to reinforcement learning suffer from the "curse of dimensionality." Moreover, most variants of a Markov decision process (MDP) are proven to have complexity ranging from P-complete (MDP) to non-deterministic exponential or NEXP (decentralized-MDP) [1,2]. However, evidence from the natural world shows that mammals outperform machines in complex task domains that can be modeled by variants of MDPs. A large body of knowledge in neuroscience indicates that brain circuits give rise to computational operations that include hierarchical data representation through clustering, embedded sequences, hash coding, reinforcement learning [3,4,5].

This paper extends findings from computational neuroscience and explores learning derived from hierarchical representation of the state-space to reduce learning complexity in agent-based tasks. Concise representation reduces the number of states that a learning agent needs to visit while keeping necessary ones and also rejects elements of the state that are not needed for learning.

C.-Y. Su, S. Rakheja, H. Liu (Eds.): ICIRA 2012, Part III, LNAI 7508, pp. 562–576, 2012.
© Springer-Verlag Berlin Heidelberg 2012

There are several ways to construct concise state representations for solving complex MDPs. One approach is based on sampling methods, and can be performed in many ways, e.g., kernels, basis functions and Gibbs sampling [6,7,8]. The central idea of these methods stems from the K-Nearest-Neighbor algorithm [9] and value function approximations [10], in which state distinctions and value approximations are based on neighboring training examples in a feature space. An issue for this type of state space construction is how to determine the resolution of the state space in advance, and thus these approaches can be impractical for complicated task domains.

Another approach is based on finding similar patterns of state features [11,12]. Starting from a mass of states, a bottom-up scheme examines state similarities based on state or MDP model features, groups similar states into a unified state, and finally partitions the state space [11]. Mean and standard deviation of a reward is used to determine the homogeneity of states in [11] while ε-homogeneity of probabilistic transition models is employed to reduce the learning complexity of a factored MDP in [12].

The concept of a hierarchical, or tree-based, state representation for reducing the complexity of large, or high dimensional learning space has been studied in [13,14,15,16,17,18,19]. In contrast to a bottom-up scheme, hierarchical state representation constructs the state space from an initial *super* state. Thus, it provides a more flexible framework for the learning agent to self-construct the state space. Tree-structured utile suffix memory (USM) is constructed to represent learning problems in [13], one of the earliest papers on hierarchical state representation. In [14], new distinctions are temporarily proposed on a leaf node and a data history is collected before the algorithm conducts a statistical test on distributions of future discounted reward and validates the distinctions. In [15,16], a data history of Q values (or ΔQ's) is collected continuously for each state and a splitting criterion is checked periodically when the data for a state is sufficient. In [19], the Q-function approximation is obtained from batch mode supervised learning consisting of several decision tree techniques. In addition, the TTree algorithm [18] utilizes both hierarchical state representation and temporally abstracted actions to solve a Semi-Markov decision problem (Semi-MDP); hierarchical state representation and action abstractions are employed in [17] to agilely solve a more complicated problem of agent-based herding introduced in [20].

This paper introduces the Q-Tree algorithm to utilize a data history of state transition information to construct hierarchical state representation for reinforcement learning. Note that all of the above methods of building hierarchical state representation (1) need to predetermine distinctions on each (categorical or continuous) state dimension as candidate subspace boundaries and (2) result in boundaries for separating the state space that are distinct on only one dimension of state-space. Observing that, we make two main contributions in this paper: (1) the proposed algorithm automatically finds new distinctions between states with respect to both the state-space and Q-space, with no need to predetermine distinctions; and (2) it constructs linear boundaries for separating subspaces that can involve distinctions on multiple dimensions of the state-space, which makes more sense for learning a complicated state representation and minimizing the total number of subspaces used to represent the state space. Additionally, the Q-Tree algorithm can provide, as a by-product, state dimension reduction when used in problems with state elements that do not contribute to learning.

The paper is organized as follows. In section 2, reinforcement learning and hierarchical state representation are first reviewed and explained, and the Q-Tree algorithm to automatically construct hierarchical state representation is then articulated. Section 3 provides and analyzes experimental results on a canonical reinforcement learning problem and discusses the application of the Q-Tree algorithm for state reduction. Finally, section 4 concludes the paper.

2   Hierarchical State Representation and the Q-Tree Algorithm

2.1   Reinforcement Learning

A Markov Decision Process (MDP) is a mathematical model for describing temporal decision-making problems in stochastic domains. An MDP of a single-agent learning system is formally defined as a tuple of $<S, A, P, R>$, where S is a set of states $s \in S$, A is a set of actions $a \in A$, available for the learning agents to choose from; P is a transition probability $P(s_{t+1}|s_t, a_t)$ that denotes the probability of transition from s_t to state s_{t+1} at time step $t+1$ when action a_t is taken by the agent at time step t, and R is the reward function, which is determined by the MDP problem under the condition of s_{t+1} and a_t. Reinforcement learning is a collection of algorithms that seek to solve MDP problems. A state in an agent's belief model is the *internal* state, also denoted by s, while the state information available to a learning agent is termed the *environmental* state, denoted in this paper by x. Generally, when solving MDP problems, we often refer to internal states; when describing MDP problems, we refer to environmental states.

Q-learning, a temporal-difference learning solution, is popular in the reinforcement learning community because it requires modest memory and is model-free [21]. Q-learning updates the Q value (state-action value) when the agent takes an action, transits to the next state, and receives a reward from the environment:

$$Q_{t+1}(s_t, a_t) = Q_t(s_t, a_t) + \alpha_{t+1}(r_{t+1} + \gamma \max_b Q_t(s_{t+1}, b) - Q_t(s_t, a_t)) \quad (1)$$

s_t and s_{t+1} are the state at time step t and $t+1$, a_t is the action taken at time step t, r_{t+1} is the reward received at time step $t+1$, $\alpha_t \in (0, 1]$ is the learning rate, and $\gamma \in (0,1)$ is the discount factor. There are generally two methods of exploiting action selection policies from Q values associated with a state: ε-greedy and softmax method [22]. The ε-greedy method selects with probability ε the action associated with the largest Q value (exploitation) and equally selects an action otherwise (exploration). The softmax method leverages the Boltzmann distribution of Q values to giving preference to actions with larger Q values while balancing exploration and exploitation. It selects an action a in state s_t at time step t with probability

$$\pi(a|s_t) = \frac{e^{Q_t(s_t, a)/\tau}}{\sum_b e^{Q_t(s_t, b)/\tau}} \quad (2)$$

2.2   Hierarchical State Representation

Conventional Q-learning uses a full lookup table to update and utilize Q values; each dimension of the state must be discretized according to a-priori knowledge and thus suffers the "curse of dimensionality." In contrast, the hierarchical state representation is concurrently learned along with the action policy from one *super* state and thus reduces state space complexity by considering only the minimum number of states required for learning [15,16,17]. It does not require initial specification of the number of states, or prior knowledge for state discretization. The hierarchical representation is based on a decision-tree structure in which visited states are clustered according to similarity of state features, e.g., Q values, change in Q values (Δ), and transition models. As illustrated in Fig. 1, it processes an external state x ("plus" mark in Fig. 1) and determines its internal state s by a sequence of judgments (the path indicated by arrows in Fig. 1) along a state hierarchy. External states are clustered using a top-down scheme; initially, there exists a single super state including all external states, the super state is separated into subspaces, and subspaces are further separated when there exists evidence for separation as learning proceeds.

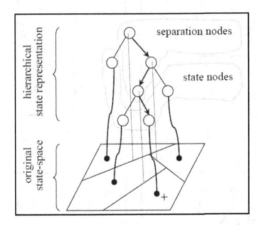

Fig. 1. Hierarchical, or tree-based, state representation

2.3   State-Space Separability w.r.t. Q-Space

Definition 1. *State-space separability*: Given two groups of states within a state space, the state space is separable if there exists a boundary separating the two groups.

Note that according to Def. 1, the boundary can be linear or nonlinear. The state-space and Q-space are paired, or mapped in the Q-learning problem such that one cannot utilize separability of either space individually to build a state representation if the other space is non-separable. Thus, in order to construct a meaningful hierarchical state representation, we seek for a separable state-space w.r.t. the Q-space. Definition 2 extends Def. 1 and captures this type of separability.

Definition 2. *State-space separability w.r.t. Q-space*: Given mapped data points in the state-space and Q-space, the state-space is separable with respect to the Q-space if there exists a grouping method such that the grouped data points make both the state-space and Q-space separable.

Figure 2 illustrates separability as described by Def. 2 for a two-dimensional state and two actions. In Fig. 2a, the state-space is non-separable while the Q-space is separable; in contrast, in Fig. 2b, the Q-space is non-separable while the state-space is separable. In Fig. 2c, the state-space and Q-space are separable (linearly separable in this case) so the state-space is considered to be separable w.r.t. the Q-space under Def. 2. In practice, the data evidence used for assessing separability has the issue that largely incomplete information describes the Q-space because the learning agent sparsely explores the outcome of actions for an external state as shown in Fig. 2d. In the following subsection, we provide a method to deal with sparse Q-space data.

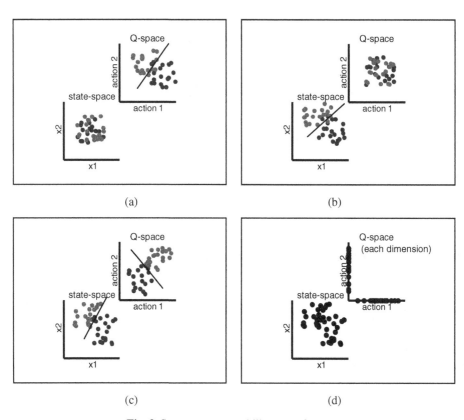

Fig. 2. State-space separability w.r.t. Q-space

2.4   Q-Tree Algorithm

The Q-Tree algorithm exploits the concept of state space separability with respect to the Q-space to automatically construct a hierarchical state representation. As discussed in section 2.1, in Q-learning, Q values are updated at each time step according to eq. (); Q values are also utilized to derive an action policy. In the Q-Tree algorithm, in addition to the original learning framework, there are phases of collecting a data history of state transition information and assessing separability periodically in order to construct a hierarchical state representation for obtaining internal states in Q-learning. However, incomplete Q-space information, as described in section 2.3, provides sparse sampling of the Q-space, and thus the following assumption is made:

Assumption 1: Given two groups of data points in the Q-space, if the Q-space is separable by Def. 1, then there exists at least one dimension on which the one-dimensional subspace is separable.

Because Q-learning is intrinsically an online learning method, Q values updated over time from some initial values do not present the appropriate information about Q-space separation but rather reflect the learning trend. Thus, the Q-Tree algorithm stores the Q value difference, or Q-difference, at each time step to determine separability:

$$\Delta_t = r_{t+1} + \gamma \max_b Q_t(s_{t+1}, b) - Q_t(s_t, a_t) \tag{3}$$

Note that eq. (3) is the second term of eq. () and describes the variation of Q values rather than unconverged Q values, as the learning proceeds and the hierarchical state representation is undergoing construction.

In the data collection phase, the algorithm gathers, at each time step, the data tuple $<x_t, \Delta_t>$ associated with a state-action pair (s, a), and counts the number $\#(s, a)$ of data tuples collected for such a pair. When all the numbers $\#(s, \cdot)$ for a state s exceed the sampling limit w, the algorithm triggers the phase of assessing state separability.

There are six steps for assessing the state-space separability w.r.t. Q-space:

(1) The Otsu method [23] is applied to conduct one-dimensional thresholding, or clustering, on Q values associated with each action and labels Q value data according to the obtained thresholds;
(2) the state-space is then also grouped based on the mapping between the external state and Q values;
(3) a linear classifier is found based on grouped external state data;
(4) external state data is separated by the proposed linear classifier, and mapped back to Q values;
(5) assessment of statistical validity to support such a separation is conducted on grouped Q value data obtained in step (4);
(6) the tested node is separated if statistical evidence supports such separation, or no separation occurs otherwise.

There are many ways to find a linear classifier (e.g., linear discriminant analysis [24], perceptron learning [25], logistic regression [26], support vector machines [27]) and to assess the separation validity (e.g., Kolmogorov-Smirnov test [28], Student's t-test, Mahalanobis distance, Pearson's correlation). In experiments reported in section 3, we use logistic regression and Kolmogorov-Smirnov test, respectively. Note that the linear classifier exists in a separation node as shown in Fig. 1, which provides a judgment for determining a query state. The boundary has a mathematical form

$w^T x + b = 0$,   where $x = [x_1, x_2 \ldots x_n]^T$ is   the   query   external   state, $w = [w_1, w_2 \ldots w_n]^T$ is the classifier's normalized weight for each dimension, and b is the intercept term. Table 1 summarizes the Q-Tree algorithm.

Table 1. Q-Tree Algorithm: Q-learning Based on Hierarchical State Representation

Algorithm QTREE()
1: **input:** tree structure $\mathcal{T}$, Q-table $Q(N_s, N_a)$
2: **Initialize:** α, γ, w
3: **for** $t = 1{:}T$ or until ISTERMINATED(s_t) **do**
4:      $a_t \leftarrow$ SELECTACTION($Q(s_t, \cdot)$)
5:      $r_t, x_{t+1} \leftarrow$ TAKEACTION(a_t)
6:      $s_{t+1} \leftarrow$ DETERMINESTATE(x_{t+1}) in $\mathcal{T}$
7:      $\Delta_t(s_t, a_t) \leftarrow r_{t+1} + \gamma \max_b Q_t(s_{t+1}, b) - Q_t(s_t, a_t)$
8:      $Q_{t+1}(s_t, a_t) \leftarrow Q_t(s_t, a_t) + \alpha \Delta_t(s_t, a_t)$
9:      $D(s_t, a_t) \leftarrow D(s_t, a_t) \cup \{tuple(x_t, \Delta_t)\}$
10:     **if** all $\#(s_t, \cdot) > w$ and ASSESSSEPARABILITY($D(s_t, \cdot)$) is true
11:         $\mathcal{T} \leftarrow \mathcal{T}^{\text{new}}$
12:     **end if**
13:     $x_t \leftarrow x_{t+1}$
14:     $s_t \leftarrow s_{t+1}$
15: **end for**
16: **output:** $\mathcal{T}, Q(N_s, N_a)$

Algorithm ASSESSSEPARABILITY($D(s, \cdot)$)
17: **input:** $\mathcal{T}, N_s, D(s, \cdot)$
18: **for** each action a
19:     $G^Q \leftarrow$ RETRIEVEQVALUE($D(s, a)$)
20:     $G^X \leftarrow$ RETRIEVEEXTERNALSTAE($D(s, a)$)
21:     $G_1^{Q+}, G_1^{Q-} \leftarrow$ OTSUTHRESHOLD(G^Q)
22:     $G_1^{X+}, G_1^{X-} \leftarrow$ QMAPTOX(G_1^{Q+}, G_1^{Q-})
23:     $L_a \leftarrow$ BUILDLINEARCLASSIFIER(G_1^{X+}, G_1^{X-})
24:     $G_2^{X+}, G_2^{X-} \leftarrow$ CLASSIFY(G^X, L_a)
25:     $G_2^{Q+}, G_2^{Q-} \leftarrow$ XMAPTOQ(G_2^{X+}, G_2^{X+})
26:     $stats(a) \leftarrow$ STATISTICALTEST(G_2^{Q+}, G_2^{Q-})
27: **end for**
28: $a_0 \leftarrow$ STRONGESTEVIDENCE($stats(\cdot)$)
29: **if** SUGGESTSEPARATION($stats(a_0)$)
30:     $separation \leftarrow$ true
31:     $\mathcal{T} \leftarrow$ MERGE($\mathcal{T}, s, L_{a_0}$)
32:     $N_s \leftarrow N_s + 1$
33: **else**
34:     $separation \leftarrow$ false
35: **end if**
36: **output:** $\mathcal{T}, N_s, separation$

3   Experimental Results and Discussion

We conduct experiments on the canonical PuddleWorld problem to investigate performance and properties of the Q-Tree algorithm. Moreover, we also test it on an extended PuddleWorld problem whose external states include additional dimensions comprised of random variables in order to investigate the ability of the Q-Tree algorithm to ignore dimensions of the state that do not contribute to learning. This section describes the PuddleWorld problem and reports findings.

3.1   PuddleWorld Problem

This problem is adapted from the description in [29]. The goal is to find the shortest path in a continuous two-dimensional world defined as $x \in [0,1]^2$, while avoiding the puddle areas. The agent is considered to reach the goal if its position satisfies the condition that $x_1 + x_2 > 1.9$. The puddles of variable depth have an oval shape with a radius of 0.1 located from (0.1, 0.75) to (0.45, 0.75) and from (0.45, 0.4) to (0.45, 0.8).

For Q-learning, an agent starts each episode from a random position uniformly distributed over the 2D world. The agent has four actions: 1: up, 2: down, 3: right, and 4: left. Each action drives an agent in the specified direction by 0.05 with additional displacement of Gaussian noise with mean 0 and standard deviation 0.01. Reward 0 is received when an agent reaches the goal area; -1 otherwise at each time step. Additionally, when an agent moves into the puddle area, it receives a penalty as -400 times the distance to the puddle fringe. Fig. 3 illustrates the PuddleWorld problem.

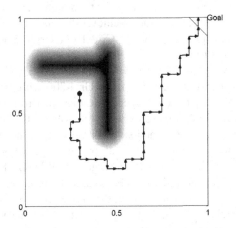

Fig. 3. Illustration of PuddleWorld problem

In order to compare performance of the Q-Tree learning with traditional Q-learning with grid-states, we conduct 30 experimental runs for the Q-Tree algorithm as well as for traditional Q-learning; in addition, in order to obtain the optimized state discretization, we conduct traditional Q-learning with different grid levels, denoted as

"Grid-X", where X denotes the number of desirable elements to discretize each state dimension. Each run consists of 500 trials, each with maximal time step 500, beyond which the episode terminates. Each run is divided into 10 equal blocks of 50 learning trials each. The performance is measured by averaging the cumulative reward within each block, and the mean and standard deviation are calculated over 30 runs as our final reported results. The parameters used in the experiments are reported in Table 2.

Table 2. Parameters used for PuddleWorld problem

	Q-Tree	Grid-X
learning rate α	0.5	0.5
discount factor γ	0.95	0.95
greediness ε	0 to 0.95^1	0.95
sampling limit w	25	----
significance level for K-S test α_{KS}	5%	----

3.2   Performance of the Q-Tree Algorithm

Fig. 4 and Table 3 show learning performance of the Q-Tree and Grid-X algorithms. Note that while Grid-10 and Grid-15 provide the best performance among traditional Q-learning with discretized state space, the best discretization level is unknown a priori. The Q-Tree algorithm finds the necessary number of states to accomplish the task as learning proceeds. At convergence, the number of states constructed by Q-Tree is in between those of Grid-10 and Grid-15. The Q-Tree algorithm starts with the lowest performance because it must collect enough data to construct the state representation; the final performance achieved by the Q-Tree algorithm has no statistical difference compared to that of Grid-10 or Grid-15 with significance level 0.05 using the Student's t-test.

Samples of state value maps are shown in Fig. 5. The "ideal" state value map (Fig. 5a) is obtained by running an experiment of Grid-200 with 100,000 trials, which is considered to be sufficient for convergence. Rather than true values in the map, the pattern of value distribution is more important to solving the control problem in that action policies give preference to actions with larger Q values regardless of the true values. The map generated by the Q-Tree algorithm (Fig. 5c) presents a more similar pattern to the "ideal" map; however, the map generated by Grid-15 (Fig. 5b) seems to learn only patterns in the half field near the goal, and there is no clear pattern far from the goal and even large inconsistency with the "ideal" map in the puddle area. Fig. 5d shows the corresponding Q-Tree state representation for the value map in Fig. 5c, where each colored polygon represents a different state (node) in the tree.

---

[1] The learning agent adopting the Q-Tree algorithm needs randomness initially to explore and construct the state representation. Thus, ε for ε-greedy action selection linearly increases from 0 to 0.95 for the Q-Tree algorithm.

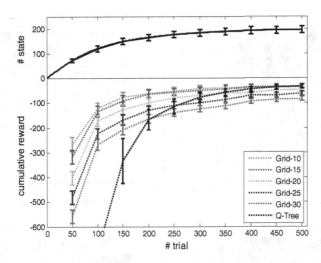

Fig. 4. Top: number of states constructed by Q-Tree over time; bottom: learning curve of Q-Tree compared to those of Grid-X algorithms for the standard PuddleWorld problem

Table 3. Performance and number of existing states in the final learning trial for the standard PuddleWorld problem

Methods	Performance	# states
Grid-10	-33.44(±8.76)	100
Grid-15	-33.21(±5.41)	225
Grid-20	-46.60(±7.34)	400
Grid-25	-62.52(±8.45)	625
Grid-30	-83.65(±11.90)	900
Q-Tree	-34.06(±7.10)	195.3(±14.0)

3.3   State Dimension Reduction Using Q-Tree Learning

To evaluate state abstraction using the Q-Tree algorithm, the standard PuddleWorld problem is recast into a three-dimensional state-space, where the third dimension is a random variable uniformly distributed from [0, 1]. This is analogous to an agent having sensors that provide data that does not aid in learning to solve the given problem. The Q-Tree algorithm should handle the noise dimension such that it will find the correct separation boundaries despite the 3D state-space. We adopt the same parameters and performance measure used in section 3.2.

Fig. 6 and Table 4 show learning performance of Q-Tree and Grid-X algorithms for this extended PuddleWorld problem. In the three-dimensional state-space, the learning speed of the Q-Tree algorithm outperforms all other Grid-X algorithms while retaining a small number of states (209.4), compared with 195 states generated for solving the standard PuddleWorld problem. In addition, experiments also show that the Q-Tree algorithm can handle the extended Puddle problem augmenting 2, 3 and 4 noise dimensions in terms of cumulative reward and the number of used states while

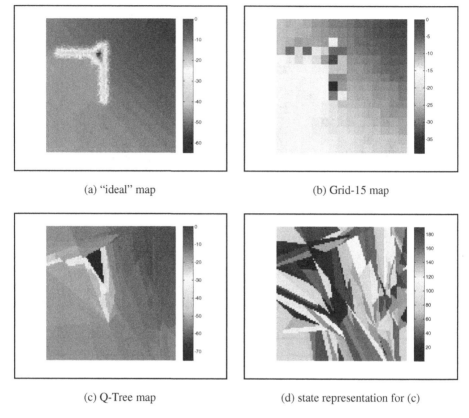

(a) "ideal" map   (b) Grid-15 map

(c) Q-Tree map   (d) state representation for (c)

Fig. 5. State value maps for the standard PuddleWorld problem

the number of trials traditional Q-learning needs to achieve the same performance level increases exponentially.

Samples of state value map for the extended PuddleWorld problem are also shown in Fig. 7. When generating the maps, a random variable uniformly distributed from [0,1] is augmented as the third dimension to the original external state to simulate the randomness caused by the noise dimension. The map generated by the Q-Tree algorithm has a more smooth learned pattern than that for the best Grid-10 does because separations are occurring less frequently for the noise dimension (Fig. 7a), and thus the value pattern is more clearly delineated in that map. In contrast, Fig. 7b shows noise patterns in many places and especially in the puddle area.

This ability to reject noise is further evidenced by examining the linear classifier weights when the Q-Tree algorithm is tested on the extended PuddleWorld problem with more noise dimensions. As described in section 2.2 and section 2.4, in the hierarchical state representation, a weight for a dimension indicates the importance of that dimension in delineating separation boundaries. The weights in learned linear classifiers in one run with 1, 2, 3, and 4 noise dimensions are analyzed as examples. Boxplots of absolute values of weights grouped by dimensions are shown in Fig. 8.

Table 4. Performance and number of existing states in the last learning block for the extended PuddleWorld problem

Methods	Performance	# states
Grid-10	-123.64(±14.66)	1000
Grid-15	-204.36(±23.46)	3375
Grid-20	-305.25(±27.35)	8000
Grid-25	-381.25(±28.57)	15625
Grid-30	-472.14(±45.22)	27000
Q-Tree	-42.71(±16.92)	209.4(±16.8)

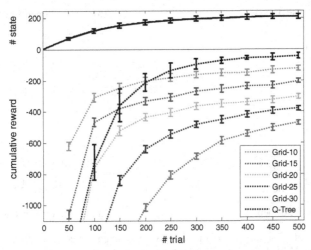

Fig. 6. Top: number of states constructed by Q-Tree over time; bottom: learning curve of Q-Tree compared to those of Grid-X algorithms for the extended PuddleWorld problem

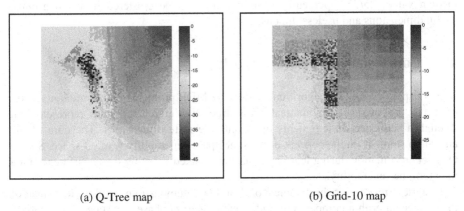

(a) Q-Tree map   (b) Grid-10 map

Fig. 7. State value maps for extended PuddleWorld problem

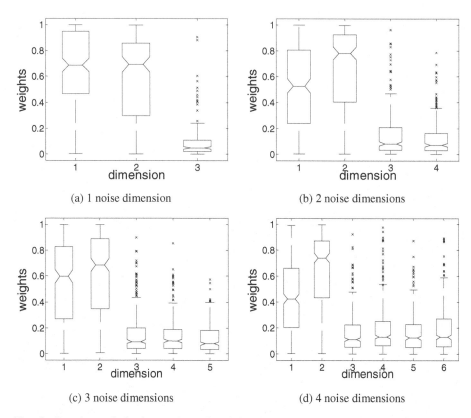

(a) 1 noise dimension   (b) 2 noise dimensions

(c) 3 noise dimensions   (d) 4 noise dimensions

Fig. 8. Boxplots of absolute value of weights in learned linear classifiers grouped by dimensions for cases with 1, 2, 3, and 4 noise dimensions

Dimensionally different features of statistical information (e.g., maximum value, median value, 25/75th percentile, outlier ratio) can be clustered into two groups: useful dimensions and useless dimensions.

4   Conclusions and Future Work

In this paper, the Q-Tree algorithm for solving MDP problems in a continuous state-space is proposed to automatically construct a hierarchical state representation through a sequence of judgments upon multiple state dimensions. The core of the algorithm stems from the concept of the state-space separability w.r.t. Q-space. Sparse Q-space information during learning is accommodated by using the Q-difference data to determine separability.

Empirical results for the PuddleWorld problem demonstrate good performance of the Q-Tree algorithm compared to traditional Q-learning based on state discretization. The algorithm is also tested on extensions of PuddleWorld problem in which noise dimensions augment the original state. The Q-Tree algorithm can find correct separation boundaries to construct the state representation, while performance of traditional Q-learning lags when noise elements exist. By analyzing weights of linear classifiers existing in separation nodes, useful and useless state dimensions can be detected using statistical information.

In order to further control the number of internal states in the state representation, techniques of state pruning and separations in kernel space (SVM-QTree) will be studied. These techniques will be evaluated on more complicated multi-agent tasks, such as herding [17] and patrolling [30].

Acknowledgements. This work is supported by the Office of Naval Research under Multi-University Research Initiative (MURI) Grant No. N00014-08-1-0693.

I also would like to thank Prof. Mark E. Borsuk from Dartmouth College for consultation on statistical testing techniques.

References

1. Bernstein, D., Givan, R., Immerman, N., Zilberstein, S.: The complexity of decentralized control of Markov decision processes. Mathematics of Operations Research 27(4), 819–840 (2002)
2. Rabinovich, Z., Goldman, C., Rosenschein, J.: The complexity of multiagent systems: the price of silence. In: 2nd Joint Conf. of Autonomous Agents and Multi-Agent Systems, Melbourne, Australia, pp. 1102–1103 (2003)
3. Granger, R.: Engines of the brain: the computational instruction set of human recognition. AI Magzine 27(2), 15–32 (2006)
4. Rodriguez, A., Whitson, J., Granger, R.: Derivation and analysis of basic computational operations of thalamocortical circuits. J. Cognitive Neuroscience 16(5), 856–877 (2004)
5. Hearn, R., Granger, R.: Learning hierarchical representations and behaviors. In: AAAI Symposium on Naturally-Inspired Artificial Intelligence (2009)
6. Ormoneit, D., Sen, S.: Kernel-based reinforcement learning in average-cost problems. IEEE Trans. Automatic Control 16(5), 1624–1636 (2002)
7. Yamaguchi, A., Takamatsu, J., Ogasawara, T.: Constructing action set from basic functions for reinforcement learning of robot control, Kobe, Japan (2009)
8. Kimura, H.: Reinforcement learning in multi-dimensional state-action sapce using random rectangular coarse coding and Gibbs sampling. In: Proc. 2009 IEEE Intl' Conf. on Robotics and Automation (ICRA), Kobe, Japan, pp. 4173–4180 (2007)
9. Cover, T., Hart, P.: Nearest neighbor pattern classification. IEEE Trans. Information Theory 13, 21–27 (1967)
10. Boyan, J., Moore, A.: Generalization in reinforcement learning: safely approximating the value function. In: Advances in Neural Information Processing Systems (NIPS), vol. 7, pp. 369–376 (1995)
11. Asada, M., Huber, M.: State space reduction for hierarchical reinforcement learning, Miami Beach, FL, USA (2004)
12. Dean, T., Givan, R., Leach, S.: Model reduction techniques for computing approximately optimal solutions for Markov decision processes. In: Proceedings of the 13th Conference on Uncertainty in Artificial Intelligence (UAI 1997), San Francisco, USA, pp. 124–131 (1997)

13. McCallum, R.: Instance-based utile distinctions for reinforcement learning with hidden state. In: Proceedings of the 20th Intl' Conf. Machine Learning, ICML 1995 (1995)
14. Jonsson, A., Barto, A.: Automated state abstraction for options using the U-Tree algorithm. In: Advances in Neural Information Processing Systems, vol. 13, pp. 1054–1060 (2001)
15. Uther, W., Veloso, M.: Tree-based discretization for continuous state space reinforcement learning. In: Proc. of 16th National Conf. on Artificial Intelligence (AAAI), Madision, WI, USA (1998)
16. Pyeatt, L., Howe, A.: Decision tree function approximation in reinforcement learning. In: Proc. 3rd Int'l Symposium on Adaptive Systems: Evolutionary Computation and Probablistic Graphical Models (2001)
17. Mao, T., Ray, L.: Hierarchical state representation and Q-learning for Agent-Based Herding. In: Proc. of Int'l Conf. on Computer and Automation Engineering (ICCAE), Chongqing, China (2011)
18. Uther, W., Veloso, M.: TTree: Tree-Based State Generalization with Temporally Abstract Actions. In: Proc. of the Symp. on Abstraction, Reformulation and Approximations, Edmonton, Canada (2002)
19. Ernst, D., Geurts, P., Wehenkel, L.: Tree-Based Batch Mode Reinforcement Learning. Journal of Machine Learning Research 6, 503–556 (2005)
20. Vaughan, R., Sumpter, N., Frost, A.: Experiments in automatic flock control. Robotics and Autonomous Systems 31, 109–116 (2000)
21. Watkins, C., Dayan, P.: Technical Note: Q-Learning. Machine Learning 8(3-4), 279–292 (1992)
22. Sutton, R., Barto, A.: Reinforcement Learning: An Introduction. MIT Press, Cambridge (1998)
23. Otsu, N.: A threshold selection method from gray-level histograms. IEEE Trans. Syst. Man Cybern 9, 62–66 (1979)
24. Seber, G.: Multivariate Observation. John Wiley & Sons, Inc., New York (1984)
25. Rosenblatt, F.: The perceptron: A probabilistic model for information storage and organization in the brain. Pyschological Rev. 65, 386–407 (1958)
26. Menard, S.: Applied Logistic Regression Analysis. Sage Publications, Thousand Oaks (2002)
27. Burges, C.: A tutorial on support vector machines for pattern recognition. Data Mining and Knowledge Discovery 2, 121–167 (1998)
28. Massey Jr., F.: The Kolmogorov-Smirnov test for goodness of fit. Journal of the American Statistics Association 46(253), 68–78 (1951)
29. Sutton, R.: Generalization in reinforcement learning: successful examples using sparse coarse coding. In: Advances in Neural Information Processing Systems, vol. 8, pp. 1038–1044 (1996)
30. Mao, T., Ray, L.: Frequency-based patrolling with heterogeneous agents and limited communication. In: WorldComp Int'l Conf. on Artificial Intelligence, Las Vegas, USA (2011)

Navigation and Localization for Autonomous Vehicle at Road Intersections with Low-Cost Sensors

Jaemin Byun[*], Myungchan Roh, Ki-In Na, Joo Chan Sohn, and Sunghoon Kim

National Institute of Electronics and Telecommunications,
Deajeon, Korea of South
{jaemin.byun,kina4147,mcroh,jcsohn,saint}@etri.re.kr

Abstract. This paper addresses the problem of navigation and global localization for intersection driving with an autonomous vehicle equipped with low-cost sensors in urban environments. The intersection driving is an important part of outdoor autonomous navigation, when it travels along structured roads and needs to reach the intended destinations. Previous almost approaches are based on the high-accuracy localization by using expensive high-performance GPS/ INS sensors. In this paper, we propose a novel approach to enhance the position accuracy of vehicle using the relative position from vehicle to lane and stop-line makings instead of them. When the vehicle autonomously approaches at the intersection, it first is able to know where the vehicle approximately is on the digital map and what the global position of lane and stop-line in the nearest intersection using a GPS and Odometer equipped. The current global position of vehicle is calculated by adding a lateral/longitudinal offset value by means of lane and stop-line detection to global position of them above obtained. This paper presents a way of generation for the optimal feasible path using Bezier Curve to safely avoid obstacles and across the intersection. We demonstrated the validation of these methods by performing experiments with a custom built autonomous vehicle using experiments conditions based on an actual intersection driving in our test site.

Keywords: Autonomous Navigation, Localization, Land Mark Detection, Intersection Driving, Path Planning.

1 Introduction

Autonomous vehicles capable of driving safely through city traffic, sharing the roads with other traffic participants, such as human-driven cars, pedestrians, bicycles, etc., have been a vision for many years. One of the most challenging remaining research task regarding the vehicles' control software, is the autonomous vehicles' ability to make intelligent real-time driving decisions, i.e. their ability to perform the most appropriate driving maneuver for any urban traffic situation. Similar to a human driver, the real-time decision making subsystem makes driving decisions based on perceived information using various sensors, knowledge about the planned route, and any other relevant information describing the vehicle's surrounding traffic environment [1-2].

---

[*] Corresponding author.

C.-Y. Su, S. Rakheja, H. Liu (Eds.): ICIRA 2012, Part III, LNAI 7508, pp. 577–587, 2012.
© Springer-Verlag Berlin Heidelberg 2012

This paper addresses a problem regarding how to enable autonomous equipped with low-cost sensors to localization and navigation about their surrounding road environment (especially at intersection). Intersection driving is one of important component for autonomous navigation in urban environments, when it travels along structured roads and needs to reach the intended destinations. Much related work on structured road navigation has been done for the DARPA Urban Challenge [3-4]. The CMU team has developed a motion planning subsystem consists of two planners, each capable of avoiding static and dynamic obstacles while achieving a desired goal. Two broad scenarios are considered: structured driving (road following) and unstructured driving (parking lots and intersections). For unstructured driving, such as entering/ exiting intersection, a planner with a four dimensional search space (position, orientation, direction of travel) is used. The Stanford team uses free-form navigation in parking lots and intersections[4]. This free-form planner uses a modified version of A*, so-called hybrid A*. It essential to get the location and heading of vehicle, so they used an Applanix POS LV-420 system provides real-time integration of multiple dual-frequency GPS receivers which includes a high performance inertial measurement unit, wheel odemetry via a distance measurement unit (DMI), and the Omni star satellite based Virtual Base Station service. The real-time position and orientation errors of this system were typically below 10 cm and 0.1 degrees, respectively.

Autonomous vehicles based on high-accuracy localization above mentioned is enable to safely accomplish intersection driving. However, it is necessary to spend a lot of cost for the high-performance GPS/INS equipment. For considering the aspect of cost, it is not reasonable to apply them to our wok with limited expense. Thus, we try to achieve all conflicting high accuracy and low costs without them. There are several approaches try to achieve the same purpose. One method of them is to extend the infrastructure by devices which allow ranging, e.g. Ultra Wide Band(UWB). Disadvantages are that such hardware is not yet available to vehicles, and that the infrastructure needs to be extended. Other works [5-8] use the information in digital maps as landmarks for positioning on the road. These approaches tried to get the more accurate location of vehicle only with respect to the lateral direction by lane detection and digital map in the normal road.

In this paper, we propose a novel approach to enhance the position accuracy of vehicle using the relative position from vehicle to lane and stop-line makings along the lateral and longitudinal directions for intersection driving. When the vehicle autonomously approaches at the intersection, it first is able to know where the vehicle approximately is on the digital map and what the global position of lane and stop-line in the near intersection using a GPS and Odometer equipped. The current global position of vehicle is able to get by adding a lateral and longitudinal offset values by means of lane and stop-line detection to global position of lane and stop-line obtained above. This paper also presents a way of generation for an optimal feasible path using Bezier Curve to safely avoid obstacles and across the intersection. The navigation regarding rest of road with well-painted lane in our site used the simple method to keep for vehicle with the constant distance from lane. In chapter 2, an overview about the vehicle localization combined with GPS, digital map and compensated with the result of detection for road markings. Chapter 3 describes the path planning and tracking and the next chapter 4 presents the results of experiment with our vehicle in practical intersections. The remainder of the paper, chapter 5, contains our conclusions.

2   Proposed Localization Method for Intersection Driving

This section shows the proposed global localization of vehicle during driving at intersection region. In short, our work uses a low-cost GPS receiver, vehicle odemetry data and a digital map which includes network and information of road. While approaching to the intersection, the global position of the vehicle is compensated by relative position and slope through offset values respectively resulted from lane and stop-line detection.

2.1   GPS and Digital Map

To get approximately where the vehicle is on the map and what the property of current road has, the vehicle is equipped with a low-cost GPS receiver with single frequency and it has the digital map described the road environment. For example, while the vehicle is moving along a normal road, the vehicle can approximately obtain the current global position by the GPS, it can also get whether the type of the current road is the intersection or parking lot though querying the current position to prior map.

The map mentioned above consists of a lot of nodes, where the node means a specific area which has road information such as road type, the number of lane, etc. However, it is not easy to select appropriate node among them corresponding current vehicle' position in the map. To do this, we use a method to calculate alternately using the Euclidean sense from current position to each node of them on the map and choose the closet one of them and also confirm whether the direction of vehicle and road is the same or not.

Our map data schema follows the definition of the map[10], which is currently under standardization. The map contains information in terms of the position of landmarks. Available landmarks are lane and stop-line markings.

2.2   Compensated Localization with Detection of the Road Markings

For autonomous navigation based on localization at intersections, it is necessary to get the more high accuracy of the global position of vehicle. While the vehicle is approaching to the intersection, our method applied to localization with the position of road markings (lane, stop-line). More specifically, as the Fig.1 has shown,

The exact global position $\left(x_g^{stop}, y_g^{stop}, \theta_g^{stop}\right)$ of stop-line in front of vehicle can easily find out by means of global current position$(x_g^{gps}, y_g^{gps}, \theta_g^{gps})$ with the GPS and the prior digital map included position information on all the areas.

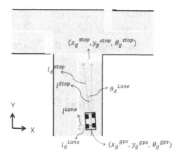

Fig. 1. Compensated localization by using lane and stop-line detection

Thus, we can definitely get the value x_g^c of global position $(x_g^c, y_g^c, \theta_g^c)$ on the lateral axis by adding the global position$(x_g^{stop})$of lane on the map and the lateral offset(l^{Lane}) generated from distance(l_d^{Lane}) as results of lane detection as follows:

$$l^{Lane} = l_d^{Lane} \cdot \cos(\theta_d^{Lane}) \tag{1}$$

$$x_g^c = x_g^{stop} + l^{Lane}. \tag{2}$$

Similarly the offset value (l^{stop}) on the longitudinal axis can easily obtain from the distance (l_d^{stop}) beteen the vehicle and stop-line and finally it should add to the global postion of stop line as follow:

$$l^{stop} = l_d^{stop} \cdot \cos(\theta_d^{Lane}) \tag{3}$$

$$y_g^c = y_g^{stop} + l^{stop} \tag{4}$$

$$\theta_g^c = \theta_g^{stop} + \theta_d^{Lane} \tag{5}$$

When the vehicle pass through the stop-line at intersection, the global position of vehicle $(x(t), y(t), \theta(t))$ is finally computed by kinematic model of car-like model with initial point $(x_g^c, y_g^c, \theta_g^c)$ in Eq. 6,7,8. Let v denote the linear velocity and $\emptyset$ denote the steering angle, the distance between the front and rear axle is represented as L.

$$x(t) = y_g^c + vt\cos\left(\theta_g^c + \theta(t)\right) \tag{6}$$

$$y(t) = y_g^c + vt\sin\left(\theta_g^c + \theta(t)\right) \tag{7}$$

$$\theta(t) = \theta_g^c + vt\frac{\tan\emptyset}{L} \tag{8}$$

Our test platform is equipped with vision system consisted of two color cameras to get the position of lane and stop-line on road. A camera of them uses aims to extract the lane in the front of vehicle. To do this, we use a simple method that it is based on edge map and extracts the candidate lines from the image with Hough Transform and finally selects the best line of them. For detection of the stop-line, we use a

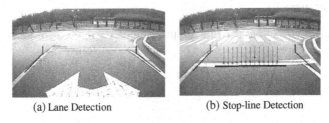

(a) Lane Detection   (b) Stop-line Detection

Fig. 2. Examples of lane (a) and stop-line(b) detection at intersection

conventional method to deal with some blob of horizontal straight edge and use template matching technology over the appearance of stop-line on the images (i.e the width and length of candidate line, the direction of edge ,etc.,) as the result of them shown in the figure 2.

Aa a step of the detection procedure, the detection of road markings is done in next one: inverse perspective mapping (IPM) for computing the lateral distance. The result of lane detection is the lateral distance transformed in metric between vehicle and lane markings, so it needs an appropriate tranformation process that the information of lane in the image coordination convert to one in the world coordinate.

We used the IPM to convert a forward facing image to a top-down view of the road image. IPM is a mathematical method to transform a coordinate system from one perspective to another. On the top-down view generated by IPM, a real physical position on road surface (x_r, y_r, x_r) has correspondence to a projection point on the image plane(u, v) as follow:

$$[x_r, y_r, x_r]^T = h[u, v]^T \tag{9}$$

To perform the transformation, the homography matrixis calculated by using the camera intrinsic (focal length and optical center) and extrinsic (pitch angle, yaw angle, and height above ground) parameters. Finally, it can obtain the lateral and longitudinal offset with the detection and transfor mation process mentioned in detail above.

3   Path Planning and Tracking

For intersection driving, this paper represents a method of path planning based on localization introduced in the previous section. Generally, for a car-like robot which has a nonho- lonomic property its constraint must be considered in planning path. To do this, we propose an approach based on Bezier curve for car-like robot. Our path planning algorithm consists of two steps. First, the algorithm generates m paths for a target state by changing two control points except the start point and the target point. And we can have k target states along the lateral offset, so the total number of the generated path is m×k. Second, the algorithm evaluates each path of them and selects an optimal path among them.

3.1   Bezier Curve

Recently, Bezier curves are used in computer aided design, graphics, and animation [11]. The Bezier curve of degree n can be generalized as follows:

$$B(t) = \sum_{i=0}^{n} \binom{n}{i} (1-t)^{n-i} t^i P_i, \quad t \in [0,1] \quad (10)$$

$$\binom{n}{i} = \frac{n!}{i!(n-i)!} \quad (11)$$

Where $\binom{n}{i}$ is the binomial coefficient that has the alternative notation in Eq.10 and P_i is the control points of the Bezier Curve. As shown Fig.3, the properties of Bezier curves are follows.

- ✓ They always pass through P_o and P_n.
- ✓ The curve is a straight line if and only if all the control points are lie on the same line.
- ✓ They always lie within the convex hull consisting of their control points.

3.2   Path Generation and Evaluation

In this step, the path planning module makes Bezier curve from $q_s = (x_s, y_s, \theta_s)$ the start configuration to the target configuration $q_t = (x_t, y_t, \theta_t)$. We can generate feasible paths by changing P_1 second, P_2 third control point. The first control P_0 and last point P_3 are located at the start point and the target one. For considering the various positions of second control point, they are propagated the constant along the line with θ_s. The third control point is accomplished with the same procedure. Therefore, the different paths for a target state can be generated.

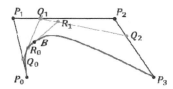

Fig. 3. Bezier curve of degree 3 at t=0.5

In the next step, the generated paths from the first step is evaluatd. The path scores each path with these criteria:

- ✓ Kinematics constraint: Since the car-like robot has the nonholonomic property due to the limited steering angle, the steering profile should not violate the steering angle constraint.
- ✓ Collision with obstacle: The optimal path should make the robot travel safely, which means that the robot was not hit by any obstacles during the travel.
- ✓ Smoothness: The smoothness of the path is defined as the sum of the absolute values of the derivatives of angle.

Finally, we can determine an optimal path among all candidated paths.

3.3   Optimal Path Tracking

Path tracking refers to a vehicle executing a generated optimal path by applying steering motions that guide the vehicle along the path. The goal of path tracking module is to minimize the lateral distance between the vehicle and the defined path, minimize the difference in the vehicle's heading and the defined path's heading, and limit steering inputs to smooth motion while maintaining stability.

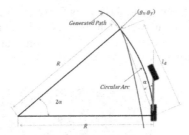

Fig. 4. The pure pursuit geometry

In this paper, we deeply consider that how good one of the tracking method is available for our vehicle platform with moving at low speed [12]. We use finally the pure pursuit method which is among the most common approaches to the path tracking problem. The pure pursuit method consist of geometrically calculation the curvature of a circular arc that connects the rear axis location to a goal point on the path ahead of the vehicle. The goal point is determined from a look-ahead distance l_d from the current rear axis position to the desired path. The goal point(g_x, g_y) is illustrated in Fig.4. The vehicle's steering angle can be determined using only the goal point location and the angle a between the vehicles heading vector and the look-ahead vector. Applying the law of sines to Fig.5 results in

$$\frac{l_d}{sin(2\alpha)} = \frac{R}{sin(\frac{\pi}{2}-\alpha)} \tag{12}$$

$$\frac{l_d}{2sin(\alpha)cos(\alpha)} = \frac{R}{cos(\alpha)} \tag{13}$$

$$R = \frac{l_d}{2sin(\alpha)} \tag{14}$$

A common simplification of an Ackerman steered vehicle used for geometric path tracking is the bicycle model as follow:

$$\tan(\delta) = \frac{L}{R} \tag{15}$$

Using Eq.14 and 15, the pure pursuit control law is given as

$$\delta(t) = \tan^{-1}(\frac{2Lsin(\alpha(t))}{l_d}) . \tag{16}$$

To track the generated optimal path safely at the intersection, the vehicle is controlled the steering angle $\delta(t)$ from Eq.16.

4   Experiments

4.1   Experimental Setup

We perform experiments on the dataset captured by our test autonomous vehicle (ESTRO) which is equipped with cameras and low-cost GPS and odemetry that are also used to get position and heading of vehicle. The test data was collect by ESTRO on the campus of our institution. This environment for experiments is suitable to represent the urban environment as shown Fig.5, we choose a three-way intersection to collect experimental data at the region 1~ 5. All roads have two lanes and a stop-line. The vehicle was autonomously driven at 10 km/h on the road and 5 km/h at intersection during the experiment.

Fig. 5. The map of ETRI campus

4.2   The Result of Localization

To compare lateral offset from the result of lane detection with the ground truth value by distance when the vehicle is approaching at intersection, we performed experiments at the region 1 ~ 5 as shown at (a) in figure 6. Figure 6 at (b) shows the positioning errors during the test driving. The error of lateral direction is less 20 cm about the all the regions. Figure 7 shows the errors of longitudinal increases by becoming far from vehicle to stop-line. However, we think that it doesn't cause serious problem since the update process repeat until reaching the stop-line.

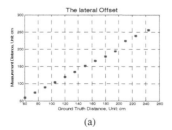
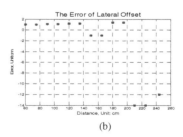

(a)   (b)

Fig. 6. (a) The result of experiment for lateral offset, (b) The error between ground true and measured values for lateral offset

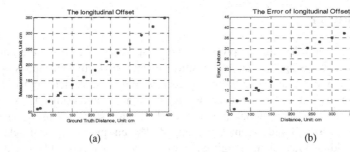

(a)   (b)

Fig. 7. (a) The result of experiment for longitudinal offset, (b) The error between ground true and measured values

Table 1. The statistical evaluation of the position error from the all regions (1~ 5).On average, the lateral position error is about 0.02m, the longitudinal is 0.51

Quantity	Mean value	Standard deviation
Lateral position error	0.02m	0.52m
Longitudinal position error	0.51m	0.45m

4.3   The Result of Path Planning and Tracking

In the performance of our path planning and tracking approaches, there is one important parameter in the path tracking, the look-ahead distance. We try to tune the proper value to our application. Since the efforts of changing the distance must be considered within the context of one of the two problems; regaining a path and maintaining the path. Figure 8 shows the results of tracking by the look-ahead distance. It is finally decided that the distance is about 2m by the more ten times experiments at the test.

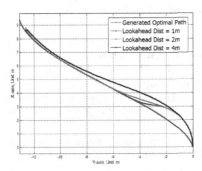

Fig. 8. The result of generated path tracking

5   Conclusion

For safely intersection driving, we propose a novel approach to enhance the position accuracy of vehicle using the relative position from vehicle to lane and stop-line makings along the lateral and longitudinal directions. When the vehicle approaches at the intersection, it first is able to know where the vehicle approximately is on the digital map and what the global position of lane and stop-line in the nearest intersection using a GPS and Odometer equipped. The current position of vehicle is able to get by adding a lateral and longitudinal offset value by means of lane and stop-line detection to global position of them obtained above. Besides, this paper presents not only a way of generation for optimal feasible path with Bezier Curve algorithm to safely avoid obstacles and across the intersection, it but also introduces the tracking method based on pure pursuit algorithm. We demonstrate these methods are feasible by performing experiments with a custom built autonomous vehicle using experiments conditions based on an actual intersection driving in our test site

References

1. Wille, J.M., Saust, F., Maurer, M.: Comprehensive Treated Sections in a Trajectory Planner for Realizing Autonomous Driving in Braunschweig's Urban Traffic. In: Proceeding of 13th International IEEE Annual Conference on Intelligent Transportation Systems (2010)
2. Wang, M., Ganjineh, T., Rojas, R.: Action Annotated Trajectory Generation for Autonomous Maneuvers on Structured Road Networks. In: Proceeding of the 5th International Conference on Automation, Robotics and Applications (2011)
3. Urmson, C., Anhalt, J., Bagnell, D., Baker, C., Bittner, R., Clark, M.N., Dolan, J., Duggins, D., Galatali, T., Geyer, C., Gittleman, M., Harbaugh, S., Hebert, M., Howard, T.M., Kolski, S., Kelly, A., Likhachev, M., McNaughton, M., Miller, N., Peterson, K., Pilnick, B., Rajkumar, R., Rybski, P., Salesky, B., Seo, Y.-W., Singh, S., Snider, J., Stentz, A., "Red" Whittaker, W., Wolkowicki, Z., Ziglar, J.: Autonomous Driving in Urban Environments: Boss and the Urban Challenge. Journal of Field Robotics 23, 425–466 (2008)
4. Johnston, D., Klumpp, S., Langer, D., Levandowski, A., Levinson, J., Marcil, J., Orenstein, D., Paefgen, J., Penny, I., Petrovskaya, A., Pflueger, M., Stanek, G., Stavens, D., Vogt, A., Thrun, S.: Junior: The Stanford Entry in the Urban Challenge. Journal of Field Robotics 23 (February 2008)
5. Toledo-Moreo, R., Betaille, D., Peyret, F., Laneurit, J.: Fusing GNSS, Dead-reckoning and Enhanced Maps for Road Vehicle Lane- Level Navigation. Journal of Selected Topics in Signal Processing (2009)
6. Selloum, A., Betaille, D., Le Carpentier, E., Peyre, F.: Lane level positioning using Particle Filtering. In: Proceedings of the 12th International IEEE Conference on Intelligent Transportation Systems (2009)
7. Mattern, N., Schubert, R., Wanielik, G.: Lane level positioning using line landmarks and high accurate maps. In: Proceedings of the 16th World Congress on Intelligent Transportation Systems (2009)

8. Heimes, F., Fleischer, K., Nagelt, H.-H.: Automatic Generation of Intersection Models from Digital Maps for Vision-Based Driving oInnercity Intersections. In: Proceedings of the IEEE Intelligent Vehicles Symposium (2000)
9. Li, M., Zhou, T.T.: Trajectory Generation based Vehicle Action Tracking for Intersection Driving Safe. In: Proceeding of IEEE Intelligent Vehicles Symposium, IV (2011)
10. Lee, Y.-C., Christiand, Park, S.-H., Yu, W., Kim, S.-H.: Topological Map Building for Mobile Robots Based on GIS in Urban. In: Proceeding of Ubiquitous Robots and Ambient Intelligence, URAI (2011)
11. Choi, J.-W., Curry, R., Elkaim, G.: Path Planning based on Bezier Curve for Autonomous Ground Vehicles. In: Proceeding of World Congress on Engineering and Computer Science (2008)
12. Choi, S., Lee, J., Yu, W.: Comparison between Position and Posture Recovery in Path Following. In: Proceeding of Ubiquitous Robots and Ambient Intelligence (URAI) (2009)

On-Road Motion Planning
for Autonomous Vehicles

Tianyu Gu* and John M. Dolan**

Carnegie Mellon University
5000 Forbes Avenue, Pittsburgh, 15213, PA, USA
tianyu@cmu.edu, jmd@cs.cmu.edu

Abstract. We present a motion planner for autonomous on-road driving, especially on highways. It adapts the idea of a on-road state lattice. A focused search is performed in the previously identified region in which the optimal trajectory is most likely to exist. The main contribution of this paper is a computationally efficient planner which handles dynamic environments generically. The Dynamic Programming algorithm is used to explore in spatiotemporal space and find a coarse trajectory solution first that encodes desirable maneuvers. Then a focused trajectory search is conducted using the "generate-and-test" approach, and the best trajectory is selected based on the smoothness of the trajectory. Analysis shows that our scheme provides a principled way to focus trajectory sampling, thus greatly reduces the search space. Simulation results show robust performance in several challenging scenarios.

Keywords: Motion Planning, Dynamic Programming, On-road Autonomous Driving.

1 Introduction

1.1 Motivation

In the last few decades, both industry and academia have put effort into developing technologies for autonomous driving. Many believe that autonomous driving will dramatically enhance driving safety, improve transportation efficiency, and even revolutionize the entire automobile industry.

Motion Planning (MP) for autonomous on-road driving is a challenging problem: (1) The optimal solution (trajectory) exists in high-dimensional space, yet real-time constraints must be met in finding it; (2) Trajectory solutions must adapt to complex and unpredictable traffic; (3) Perception data, which are critical to high-speed driving, are partially observed, noisy, and lagging.

---

* Tianyu Gu is with the Department of Electrical and Computer Engineering.
** John M. Dolan is with Dept. ECE and Robotics Institute, School of Computer Science.

C.-Y. Su, S. Rakheja, H. Liu (Eds.): ICIRA 2012, Part III, LNAI 7508, pp. 588–597, 2012.
© Springer-Verlag Berlin Heidelberg 2012

1.2   Related Work

Much research has been conducted on motion planning of various robots [9][5]. Dijkstra's Algorithm, the A* Algorithm and their derivatives[12][8] have been used intensively for path planning on a grid-like space. The resulting paths, however, do not satisfy the non-holonomic constraints of a car-like vehicle. To address this, [1] introduced a non-holonomic path generation method.

To inspire the development of autonomous driving technologies, DARPA organized the Urban Challenge in 2007. To deal with on-road driving, many teams [2][3] performed lane-based trajectory generation by rolling out trajectories based on lateral shifts from the lane centerline. This scheme worked well in the low-density, low-speed (up to 30 mph) competition environment, but was too naive for realistic on-road driving in complex dynamic environments.

Several on-road motion planners have used an on-road state lattice. Artificial heuristics were developed in a few works to narrow down the exploration region in the lattice. [13] proposed a method that connected lattice nodes to generate paths that complied with certain speed heuristics. A directed acyclic graph search algorithm was used to search for the shortest path on the grid. [6] proposed an on-road planner that solved optimal lateral and longitudinal control problems in a Frenet Frame. Different heuristic functionals were devised for maneuvers like road following and lane merging. The disadvantage of heuristics-based approaches is that it is unrealistic to find a complete set of heuristics that are applicable in all cases.

An alternative solution is to exhaustively iterate over all possible solutions by conducting dense trajectory sampling. [4] proposed a planner that sampled trajectories on a road lattice. To prevent exponential blowup of trajectories, the author adopted a scheme to trim trajectories that ended at a similar vehicle state. Based on this work, [7] reduced the computation by sampling fewer paths but post-optimizating the trajectories. The disadvantage of sampling-based approaches is that effort is wasted, since most of the trajectories generated will eventually be discarded. Our proposed approach addresses these issues. A sequence of high-level actions that encrypts desirable maneuvers is found first and serves as guidance to a focused yet modest amount of trajectory sampling and search.

The rest of this paper is structured as follows. Section 2 presents a few assumptions to focus our work on motion planning. Section 3 introduces an action-based coarse trajectory-planning scheme amenable to Dynamic Programming. Section 4 explains focused trajectory search for fine trajectory planning. Section 5 explains the implementation details and compares our algorithm with state-of-the-art alternatives. Section 6 presents simulation results in our test scenarios.

2   Assumptions

In order to focus our work on motion planning, we will make the following assumptions.

Assumption 1. *Perfect Perception*

Perception is perfect in the sense that static obstacles are stable, and dynamic obstacles can be precisely predicted.

We use the road state lattice for our planer. It is convenient to use a road coordinate system, so that every interesting point can be indexed by station and latitude. Moreover, vehicle shape has been convolved to the map, so that we can plan a trajectory for a fixed point on the car body without evaluating the entire trajectory for collision checking of the sides and front/rear bumper.

Assumption 2. *Perfect Tracker*

A low-level tracking module that perfectly executes the planned trajectory is assumed, so that the safety is guaranteed if the trajectory is safe.

3 Action-Based Coarse Trajectory Planning

A human driver doesn't have a precise trajectory in mind when driving; instead, s/he would normally have a rough idea about how to avoid an obstacle, or how fast to overtake the vehicle in front. Based on this insight, we would like our planner to find a sequence of actions that describes a rough maneuver first.

Time-dimension discretization naturally gives us stages of the planning process at each time increment. The state space (manifold) is defined that describes the vehicle's state at every stage. The process now only demands choosing an action at each stage. The above two characteristics (staged & action-based) satisfy the requirements of applying Dynamic Programming (DP) algorithms.

3.1 State and Action Space

The state space includes station (s) and latitude (l) dimensions to represent the vehicle's location in road coordinates, Fig.1. Given the discretized centerline,

$$\left[x_c(s) \ y_c(s) \ \theta_c(s) \ \kappa_c(s) \right]$$

the following equations are used to construct the on-road state lattice according to the centerline:

$$\begin{aligned}
x(s,l) &= x_c(s) + l \cdot cos(\theta_c(s)) \\
y(s,l) &= y_c(s) + l \cdot sin(\theta_c(s)) \\
\theta(s,l) &= \theta_c(l) \\
\kappa(s,l) &= (\kappa_c(l)^{-1} + l)^{-1}
\end{aligned} \tag{1}$$

where s is the station, l is the lateral offset from the centerline.

For highway driving, the longitudinal velocity component dominates the lateral velocity component. We introduce longitudinal velocity (v_{lon}) as another dimension in state space. The addition of the velocity dimension diversifies our

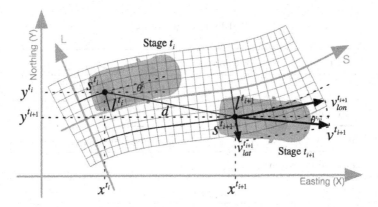

Fig. 1. Cordinates and Parameters

state space, hense The optimization process becomes more informed, since velocity serves as one of the most important indicators of the quality of driving.

Define $\mathcal{M}^{t_i}$ as a three-dimensional state manifold at stage t_i, and state X^{t_i}, where

$$X^{t_i} = \begin{bmatrix} s^{t_i} & l^{t_i} & v_{lon}^{t_i} \end{bmatrix}^T, \ X^{t_i} \in \mathcal{M}^{t_i} \tag{2}$$

An action A^{t_i} is a function of state, $A^{t_i} \in \mathcal{U}(X^{t_i})$. It leads to a state transition, represented as $T(X^{t_i}, A^{t_i}) : X^{t_i} \xrightarrow{A^{t_i}} X^{t_{i+1}}$

3.2 Cost Functions

For each state transition $T(X^{t_i}, A^{t_i})$, a cost criterion $C(X^{t_i}, A^{t_i})$ is specified to penalize undesirable action effects. The optimality achieved by the DP algorithm is with respect to the linear addition of the cost terms in table 1:

$$C(X^{t_i}, A^{t_i}) = c_d + c_{offset} + c_{v_{lon}} + c_{a_{lon}} + c_{a_{lat}} + c_{obstacle} \tag{3}$$

A few cost terms are devised to characterize good behavior. The philosophy is to create as few and as decoupled cost terms as possible so that the tuning can be intuitive.

3.3 Dynamic Programming Algorithm

The solution to a DP problem is a sequence of actions $\{A^{t_i}\}$ that minimize

$$\sum_{t=t_0}^{t_{N_{time}}} \beta^t C(X^t, A^t) \tag{4}$$

where state transitions are subject to

$$X^{t_{i+1}} = T(X^{t_i}, A^{t_i}) \tag{5}$$

Table 1. Cost Terms

Description	Parameter c	Expression
Distance	$w_d \cdot d$	$d = \sqrt{(x^{t_{i+1}} - x^{t_i})^2 + (y^{t_{i+1}} - y^{t_i})^2}$
Lateral Offset	$w_{offset} \cdot offset$	$offset = \frac{l^{t_{i+1}} + l^{t_i}}{2}$
Longitudinal Velocity	$w_{v_{lon}} \cdot v_{lon}$	$v_{lon} = v_{horizon} - \frac{v^{t_{i+1}} + v^{t_i}}{2}$
Longitudinal Acceleration	$w_{a_{lon}} \cdot a_{lon}$	$a_{lon} = a^{t_i}$
Lateral Acceleration	$w_{a_{lat}} \cdot a_{lat}$	$a_{lat} = \frac{\kappa^{t_{i+1}} + \kappa^{t_i}}{2} \cdot (\frac{v^{t_{i+1}} + v^{t_i}}{2})^2$
Obstacle	$w_{obstacle} \cdot obstacle$	$obstacle = Status(s^{t_{i+1}}, l^{t_{i+1}})$

We find it reasonable to treat planning as a stateless process over time. Again, taking the human driver as an example, s/he rarely (almost never) plans from the past, e.g considering the path s/he has travelled. Human drivers always look at the road in front and plan from the current state into the future.

This means that choosing actions in a given state is completely independent of the past states. Statelessness (the Markov Property) allows us to exploit Bellman's Principle of Optimality to solve our dynamic programming problem. Define

$$\Omega_i = min\{ \sum_{t=t_i}^{t_{N_{time}}} \beta^t C(X^t, A^t)\}, i = 0, 1, 2, ..., t_{N_{time}} \tag{6}$$

Note that

$$\Omega_{N_{time}} = \beta^{t_{N_{time}}} C(X^{t_{N_{time}}}, A^{t_{N_{time}}}), A^{t_{N_{time}}} \text{ is NULL} \tag{7}$$

specifies the cost distribution on the manifold at stage $t_{N_{time}}$. By assigning a different distribution, we can specify the most desirable state at the final stage.

The Principle of Optimality tells us,

$$\Omega_i = min\{\beta^{t_i} C(X^{t_i}, A^{t_i}) + \sum_{t=t_{i+1}}^{t_{N_{time}}} \beta^t C(X^t, A^t)\} \tag{8}$$

$$= min(\beta^{t_i} C(X^{t_i}, A^{t_i})) + \Omega_{i+1} \tag{9}$$

After recursively finding the optimal actions for all state transitions, we can quickly backtrace a sequence of actions from A^{t_0} to $A^{t_{N_{time}-1}}$ by feeding the inital state.

3.4   Algorithm Features

Tuning parameters to get desirable maneuvers is an iterative learning process. But with decoupled cost weight terms, this process is very intuitive.

The discount factor β plays an important role in the optimization process. If the factor is small, so that transition costs from future states are very close to zero, the trajectory ends very early. The implication is that the future states are becoming untrustworthy such that the optimization would make no difference for whether to continue or not. If the factor is close to 1, on the other hand, the trajectory becomes aggressive.

To mitigate the "Curse of Dimensionality", our formulation constructs state space with relatively low dimensionality and coarse resolution, and also a modest action space. Yet it retains enough diversity to represent desirable on-road maneuvers.

4 Focused Fine Trajectory Planning

The result of the previous section is a global plan in the form of a sequence of desirable maneuvers, and a sequence of safe vehicle poses. Once this is given, we need to generate one dynamically feasible smooth trajectory for the vehicle to execute.

4.1 Path Generation

A path that satisfies nonholonomic constraints is given by

$$x(\tilde{s}) = x(0) + \int_0^{\tilde{s}} cos(\theta(\tau))d\tau$$

$$y(\tilde{s}) = y(0) + \int_0^{\tilde{s}} sin(\theta(\tau))d\tau \tag{10}$$

$$\theta(\tilde{s}) = \theta(0) + \dot{\kappa}(\tilde{s})$$

$$\kappa(\tilde{s}) = p_0 + p_1\tilde{s} + p_2\tilde{s}^2 + p_3\tilde{s}^3 (+p_4\tilde{s}^4 + p_5\tilde{s}^4)$$

where $\tilde{s}$ is the arc-length of the path, and the unknown parameters $p_0...p_5$ and s_f. To solve the unknowns, we use the method proposed in [1].

[11] proved that quintic polynomial curvature guarantees the continuity of both the curvature's rate of change and its derivative, which leads to smooth robot motions. While quintic polynomial paths are suitable for high-speed trajectories, cubic polynomials are sufficient, even ideal, for low-speed trajectories in that they will result in paths that are quicker in turning [10].

4.2 Velocity Profile Generation

Instead of using linear velocity profiles, as do many prior works, we use a cubic function of time, which is smoother.

$$v(t) = q_0 + q_1 t + q_2 t^2 + q_3 t^3 \tag{11}$$

This relation naturally gives us analytical expressions for both acceleration and length by differentiation and integration respectively. Given the travel time t_f, start velocity v_0, start acceleration a_0, end velocity v_f and path length s_f, we can analytically express the remaining unknowns.

4.3   Focused Trajectory Sampling and Evaluation

Unlike prior work [4][7], we don't want to generate a large number of trajectories that eventually will be discarded, nor do we want to generate trajectories that are too long, and will not have the chance to be executed, since the planner is replanning very fast.

A sampling center that guides the focused trajectory sampling must be determined. A sampling center is chosen as any of the states in the sequence of state transitions solved by previous planning. We have two rules in choosing:

(1) The trajectory should last at least T seconds. T should be greater than the planner's replanning period, so that we will always have a safe trajectory. We pick T = 1sec.

(2) The trajectory should be at least S meters long. S should be long enough so that the path does not have undesirable features, e.g. the curvature and the derivative of curvature may increase dramatically in the middle of a too-short path. We pick S = 5m.

Once the sampling center is picked, we conduct a random path and velocity profile sampling and evaluation within this small region, and pick the best trajectory with the minimum integral of the squared jerk.

5   Implementation and Analysis

5.1   Implementation

As explained in section 3, the states contain three components: station, lateral offset and speed.

States are discretized to adapt the need for mimicking on-road driving maneuvers. $\Delta T, \Delta S, \Delta L, \Delta V$, are the units of our system discretization. Their values need to be carefully specified. Starting with ΔT, we believe a second-level discretization will be enough for a coarse on-road trajectory plan, $\Delta T = 1s$. ΔV is the minimum speed difference of sampled speeds. Any $v_{lon} = n \cdot \Delta V$, where integer $n \in [0, N_V)$. The finer ΔV is, the more accurate speed we can express. For our purpose, we found that $\Delta V = 3m/s$ is a reasonable value. To decide ΔS, we notice that for any $v_{lon}^{t_i} = n_1 \cdot \Delta V$, $v_{lon}^{t_{i+1}} = n_2 \cdot \Delta V$, where n_1, n_2 are integers. the difference $\|v_{lon}^{t_{i+1}} - v_{lon}^{t_i}\| = \|n_1 - n_2\| \cdot \Delta V$ is always a multiple of ΔV. Thus the minimum traversing station (other than zero) between two stages is $\Delta S = \frac{\Delta V \cdot \Delta T}{2} = 1.5m$. For on-road driving, the lateral speed is much smaller than the longitudinal component. We assume the maximum lateral velocity to be 0.5m/s, thus set $\Delta L = 0.5 \cdot \Delta T = 0.5m$.

The details are listed in Table 2.

An action on states takes effect on all three components. Particularly, a_1 affects longitudinal velocity, a_2 lateral offset, and a_3 longitudinal velocity.

$$T(v_{lon}^{t_i}, A^{t_i}) : v_{lon}^{t_{i+1}} = v_{lon}^{t_i} + a_1^{t_i} \cdot \Delta T$$
$$T(l^{t_i}, A^{t_i}) : l^{t_{i+1}} = l^{t_i} + a_2^{t_i} \cdot \Delta T \tag{12}$$
$$T(s^{t_i}, A^{t_i}) : s^{t_{i+1}} = s^{t_i} + a_3^{t_i} \cdot \Delta T$$

Table 2. Dimension Discretization List

Dimensions	Time(s)	Station(m)	Lattitude(m)	Velocity(m/s)
Horizon	$H_T = 10$	$H_S = 60$	$H_L = 5$	$H_V = 27$
Discretization	$\Delta T = 1$	$\Delta S = 1.5$	$\Delta L = 0.5$	$\Delta V = 3$
Increments	$N_T = 10$	$N_S = 40$	$N_L = 10$	$N_V = 10$

To constrain the action space, we let $a_1^{t_i} = n_1 \frac{\Delta V}{\Delta T}$, where integer $n_1 \in [-2, 1]$ and $a_2^{t_i} = n_2 \frac{\Delta L}{\Delta T}$, where integer $n_2 \in [-1, 1]$ and $a_3^{t_i} = \frac{v_{lon}^{t_{i+1}} + v_{lon}^{t_i}}{2}$.

Let P represent the number of possible state transitions from each state. We use approximate equality, since these actions are not available to all states.

$$P \approx num(n_1) \cdot num(n_2) = 12 \qquad (13)$$

5.2 Analysis

For the heuristics-based approaches [13][6], it is hard to perform a direct comparison on computation, since the authors did not provide a detailed computation cost. On the other hand, we can compare to the sampling-based approaches [4] [7], since the authors have provided the number of trajectories they evaluated for each planning cycle.

Typically, trajectory evaluation is conducted in the following steps: (1) sample on the trajectory; (2) perform collision checking for each sampled point; (3) calculate the cost for each of the sampled points; (4) accumulate the cost for each of the sampled points. For a fair comparison, we assume the same discretization resolution, and suppose a realistic 10 points/trajectory sampling.

[7] specified the full search space at every cycle, thus suffered the "Curse of Dimensionality" with our resolution: 1,000,000 trajectories/cycle = 10,000,000 points/cycle.

[4] used a clever trimming scheme that constrains the search space while the search proceeds, so that the search space does not blow up. Still, the author had to maintain a complex data structure and had to evaluate about: 400,000 trajectories/cycle = 4,000,000 points/cycle.

For our approach, the focused fine planning only selects a fixed and small number of trajectory samples (about 100), which is a trivial overhead. The major computation occurs in calculating state transition in the action-based coarse planning. The number of state transitions is given by $[(N_S \cdot N_L \cdot N_V) \cdot P] \cdot N_T$ = 480,000 transitions/cycle.

The computation required to calculate a state transition is similar to that of conducting collision checking and calculating cost for a point. Comparing to [4] and [7], we have a 8.3X and 20.8X speed-up respectively.

Actually, it is nearly as efficient as if we were doing trajectory evaluation with only one sample point, that is saving $\frac{N-1}{N}\cdot 100\%$ computations for each trajectory evaluation, where N stands for the number of sampling points. In this sense, our approach obviously wins out over the brute force sampling approaches.

6   Simulation Result

Four on-road situations were tested in simulation (Fig. 2).

Road Blockage: The car can reach a full stop just in time to avoid collision with the blocking obstacle.

Static Obstacle Avoidance: The car will slightly nudge to the left, and decrease the speed a little bit to avoid collision.

Oncoming Vehicle Avoidance: The car will veer slightly to the right, and meanwhile decrease the speed until the oncoming vehicle drives away.

Aggressive Merging Vehicle Avoidance: This scenario shows a rogue vehicle trying to cross our lane. Our car comes to a stop smoothly, and gets back to on-road driving when the moving vehicle is out of the way.

All sub-figures in Fig. 2 came from the same setting of the cost weights and discount parameter.

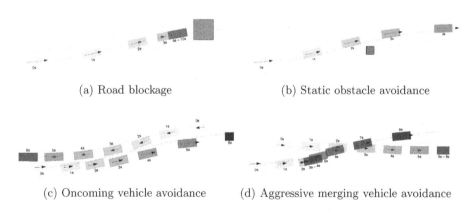

(a) Road blockage   (b) Static obstacle avoidance

(c) Oncoming vehicle avoidance   (d) Aggressive merging vehicle avoidance

Fig. 2. Simulation Results with Time Steps Indicated

7   Conclusion

Most prior on-road motion planners have wasted a large amount of computation on arbitrary and unfocused sampling of trajectories. We provide a two-step scheme that plans coarsely first, attempting to capture the gist of how human drivers drive, namely not knowing the precise plan, but having a global sense of how they should drive. Simulation has shown that our method can robustly handle different dynamic on-road driving scenarios, some of which are challenging even to human drivers.

Our immediate next step is to implement and test our planner on a real vehicle, then robustify the scheme by making it capable of handling more complex and realistic scenarios, for example, planning lane changes.

References

1. Kelly, A., et al.: Reactive nonholonomic trajectory generation via parametric optimal control. International Journal of Robotics Research 22(7), 583–601 (2003)
2. Urmson, C., et al.: Autonomous driving in urban environments: Boss and the urban challenge. J. Field Robotics 25(8), 425–466 (2008)
3. Montemerlo, M., et al.: Junior: The stanford entry in the urban challenge. J. Field Robotics 25(9), 569–597 (2008)
4. McNaughton, M., et al.: Motion Planning for Autonomous Driving with a Conformal Spatiotemporal Lattice. In: IEEE International Conference on Robotics and Automation, vol. 1, pp. 4889–4895 (2011)
5. Pivtoraiko, M., et al.: Differentially constrained mobile robot motion planning in state lattices. Journal of Field Robotics 26(3), 308–333 (2009)
6. Werling, M., et al.: Optimal trajectory generation for dynamic street scenarios in a frenét frame. In: ICRA, pp. 987–993 (2010)
7. Xu, W., et al.: A real-time motion planner with trajectory optimization for autonomous vehicles. In: ICRA (2012)
8. Koenig, S., Likhachev, M., Furcy, D.: Lifelong planning a*. Artif. Intell. 155(1-2), 93–146 (2004)
9. LaValle, S.M.: Planning algorithms. Cambridge University Press, Cambridge (2006), http://planning.cs.uiuc.edu/
10. McNaughton, M.: Parallel algorithms for real-time motion planning. Ph.D. thesis, Robotics Institute, Carnegie Mellon University, Pittsburgh, PA (July 2011)
11. Piazzi, A., Bianco, C.G.L.: Quintic G2-splines for trajectory planning of autonomous vehicles. In: IEEE Intelligent Vehicles Symposium (2000)
12. Stentz, A.: The focussed d* algorithm for real-time replanning (1995)
13. Ziegler, J., Stiller, C.: Spatiotemporal state lattices for fast trajectory planning in dynamic on-road driving scenarios. In: The International Conference on Intelligent Robots and Systems (2009)

On the Development of an Open-Source Vehicle Dynamics Simulation

Bruce P. Minaker

University of Windsor, Windsor ON N9B 3P4, Canada
bminaker@uwindsor.ca
www.uwindsor.ca/minaker

Abstract. The paper describes the vehicle modeling software under development at the University of Windsor Vehicle Dynamics and Control research group. The intent is to develop a simulation environment for vehicle dynamics and control applications. It should be noted that the software development is ongoing, and that the code described in the paper is a work-in-progress. Nevertheless, there are a number of components that are well developed and useful for the analysis of the motion of a vehicle, or other similar mechanical systems. The first and most mature component is an automatic equation of motion generator. The code generates the linearized non-holonomic equations of motion in state space form from an input file describing the locations, inertial properties, etc., of the various bodies in the system. As an extension to the linear equation generator, a 'semi-linearized' time domain solver is under development, to allow solution of the linear equations in a moving global reference frame. Finally, a track mapping utility is described. Based on a set of points describing the track centreline, the code discretizes the track into blocks of finite length and width, and determines the coefficients of a smooth interpolating polynomial.

Keywords: automatic generation equations of motion, vehicle dynamics, track mapping, simulation, software.

1 Introduction

This paper details some of the software development that has taken place at the University of Windsor by the Vehicle Dynamics and Control research group. The group is developing its own vehicle simulation software, designed to be freely distributable to any interested party, but aimed at university-level engineering students or researchers, or practising engineers with an interest in expanding their understanding of vehicle dynamics on a fundamental, theoretical level. The intention of the group is to provide a fully open-source and freely distributable vehicle dynamics and control simulation software.

The group, led by the author, focuses on three principles with its vehicle modeling software. First, the code is free and open-source wherever possible, and published under a public license. This enables easy distribution, and promotes exposure to vehicle modeling and simulation, particularly among students.

C.-Y. Su, S. Rakheja, H. Liu (Eds.): ICIRA 2012, Part III, LNAI 7508, pp. 598–607, 2012.
© Springer-Verlag Berlin Heidelberg 2012

Second, the code is designed to be modular and expandable, with the intention that users may wish to experiment with their own methods or algorithms. Finally, the code should be flexible — one should be able to generate models for systems ranging in complexity from a simple single DOF mass and spring, to a three-dimensional multibody vehicle model.

The motivation for the development of the code comes from the author's own research interests, and in part, from previous experience in the senior undergraduate vehicle dynamics course in the University of Windsor Mechanical Engineering program. In the past, the course has used a 'virtual Grand Prix' to provide a competitive design experience to the students.

1.1   Formula 463

The virtual racing competition, dubbed 'Formula 463', after the course code, was created in order incorporate a design component to the course, where the scoring would be entirely objective, based on the performance of the vehicle design produced by the students. The students were given a set of known and fixed parameters for the virtual vehicles, and a track of known dimensions. All the vehicles used the same driver model, so the event was a contest in vehicle design, not driver skill. Students would then choose the remaining vehicle parameters for maximum performance in a series of virtual events. For more details, see Johnston and Minaker[1], and Rieveley and Minaker[2],[3].

The course built on models of increasing complexity, where initially only longitudinal performance was tested, with cornering and vertical disturbances added in steps. The students would typically write their own simulation codes to model these relatively simple cases, before submitting their design for evaluation. For the final event, the full vehicle model on the circuit, the students would submit their design parameters, and the instructors would simulate the vehicle model using a commercial simulation code (CarSim[4], developed by the Mechanical Simulation corporation).

This produced generally good results, with high interest, and positive feedback from the students. The objective comparison of the results, through overlaid animations of individual vehicles, promoted competitive but friendly rivalry. However, there were several shortcomings. First, the students had relatively fewer tools to predict their performance on the circuit test, as most were not capable or experienced enough with software development to produce a full vehicle simulator in the necessarily short time frame. Secondly, even if it were more widely available to the students, the commercial simulation code was a 'black box'; that is, the students had no access to the source code, to understand exactly how the numerical results were generated. Finally, it was especially time consuming for the instructors, who, even with the assistance of several utilities to allow batches of simulations, often faced numerical issues resulting from unexpected and unrealistic choices of parameters from the students.

1.2 Software Development

In an effort to alleviate this situation, an open-source vehicle simulator that could be both freely distributed and dissected was sought. A number of open-source codes were identified; the candidates generally fall into one of three categories: those intended for engineering analysis of the motion of general mechanical systems; codes developed specifically for vehicle dynamics; and 'physics engines'.

Of the open-source dynamics codes intended for engineering analysis, two notable examples are MBDyn[5], developed at the Politecnico di Milano, and DynaMechs[6], developed at The Ohio State University. MBDyn is a time domain multibody dynamics solver, with a command line interface and an impressive array of multi-physics capabilities. It an active project and has an extensive team of developers. DynaMechs is a C^{++} library of routines similar in intent to MBDyn. However, in contrast to MBDyn, the code appears to have been unmaintained for a number of years.

A number of open-source driving simulator projects also exist[7],[8], and while they contain relatively sophisticated vehicle models, they are generally intended for entertainment purposes, and the structure of the internal model is not easily modified to simulate other types of vehicles (e.g., bicycles, truck-trailer combinations, etc.).

In addition, there are a number of open-source physics engines designed to model motion of general systems of bodies, including vehicle motion. The most popular are the Bullet[9] engine, the Open Dynamics Engine (ODE)[10], and the Newton Game Dynamics[11] engine. While all are quite sophisticated, these physics engines are also intended primarily for gaming software, and not for engineering analysis. They are optimized to provide animations of time domain solutions as efficiently as possible, and are not easily utilized by students unfamiliar with software development.

The above mentioned codes all share one characteristic that is particularly at odds with the needs of the author's research group: they focus on generating time history solutions to the equations of motion, and provide the user with much less information about the actual equations used to generate these solutions. As a result, the group has decided to produce their own code for vehicle modeling and simulation. The code is designed from the outset to generate linear or linearized equations of motion, with the intention of providing the actual equations, independent of the solution. As a consequence, it is less accurate for describing certain types of behaviour, and therefore not the ideal tool for predicting specific results, such as lap times, etc. However, the linearization of the equations of motion allow a more qualitative solution, independent of the initial state of the system. The specifics of the mechanical system or vehicle in question determine its behaviour, and using a linear model allows a more general characterization of this behaviour.

This paper describes three codes that have been developed by the University of Windsor Vehicle Dynamics and Control research group: a multibody equation of motion generator, referred to as EoM, that automatically produces a state space description of the equations of motion from a descriptive input file; second, an extension of the equation generator that provides time history solutions when desired, simultaneously capturing the non-linear inertial terms that result from large rotations; and finally, a mapping algorithm that is developed to describe the track, and the vehicle's intended path relative to the track.

The codes described above have been used by the group in the analysis of a proposed vehicle dynamics control system that utilizes individual wheel torque control, see Rieveley[12], as well as in numerous other projects. Other software components that have been developed by the group are not described in this paper, for various reasons. For example, the group has developed a driver model that is not yet mature, but has produced very good results, as well as a suspension kinematics solver used in the Formula 463 project that is no longer under active development.

2   Automatic Generation of the Equations of Motion

The automatic equation of motion generator (EoM) will now be described in detail.

2.1   Kinematic Differential Equations, Newton-Euler Equations

The foundation of the method is the linearized Newton-Euler equations, combined with the linearized kinematic differential equations, as given in Equation (1). The equations of motion are written in physical coordinates, representing the location of each bodies' centre of mass, and the orientation of a body fixed reference frame. The positions and orientations (p) are expressed in a fixed global frame, where the velocities and angular velocities (w) are given in the body fixed moving reference frame. The orientations are assumed to be small angles, allowing representation as a three coordinate orientation vector. Combining the equations in this fashion results in a first order form.

$$\begin{bmatrix} I & 0 \\ 0 & M \end{bmatrix} \begin{Bmatrix} \dot{p} \\ \dot{w} \end{Bmatrix} + \begin{bmatrix} V & -I \\ K & C \end{bmatrix} \begin{Bmatrix} p \\ w \end{Bmatrix} = \begin{Bmatrix} 0 \\ f_c + f_a \end{Bmatrix} \tag{1}$$

The motion at equilibrium is assumed to be composed of a translation component, and a rotation component. Of course, any large rotational speed at equilibrium would violate the assumption of small orientation angles. Non-zero angular speeds at the point of linearization are accommodated by allowing rotation around an axisymmetric axis, relative to the moving reference frame. In this case, the orientation angles represent the orientation of the reference frame, rather than the body itself. The V matrix resulting from the linearization of the kinematic differential equations contains the skew symmetric matrix of the translational velocities of the bodies, arranged in the upper right 3x3 sub-matrix of the set of 6x6 matrices arranged along the diagonal. All other entries are zero. The C matrix contains the traditional viscous damping matrix, plus terms due to the inertia forces, i.e., centripetal forces and gyroscopic moments. The stiffness matrix K is the sum of terms resulting from deflection of elastic elements, and additional tangent stiffness matrix terms. These tangent stiffness terms result from preloads or other constant external forces acting on the system, and are key to capturing the tilting behaviour of bicycles or motorcycles. The mass matrix $\mathbf{M}$ results from Newton's Laws, and is tri-diagonal as is typical. The externally applied and constraint forces appear in the right hand side. For further details on the derivation of the equations, see Minaker and Rieveley[13].

2.2 Constraint Equations

Constraints are imposed through six sets of equations. Because the positions and velocities are given as separate states, the holonomic constraint equations are applied twice; first in their original form, and again, in differentiated form. The choice of coordinates results in repetition of the coefficients when the constraints are applied to the state vector of global position/local velocity, and when they are applied to the derivative of the state vector, (i.e., global velocity/local acceleration). There is some redundancy in the constraints at the velocity level, due to the way the kinematic differential equations are incorporated. However, this redundancy does not influence the number or type of the final set of coordinates, and thus does not pose a problem. Nonholonomic constraints are applied to velocity and acceleration only. The combined constraint equations are given in Equation (2), where the $\mathbf{B}_h$ and $\mathbf{B}_{nh}$ matrices represent the holonomic and nonholonomic constraint equations, respectively.

$$
\begin{bmatrix} \mathbf{B}_h & 0 \\ -\mathbf{B}_h\mathbf{V} & \mathbf{B}_h \\ 0 & \mathbf{B}_{nh} \end{bmatrix} \begin{bmatrix} \dot{p} & p \\ \dot{w} & w \end{bmatrix} = \begin{bmatrix} 0 & 0 \\ 0 & 0 \\ 0 & 0 \end{bmatrix} \tag{2}
$$

In order to eliminate the constraint equations, a new state vector z that will always satisfy the constraints is defined, using an orthogonal complement $\mathbf{R}$. The orthogonal complement is not unique, and depends on the method used for its evaluation. In the author's implementation, the standard null space routines in $\text{MATLAB}^{\text{TM}}$, which are based on a singular value decomposition approach, are used.

$$
\left\{ \begin{array}{c} p \\ w \end{array} \right\} = \mathbf{R}z \; \left| \; \begin{bmatrix} \mathbf{B}_h & 0 \\ -\mathbf{B}_h\mathbf{V} & \mathbf{B}_h \\ 0 & \mathbf{B}_{nh} \end{bmatrix} \mathbf{R} = 0 \Rightarrow \begin{bmatrix} \mathbf{B}_h & 0 \\ -\mathbf{B}_h\mathbf{V} & \mathbf{B}_h \\ 0 & \mathbf{B}_{nh} \end{bmatrix} \left\{ \begin{array}{c} p \\ w \end{array} \right\} = \left\{ \begin{array}{c} 0 \\ 0 \\ 0 \end{array} \right\} \tag{3}
$$

To reduce the equations to a minimal dimension, and eliminate the forces of constraint, the matrix $\mathbf{L}$ is formed from as the orthogonal complement as shown in Equation (4).

$$
\begin{bmatrix} \mathbf{B}_h & 0 \\ 0 & \mathbf{B}_h \\ 0 & \mathbf{B}_{nh} \end{bmatrix} \mathbf{L} = 0 \Rightarrow \mathbf{L}^{\text{T}} \left\{ \begin{array}{c} 0 \\ f_c \end{array} \right\} = \left\{ \begin{array}{c} 0 \\ 0 \end{array} \right\} \tag{4}
$$

The resulting first order form is shown in Equation (5). From here, the equations can easily be manipulated into the standard form for eigenvalue or frequency response analysis.

$$\mathbf{L}^{\mathrm{T}} \begin{bmatrix} \mathbf{I} & \mathbf{0} \\ \mathbf{0} & \mathbf{M} \end{bmatrix} \mathbf{R}\dot{z} + \mathbf{L}^{\mathrm{T}} \begin{bmatrix} \mathbf{V} & -\mathbf{I} \\ \mathbf{K} & \mathbf{C} \end{bmatrix} \mathbf{R}z = \mathbf{L}^{\mathrm{T}} \left\{ \begin{matrix} \mathbf{0} \\ f_{\mathrm{c}} + f_{\mathrm{a}} \end{matrix} \right\} \tag{5}$$

The algorithm described above has been implemented in software, and has been used to generate results for a number of vehicle systems, see Minaker and Rieveley[13],[14], and Minaker[15]. The results have been compared against benchmarks from the literature, including the yaw plane vehicle model, the yaw plane truck and trailer, the rigid-rider bicycle, and a model of the Iltis off-road military vehicle described by Kortüm and Sharp[16]. The results of an eigenvalue analysis of the benchmark bicycle described by Meijaard et. al.[17], produced using the EoM software, are shown in Figure 1.

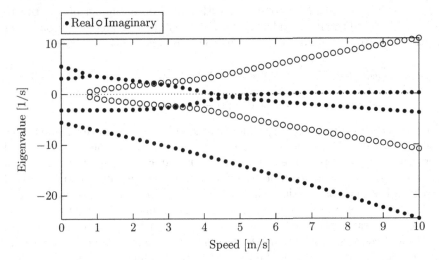

Fig. 1. Eigenvalues vs. Speed

3 Extension to Circuit Lap Time Simulations

While the EoM software is able to generate equations of motion for complex three dimensional multibody systems, its linearization of these equations makes them ill-suited for accurate time history solutions in certain situations, e.g., a full lap of a vehicle on a circuit. In order to allow this important component of vehicle simulation to be included, the research group is exploring a number of extensions to allow simulations of this type. The first is the use of a moving global reference frame, and the second is an efficient means of defining a circuit and the ideal 'driving line' of the vehicle on that circuit.

3.1 Moving Reference Frames

When a vehicle is in motion, its range of operating conditions is such that the fundamental equations describing that motion become non-linear differential equations. One of the primary sources of non-linearity is in the kinematic differential equations that relate the global ground fixed reference frame and the local co-ordinate frames attached to each body. As a result, the linearized equations of motion cannot describe the vehicle as it changes its orientation through large rotations, as it would on a circuit. However, the relative motion of the compo-nents of the vehicle, or the deflection and vibration of the vehicle itself, is often very well described by a set of linear or linearized equations.

Expressing the equations of motion in a moving global reference frame that is not attached to any of the bodies in the system, but rather follows a path near the vehicle, provides a solution. Essentially, it provides a 'semi-linearized' approach, where the non-linear inertial terms due to the motion of the reference frame are captured as external forces, which then act on a set of linearized equations. These inertial forces and moments are given in Equations (6) and (7). If desired, these inertial terms can be combined with a non-linear model of the tire to provide increased tire model fidelity. Even so, the linearized kinematic constraint relationships are still maintained, so the solution is not fully non-linear.

$$f_{\text{inertial}} = -m(\dot{\omega} \times r + \omega \times (\omega \times r) + 2\omega \times \dot{r} + \omega \times v + \dot{v}) \tag{6}$$

$$m_{\text{inertial}} = -\mathbf{I}(\omega \times \dot{\theta} + \dot{\omega}) - ((\omega + \dot{\theta}) \times \mathbf{I}(\omega + \dot{\theta})) \tag{7}$$

The terms $v, \omega, \dot{v}, \dot{\omega}$ represent the linear and angular velocity of the global frame, respectively, and their time derivatives, measured in the frame. The mass and inertia matrix are represented as m and $\mathbf{I}$; r and $\dot{r}$ represent the location of the centre of mass and its time derivative, and $\dot{\theta}$ represents the time rate of change of the small orientation angles of the individual bodies measured relative to the rotating reference frame. As all the inertial terms require knowledge of the locations and rates measured in the frame, these must be computed from the set of minimal coordinates. The inertial forces and moments are also expressed in physical coordinates, and must be reduced to the minimal coordinate set before they can be included.

One of the major challenges in the use of a moving global reference frame is determining the best choice of motion for the frame. One possibility is that the motion of the frame is such that its orientation and lateral location converge to align with the desired vehicle path, and the longitudinal location converges toward the location of the vehicle chassis mass centre. The effect of the algorithm that determines the reference frame motion is a current topic of investigation.

3.2   Track Mapping

In order to produce a simulation of a vehicle lapping on a track, a means of mapping the path of the vehicle, relative to a track or roadway, must be defined. An approach similar to the concept of finite elements has been chosen. At present, only flat and level tracks have been considered, but the method can be extended to three dimensions if warranted. The process is as follows: first, the track is defined using a series of points that describe it's centreline. Then, using the direction from each point to the next, and to the previous, the average direction of the track can be found; from this and the width of the track, the set of points defining the edges of the track can be found.

Next, the track is broken into segments, using two sets of two edge points, as shown in Figure 2. The four points do not generally form a regular shape, but are mapped into a '2x2' space, where (x, y) denotes the location of a point in physical space, and (s, t) denotes the location of the point in the mapped space. Using this approach, any point in the new space can quickly and easily be translated back to its location in physical space, given the four corners in physical space. Care must be taken to ensure that the corner points are defined consistently, as shown in Figure 2.

$$\begin{Bmatrix} x \\ y \end{Bmatrix} = 1/4 \begin{bmatrix} x_1 & x_2 & x_3 & x_4 \\ y_1 & y_2 & y_3 & y_4 \end{bmatrix} \begin{bmatrix} (1-s)(1-t) \\ (1-s)(1+t) \\ (1+s)(1-t) \\ (1+s)(1+t) \end{bmatrix} \tag{8}$$

A set of four Hermite interpolating polynomials is then used to describe the desired path of the vehicle, in each particular segment of track. The four polynomials are defined in terms of the lateral displacement at the start and at the end the interval, and the slope at the start and end of the interval. Each of the four polynomials has a unit value of slope or displacement at one end, and zero everywhere else; the four polynomials cover all four possible cases. A linear combination of the four polynomials then defines the desired path.

In this way, only four values are required to define the path in a particular segment; those four values simultaneously being the offsets and slopes at the ends, and the weights of each polynomial. Allowing that the path must be smooth and continuous requires that the offsets and slopes at the end of one segment must match the values at the start of next, which reduces the number of values to just two per segment. Defining the path in st space as a cubic allows the coefficients to be found from the values of t and t' at the start and end of the mapped segment.

$$t = as^3 + bs^2 + cs + d \tag{9}$$

$$\begin{Bmatrix} a \\ b \\ c \\ d \end{Bmatrix} = \begin{bmatrix} 1/4 & 1/4 & -1/4 & 1/4 \\ 0 & -1/4 & 0 & 1/4 \\ -3/4 & -1/4 & 3/4 & -1/4 \\ 1/2 & 1/4 & 1/2 & -1/4 \end{bmatrix} \begin{Bmatrix} t(-1) \\ t'(-1) \\ t(1) \\ t'(1) \end{Bmatrix} \tag{10}$$

Of course, the s axes of adjoining track segments do not usually align, and so while matching values of t across segment boundaries will ensure a continuous path, it will not necessarily be smooth. The values of the slope at the end of each segment must be adjusted in st space to accommodate the change in orientation of each segment. The desired slope of the curve in st space is found by starting with the unit normal in xy space, and rotating it through the desired path angle, and then using the Jacobian matrix to relate the slopes between the two spaces.

$$\begin{Bmatrix} ds \\ dt \end{Bmatrix} = \begin{bmatrix} \frac{\partial x}{\partial s} & \frac{\partial x}{\partial t} \\ \frac{\partial y}{\partial s} & \frac{\partial y}{\partial t} \end{bmatrix}^{-1} \begin{bmatrix} \cos(\theta) & -\sin(\theta) \\ \sin(\theta) & \cos(\theta) \end{bmatrix} \begin{Bmatrix} \hat{u}_x \\ \hat{u}_y \end{Bmatrix} \tag{11}$$

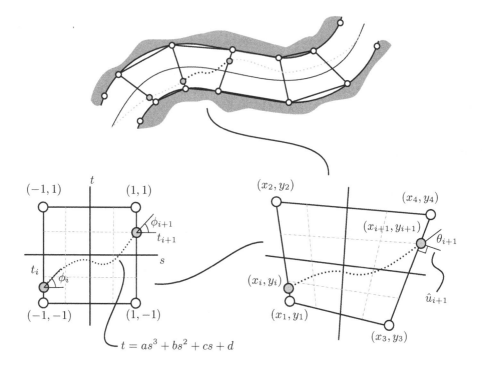

mapped element   global element

Fig. 2. Mapped track segments (figure adapted from Rieveley[12])

The Jacobian can be found using the following relationship:

$$
\begin{bmatrix} \frac{\partial x}{\partial s} & \frac{\partial x}{\partial t} \\ \frac{\partial y}{\partial s} & \frac{\partial y}{\partial t} \end{bmatrix} = \frac{1}{4} \begin{bmatrix} x_1 & x_2 & x_3 & x_4 \\ y_1 & y_2 & y_3 & y_4 \end{bmatrix} \begin{bmatrix} t-1 & s-1 \\ -(t+1) & 1-s \\ 1-t & -(s+1) \\ t+1 & s+1 \end{bmatrix}
\tag{12}
$$

$$
\tan(\phi) = \frac{dt}{ds}
\tag{13}
$$

At this point, a smooth and continuous desired path of a vehicle around at track can now be defined using only the points describing the centreline, and the desired values of the offset and angle at each segment boundary. The actual location of the vehicle can then be compared to the desired path of the vehicle, and this information can be used by the driver model to determine the inputs to the vehicle model.

4   Conclusion

The paper has presented some of the technical details of the vehicle simulation software under development at the University of Windsor Vehicle Dynamics and Control research group. For more information about the software, or the research group, please visit the website at www.uwindsor.ca/vdc.

References

1. Johnston, M., Minaker, B.P.: The Design of a Digital Vehicle for Use in a Student Virtual Race. In: Proceedings of the 22nd Canadian Congress of Applied Mechanics, alifax, Nova Scotia, pp. 205–206 (2009)
2. Rieveley, R.J., Minaker, B.P.: Virtual Motorsports In Project-Based Engineering Education. In: Proceedings of the 22nd Canadian Congress of Applied Mechanics, Halifax, Nova Scotia, pp. 104–105 (2009)
3. Rieveley, R.J., Minaker, B.P.: Virtual Motorsports as a Vehicle Dynamics Teaching Tool. SAE International Journal of Passenger Cars - Mechanical Systems V117-6 (SAE paper 2008-01-2967), 1325–1333
4. CarSim, Mechanical Simulation, http://www.carsim.com
5. MBDyn, http://mbdyn.org
6. DynaMechs, http://dynamechs.sourceforge.net
7. The Open Race Car Simulator, http://torcs.org
8. VDrift, http://vdrift.net/
9. Bullet Game Physics, http://bulletphysics.org
10. Open Dynamics Engine, http://ode.org
11. Newton Game Dynamics, http://newtondynamics.com
12. Rieveley, R.J.: The Effect of Direct Yaw Moment on Human Controlled Vehicle Systems. PhD Thesis, Dept. of Mech., Auto., & Mat'ls Eng., University of Windsor (2010)
13. Minaker, B.P., Rieveley, R.J.: Automatic Generation of the Non-holonomic Equations of Motion for Vehicle Stability Analysis. Vehicle System Dynamics 48(9), 1043–1063 (2010)
14. Minaker, B.P., Rieveley, R.J.: Dynamic Behaviour of a Narrow Tilting Vehicle. In: Proceedings of the 23rd Canadian Congress of Applied Mechanics, Vancouver, British Columbia, pp. 535–538 (2011)
15. Minaker, B.P.: Automatic Generation of Linearised Equations of Motion for Moving Vehicles. In: Proceedings, Bicycle and Motorcycle Dynamics, Delft, The Netherlands (2010)
16. Kortüm, W., Sharp, R.S.: Multibody Computer Codes In Vehicle System Dynamics. Supp. to Vehicle Dynamics 22 (1993)
17. Meijaard, J.P., Papadopoulos, J.M., Ruina, A., Schwab, A.L.: Linearised dynamics equations for the balance and steer of a bicycle: a benchmark and review. Proc. Roy. Soc. A 463, 1955–1982 (2007)

A Study of New Path Planning Algorithm Using Extended A* Algorithm with Survivability

Min-Ho Kim[1], Hee-Mu Lee, Yuanlong Wei[1], and Min-Cheol Lee[1]

[1] Control and Automation Systems Division, Pusan National University,
Busan, South Korea
{xho1995,ylwei860101}@gmail.com, slm1023@nate.com,
mclee@pusan.ac.kr

Abstract. There are a lot of researches on the path planning algorithm of the unmanned vehicle. Previous researches related to the path planning mainly focused on finding the shortest path on the given map. However, on the battle field, if the vehicle just moves along the shortest path, it could not reach the goal, because of the enemy's attack. Therefore it's necessary that the new path planning algorithm for the unmanned vehicle on the battle field.
In this paper, we will suggest a new path planning algorithm for the vehicle on the battle field using extended A* algorithm with survivability. For this, we will define the survivability and develop the additional cost function to find the optimal path in this situation. To verify the proposed algorithm, we developed the simulation program and the results will be shown.

Keywords: unmanned vehicle, path planning, battle filed simulation, A*.

1 Introduction

Recently USA has developed the future combat system. One component of the combat system is the unmanned ground vehicle which can travel, observe, and sometimes battle on the battle field automatically. Since this system's research had been started, researches about the unmanned vehicle have increased. This vehicle has to avoid the obstacle and the hidden enemies in the unknown environment. To reach the goal position under these conditions, the improved path planning algorithm is needed because the conventional path planning algorithms like as the A* find only the shortest path to the goal position and do not consider whether the vehicle will be alive or not. If the vehicle should be alive on the battle field and reach the goal, the path planning algorithm must consider about the survivability of the vehicle.

In this paper, an improved path planning algorithm considering the survivability is suggested. First, the survivability is defined and the additional cost function is developed with this, and then the extended A* algorithm is proposed by combining the normal A* algorithm and the cost function. To evaluate the proposed path planning algorithm, the simulation program is developed. The simulation results will show the proposed algorithm give the vehicle the safer path to avoid the obstacles and the enemies on the battle field.

C.-Y. Su, S. Rakheja, H. Liu (Eds.): ICIRA 2012, Part III, LNAI 7508, pp. 608–617, 2012.
© Springer-Verlag Berlin Heidelberg 2012

2   The Survivability for the Additional Cost Function

Before define the survivability, first we describe the grid map used in the path planning algorithm and check out the environment in which the unmanned vehicle moves around. That's shown as the Fig. 1.

In the Fig. 1, A_i means an unmanned vehicle called by 'Agent'. An agent can only move to its adjacent cells. Each cell of the grid map has a cost value, and usually the shortest path can be determined with comparing those cost function values. But on the battle field, there are the enemies which can attack the agent shown as Fig. 1. So if the agent only move along the shortest path, it might not reach the goal, especially the path goes through the enemy's attack range. However, if we know the survivability of the agent, then we can choose safer path, and it may be more optimal path in this case.

Now the survivability will be defined. The survivability is the probability that shows the vehicle could be alive until it reaches the goal position. There might be a lot of methods to define the survivability. In this paper, the classic definition of the probability is used to define the survivability, it's shown as; [1]

$$P(A) = \frac{N_A}{N} \tag{1}$$

In the equation (1), P(A) is the probability of an event A, N is the number of possible outcomes and N_A is the number of outcomes that are favorable to the event A. From this simple theory, the survivability and the additional cost function will be built up to extend the A* algorithm.

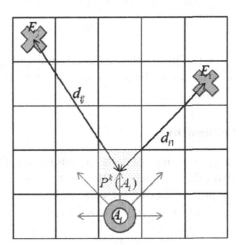

Fig. 1. A_i is an i-th agent, E_1, ... , E_j are the enemies, and d_{i1}, ... , d_{ij} are the distances between agent and the enemies. $P^k(A_i)$ is the survivability of A_i at the k-th unit time.

2.1   The Definition of the Survivability

Using the definition of probability in equation (1), the survivability is defined as

$$P_s(A_i) = \frac{L_i - D_i}{L_i} = 1 - \frac{D_i}{L_i} \tag{2}$$

Where, Ps(Ai) is the survivability of i-th agent, Li is the amount, called by 'Life', for the Ai to be able to resist the enemy's attack, and Di is the amount which the enemies can damage the Ai. In the equation (2), we can define the damaged probability of the Ai like as;

$$P_d(A_i) = \frac{D_i}{L_i} \tag{3}$$

So, the survivability can be defined as 1 minus the damaged probability;

$$P_s(A_i) = 1 - P_d(A_i) \tag{4}$$

And the survivability has the value of 0 to 1 like as the equation (5). If D_i is bigger than the L_i, then the agent must be killed and it's ignorable.

$$P_s(A_i) = \begin{cases} 1 & D_i = 0 \\ \alpha & 0 < D_i < L_i \\ 0 & D_i \geq L_i \end{cases} \tag{5}$$

According to the equation (4), to calculate the survivability of the Ai, the damaged probability should be calculated. Next chapter, we will define the damaged probability of the Ai.

2.2   The Damaged Probability

The damaged probability shows the possibility which the agent can be attacked by enemies. It's already defined in equation (3). However, to determine the optimal path we should compare the probabilities on the adjacent cells at a time. So we should calculate the damaged probability at a certain time k like as;

$$P_d^k(A_i) = \frac{D_i^k}{L_i} \tag{6}$$

If there are several enemies, then using total probability theorem, we can explain the equation like this;

$$P_d^k(A_i) = P_d^k(A_i|E_1)P^k(E_1) + \cdots + P_d^k(A_i|E_m)P^k(E_m) \tag{7}$$

Here, m is the number of enemy. $P_d(A_i|E_j)$ means the damaged probability when the j-th enemy E_j attacks the A_i. $P^k(E_j)$ mean the probability whether the E_j attacks the A_i or not. So, if there is only one agent, then $P^k(E_j)$ is always 1. Thus the damaged probability at the k-th unit time is like this;

$$P_d^k(A_i) = \sum_{j=1}^{m} P_d^k(A_i|E_j) = \frac{D_i^k}{L_i} \tag{8}$$

In this paper, we defined the D^k like as;

$$D_i^k = \sum_{j=1}^{m} \beta_j P_h(A_i) \tag{9}$$

Here, β_j is the coefficient of the power of the j-th enemy's weapon, $P_h(A_i)$ is the probability that the enemy's attack can hit the A_i so called by 'the hit probability'. Finally, we've got the damaged probability at the k-th unit time like this;

$$P_d^k(A_i) = \sum_{j=1}^{m} \frac{\beta_j P_h(A_i)}{L_i} \tag{10}$$

2.3   The Hit Probability

The hit probability is the related with the enemy's aim. And it can be described with the Gaussian distribution like as;

$$P_h(A_i) = \int_{-z}^{+z} \frac{1}{\sqrt{2\pi}} e^{-\frac{z^2}{2}} \tag{11}$$

And with the equation (10) and (11), we rebuild the damaged probability like as;

$$P_d^k(A_i) = \frac{1}{L_i} \sum_{j=1}^{m} \beta_j \int_{-z_{ij}}^{+z_{ij}} \frac{1}{\sqrt{2\pi}} e^{-\frac{z_{ij}^2}{2}} \tag{12}$$

Approximation. However, there is no direct solution of the integral of the normal distribution. Thus we use the approximation of the normal distribution. There might be a lot of better approximations, but our approximation would be applied on the grid map, so the ruff approximation shows not bad result. Therefore, we choose the simplest equation developed by Arvind K. Shah. [2]

$$P_h(A_i) = \begin{cases} z(4.4-z)/10 & 0 \le z \le 2.2 \\ 0.49 & 2.2 < z < 2.6 \\ 0.5 & z \ge 2.6 \end{cases} \tag{13}$$

3   The Extended A* Algorithm with the Survivability

Until now the survivability has been defined. Using this probability, the normal A* algorithm is extended to be able to apply to the unmanned vehicle on the battle field. The extended A* algorithm will find the safer path on the map.

3.1   The Normal A* Algorithm

The A* algorithm is one of the graph/tree search algorithm using the heuristic estimate function. It searches the cell which has the minimum cost function value. If the reasonable heuristic function is chosen, it shows the optimal path on the given grid map. And it's a kind of depth-first search algorithm. The cost function of the normal A* algorithm is shown as; [3, 4]

$$F(n) = g(n) + h(n) \tag{14}$$

Where, the $F(n)$ is the total cost function of A* algorithm, the $g(n)$ is the cost function from the start position to the current position which is on the n-th node on the grid map, and the $h(n)$ is the heuristic cost function from the current position to the goal. In the equation (14), the cost function manly consists of the distance between the start and the goal. Therefore, it's hard to put the survivability into the cost function. Therefore, the additional cost function is developed to evaluate the safest path of the vehicle on the map.

3.2   The Additional Cost Function of the Extended A* Algorithm

In the previous chapter, the survivability and the damaged probability were defined. However to apply to the proposed algorithm, the probability should be accumulated along the path. The total damaged probability is shown as;

$$P_d^t(A_i) = \sum_{k=0}^{t} P_d^k(A_i) \tag{15}$$

Where, $P_d^t(A_i)$ means the damaged probability that is accumulated along the path with respect to the time interval [0, t]. with the equation (8) and (12), the total damaged probability can be calculated as;

$$P_d^t(A_i) = \sum_{k=0}^{t}\sum_{j=1}^{m} P_d^k(A_i|E_j) = \frac{1}{L_i}\sum_{k=0}^{t}\sum_{j=1}^{m}\beta_j\int_{-z_{ij}}^{+z_{ij}}\frac{1}{\sqrt{2\pi}}e^{-\frac{z_{ij}^2}{2}} \tag{16}$$

And the total survivability is shown as;

$$P_s^t(A_i) = 1 - \sum_{k=0}^{t}\sum_{j=1}^{m} P_d^k(A_i|E_j) \tag{17}$$

This equation is the additional cost function of the extended A* algorithm. Fig. 2 shows the mechanism of this cost function. To compare these function values of the cells, the proposed algorithm can find the safest path of the vehicle on battle field. Next the workflow of the proposed algorithm will be explained.

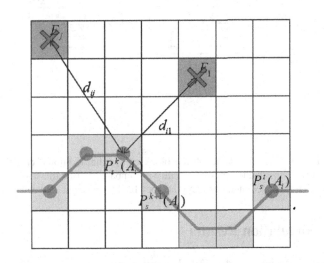

Fig. 2. The red line means the path. $P^k(A_i)$ is the survivability of A_i at the k-th unit time. And $P^t(A_i)$ is the survivability in the time interval [0, t]. if there is the path which has the maximum $P^t(A_i)$ value, then it's the safest path on the map.

3.3   The Work Flow of the Extended A* Algorithm

Fig. 3 shows the work flow of the extended A* algorithm. It compares the cost value twice times, first is the survivability and second is the normal cost value. The additional cost function is shown in the Fig. 3 as the dark colored block. Actually it changes the priority of the cells on the grid map. Normally the cell which has the lowest cost value would have the highest priority, but in the proposed algorithm, the maximum survivability has the highest priority.

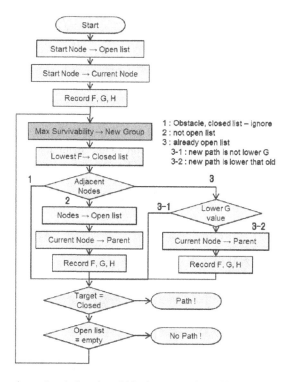

Fig. 3. In this flowchart, the dark colored block means the additional cost function. Before compare the normal cost value, the survivability is compared to find the safest path on the map. The closed list has the calculated cells and the open list has the candidate cells.

4   The Simulation Results

To verify our algorithm, we developed the simulation program and the results will be shown. In this paper, there is only one agent on the battle field and the agent and the enemy can't be the same grid at a time.

4.1   The Simulation Program

The simulation program is developed with C++ builder 2007 on the windows 7 environment. And the main algorithm is developed with STL (Standard Template Library) and advised from the website 'A* Pathfinding for Beginners'. [4, 5, 6]

4.2   The Results

The one of results of the proposed path planning algorithm are shown in the Fig. 4. The vehicle moves from the start position 'S' to the goal 'G', and the enemy is at the position 'E'. There are two different paths. '1' is the result of the normal A* algorithm and '2' is of the proposed algorithm. Fig. 4 shows that the normal A* algorithm finds the path along which the vehicle goes through the enemy's attack range, because the algorithm just finds the shortest path to the goal. However, with the proposed algorithm, the vehicle can avoid the dangerous situation. Out of the enemy's range, the proposed algorithm shows the same path as the normal A*, because it's actually same as the A* in the normal environment. Thus the result path is the fastest and safest path. The extended A* algorithm can be called 'the conditional optimal path planning algorithm'.

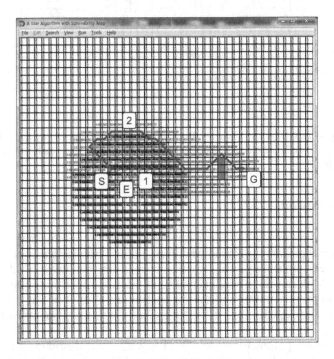

Fig. 4. 'S' means the start node, and 'G' means the goal. The box number '1' is the result of normal A* algorithm and '2' is one of the extended A* algorithm. 'E' is the center of the enemy position. The gray boxes are the obstacles.

Fig. 5 shows the result of the general environment in which the unmanned vehicle should avoid the obstacles and the enemy. Before the vehicle meets the enemy the paths are same, and after the enemy is detected, the proposed algorithm suggests the different path shown as the path '2' in the Fig. 5. The path is the safest path and possibly the fastest path, too.

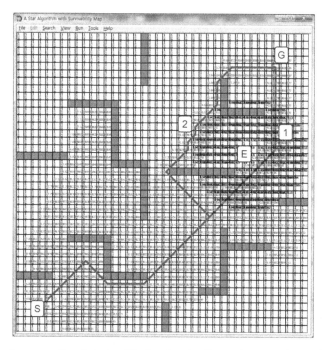

Fig. 5. The gray boxes are the obstacles. Black colored cells are the enemy's attack range, and light gray colored cells are calculated cells. The path '2' is the fastest path which satisfies the survival conditions.

5   Conclusion

In this paper, the extended A* algorithm was proposed for the unmanned vehicle to find the optimal path on the battled field. First, the survivability was defined using the total damaged probability which was obtained as the sum of the damaged probabilities with respect to time interval [0, t]. Each damaged probability consists of the enemy's weapon power and the hit probability. And then the additional cost function was developed to apply the survivability into the proposed path planning algorithm.

The simulation program was developed to verify the algorithm. And the results were shown. The results showed that the proposed algorithm can find the safest path which is the optimal path in these environments. However there is only one agent in the simulation, in further work the optimal path planning of the multi-agent system in the battle field will be researched.

Acknowledgments. The Authors gratefully acknowledge the support from UTRC (Unmanned technology Research Center) at KAIST (Korea Advanced Institute of Science and Technology), originally funded by DAPA, ADD.

References

1. Papoulis, A., Unnikrishna Pillai, S.: Probability, Random Variables and Stochastic Processes. McGraw-Hill Higher Education (2002)
2. Arvind, K.,, S.: A Simpler Approximation for Areas Under the Standard Normal Curve. The American Statistician 39(1), 80 (1985)
3. Peter, E., Hart, N.J.: Nilsson, Bertram Raphael: A Formal Basis for the Heuristic Determination of Minimum Cost Paths. IEEE Transactions of Systems Science and Cybernetics ssc-4(2), 100–107 (1968)
4. Lester, P.: A* Pathfinding for Beginners,
   http://www.policyalmanac.org/games/aStarTutorial.htm
5. Gamma, E., Helm, R., Johnson, R., Vlissides, J.: Design Patterns. Addison-Wesley (1995)
6. Musser, D.R., Derge, C.J., Saini, A.: STL Tutorial and Reference Guide, 2nd edn. Addison-Wesley (2001)

Author Index